W9-CFZ-871

Frommer's®
Los Angeles

My Los Angeles
by Matthew R. Poole

I HAVE A CONFESSION TO MAKE: I USED TO HATE LA. I WAS RAISED IN

Northern California where it's considered a birthright to look down your nose at the Los Angelenos. Then one day I ate my hubris for lunch and moved here. I was offered a job and needed the money. And, however grudgingly, I found myself increasingly amused by this vast circus-without-a-tent, where every neighborhood is a veritable sideshow of cultural spontaneity. Wherever you go in San Francisco always looks and feels like San Francisco. In LA it's the opposite: drive 5 miles in any direction and you feel like Francisco Pizarro on speed.

How do you get to Roscoe's Chicken and Waffles? Head toward Korea, turn right at Samoa, go straight through Armenia, past lower Moscow, then park in Mexico City. You could spend 10 lifetimes in LA and finally notice that Peruvian restaurant across the street from your gym.

But what finally melted my icy attitude toward Los Angeles was the miles and miles of cathartic gold-sand beaches. A morning run along the shore—with pelicans skimming the waves, dolphins swimming past you, warm sunshine on your face—will melt your daily anxieties.

Check out these photos, then skim my "Best Of" chapter, and you'll see why crow is such a popular dish among us Northern Californians.

© Tim Street Porter/The Standard, Downtown LA

Pack black, because you haven't really experienced LA until you've mingled with the dig-me crowd at the city's uber-hip clubs and bars. Don't bother standing in line—if you're not on a list at the hottest places you'll never get in. My advice: Head to the **STANDARD DOWNTOWN'S ROOFTOP BAR (left),** order a Cosmo, and strike a pose—there's nothing to it.

My all-time favorite LA activity is to take a leisurely bicycle ride on the 8-mile **BEACHSIDE BIKE PATH (above)** that runs along Santa Monica and Venice Beach. Everyone always appears healthy and happy as they jog, skate, walk, and ride in the sunshine as a cool breeze blows in off the Pacific.

© Peter Bennett/Ambient Images Inc./Alamy

Los Angeles is all about entertainment, so it's no surprise that the city's numerous museums and galleries are designed to keep you endlessly enthralled. Even a pool of stinky tar—the famous **LA BREA TAR PITS** (left)—is livened up with massive woolly mammoths in the throes of certain death. Kids will marvel at all the menacing dinosaurs on display at the **NATURAL HISTORY MUSEUM** (below) and at the tar pit's Page Museum.

The "Happiest Place on Earth" is a mere 40-minute drive from downtown LA. The original **DISNEYLAND RESORT** (above right) in Anaheim still opens its gates every day to thousands of Mickey fans of all ages. It's so popular that we've included an entire chapter that tells you how to get the best Disney experience.

In addition to the Disneyland Resort, the LA region hosts three other destinations for thrill-seekers: Six Flags California, Universal Studios, and **KNOTT'S BERRY FARM** (below right). That's 4 days of guaranteed fun in the sun.

© Richard Cummins/Corbis

Go on, admit it: You want to see the street where *Desperate Housewives* is filmed. Touring the backlots of **UNIVERSAL STUDIOS (left)**, Paramount Pictures, Warner Brothers, and the other major studios is a classic LA experience. These aren't fake tours—you'll see real sets from TV shows and movies—and there's always the chance of spotting a celebrity at work. This *Jurassic Park*–inspired ride is just one small part of what you might experience.

Some of the biggest stars in show business have their noses (Bob Hope), hair (Whoopi Goldberg), cigars (George Burns), wheels (R2-D2), hands, feet, and signatures immortalized at the famous **ENTRY COURT TO SID GRAUMAN'S CHINESE THEATER (below)**. I drop by once in a while just to admire Betty Grable's gams.

You never know who you'll bump into while visiting Los Angeles (last year I spent 2 hours chatting with Roseanne Barr at a hotel bar). This city's so chock full of **CELEBRITIES (like Tom Cruise above)**, you're bound to spot someone famous— you just need to know where to look.

It'll cost you $15,000 to buy your own star on the **HOLLYWOOD WALK OF FAME (right)**, but first you need to get famous. More than 2,500 celebrities from the worlds of film, radio, television, theater, and music are immortalized in Italian marble along Hollywood Boulevard. It seems sort of a sacrilege to step on Elvis, and poor Rodney Dangerfield still can't get any respect.

The birthplace of America's surfing culture (and, of course, the Beach Boys), **SOUTHERN CALIFORNIA'S SURF BREAKS** (left) are legendary. But why be a spectator when you can be a participant? The fabled beaches along the Los Angeles coastline—Malibu, Redondo, Manhattan—host numerous surfing schools that guarantee you'll stand up and ride a wave in a single lesson (really, it's true).

Architectural buffs from around the world come to Los Angeles just to see the **WALT DISNEY CONCERT HALL** (above), a triumph of art, acoustics, and design. Architect Frank Gehry's undulating stainless-steel facade is mesmerizing— you can't stop staring at it—and the self-guided audio tour is excellent. Purchase tickets well in advance to experience the world's finest concert hall acoustics.

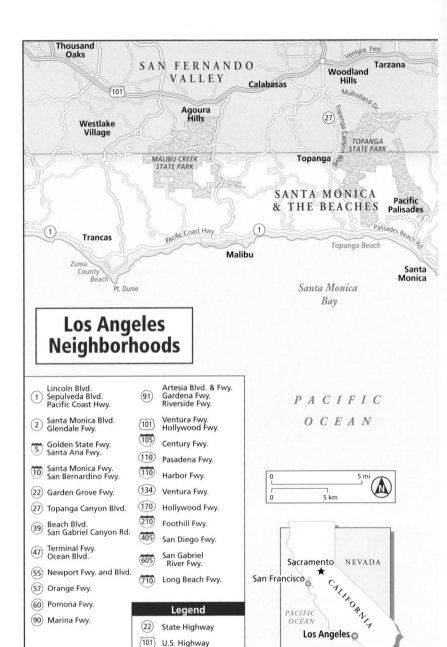

Los Angeles Neighborhoods

Legend

22 State Highway

101 U.S. Highway

210 Interstate Highway

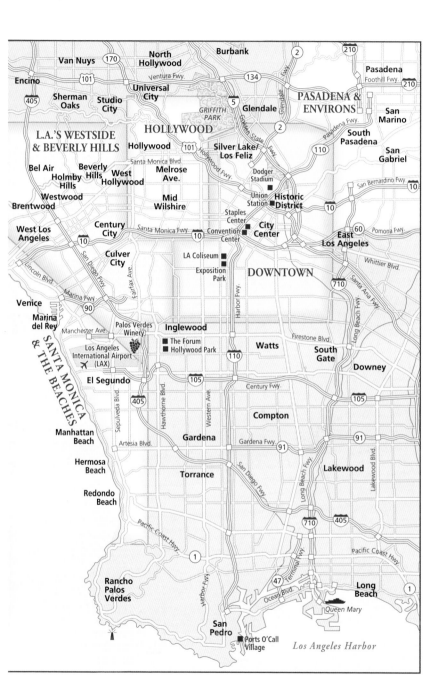

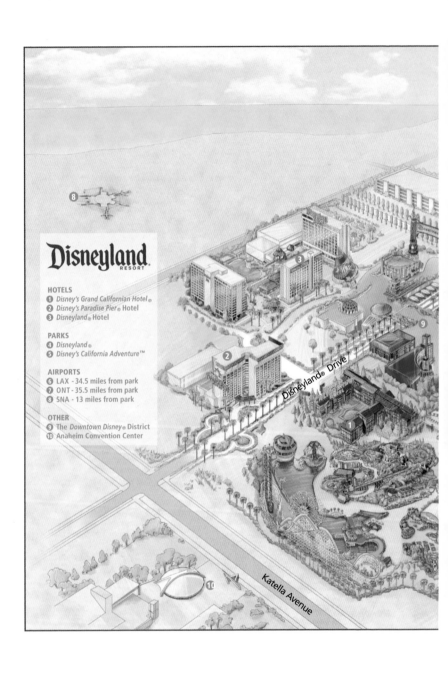

Disneyland
RESORT®

HOTELS
① Disney's Grand Californian Hotel®
② Disney's Paradise Pier® Hotel
③ Disneyland® Hotel

PARKS
④ Disneyland®
⑤ Disney's California Adventure™

AIRPORTS
⑥ LAX - 34.5 miles from park
⑦ ONT - 35.5 miles from park
⑧ SNA - 13 miles from park

OTHER
⑨ The Downtown Disney® District
⑩ Anaheim Convention Center

Disneyland® Drive

Katella Avenue

I-5

Ball Road

Harbor Boulevard

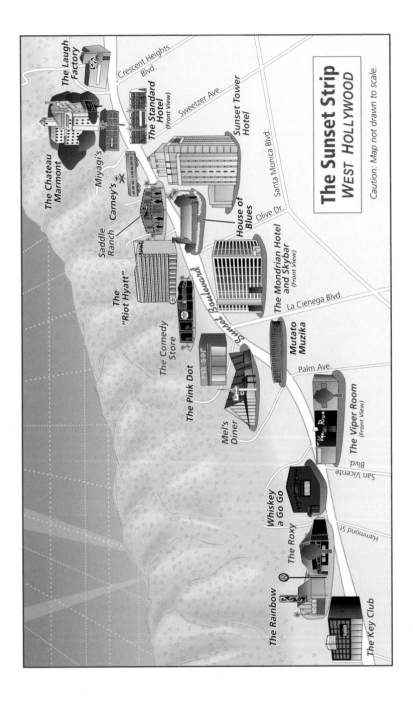

The Sunset Strip
WEST HOLLYWOOD

Caution: Map not drawn to scale.

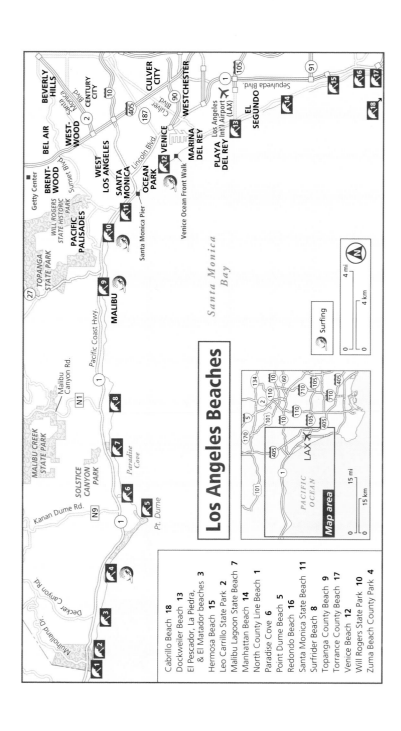

Los Angeles Beaches

Cabrillo Beach **18**
Dockweiler Beach **13**
El Pescador, La Piedra, & El Matador beaches **3**
Hermosa Beach **15**
Leo Carrillo State Park **2**
Malibu Lagoon State Beach **7**
Manhattan Beach **14**
North County Line Beach **1**
Paradise Cove **6**
Point Dume Beach **5**
Redondo Beach **16**
Santa Monica State Beach **11**
Surfrider Beach **8**
Topanga County Beach **9**
Torrance County Beach **17**
Venice Beach **12**
Will Rogers State Park **10**
Zuma Beach County Park **4**

Santa Monica Bay

Surfing

PACIFIC OCEAN

Map area

LAX

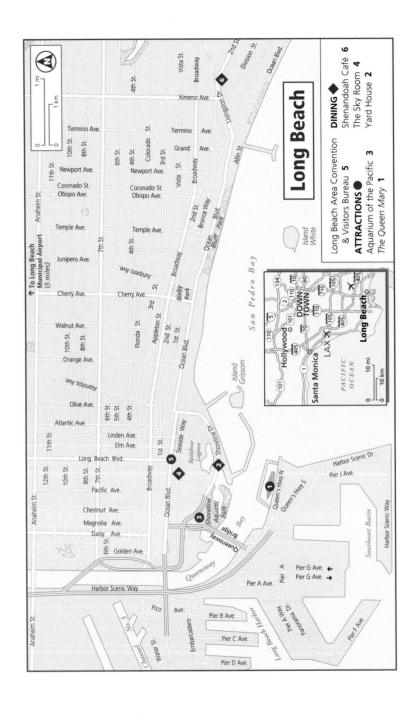

Long Beach

DINING ◆
Shenandoah Café **6**
The Sky Room **4**
Yard House **2**

Long Beach Area Convention
& Visitors Bureau **5**
ATTRACTIONS ●
Aquarium of the Pacific **3**
The Queen Mary **1**

Frommer's®

Los Angeles

2009

by Matthew Richard Poole

Here's what the critics say about Frommer's:

"Amazingly easy to use. Very portable, very complete."

—*Booklist*

"Detailed, accurate, and easy-to-read information for all price ranges."
—*Glamour Magazine*

"Hotel information is close to encyclopedic."
—*Des Moines Sunday Register*

"Frommer's Guides have a way of giving you a real feel for a place."
—*Knight Ridder Newspapers*

WILEY
Wiley Publishing, Inc.

About the Author

Matthew Richard Poole, a native Californian, has authored more than two dozen travel guides to California, Hawaii, and abroad, and is a regular contributor to radio and television travel programs, including numerous guest appearances on the award-winning *Bay Area Backroads* television show. Before becoming a full-time travel writer and photographer, he worked as an English tutor in Prague, a ski instructor in the Swiss Alps, and a scuba instructor in Maui and Thailand. He currently lives in San Francisco, but spends most of his time on the road searching for new adventures. His other Frommer's titles include *California, San Francisco,* and *Portable Disneyland®*.

Published by:

Wiley Publishing, Inc.

111 River St.
Hoboken, NJ 07030-5774

ISBN 978-0-470-28769-9
Editor: Linda Barth
Production Editor: Katie Robinson
Cartographer: Anton Crane
Photo Editor: Richard Fox
Production by Wiley Indianapolis Composition Services

Front cover photo: Venice Beach mural
Back cover photo: Men playing beach volleyball

For information on our other products and services or to obtain technical support, please contact our Customer Care Department within the U.S. at 800/762-2974, outside the U.S. at 317/572-3993 or fax 317/572-4002.

Wiley also publishes its books in a variety of electronic formats. Some content that appears in print may not be available in electronic formats.

Manufactured in the United States of America

5 4 3 2 1

Contents

List of Maps

Acknowledgments

I would like to acknowledge the following people for their time and effort in helping me complete this 2009 edition: Lesley Balla, Alison Branch, Bryan Lane, Billy Ruvelson, Jannis Swerman, Arlene Winnick, Susan Bejeckian, Kim Sudhalter, and my ever-patient editor, Linda Barth.

—Matthew R. Poole

An Invitation to the Reader

In researching this book, we discovered many wonderful places—hotels, restaurants, shops, and more. We're sure you'll find others. Please tell us about them, so we can share the information with your fellow travelers in upcoming editions. If you were disappointed with a recommendation, we'd love to know that, too. Please write to:

Frommer's Los Angeles 2009
Wiley Publishing, Inc. • 111 River St. • Hoboken, NJ 07030-5774

An Additional Note

Please be advised that travel information is subject to change at any time—and this is especially true of prices. We therefore suggest that you write or call ahead for confirmation when making your travel plans. The authors, editors, and publisher cannot be held responsible for the experiences of readers while traveling. Your safety is important to us, however, so we encourage you to stay alert and be aware of your surroundings. Keep a close eye on cameras, purses, and wallets, all favorite targets of thieves and pickpockets.

Frommer's Star Ratings, Icons & Abbreviations

Every hotel, restaurant, and attraction listing in this guide has been ranked for quality, value, service, amenities, and special features using a **star-rating system.** In country, state, and regional guides, we also rate towns and regions to help you narrow down your choices and budget your time accordingly. Hotels and restaurants are rated on a scale of zero (recommended) to three stars (exceptional). Attractions, shopping, nightlife, towns, and regions are rated according to the following scale: zero stars (recommended), one star (highly recommended), two stars (very highly recommended), and three stars (must-see).

In addition to the star-rating system, we also use **seven feature icons** that point you to the great deals, in-the-know advice, and unique experiences that separate travelers from tourists. Throughout the book, look for:

Finds	Special finds—those places only insiders know about
Fun Fact	Fun facts—details that make travelers more informed and their trips more fun
Kids	Best bets for kids and advice for the whole family
Moments	Special moments—those experiences that memories are made of
Overrated	Places or experiences not worth your time or money
Tips	Insider tips—great ways to save time and money
Value	Great values—where to get the best deals

The following **abbreviations** are used for credit cards:

AE	American Express	DISC Discover	V Visa
DC	Diners Club	MC MasterCard	

Frommers.com

Now that you have this guidebook to help you plan a great trip, visit our website at **www. frommers.com** for additional travel information on more than 4,000 destinations. We update features regularly to give you instant access to the most current trip-planning information available. At Frommers.com, you'll find scoops on the best airfares, lodging rates, and car rental bargains. You can even book your travel online through our reliable travel booking partners. Other popular features include:

- Online updates of our most popular guidebooks
- Vacation sweepstakes and contest giveaways
- Newsletters highlighting the hottest travel trends
- Podcasts, interactive maps, and up-to-the-minute events listings
- Opinionated blog entries by Arthur Frommer himself
- Online travel message boards with featured travel discussions

What's New in Los Angeles

Los Angeles and Madonna have a lot in common: They're always one step ahead of trends. Trying to keep up with the constant changes in this amorphous metropolis is a full-time job because what was "in" last year is probably out this year. Here's a short list of what's new in L.A. that's worth checking out (or checking into).

HOTELS If you haven't already made a hotel reservation, I've got some great recommendations for you. If you want to be entrenched in the Hollywood scene, you have to stay at the **Roosevelt Hotel, Hollywood** (© 800/950-7667; www. hollywoodroosevelt.com). The hotel just completed a $30-million renovation and is now *the* place to stay and play in the city. Hanging out by the pool and being served cocktails by models/actresses is a classic L.A. experience. Also playing into the narcissistic Hollywood theme is the swanky new **Hotel Palomar Los Angeles** (© 800/472-8556; www.hotelpalomar-lawestwood.com), where the modus operandi is to treat each guest like a celebrity V.I.P. by offering such perks as personal trainers and 24-hour in-room yoga and Pilates on your flatscreen TV.

If you would rather stay near the beach, I have two new insider tips for you: the **Marina del Rey Marriott** (© 800/228-9290; www.marriott.com) and the **Best Western Marina Pacific Hotel & Suites** (© 800/786-7789; www.mphotel. com). Yes, two chain hotels, but this is L.A., where nothing is quite as it seems. At the Marriott, for example, a subtle aromatherapy mixture called Zanzibar Mist and a soundtrack of ambient world beats circulate throughout the lobby, and the hotel's outdoor lounge is ranked as one of the top hotel lounges in the country by *Playboy* magazine. The newly renovated Best Western, meanwhile, has a groovy rock-'n'-roll theme, great rates, and oceanview rooms, and is within easy walking distance of Venice Beach.

Then again, if all you really want is a really nice room at a reasonable rate without any mist or models, the newly renovated boutique-style **Elan Hotel** (© 323/658-6663; www.elanhotel.com) is my top choice. They did a fantastic job with the decor, the staff is wonderful, and the central location makes driving around the city very convenient.

ATTRACTIONS The big news this year is the opening of **L.A. LIVE** (© 866/548-3452; www.lalive.com) in Downtown Los Angeles, a $2.5-billion mega-entertainment complex that's being optimistically hailed as Times Square West ("You, sir, are no Times Square."). Anchored by the Nokia Theatre and the STAPLES Center, the 6-square-block complex is crammed with restaurants, clubs, luxury condos, two hotels, a movie theater, and even a bowling alley. It's all part of the city's pricey push to revitalize the Downtown area and increase convention business.

At the **Los Angeles Zoo** (© 323/644-4200; www.lazoo.org) they've finally completed the new $19-million **Campo Gorilla Reserve,** a habitat for six African lowland gorillas that's designed to resemble their native West African homeland. Visitors walk along a misty, forested pathway that has glass viewing areas for close-up views of the gorillas. Over at the wonderful **Natural History Museum** (© 213/763-DINO [213/763-3466]; www.nhm.org), the inspiring new **Thomas the *T. rex* Lab** is ready for budding paleontologists. It's a specially designed workroom where visitors can watch the work of real paleontologists as they prepare and assemble the fossils of a 66-million-year-old *Tyrannosaurus rex* nicknamed "Thomas." It's one of many interactive exhibits that kids will find really cool.

The city has added some introspective attractions as well this year. At the **Los Angeles County Museum of Art** (© 323/857-6000; www.lacma.org), the highly anticipated **Broad Contemporary Art Museum** (also known as BCAM) has finally opened. The $56-million, three-story museum is one of the largest column-free art spaces in the U.S., hosting opening installations by such artists as Richard Serra, Andy Warhol, and Roy Lichtenstein. And at the **Huntington Library, Art Collections & Botanical Gardens** (© 626/405-2100; www.huntington.org), they've added a new **Chinese Garden** that is the largest classical garden outside mainland China and is landscaped with 12 acres of plants native to China.

RESTAURANTS The big news this year is the opening of **Katsuya Hollywood** (© 323/871-8777; www.sbe.com/katsuya), a collaboration between designer Philippe Starck and Master Sushi Chef Katsuya Uechi. If you want to spot celebrities on your vacation it's a good place to start (assuming you can get a reservation). But if you're more into food than famous people, my top two picks this year are **Osteria Mozza** (© 323/297-0100; www.mozza-la.com) and **Fraîche** (© 310/

839-6800; www.fraicherestaurantla.com). The former is my new favorite restaurant in the city, and the latter is one of the most popular new restaurants in the city (and deservedly so).

If you're more into value with a side of kitsch, I highly recommend **Luckyfish** (© 310/274-9800; www.luckyfishsushi.com) in Beverly Hills and the **Waffle** (© 323/465-6901; www.thewaffle.us) in Hollywood. Luckyfish is a lively sushi restaurant that uses an ultramodern conveyer belt system to deliver mini-size plates of fresh fish, while the Waffle is a modern take on a diner classic, serving cornmeal jalapeño waffles and maple syrup martinis to a hip crowd.

NIGHTLIFE The irony of clubs in L.A. is that you can't get in the ones everyone talks about. If you're under 30 and have the look, you probably won't have any problem getting into some of the newer clubs, such as **Green Door** (© 323/463-0008) in Hollywood or **Winston's** (© 323/654-0105) in West Hollywood. Of course, you'll need the address because they don't have signage.

But if standing in line so a bouncer can determine your eligibility isn't your idea of a fun night out, here are a few hip alternatives that still provide that only-in-L.A. experience: The new **Bar Nineteen12** (© 310/273-1912; www.barnineteen12.com) within the Beverly Hills Hotel doubles as a good excuse to check out the legendary hotel and is an easy way to spot celebrities; **Nic's Beverly Hills** (© 310/550-5707; www.nicsbeverlyhills.com) serves the city's best martinis in a lively, snob-free setting, despite its central B.H. location; and **Glow** (© 310/578-4152; www.glow-bar.com) at the Marriott in Marina Del Rey is the sexiest hotel lounge I've ever seen. All three are good bets for a fun night in L.A.

The Best of Los Angeles

Like Las Vegas, the allure of L.A.—for better or for worse—is undeniable. Angelenos know their city will never have the sophisticated style of Paris or the historical riches of London, but they cheerfully lay claim to living in the most entertaining city in the United States, if not the world. It really is warm and sunny most days of the year, movie stars actually do live and dine among the commoners, and you can't swing a cellphone without hitting a rollerblading blonde at the beach.

This part of the L.A. mystique—however exaggerated it may be—truly does exist, and it's not hard to find. In fact, it's fitting that L.A. is home to the world's first amusement park because it regularly feels like one, as the line between fantasy and reality is often obscured. From the anachronistic glamour of Beverly Hills to the vibrant street energy of the Venice Boardwalk, each of the city's diverse neighborhoods is like a mini–theme park, offering its own kind of unique adventure. Drive down Sunset Boulevard and you'll see what I mean: The billboards are racier, the fashions trendier, the cars fancier, the bodies sexier, the sun brighter, and the energy higher than any place you've ever been. Darlin', you ain't in Kansas anymore—you're in La-La Land. Let's go play.

1 The Most Unforgettable Travel Experiences

- **Cruising Along the Coast:** Driving along the sunny coastline with the top down and your hair blowing in the warm wind is the quintessential Southern California experience—one that never loses its appeal, even for locals. Stop and visit whatever interests you: a Malibu cantina, the famous Santa Monica pier, or a South Bay beach—a casual cruise along the shoreline is good for the soul (B.Y.O. Mustang convertible). See chapter 11, "Side Trips from Los Angeles," for destination ideas.

- **Visiting Venice Beach's Ocean Front Walk:** You haven't visited L.A. properly until you've rented some skates in Venice and embarrassed yourself in front of thousands while taking in the human carnival around you. Nosh on a Jody Maroni's "haute dog," buy some knockoff sunglasses, and realize how pathetically out of shape you are compared to all the tan and trim locals—all while enjoying the wide beach, blue sea, and assorted performers along the boardwalk. Can't skate? Cowards can rent a bicycle and pedal along the bike path. See p. 172.

- **Basking at the Beach:** This is, after all, L.A.—so get thy buttocks to a beach. Watch a volleyball tournament at Hermosa Beach, take surf lessons at Manhattan Beach, or gawk at the world's vainest weight lifters pumping iron at Venice Beach. Surfers are always spotted at the Malibu beaches, and local families prefer to pitch their umbrellas at Zuma Beach. See chapter 7.

- **Visiting the "Happiest Place on Earth," the Disneyland Resort:** The resort's worldwide appeal is evident in the virtual United Nations of revelers traipsing through Adventureland, Fantasyland, Tomorrowland, and Disney's California Adventure park. It won't be long before the song "It's a Small World" seems permanently stuck in your head. See chapter 8.

- **Dining at Spago (or the Ivy or the Palm):** Dining at one of L.A.'s über-trendy A-list celebrity haunts is an experience to be filed under "Only in L.A." Hear dialogue straight out of *Entourage* while eating fine food prepared for the world's pickiest eaters ("I can't eat *that!* Take it away."). See chapter 6.

- **Cruising Sunset Boulevard:** It's a must for first-time visitors because you'll see a cross section of everything that is L.A.: legendary clubs, studios, and hotels that you'll instantly recognize from the silver screen and TV shows. The journey ends with a trip to Malibu's fabled beaches, where those classy *Baywatch* episodes were filmed (how perfect). See p. 169.

- **Touring the Getty Center:** See the result of unlimited funds and very expensive tastes at this multifaceted cultural center looming large over the city. The ultramodern facility, more airy and inviting than it looks from below, features a museum housing the impressive art collection of deep-pocketed industrialist J. Paul Getty, a postmodern garden, and breathtaking views of L.A. A sleekly high-tech funicular whisks you from freeway level to this virtual city in the clouds. See p. 159.

- **Spending a Day Downtown:** If you're looking for a healthy dose of ethnic culture, you'll find it in Downtown L.A. Take a self-guided tour of the mind-blowing Walt Disney Concert Hall (p. 172) or cutting-edge Museum of Contemporary Art (p. 180), stop in for a snack at the bustling Grand Central Market (p. 250), pick up some inexpensive Mexican handicrafts along colorful and historic Olvera Street, and have dim sum in Chinatown. See chapter 7.

- **Power Shopping:** You'll see "I'd Rather Be Shopping at Nordstrom" license-plate frames on Lexuses all over L.A., evidence that spending money is a major pastime here. Whether it's $5 vintage bowling shirts, $10,000 Beverly Hills baubles, or anything in between, you're sure to find it in L.A.'s cornucopia of consumerism. My favorite shopping zones are the eclectic shops along Abbot Kinney Boulevard, the endless ethnic oddities at the Grand Central Market in Downtown L.A., and the ultratrendy stores such as GR2 and Giant Robot along Sawtelle Boulevard in Japantown (p. 245). (Also, check out the sidebar "Where to Find Hollywood's Hand-Me-Downs" on p. 260.) See chapter 9.

- **Strolling Wilshire Boulevard's Museum Row:** Natural history meets pop culture meets modern art along Museum Row. La Brea Tar Pits, Petersen Automotive Museum, Craft & Folk Art Museum, and Los Angeles County Museum of Art are all shoulder-to-shoulder in the heart of L.A. The only problem is that it's too much to see in a single day. See chapter 7.

- **Taking a Gourmet Picnic to the Hollywood Bowl:** What better way to spend a typically warm L.A. evening than under the stars with a picnic basket, a bottle of wine, and some world-class entertainment? In addition to being the summer home of the Los Angeles Philharmonic, the

Bowl hosts visiting performers ranging from chamber music quartets to jazz greats to folk humorists. The imposing white Frank Lloyd Wright–designed band shell always elicits appreciative gasps from first-time Bowl-goers. See p. 278.

- **Taking a Tour of the Walt Disney Concert Hall:** Built with a lot of Disney money but without a trace of goofiness, this stunning accomplishment of art and architecture is the crown jewel of Downtown. You'd have to fly to Spain to see architect Frank Gehry's similar architectural masterpiece, the Guggenheim Bilbao. The dramatically curvaceous stainless-steel exterior houses one of the most acoustically perfect concert halls in the world. The self-guided audio walking tour, narrated by actor John Lithgow, is superb. See p. 187.

- **Taking a Studio Tour:** This is why you're vacationing in L.A.—to see where movie magic is being made. Studio tours are an entertaining opportunity to get a peek at the stage sets for sitcom and talk shows (sometimes during filming), and you never know who you're going to see emerging from his or her Star Wagon. See the "Studio Tours" section on p. 199.

- **Visiting Santa Catalina Island:** Taking a day trip to Catalina makes for a most adventurous day: a scenic boat ride; oodles of shopping, snorkeling, and scuba diving; golf; hiking trails; waffle cones; sunburns; and DUI-free barhopping. *Tip:* The helicopter taxi is a lot cheaper than you'd expect. See chapter 11.

2 The Best Splurge Hotels

- **Beverly Hills Hotel and Bungalows** (9641 Sunset Blvd., Beverly Hills; ✆ 800/283-8885): Spending at least 1 night at this Hollywood icon is well worth the heavy hit to your credit card. Take afternoon tea in the famous Polo Lounge next to Ozzy Osbourne, swim laps in the same pool Katharine Hepburn once dove into fully clothed, and eat pancakes in the fabled Fountain Coffee Shop. Ah, yes, the Pink Palace is still the place to relive Hollywood's Golden Age. See p. 82.

- **Chateau Marmont** (8221 Sunset Blvd., West Hollywood; ✆ 800/242-8328): Modeled after an elegant Loire Valley castle, the 1920s-era Chateau oozes Old Hollywood. Secreted above the Sunset Strip, it has ghosts from the past that include Greta Garbo, Errol Flynn, Natalie Wood, Marlon Brando, James Dean, Marilyn Monroe, Clark Gable, and Jean Harlow. See p. 89.

- **Sunset Tower Hotel** (8358 Sunset Blvd., West Hollywood; ✆ 800/225-2637): Elizabeth Taylor, Joan Crawford, John Wayne, Frank Sinatra—they've all been tenants at the storied Sunset Tower Hotel. The Tower has everything you could hope for in a Los Angeles hotel: elegance, impeccable service, beautiful views, Deco-era decor, and the ideal Sunset Strip location. See p. 92.

- **Millennium Biltmore Hotel Los Angeles** (506 S. Grand Ave., Downtown; ✆ 800/245-8673): Eye-poppingly magnificent, the Biltmore has been hosting royalty, U.S. presidents, and international celebs since 1923. You've seen it in *Chinatown, Ghostbusters, Bugsy,* and *Beverly Hills Cop*—now see it for real. See p. 102.

- **The Mosaic Hotel Beverly Hills** (125 S. Spalding Dr., Beverly Hills; ✆ 800/463-4466): You'll want to redecorate your own bedroom by the time you check out of this gorgeous boutique hotel. Huge rainforest shower heads, Frette linens, Bulgari bath products, Wolfgang Puck refreshments, and piles of pillows all add up to hotel heaven. It's the perfect blend of art, luxury, service, prime location, and value. See p. 91.

- **Shutters on the Beach** (1 Pico Blvd., Santa Monica; ✆ **800/334-9000**): If a luxurious oceanfront room at Shutters doesn't add romance to your relationship, it's hard to imagine what will. It's like staying at a really rich friend's East Coast beach house. See p. 74.

- **Casa del Mar** (1910 Ocean Way, Santa Monica; ✆ **800/898-6999**): This impeccably restored Renaissance Revival–style hotel is the grande dame of L.A.'s beachfront hotels, ideally situated in the midst of the Santa Monica scene and offering panoramic views of the ocean from every room. Be sure to book the "All About Me" spa package for ultimate indulgence. See p. 69.

- **Huntley Santa Monica Beach** (1111 2nd St., Santa Monica; ✆ **310/394-5454**): Tucked away on the edge of a quiet Santa Monica neighborhood is my favorite Santa Monica hotel, one that combines a superb location with excellent service and strikingly stylish decor. The Huntley's 18th-floor **Penthouse** restaurant, bar, and lounge has the best nightlife scene in Santa Monica. See p. 78.

- **The Ambrose** (1255 20th St., Santa Monica; ✆ **310/315-1555**): Take a break from the fast-paced L.A. scene at this stylish 77-room boutique Arts and Crafts hideaway that offers a soothing, peaceful environment—tranquil Japanese garden, koi pond, trickling fountains—and plenty of free perks (including complimentary taxi shuttle service). See p. 77.

- **Raffles L'Ermitage** (9291 Burton Way Beverly Hills; ✆ **800/768-9009**). The melding of luxury, service, and business perks is incomparable. Extra-large executive work desks, personal cellphones, and complimentary stationery with your personal direct-dial number printed on it are all part of the package. See p. 87.

- **Beach House Hotel Hermosa Beach** (1300 The Strand, Hermosa Beach; ✆ **888/895-4559**): Romance-seeking couples will never want to leave this beautiful boutique resort offering plush, luxury-laden studio suites. Book one overlooking the sand and sunbathers for the ultimate beach getaway. See p. 75.

3 The Best Moderately Priced Hotels

- **Casa Malibu** (22752 Pacific Coast Hwy., Malibu; ✆ **800/831-0858**): This well-maintained hotel has a terrific beachfront location. Innkeepers don't come any friendlier, and oceanfront Malibu accommodations don't get more affordable. See p. 80.

- **The Hotel California** (1670 Ocean Ave., Santa Monica; ✆ **866/571-0000**): You'll like livin' it up at this hacienda-style beachfront motel that charges less than half the price of its fancy-pants neighbors. You'll dig the hotel's surfer/sun-worshiper ambience, cheery rooms with California-themed decor, and direct access to the sand via a private path. See p. 77.

- **Carlyle Inn** (1119 S. Robertson Blvd.; ✆ **800/322-7595**): This hidden gem, cleverly tucked away in the heart of West L.A., offers a pleasing courtyard setting, a dash of Deco-inspired style in the guest rooms, and abundant freebies—including a generous breakfast spread and weekday wine and hors d'oeuvres. It's a real find for those in search of value-priced comforts. See p. 93.

- **Elan Hotel** (8435 Beverly Blvd., Los Angeles; (C) **888/611-0398**): This former retirement home has been transformed into one of L.A.'s best boutique-style hotels (and one of the city's best values). Its Beverly Boulevard location isn't pretty, but it's within walking distance of dozens of restaurants and Hollywood attractions. See p. 94.
- **Inn at Playa del Rey** (435 Culver Blvd., Playa del Rey; (C) **310/574-1920**): If you crave the slower pace and personal attention that only a bed-and-breakfast can offer, book a room at this inn, which merges easy airport access with a one-of-a-kind

natural setting, thoughtful service, and luxury comforts. The spacious View Suites—complete with a two-sided fireplace that casts a romantic glow on the king-size bed and the Jacuzzi for two—are the ideal choice for celebrating couples. See p. 76.

- **Figueroa Hotel** (939 S. Figueroa St., Los Angeles; (C) **800/421-9092**): My favorite Downtown lodging is this venerable 1925 building re-created as a Spanish colonial–Gothic palace. Fun and funky, the exotically decorated guest rooms have far more style than your average hotel; what's more, this gentrified corner of Downtown offers easy, car-free Metro Line access to Hollywood and Universal Studios. See p. 100.

4 The Most Unforgettable Dining Experiences

- **Grace** (7360 Beverly Blvd., Los Angeles; (C) **323/934-4400**): The best overall dining experience in Los Angeles. Iron Chef Neal Fraser was trained by America's finest chefs, and it shows (the foie gras served two ways alone is worth the trip). Sophisticated yet unpretentious, Grace is a splurge worth making. See p. 138.
- **Pizzeria Mozza & Osteria Mozza** (641 N. Highland Ave., Los Angeles; (C) **323/297-0101;** and 6602 Melrose Ave., Los Angeles (C) **323/297-0100**): I would marry celeb-chef Nancy Silverton in a heartbeat just to have an excuse to never leave at her two restaurants: Pizzeria Mozza and Osteria Mozza. Every time I eat here I spend the next few days dreamily contemplating how simple yet brilliant my meal was. See p. 142 and 143.
- **Koi** (730 N. La Cienega Blvd., West Hollywood; (C) **310/659-9449**): The combination of soothing feng shui ambience and superb Asian fusion cuisine has made Koi one of the hottest restaurants in L.A. Hollywood's

biggest celebrities—George Clooney, Jennifer Garner, Lindsay Lohan, Demi and Ashton—dine here often to nosh on addictive dishes such as baked crab rolls with edible rice paper and miso-bronzed black cod. See p. 133.

- **Saddle Peak Lodge** (419 Cold Canyon Rd., Calabasas; (C) **818/222-3888**): In L.A., a romantic restaurant is one without cellphone service (that would be in the hills above Malibu). This converted hunting lodge is quite the quixotic setting for a meaty meal for two. Candlelit tables, a crackling fireplace, and a *Wine Spectator*–award-winning wine list are sure bets for creating *la mood d'amour*. See p. 143.
- **The Little Door** (8164 W. 3rd St., Los Angeles; (C) **323/951-1210**): Consistently voted one of L.A.'s most romantic restaurants is this French/Mediterranean charmer hidden behind a little door on 3rd Street. Sit at the shaded patio among the fragrant bougainvillea while sipping champagne and you'd swear you're in Provence. See p. 141.

- **Beacon** (3280 Helms Ave., Culver City; ☎ **310/838-7500**): Chef Kazuto Matsusaka serves Spago-quality Asian fusion at a fraction of the price at this humble Culver City hot spot. The warm crispy oysters in lettuce cups, stir-fried mushroom salad, and miso-marinated black cod are fantastic. See p. 130.
- **Mastro's Steakhouse** (246 N. Canon Dr., Beverly Hills; ☎ **310/888-8782**): You'll find Fred Flintstone–size slabs of hand-cut USDA beef, oysters the size of your palm, and a big pile of creamy mashed potatoes mixed with sour cream, chives, bacon, and butter. God bless America. See p. 128.
- **La Cachette** (10506 Santa Monica Blvd., Century City; ☎ **310/470-4992**): Jean François Meteigner, owner and executive chef of this *tres romantique* restaurant, is one of America's most influential French chefs, and his *cuisine naturelle* menu is full of flavor while 90% free of cream and butter. See p. 127.
- **The Hump** (3221 Donald Douglas Loop Rd., Santa Monica; ☎ **310/313-0977**): Claim a sushi bar as L.A.'s best—and I think this is the best—and you're sure to start an argument. The chefs at the Hump are deadly serious about their sushi: Flown in daily from Tokyo's Tsukiji and Fukuoka fish markets in oxygen-filled containers, it's so fresh that there's a sign at the entrance warning the faint-of-heart that the meat's still moving. See p. 117.
- **Restaurant Hama** (213 Windward Ave., Venice; ☎ **310/396-8783**): It's the always-festive atmosphere that makes everyone feel welcome at this lively Japanese restaurant. Party along with the six cheery sushi chefs as they slice, dice, and drink many rounds of beers and sake. By closing time, everyone's singing along to "Hotel California." See p. 121.
- **Frida** (236 S. Beverly Dr., Beverly Hills; ☎ **310/278-7666**): This Mexican restaurant's cuisine is so authentic the executive chef's ancestors are responsible for the recipes (the mole dishes alone are worth the drive over here). Bite into a handmade soft taco brimming with sautéed shrimp bathed in a dark, tangy pasilla-orange sauce, and you'll see what I mean. See p. 132.
- **Providence** (5855 Melrose Ave., Los Angeles; ☎ **323/460-4170**): Chef Michael Cimarusti serves the city's best seafood at this sleek, modern newcomer. I didn't even know I liked sea urchin until I tasted Michael's masterpieces. See p. 129.
- **House of Blues Gospel Brunch** (8430 Sunset Blvd., West Hollywood; ☎ **323/848-5100**): For more than a decade the HOB has hosted a raucous Sunday brunch that's simmering with high-energy gospel music and all-you-can-eat Southern home cookin'. It's a booty-shaking brunch. See p. 144.

5 The Best Things to Do for Free (or Almost)

- **Watching One of Your Favorite TV Sitcoms Being Taped:** Alternately boring and fascinating (the old hurry-up-and-wait syndrome), being an audience member gives you the chance to wander the soundstage, marvel at the cheesy three-wall sets that look so real on TV, and get an inside look at the bloopers that never make it to broadcast—and are often far more entertaining than the scripted dialogue. See "Live-Audience TV Tapings" on p. 202.

- **Going to the Getty Center:** I already mentioned it above and I'll mention it again here because one of L.A.'s best attractions is absolutely free (JPG doesn't need your money). See p. 159.

- **Paying Your Respects at the Cemeteries of the Stars:** Spend some downtime with Humphrey Bogart, Clark Gable, Karen Carpenter, and all their famous pals at L.A.'s most enduring celebrity hangouts. Six public cemeteries showcase the final performances of Bette Davis, Lucille Ball, Marilyn Monroe, and dozens more famous names. See p. 204.

- **Cruising Mulholland Drive:** Ride past the homes with million-dollar views, and then pull over at the public viewing pullouts to see the splayed-out city in all its smoggy glory. It's even more romantic at night, when the lights of the city and the valley twinkle below. See p. 198.

- **Free Admission Days to L.A.'s Museums:** If it's free, baby, it's for me. Almost all of L.A.'s art galleries and museums are open free to the public 1 day of the week or month (or both), and several never charge admission. See p. 175.

- **Evening Jazz Performances:** The Los Angeles County Museum of Art offers free jazz concerts every Thursday and Friday evening. It's the perfect coda to a satisfying day of art appreciation. See p. 270.

- **Hollywood Bowl Rehearsals:** Few people know about the Bowl's morning rehearsals, which are open to the public and absolutely free. Bring coffee and doughnuts and enjoy the best seats in the house. See p. 281.

6 The Best Outdoor Experiences

- **Learning How to Surf:** What could be more fun during your L.A. vacation than learning how to surf on the same breaks that the Beach Boys surfed? Surfing schools such as **Learn to Surf L.A.** in Manhattan Beach will guarantee you'll get up on a longboard and be surfing the easy waves in one short lesson. See p. 215.

- **Flying a World War II Fighter Aircraft:** Don your parachute, strap yourself into the 600-horsepower fighter aircraft, and prepare to have your mind blown as you (yes, you) perform aerobatic maneuvers—loops, rolls, lazy-8s—high above the California coastline. There's an aviation company in Carlsbad that gives nonpilots the chance to fly in a 1920s-era biplane ride, and to actually fly—as in control the stick—other toys on the tarmac, including a pair of modern prop-driven dogfighters. It's an experience you'll never forget. See p. 295.

- **Dining by Helicopter:** Impress your sweetie with a helicopter tour of the city that ends with a front-door drop-off at a romantic restaurant. Get that ring ready. See p. 201.

- **Taking a Sunset Margarita Horse Ride:** Whoever thought this one up is a genius: Drive to Sunset Ranch Hollywood Stables in Griffith Park, hop on a big ol' horse, and take a scenic ride through the park to a Mexican restaurant in Burbank. Eat, drink, and be merry; then ride back to the ranch under warm, starry skies. See p. 165.

- **Watching a Polo Match:** Mid-April through early October, polo matches are held on weekends at the Will Rogers Polo Club. Enjoy a leisurely picnic lunch among the wide green fields, mighty oaks, and whitewashed fences. See p. 218.

7 The Best Offbeat Experiences

- **Dining in the Dark** (© **800/710-1270;** www.darkdining.com): Only in L.A. would you have the opportunity to experience a three-course dinner served by sight-impaired waitstaff in pitch blackness. Yes, it's as weird as it sounds and an evening you'll never forget. See p. 140.

- **Attending Movie Screenings in a Cemetery:** Pack a picnic basket and head to the Hollywood Forever Cemetery for a summer Saturday evening of classic cinema projected onto the mortuary wall. Arrive early, because people are just dying to get here. (6000 Santa Monica Blvd., Hollywood; www.cinespia.org). See p. 283.

- **Auditioning as a Game Show Contestant:** You too could be the next contestant on *The Price Is Right* or *Wheel of Fortune.* Fame and fortune are just a phone call away, so set up that audition before you arrive in L.A. See p. 203.

- **Going to ArcLight Cinemas** (6360 W. Sunset Blvd., Hollywood; © **323/464-4226**): "The World's Most Private Public Theater" hosts 21-and-over movie screenings where you can sip cocktails while watching first-run flicks. Seats are reserved in advance, ushers keep it quiet, late arrivals are forbidden, and there's even a lounge serving appetizers. See p. 284.

- **Visiting Roscoe's House of Chicken 'n' Waffles** (1514 N. Gower St., Hollywood; © **323/466-7453**): You haven't seen everything until you've seen Southern-fried chicken and waffles on the same plate. Roscoe's is a Hollywood institution where a polyglot of L.A.'s population comes for chicken-and-cheese omelets and sweet-potato pie. The friendly atmosphere and creative combinations make for a fun, adventuresome, and inexpensive dining experience. See p. 145.

- **Listening to Jon Brion:** Make reservations far in advance to see producer, songwriter, and multi-instrumentalist legend Jon Brion play at the Largo supper club (432 N. Fairfax Ave., Los Angeles; © **323/852-1073;** www.largo-la.com). His ability to make up songs on the spot from titles shouted from the audience is mind-blowing. See p. 268.

- **Eating Crickets:** If you want to train for a *Survivor* tryout, try several servings of stir-fried Taiwanese spicy crickets, dried Manchurian ants, and Thai-style crispy white sea worms at **Typhoon** (3221 Donald Douglas Loop Rd., Santa Monica; © **310/390-6565**). See p. 117.

2

Los Angeles in Depth

Los Angeles ranks as the second-largest city in the nation; its citizens hail from 140 countries and speak 86 different languages. In fact, Los Angeles is one of only two U.S. cities without a majority population.

But unlike many of the world's greatest metropolitan destinations, L.A. is seen more in the context of the present—even the future—than the past. This young city is all the more intriguing because that past is fresh and easily excavated (both figuratively and literally); the sense of simultaneously having one foot in yesterday and one in tomorrow is part of what makes discovering L.A. so rewarding. In this chapter, we give you a little rundown on the history of El Pueblo de Nuestra Senora la Reina de Los Angeles (the Town of Our Lady the Queen of the Angels), along with some other useful background on the local views and customs that give an insight into the city and its inhabitants.

1 Los Angeles Today

Having survived a long, leisurely pioneering infancy, and a slightly uncouth adolescence, Los Angeles has blossomed into one of the world's major cultural centers. The movies, TV, and music produced here are seen and heard throughout the world; the pop products of the city's efforts govern who we are, how we spend our time, and how we think more than we like to admit.

As Los Angeles hurtles into the 21st century, the city is going through some drastic changes. Intense growth and increased ethnic diversity have fueled a climate of political and philosophical change; in many ways, there are two L.A.s, existing in parallel universes. There's the beautiful showbiz town, home of starlets and hunks who cruise palm-tree-lined streets in sleek convertibles on their way to the studio. The other universe is a multi-ethnic Pacific Rim metropolis, swelling uncomfortably from the influx of new residents, yet enriching the city with cultural diversity. In this other L.A., you'll encounter Vietnamese, Ethiopian, Russian, and Ecuadorian enclaves in formerly run-down parts of town. You'll find a city straining to grow technologically into a new century, right next to the town eager to preserve its golden (and sometimes isolationist) roots.

2 Looking Back at Los Angeles

IN THE BEGINNING

Los Angeles was founded by the Spanish on the site of a Native American village in 1781, but it wasn't until after the first film studio was established, in 1911, that Los Angeles really took off. Within 5 years, movies such as D. W. Griffith's *Birth of a Nation* were being produced by the hundreds. By World War I, the Hollywood studio system was firmly entrenched, with the young trio of Charlie Chaplin, Douglas Fairbanks, and "America's Sweetheart," Mary Pickford, at its fore.

As the box office boomed in the 1920s and 1930s, so did the population of Los Angeles. Easterners came to the burgeoning urban paradise in droves in order to find their fortunes. The world-famous Hollywood sign, erected in 1923, was built as an advertisement for just one of many fledgling real-estate developments that began to crop up on the "outskirts" of the city. Los Angeles, and Hollywood, was even more alluring during the Great Depression. As Americans ached for an escape from their less-than-inspiring reality, Hollywood's cinematic fantasies were there to oblige. With each glamorous, idyllic portrayal of California, Los Angeles's popularity—and population—grew.

QUEST FOR WATER As the city expanded, so did the need for water. Most great American cities grew from small settlements on rivers or lakes, freshwater sources vital to everyday life and commerce. Not L.A.—it was founded in the middle of an arid basin. The Los Angeles River has always been too unpredictable to support the city's growth, and today it is merely a series of flood-control channels operated by the Department of Water and Power. The quest for water has provided some of L.A.'s most gripping real-life drama. As early as 1799, Spanish padres at the new Mission San Fernando dammed the river to provide for their water needs, causing an uprising among settlers downstream. Disputes continued up to the incidents that inspired the movie *Chinatown,* about the early battle for the rights to the Owens Valley's abundant water, which William Mulholland and Fred Eaton "stole" with their new California aqueduct. Resentment from Northern California continues up to the present time, as L.A. residents continue to reap the agricultural, domestic, and electrical benefits of what many claim is never rightfully theirs.

THE TRIUMPH OF CAR CULTURE
The opening of the Arroyo Seco Parkway in 1940, linking Downtown L.A. and Pasadena with the first of what would be a network of freeways, ushered in a new era for the city. From that time on, car culture flourished in Los Angeles, becoming perhaps the city's most distinctive feature. (For more on this subject, see "From Horseless Carriages to Hot Rods," below.) America's automotive industry successfully conspired to undermine Los

Timeline

- **1781** Los Angeles is founded.
- **1821** Spain grants independence to Mexico and, therefore, to California.
- **1850** California becomes the 31st state.
- **1875** The Santa Fe Railroad reaches Los Angeles.
- **1881** The *Los Angeles Times* begins publication.

- **1892** Oil is discovered in Downtown Los Angeles.
- **1900** The population of California approaches 1.5 million; Los Angeles has more than 102,000 residents.
- **1902** The first movie house, the Electric Theatre, opens.
- **1909** Santa Monica Pier is erected to accommodate cargo and passenger ships.
- **1911** Hollywood's first film studio is established.

- **1912** More than 16 motion-picture companies are operating out of Hollywood.
- **1913** Cecil B. DeMille directs the film industry's first full-length feature, *The Squaw Man.*
- **1923** The Hollywood sign (which at the time read HOLLYWOODLAND) is erected to advertise a real-estate development.

Angeles's public transportation system by halting the trolley service that once plied Downtown and advocating the construction of auto-friendly roads. The growth of the freeways led to the development of L.A.'s suburban sprawl, turning Los Angeles into a city without a single geographical focus. The suburbs became firmly entrenched in the L.A. landscape during World War II, when shipyards and munitions factories, as well as aerospace giants McDonnell Douglas, Lockheed, Rockwell, and General Dynamics, opened their doors in Southern California and the workers who flocked here needed affordable housing.

THE POSTWAR ERA   After the war, the threat of television put the movie industry into a tailspin. But instead of being destroyed by the "tube," Hollywood was strengthened when that industry made its home here as well. Soon afterward, in the 1950s and 1960s, the avant-garde discovered Los Angeles, too; the city became popular with artists, beatniks, and hippies, many of whom settled in Venice.

The 1970s gave rise to a number of exotic religions and cults that found eager adherents in Southern California. The spiritual "New Age" born in the "Me" decade found life into the 1980s, in the face of a population growing beyond manageable limits, an increasingly polluted environment, and escalating social ills. At the same time, California became very rich. Real-estate values soared, banks and businesses prospered, and the entertainment industry boomed.

THE NEW MILLENNIUM   Today, as always, Angelenos are on the leading edge of American pop culture. But they've discovered, as the world wags its finger and shakes its collective head, that success isn't always all it's cracked up to be. The nation's economic, social, and environmental problems have become the city's own, and even become amplified in this larger-than-life arena. The 1991 Rodney King beating and subsequent 1992 rioting, the 1994 Northridge earthquake, the 1996 acquittal of O. J. Simpson, the 1998 *El Niño* floods, the LAPD Rampart scandal in 2000—half the city proclaimed these disasters as signaling the beginning of the end, declaring each time that L.A. would never fully recover. The other half optimistically predicted that adversity would unite the fragmented city and it would emerge, phoenix-like, stronger than ever. Both factions were partially correct—but mostly the city has just gone on with the business of being L.A.

- **1927** The first "talkie" is released: *The Jazz Singer* with Al Jolson.
- **1929** The Academy of Motion Picture Arts and Sciences bestows its first Oscar.
- **1940** L.A.'s first freeway, the Arroyo Seco Parkway, connects Hollywood and Pasadena.
- **1947** The first TV station west of the Mississippi, KTLA, begins broadcasting.
- **1950** L.A.'s population is nearly two million.

- **1955** Disneyland opens.
- **1961** Hollywood's Walk of Fame is started by the Hollywood Chamber of Commerce.
- **1962** California overtakes New York as the nation's most populous state.
- **1965** Tension between white LAPD officers and the black community fuels riots in Watts.
- **1968** Robert F. Kennedy is fatally shot at the Ambassador Hotel after winning

California's Democratic Party presidential primary.
- **1980** L.A.'s population is nearly three million.
- **1984** Los Angeles hosts the Summer Olympic Games.
- **1992** More than 40 die and hundreds are injured in the race riots resulting from the acquittal of the police officers involved in the Rodney King hearing.

continues

3 Art & Architecture

The movie industry, more than anything else, has defined Los Angeles. The process of moviemaking has never been confined to studio offices and back lots; it spills into the city's streets and other public spaces. The city itself is an extension of the movie set, and Angelenos have always seen it that way. All of Los Angeles has an air of Hollywood surreality (or disposability), even in its architecture. The whole city seems a bit larger than life. As a result, L.A. is a veritable Disneyland of architecture and is home to an amalgam of distinctive styles, from Art Deco to Spanish Revival, to coffee-shop kitsch, to suburban ranch, to postmodern—and much more.

Between 1945 and 1966, *Arts & Architecture* magazine focused the design world's attention on L.A. with its series of "Case Study Houses," prototypes for postwar living, which were designed by prominent émigrés like Pierre Koenig, Richard Neutra, and Eero Saarinen. Los Angeles has taken some criticism for not being a "serious" architectural center, but in terms of innovation and style, the city gets high marks.

Although much of it is gone, you can still find some prime examples of the kitschy roadside art that defined L.A. in earlier days. The famous Brown Derby is no more, but you can still find a neon-lit **1950s gas station/spaceship** (at the corner of Little Santa Monica Blvd. and Crescent Dr. in Beverly Hills), in addition to some newer structures carrying on the tradition, such as the **Chiat/Day offices** in Venice (see below).

SANTA MONICA & THE BEACHES
When you're strolling the historic canals and streets of Venice, be sure to check out the **Chiat/Day** offices at 340 Main St. What would otherwise be an unspectacular contemporary office building is made fantastic by a **three-story pair of binoculars** that frames the entrance. The sculpture is modeled after a design created by Claes Oldenburg and Coosje van Bruggen.

The spacey *Jetsons*-style **Theme Building,** which has always loomed over Los Angeles International Airport, has been joined by a more recent silhouette. The main LAX **control tower,** designed by local architect Kate Diamond to evoke a stylized palm tree, is tailored to present Southern California in its best light. You can go inside to enjoy the view from the Theme Building's observation deck, or have a space-age cocktail at the Technicolor bachelor pad that is the **Encounter at LAX** restaurant.

- **1994** An earthquake measuring 6.8 on the Richter scale shakes the city.
- **1996** At the conclusion of the "Crime of the Century" trial, O. J. Simpson is found not guilty of the murders of Nicole Brown Simpson and Ron Goldman.
- **1997** The J. Paul Getty Center opens on a Brentwood hilltop overlooking L.A.
- **1998** *El Niño* conditions over the Pacific bring torrential rain, flooding, and landslides to Southern California.
- **2000** The country's largest police scandal erupts in L.A., with dozens of Rampart Division officers incriminated in illegal activity.
- **2005** Antonio Villaraigosa is elected mayor of Los Angeles—he is the first Latino mayor since Cristobal Aguilar in 1872.
- **2006** The Griffith Observatory reopens in November after a $93-million, 4-year renovation.

Constructed on a broad cliff with a steep face, the **Wayfarers Chapel** in Rancho Palos Verdes enjoys a fantastic spot overlooking the waves of the Pacific. It was designed by Lloyd Wright, son of celebrated architect Frank Lloyd Wright. Known locally as the "glass church," Wayfarers is a memorial to Emanuel Swedenborg, an 18th-century Swedish philosopher who claimed to have visions of spirits and heavenly hosts. The church is constructed of glass, redwood, and native stone.

L.A.'S WESTSIDE & BEVERLY HILLS The bold architecture and overwhelming scale of the **Pacific Design Center,** designed by Argentine architect Cesar Pelli, aroused controversy when it was erected in 1975. Sheathed in gently curving cobalt-blue glass, the seven-story building houses more than 750,000 square feet of wholesale interior-design showrooms and is known to locals as "the Blue Whale." In 1988, a second boxlike structure, dressed in equally dramatic Kelly green, was added to the design center and surrounded by a protected outdoor plaza.

A protégé of Frank Lloyd Wright and contemporary of Richard Neutra, Austrian architect Rudolph Schindler designed the innovative **Schindler House** for himself in 1921 and 1922. It's now home to the Los Angeles arm of Austria's Museum of Applied Arts (MAK). The house is noted for its complicated interlocking spaces; the interpenetration of indoors and out; simple, unadorned materials; and technological innovations. Docent-guided tours are conducted at no additional charge on weekends.

HOLLYWOOD Opened in 1956, the 13-story **Capitol Records Building** tower, just north of the legendary intersection of Hollywood and Vine, is one of the city's most recognizable buildings. The world's first circular office building is often, but incorrectly, said to have been made to resemble a stack of 45s under a turntable stylus.

Conceived by grandiose impresario Sid Grauman, the **Egyptian Theatre** is just down the street from his better-known **Chinese Theatre,** but it remains less altered from its original design, which was based on the then-headline-news discovery of hidden treasures in Pharaohs' tombs—hence the hieroglyphic murals and enormous scarab decoration above the stage. Hollywood's first movie premiere, *Robin Hood,* starring Douglas Fairbanks, was shown here in 1922. The building recently underwent a sensitive restoration by American Cinematheque, which now screens rare, classic, and independent films (see section 6 in chapter 10, "Los Angeles After Dark.").

Frank Lloyd Wright's **Freeman House,** built in 1924, was designed as an experimental prototype of mass-produced affordable housing. The home's richly patterned "textile-block" exterior is the most famous aspect of the home's design. Situated on a dramatic site overlooking Hollywood, Freeman House is built with the world's first glass-to-glass corner windows. Dancer Martha Graham, bandleader Xavier Cugat, art collector Galka Sheye, photographer Edward Weston, and architects Philip Johnson and Richard Neutra all lived or spent significant time at this house.

DOWNTOWN For a taste of what Downtown's Bunker Hill was like before the bulldozers, visit the residential neighborhood of **Angelino Heights,** near Echo Park. Entire streets are still filled with stately gingerbread Victorian homes; most still enjoy the beautiful views that led early L.A.'s elite to build here. The 1300 block of Carroll Avenue is the best preserved. Don't be surprised if a film crew is scouting locations while you're there—these blocks often appear on the silver screen.

The **Bradbury Building,** a National Historic Landmark, built in 1893 and designed by George Wyman, is Los Angeles's oldest commercial building and one of the city's most revered architectural achievements. Legend has it that an inexperienced draftsman named George Wyman accepted the $125,000 commission after communicating with his dead brother through a Ouija board. Capped by a magical five-story skylight, Bradbury's courtyard combines glazed brick, ornate Mexican tile floors, rich Belgian marble, Art Nouveau grillwork, handsome oak paneling, and lacelike wrought-iron railings—it's one of the great interior spaces of the 19th century. The glass-topped atrium is often used as a movie and TV set; you've probably seen it before in *Chinatown* and *Blade Runner.*

The **Cathedral of Our Lady of the Angels,** completed in September 2002 at a cost of $163 million and built to last 500 years, is one of L.A.'s newest architectural treasures and the third-largest cathedral in the world. It was designed by award-winning Spanish architect Jose Rafael Moneo and features a 20,000-square-foot plaza with a meditation garden, more than 6,000 crypts and niches (making it the largest crypt mausoleum in the U.S.), mission-style colonnades, biblically inspired gardens, and numerous artworks. The exterior of this austere, sand-colored structure is rather uninspiring and uninviting but the interior is breathtaking: 12,000 panes of translucent alabaster, and larger-than-life tapestries lining the walls create an awe-inspiring sense of magnificence and serenity. The 25,000-pound bronze doors, created by sculptor Robert Graham, pay homage to Ghiberti's bronze baptistery door in Florence. Free self-guided tours are available, and there's a small cafe and gift shop as well.

Built in 1928, the 27-story **Los Angeles City Hall** was the tallest building in the city for more than 30 years. The structure's distinctive ziggurat tower was designed to resemble the Mausoleum at Halicarnassus, one of the seven wonders of the ancient world. The building has been featured in numerous films and television shows, but it is probably best known as the headquarters of the *Daily Planet* in the *Superman* TV series. When it was built, City Hall was the sole exception to an ordinance outlawing buildings taller than 150 feet. Take the elevator to the rarely used 27th-floor Observation Deck—on a clear day you can see to Mount Wilson 15 miles away.

The **L.A. Central Library** is one of L.A.'s early architectural achievements and the third-largest library in the United States. The city rallied to save the library when arson nearly destroyed it in 1986; the triumphant restoration has returned much of its original splendor. Working in the early 1920s, architect Bertram G. Goodhue employed the Egyptian motifs and materials popularized by the discovery of King Tut's tomb, and combined them with a more modern use of concrete block to great effect. Walking tours are the best way to explore this old beauty; they're led Monday through Friday at 12:30pm, Saturday at 11am and 2pm, and Sunday at 2pm.

Union Station, completed in 1939, is one of the finest examples of California mission-style architecture and one of the last of America's great rail stations. With its cathedral-like size and richly paneled ticket lobby and waiting area, it has the attention to detail that characterizes 1930s WPA projects. When you're strolling through these grand historic halls, it's easy to imagine the glamorous movie stars who once boarded *The City of Los Angeles* and *The Super Chief* to journey back East during the glory days of rail travel; it's also easy to picture the many heartfelt reunions between returning soldiers and loved ones following the end of World War II, in the station's heyday.

Movies shot here include *Bugsy, The Way We Were,* and *Blade Runner.*

Designed by renowned architect I. M. Pei, **US Bank Tower** (also known as **Library Tower**) is L.A.'s most distinctive skyscraper (it's the round one) and is the tallest building between Chicago and Singapore. Built in 1989 at a cost of $450 million, the 76-story monolith is both square and rectangular, rising from its 5th Street base in a series of overlapping spirals and cubes. The Bunker Hill Steps wrapping around the west side of the building were inspired by Rome's Spanish Steps. The glass crown at the top—illuminated at night—is the highest building helipad in the world.

WATTS   Watts became notorious as the site of riots in the summer of 1965, during which 34 people were killed and more than 1,000 were injured. Today, a visit to the **Watts Towers & Art Center** is a lesson in inner-city life. Watts is a high-density land of gray strip malls, well-guarded check-cashing shops, and fast-food restaurants; but it's also a neighborhood of hardworking families struggling to survive in the midst of gangland. Although there's not much for the casual tourist here, the Watts Towers are truly a unique attraction, and the adjoining art gallery illustrates the fierce determination of area residents to maintain cultural integrity.

The Towers—the largest piece of folk art created by a single person—are colorful, 99-foot-tall cement and steel sculptures ornamented with mosaics of bottles, seashells, cups, plates, pottery, and ceramic tiles. They were completed in 1955 by folk artist Simon Rodia, an immigrant Italian tile-setter who worked on them for 33 years in his spare time. Closed in 1994 due to earthquake damage, the towers were reopened in 2001 and now attract more than 20,000 visitors annually. Tours are by request.

PASADENA & ENVIRONS   The two-story **Gamble House,** built in 1908 as a California vacation home for the wealthy family of Procter and Gamble fame, is a sublime example of Arts and Crafts architecture. The interior, designed by the famous Pasadena-based Greene & Greene architectural team, abounds with hand-craftsmanship, including intricately carved teak cornices, custom-designed furnishings, elaborate carpets, and a fantastic Tiffany glass door.

Additional elegant Greene & Greene houses (still privately owned) abound 2 blocks away along **Arroyo Terrace,** including nos. **368, 370, 400, 408, 424,** and **440.** The Gamble House bookstore can give you a walking-tour map and also conducts guided neighborhood tours by appointment.

In the late 18th century, Franciscan missionaries established 21 missions up the California coast, from San Diego to Sonoma. Each uniquely beautiful mission was built 1 day's trek from the next, along a path known as El Camino Real ("the Royal Road"), remnants of which still exist. The missions' construction marked the beginning of European settlement of California and the displacement of the Native American population. The two L.A.-area missions are located in the valleys that took their names: the San Fernando Valley and the San Gabriel Valley. A third mission, San Juan Capistrano, is located in Orange County.

Established in 1797, **Mission San Fernando** once controlled more than 1½ million acres, employed 1,500 Native Americans, and boasted more than 22,000 head of cattle and extensive orchards. The fragile adobe mission complex was destroyed several times but was always faithfully rebuilt with low buildings surrounding grassy courtyards. The aging church was replaced in the 1940s and again in the 1970s after an earthquake. The **Convento,** a 250-foot-long colonnaded structure dating from 1810, is the compound's oldest remaining building. Some of the mission's rooms, including the old library and the private salon of the first bishop of California, have been restored to their late-18th-century appearance. A half-dozen padres and many hundreds of Shoshone Indians are buried in the adjacent cemetery.

Founded in 1771, **Mission San Gabriel Arcangel** retains its original facade, notable for its high oblong windows and large capped buttresses said to have been influenced by the cathedral in Cordova, Spain. The mission's self-contained compound encompasses an aqueduct, a cemetery, a tannery, and a working winery. Within the church stands a copper font with the distinction of being the first one used to baptize a Native Californian. The most notable contents of the mission's museum are Native American paintings depicting the Stations of the Cross, done on sailcloth, with colors made from crushed desert flower petals.

4 Los Angeles in Popular Culture: Books & Automobiles

LOS ANGELES ON THE PAGE

NONFICTION In vivid detail, Edward Jay Epstein's *The Big Picture: The New Logic of Money and Power in Hollywood* (Random House, 2005) delves deep into the modern moviemaking machine with a behind-the-scenes glimpse into the "sexopoly": the six mega-media companies that control motion picture entertainment (it's a real myth-buster). Love 'em or hate 'em, the saga of the L.A. Lakers makes for good reading in *The Last Season: A Team In Search of Its Soul* by Lakers coach Phil Jackson (Penguin Press, 2004). It's a pro-athlete opera of rape charges, spoiled superstars, team meltdowns, and public feuds. Former Crips gang member Sanyika Shakur documents his life of violence, drugs, and redemption growing up in the streets of South Central L.A. in *Monster: Autobiography of an L.A. Gang Member* (Penguin Books, 1998). *L.A. Exposed: Strange Myths and Curious Legends in the City of Angels* by Paul Young (St. Martin's Press, 2002) is a compelling compendium of dispelled myths, verified rumors, crime lore, conspiracy legends, tall tales, blatant lies, political scandal, and various other fascinating accounts of past and present Los Angeles. Equally titillating is Matt Maranian and Anthony Lovett's *L.A. Bizarro: The Insiders Guide to the Obscure, the Absurd and the Perverse in Los Angeles* (St. Martin's Griffin, 1997), 192 pages of murder sites, sex shops, curiosity shops, dive bars, and various other Southern California scurrility.

FICTION Since the book's almost always better than the movie, try a few of these novels that have been adapted into successful films: James Ellroy's epic crime novel *L.A. Confidential* (Mysterious Press, 1990), Joan Didion's profoundly disturbing *Play It as It Lays* (Farrar, Straus and Giroux, 1990), Joseph Wambaugh's gripping LAPD chronicles such as *The Onion Field* (Dell, 1974), John Gregory Dunne's cynical and hard-boiled *True Confessions* (Bookthrift Co., 1977), Elmore Leonard's Hollywood-based bestseller *Get Shorty* (HarperTorch, 2002), and Michael Tolkin's absorbing mystery/thriller *The Player* (Grove Press, 1997). And, of course, anything by Raymond Chandler: *Farewell My Lovely, The Big Sleep, The Long Goodbye, The Lady in the Lake,* and *The Postman Always Rings Twice.*

FROM HORSELESS CARRIAGES TO HOT RODS

The Southern California lifestyle is so closely tied to the automobile that it has given rise to a whole subculture of the car. Since its introduction to the infant city it would grow up with, the automobile has become a pop phenomenon all its own, inextricably intertwined with the personality of L.A.—and the identities of its residents. Although the first "horseless carriages" emerged from the Midwest, it's been Hollywood's influence that has defined the entire nation's passion for the car.

During the early 1920s, movie comedians Laurel and Hardy and the Keystone Cops began to blend their brand of physical humor with the popular Ford Model T. And a visionary coach builder named Harley Earl was busy in his shop on South Main Street, building special vehicles for the movies—the Ben Hur racing chariots—and designing flamboyant custom cars for wealthy movie stars. Earl would later be recruited by General Motors, bringing along with him from Hollywood to Detroit an obsession with style over substance that would culminate in the legendary tail fins of the 1950s.

As movie director Cecil B. DeMille once said, both cars and movies capture Americans' love of motion and speed. Car culture as it was depicted in motion pictures continued to set the pace for the country. In *Rebel Without a Cause,* James Dean's troubled teenager and his hot-rodding buddies assert their independence through their jalopies in scenes filmed on the roads around the Griffith Observatory in the Hollywood Hills. As authorities cracked down on dangerous street racing, locally based *Hot Rod Magazine* helped spawn the movement to create legal drag strips, and the sport of professional drag racing was born. The art of auto-body customizing also came into being here, pioneered by George Barns, the "King of Kustomizers."

The world watched Southern California's physical landscape change to accommodate the four-wheeled resident. In postwar suburban tracts, the garage, which had traditionally been a separate shed, grew attached to the house and became the family's main entrance. The Arroyo Seco Parkway (now the Pasadena Fwy.) opened in 1940; its curvaceous lanes modeled after the landscaped parkways of the New York City metropolitan area, each turn placed to open up a series of scenic vistas for the driver. (Later L.A. freeways, reflecting a greater concern with speed, were modeled after the straight, efficient autobahns of Europe.)

Meanwhile, businesses in town built signs in an attempt to catch the eye of the driving customer; as the cars got faster, the signs got larger and brighter. A look at the gargantuan billboards on the Sunset Strip shows where that trend ended up. Another scourge of the modern landscape, the minimall, actually started innocently enough in 1927 with the first "supermarket." The term was coined by Hattem's (at the corner of Western Ave. and 43rd St.), where several grocers lined up side by side, set back from the street to provide plentiful parking and one-stop convenience for their customers.

But perhaps the most enduring feature to arise from the phenomenon of the automobile is the drive-up, drive-in, and drive-through business. In the mid-1920s, someone thought to punch through their outer wall in order to serve the motoring customer. By the next decade, Los Angeles boasted the world's largest collection of establishments that you could patronize from the privacy and comfort of your car. There were drive-up bank-teller windows, drive-through florists and dry cleaners, drive-through dairies (Alta Dena still maintains several in the Southland), and drive-up restaurants. These weren't the impersonal fast-food joints of today, but real restaurants (like the popular Dolores Drive-In chain) with cheerful carhops bringing your freshly made order to you on a window tray.

Perhaps the most popular of these drive-in landmarks are the movie theaters. Los Angeles had the second one built in the country (at the corner of Pico and Westwood boulevards). Long established as a teenage make-out haven, one theater gained popularity in a more spiritual way when Reverend Robert Schuller began to deliver Sunday-morning sermons to a comfortably parked audience at the Orange County Drive-In. His slogan: "Come as you are, in the family car."

The trend to view the car as an extension of the home persists today, with the marketing of telephones, fax machines, electric shavers, VCRs, and more, all capable of plugging in and functioning inside your car (or even coming as standard equipment). What more could the auto-loving Angeleno ask for?

5 Eating or Drinking in Los Angeles

Once upon a time, the culinary culture of Los Angeles was defined by the city's dominant Midwestern heritage. It was mostly a basic meat-and-potatoes fare, or else bad imitations of what passed for good eating in New York or Chicago. Sure, there was always Mexican and Chinese food around, but ethnic cuisine was only acceptable if it was toned down—the spices reduced and the dishes emasculated to fit in with Angelenos' bland-is-best sensibilities. In fact, for far too long the most reliable meal in the city was a burger, a side order of greasy fries, and a drink.

Happily for those seeking more civilized dining, the city's movable feast is now globally varied. As one might expect, the culinary cartography of L.A. parallels the metastasized character of our ethnic communities, with flare-ups of great food emerging in the least expected places: tucked away in anonymous strip malls and bracketed by a liquor store and a laundry, or hidden in decrepit sections of the inner city. It's no coincidence that the traditional DMZ between the East Side and the Westside, La Cienega Boulevard, is known as Restaurant Row. It used to be that the wealthy gourmands of Beverly Hills and West L.A. would head east for something a little out of the ordinary, and this was as far as they would drive. Conversely, when the citizens of the East Side wanted to splurge and step up for the night, they'd head west, winding up in the same place.

The culinary scene remained in this stalemate until the '70s when California Cuisine first hit the streets, drifting south from Alice Waters's Chez Panisse in Berkeley, daring local chefs to explore the fresh and foreign. Throw in the cacophony of herbs and spices brought to the city by the Pacific Rim immigrants, and you begin to get an idea of what's on the menu at L.A.'s forward-thinking restaurants.

Who are kitchen gods of L.A.? For starters: Wolfgang Puck, Nobu Matsuhisa, Joaquim Splichal, Tommy Tang, Nancy Silverton and Mark Peel, Toribio Prado, and Mary Sue Milliken and Susan Feniger. What's new? Dining alfresco, Indian-Asian fusion, and Mexican comfort food. Thanks to the new smoking laws, diners who have to have nicotine with their food have a whole new world to explore, in backyard patios or sidewalk tables that offer ringside seats from which to eye the busy streams of cars jockeying for position between slow red lights.

And if you're wondering about those A, B, and C ratings you see in the windows of our local eateries, they're the work of the County Public Health Department, which started rating the county's 34,000 food outlets in 1998. Food-selling establishments get inspected four times a year and more than 75% of them get an A grade, while only 3% get a C grade. But if you're worried about mouse poop in your pasta, check out www.lapublichealth.org/rating so you don't have any reservations about making your reservations.

3

Planning Your Trip to Los Angeles

Although the best vacations are the ones that allow for spontaneity, there's no substitute for a little pre-trip research when it comes to planning a great vacation. Ergo, this entire chapter contains practical information to help you prepare the perfect trip to L.A., including topical websites, recommended pre-trip arrangements, ideal times to visit, and local resources for those with specialized needs.

For additional help in planning your trip and for more on-the-ground resources in Los Angeles, please see the "Fast Facts, Toll-Free Numbers & Websites" appendix on p. 321.

1 Visitor Information

If you'd like free visitor information before you go, contact **LA INC.**, which is the snazzy moniker for the **Los Angeles Convention & Visitors Bureau** (© 800/ 228-2452 or 213/624-7300; www.discover losangeles.com). Staffers will send you a free visitor's kit, provide a schedule of upcoming events, and answer questions over the phone. They also have two walk-in visitor centers: Downtown at 685 S. Figueroa St. at West 7th Street, and in Hollywood at 6801 Hollywood Blvd. at Highland Avenue.

In addition, almost every municipality and district in Los Angeles has a dedicated tourist bureau or chamber of commerce that will be happy to send you information on a particular area.

To read numerous blogs about the Los Angeles scene, log onto **LA.COM's** blog page at www.la.com/blog, a popular travel blog site. For a more esoteric array of L.A.-based blogs, try **Metroblogging Los Angeles** at http://la.metblogs.com.

2 Entry Requirements

PASSPORTS

New regulations issued by the Department of Homeland Security now require virtually every air traveler entering the U.S. to show a passport. As of January 23, 2007, all persons, including U.S. citizens, traveling by air between the United States and Canada, Mexico, Central and South America, the Caribbean, and Bermuda are required to present a valid passport. As of January 31, 2008, U.S. and Canadian citizens entering the U. S. at land and sea ports of entry from within the Western Hemisphere need to present government-issued proof of citizenship, such as a birth certificate, along with a

Website-Seeing: The Best of L.A. Online

Keep in mind that this is a press-time snapshot of leading websites—some may have crashed, evolved, changed, or moved by the time you read this. My favorite? The **losangeles.citysearch.com** website—it has the best written, unbiased reviews and candid reader opinions of just about every hotel, restaurant, and club. **LA.com** is also excellent for planning a trip and seeing what's going on while you're in town.

- **losangeles.citysearch.com:** The local City Search site features movie/sports/entertainment listings, specialty guides like "Destination: Disney" and "Weekend Planner," online drawings for tickets and prizes, and an interactive match engine for singles.
- **la.com:** If it's open to the public in L.A., it's listed somewhere on this huge website that hosts everything from an entire "Shopping & Spas" section to a LA.COMfidential blog page filled with juicy gossip. Browsing this website alone will make you want to visit L.A.
- **theguide.latimes.com:** Hosted by the *L.A. Times,* the **Guide** is loaded with entertainment and nightlife reviews and listings in greater Los Angeles. Use the pull-down menu for categories ranging from "Theater & Dance" to "Family & Festivals." Other topics include restaurants, art and museums, and Southern California side trips. Use the search box to zoom in on whatever you're seeking. Online ticket purchasing via Ticketmaster is available as well.
- **www.at-la.com:** This is the home page of **@LA,** whose exceptional search engine provides links to close to 60,000 sites in thousands of categories relating to all of Southern California.
- **Lamag.com:** This online edition of *Los Angeles* magazine offers "The Guide," an oft-updated listing of L.A.'s theater, music scene, museums, and more, as well as an excellent "Dining Out" guide listing hundreds of restaurants organized geographically.
- **www.discoverlosangeles.com:** The **L.A. Convention & Visitors Bureau** (also known as LA INC.) lets you browse its site by region or category; view sample itineraries keyed to selected neighborhoods, activities, ethnic themes, or type of visitor; and use the "Plan Your Vacation" section to assemble a hotel/rental car/activity itinerary based on your interests.
- **www.santamonica.com:** Everything you could possibly want to know about travel and tourist information in Santa Monica is covered in this vibrant website hosted by the Convention & Visitors Bureau. Also available is an online reservation system with comprehensive information on hotels and motels.
- **www.beverlyhillscvb.com:** This official site of the Beverly Hills Visitors Bureau is as perfectly manicured as Beverly Hills itself, offering tons of practical information (including an indispensable map of parking lots, complete with rates), plus extras like a short historical walking tour, and a list of spas and salons as long as Cher's wigs.

- **www.TheatreLA.org**: Theatre L.A. is an association of live theaters and producers in Los Angeles (and the organization that puts on the yearly Ovation Awards, L.A.'s answer to Broadway's Tonys). The website is a great place to look for small and midsize productions, plus information on what's currently on sale at the half-price ticket booth (Times Tix) in West Hollywood.
- **www.visitwesthollywood.com**: The West Hollywood Convention & Visitors Bureau hosts this frequently updated guide to everything to see/do/eat/buy in WeHo, as it's come to be known. Learn about the Avenues of Art & Design (a district of L.A.'s best galleries and showrooms), plus browse extensive activity and service guides for WeHo's prominent gay and lesbian community.
- **www.tvtickets.com**: This is your online source for free tickets to dozens of sitcoms and talk shows. The site, hosted by Audiences Unlimited, Inc., includes a taping schedule, studio information, news about shows, updates on specials, and just about everything else you need to help you figure out what show you'd like to catch.
- **www.disneyland.com**: Check out the resorts, dining facilities, travel-package options, and activities and rides in the Magic Kingdom at Disneyland's official website. Get specific hours and ride closures in advance by selecting the day of your visit; this site is guaranteed to rev up your enthusiasm level. Also visit **Disneyland: Inside & Out (www.intercot west.com)**, an independent guide to Disneyland with updates on activities, rides, entertainment, and the ever-expanding Disneyland resort; consult tips on what to bring, best times of year to visit, and more.
- **www.universalstudioshollywood.com**: Take a virtual tour of the Universal Studios Hollywood attractions, view current show schedules, check out special ticket offers (and purchase tickets online), or play games based on Universal's most popular rides.
- **www.laweekly.com**: Straight from the pages of the alternative *L.A. Weekly* paper, this site combines listings with social commentary. It has an events calendar, arts listings and critiques, and restaurant reviews.
- **www.losangeles.com**: This is the L.A. feature of Boulevards New Media, whose national alternative websites emphasize travel, arts, entertainment, contemporary culture, and politics.
- **www.musictoday.com**: This is a great source of information for local music, including venues and artists (click "login," then type "Los Angeles" in the Search For Tour Dates box, and search by City). You can also purchase tickets here.
- **www.festivalfinder.com** or **www.festivalusa.com**: These sites can locate music festivals in and around Los Angeles.

government-issued photo ID, such as a driver's license. A passport is not required for U.S. or Canadian citizens entering by land or sea, but you are highly encouraged to carry one.

For information on how to obtain a passport, see "**Passports**" in the "**Fast Facts, Toll-Free Numbers & Websites**" appendix (p. 321).

VISAS

The U.S. State Department has a **Visa Waiver Program (VWP)** allowing citizens of the following countries to enter the United States without a visa for stays of up to 90 days: Andorra, Australia, Austria, Belgium, Brunei, Denmark, Finland, France, Germany, Iceland, Ireland, Italy, Japan, Liechtenstein, Luxembourg, Monaco, the Netherlands, New Zealand, Norway, Portugal, San Marino, Singapore, Slovenia, Spain, Sweden, Switzerland, and the United Kingdom. (*Note:* This list was accurate at press time; for the most up-to-date list of countries in the VWP, consult www.travel.state.gov/visa.) Canadian citizens may enter the United States without visas; they will need to show passports (if traveling by air) and proof of residence, however. *Note:* Any passport issued on or after October 26, 2006, by a VWP country must be an **e-Passport** for VWP travelers to be eligible to enter the U.S. without a visa. Citizens of these nations also need to present a round-trip air or cruise ticket upon arrival. E-Passports contain computer chips capable of storing biometric information, such as the required digital photograph of the holder. (You can identify an e-Passport by the symbol on the bottom center cover of your passport.) If your passport doesn't have this feature, you can still travel without a visa if it is a valid passport issued before October 26, 2005, and includes a machine-readable zone, or between October 26, 2005, and October 25, 2006, and includes a digital photograph. For more information, go to **www.travel.state.gov/visa**.

Citizens of all other countries must have (1) a valid passport that expires at least 6 months later than the scheduled end of their visit to the U.S., and (2) a tourist visa, which may be obtained without charge from any U.S. consulate.

As of January 2004, many international visitors traveling on visas to the United States are being photographed and fingerprinted on arrival at Customs in airports and on cruise ships in a program created by the Department of Homeland Security called **US-VISIT.** Exempt from the extra scrutiny are visitors entering by land or those (mostly in Europe; see above) that don't require a visa for short-term visits. For more information, go to the Homeland Security website at **www.dhs.gov/dhspublic**.

For specifics on how to get a visa, see "**Visas**" in the "**Fast Facts, Toll-Free Numbers & Websites**" appendix (p. 321).

MEDICAL REQUIREMENTS

Unless you're arriving from an area known to be suffering from an epidemic (particularly cholera or yellow fever), inoculations or vaccinations are not required for entry into the United States.

CUSTOMS
WHAT YOU CAN BRING INTO THE U.S.

Every visitor more than 21 years of age may bring in, free of duty, the following: (1) 1 liter of wine or hard liquor; (2) 200 cigarettes, 100 cigars (but not from Cuba), or 3 pounds of smoking tobacco; and (3) $100 worth of gifts. These exemptions are offered to travelers who spend at least 72 hours in the United States and who have not claimed them within the preceding 6 months. It is forbidden to bring into the country almost any meat products (including canned, fresh, and dried meat products such as bullion, soup mixes, and so on). Generally, condiments including vinegars, oils, spices, coffee, tea, and some cheeses and baked goods are permitted. Avoid rice products, as rice can often harbor insects. Bringing fruits and vegetables is not advised, though not prohibited. Customs will allow produce depending on where you got it and where you're going after you arrive in the U.S. Foreign tourists may carry in or out up to $10,000 in U.S. or foreign currency with no formalities; larger sums must be declared to U.S. Customs on entering or leaving, which includes filing form CM 4790. For details regarding U.S. Customs and Border Protection, consult your nearest U.S. embassy or consulate, or **U.S. Customs** (www.customs.ustreas.gov).

WHAT YOU CAN TAKE HOME FROM LOS ANGELES

Canadian Citizens: For a clear summary of Canadian rules, write for the booklet *I Declare,* issued by the Canada Border Services Agency (© **800/461-9999** in Canada, or 204/983-3500; www.cbsa-asfc.gc.ca).

U.K. Citizens: For information, contact **HM Customs & Excise** at © **0845/010-9000** (from outside the U.K., 020/8929-0152), or consult their website at **www.hmce.gov.uk**.

Australian Citizens: A helpful brochure available from Australian consulates or Customs offices is *Know Before You Go.* For more information, call the **Australian Customs Service** at © **1300/363-263,** or log on to **www.customs.gov.au**.

New Zealand Citizens: Most questions are answered in a free pamphlet available at New Zealand consulates and Customs offices: *New Zealand Customs Guide for Travellers, Notice no. 4.* For more information, contact **New Zealand Customs,** The Customhouse, 17–21 Whitmore St., Box 2218, Wellington (© **04/473-6099** or 0800/428-786; **www.customs.govt.nz**).

3 When to Go

Many visitors don't realize that Los Angeles—despite its blue ocean, swaying palm trees, green lawns, and forested foothills—is actually the high desert. But with the desert climes tempered by sea breezes, and the landscape kept green with water carried by aqueducts from all around the West, L.A. might be the most accommodating desert you've ever visited. No matter how hot it gets, low humidity usually keeps things dry and comfortable.

Tourism peaks during **summer,** when coastal hotels fill to capacity, restaurant reservations can be hard to get, and top attractions are packed with visitors and locals off from work or school. Summer can be miserable in the inland valleys, where daytime temperatures—and that famous L.A. smog—can be stifling, but the beach communities almost always

remain comfortable. Moderate temperatures, fewer crowds, and lower hotel rates make travel to L.A. most pleasurable during the **winter.** The city is at its best from early autumn to late spring, when the skies are less smoggy. Rain is rare in Los Angeles—about 34 days a year, on average—but it can cause flooding when it does sneak up on the unsuspecting city; precipitation is most likely from February to April and is virtually unheard of between May and November. Even in January, daytime temperatures reach into the 60s (teens Celsius) and higher—sometimes up to the 80s (high 20s Celsius).

Pundits claim L.A. has no seasons; it might be more accurate to say the city has its own unique seasons. Two of them are "June Gloom" and "the Santa Anas." The first refers to the ocean fog that keeps the beach cities (and often all of L.A.) overcast into early afternoon; it's most common in June but can occur any time between March and mid-August. The middle of autumn (Oct and Nov) often brings the "Santa Anas," strong, hot winds from across the desert that increase brush-fire danger (surfers love the offshore conditions they usually create).

Winds and coastal fog aside, Los Angeles remains relatively temperate year-round, with an average of 292 sunny skies each year and an average mean temperature of 66°F (19°C). It's possible to sunbathe throughout the year, but only die-hard enthusiasts and wet-suited surfers venture into the ocean in winter, when water temps hover around 50° to 55°F (10°–13°C). The water is warmest in summer and fall, usually about 65° to 70°F (18°–21°C), but, even then, the Pacific can be too chilly for many.

LOS ANGELES–AREA CALENDAR OF EVENTS

January

Tournament of Roses, Pasadena. A spectacular parade marches down Colorado Boulevard, with lavish floats, music, and extraordinary equestrian entries, followed by the Rose Bowl football game and a nightlong party along Colorado Boulevard. Call © 626/449-4100 or see www.tournamentof roses.com for details. January 1.

Native American Film Festival, Los Angeles. Cinematic works by or about Native Americans express their visions, diversity, and ideas. Call the Southwest Museum at © 323/221-2164 for the schedule and details. Mid-January.

Martin Luther King, Jr. Parade, Long Beach. This annual parade down Alameda and 7th streets ends with a festival in Martin Luther King, Jr. Park. For more information, contact the city manager at © 562/570-6711. Third Monday in January.

Bob Hope Chrysler Classic, Palm Springs area. Celebrating its 49th year in 2008, this PGA golf tournament classic raises money for charity and includes a celebrity-studded Pro-Am. For spectator information and tickets, call © 760/346-8184. Mid- to late January.

February

National Date Festival, Indio (Palm Springs area). Crowds gather for 2 weeks to celebrate the Coachella Valley desert's most beloved cash crop with events like camel and ostrich races, the Blessing of the Date Garden, and festive Arabian Nights pageants. Plenty of date-sampling booths are set up, along with rides, food vendors, and other county-fair trappings. Call © 800/811-3247 or 760/863-8247, or visit www.datefest.org. Two weeks in February.

Chinese New Year & Golden Dragon Parade, Los Angeles. Dragon dancers and martial arts masters parade through the streets of Downtown's Chinatown. Chinese opera and other events are scheduled. For this year's schedule, contact the Chinese Chamber of Commerce at © 213/617-0396 or visit www.lachinesechamber.org. Late January or early February.

Nissan L.A. Open Golf Tournament, Pacific Palisades. The PGA Tour makes its only Tinseltown appearance at the Riviera Country Club overlooking the ocean. Expect to see stars in attendance. For information, call the Los Angeles Junior Chamber of Commerce at © 213/482-1311. Mid-February.

Mardi Gras, West Hollywood. The festivities—including live jazz and lots of food—take place along Santa Monica Boulevard, from Doheny Drive to La Brea Avenue, and in the alley behind Santa Monica Boulevard. Contact the West Hollywood Convention & Visitors Bureau at © 800/368-6020 for details. Late February or early March.

March

Los Angeles Marathon, Downtown. This 26-mile run attracts thousands of participants, from world champions to the guy next door; the big day also features a 5K run/walk and a bike marathon on the same route. The run starts in Downtown Los Angeles. Call ℂ **310/444-5544** or visit www.la marathon.com for registration or spectator information. First weekend in March.

Santa Barbara International Film Festival, Santa Barbara. For 10 days each March, Santa Barbara does its best impression of Cannes. There's a flurry of foreign and independent film premieres, appearances by actors and directors, and symposia on cinematic topics. For a rundown of events, call ℂ **805/963-0023.** Early to mid-March.

California Poppy Blooming Season, Antelope Valley. Less than an hour's drive north of Los Angeles lies the California Poppy Reserve, part of the state park system. In spring, miles of hillside blaze with brilliant hues of red and orange, dazzling the senses of motorists who flock to witness the display. For information and directions, call ℂ **661/723-6077.** Mid-March to mid-May. For information on the annual **California Poppy Festival,** held at full bloom (usually in late Apr), call ℂ **661/723-6077** or visit www.poppyfestival.com.

Nabisco Dinah Shore, Rancho Mirage (Palm Springs area). This LPGA golf tournament takes place near Palm Springs during the last week of March. After the celebrity Pro-Am early in the week, the best female pros get down to business. For further information, call ℂ **760/324-4546.** Other special-interest events for women usually take place around the Dinah Shore, including the White Party, the country's largest annual lesbian gathering.

American Indian Festival and Market, Los Angeles Natural History Museum. At this showcase of Native American arts and culture, the fun includes traditional dances, storytelling, and arts and crafts, as well as a chance to sample Native American foods. Admission to the museum includes festival tickets. For further details, call ℂ **213/744-DINO** (213/744-3466). Late March.

April

Toyota Grand Prix, Long Beach. An exciting weekend of Indy-class auto racing and entertainment in and around downtown Long Beach draws world-class drivers from the United States and Europe, plus many celebrity contestants and spectators. Contact the Grand Prix Association at ℂ **888/82-SPEED** (888/827-7333) or www.longbeachgp.com. Mid-April.

Renaissance Pleasure Faire, San Bernardino. This annual event in the relatively remote Glen Helen Regional Park is one of America's largest Renaissance festivals. It features an Elizabethan marketplace with costumed performers. The fair provides an entire day's activities, including shows, food, and crafts. You're encouraged to come in period costume. For ticket information, call ℂ **800/52-FAIRE** (800/523-2473), or log on to the national website, http://renaissance-faire.com. Weekends from late April to Memorial Day.

May

Cinco de Mayo, Los Angeles. A week-long celebration of the Mexican victory over the French Army in 1862 takes place throughout the city. There's a carnival atmosphere with large crowds, live music, dancing, and food. The main festivities are held at El Pueblo de Los Angeles State Historic Park, Downtown; call ℂ **213/628-1274** for information. Other events are held around the city. The week surrounding May 5.

National Orange Show, San Bernardino. An Inland Empire tradition since 1911—when there were more orange groves than houses in Southern California—this weeklong county fair includes stadium events, celebrity entertainment, livestock shows, crafts and food booths, and carnival rides. Call ℂ **909/888-6788.** Second half of May.

Venice Art Walk, Venice Beach. This annual weekend event, which celebrated its 25th anniversary in 2004, gives visitors a chance to take docent-guided tours of galleries and studios, plus a Sunday self-guided art walk through the private home studios of more than 50 emerging and well-known artists. For details, call the Venice Family Clinic, which coordinates the event (ℂ **310/392-WALK** [310/392-9255]), or visit its website at www.venicefamilyclinic.org. Second half of May.

Long Beach Lesbian & Gay Pride Parade and Festival, Shoreline Park, Long Beach. There are health-awareness booths, rock and country music, dancing, food, and more than 100 decorated floats. Call ℂ **562/987-9191.** Second half of May.

Doheny Blues Festival, Doheny State Beach, Dana Point. This festival features great live music (past acts have included the likes of Little Richard, Bo Diddley, and Chuck Berry) on three stages—blues, rock, and soul—at a waterfront grass park with two stages at opposite ends of the venue. Arts and crafts vendors, memorabilia, and unique displays surround the International Food Court, with restaurants and beverages of all types. Proceeds benefit the Surfrider Foundation, San Clemente Chapter. Call ℂ **949/262-2662** or log on to www.omegaevents. com. Mid- to late May.

June

Playboy Jazz Festival, Los Angeles. Bill Cosby is the traditional master of ceremonies, presiding over the top jazz musicians at the Hollywood Bowl. Call ℂ **213/480-3232.** Mid-June.

Christopher Street West Festival & Parade, West Hollywood. In its 38th year in 2008, this West Hollywood event is one of the largest lesbian and gay pride festivals and parades in the world. Outdoor stages, disco- and Western-dance tents, food, and revelry culminate in Sunday's parade down Santa Monica Boulevard. Call ℂ **323/969-8302** or log on to www.lapride. org. Third week in June.

Los Angeles Film Festival, Los Angeles. With an attendance of over 60,000, the festival showcases more than 175 American and international indies, short films, and music videos during a 10-day event in late June. Call ℂ **866/345-6337** or log onto www. lafilmfest.com.

Mariachi USA Festival, Los Angeles. At this 2-day family-oriented celebration of Mexican culture and tradition at the Hollywood Bowl, festivalgoers pack their picnic baskets and enjoy music, folkloric ballet, and related performances by top *grupos.* The all-day, all-night celebration is one of the largest mariachi festivals in the world. For tickets, call ℂ **800/MARIACHI** (800/627-4224) or 323/850-2000 (the Hollywood Bowl), or log on to www. mariachiusa.com. Late June.

July

Lotus Festival, Echo Park. Celebrants gather to witness the spectacular blooms of Echo Lake's floating lotus grove. In keeping with an Asian and South Pacific islands theme, the festivities include tropical music and entertainment, ethnic foods, exotic birds, and plenty of lotus-inspired arts and crafts for sale. Admission is free. Call © 213/485-8743 for information, or log on to www.laparks.org/grifmet/lotus.htm. Second weekend of July.

Beach Festival, Huntington Beach. Two weeks of fun in the sun featuring two surfing competitions—the U.S. Open of Surfing and the world-class Pro of Surfing—plus extreme sports like BMX biking, skateboarding, and more. The festival includes entertainment, food, tons of product booths and giveaways—and plenty of tanned, swimsuit-clad bodies of both sexes. For more information, call © 714/969-3492 or log on to www.surfcityusa.com. End of July.

Festival of Arts & Pageant of the Masters, Laguna Beach. A 60-plus-year tradition in artsy Laguna, this festival centers on a fantastic performance-art production in which actors re-create famous old masters paintings. Other festivities include live music, crafts sales, art demonstrations and workshops, and the grass-roots Sawdust Festival across the street. Grounds admission is $3 to $5; pageant tickets range from $15 to $80. Call © 800/487-FEST (800/487-3378) or 949/494-1145; there's online info at www.foapom.com. July through August.

August

Nisei Week Japanese Festival, Los Angeles. This weeklong celebration of Japanese culture and heritage—and L.A.'s oldest ethnic festival—is held in the Japanese American Cultural and Community Center Plaza in Little Tokyo. Festivities include parades, food, Taiko Drum performances, arts, and crafts. Call © 213/687-7193 or log on to www.niseiweek.org. Mid-August.

African Marketplace and Cultural Fair, Los Angeles. African arts, crafts, food, and music are featured at this cultural-awareness event. It's one of the largest festivals in the world celebrating the cultures of Africa and the African Diaspora. It's spread over 3 weekends at Rancho La Cienega Park, 5001 Rodeo Rd. Call © 323/734-1164 or visit www.africanmarketplace.org. Weekends from mid-August to Labor Day.

September

Los Angeles County Fair, Pomona. Horse racing, arts, agricultural displays, celebrity entertainment, and carnival rides are among the attractions at one of the largest county fairs in the world, held at the Los Angeles County Fair and Exposition Center. Call © 909/623-3111 or visit www.fairplex.com for information. Throughout September.

Long Beach Blues Festival, Long Beach. Great performances by blues legends such as Etta James, Dr. John, and the Allman Brothers make this an event you won't want to miss if you love the blues. Located in the middle of the athletic field at Long Beach State, the event serves cold beer, wine, and food throughout. Call © 562/985-5566 or log on to www.kkjz.org. Labor Day weekend.

Simon Rodia Watts Towers Jazz Festival, Los Angeles. This event pays tribute to the roots of jazz in gospel and blues, as well as celebrating the avant-garde and Latin jazz scene. It's also a great opportunity to visit the Watts Towers. Call © 213/847-4646 or log on to www.trywatts.com or www.wattstowers.net. Late September.

October

Catalina Island Jazz Trax Festival, Catalina Island. Contemporary jazz greats play at Avalon's legendary Casino Ballroom. This enormously popular festival takes place over 2 consecutive 3-day weekends. Call ✆ **760/323-1171** or see www.jazztrax.com for advance ticket sales and a schedule of performers. Early October.

Hollywood Film Festival, Hollywood. More than 50 films from the U.S. and abroad are screened, with celebrities in abundance. There's also a variety of workshops and marketplaces for aspiring actors and filmmakers. Call ✆ **310/288-1882** or visit www.hollywoodawards.com for info and tickets. Mid-October.

West Hollywood Halloween Costume Carnaval, West Hollywood. This is one of the world's largest Halloween parties. Over 400,000 people, many dressed in outlandish drag couture, party all night along Santa Monica Boulevard. Call ✆ **310/289-2525** or visit www.visitwesthollywood.com for info. October 31.

November

American Film Institute's Los Angeles International Film Festival, Los Angeles. Some of the biggest names in the international film community gather to see new movies from around the world. Call ✆ **866/AFI-FEST** (866/234-3378) or visit www.afifest.com for info and tickets. Early November.

Catalina Island Triathlon, Catalina Island. This is one of the top triathlons in the world. Participants run on unpaved roads, swim in the cleanest bay on the West Coast, and bike on challenging trails. There's also a "kid's tri." Call Pacific Sports at ✆ **714/978-1528** or visit www.PacificSports LLC.com. Early November.

Doo Dah Parade, Pasadena. This outrageous spoof of the Rose Parade features such participants as the Briefcase Precision Drill Team and a kazoo-playing marching band. Call ✆ **626/440-7379** or visit www.pasadenadoodahparade.info. Near Thanksgiving.

Hollywood Christmas Parade, Hollywood. This spectacular, star-studded parade marches through the heart of Hollywood. For information, call ✆ **323/469-2337.** Sunday after Thanksgiving.

December

Christmas Boat Parade of Lights. Sailors decorate their crafts with colorful lights. Several Southern California harbors hold nighttime parades. Participants range from tiny dinghies with a single strand of lights to showy yachts with Nativity scenes twinkling on deck. Call the following for information: Ventura Harbor, ✆ **805/382-3001;** Long Beach, ✆ **562/435-4093;** Huntington Harbour, ✆ **714/840-7542.**

Los Angeles's Average Temperatures (°F/°C)

	Jan	Feb	Mar	Apr	May	June	July	Aug	Sept	Oct	Nov	Dec
Avg. High	66/19	68/20	69/21	71/22	73/23	77/25	82/28	84/29	82/28	78/26	73/23	68/20
Avg. Low	48/9	50/10	51/11	54/12	57/14	60/16	63/17	64/18	63/17	59/15	53/12	50/10

4 Getting There & Getting Around

GETTING TO LOS ANGELES
LAX & OTHER AIRPORTS

There are five airports in the Los Angeles area. Most visitors fly into **Los Angeles International Airport** (✆ **310/646-5252;** www.lawa.org/lax), better known as LAX. This behemoth—ranked fifth in the world for number of passengers handled—is situated oceanside, between Marina del Rey and Manhattan Beach. LAX is a convenient place to land; it's located within minutes of Santa Monica and the beaches, and not more than a half-hour from Downtown, Hollywood, and the Westside (depending on traffic, of course). Despite its huge size, the nine-terminal airport has a straightforward, easy-to-understand design. Free blue, green, and white **shuttle buses** connect the terminals and stop in front of each ticket building. Special minibuses accessible to travelers with disabilities are also available. **Travelers Aid of Los Angeles** (✆ 310/646-2270; www.travelersaid. org) operates booths in each terminal.

There are eight short-stay (and expensive) parking lots within the main concourse building and a long-stay park situated on 96th Street and Sepulveda Boulevard. A free bus service runs between this car park and the terminals. There's also a free 24-hour **Cell Phone Waiting Lot** at 9011 Airport Blvd. for drivers picking up passengers. You can find extensive information about LAX—including maps, parking, shuttle-van information, and links to weather forecasts—online at **www.lawa.org**. All car-rental agencies are in the neighborhood surrounding LAX, within a few minutes' drive; each provides a complimentary shuttle to and from the airport.

For some travelers, one of the area's smaller airports might be more convenient than LAX. **Bob Hope Airport** (2627 N. Hollywood Way, Burbank; ✆ 818/840-8840; www.bobhopeairport.com) is the best place to land if you're headed for Hollywood or the valleys—and it's even closer to Downtown L.A. than LAX. The small airport has especially good links to Las Vegas and other southwestern cities. **Long Beach Municipal Airport** (4100 Donald Douglas Dr., Long Beach; ✆ 562/570-2600; www.lgb.org), south of LAX, is the best place to land if you're visiting Long Beach or northern Orange County and want to avoid L.A. **John Wayne Airport** (19051 Airport Way N., Anaheim; ✆ 949/252-5200; www.ocair.com) is closest to Disneyland, Knott's Berry Farm, and other Orange County attractions. **Ontario International Airport** (Terminal Way, Ontario; ✆ 909/937-2700; www.lawa.org/ont) is not a popular airport for tourists; businesspeople use it to head to San Bernardino, Riverside, and other inland communities. However, it's convenient if you're heading to Palm Springs, and also a viable choice if you're staying in Pasadena.

Arriving at the Airport

IMMIGRATION & CUSTOMS CLEARANCE International visitors arriving by air, no matter what the port of entry, should cultivate patience and resignation before setting foot on U.S. soil. U.S. airports have considerably beefed up security clearances in the years since the September 11, 2001, terrorist attacks, and clearing Customs and Immigration can take as long as 2 hours.

Getting into Town from the Airport

BY CAR To reach Santa Monica and other northern beach communities, exit the airport, take Sepulveda Boulevard north, and follow the signs to California 1 (Pacific Coast Hwy., or PCH) north. You *can* take the I-405 north, but you'll be sorry you did—that stretch of freeway is always heavily congested.

To reach Redondo, Hermosa, Newport, and the other southern beach communities, take Sepulveda Boulevard south and then follow the signs to California 1 south.

To reach Beverly Hills or Hollywood, exit the airport via Century Boulevard and then take I-405 north to Santa Monica Boulevard east.

To reach Downtown or Pasadena, exit the airport, take Sepulveda Boulevard south, then take I-105 east to I-110 north.

Tip: If you're going to rent a car at LAX, avoid arriving at the midweek morning or evening rush hour, particularly if you have to get on dreaded I-405. You'll save yourself several hours of stop-and-go misery if you time it right.

BY SHUTTLE   Many city hotels provide free shuttles for their guests; ask when you make reservations. **SuperShuttle** (© **800/258-3826** or 310/782-6600; www.supershuttle.com) offers regularly scheduled minivans from LAX to any location in the city, as does **Prime Time Shuttle** (© **800/RED-VANS** [800/733-8267] or 310/536-7922; www.prime timeshuttle.com). Fares can range from about $15 to $35 per person, depending on your destination. It's cheaper to cab it to most places if you're a group of three or more, but you might have to stop at other passengers' destinations before you reach your own. Reservations aren't needed for your arrival but are required for a return to the airport.

BY TAXI   Taxis are located at the Arrivals level under the yellow sign outside each terminal. Be sure to ask for a list of prices to various major destinations before setting off. There's a flat price of $42 between LAX and Downtown Los Angeles. For other destinations, expect to pay at least $35 to Hollywood, $25 to Beverly Hills, $20 to Santa Monica, and $50 to $60 to the Valley and Pasadena. But wait, there's more—you'll also have to pay an airport surcharge of $2.50 for trips originating from LAX.

BY RAIL   Budget-minded travelers heading to Downtown, Universal City, or Long Beach can take L.A.'s Metro Rail service from LAX. An airport shuttle can take you to the Green Line light-rail station; from there, connections on the Blue, Gold, and Red lines can get you where you're headed. It's a good idea to contact your hotel for advice on the closest station. The service operates from 5am to midnight, and the combined fare is under $2—but you should be prepared to spend 1 to 2 hours in transit. Call the **Los Angeles County Metropolitan Transit Authority (MTA)** at © **800/ COMMUTE** (800/266-6883), or see www.mta.net for information.

Tips A Shortcut to LAX

One of the city's busiest interchanges is from the Santa Monica Freeway (I-10) to the San Diego Freeway (I-405) on the way to LAX—many a tourist has missed a flight because of this beastly bottleneck. Therefore, if you're heading to LAX for your flight home, the scenic route may prove to be the fastest. From the Santa Monica Freeway (I-10) westbound, exit south to La Brea Avenue. Go right on Stocker Street and then left on La Cienega Boulevard. Veer right on La Tijera Boulevard and left on Airport Boulevard, then follow the signs. You can use this trick from West Hollywood and Beverly Hills as well—simply take La Cienega south, continuing as above.

Tips **Disneyland Express**

If you're headed directly to **Disneyland,** Gray Line's **Disneyland Resort Express** (℗ **714/978-8855;** www.graylineanaheim.com) runs a shuttle service from LAX from 6:30am to 12:30am, 7 days a week. The buses are located under the green sign on the Arrivals level of every terminal. Reservations aren't required but you can book tickets in advance at their website. A round-trip ticket is $30 for adults and $22 for kids.

BY PUBLIC BUS   The city's MTA buses also go between LAX and many parts of the city. Phone **MTA Airport Information** (℗ **800/COMMUTE** [800/ 266-6883]; www.mta.net) for the schedules and fares. If you're arriving at LAX and your hotel is in Santa Monica, you can hop aboard the city's **Big Blue Bus** (℗ **310/451-5444;** www.bigbluebus. com). It's a slow ride, but the price, 75¢, is hard to beat. Bus information is available in the baggage claim area of each LAX terminal.

BY CAR

Los Angeles is well connected to the rest of the United States by several major highways—in fact, L.A. has the highest rate of bank robberies in the U.S. because it's so easy to make a fast getaway. Among them are Interstate 5, which enters the state from the north; Interstate 10, which originates in Jacksonville, Florida, and terminates in Los Angeles; and U.S. 101, a scenic route that follows the western seaboard from Los Angeles north to the Oregon state line.

If you're driving **from the north,** you have two choices: the quick route, along I-5 through the middle of the state; or the scenic route along the coast. Heading south along I-5, you'll pass a small town called Grapevine. This marks the start of the mountain pass with the same name. Once you've reached the southern end of the pass, you'll be in the San Fernando Valley, which is the start of Los Angeles County. To reach the beach communities

and L.A.'s Westside, take I-405 south (Hello traffic!); to get to Hollywood, take California 170 south to U.S. 101 south (this route is called the Hollywood Fwy. the entire way); I-5 will take you along the eastern edge of Downtown and into Orange County.

If you're taking the **scenic coastal route** from the north, take U.S. 101 to I-405 or I-5, or stay on U.S. 101, following the instructions above to your destination.

If you're approaching **from the east,** you'll be coming in on I-10. For Orange County, take California 57 south. I-10 continues through Downtown and terminates at the beach. If you're heading to the Westside, take I-405 north. To get to the beaches, take California 1 (PCH) north or south, depending on your destination.

From the south, head north on I-5 at the southern end of Orange County. I-405 splits off to the west; take this road to the Westside and beach communities. Stay on I-5 to reach Downtown and Hollywood.

Here are some **driving times** if you're on one of those see-the-USA car trips: From Phoenix, it's about 350 miles, or 6 hours (okay, 7 if you drive the speed limit) to Los Angeles via I-10. Las Vegas is 265 miles northeast of Los Angeles (about a 4- or 5-hr. drive). San Francisco is 390 miles north of Los Angeles on I-5 (6–7 hr.), and San Diego is 115 miles south (about 2 hr.).

If you're visiting from abroad and plan to rent a car in the United States, you probably won't need the services of an additional automobile organization. If you plan to buy or borrow a car, automobile-association membership is recommended. **AAA,** the **American Automobile Association** (© **800/222-4357;** http://travel.aaa.com), is the country's largest motor club and supplies its members with maps, insurance and, most importantly, emergency road service. *Note:* Foreign driver's licenses are usually recognized in the U.S., but you should get an international one if your home license is not in English.

For listings of the major car rental agencies in Los Angeles, please see "Toll-Free Numbers & Websites" in the appendix (p. 328).

BY TRAIN

Amtrak (© **800/USA-RAIL** [800/872-7245]; www.amtrak.com) connects Los Angeles with about 500 American cities. As with plane travel along popular routes, fares fluctuate depending on the season and special promotions. As a general rule, heavily restricted advance tickets are competitive with similar airfares. Remember, however, that those low fares are for coach travel in reclining seats; private sleeping accommodations cost substantially more.

The *Sunset Limited* is Amtrak's regularly scheduled transcontinental service, originating in Florida and making 52 stops along the way as it passes through Alabama, Mississippi, Louisiana, Texas, New Mexico, and Arizona before arriving in Los Angeles 2 days later. Amtrak's *Coast Starlight* travels along the Pacific Coast between Seattle and Los Angeles. This stylish train (with its wonderfully scenic route) has been steadily growing in popularity.

Amtrak also runs trains along the California coast, connecting San Diego, Los Angeles, San Francisco, and all points in between. There are multiple trains each day. One-way fares for popular segments

can range from $22 (Los Angeles–Santa Barbara) to $25 (Los Angeles–San Diego) to $87 (San Francisco–Los Angeles) but, again, fares fluctuate.

Ask about special family plans, tours, and other money-saving promotions. You can call for a brochure outlining routes and prices for the entire system; up-to-date schedules and fares are also available on Amtrak's comprehensive—but often unwieldy—website (www.amtrak.com). Better yet, log on to Amtrak's California website: **www.amtrakcalifornia.com**. It's far more user-friendly and lists only California schedules and special fares.

The L.A. train terminus is **Union Station,** 800 N. Alameda (© **213/617-0111**), on Downtown's northern edge. Completed in 1939, this was the last of America's great train depots—a unique blend of Spanish Revival and Streamline Moderne architecture (see "Architectural Highlights," in chapter 7). From the station, you can take one of the taxis that line up outside; board the Metro Red Line to Hollywood or Universal City; or take the Metro Blue Line to Long Beach. If you're headed to the San Fernando Valley or Anaheim, Metrolink commuter trains leave from Union Station; call © **800/371-LINK** (800/371-5465), or visit www.metrolinktrains.com.

International visitors can buy a USA Rail Pass, good for 15 or 30 days of unlimited travel on Amtrak (© **800/USA-RAIL** [800/872-7245]; www.amtrak.com). The pass is available through many overseas travel agents. See Amtrak's website for the cost of travel within the western, eastern, or northwestern United States. With a foreign passport, you can also buy passes directly from some Amtrak locations, including San Francisco, Los Angeles, Chicago, New York, Miami, Boston, and Washington, D.C. Reservations are generally required and should be made as early as possible. Regional rail passes are also available.

GETTING AROUND
BY CAR

Need I tell you that Los Angeles is a car-crazed city? L.A. is a sprawling metropolis, so you're really going to need some wheels to get around easily (there *is* public transportation in L.A., but you probably don't want to rely on it). An elaborate network of well-maintained freeways connects this urban sprawl, but you have to learn how to make sense of the system and cultivate some patience for dealing with the traffic—purchasing one of those plastic-covered fold-out maps is a smart investment. For an detailed view of L.A.'s freeway system, see the tear-out map tucked inside the back cover.

L.A.'S MAIN FREEWAYS

L.A.'s extensive system of toll-free, high-speed freeways connects the city's patchwork of communities, though most visitors spend the bulk of their time either along the coastline or on the city's ever-trendy Westside (see "Neighborhoods in Brief," in chapter 4, for complete details on all of the city's sectors). The system works well to get you where you need to be, although rush-hour (roughly 6–9am and 3–7pm) traffic is often bumper-to-bumper, particularly on the dreaded I-405. Here's an overview of the city's main freeways (best read with an L.A. map in hand):

U.S. 101, called the Ventura Freeway in the San Fernando Valley and the Hollywood Freeway in the city, runs across L.A. in a roughly northwest-southeast direction, from the San Fernando Valley to the center of Downtown. You'll encounter heavy rush-hour traffic.

California 134 continues as the Ventura Freeway after U.S. 101 reaches the city and becomes the Hollywood Freeway. This branch of the Ventura Freeway continues directly east, through the valley towns of Burbank and Glendale, to I-210 (the Foothill Fwy.), which takes you through Pasadena and out toward the eastern edge of Los Angeles County.

I-5, otherwise known as the Golden State Freeway north of I-10 and the Santa Ana Freeway south of I-10, bisects Downtown on its way from Sacramento to San Diego.

I-10, labeled the Santa Monica Freeway west of I-5 and the San Bernardino Freeway east of I-5, is the city's major east-west freeway, connecting the San Gabriel Valley with Downtown and Santa Monica.

I-405, known as the San Diego Freeway, runs north-south through L.A.'s Westside, connecting the San Fernando Valley with LAX and southern beach areas. *Tip:* This is one of the area's busiest freeways; avoid it as much as possible (and like the plague during rush hour).

I-105, Los Angeles's newest freeway—called the Century Freeway—extends from LAX east to I-605.

I-110, commonly known as the Harbor Freeway, starts in Pasadena as California 110 (the Pasadena Fwy.); it becomes an interstate in Downtown Los Angeles and runs directly south, where it dead-ends in San Pedro. The section that is now the Pasadena Freeway was Los Angeles's first freeway, known as the Arroyo Seco when it opened in 1940.

⌒Tips Stay Away from Santa Monica Boulevard

If you're driving to or from Santa Monica and the Westside communities—Beverly Hills, West Hollywood, Century City—try to avoid Santa Monica Boulevard during rush hour. Both Wilshire and Pico boulevards parallel Santa Monica Boulevard and are usually far less congested. (Pico Blvd. is my savior.)

⸤Tips⸣ Freeway Names & Numbers

Locals refer to L.A. freeways by both their numbers and their names. For example, I-10 is both "the 10" and "the Santa Monica Freeway."

I-710, also known as the Long Beach Freeway, runs in a north-south direction through East Los Angeles and dead-ends at Long Beach. Crammed with big rigs leaving the port in San Pedro in a rush, this is the ugliest and most dangerous freeway in California.

I-605, the San Gabriel River Freeway, runs from the I-405 near Seal Beach to the I-210 interchange at Duarte. It follows the San Gabriel River (hence the moniker), roughly paralleling the I-710 to the east. Most importantly, it gets you through the San Gabriel Valley up to the edge of the San Gabriel Mountains.

California 1—called Hwy. 1, the Pacific Coast Highway, or simply PCH— is more of a scenic parkway than a freeway. It skirts the ocean, linking all of L.A.'s beach communities, from Malibu to the Orange Coast. It's often slow going due to all the stoplights but is far more scenic than the freeways.

A complex web of surface streets complements the freeways. From north to south, the major east-west thoroughfares connecting Downtown to the beaches are **Sunset, Santa Monica, Wilshire, Olympic, Pico,** and **Venice boulevards.**

DRIVING

You may turn right at a red light after stopping unless a sign says otherwise. Likewise, you may turn left on a red light from a one-way street onto another one-way street after coming to a full stop. Also, California has a seat-belt law for both drivers and passengers, so buckle up before you venture out.

Many Southern California freeways have designated **carpool lanes,** also known as High Occupancy Vehicle (HOV) lanes or "white diamond" lanes

(after the large diamonds painted on the blacktop along the lane). Most require two passengers (others three), and they have rigidly enforced zones where you can't leave the HOV lane for several miles at a time (I've missed many an exit because of this rule). Most on-ramps are metered during even light congestion to regulate the flow of traffic onto the freeway; cars in HOV lanes can pass the signal without stopping. Although there are tales of drivers sitting life-size mannequins next to them in order to beat the system, don't use the HOV lane unless you have the right numbers—fines begin at $271.

Here are a few more tips for driving around:

- **Allow more time than you think it will actually take to get where you're going.** You need to make time for traffic and parking. Double your margin in weekday rush hours, from 7 to 9am and again from 3 to 7pm. Also, the freeways tend to be much more crowded than you'd expect all day on Saturdays, especially heading toward the ocean on a sunny day.

- **Plan your exact route before you set out.** Know where you need to exit the freeway and/or make turns— especially lefts—and merge well in advance. Otherwise, you're likely to find yourself waving at your freeway exit from an inside lane or your turnoff from an outside one. Pulling over and whipping out your map if you screw up is never easy, and it's near impossible on the freeways.

- **Pedestrians in Los Angeles have the right of way at all times,** so stop for people who have stepped off the curb.

- **Get detailed driving directions to your hotel.** Save yourself the frustration of trying to find your hotel—plot it on a map and call the hotel for the best route.

PARKING

Explaining the parking situation in Los Angeles is like explaining the English language—there are more exceptions than rules. In some areas, every establishment has a convenient free lot or ample street parking; other areas are pretty manageable, as long as you have a quick eye and are willing to take a few turns around the block, but there are some frustrating parts of town (particularly around restaurants after 7:30pm) where you might have to give in and use valet parking. Whether there's valet parking depends more on the congestion of the area than on the elegance of the establishment; the size of an establishment's lot often simply won't allow for self-parking. Restaurants and nightclubs sometimes provide a complimentary valet service, but more often they charge between $5 and $7. Some areas, like Santa Monica and Beverly Hills, offer self-park lots and garages near the neighborhood action; costs range from $2 to $10. Most of the hotels that are listed in this book offer both self-parking (often free) and/or valet parking, which ranges from $10 to $30 per day.

Here are a few more parking tips to remember:

- **Beware of parking in residential neighborhoods.** Many areas allow only permit parking, so you will be ticketed and possibly towed (especially in the Westside and Beverly Hills neighborhoods).
- **Have plenty of quarters on hand.** Angelenos scrounge for parking-meter quarters like New Yorkers do for laundry quarters: They are the equivalent of pure gold. Save yourself some hassle and just buy a roll or two at your bank before you leave home.

- **Be creative.** Case the immediate area by taking a turn around the block. In many parts of the city, you can find an unrestricted street space less than a block away from eager valets.
- **Read posted restrictions carefully.** You can avoid a ticket if you pay attention to the signs, which warn of street-cleaning schedules and those sneaky rush-hour "no parking" zones.
- **Don't lose your car in a parking garage.** This seems like obvious advice, but you'd be surprised how easily you can lose your car at a L.A. megamall. Most garage levels and subsections are letter-, number-, and color-coded, so make a mental note after you lock your car.

RENTALS

Los Angeles is one of the cheapest places in America to rent a car. Major national car-rental companies usually rent economy- and compact-class cars for about $40 per day and $130 per week, with unlimited mileage.

All the major car-rental agencies have offices at the airports and in the larger hotels; I highly recommend booking a car online before you arrive. If you're thinking of splurging on a dig-me road machine such as a Maserati, Ferrari, Rolls-Royce, Lamborghini, or Hummer, the places to call are either **Budget Beverly Hills Car Collection,** 9815 Wilshire Blvd. (🅒 **800/227-7117** or 310/881-2335; www.budgetbeverlyhills.com); or **Beverly Hills Rent-A-Car,** 9732 Little Santa Monica Blvd., Beverly Hills (🅒 **800/479-5996** or 310/337-1400; www.bhrentacar.com). Both car-rental companies have additional locations in Santa Monica, LAX, Orange County, and Newport Beach, and both offer complimentary delivery to local hotels or pickup service at LAX.

SAVING MONEY ON A RENTAL CAR Car-rental rates vary even more than airline fares. The price you pay will depend on the size of the car, where and when you pick it up and drop it off, the length of the rental period, where and how far you drive it, whether you purchase insurance, and a host of other factors. A few key questions could save you hundreds of dollars:

- **Are weekend rates lower than weekday rates?** Ask if the rate is the same for pickup Friday morning, for instance, as it is for Thursday night.
- **Does the agency assess a drop-off charge** if you don't return the car to the location where you picked it up?
- **Are special promotional rates available?** If you see an advertised price in your local newspaper, be sure to ask for that specific rate; otherwise, you may be charged the standard cost. Terms change constantly.
- **Are discounts available** for members of AARP, AAA, frequent-flier programs, or trade unions? If you belong to any of these organizations, you may be entitled to discounts of up to 30%.
- **How much tax will be added to the rental bill?** Local tax? State use tax?
- **How much does the company charge for gas** if you return with the tank less than full? Though most companies claim these prices are "competitive," you will almost always

save money if you refill the car yourself before you return it. Some offer "refueling packages," in which you pay for an entire tank of gas upfront. The price is usually fairly competitive with local prices, but you don't get credit for any gas remaining in the tank. If you fear that a stop at a gas station on the way to the airport will make you miss your plane, take advantage of the fuel purchase option; otherwise, skip it.

BY PUBLIC TRANSPORTATION

There are visitors who successfully tour Los Angeles entirely by public transportation (I've met them both), but we can't honestly recommend that plan for most readers. L.A. is a metropolis that's grown up around—and is best traversed by—the automobile, and many areas are inaccessible without one. As a result, an overwhelming number of visitors rent a car for their stay. Still, if you're in the city for only a short time, are on a very tight budget, or don't expect to be moving around a lot, public transport might be for you.

The city's trains and buses are operated by the **Los Angeles County Metropolitan Transit Authority (MTA)** (✆ 213/922-2000; www.mta.net), and MTA brochures and schedules are available at every area visitor center.

⟮Tips⟯ Hogging the Roads, Harley Style

Instead of renting a boring ol' car to cruise Sunset Strip, why not rent a motorcycle? Even better, why not rent a Harley? **EagleRider** (11860 S. La Cienega Blvd.; ✆ **800/501-8687** or 310/536-6777; www.eaglerider.com), the world's largest motorcycle rental and tour company, will rent you a mild-mannered Sportster 883cc for about $80 per day. Leather chaps are optional, but a motorcycle license is required. Other quality L.A.-based Harley motorcycle-rental companies include **Route 66 Riders** (4161 Lincoln Blvd. in Marina Del Rey; ✆ **888/434-4473** or 310/578-0112; www.route66riders.com) and **Ride Free Motorcycle Tours** (4848 W. 136th St., Hawthorne; ✆ **310/487-1047**; www.ridefree.com). Keep the rubber side down.

Tips **Public Transport Tip**

The **L.A. County Metropolitan Transit Authority (MTA)** website, **www.mta.net,** provides all the practical information you need—hours, routes, fares—for using L.A.'s nearly invisible network of public transportation (buses, subways, light rail).

By Bus

Spread-out stops, sluggish service, and frequent transfers make extensive touring by bus impractical. For short hops and occasional jaunts, however, buses are economical and environmentally correct. However, I don't recommend riding buses late at night.

The basic bus fare is $1.25 for all local lines, with transfers costing 25¢. A Metro Day Pass is $5 and gives you unlimited bus and rail rides all day long; these can be purchased while boarding any Metro Bus (exact change is needed) or at the self-service vending machines at the Metro Rail stations. *Note:* Two kids 4 and under may travel free with each fare-paying adult.

The **Downtown Area Short Hop (DASH)** shuttle system operates buses throughout Downtown, Hollywood, and the Westside of L.A. Service runs every 5 to 20 minutes, depending on the time of day, and costs just 25¢. Contact the Department of Transportation (✆ **213/ 808-2273;** www.ladottransit.com) for schedules and route information (it's pretty confusing—you'll definitely need a weekday *and* weekend map).

The **Cityline** shuttle is a great way to get around West Hollywood on weekdays (9am–4pm) and Saturday (10am–7:30pm). For 50¢, it'll take you to most of the major shops and restaurants throughout WeHo (very handy if you park your car in a flat-fee lot). For more information, call ✆ **800/ 447-2189.**

By Rail & Subway

The **MetroRail** system is a sore subject around town. For years, the MTA has been digging up the city's streets, sucking in huge amounts of tax money, and pushing exhaust vents up through peaceful parkland—and for what? Let's face it, L.A. will never have New York's subway or San Francisco's BART. Today the system is still in its infancy, mainly popular with commuters from outlying suburbs. Here's an overview of what's currently in place:

The **Metro Blue Line,** an above-ground rail line, connects Downtown Los Angeles with Long Beach. Trains operate daily from 6am to 9pm.

The **Metro Red Line,** L.A.'s first subway, has been growing since 1993 and opened a highly publicized Hollywood–Universal City extension in 2000. The line begins at Union Station, the city's main train depot, and travels west underneath Wilshire Boulevard, looping north into Hollywood and the San Fernando Valley. Discount tokens are available at Metro service centers and many area convenience stores.

The **Metro Purple Line** subway starts at Union Station, shares six stations with the Red Line Downtown, and continues to the Mid-Wilshire area.

The **Metro Green Line** runs for 20 miles along the center of I-105, the Glenn Anderson (Century) Freeway, and connects Norwalk in eastern Los Angeles County to LAX and Redondo Beach. A connection with the Blue Line offers visitors access from LAX to Downtown L.A. or Long Beach.

The **Metro Gold Line** is a 14-mile link between Pasadena and Union Station in Downtown L.A. Stops include Old Pasadena, the Southwest Museum, and Chinatown.

The base Metro fare is $1.25 for all lines. A Metro Day Pass is $5 and weekly passes are $17. Passes are available at Metro Customer Centers and local convenience and grocery stores. For more information on public transportation—including construction updates, timetables, and details on purchasing tokens or passes—call **MTA** at (© **213/922-2000** or, better yet, log on to their handy website at **www.mta.net**.

BY TAXI

Distances are long in Los Angeles, and cab fares are high; even a short trip can cost $20 or more. Taxis currently charge $2.65 at the flag drop, plus $2.45 per mile. A service charge of $2.50 is added to fares originating from LAX.

Except in the heart of Downtown, cabs will usually not pull over when hailed. Cabstands are located at airports, at Downtown's Union Station, and at major hotels. To ensure a ride, order a taxi in advance from **Checker Cab** (© **323/654-8400**), **L.A. Taxi** (© **213/627-7000**), or **United Taxi** (© **213/483-7604**).

5 Money & Costs

It's always advisable to bring money in a variety of forms on a vacation: a mix of cash, credit cards, and ATM cards. You should also have enough petty cash upon arrival to cover airport incidentals, tipping, and transportation to your hotel before you leave home. You can always withdraw money upon arrival at an airport ATM, but you'll still need to make smaller change for tipping.

The most common bills in the U.S. are the $1 (a "buck"), $5, $10, and $20 denominations. There are also $2 bills (seldom encountered), $50 bills, and $100 bills. (The last two are usually not welcome as payment for small purchases.)

Coins come in seven denominations: 1¢ (1 cent, or a penny); 5¢ (5 cents, or a nickel); 10¢ (10 cents, or a dime); 25¢ (25 cents, or a quarter); 50¢ (50 cents, or a half dollar); the gold-colored Sacagawea coin, worth $1; and the rare silver dollar.

ATMs

In the land of shopping malls and immediate gratification, there's an ATM on almost every block—often droves of them. In fact, finding a place to withdraw cash is one of the easiest tasks you'll partake in while visiting Los Angeles.

Nationwide, the easiest and best way to get cash away from home is from an ATM (automated teller machine), sometimes referred to as a "cash machine" or "cashpoint." The **Cirrus** (© **800/424-7787**; www.mastercard.com) and **PLUS** (© **800/843-7587**; www.visa.com) networks span the country; you can find them even in remote regions. Go to your bank card's website to find ATM locations at your destination. Be sure you know your daily withdrawal limit before you depart.

Note: Many banks impose a fee every time you use a card at another bank's ATM, and that fee is often higher for international transactions (up to $5 or more) than for domestic ones (where they're rarely more than $2). In addition, the bank from which you withdraw cash may charge its own fee. To compare banks' ATM fees within the U.S., use **www.bankrate.com**. Visitors from outside the U.S. should also find out whether their bank assesses a 1% to 3% fee on charges incurred abroad.

Tip: One way around these fees is to ask for cash back at grocery, drug, and convenience stores that accept ATM cards and don't charge usage fees (be sure to ask). Of course, you'll have to purchase something first.

What Things Cost in Los Angeles	US$
Taxi from the airport to Downtown	42.00
SuperShuttle from LAX to West Hollywood area	25.00
Fine for expired parking meter	35.00–60.00
Double room at the Beverly Hills Hotel (absurdly expensive)	500.00
Double room at the Beach House at Hermosa Beach (expensive)	349.00
Double room at the Standard (moderate)	175.00
Double room at the Sea Shore Motel (inexpensive)	90.00
Lunch for one at Cafe Pinot (moderate)	22.00
Bacon Chili Cheese Dog at Pink's	4.30
Dinner for one, without wine, at Koi (expensive)	45.00
Dinner for one, without wine, at Border Grill (moderate)	25.00
Dinner for one, without wine, at Good Stuff (inexpensive)	12.00
Cup of coffee at Philippe The Original	.09
Cup of coffee at the Peninsula Hotel	3.25
2-hour StarLine Movie Star's Home Tour	37.00
Admission to the Hollywood Wax Museum	16.00
Admission to the Getty Museum	Free
Full-price movie ticket	11.50

CREDIT CARDS & DEBIT CARDS

Credit cards are the most widely used form of payment in the United States: **Visa** (Barclaycard in Britain), **Master-Card** (Eurocard in Europe, Access in Britain, Chargex in Canada), **American Express, Diners Club,** and **Discover.** They also provide a convenient record of all your expenses, and offer relatively good exchange rates. You can withdraw cash advances from your credit cards at banks or ATMs, but high fees make credit card cash advances a pricey way to get cash.

It's highly recommended that you travel with at least one major credit card. You must have a credit card to rent a car, and hotels and airlines usually require a credit card imprint as a deposit against expenses.

ATM cards with major credit card backing, known as **"debit cards,"** are now a commonly acceptable form of payment in most stores and restaurants. Debit cards draw money directly from your checking account. Some stores enable you to receive cash back on your debit-card purchases as well. The same is true at most U.S. post offices.

TRAVELER'S CHECKS

Traveler's checks are something of an anachronism from the days before the ATM made cash accessible at any time. Traveler's checks used to be the only sound alternative to traveling with dangerously large amounts of cash. They were as reliable as currency, but, unlike cash, could be replaced if lost or stolen.

These days, traveler's checks are less necessary because most cities have 24-hour ATMs that allow you to withdraw small amounts of cash as needed. However, keep in mind that you will likely be charged an ATM withdrawal fee if the bank is not your own, so if you're withdrawing money every day, you might be better off with traveler's checks—provided that you don't mind showing identification every time you want to cash one. Visitors should make sure that traveler's checks are denominated in U.S. dollars; foreign-currency checks are often difficult to exchange.

You can buy traveler's checks at most banks. Most are offered in denominations of $20, $50, $100, $500, and sometimes $1,000. Generally, you'll pay a service charge ranging from 1% to 4%.

The most popular traveler's checks are offered by **American Express** (© **800/807-6233,** or 800/221-7282 for cardholders—this number accepts collect calls, offers service in several foreign languages, and exempts Amex gold and platinum cardholders from the 1% fee); **Visa** (© **800/732-1322**)—AAA members can obtain Visa checks for a $9.95 fee (for checks up to $1,500) at most AAA offices or by calling © **866/339-3378**; and **MasterCard** (© **800/223-9920**).

Be sure to keep a copy of the traveler's checks' serial numbers separate from your checks in the event that they are stolen or lost. You'll get a refund faster if you know the numbers.

Another option is the new **prepaid traveler's check cards,** reloadable cards that work much like debit cards but aren't linked to your checking account. The **American Express Travelers Cheque Card,** for example, requires a minimum deposit ($300), sets a maximum balance ($2,750), and has a one-time issuance fee of $15. You can withdraw money from an ATM ($2.50 per transaction, not including bank fees), and the funds can be purchased in dollars, euros, or pounds. If you lose the card, your available funds will be refunded within 24 hours.

6 Health

STAYING HEALTHY

Contact the **International Association for Medical Assistance to Travelers (IAMAT)** (© 716/754-4883 or, in Canada, 416/652-0137; www.iamat. org) for tips on travel and health concerns in the countries you're visiting, and for lists of local, English-speaking doctors. The United States **Centers for Disease Control and Prevention** (© 800/311-3435; www.cdc.gov) provides up-to-date information on health hazards by region or country and offers tips on food safety. The website **www.tripprep.com,** sponsored by a consortium of travel medicine practitioners, **Travel Health Online,** may also offer helpful advice on traveling abroad. You can find listings of reliable clinics overseas at the **International Society of Travel Medicine** (www.istm.org).

WHAT TO DO IF YOU GET SICK AWAY FROM HOME

If you worry about getting sick away from home, you may want to consider **medical travel insurance** (see "Insurance" in the **"Fast Facts, Toll-Free Numbers & Websites"** appendix). In most cases, however, your existing health plan will provide all the coverage you need, and Los Angeles has two of the best hospitals in the nation: Cedar Sinai and UCLA medical centers. In fact, people travel to L.A. *because* they're sick. I list **hospitals** and **emergency numbers** under "Fast Facts: Los Angeles," p. 321. Also, be sure to carry your identification card in your wallet.

If you suffer from a chronic illness, consult your doctor before your departure. Pack **prescription medications** in your carry-on luggage, and carry them in their original containers, with pharmacy labels—otherwise they won't make it through airport security. Visitors from outside the U.S. should carry generic names of prescription drugs. For U.S. travelers, most reliable healthcare plans provide coverage if you get sick away from home. Foreign visitors may have to pay all medical costs upfront and be reimbursed later.

7 Specialized Travel Resources

TRAVELERS WITH DISABILITIES

Los Angeles' spirit of tolerance and diversity has made it a welcoming place for travelers with disabilities. Strict building codes make most public facilities and attractions extremely accessible (though some historic sites and older buildings simply can't accommodate drastic remodeling), and the city provides many services for those with disabilities.

The **Los Angeles County Commission on Disabilities** (© 213/974-1053) provides telephone referrals and information about L.A. for those with physical disabilities. The **Junior League of Los Angeles,** Farmers Market, 3rd and Fairfax streets, Gate 12, Los Angeles, CA 90036 (© 323/957-4280; www.jlla.org), distributes *Around the Town with Ease,* a free brochure detailing the accessibility of various Los Angeles sites. There's a $2 handling fee for mail orders.

Organizations that offer a vast range of resources and assistance to travelers with limited mobility include **MossRehab** (© 800/CALL-MOSS [800/225-5667]; www.mossresourcenet.org); the **American Foundation for the Blind (AFB)** (© 800/232-5463; www.afb.org); and **SATH** (Society for Accessible Travel & Hospitality) (© 212/447-7284; www.sath.org). **AirAmbulanceCard.com** is now partnered with SATH and allows you to preselect top-notch hospitals in case of an emergency.

Access-Able Travel Source (© 303/232-2979; www.access-able.com) offers a comprehensive database on travel agents from around the world with experience in accessible travel; destination-specific access information; and links to such resources as service animals, equipment rentals, and access guides.

Many travel agencies offer customized tours and itineraries for travelers with disabilities. Among them are **Flying Wheels Travel** (© 507/451-5005; www.flying wheelstravel.com); and **Accessible Journeys** (© 800/846-4537 or 610/521-0339; www.disabilitytravel.com).

Flying with Disability (www.flying-with-disability.org) is a comprehensive information source on airplane travel. **Avis Rent a Car** (© 888/879-4273) has an "Avis Access" program that offers services for customers with special travel needs. These include specially outfitted vehicles with swivel seats, spinner knobs, and hand controls; mobility scooter rentals; and accessible bus service. Be sure to reserve well in advance.

Also check out the quarterly magazine *Emerging Horizons* (www.emerging horizons.com), available by subscription ($17 per year U.S.; $22 outside the U.S.).

The "Accessible Travel" link at **Mobility-Advisor.com** offers a variety of travel resources to people with limited mobility.

British travelers should contact **Holiday Care** (© 0845-124-9971 in the U.K. only; www.holidaycare.org.uk) to access a wide range of travel information and resources for travelers with limited mobility and seniors.

GAY & LESBIAN TRAVELERS

When the city of **West Hollywood** was incorporated in 1984, it elected a lesbian mayor and a predominantly gay city council. West Hollywood, also known as

WeHo, has been waving the rainbow flag ever since. While L.A.'s large gay community is too vast to be contained in this 2-square-mile city, West Hollywood has the largest concentration of gay- and lesbian-oriented businesses and services. Santa Monica, Venice, Silver Lake, and Studio City are other lesbian and gay enclaves.

GUIDES & PUBLICATIONS There are many gay-oriented publications with information and up-to-date listings, including *Frontiers,* a Southern California–based biweekly; and *Nightlife,* a local weekly with comprehensive entertainment listings, complete with maps. The periodicals above are available at most newsstands citywide and at **A Different Light Bookstore** (8853 Santa Monica Blvd., West Hollywood; ℂ 310/854-6601; www.adlbooks.com), L.A.'s largest and best gay-oriented bookshop. Its website is also enormously helpful.

The **International Gay and Lesbian Travel Association (IGLTA)** (ℂ 800/448-8550 or 954/776-2626; www.iglta.org) is the trade association for the gay and lesbian travel industry, and offers an online directory of gay- and lesbian-friendly travel businesses and tour operators.

Many agencies offer tours and travel itineraries specifically for gay and lesbian travelers. **Above and Beyond Tours** (ℂ 800/397-2681; www.abovebeyond tours.com) are gay Australia tour specialists. San Francisco–based **Now, Voyager** (ℂ 800/255-6951; www.nowvoyager.com) offers worldwide trips and cruises. **Olivia** (ℂ 800/631-6277; www.olivia.com) offers lesbian cruises and resort vacations.

Gay.com Travel (ℂ 800/929-2268 or 415/644-8044; www.gay.com/travel or www.outandabout.com), is an excellent online successor to the popular *Out & About* print magazine. It provides regularly updated information about gay-owned, gay-oriented, and gay-friendly lodging, dining, sightseeing, nightlife, and shopping establishments in every important destination worldwide. British travelers should click on the "Travel" link at **www.uk.gay.com** for advice and gay-friendly trip ideas.

The following travel guides are available at many bookstores, or you can order them from any online bookseller: *Spartacus International Gay Guide, 35th Edition* (Bruno Gmünder Verlag; www.spartacusworld.com/gayguide) and *Odysseus: The International Gay Travel Planner, 17th Edition;* and the *Damron* guides (www.damron.com), with separate, annual books for gay men and lesbians.

SENIOR TRAVEL

Nearly every attraction in Los Angeles offers a senior discount; age requirements vary, and specific prices are listed in chapter 7. Public transportation and movie theaters also have reduced rates. Don't be shy about asking for discounts, but always carry some kind of identification, such as a driver's license, that shows your date of birth.

Members of **AARP,** 601 E St. NW, Washington, DC 20049 (ℂ 888/687-2277; www.aarp.org), get discounts on hotels, airfares, and car rentals. AARP offers members a wide range of benefits, including *AARP The Magazine* and a monthly newsletter. Anyone 50 and over can join.

Recommended publications offering travel resources and discounts for seniors include the quarterly magazine *Travel 50 & Beyond* (www.travel50andbeyond.com) and the bestselling paperback *Unbelievably Good Deals and Great Adventures That You Absolutely Can't Get Unless You're Over 50 2005–2006, 16th Edition* (McGraw-Hill), by Joann Rattner Heilman.

Kids Baby Gear & Babysitters

Babyland rents strollers, cribs, car seats, and the like from its store located at 7134 Topanga Canyon Blvd. (© **310/836-2222**). Rates vary; expect to spend around $35 per week for strollers and $72 per week (plus a deposit) for a crib. If you need a babysitter in L.A., contact the **Baby-Sitters Guild** (© **818/552-2229** or 310/837-1800), named the city's best by *Los Angeles* magazine. The concierge at larger hotels can also often recommend a reliable sitter.

FAMILY TRAVEL

If you have enough trouble getting your kids out of the house in the morning, dragging them thousands of miles away may seem like an insurmountable challenge. But family travel can be immensely rewarding, giving you new ways of seeing the world through smaller pairs of eyes.

To make things easier for families vacationing in L.A., I've included three family-friendly sidebars that highlight the best hotels (p. 104), restaurants (p. 126), and attractions (p. 183) for parents and kids. Also watch for the *Kids* icon throughout this guide.

Recommended family travel websites include **Family Travel Forum** (www.familytravelforum.com), a comprehensive site that offers customized trip planning; **Family Travel Network** (www.familytravelnetwork.com), an online magazine providing travel tips; and **Travel WithYourKids.com** (www.travelwithyourkids.com), a comprehensive site written by parents for parents offering sound advice for long-distance and international travel with children.

TRAVELING WITH PETS

If you're thinking of taking your pet along with you to romp on a California beach, make sure you do a little research. For one thing, dogs are restricted from most public beaches in the L.A. area. To find out where you can bring man's best friend, check out the online **Pets Welcome** service (www.petswelcome.com), which lists accommodations that allow pets. The site also lists pet-related publications, medical travel tips, and links to other pet-related websites.

A good book to carry along is *The California Dog Lover's Companion: The Insider's Scoop on Where to Take Your Dog* (Avalon Travel Publishing), a 900-page source for complete statewide listings of fenced dog parks, dog-friendly beaches, and other indispensable information.

Los Angeles has strict leash laws (including stiff penalties for failing to pick up waste), prompting the formation of a dog owner/supporter group called **Freeplay** (© **310/301-1550;** www.freeplay.org). Contact them for the latest developments on dog-related issues, including information on off-leash parks around town.

In the event that your pet requires medical care while you're visiting, call or visit the **California Animal Hospital,** 1736 S. Sepulveda Blvd., Suite D (south of Santa Monica Blvd.), Los Angeles (© **310/478-0248**). The **Animal Emergency Facility** (© **310/473-1561**), located in adjoining Suite A, is open 24 hours a day. The **www.petplace.org** website is another good source for emergency animal clinics.

8 Sustainable Tourism

Sustainable tourism is conscientious travel. It means being careful with the environments you explore, and respecting the communities you visit. Two overlapping components of sustainable travel are **ecotourism** and **ethical tourism.** The **International Ecotourism Society** (TIES) defines ecotourism as responsible travel to natural areas that conserves the environment and improves the well-being of local people. TIES suggests that ecotourists follow these principles:

• Minimize environmental impact.
• Build environmental and cultural awareness and respect.
• Provide positive experiences for both visitors and hosts.
• Provide direct financial benefits for conservation and for local people.
• Raise sensitivity to host countries' political, environmental, and social climates.
• Support international human rights and labor agreements.

You can find some eco-friendly travel tips and statistics, as well as touring companies and associations—listed by destination under "Travel Choice"—at the **TIES** website, www.ecotourism.org. Also check out **Ecotravel.com**, which lets you search for sustainable touring companies in several categories (water-based, land-based, spiritually oriented, and so on).

While much of the focus of ecotourism is about reducing impacts on the natural environment, ethical tourism concentrates on ways to preserve and enhance local economies and communities, regardless of location. You can embrace ethical tourism by staying at a locally owned hotel or shopping at a store that employs local workers and sells locally produced goods.

Responsible Travel (www.responsible travel.com) is a great source of sustainable travel ideas; the site is run by a spokesperson for ethical tourism in the travel industry. **Sustainable Travel International** (www.sustainabletravelinternational.org) promotes ethical tourism practices, and manages an extensive directory of sustainable properties and tour operators around the world.

In the U.K., **Tourism Concern** (www.tourismconcern.org.uk) works to reduce social and environmental problems connected to tourism. The **Association of Independent Tour Operators (AITO)** (www.aito.co.uk) is a group of specialist operators leading the field in making holidays sustainable.

Volunteer travel has become increasingly popular among those who want to venture beyond the standard group-tour experience to learn languages, interact with locals, and make a positive difference while on vacation. Volunteer travel usually doesn't require special skills—just a willingness to work hard—and programs vary in length from a few days to a number of weeks. Some programs provide free housing and food, but many require volunteers to pay for travel expenses, which can add up quickly.

For general info on volunteer travel, visit **www.volunteerabroad.org** and **www.idealist.org**. Before you commit to a volunteer program, it's important to make sure any money you're giving is truly going back to the local community, and that the work you'll be doing will be a good fit for you. **Volunteer International** (www.volunteerinternational.org) has a helpful list of questions to ask to determine the intentions and the nature of a volunteer program.

Tips It's Easy Being Green

Here are a few simple ways you can help conserve fuel and energy when you travel:

- Each time you take a flight or drive a car, greenhouse gases release into the atmosphere. You can help neutralize this danger to the planet through "carbon offsetting"—paying someone to invest your money in programs that reduce your greenhouse gas emissions by the same amount you've added. Before buying carbon offset credits, just make sure that you're using a reputable company, one with a proven program that invests in renewable energy. Reliable carbon offset companies include **Carbonfund** (www.carbonfund.org), **TerraPass** (www.terrapass.org), and **Carbon Neutral** (www.carbonneutral.org).

- Whenever possible, choose nonstop flights; they generally require less fuel than indirect flights that stop and take off again. Try to fly during the day—some scientists estimate that nighttime flights are twice as harmful to the environment. And pack light—each 15 pounds of luggage on a 5,000-mile flight adds up to 50 pounds of carbon dioxide emitted.

- Where you stay during your travels can have a major environmental impact. To determine the green credentials of a property, ask about trash disposal and recycling, water conservation, and energy use; also question if sustainable materials were used in the construction of the property. The website **www.greenhotels.com** recommends green-rated member hotels around the world that fulfill the company's stringent environmental requirements. Also consult **www.environmentallyfriendlyhotels.com** for more green accommodations ratings.

- At hotels, request that your sheets and towels not be changed daily. (Many hotels already have programs like this in place.) Turn off the lights and air-conditioner (or heater) when you leave your room.

- Use public transport where possible—trains, buses, and even taxis are more energy-efficient forms of transport than driving. Even better is to walk or cycle; you'll produce zero emissions and stay fit and healthy on your travels.

- If renting a car is necessary, ask the rental agent for a hybrid, or rent the most fuel-efficient car available. You'll use less gas and save money at the tank.

- Eat at locally owned and operated restaurants that use produce grown in the area. This contributes to the local economy and cuts down on greenhouse gas emissions by supporting restaurants where the food is not flown or trucked in across long distances. Visit **Sustain Lane** (www.sustainlane.org) to find sustainable eating and drinking choices around the U.S.; also check out **www.eatwellguide.org** for tips on eating sustainably in the U.S. and Canada.

Frommers.com: The Complete Travel Resource

Planning a trip or just returned? Head to **Frommers.com**, voted Best Travel Site by *PC Magazine*. We think you'll find our site indispensable before, during, and after your travels—with expert advice and tips; independent reviews of hotels, restaurants, attractions, and preferred shopping and nightlife venues; vacation giveaways; and an online booking tool. We publish the complete contents of over 135 travel guides in our **Destinations** section, covering over 4,000 places worldwide. Each weekday, we publish original articles that report on **Deals and News** via our free **Frommers.com Newsletters**. What's more, **Arthur Frommer** himself blogs 5 days a week, with cutting opinions about the state of travel in the modern world. We're betting you'll find our **Events** listings an invaluable resource; it's an up-to-the-minute roster of what's happening in cities everywhere—including concerts, festivals, lectures, and more. We've also added weekly **podcasts, interactive maps,** and hundreds of new images across the site. Finally, don't forget to visit our **Message Boards,** where you can join in conversations with thousands of fellow Frommer's travelers and post your trip report once you return.

9 Packages for the Independent Traveler

Package tours are simply a way to buy the airfare, accommodations, and other elements of your trip (such as car rentals, airport transfers, and sometimes even activities) at the same time and often at discounted prices.

One good source of package deals is the airlines themselves. Most major airlines offer air/land packages, including **American Airlines Vacations** (© 800/321-2121; www.aavacations.com), **Delta Vacations** (© 800/654-6559; www.deltavacations.com), **Continental Airlines Vacations** (© 800/301-3800; www.covacations.com), and **United Vacations** (© 888/854-3899; www.unitedvacations.com). Several big **online travel agencies** —Expedia, Travelocity, Orbitz, Site59, and Lastminute.com—also do a brisk business in packages.

Travel packages are also listed in the travel section of your local Sunday newspaper. Or check ads in the national travel magazines such as *Arthur Frommer's Budget Travel Magazine, Travel + Leisure, National Geographic Traveler,* and *Condé Nast Traveler.*

For more information on Package Tours and for tips on booking your trip, see frommers.com.

10 Escorted General-Interest Tours

Escorted tours are structured group tours, with a group leader. The price usually includes everything from airfare to hotels, meals, tours, admission costs, and local transportation.

Despite the fact that escorted tours require big deposits and predetermined hotels, restaurants, and itineraries, many people derive security and peace of mind from the structure they offer. Escorted tours—whether they're navigated by bus, motorcoach, train, or boat—let travelers sit back and enjoy the trip without having to drive or worry about details. They take you to the maximum number of sights in the minimum amount of time with the least amount of hassle. They're particularly convenient for people with limited mobility and they can be a great way to make new friends.

On the downside, you'll have little opportunity for serendipitous interactions with locals. The tours can be jampacked with activities, leaving little room for individual sightseeing, whim, or adventure—plus they often focus on the heavily touristed sites, so you miss out on many a lesser-known gem.

For more information on Escorted General-Interest Tours, including questions to ask before booking your trip, see frommers.com.

11 Staying Connected

TELEPHONES

Generally, hotel surcharges on long-distance and local calls are astronomical, so you're better off using your **cellphone** or a **public pay telephone.** Many convenience groceries and packaging services sell **prepaid calling cards** in denominations up to $50; for international visitors these can be the least expensive way to call home. Many public pay phones at airports now accept American Express, MasterCard, and Visa credit cards. **Local calls** made from pay phones in most locales cost either 25¢ or 35¢ (no pennies, please).

Most long-distance and international calls can be dialed directly from any phone. **For calls within the United States and to Canada,** dial 1 followed by the area code and the seven-digit number. **For other international calls,** dial 011 followed by the country code, city code, and the number you are calling.

Calls to area codes **800, 888, 877,** and **866** are toll-free. However, calls to area codes **700** and **900** (chat lines, bulletin boards, "dating" services, and so on) can be very expensive—usually a charge of 95¢ to $3 or more per minute, and they sometimes have minimum charges that can run as high as $15 or more.

For **reversed-charge or collect calls,** and for person-to-person calls, dial the number 0 then the area code and number; an operator will come on the line, and you should specify whether you are calling collect, person-to-person, or both. If your operator-assisted call is international, ask for the overseas operator.

For **local directory assistance** ("information"), dial 411; for long-distance information, dial 1, then the appropriate area code and 555-1212.

CELLPHONES

Just because your cellphone works at home doesn't mean it'll work everywhere in the U.S. (thanks to our nation's fragmented cellphone system). It's a good bet that your phone will work in major cities, but take a look at your wireless company's coverage map on its website before heading out; T-Mobile, Sprint, and Nextel are particularly weak in rural areas. If you need to stay in touch at a destination where you know your phone won't work, **rent** a phone that does from **InTouch USA** (© **800/872-7626;** www.intouch global.com) or a rental car location, but be aware that you'll pay $1 a minute or more for airtime.

If you're not from the U.S., you'll be appalled at the poor reach of our **GSM (Global System for Mobile Communications) wireless network,** which is used by much of the rest of the world. Your

> **Tips Wireless West Hollywood**
>
> If you're bringing along your PDA or laptop to L.A. (geek), you might want to hang out in West Hollywood, which has gone wireless. The City of West Hollywood is keeping visitors connected to the Web with free outdoor high-speed wireless Internet access. The pilot project area encompasses Santa Monica Boulevard between La Brea and Fairfax avenues.

phone will probably work in most major U.S. cities; it definitely won't work in many rural areas. To see where GSM phones work in the U.S., check out www.t-mobile.com/coverage/national_popup.asp. And you may or may not be able to send SMS (text messaging) home.

For visitors arriving via LAX airport, a phone rental company called **Triptel** has a rental kiosk located on the arrival level of the international terminal. The daily rental fee is $3, and nationwide coverage is $1.25 per minute. At the end of your stay the phones can be dropped off at the airport or shipped back via Federal Express for an additional fee. For more information call © **877/TRI-PTEL** (877/ 874-7835) or log onto www.triptel.com.

INTERNET/E-MAIL
WITHOUT YOUR OWN COMPUTER

To find cybercafes in your destination check **www.cybercaptive.com** and **www. cybercafe.com**.

Most major airports have **Internet kiosks** that provide basic Web access for a per-minute fee that's usually higher than cybercafe prices. Check out copy shops like **Kinko's** (FedEx Kinkos),

which offers computer stations with fully loaded software (as well as Wi-Fi).

WITH YOUR OWN COMPUTER

More and more hotels, resorts, airports, cafes, and retailers are going Wi-Fi (wireless fidelity), becoming "hotspots" that offer free high-speed Wi-Fi access or charge a small fee for usage. Wi-Fi is even found in campgrounds, RV parks, and even entire towns. Most laptops sold today have built-in wireless capability. To find public Wi-Fi hotspots at your destination, go to **www.jiwire.com**; its Hotspot Finder holds the world's largest directory of public wireless hotspots.

For dial-up access, most business-class hotels in the U.S. offer dataports for laptop modems, and a few thousand hotels in the U.S. and Europe now offer free high-speed Internet access.

Wherever you go, bring a **connection kit** of the right power and phone adapters, a spare phone cord, and a spare Ethernet network cable—or find out whether your hotel supplies them to guests.

For information on electrical currency conversions, see "Electricity," in the "Fast Facts: Los Angeles" section of the appendix.

4

Suggested Los Angeles Itineraries

If you've left your brain at the office and want someone else to make the tough decisions during your vacation, you'll love this chapter. It's where I tell you what *I* think you should see and do during your time in L.A. The itineraries are broken down into 1-, 2-, and 3-day sections, depending on how long you're in town. If you've already made your way through "The Best of Los Angeles in 1 Day," the 2-day tour starts where the 1-day schedule left off, and so on.

But if you really want to enjoy even a fraction of what L.A. has to offer, you should plan on staying at least 3 days, preferably a week (besides, it'll increase your chances of getting discovered). And this might seem obvious, but you'll need a car to get around—public transportation in L.A. is terrible.

1 Orientation

VISITOR INFORMATION CENTERS

The **Los Angeles Convention and Visitors Bureau** (or **LA INC.;** © 800/228-2452 or 213/624-7300; www.discoverlosangeles.com) is the city's main source for information. In addition to maintaining an informative website, answering telephone inquiries, and sending free visitors kits, the bureau provides two **walk-in visitor centers:** Downtown at 685 S. Figueroa St. at West 7th Street (Mon–Fri 9am–5pm), and in Hollywood at the Hollywood & Highland Center, 6801 Hollywood Blvd. at Highland Avenue (daily 10am–11pm).

Many Los Angeles–area communities also have their own information centers and often maintain detailed and colorful websites that are loaded with timely information. These include the following:

- The **Beverly Hills Visitors Bureau,** 239 S. Beverly Dr. (© 800/345-2210 or 310/248-1015; www.beverlyhillscvb.com), is open Monday through Friday from 8:30am to 5pm.
- The **Hollywood Arts Council,** P.O. Box 931056, Dept. 1995, Hollywood, CA 90093 (© 323/462-2355; www.discoverhollywood.com), publishes the magazine *Discover Hollywood,* a biannual publication that contains listings and schedules for the area's many theaters, galleries, music venues, and comedy clubs; the current issue is always available online. You can also load up on info at the **Hollywood Visitor Center,** 6801 Hollywood Blvd., Ste. 237 (© 323/467-6412), on the second level of the Hollywood & Highland mall (btw. Babylon Court and Awards Walk).

- The **West Hollywood Convention and Visitors Bureau,** 8687 Melrose Ave., M-26, West Hollywood, CA 90096 (© **800/368-6020** or 310/289-2525; www.visit westhollywood.com), is located in the Pacific Design Center and is open Monday through Friday from 9am to 6pm.
- The **Santa Monica Convention and Visitors Bureau** (© **800/544-5319** or 310/393-7593; www.santamonica.com) is the best source for information about Santa Monica. The Palisades Park walk-up center is located near the Santa Monica Pier, at 1400 Ocean Ave. (btw. Santa Monica Blvd. and Broadway), and is open daily from 10am to 4pm. Also check out **www.malibu.org** for information about Malibu, to the northwest.
- The **Pasadena Convention and Visitors Bureau,** 171 S. Los Robles Ave. (© **626/795-9311;** www.pasadenacal.com), is open Monday through Friday from 8am to 5pm and Saturday from 10am to 4pm.

OTHER INFORMATION SOURCES

Local tourist boards are great for information regarding attractions and special events, but they often fail to keep a finger on the pulse of what's "in" in L.A., especially with regard to dining, culture, and nightlife. Several city-oriented newspapers and magazines offer more up-to-date info. *L.A. Weekly* (www.laweekly.com), a free listings magazine, is packed with information on current events around town. It's available from sidewalk news racks and in many stores and restaurants around the city.

The *Los Angeles Times* "Calendar" section of the Sunday paper, an excellent guide to the world of entertainment in and around L.A., includes listings of what's doing and where to do it. The *Times* also maintains a comprehensive website at www.theguide.latimes.com. Information is culled from the newspaper's many departments and is always up-to-date. If you want to check out L.A.'s most immediate news, the *Times*'s main website is **www.latimes.com**.

Los Angeles magazine (**www.lamag.com**) is a glossy city-based monthly full of real news and pure gossip, plus guides to L.A.'s art, music, and food scenes. Its calendar of events gives an excellent overview of goings-on at museums, art galleries, musical venues, and other places. The magazine is available at newsstands around town and in other major U.S. cities; you can also access stories and listings from the current issue on the Internet. Cybersurfers should visit @ L.A.'s website, **www.at-la.com**; its exceptional search engine provides links to more than 23,000 sites relating to the L.A. area, including many destinations covered in chapter 11.

CITY LAYOUT

Los Angeles isn't a single compact city like San Francisco, but a sprawling suburbia comprising dozens of disparate communities located either on the ocean or on the flatlands of a huge desert basin. Ocean breezes push the city's infamous smog inland and through mountain passes into the sprawl of the San Fernando and San Gabriel valleys. Downtown L.A. is in the center of the basin, about 12 miles east of the Pacific Ocean. Most visitors spend the bulk of their time either along the coastline or on the city's ever-trendy Westside.

NEIGHBORHOODS IN BRIEF
Santa Monica & the Beaches

These are nearly everyone's favorite L.A. communities and get my highest recommendation as the premier place to book a hotel during your vacation. The 60-mile beachfront stretching from Malibu to the Palos Verdes peninsula has milder weather and less smog than the inland communities, and traffic is lighter, except on summer weekends. The towns along the coast each have a distinct mood and charm, and most are connected via a walk/bike path. They're listed below from north to south.

Malibu At the northern border of Los Angeles County, 25 miles from Downtown, Malibu was once a privately owned ranch—purchased in 1857 for 10¢ an acre and now the most expensive real estate in L.A. Today its 27 miles of wide beaches, beachfront cliffs, sparsely populated hills, and relative remoteness from the inner city make it popular with rich recluses such as Cher and Mel Gibson. Indeed, the resident lists of Malibu Colony and nearby Broad Beach—oceanfront strips of closely packed mansions—read like a who's who in Hollywood. With plenty of green space and dramatic rocky outcroppings, Malibu's rural beauty is unsurpassed in L.A., and surfers flock to "the 'Bu" for great, if crowded, waves.

Santa Monica Los Angeles's premier beach community, Santa Monica is known for its festive ocean pier, stylish oceanfront hotels, artsy atmosphere, and large population of homeless residents (I know, that's an oxymoron, but it fits). Shopping is king here, especially along the Third Street Promenade, a pedestrian-only outdoor mall lined with dozens of shops and restaurants.

Venice Beach Created by tobacco mogul Abbot Kinney (who set out in 1904 to transform a worthless marsh into a resort town modeled after Venice, Italy), Venice Beach has a series of narrow canals connected by one-lane bridges that you'll see as you explore this refreshingly eclectic community. It was once infested with grime and crime, but regentrification has brought scores of great restaurants, boutiques, and rising property values for the canal-side homes and apartment duplexes. Even the movie stars are moving in: Dennis Hopper, Anjelica Huston, Nicolas Cage, and Julia Roberts reside here. Some of L.A.'s most innovative and interesting architecture lines funky Main Street. But without question, Venice Beach is best known for its Ocean Front Walk, a nonstop Mardi Gras of thong-wearing skaters, fortunetellers, street musicians, and poseurs of all ages, colors, types, and sizes.

Marina del Rey Just south of Venice, Marina del Ray is a somewhat quieter, more upscale waterside community best known for its man-made small-craft harbor, the largest of its kind in the world. Fittingly, it offers a wide variety of public boating opportunities, including fishing trips, harbor tours, dinner cruises, and private sailing charters.

Manhattan, Hermosa & Redondo beaches These are laid-back, mainly residential neighborhoods with modest homes (except for oceanfront real estate), mild weather, and residents happy to have fled the L.A. hubbub. There are excellent beaches for volleyball, surfing, and tanning here, but when it comes to cultural activities, pickings can be slim. The restaurant

L.A. Neighborhoods in Brief

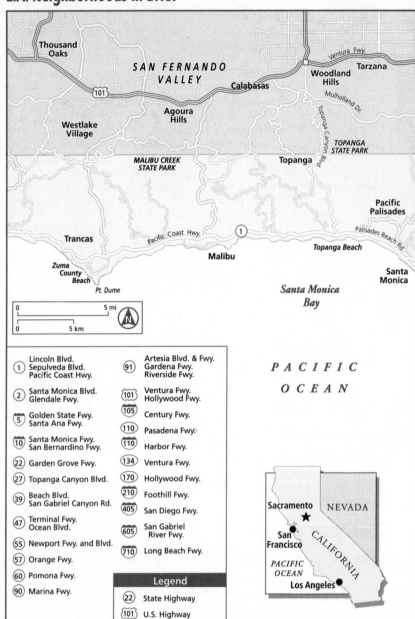

Lincoln Blvd.
1 Sepulveda Blvd.
Pacific Coast Hwy.

2 Santa Monica Blvd.
Glendale Fwy.

5 Golden State Fwy.
Santa Ana Fwy.

10 Santa Monica Fwy.
San Bernardino Fwy.

22 Garden Grove Fwy.

27 Topanga Canyon Blvd.

39 Beach Blvd.
San Gabriel Canyon Rd.

47 Terminal Fwy.
Ocean Blvd.

55 Newport Fwy. and Blvd.

57 Orange Fwy.

60 Pomona Fwy.

90 Marina Fwy.

91 Artesia Blvd. & Fwy.
Gardena Fwy.
Riverside Fwy.

101 Ventura Fwy.
Hollywood Fwy.

105 Century Fwy.

110 Pasadena Fwy.

110 Harbor Fwy.

134 Ventura Fwy.

170 Hollywood Fwy.

210 Foothill Fwy.

405 San Diego Fwy.

605 San Gabriel
River Fwy.

710 Long Beach Fwy.

Legend

22 State Highway

101 U.S. Highway

210 Interstate Highway

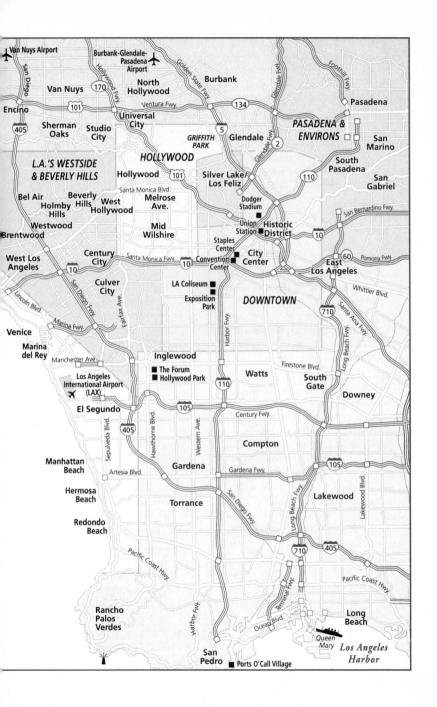

scene, while limited, has been improving steadily, and some great new bars and clubs have opened near their respective piers.

L.A.'s Westside & Beverly Hills

The **Westside,** sandwiched between Hollywood and the city's coastal communities, includes some of Los Angeles's most prestigious neighborhoods, virtually all with names you're sure to recognize:

Beverly Hills Politically distinct from the rest of Los Angeles, Beverly Hills is a famous enclave best known for its palm tree–lined streets of palatial homes, famous residents (Jack Nicholson, Warren Beatty and Annette Bening), and high-priced shops. But it's not all glitz and glamour; the healthy mix of filthy rich, wannabes, and tourists that peoples downtown Beverly Hills creates a unique—and often snobby-surreal—atmosphere.

West Hollywood This key-shaped community's epicenter is the intersection of Santa Monica and La Cienega boulevards. Nestled between Beverly Hills and Hollywood, this politically independent—and blissfully fast food free—town is home to some of the area's best restaurants, clubs, shops, and art galleries. WeHo, as it's come to be known, is also the center of L.A.'s gay community—you'll know you've arrived when you see the risqué billboards. Encompassing about 2 square miles, it's a pedestrian-friendly place with plenty of metered parking. Highlights include the 1½ miles of Sunset Boulevard known as Sunset Strip, the chic Sunset Plaza retail strip, and the liveliest stretch of Santa Monica Boulevard.

Bel Air & Holmby Hills Located in the hills north of Westwood and west of Beverly Hills, these are old-money residential areas that are featured prominently on most maps to the stars' homes.

Brentwood Brentwood is best known as the famous backdrop to the O. J. Simpson melodrama. The neighborhood itself is generic, a relatively upscale mix of tract homes, restaurants, and strip malls. The Getty Center looms over Brentwood from its hilltop perch next to I-405.

Westwood An urban village founded in 1929 and home to the University of California at Los Angeles (UCLA), Westwood used to be a hot destination for a night on the town, but it lost much of its appeal in the past decade due to overcrowding and even some minor street violence. Although Westwood is unlikely to regain its old charm, the vibrant culinary scene has brought new life to the village. Combined with the high concentration of movie theaters, Westwood is now the premier L.A. destination for dinner and a flick.

Century City This a compact and rather bland area sandwiched between West Los Angeles and Beverly Hills. The primary draws here are the 20th Century Fox studios, Shubert Theatre, and the Westside Pavilion, a huge open-air shopping mall. Century City's three main thoroughfares are Century Park East, Avenue of the Stars, and Century Park West.

West Los Angeles West Los Angeles is a label that generally applies to everything that isn't one of the other Westside neighborhoods. It's basically the area south of Santa Monica Boulevard, north of Venice Boulevard, east of Santa Monica and Venice, and west and south of Century City.

Hollywood

Yes, they still come to the mecca of the film industry—young hopefuls with stars in their eyes gravitate to this historic heart of L.A.'s movie production like moths fluttering to the glare of neon lights. But today's Hollywood is more illusion than industry. Many of the neighborhood's former movie studios have moved to more spacious venues in Burbank, the Westside, and other parts of the city.

Despite the downturn, visitors continue to flock to Hollywood's landmark attractions, such as the star-studded Walk of Fame and Grauman's Chinese Theatre. And now that the city's $1-billion, 30-year revitalization project is in full swing, Hollywood Boulevard is, for the first time in decades, showing signs of rising out of a seedy slump, with refurbished movie houses and stylish restaurants and clubs making a fierce comeback. The centerpiece Hollywood & Highland complex anchors the neighborhood, with shopping, entertainment, and a luxury hotel built around the beautiful Kodak Theatre designed specifically to host the Academy Awards (really, you'll want to poke your head into this gorgeous theater).

Melrose Avenue Scruffy but fun, Melrose Avenue is the city's funkiest shopping district, catering to often-raucous youth with secondhand and avant-garde clothing shops. There are also several good restaurants.

The stretch of Wilshire Boulevard running through the southern part of Hollywood is known as the **Mid-Wilshire** district, or the Miracle Mile. It's lined with tall, contemporary apartment houses and office buildings. The section just east of Fairfax Avenue, known as Museum Row, is home to almost a dozen museums, including the Los Angeles County Museum of Art, the La Brea Tar Pits, and that shrine to L.A. car culture, the Petersen Automotive Museum.

Griffith Park Up Western Avenue in the northernmost part of Hollywood, this is one of the country's largest urban parks, home to the Los Angeles Zoo, the famous Griffith Observatory, and the outdoor Greek Theater.

Downtown

Despite the relatively recent construction of several major cultural and entertainment centers (such as the Walt Disney Concert Hall, L.A. LIVE, and Cathedral of Our Lady of the Angels) and a handful of trendy restaurants, L.A.'s Downtown isn't the tourist hub it would be in most cities. When it comes to entertaining visitors, the Westside, Hollywood, and beach communities are all far more popular.

Easily recognized by the tight cluster of high-rise offices—skyscrapers bolstered by earthquake-proof technology—the business center of the city is eerily vacant on weekends and evenings, but the outlying residential communities, such as Koreatown, Little Tokyo, Chinatown, and Los Feliz, are enticingly ethnic and vibrant. If you want a tan, head to Santa Monica, but if you want a refreshing dose of non-90210 culture, come here.

El Pueblo de Los Angeles Historic District This is a 44-acre ode to the city's early years and is worth a visit. **Chinatown** is small and touristy, but can be plenty of fun for souvenir hunting or traditional dim sum. **Little Tokyo,** on the other hand, is a genuine gathering place for the Southland's Japanese population, with a wide array of shops and restaurants with an authentic flair.

Silver Lake This residential neighborhood just north of Downtown and adjacent to **Los Feliz** (home to the Los Angeles Zoo and Griffith Park), just to the west, has arty areas with unique cafes, theaters, graffiti, and art galleries—all in equally plentiful proportions. The local music scene has been burgeoning of late.

Exposition Park South and west of Downtown is home to the Los Angeles Memorial Coliseum and the L.A. Sports Arena, as well as the Natural History Museum, the African-American Museum, and the California Science Center. The University of Southern California (USC) is next door.

The San Fernando Valley

The San Fernando Valley, known locally as "the Valley," was nationally popularized in the 1980s by the notorious mall-loving "Valley Girl!" stereotype. Sandwiched between the Santa Monica and the San Gabriel mountain ranges, most of the Valley is residential and commercial and off the beaten track for tourists. But some of its attractions are bound to draw you over the hill. **Universal City,** located west of Griffith Park between U.S. 101 and California 134, is home to Universal Studios Hollywood and the supersize shopping and entertainment complex CityWalk. About the only reason to go to **Burbank,** west of these other suburbs and north of Universal City, is to see one of your favorite TV shows being filmed at NBC or Warner Brothers Studios. There are also a few good restaurants and shops along Ventura Boulevard, in and around Studio City.

Glendale Glendale is a largely residential community north of Downtown between the Valley and Pasadena. Here you'll find Forest Lawn, the city's best cemetery for very retired movie stars.

Pasadena & Environs

Best known as the site of the Tournament of Roses Parade each New Year's Day, **Pasadena** was spared from the tear-down epidemic that swept L.A., so it has a refreshing old-time feel. Once upon a time, Pasadena was every Angeleno's best-kept secret: a quiet community whose slow and careful regentrification meant nonchain restaurants and boutique shopping without the crowds, in a revitalized downtown respectful of its old brick and stone commercial buildings. Although the area's natural and architectural beauty still shines through—so much so that Pasadena remains Hollywood's favorite backyard location for countless movies and TV shows—Old Town has become a pedestrian mall similar to Santa Monica's Third Street Promenade, complete with huge crowds, midrange chain eateries, and standard-issue mall stores. It still gets our vote as a scenic alternative to the congestion of central L.A., but it has lost much of its small-town charm.

Pasadena is also home to the famous California Institute of Technology (CalTech), which boasts 22 Nobel prize winners among its alumni. The CalTech-operated Jet Propulsion Laboratory was the birthplace of America's space program, and CalTech scientists were the first to report earthquake activity worldwide in the 1930s.

The residential neighborhoods in Pasadena and its adjacent communities—**Arcadia, La Cañada–Flintridge, San Marino,** and **South Pasadena**—are renowned for well-preserved historic homes, from humble bungalows to lavish mansions. These areas feature public gardens, historic neighborhoods, house museums, and quiet bed-and-breakfast inns.

2 The Best of Los Angeles in 1 Day

Seeing the top sights of Los Angeles in a single day requires an early start and a bit of stamina, but it's quite doable. This "greatest hits" itinerary begins with L.A.'s sine qua non attraction, Hollywood. After lunch, you'll cruise along Sunset Boulevard to the beach and spend a few hours on foot touring the Santa Monica Pier and Venice Beach. You'll conclude your, like, most excellent day with a live performance under the stars at the legendary Hollywood Bowl. ***Start:*** *Corner of Gower Street and Hollywood Boulevard, and walk west.*

❶ Hollywood Walk of Fame 🅐🅐

Forget the culture/museum stuff—it's time to see for yourself all those famous Hollywood sites you've watched on TV since you were a toddler. Start the day by spending the morning on Hollywood Boulevard, following the path of bronze-and-marble stars along the Walk of Fame. Since 1960, more than 2,000 celebrities have been honored along the world's most famous sidewalk, but you'll need an old-timer to explain who a lot of the now-long-dead entertainers were. For a few bucks you can buy a map that lists every star; better yet, log on to www.hollywoodchamber.net and plan your own "Favorite Celebrities" route. See p. 164.

On Hollywood Boulevard, between Highland Avenue and La Brea Avenue, you'll find:

❷ Grauman's Chinese Theatre 🅐

It's sort of a tourist rite of passage to compare your hands and feet with the famous prints set in cement at the entrance court to Grauman's Chinese Theatre, a tradition started when silent film star Norma Talmadge "accidentally" stepped in wet cement during the premiere of Cecil B. DeMille's *King of Kings*. Because it's along the Hollywood Walk of Fame, you're already here. Go ahead—compare your shoes to footprints left by Humphrey Bogart or Marilyn Monroe. There are about 160 celebrity squares to scrutinize: See if you can find Whoopi Goldberg's dreadlocks, Bob Hope's nose, Betty Grable's gams, and R2D2's wheels. See p. 163.

Stay at Grauman's for the:

❸ Movie Stars' Homes Tour 🅐

Oh, c'mon! You know you want to do it. It's not like you're the only one who feels slightly guilty by paying to peek into the private lives of Harrison Ford, Barbra Streisand, and Richard Gere (hey, nobody forced them buy a home around Hollywood). Besides, you're already here—the 2-hour tours leave every half-hour between 9:30am and 5:30pm in front of Grauman's Chinese Theatre. Just buy a ticket at the Starline kiosk in front of you, hop into an air-conditioned minibus, and let the voyeurism begin. See p. 200.

❹ MUSSO & FRANK GRILL 🅐🅐

Time for lunch. Walk down the street to Musso & Frank Grill, Hollywood's oldest restaurant (since 1919) and a paragon of Hollywood's halcyon-era grillrooms. Part restaurant, part museum, this is where Faulkner, Hemingway, and Orson Welles derived liquid inspiration during their screenwriting days. Slither into one of the red-leather booths, order one of the legendary martinis or bloody marys from the gruff red-coated waiters, and work on that Atkins diet with a fat rib-eye. 6667 Hollywood Blvd. (at Cherokee Ave.). ☎ 323/467-7788. See p. 142.

After lunch, waddle to your rented convertible red Mustang (you did rent a convertible red Mustang, didn't you?), put in a *Best of the Beach Boys* CD, and slowly cruise the legendary:

L.A. Suggested Itineraries

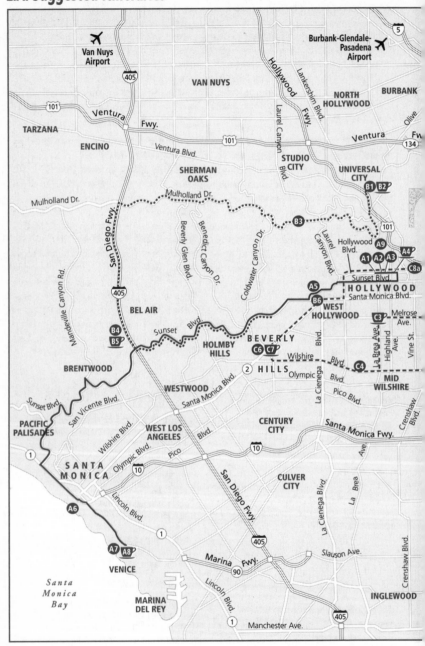

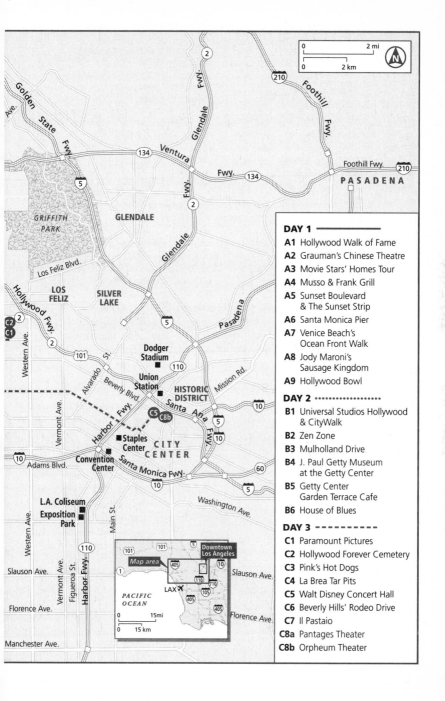

DAY 1 ———

- **A1** Hollywood Walk of Fame
- **A2** Grauman's Chinese Theatre
- **A3** Movie Stars' Homes Tour
- **A4** Musso & Frank Grill
- **A5** Sunset Boulevard & The Sunset Strip
- **A6** Santa Monica Pier
- **A7** Venice Beach's Ocean Front Walk
- **A8** Jody Maroni's Sausage Kingdom
- **A9** Hollywood Bowl

DAY 2 ···············

- **B1** Universal Studios Hollywood & CityWalk
- **B2** Zen Zone
- **B3** Mulholland Drive
- **B4** J. Paul Getty Museum at the Getty Center
- **B5** Getty Center Garden Terrace Cafe
- **B6** House of Blues

DAY 3 ----------

- **C1** Paramount Pictures
- **C2** Hollywood Forever Cemetery
- **C3** Pink's Hot Dogs
- **C4** La Brea Tar Pits
- **C5** Walt Disney Concert Hall
- **C6** Beverly Hills' Rodeo Drive
- **C7** Il Pastaio
- **C8a** Pantages Theater
- **C8b** Orpheum Theater

❺ Sunset Boulevard & The Sunset Strip ⭐⭐

This 45-minute-or-so drive takes you from sorta-seedy Hollywood to flamboyant West Hollywood, past the moneyed mini-mansions of Beverly Hills, through neighborhoods most people can't afford to live in such as Westside and Brentwood, winding your way into the secluded enclave of Pacific Palisades toward Malibu, and finally the Pacific Coast Highway ("PCH," if you're hip). The entire drive takes you through a cross section of nearly everything the western side of Los Angeles has to offer. See p. 169 for an itinerary of the Strip.

Drive south on the PCH into the big-city beach town of Santa Monica, and park at the:

❻ Santa Monica Pier ⭐⭐

Built in 1908 for passenger and cargo ships, the pier does a pretty good job of recapturing the glory days of Southern California. Buy an ice-cream cone at one of the snack shacks and stroll seaward past the wooden carousel, roller coaster, and arcades, then buy a ticket to ride the Ferris wheel (when's the last time you rode on a Ferris wheel?). See p. 166.

From the pier, walk south to the carnival-like stretch known as:

❼ Venice Beach's Ocean Front Walk ⭐⭐⭐

For first-timers, this pseudo-bohemian scene is a bit of a shock to the senses: a surreal assemblage of street performers, musicians, musclemen pumping serious iron, apocalyptic evangelists, break dancers, stoned drummers, and endless schlock shops. By now your feet are probably talking to you, so stop at one of the outdoor cafes and have a beer while taking in the scene. This is also where you can rent a bike and cruise along the 8-mile bike path that runs along the beach.

---

❽ JODY MARONI'S SAUSAGE KINGDOM ⭐⭐

Along the Ocean Front Walk is a brightly colored food stand called Jody Maroni's Sausage Kingdom (look for the line), a favorite among sausage-worshiping locals. The all-natural, preservative-free "haute dogs" come in all sorts of flavors—Toulouse garlic, Bombay curried lamb, orange-garlic-cumin—served on a freshly baked onion roll and smothered with grilled onions and peppers. No matter which one you choose, they're all wieners. 2011 Ocean Front Walk (north of Venice Blvd.). ☎ 310/822-5639. See p. 121.

Pile into the convertible and cruise northeast on Santa Monica Boulevard all the way across town (or take the I-10 east to Hwy. 110 north to Hwy. 101 north) to the:

❾ Hollywood Bowl ⭐⭐⭐

I've saved the best for last: the Hollywood Bowl. I've yet to meet anyone who hasn't had a wonderful experience at the Bowl, an elegant Greek-style natural outdoor amphitheater cradled in a small canyon northeast of Hollywood. Truly, it's one of L.A.'s grandest traditions, watching a live performance under the stars on a warm summer night while noshing on caviar and champagne. It's the summer home of the Los Angeles Philharmonic and Hollywood Bowl orchestras, and often hosts internationally known conductors, soloists, and popular acts ranging from Radiohead to Garrison Keillor. Here's how you do the Bowl right: Reserve a box seat section as far in advance as possible, then preorder a gourmet picnic basket filled with hot and cold dishes, desserts, and fine wines from the excellent on-site catering department, which will deliver the goodies to your box once you arrive. See p. 278.

3 The Best of Los Angeles in 2 Days

On your second day you'll continue seeing L.A.'s biggest attractions: Universal Studios Hollywood (the most popular attraction in L.A.), the massive gazillion-dollar Getty Center, and the rockin' Sunset Strip House of Blues. It's another full day on your feet, so wear comfortable shoes and make that coffee drink a double. Also, you'll want to make advance reservations: Buy tickets online for Universal Studios, and reserve a table at the House of Blues. *Start: Universal Studios.*

❶ Universal Studios Hollywood & CityWalk 🏛🏛

A visit to Universal Studios Hollywood will accomplish three classic L.A. experiences in one swoop: taking a studio tour, visiting an amusement park, and strolling through an outdoor megamall. Start with the 1-hour guided tram ride around the studio's 420 acres of actual movie sets, then hit the movie-themed thrill rides and shows, and end with an amble through Universal CityWalk, a 3-block-long Disney-like promenade crammed with flashy name-brand stores and restaurants (but don't have lunch yet—save that for the Getty Center). Even with an early start this should take you at least half a day. Also, be sure to splurge on a Front of Line Pass, which could save you hours of standing in lines. See p. 169.

❷ ZEN ZONE

I'm supposed to recommend a dining option here, but I have something you'll like a whole lot better. Along the CityWalk is a place called the Zen Zone, where you can get an inexpensive 20-minute "aqua massage." You lay down fully clothed in what looks like a tanning bed, and strong rotating jets of water massage your backside from neck to toe (a blue rubber sheet keeps you dry). The sensation is a bit weird at first, but after it's over you'll feel incredibly refreshed. Universal City. ✆ 818/487-7889. See p. 172.

Hop in the convertible, cross over the freeway, turn left on Cahuenga Boulevard, then right onto the famous:

❸ Mulholland Drive 🏛

This winding scenic road follows the peaks and canyons of Hollywood Hills (all festooned with seriously huge homes of people who make way too much money). Not only does it offer amazing views of Los Angeles and the San Fernando Valley—you'll find several scenic viewing areas along the drive—it takes you directly to Interstate 405 and our next stop. See p. 198.

Head south on I-405, and just a few miles down the freeway on your right side is the exit for the:

❹ J. Paul Getty Museum at the Getty Center 🏛🏛

Perched on a hillside in the Santa Monica Mountains and swathed in Italian travertine marble, the Getty Center is stunning both in design and construction cost (roughly $1 billion). Everything about this postmodernist complex elicits oohs and aahs, from Paul Getty's enormous collection of art (including van Gogh's *Irises*), gorgeous landscaped gardens, and postcard views of Los Angeles and the Pacific Ocean. What's more, entrance to the Getty Center is free—they don't need your money—but parking reservations are required weekdays. If you're like me and don't remember a thing from your college art appreciation class, spend a few bucks for a self-guided audio tour that gives a brief overview of the 250-plus works in the collection. See p. 159.

⑤ GETTY CENTER GARDEN TERRACE CAFE ⭑

Dining options at the Getty Center range from a self-service cafe to the elegant (though informal) **Restaurant,** but my favorite place to take a break is the Garden Terrace Cafe, which serves lunch in a beautiful outdoor setting overlooking the Central Garden. You can also pick up a picnic lunch on the Plaza Level and head down to the flower-filled picnic area. 1200 Getty Center Dr. ℂ **310/440-7300.** See p. 159 for more about the Getty Center.

Head south again on I-405 (it's rush hour now, so you'll have plenty of time to give your feet and brain a rest), and about a mile down the freeway take the Sunset Boulevard exit. Head east on Sunset until you reach the Sunset Strip and the:

⑥ House of Blues ⭑

After sitting in traffic on I-405, it's time for another classic L.A. experience: dinner and a show at the House of Blues. This being L.A., the Sunset Strip HOB consistently books top-tier musicians who live here anyway. If you can make it past the three bars, the upstairs restaurant serves great Southern-style comfort food (the slow-smoked baby back ribs with Jim Beam barbecue sauce are addictive). Reservations are a must, so plan ahead. By the time the show's over, the action on the Strip will keep you entertained well past midnight. See p. 267.

4 The Best of Los Angeles in 3 Days

On your third day just lay in bed all day, watch TV, and order room service. Or not. There are plenty of top attractions in L.A. you still haven't seen, and hopefully there's still room on your credit card. Try to make the 9am tour of Paramount Pictures, because you're in for another full day of only-in-L.A. experiences: seeing famous dead people, eating famous chili dogs, staring at a famous pit of tar (heart be still), laughing at price tags along famous Rodeo Drive, and taking a tour of the will-be-famous-one-day Walt Disney Concert Hall. Again, be ready with comfy shoes, strong coffee, and a red convertible. *Start: 5555 Melrose Ave.*

① Paramount Pictures ⭑⭑

Yes, another studio tour, but this one's my favorite. Paramount is the only major studio still located in Hollywood, so its hallowed grounds are oozing with Hollywood history. The 2-hour walking tour (screw the trams) is both a historical ode to filmmaking and a real-life, behind-the-scenes look at working movie and television facilities in day-to-day operation; ergo, no two tours are alike, and chances of spotting a celebrity are pretty good. What you'll get to see depends on what's being filmed while you're there, but it's cool just to hang out on the other side of that big wall. See p. 199.

Right behind Paramount Pictures on Santa Monica Boulevard is the main entrance to:

② Hollywood Forever Cemetery

This is the "resting place of Hollywood immortals" (whatever). It's 60 minutes well spent walking around the meticulously manicured lawns, searching for familiar names such as Rudolph Valentino, Douglas Fairbanks (Sr. and Jr.), Peter Lorre, and Jayne Mansfield. Fittingly, there's a terrific view of the Hollywood sign from here. You can pick up a map of the stars' burial sites at the flower shop. See p. 204.

For a lunch break, drive about a mile east on Melrose Avenue to La Brea Avenue for:

3 PINK'S HOT DOGS

Why anyone would stand in line for an hour to buy a hot dog is way beyond me, but on weekends the line wraps around the building at Pink's Hot Dogs, an L.A. icon that's been dishing dogs since 1939. About 2,000 of them are served every day in 24 varieties, including a heartburn-inducing chili dog made from a secret chili formula that will stick with you for days. If the line's doable, give it a try. 709 N. La Brea Ave. (at Melrose Ave.). ☎ 323/931-4223. See p. 145.

Drive south on La Brea Avenue for about a mile, then turn right (west) onto Wilshire Boulevard. About 10 blocks down on your right side is:

4 La Brea Tar Pits 🐾🐾

There's something about this odorous swamp of gooey asphalt oozing to the earth's surface that's fascinating. Perhaps it's the location: smack-dab in the middle of Los Angeles, the last place you'd expect to find this truly bizarre primal pool of hot tar that's been bubbling from the earth for more than 40,000 years. Nearly 400 species of mammals, birds, amphibians, and fish—many of which are now extinct—walked, crawled, landed, swam, or slithered into the sticky sludge, got stuck in the worst way, and stayed forever. It looks like a fake Disney set, complete with cement mastodons in the throes of certain death, wailing from hidden speakers. If you have time, stop in the adjacent Page Museum, which houses the largest and most diverse collection of Ice Age plants and animals in the world. See p. 165.

Head east on Wilshire Boulevard to the Downtown area, turn left on South Figueroa Street, then right on West 1st Street. At South Grand Avenue between 1st and 2nd streets is the:

5 Walt Disney Concert Hall 🐾🐾🐾

The strikingly beautiful Walt Disney Concert Hall is a masterpiece of design by world-renowned architect Frank Gehry. Even if you don't have the slightest interest in architecture, you will experience shock and awe the first time you see the impossibly curvaceous stainless-steel exterior. The 45-minute self-guided audio tour is excellent: Narrated by actor John Lithgow, it takes you all over the building and includes interviews with Gehry. Within is a dazzling 2,273-seat auditorium, but you can't see it unless you attend a performance (which I strongly recommend). See p. 172.

Get back on Wilshire Boulevard, and head west about 9 miles to Beverly Hills. Just before Santa Monica Boulevard on your right-hand side is:

6 Beverly Hills' Rodeo Drive 🐾🐾

Okay, that's enough sightseeing for today—let's go shopping along one of the wealthiest and most famous shopping streets in the world: Rodeo Drive. Within Beverly Hills' Golden Triangle—a 16-square-block area surrounding Rodeo Drive—are the couture shops from high fashion's Old Guard: Gucci, Armani, Yves Saint Laurent, Christian Dior, Ralph Lauren, Cartier, Tiffany, and all the rest. If $15,000 is a bit out of your price range for a suit, the shops off Rodeo are generally not as name-conscious as those on the strip, and you might actually be able to afford something. Surprisingly, parking is a bargain, with nine city-run lots offering 2 hours of free parking.

7 IL PASTAIO 🐾🐾

This corner restaurant within the Golden Triangle is *the* place to take a break from shopping and dine on superb Italian food. Ask for a sidewalk table, then order a bottle of chianti, the *arancini* appetizer (trust me), the pumpkin tortelloni in a light sage-and-cream sauce, and for the finale the silkiest panna cotta you'll ever swoon over. 400 N. Canon Dr. ☎ 310/205-5444. See p. 132.

Now you have two options. To get to the Pantages Theater from Beverly Hills, head east on Santa Monica Boulevard, turn left onto North Fairfax Avenue, then right onto Hollywood Boulevard. Head east about 2 miles to 6233 Hollywood Blvd.

To get to the Orpheum Theatre from Beverly Hills, take I-10 east to Hwy. 110 north, exit at 8th Street/9th Street, and take 9th Street eastward. Turn left onto Broadway, and the theater is on the right side of the street.

❽ Pantages & Orpheum Theaters

You really should end your vacation with a grand show at one of L.A.'s major playhouses, preferably the Pantages or Orpheum theaters, historical and cultural landmarks that have been meticulously restored. Opened in 1930, the Pantages was the first Art Deco movie palace in the U.S. and site of the Academy Awards from 1949 to 1959. Built in 1926, the Orpheum has hosted performances ranging from Judy Garland's 1933 vaudeville act to Ella Fitzgerald and Duke Ellington. Just being inside either of these historic theaters is a thrill, and seeing a show here is a fitting end to your vacation at the film and entertainment capital of the world. See p. 280.

5

Where to Stay

In sprawling Los Angeles, location is everything. The neighborhood you choose as a base can make or break your vacation. If you plan to spend your days at the beach but stay Downtown, for example, you're going to lose a lot of valuable relaxation time on the freeway. For business travelers, choosing a location is easy: Pick a hotel near your work event—don't get on the freeways if you don't have to. For vacationers, though, the decision about where to stay is more difficult. Consider where you want to spend most of your time before you commit yourself to a base. But wherever you stay, count on doing a good deal of driving—no hotel in Los Angeles is convenient to everything.

The relatively smog-free beach communities such as **Santa Monica** and **Venice** are understandably popular with visitors—just about everybody loves to stay at the beach. Book ahead because hotels fill up quickly, especially in summer.

If they're not at one of the beach communities, most visitors stay on the city's **Westside,** a short drive from the beach and close to most of L.A.'s colorful sights. The city's most elegant and expensive accommodations are in **Beverly Hills** and **Bel Air;** a few of the hotels in these neighborhoods, such as the Beverly Hills Hotel, have become visitor attractions unto themselves. As well as being one of the focal points of L.A. nightlife, **West Hollywood** is also home to the greatest range and breadth of hotels, from $300-plus-per-night boutique spots to affordably priced motels.

There are fewer hotels in **Hollywood** than you might expect. Accommodations are generally moderately priced and well maintained but unspectacular. Centrally located between Downtown and Beverly Hills, just a stone's throw from Universal Studios, Hollywood makes a convenient base if you're planning to do a lot of exploring, but it has more tourists and is less visually appealing than some other neighborhoods.

Downtown hotels are generally business-oriented, but thanks to direct Metro (L.A.'s subway) connections to Hollywood and Universal Studios, the demographic has begun to shift. The top hotels offer excellent deals on weekend packages. But chances are good that Downtown doesn't embody the picture of L.A. you've been dreaming of; you need a coastal or Westside base for that.

Families might want to head to **Universal City** to be near Universal Studios, or straight to **Anaheim and Disneyland** (see chapter 8). **Pasadena** offers historical charm, small-town ambience, easy access to Downtown L.A., and Stepford-wives beauty, but driving to the beach can take forever.

RACK RATES The **rates** quoted in the listings that follow are the rack rates—the maximum rates that a hotel charges for rooms. But rack rates are only guidelines, and there are often many ways around them. *Always* **check each hotel's website for package deals and special Internet rates.**

The hotels listed in this chapter have provided their best estimates for 2008. **Be aware that rates can change at any time** and are subject to availability, seasonal fluctuations, and plain ol' increases.

PET POLICIES   I indicate in the listings below those hotels that generally accept pets. However, these policies may have limitations, such as weight and breed restrictions; may require a hefty deposit and/or a signed waiver against damages; and may be revoked at any time. Always inquire when booking if you're bringing Bowser along—*never* just show up with a pet in tow.

1 Best Hotel Bets

Note: In addition to the best hotel bets below, be sure to check out "The Best Splurge Hotels" and "The Best Moderately Priced Hotels" in chapter 1. For additional help in choosing a location, take a look at "Neighborhoods in Brief" on p. 53.

- **Best for Families:** With a great location close to both beach and boardwalk, a terrific oceanview pool, and a kids-stay-free policy (plus welcome goodies and special menus for young ones), **Loews Santa Monica Beach Hotel,** 1700 Ocean Ave., Santa Monica (© **800/235-6397** or 310/458-6700), tops my list as L.A.'s best family hotel. See p. 73. Families on a tighter budget might prefer **Best Western Marina Pacific Hotel & Suites,** 1697 Pacific Ave., Venice (© **800/786-7789** or 310/452-1111), located right next to the carnival-like Venice Beach and boardwalk. You get free continental breakfast and indoor parking, and large suites with full kitchens and a pullout sofa. See p. 79. If you're heading to Universal Studios, stay at the **Sheraton Universal Hotel,** 333 Universal Hollywood Dr., Los Angeles (© **800/325-3535** or 818/980-1212), which offers free shuttle service to the theme park and adjacent Universal CityWalk, both just a minute away. See p. 106.
- **Best for Business Travelers:** With an oversize work desk, a fax machine, two-line phones, a terrific business/copy center, extensive recreational facilities, plus 24-hour room service and a wet bar for late-night, report-due-in-the-morning munchies, the guest office suites at **Westin Bonaventure Hotel & Suites,** 404 S. Figueroa St. (© **800/WESTIN-1** [800/937-8461] or 213/624-1000), are Downtown's best accommodations for business travelers. See p. 103.
- **Best Budget Hotel:** The bargain of the beach is the friendly, family-run **Sea Shore Motel,** 2637 Main St., Santa Monica (© **310/392-2787**), whose motel-basic but beautifully kept rooms couldn't be better located, in the heart of stylish Main Street shopping and dining, and just a stone's throw from Santa Monica's pier and sand. See p. 80.
- **Best for Travelers with Disabilities:** With 25 accessible rooms, the **Sheraton Universal Hotel,** 333 Universal Hollywood Dr., Universal City (© **800/325-3535** or 818/980-1212), offers the most extensive facilities for wheelchair-using and vision-impaired visitors. Two bathrooms have roll-in showers; the rest have tubs with available benches, lowered closet rods and peepholes, and raised vanities and toilets. There are also strobe kits for door and phone, and Braille symbols on the restaurant menus and on all public facilities. See p. 106. Downtown, the **Westin Bonaventure Hotel & Suites,** 404 S. Figueroa St. (© **800/WESTIN-1** [800/937-8461] or 213/624-1000), boasts 39 rooms with similarly extensive auxiliary aids, 15 with roll-in showers. See p. 103. For more information on resources for travelers with disabilities, see "Travelers with Disabilities," in chapter 3.

> *Tips* **More Important Advice on Accommodations**
>
> The prices given in this book do not include state and city **hotel taxes,** which run from 12% to 17%, depending upon which municipality the hotel is based in. Most hotels in densely populated parts of the city charge for **parking** (with in-and-out privileges). Also, some provide a **free airport shuttle;** if you're not renting a car, check to see what your hotel offers before you call a cab.

- **Best Hotel Nightlife Scene:** The gorgeous 18th-floor **Penthouse** restaurant, bar, and lounge at the **Huntley Santa Monica Beach,** 1111 2nd St., Santa Monica (© **310/394-5454**), is my new favorite hotel hangout. It has everything you need for a great night out: a lively bar scene, great food, beautiful views, and plenty of eye candy. All this and no lines, cover charge, or snobby attitude. See p. 78.

2 Santa Monica & the Beaches

If surf, sand, and sunshine are what you're craving on this vacation, don't consider staying anywhere but here. Not only will you avoid the traffic crush as everyone from the rest of the city flocks to the seaside on clear, sunny days, but you can also soak up the laid-back vibe that only beach communities have.

With its wide beach, amusement pier, abundant dining and shopping, and easy freeway access, Santa Monica is the glittering jewel of the L.A. coast. A Venice location puts you at the heart of the wild, colorful human carnival that is Venice Beach, while Marina del Rey is the destination for those who want a sparkling, serene marina scene. World-famous Malibu is the ultimate symbol of the star-studded, sun-soaked coastal L.A. lifestyle, and offers good surf to boot—but be prepared to spend lots of time in the car, as this high-rent enclave is at least a half-hour drive from everything.

LAX is also near the coast, so airport-area accommodations are found in this section as well.

VERY EXPENSIVE

Casa del Mar ✿✿✿   Housed in a former 1920s Renaissance Revival beach club, this Art Deco stunner is a real dream of a resort hotel, equal in every respect to its sister resort, Shutters, located across the street (see below). Which one you prefer depends on your personal sense of style. While Shutters is outfitted like a chic East Coast beach house, this impeccable, U-shape villa-like structure radiates period glamour. The building's shape awards ocean views to most of the guest rooms. You're unlikely to be too disappointed, thanks to the gorgeous, summery, European-inspired decor in golds and sea-grass hues, plus abundant luxuries that include sumptuously dressed beds and big Italian marble bathrooms with extra-large whirlpool tubs and separate showers. Rooms are laid out for relaxation, not business, so travelers with work on their minds should stay elsewhere.

Downstairs you'll find a big, elegant living room with ocean views, a stylish veranda lounge, and the **Catch Restaurant,** which has earned justifiable kudos (and more than a few celebrity fans) for its beautiful setting, great service, and finest seasonal seafood. The hotel's spa features the exclusive product line of Dr. Howard Murad, one of the country's foremost authorities on skin care.

Where to Stay in Santa Monica & the Beaches

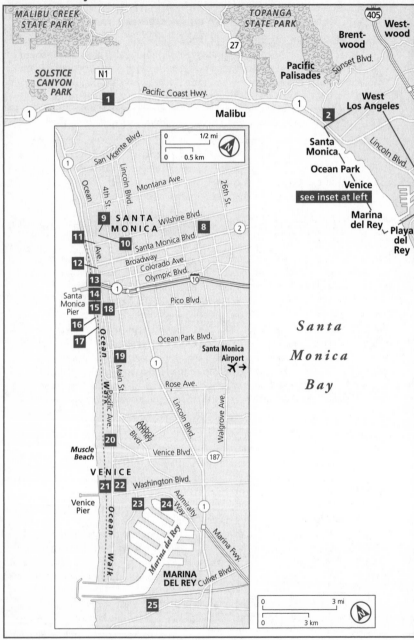

MALIBU CREEK STATE PARK

TOPANGA STATE PARK

Brent-wood

West-wood

405

27

SOLSTICE CANYON PARK

N1

Pacific Coast Hwy.

Pacific Palisades

Sunset Blvd.

1

Malibu

1

West Los Angeles

2

Santa Monica

Lincoln Blvd.

Ocean Park

Venice

see inset at left

Marina del Rey

Playa del Rey

0   1/2 mi
0   0.5 km

San Vicente Blvd.

1

Ocean

4th St.

Lincoln Blvd.

Montana Ave.

26th St.

9   SANTA MONICA

Wilshire Blvd.

8

2

11

10

Santa Monica Blvd.

Ave.

12

Broadway

Colorado Ave.

13

Olympic Blvd.

10

1

14

Santa Monica Pier

Pico Blvd.

15   18

16

Ocean Walk

17

Ocean Park Blvd.

19

Santa Monica Airport

1

Main St.

Rose Ave.

Santa Monica Bay

Lincoln Blvd.

Walgrove Ave.

Abbot Blvd.

Pacific Ave.

20

Venice Blvd.

187

Muscle Beach

VENICE

21   22

Washington Blvd.

Venice Pier

23

24

Admiralty Way

1

Ocean Walk

Marina del Rey

Marina Fwy.

MARINA DEL REY

Culver Blvd.

25

0   3 mi
0   3 km

70

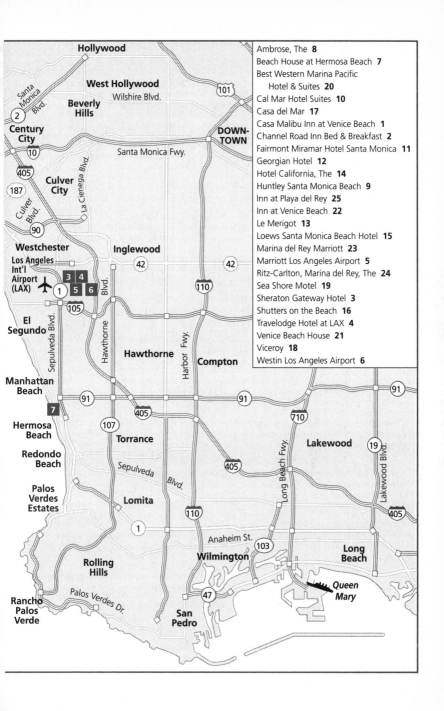

Ambrose, The **8**
Beach House at Hermosa Beach **7**
Best Western Marina Pacific
   Hotel & Suites **20**
Cal Mar Hotel Suites **10**
Casa del Mar **17**
Casa Malibu Inn at Venice Beach **1**
Channel Road Inn Bed & Breakfast **2**
Fairmont Miramar Hotel Santa Monica **11**
Georgian Hotel **12**
Hotel California, The **14**
Huntley Santa Monica Beach **9**
Inn at Playa del Rey **25**
Inn at Venice Beach **22**
Le Merigot **13**
Loews Santa Monica Beach Hotel **15**
Marina del Rey Marriott **23**
Marriott Los Angeles Airport **5**
Ritz-Carlton, Marina del Rey, The **24**
Sea Shore Motel **19**
Sheraton Gateway Hotel **3**
Shutters on the Beach **16**
Travelodge Hotel at LAX **4**
Venice Beach House **21**
Viceroy **18**
Westin Los Angeles Airport **6**

1910 Ocean Way (next to the Santa Monica Pier), Santa Monica, CA 90405. ℂ **800/898-6999** or 310/581-5533. Fax 310/581-5503. www.hotelcasadelmar.com. 129 units. $460–$735 double; from $1,085 suite. AE, DC, DISC, MC, V. Valet parking $26. **Amenities:** Oceanfront restaurant; lobby lounge for cocktails and light fare; cafe for daytime dining; heated outdoor Roman-style pool; plunge pool; state-of-the-art health club w/spa services; Jacuzzi overlooking Santa Monica Beach; 24-hr. concierge; virtual business center; 24-hr. room service; laundry service; dry cleaning. *In room:* A/C, TV/DVD, high-speed Internet, minibar, hair dryer, iron, laptop-size safe, iPod stations.

Fairmont Miramar Hotel & Bungalows 🐱🐱

So well hidden that I passed it for 2 years without noticing it was even there, the Fairmont Miramar is for people who prefer their luxury hotels low-key and unobtrusive, yet within walking distance of the area's best attractions. Which explains why it has served as temporary residence of numerous celebrities and politicians: Cary Grant, Greta Garbo, J.F.K., Marilyn Monroe, Eleanor Roosevelt . . . . It's almost ironic that this hidden gem is located on one of the busiest blocks in Santa Monica—a block from the beach and at the north end of Santa Monica's perpetually crowded Third Street Promenade. But through clever use of extensive landscaping and high walls, hotel guests are blissfully unaware of the hubbub that surrounds them.

The hotel consists of two towers and a bevy of bungalows on 5 acres of grounds. The older, larger rooms in the Palisades Building are ideal for families, but I prefer the newer, more modern rooms in the taller Ocean Tower—particularly the corner rooms on the 8th through 10th floors overlooking the Santa Monica Pier or Malibu coastline. All rooms are well-appointed with such luxuries as goose-down duvets and soundproof windows; rooms in the Ocean Tower have balconies. If you're in a splurging mood, I highly recommend one of the über-romantic garden bungalows, each outfitted with hardwood floors, deep soaking tubs, and original artwork (they're almost as nice as the Beverly Hills Hotel bungalows and far less expensive). Other incentives for staying here include an outdoor pool and whirlpool, a pretty outdoor lounge serving drinks and food, and a fitness center and day spa.

101 Wilshire Blvd. (at Ocean Ave.), Santa Monica, CA 90401. ℂ **800/257-7544** or 310/576-7777. Fax 310/458-7912. www.fairmont.com/santamonica. 270 units, 32 bungalows. $319–$769 double; $579–$1,429 bungalow. AE, DC, DISC, MC, V. Valet parking $30. **Amenities:** Restaurant; outdoor lounge; lobby lounge; heated outdoor pool and whirlpool; 24-hr. health and fitness center; Exhale Spa; 24-hr. concierge; business center; 24-hr. room service; laundry service; dry cleaning; Wi-Fi access in lobby. *In room:* A/C, TV/DVD, high-speed Internet, minibar, hair dryer, iron, safe, terry-cloth robes.

Georgian Hotel 🐱🐱 *Finds*

This eight-story Art Deco beauty offers luxury comforts, loads of historical charm, and a terrific oceanview location, just across the street from Santa Monica's beach and pier, with prime Ocean Avenue dining just steps away. Established in 1933, the Georgian was popular among Hollywood's golden age elite; it even had its own speak-easy, rumored to have been established by Bugsy Siegel. Today the elegant classic revival architecture is beautifully accented with a well-chosen palette of bold pastels (a la Miami Beach's hotels of the same era). A wonderful veranda with handsome teak furnishings and unobstructed ocean views opens onto a light and airy lobby with comfortable seating nooks. Two swift antique elevators lead to guest rooms that are an ideal blend of nostalgic style and modern-day amenities such as complimentary Wi-Fi Internet access and flatscreen TVs in all the suites. Fittings include furnishings upholstered in gorgeous nubby textiles, mattresses dressed in goose-down comforters, and ceiling fans; suites have sleeper sofas and clock radios with MP3 capability. The hotel has an unobstructed coastal vista, so most rooms have at least a partial or full ocean view; the best views are above the third floor. The rooms facing the ocean can be a bit small and noisy, so ask for a Malibu view for the best of both worlds. The back-facing rooms are best for light sleepers—be sure to request one that has a city view.

1415 Ocean Ave. (btw. Santa Monica Blvd. and Broadway), Santa Monica, CA 90401. (©) **800/538-8147** or 310/395-9945. Fax 310/451-3374. www.georgianhotel.com. 84 units. $250 double; from $450 suite. Inquire about packages. AE, DC, DISC, MC, V. Valet parking $21. **Amenities:** Breakfast and lunch on the veranda; lobby bar w/signature *Georgini* martini; exercise room; concierge service; activities desk; 24-hr. room service; 24-hour laundry service; dry cleaning. *In room:* TV w/pay movies and Nintendo, dataport, Wi-Fi, minibar, coffeemaker, hair dryer, iron, laptop-size safe.

Le Merigot ✹✹ If you're accustomed to hotels that are roomier and more contemporary than the historic Georgian, yet not as pricey and prestigious as the Shutters or Casa del Mar properties, the porridge that's just right is Le Merigot, a low-key luxury hotel and spa that doesn't try to be anything other than a comfortable place in which to spend your seaside vacation. Ideally situated on the sandy side of Ocean Avenue in the heart of Santa Monica's beach scene, the 175-room property houses a well-regarded French-California restaurant, **Cézanne,** and the 5,500-square-foot SPA Le Merigot, which offers a full range of services along with an outdoor pool and a state-of-the-art fitness center. Some of the contemporary-style guest rooms offer partial ocean views, and all are furnished with plush carpeting, marble-tiled bathrooms, over-size lounge chairs, and pillow-top beds with Italian cotton linens, down comforters, and feather pillows. What I really like about this hotel, however, are the clever package deals, such as the "California Dreamin'," which includes your choice of a convertible Porsche Boxster or a BMW Z4 Roadster rental car; and the "California Surfin' Safari," a deluxe package, a 2-hour surf lesson, a rejuvenating full-session Swedish massage, and celebratory Blue Crush graduation martinis (how very L.A.).

1740 Ocean Ave., Santa Monica, CA 90401. (©) **877/MER-IGOT** (877/637-4468) or 310/395-9700. Fax 310/395-9200. www.lemerigothotel.com. 175 units. $340–$635 double; from $800 suite. AE, DISC, MC, V. Valet parking $28. **Amenities:** Full-service restaurant; lobby bar; outdoor pool; fitness facilities and spa; concierge; business services; 24-hr. room service; gift shop; choice of morning newspaper. *In room:* A/C, cable TV, fax machine on request, high-speed Internet, minibar, iron/ironing board, laptop safe, 3 dual-line phones w/voice mail.

Loews Santa Monica Beach Hotel ✹✹ *(Kids)* L.A.'s finest family-friendly hotel is also a great choice for anybody looking for comfortable accommodations, an A-1 Santa Monica location, outstanding service, and a wealth of first-rate facilities. Loews isn't exactly beachfront—it's on a hill less than a block away—but the unobstructed ocean views are fabulous. Immediately upon entering, guests are wowed by the dramatic atrium lobby with its playful SoCal style (including dual rows of huge palm trees), which serves as a great backdrop for the spectacular ocean views. The guest rooms have an inviting, clean-lined contemporary style in light, earthy colors. But the best news is still the top-rated facilities, which include an excellent heated pool, plus the fitness center and spa with a state-of-the-art gym, yoga and Pilates classes, health and fitness counseling, and full slate of spa and salon services.

The restaurant **Ocean & Vine** is one of the newest additions to the hotel, offering California farm-to-table cuisine and expertly paired wines to match. The stunning patio has fire pits, lounge chairs, and the picturesque backdrop of the beach and Santa Monica pier. The Papillon Lobby Bar is a classy spot for a drink.

1700 Ocean Ave. (south of Colorado Blvd.), Santa Monica, CA 90401. (©) **800/235-6397** or 310/458-6700. Fax 310/458-6761. www.santamonicaloewshotel.com. 340 units. $349–$489 double; from $850 suite. Ask about corporate rates, Internet offers, and other discounts. Children 17 and under stay free in parent's room. AE, DC, DISC, MC, V. Valet parking $31. Pets welcome. **Amenities:** Restaurant; bar; poolside lunch service; oceanview outdoor heated pool and whirlpool; full-service spa; state-of-the-art workout room, steam, and sauna; bike and skate rentals; concierge; Hertz car-rental desk; executive business center; salon; 24-hr. room service; laundry service; dry cleaning. *In room:* A/C, TV, dataport, minibar, hair dryer, iron, CD player, daily newspaper.

The Ritz-Carlton, Marina del Rey ★★   There are three reasons to stay at the Ritz-Carlton in Marina del Rey: 1) You're a watercraft cognoscenti and you desire a serene view of more than 5,000 beautiful sailboats and yachts from your private balcony; 2) You want to take advantage of this business hotel's reduced weekend rates; or 3) You want to stay in style near the airport (a traffic-free, 10-min. ride). In typical Ritz-Carlton fashion, the hotel is swathed in soothingly sophisticated decor—Italian marble bathrooms, French doors leading to private balconies, 32-inch plasma-screen televisions, and the most comfortable goose-down feather bed I've ever slept in. The two top floors consist of the Ritz-Carlton Club Lounge, with a dedicated concierge, on-the-house cocktails, and complimentary gourmet spreads all day (including breakfast). Thanks to its marina location, the hotel offers yacht and sailing charters, and reserves several slips for boat-bound customers. Venice Beach is about a 15-minute walk, but it's easier to rent a bicycle from the hotel. And to keep up with the competition, the hotel has recently added a full-service boutique spa as well. *Tip:* Request one of the "27 series" rooms, which are junior suites that are larger and have the best views. The hotel's restaurant, **Jər-nē Restaurant + Bar** (pronounced "journey"), serves superb New World cuisine in a stylishly modern setting—although I prefer a table on the deck overlooking the harbor—and they've recently opened their new **Boutique Spa at The Ritz-Carlton,** featuring eight treatment rooms, manicure and pedicure services, steam room experiences, a spa retail shop, and a new state-of-the-art cardio/weight studio furnished with high-tech equipment.

4375 Admiralty Way, Marina del Rey, CA 90292. (℃) **800/241-3333** or 310/823-1700. Fax 310/823-2403. www.ritz carlton.com. 304 units. $369–$609 double; from $669 suite. Discount packages always available. AE, DC, MC, V. Valet parking $10 day, $29 overnight. Pets accepted. **Amenities:** 2 restaurants; bar and lounge; heated outdoor pool and whirlpool; 2 lighted tennis courts; fitness center; spa; bike rentals; concierge; 24-hr. room service; babysitting; laundry service; dry cleaning; basketball court. *In room:* A/C, plasma-screen TV w/pay movies, dataport, high-speed Internet, minibar, hair dryer, iron, laptop-size safe, CD player.

Shutters on the Beach ★★★   This Cape Cod–style luxury hotel enjoys one of the city's most prized locations: directly on the beach, a block from Santa Monica Pier. Only the Shutters' sister property—Casa del Mar (above) can compete, but Shutters bests the Casa by attaching alfresco balconies to every guest room and having a more personal boutique hotel–like ambience. The views and sounds of the ocean are the most outstanding qualities of the spacious, luxuriously outfitted, Cape Cod–inspired rooms, some of which have fireplaces and/or whirlpool tubs; all have floor-to-ceiling windows that open. The elegant marble bathrooms come with generous counter space and welcome whimsies that include waterproof radios and toy whales. A relaxed ambience pervades the contemporary art–filled public spaces, which feel like the common areas of a deluxe Montauk beach house. The small swimming pool and the sunny lobby lounge overlooking the sand are two great perches for spotting the celebrities who swear by Shutters as an alternative hangout to smoggy Hollywood. **One Pico,** the hotel's premier restaurant, serves modern American cuisine in a seaside setting; the best meals at the more casual **Coast Beach Café & Bar** come from the wood-burning grill. The hotel's **ONE** spa offers guests facials, massages, body scrubs and body treatments, manicures, pedicures, and waxing. *Tip:* The beach-cottage rooms overlooking the sand are more desirable and no more expensive than those in the towers.

1 Pico Blvd., Santa Monica, CA 90405. (C) **800/334-9000** or 310/458-0030. Fax 310/458-4589. www.shuttersonthe beach.com. 198 units. $490–$785 double; from $1,175 suite. AE, DC, DISC, MC, V. Valet parking $26. **Amenities:** Restaurant; cafe; lobby lounge; outdoor heated pool and Jacuzzi; health club w/spa services; sauna; extensive beach-equipment rentals; concierge; courtesy car; activities desk; business center w/secretarial services; 24-hr. room service; babysitting; laundry service; dry cleaning; video library; Wi-Fi throughout property. *In room:* TV/DVD, minibar, hair dryer, iron, laptop-size safe, iPod station.

Viceroy 𝆕𝆕 Still near the top of L.A.'s coveted "in" list is this über-chic hotel on the sea side of Santa Monica. Of course, part of being "in" is breaking new ground, and that's certainly what designer Kelly Wearstler has achieved with her "Modern Colonialism" makeover. It's the startling color scheme that first grabs your attention as you enter the lobby—a rather unorthodox blend of parrot green, driftwood gray, and wave-crest white with chrome, silver, and ebony highlights. Then there's the dish thing: hundreds of custom-made china arranged in symmetrical patterns throughout the hotel and guest rooms. (Where's The Who when you really need them?) The array of white patent-leather chaises in the lobby seems more for form than function; most guests prefer more conventional seating in the Cameo bar or private poolside cabanas. The edgy-English theme is applied to each guest room as well, along with an array of high-tech toys (27-in. flatscreen TV, another flatscreen TV in the marble-laden bathrooms, a CD/DVD player, and T1 Internet access), custom-made furnishings, and luxuries such as Miscioni linens and bathrobes, Aromatherapy & Associates products, and down comforters and pillows. The Viceroy's restaurant, **Whist,** serves superb contemporary cuisine. You'll enjoy the location as well—a short walk to the beach and in the thick of the shopping, entertainment, and restaurant scene. Full spa services are offered either in-room or poolside. *Tip:* Splurge for an oceanview room; your only other view choice is the hotel parking lot.

1819 Ocean Ave., Santa Monica, CA 90401. (C) **866/891-0947** or 310/260-7500. Fax 310/260-7515. www.viceroy santamonica.com. 162 units. $359 double; from $559 suite. AE, DC, DISC, MC, V. Valet parking $24. **Amenities:** Restaurant; bar; lounge; 2 heated outdoor pools; fitness center; concierge; 24-hr. room service; in-room massage; laundry service; dry cleaning; newspaper delivery; videos available. *In room:* TV w/pay movies and video games, dataport, high-speed Internet, minibar, hair dryer, safe, CD/DVD player.

EXPENSIVE

Beach House Hotel Hermosa Beach 𝆕𝆕 *Finds* Sporting a Cape Cod style that suits the on-the-sand location, this luxurious, romantic inn is comprised of beautifully designed and outfitted split-level studio suites. Every bright, sunny unit comes with a plush, furnished living room with a wood-burning fireplace (Duraflame logs provided) and entertainment center; a microkitchen with china and flatware for four; an elevated sleeping niche with a down-dressed king-size bed, a second TV, and a generous work area; an extra-large bathroom with an extra-deep soaking tub, a separate shower, cotton robes, and Aveda products. There are even furnished balconies, many of which overlook the beach. (Believe me—it's worth the extra money to score a beachfront room.) While sofas convert into second beds, the unit configuration is best suited to couples rather than families; more than three is too many. Despite the summertime carnival atmosphere of The Strand, the Beach House keeps serene with double-paned windows and noise-insulated walls. The hotel's small spa offers a wide range of services, including massage treatments (in-room if you prefer), wraps, facials, waxing, and yoga sessions on the beach. An excellent light breakfast is served in the sunny breakfast room overlooking The Strand. The attentive staff has an easygoing attitude that suits the property perfectly. While L.A.'s city center is at least a half-hour drive away, Hermosa is airport-convenient and ideal for a beach getaway. And, the hotel has Wi-Fi for your computer needs and there is a computer/printer station in the lobby for guests to use.

1300 The Strand, Hermosa Beach, CA 90254. © **888/895-4559** or 310/374-3001. Fax 310/372-2115. www.beach-house. com. 96 units. $329–$459 double. Rates include continental breakfast. AE, DC, DISC, MC, V. Valet parking $22. **Amenities:** Spa; concierge; room service from nearby restaurant; laundry service; dry cleaning. *In room:* A/C, 2 TVs, dataport, stocked kitchenette w/microwave and stovetop, fridge, coffeemaker, hair dryer, iron, stereo w/5-disc CD changer.

Channel Road Inn ★★

The innkeeper has used her eye for design to outfit this beautiful 1910 Colonial Revival house in gracious period style. The individually appointed rooms range from "shabby chic" to antique, and all have top-quality textiles and linens, VCRs, and spacious, nicely renovated bathrooms. Some have four-poster beds covered with hand-sewn Amish quilts; others have fireplaces, and still others feature whirlpool tubs. Don't expect much from the promise of an ocean view, however; you'll overlook a busy street, wires, and rooftops for your sliver of blue. The outdoor areas include a quiet rose garden and private hillside hot tub on the upper lawn. Dominated by an impressive Batchelder tile fireplace, the impeccably decorated living room makes an ideal place to curl up with a book. If you'd rather head outside, the staff will provide bicycles, beach chairs, and towels for your use—the beach is a short walk away. I prefer Channel Road's sister property, the Inn at Playa del Rey (see below); still, this is a beautiful, comfortable, and well-run B&B in a terrific location for beach lovers.

219 W. Channel Rd., Santa Monica, CA 90402. © **310/459-1920.** Fax 310/454-9920. www.channelroadinn.com. 15 units. $225–$325 double; from $385 suite. All rates include full breakfast and afternoon tea, wine, and hors d'oeuvres. AE, MC, V. Free parking. **Amenities:** Access to nearby health club; outdoor Jacuzzi; business center; video library. *In room:* A/C, TV/VCR, Wi-Fi, hair dryer, iron.

Inn at Playa del Rey ★★ *Finds*

A half-hour drive from L.A. proper, my favorite L.A. B&B is less than ideal for sightseers with packed itineraries, but great for those looking for romance, a relaxed small-town vibe, or airport convenience. Only 5 minutes from LAX, the pampering inn is as much a sanctuary from the city as it is for the protected wetlands outside the back door. From the street, the contemporary structure looks like a set of condos; inside, it glows with its true character. Fresh salty breezes and the soft chatter of waterfowl fill a spacious yet cozy fireplace lounge, whose long veranda overlooks peaceful marshland. Hiking trails wind through the wildlife preserve; a wooden observation platform 50 yards out is ideal for contemplation, bird-watching, or spying on sailboats that pass through the channel. A beach suitable for swimming is a short walk away, and bicycles are on hand for cruising a coastal path.

The impeccably decorated, amenity-laden guest rooms are outfitted in a classy-yet-casual, sophisticated style that evokes the best of Nantucket or Santa Barbara. Country-chic furnishings, snuggly comforters, and plush bathrobes and towels are on hand. Luxuries include televisions hidden in handsome armoires and bathrooms. Most rooms have balconies; other options include whirlpool tubs and fireplaces. The ultimate in romance are the spacious View Suites, whose two-sided fireplaces cast a heavenly glow on both the luxuriously made bed and the inviting double Jacuzzi. A garden hot tub is available for those booking simpler accommodations.

435 Culver Blvd., Playa del Rey, CA 90293. © **310/574-1920.** Fax 310/574-9920. www.innatplayadelrey.com. 21 units. $195–$290 double; from $325 suite. Midweek discounts available. Rates include full breakfast and afternoon wine and cheese. AE, MC, V. Free parking. From LAX, take Sepulveda Blvd. north, veering left onto Lincoln Blvd.; turn left at Jefferson Blvd., which turns into Culver Blvd. **Amenities:** Access to nearby health club; small gym; outdoor

Jacuzzi; complimentary bikes; business center; massage; video library. *In room:* A/C, TV/VCR w/free movies, dataport, hair dryer, iron, safe.

MODERATE

The Ambrose 𝒢𝒢   If being within walking distance of the ocean isn't crucial, but a soothing, peaceful environment is, I've found your hotel. Located in a residential Santa Monica neighborhood, the 77-room Ambrose is quickly becoming a favorite boutique hideaway for CEOs who are tired of the megahotel experience and just want a relaxing place to hang their coats and unwind. The Ambrose's unique architecture blends the Arts and Crafts movement with soothing Asian influences—a tranquil Japanese garden, a koi pond, trickling fountains, beautiful artwork, and a profusion of dark woods and mossy palates. The serene, natural setting isn't just a facade: The hotel has been designated a "green" property, meaning that it's committed to conserving the state's natural resources and to low-impact living. In short: You can feel good about staying here. The majority of the guest rooms are on the small side—if you're not satisfied with the size, feel free to ask for another—but are luxuriously appointed with Matteo Italian bedding, Frette cotton kimonos and bath linens, oversize goose-down pillows, and surround-sound CD/DVD music systems. Studio rooms are the most luxurious and come with terraces or balconies. It's the many complimentary amenities that really sold me on the Ambrose (a strategy I wish more hotels would follow): underground parking with direct elevator access, wireless Internet access, access to the community computer, breakfast provided by a local gourmet restaurant, a 24-hour fitness room filled with top-of-the-line equipment, and even shuttle service around Santa Monica via the hotel's cute-as-all-get-out London taxi (trust me, you'll love this car). Other perks include a 24-hour in-room dining menu and Aveda bath products.

1255 20th St. (at Arizona Ave.), Santa Monica, CA 90404. © **877-AMBROSE** (877/262-7673) or 310/315-1555. Fax 310/315-1556. www.ambrosehotel.com. 77 units. From $229. Rates include continental breakfast. AE, DC, DISC, MC, V. Free valet parking. **Amenities:** Fitness center; complimentary local transportation; 24-hr. room service. *In room:* TV/VCR, dataport, Wi-Fi, minibar, hair dryer, safe, daily newspaper, CD/DVD w/surround sound.

The Hotel California 𝒢𝒢 *Finds*   Situated on enviable real estate along Ocean Avenue—right next door to the behemoth Loews—this welcoming hacienda-style beachfront motel embodies the surfer/sun-worshiper ambience you'd expect from a Santa Monica lodging. The well-tended complex sits above and across an alley from the beach but offers excellent views and direct access to the sand via a private path. The inn offers cheery rooms with California-themed decor—including beds with down comforters, Egyptian-cotton sheets, and surfboard headboards—hardwood floors, and Spanish-tiled bathrooms. Five one-bedroom suites also have kitchenettes and trundle beds that make them great for families or longer stays; all rooms have minifridges, 27-inch TVs, and ceiling fans, as well as free wireless Internet. A handful of rooms have only showers in the bathrooms, so be sure to request a room with a tub from the friendly front-desk staff if it matters to you. (And no, it's not the hotel from the Eagles' hit—that hotel is rumored to be in Mexico and the album's cover photo is of the Beverly Hills Hotel.) *Tip:* Pay a few bucks extra for a courtyard view, as the cheapest rooms face the parking lot and noisy Ocean Avenue. And be sure to check their website for specials.

1670 Ocean Ave. (south of Colorado Ave.), Santa Monica, CA 90401. © **866/571-0000** or 310/393-2363. Fax 310/393-1063. www.hotelca.com. 26 units. $179–$279 double or suite. AE, DISC, MC, V. Self-parking $20. **Amenities:** Jacuzzi; activities desk; discount car-rental desk; high-speed Internet access, fax/copier, and coffeemaker in front office. *In room:* TV/VCR, Wi-Fi, fridge, hair dryer, iron.

Huntley Santa Monica Beach ★★ *Finds*   If you're looking for a hotel that's on the beach and you can afford it, stay at Shutters; otherwise, the Huntley is my top choice for vacationing in style in Santa Monica. Even though it's housed in one of Santa Monica's tallest buildings (18 floors), the Huntley is a hidden gem—tucked away behind the Fairmont on the edge of a quiet neighborhood, yet close to Third Street Promenade dining and shopping and just a short walk from the beach. I love everything about this hotel, from its strikingly stylish lobby decor to the non-snobbish staff and clientele, but the coup de grâce is the new 18th-floor **Penthouse** restaurant, bar, and lounge. I'm still floored at what an incredible job designer Thomas Schoos did with the makeover—you can't help but wander around in awe of his talent. Combine the incredible views of the Santa Monica skyline, a lively bar scene, and great Contemporary American cuisine, and it's no surprise that hotel guests rarely venture elsewhere for dinner and drinks. The Huntley's modern, earth-toned guest rooms offer either ocean or mountain views, good work desks, 42-inch flatscreen TVs, pillow-top beds with Egyptian cotton linens, and bathrooms with Italian marble tile. If you want an ocean view be sure to book a room on floors 9 to 17. *Fun tip:* Take a thrilling ride in the oceanside glass elevator (acrophobes will prefer the interior lobby elevators).

1111 2nd St. (north of Wilshire Blvd.), Santa Monica, CA 90403. (📞) 310/394-5454. Fax 310/458-9776. www.the huntleyhotel.com. 209 units. $289–$335 double. AE, DC, DISC, MC, V. Valet parking $18. **Amenities:** Restaurant and bar; lobby cafe; fitness center; concierge; business center; 24-hr. room service; laundry; dry cleaning; wireless Internet. *In room:* A/C, flatscreen TV w/DVD, dataport, coffeemaker, hair dryer, iron, CD player, daily newspaper.

Marina del Rey Marriott ★★ *Finds*   This is not your average Marriott. In order to attract a more L.A.-hip clientele, this particular Marriott in Marina del Rey has made some rather unorthodox modifications to what would typically be a boring business hotel. As soon as you enter the lobby, three of your senses are subliminally put at ease: inhale the Zanzibar Mist, an subtle aromatherapy mixture that circulates throughout the hotel; hear the faint soundtrack of ambient world beats; gaze into the hypnotic tiers of fire at Glow, their outdoor lounge that's ranked as one of the top hotel lounges in the country (p. 275). Okay, so things get a bit more utilitarian when you enter your guest room, but each is soothingly spacious and comfortably appointed with down comforters and pillows, 32-inch HDTVs, bathrobes, Jacuzzi-style tubs, a work desk, and small balconies with stress-relieving views of the marina or Pacific Ocean. The 10-story hotel's location is excellent as well—across the street from Marina del Rey's glimmering harbor and footpath, within walking distance of several Marina del Rey restaurants and Venice Beach, a short drive to Santa Monica, and easy freeway access to Hollywood, Downtown, and the airport. The hotel has a steakhouse, but you're better off noshing on small plates and swilling martinis at Glow, canceling your plans for the night because you're so relaxed you can't be bothered to drive anywhere. Best of all, this is mainly a business hotel so the weekend rates are often heavily discounted (be sure to check their website for deals).

4100 Admiralty Way (at the north end of the marina), Marina del Rey, CA 90292. (📞) 800/228-9290 or 310/301-3000. Fax 310/448-4870. www.marriott.com. 370 units. AE, DC, DISC, MC, V. Valet parking $26. **Amenities:** Restaurant; lobby bar; Glow outdoor lounge; pool; fitness center; whirlpool; business center; room service; laundry service; dry cleaning; barber/beauty shop. *In room:* A/C, HDTV, high-speed Internet, coffeemaker, hair dryer, safe, iron.

Venice Beach House ★★ *Finds*   Listed on the National Register of Historic Places, this two-story, ivy-covered 1911 Craftsman bungalow is now a homey bed-and-breakfast on one of funky Venice's unique sidewalk streets, just a block from the beach. The interior has a homey lived-in look—shelves of vintage books, antique furnishings, hardwood floors, faded Oriental rugs—that adds charm for romantics but won't live up to the expectations of travelers who like their lodgings to be flawless (or who aren't keen on possibly sharing a bathroom). What's more, the inn hums noisily with activity when there's a full house—seekers of absolute quiet and designer appointments will *not* be comfortable here. Still, the huge repeat clientele base doesn't seem to mind these minor caveats. My favorite room is the upstairs Venice Pier Suite—light and airy, with a wood-burning fireplace, king-size bed, private bathroom, and sunny sitting room. An expanded continental breakfast with homemade baked goods is served in the sunroom overlooking a splendid garden.

15 30th Ave. (at Speedway, 1 block west of Pacific Ave.), Venice, CA 90291. ✆ **310/823-1966.** Fax 310/823-1842. www.venicebeachhouse.com. 9 units (5 with private bathroom). $145 double with shared bathroom; $170–$235 double with private bathroom. Extra person after 2 people $20. Rates include expanded continental breakfast. AE, MC, V. On-site parking $12 a day. **Amenities:** Jacuzzi (some rooms). *In room:* TV, high-speed Internet, fireplace (some rooms).

INEXPENSIVE

Best Western Marina Pacific Hotel & Suites ☆☆ (Value (Kids)
This coastal hotel is a haven of smart value, and with a recent renovation and expansion it's only gotten better. Located just off the Venice boardwalk and 200 feet from the beach, the hotel's spacious rooms are brightened with beachy colors and dutifully equipped with chain-standard furnishings, fridges, and two-line phones. The one-bedroom suites are terrific for families, offering master bedrooms with king-size beds, fully outfitted kitchens with microwave and dishwasher, dining areas, queen-size sofa sleepers, balconies, and fireplaces. Photos of local scenes and rock-'n'-roll legends along with works by local artists give the public spaces a cool L.A. vibe, and many rooms have at least partial ocean views (the best views are from the top-floor rooms facing the ocean). Additional incentives include complimentary continental breakfast, free local shuttle service, and secured covered parking. Stay elsewhere if you need a lot in the way of service or if you don't relish the party-hearty human carnival of Venice Beach (Santa Monica is generally quieter, safer, and more refined).

1697 Pacific Ave. (at 17th Ave.), Venice, CA 90291. ✆ **800/786-7789** or 310/452-1111. Fax 310/452-5479. www.mp hotel.com. 88 units. $189–$309 double; $209–$429 suite. Rates include continental breakfast. Extra person $10. Children 12 and under stay free in parent's room. Ask about AAA, senior, and other discounts; weekly and monthly rates also available. AE, DC, DISC, MC, V. Self-parking $9. **Amenities:** Continental breakfast; free shuttle to Santa Monica and Marina del Rey; coin-op laundry; laundry service; dry cleaning. *In room:* A/C, cable TV w/HBO, high-speed Internet, fridge, coffeemaker, hair dryer, iron.

Cal Mar Hotel Suites ☆☆ (Value
Tucked away in a residential neighborhood just 2 blocks from the ocean, this garden apartment complex delivers a lot of bang for your vacation buck. Each unit is an apartment-style suite with a living room and pullout sofa, a full-size kitchen with utensils, and a separate bedroom; most are spacious enough to accommodate four in comfort. The building was constructed in the 1950s with an eye for quality (attractive tile work, large closets). While the furnishings aren't luxurious, they're all quite modern and very clean, and everything is well kept. It's easy to be comfortable here for stays of a week or more, especially since it's so well located, a mere block from the Third Street Promenade and a short walk to the beach. The staff is attentive and courteous, which helps account for the high rate of repeat guests. The garden courtyard has an inviting swimming pool and plenty of chaises for lounging. *Tip:* Request a room on the second floor to avoid the sound of stomping feet.

220 California Ave., Santa Monica, CA 90403. ✆ **800/776-6007** or 310/395-5555. Fax 310/451-1111. www.calmar hotel.com. 36 units. $129–$229 suite. Extra person $10. Children 9 and under stay free in parent's room. AE, DC, DISC,

MC, V. Free parking. **Amenities:** Heated outdoor pool; coin-op laundry. *In room:* TV, full kitchen w/fridge and coffeemaker, hair dryer, iron, CD sound system.

Casa Malibu *(kids)* *(Finds)*   Sitting right on its very own beach, this leftover jewel from Malibu's golden age doesn't try to play the sleek resort game (and what a refreshing exception). Instead, the modest, low-rise inn has a traditional California-beach-cottage look that's cozy and timeless.

Wrapped around a palm-studded inner courtyard brightened with well-tended flower beds and climbing *cuppa d'oro* vines, the 21 rooms are comfortable and thoughtfully outfitted. Many have been upgraded with tile bathrooms, air-conditioning (almost never needed on the coast), and DVDs, but even the older ones are in great shape and boast top-quality bedding and bathrobes. Depending on which you choose, you might also find a fireplace, a kitchenette (in a half-dozen or so), a CD player (in suites), a tub (instead of shower only), and/or a private deck over the sand. The upstairs Catalina Suite (Lana Turner's old hide-out) has the best view, while the gorgeous Malibu Suite—the best room in the house and, like the beachfront rooms, located right on the beach—offers state-of-the-art pampering. More than half have ocean views, but even those facing the courtyard are quiet and offer easy beach access via wooden stairs to the private stretch of beach, which is raked smooth each morning. There's also a handsome, wind-shielded brick sun deck, which extends directly over the sand, allowing everyone to enjoy the blue Pacific even in cool months. Book well ahead for summer—this one's a favorite of locals and visitors alike.

22752 Pacific Coast Hwy. (about ¼ mile south of Malibu Pier), Malibu, CA 90265. © **800/831-0858** or 310/456-2219. Fax 310/456-5418. 21 units. $129–$229 garden or oceanview double; $289–$299 beachfront double; $269–$429 suite. Rates include continental breakfast. Extra person $15. AE, MC, V. Free parking. **Amenities:** Access to nearby private health club; room service for lunch and dinner; in-room massage; laundry service; dry cleaning; private beach. *In room:* TV w/DVD, Wi-Fi, fridge, coffeemaker, hair dryer, iron, 2-line telephone.

Inn at Venice Beach *(kids)*   This cheery motel at the (relatively) quiet residential south end of Venice is a good choice for travelers who want a near-the-beach, near-the-boardwalk location without being at the center of the fray. Rooms are cheerily colorful (lots of blues and yellows); open-beam ceilings add to the spacious feel. All rooms overlook a cobblestone courtyard, where complimentary continental breakfast is served on warm mornings. It all adds up to a reasonable value for budget-minded travelers (the bi-level loft suites are a great value if there's more than two of you). Because the hotel is just 3 blocks from the ocean on the border between Venice and Marina del Rey, there's an endless parade of people exploring the marina, the beach, or the nearby canals on foot, bike, or in-line skates (rentals are 2 blocks away). About the only thing missing is a pool, but the staff will lend you beach towels for an ocean dip.

327 Washington Blvd., Venice, CA 90291. © **800/828-0688** or 310/821-2557. Fax 310/827-0289. www.innatvenice beach.com. 43 units. $135–$179 double; $219 suite. Extra person $10. Rates include continental breakfast. Ask for AAA, AARP, corporate, and other available discounts. AE, DC, DISC, MC, V. Parking $4. **Amenities:** Fitness center; activities desk; laundry service; dry cleaning. *In room:* A/C, TV, free Wi-Fi, fridge, coffeemaker, hair dryer, iron, safe, daily paper.

Sea Shore Motel *(Value)*   Located in the heart of Santa Monica's Main Street dining and shopping sector, this small, friendly, family-run motel is one of the best bargains near the beach. The Sea Shore is such a well-kept secret that most denizens of stylish Main Street are unaware of the incredible value in their midst. Arranged around a parking courtyard, rooms are small and unremarkable from the outside, but the conscientious management has done a nice job with the interiors, installing attractive terra-cotta floor tiles, granite countertops, and conveniences like voice mail and data-jack phones. Complete with a living room and full kitchen, the 800-square-foot suites that sleep up to six are a phenomenal deal; book them as far in advance as possible. With a full slate of restaurants out the front door and the Santa Monica Pier and beach just a couple of blocks away, it's a terrific bargain base for exploring the sandy side of the city.

2637 Main St. (south of Ocean Park Blvd.), Santa Monica, CA 90405. ✆ **310/392-2787.** Fax 310/392-5167. www.seashoremotel.com. 24 units. $110–$145 double; $160–$260 suite. Extra person $5. Children 11 and under stay free in parent's room. Midweek discounts available. AE, DISC, MC, V. Free parking. Pets accepted for $10-per-night fee. **Amenities:** Deli; coin-op laundry; sun deck; complimentary wireless Internet. *In room:* TV, 27-in. flatscreen HDTV, dataport, fridge, coffeemaker, iron.

ACCOMMODATIONS NEAR LAX
EXPENSIVE
Westin Los Angeles Airport ⚘   This massive 12-story hotel stands a cut above the rest, thanks to an invention that borders on miracle status: Westin's own Heavenly Bed. Touted as "10 layers of heaven"—from the custom pillow-top mattress to the fluffy down comforter and a family of pillows—the Heavenly Bed is the best hotel bed in the business. The like-new rooms are nicely outfitted in chain-standard style, and some have balconies (don't expect anything resembling a view). All of the conveniences are on hand, including a free airport shuttle and a very nice pool and fitness center.

5400 W. Century Blvd., Los Angeles, CA 90045. ✆ **800/937-8461** or 310/216-5858. Fax 310/417-4545. www.westin.com/losangelesairport. 740 units. $189–$299 double; from $349 suite. Discounted rates can go as low as $139. AE, DC, DISC, MC, V. Parking $15. Small pets allowed. **Amenities:** California-style restaurant; lobby court for cocktails; heated outdoor pool and whirlpool; exercise room; Westin Kids Club; 24-hr. concierge; free airport shuttle; business center; secretarial services; 24-hr. room service; laundry service; dry cleaning. *In room:* A/C, TV w/pay movies, dataport, Wi-Fi, minibar, coffeemaker, hair dryer, iron.

MODERATE
Marriott Los Angeles Airport   This huge 18-story Marriott is a good airport choice, designed for travelers on the fly. Rooms are decorated in standard chain-hotel style; some have balconies, and a select few are designed expressly for business travelers with voice mail, two-line phones, and (for $13) both high-speed Internet and unlimited long-distance calls.

5855 W. Century Blvd. (at Airport Blvd.), Los Angeles, CA 90045. ✆ **800/228-9290** or 310/641-5700. Fax 310/337-5358. www.marriott.com. 1,026 units. $119–$251 double. Ask about discounted AAA and AARP rates, as well as bed-and-breakfast packages. AE, DC, DISC, MC, V. Valet parking $23; self-parking $19. **Amenities:** 2 restaurants; coffee shop; sports bar; outdoor heated pool; exercise room; whirlpool; sauna; concierge; Hertz car-rental desk; free airport shuttle; business center; secretarial services; 24-hr. room service; coin-op laundry; laundry service; dry cleaning. *In room:* A/C, TV w/pay movies, dataport, Wi-Fi, minibar, coffeemaker, hair dryer, iron.

Sheraton Gateway Hotel Los Angeles Airport   This 15-story hotel is so close to the Los Angeles Airport that it literally overlooks the runway. Rooms have a stylish boutique look with new furnishings, Sheraton "Sweet Sleeper" beds, and triple-pane windows that block out even the loudest takeoffs.

6101 W. Century Blvd. (near Sepulveda Blvd.), Los Angeles, CA 90045. ✆ **800/325-3535** or 310/642-1111. Fax 310/645-1414. www.sheratonlosangeles.com. 802 units. $199–$295 double. AE, DC, DISC, MC, V. Valet parking $14; self-parking $11. **Amenities:** 2 restaurants; cocktail lounge; heated outdoor pool w/cabanas; exercise room; whirlpool; concierge; car-rental desk; free airport shuttle; business center; 24-hr. room service; laundry service; dry cleaning; executive-level rooms. *In room:* A/C, TV w/pay movies, dataport, Wi-Fi, minibar, coffeemaker, hair dryer, iron, safe.

INEXPENSIVE

Travelodge Hotel at LAX *(Value)*   The lobby is nondescript and the rooms are standard, but there's a beautiful tropical garden surrounding the pool area, and amenities extend beyond the budget-motel standard, such as courtesy airport/car-rental shuttle service and a free morning paper. Some units have terraces; about two-thirds of the rooms have showers only, so request a tub if you require one. A 24-hour Denny's adjoins the hotel. If you've brought the kids along, request the Sleepy Bear Den, a separate sleeping room designed for children.

5547 W. Century Blvd., Los Angeles, CA 90045. © **800/421-3939** or 310/649-4000. Fax 310/649-0311. www. travelodgelax.com. 147 units. $65–$99 double. Rates include continental breakfast. Extra person $8; children 17 and under stay free in parent's room. AE, DC, DISC, MC, V. Free parking. Pet fee is $10. **Amenities:** Restaurant; outdoor heated pool; exercise room; activities desk; car-rental desk; free 24-hr. airport shuttle; business center; room service (6am–10pm); babysitting; coin-op laundry; laundry service; dry cleaning. *In room:* A/C, TV w/pay movies and Nintendo, dataport, coffeemaker, hair dryer, iron.

3 L.A.'s Westside & Beverly Hills

These are the city's most centrally located, star-studded, and dining/shopping/ nightlife-rich communities. As such, hotels tend toward the pricey end of the scale— this is where you can find L.A.'s largest concentration of luxury hotels, many of which you've no doubt seen on TV or the big screen. There aren't many bargains to be found, so travelers in search of the best values shouldn't set their hearts on a Westside location. Even so, I've managed to ferret out a few good midpriced and budget options.

VERY EXPENSIVE

Beverly Hills Hotel and Bungalows ★★★   Behind the famous facade (remember the Eagles' *Hotel California* album?) lies this star-studded haven where legends were, and still are, made: The "Pink Palace" was center stage for both deal- and star-making in Hollywood's golden days. Today stars and industry hotshots or, as one member of the staff joked, "all the current rulers of the universe," can still be found lounging around the Olympic-size pool (into which Katharine Hepburn once dove fully clothed) or digging into Dutch apple pancakes in the iconic **Polo Lounge,** where Hunter S. Thompson kicked off his adventure to Las Vegas. I had the pleasure of staying here recently and was so impressed with the entire experience that the Beverly Hills Hotel has become my new favorite among every other hotel in Los Angeles. It is a truly world-class property.

Following a $100-million restoration a few years back, the hotel's grand lobby and impeccably landscaped grounds retain their over-the-top glory, while the lavish guest rooms—each uniquely decorated in a subdued palate of pinks, greens, apricots, and yellows—boast every state-of-the-art luxury, including extra-large bathrooms with double Grecian marble sinks and TVs. The management has assembled a refreshingly unpretentious, service-oriented staff who seem genuinely bent on guest comfort, and the best original touches have been retained, like butler service at the touch of a button. Many rooms feature private patios, Jacuzzi tubs, kitchens, fireplaces, and/or dining rooms. The 21 bungalows are more luxurious than ever, and the lush, tropical-like grounds are brimming with exotic trees and flowers that emit divine aromas. Even the outdoor pathways are carpeted, to keep noise to a minimum. Adding one more layer of luxury to the hotel, the **Beverly Hills Hotel Spa by La Prairie** offers European and Asian-influenced massage and expert facials.

Where to Stay in L.A.'s Westside & Beverly Hills

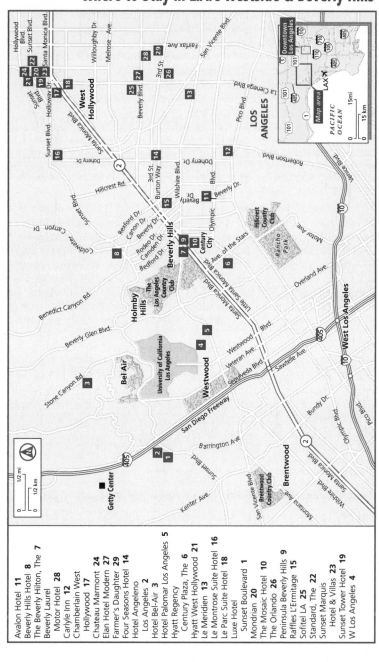

Avalon Hotel **11**
Beverly Hills Hotel **8**
The Beverly Hilton, The **7**
Beverly Laurel
    Motor Hotel **28**
Carlyle Inn **12**
Chamberlain West
    Hollywood **17**
Chateau Marmont **24**
Elan Hotel Modern **27**
Farmer's Daughter **29**
Four Seasons Hotel **14**
Hotel Angeleno
    Los Angeles **2**
Hotel Bel-Air **3**
Hotel Palomar Los Angeles **5**
Hyatt Regency
    Century Plaza, The **6**
Hyatt West Hollywood **21**
Le Meridien **13**
Le Montrose Suite Hotel **16**
Le Parc Suite Hotel **18**
Luxe Hotel
    Sunset Boulevard **1**
Mondrian **20**
The Mosaic Hotel **10**
The Orlando **26**
Peninsula Beverly Hills **9**
Raffles L'Ermitage **15**
Sofitel LA **25**
Standard, The **22**
Sunset Marquis
    Hotel & Villas **23**
Sunset Tower Hotel **19**
W Los Angeles **4**

If you feel like drinking like one of the Hollywood elite, stop by Bar NINE-TEEN12. Named in honor of the year the hotel first opened, the bar has an inside area with a living-room feel and a lighted terrace. Drink prices can run pretty high here. Tableside bottle service can cost anywhere from $475 to $23,000. But, you never know who might be there talking business over drinks. *Tip:* For a more affordable time, try the inexpensive, informal, and groovily retro-chic **Fountain Coffee Shop,** open daily 7am to 7pm. Either place is a great excuse to visit the hotel.

9641 Sunset Blvd. (at Rodeo Dr.), Beverly Hills, CA 90210. (C) 800/283-8885 or 310/276-2251. Fax 310/887-2887. www.beverlyhillshotel.com. 204 units. $485–$665 double; from $1,025 suite or bungalow. AE, DC, MC, V. Parking $23. Pets accepted in bungalows only. **Amenities:** 3 restaurants; 2 bars; 2 lounges; Olympic-size outdoor heated pool; 2 outdoor tennis courts (lit for night play); fitness center; full spa services; whirlpool; concierge; car-rental desk; courtesy limo; business center w/computers; 24-hr. room service; in-room or poolside massage; babysitting; laundry service; dry cleaning; video rentals. *In room:* A/C, TV/VCR, fax/copier/scanner, high-speed Internet, minibar, hair dryer, safe, CD player.

Four Seasons Hotel Los Angeles at Beverly Hills ★★

This intimate-feeling 16-story hotel attracts a mix of A-list jet-setters loyal to the Four Seasons brand and an L.A. showbiz crowd who cherish the hotel as an après-event gathering place. The small marbled lobby is anchored by an always-stunning floral extravaganza, and lush gardens will help you forget you're in the heart of the city. Four Seasons operates terrific hotels, with a concierge that's famously well connected and service that goes the distance. Guest rooms are sumptuously furnished in traditional style and pastel hues. Luxuries include custom extra-stuffed Sealy mattresses with heavenly linens and pillows, marble bathrooms with vanity TV, and French doors leading to private balconies. Room rates rise with the elevator, so bargain hunters need to sacrifice the view; ask for a corner room to get extra space at no additional cost.

Since you're already in for a penny, get the pounding as well: a California Sunset Massage at one of the private candlelit poolside cabanas. Along with a full-service spa, the view-endowed fourth-floor deck features a lap pool, poolside grill, and glass-walled fitness center. **Gardens** is a refined and excellent California-French restaurant often overlooked by locals.

300 S. Doheny Dr. (at Burton Way), Los Angeles, CA 90048. (C) 800/819-5053, 800/332-3442, or 310/273-2222. Fax 310/859-3824. www.fourseasons.com/losangeles. 285 units. $395–$475 double; from $595 suite. AE, DC, DISC, MC, V. Valet parking $21. Pets 15 lb. and under welcomed (no charge). **Amenities:** Restaurant; lounge; poolside grill; rooftop heated pool; exercise room; full-service spa; Jacuzzi; children's program; concierge; courtesy limo within 2-mile radius; business center; 24-hr. room service; in-room massage; laundry service; dry cleaning. *In room:* A/C, TV/DVD w/pay movies (suites have DVD), dataport, free Wi-Fi, minibar, hair dryer, iron, safe, CD player.

Hotel Bel-Air ★★★

Spread over 12 luxuriant garden acres, this stunning mission-style hotel is one of the most beautiful, romantic, exclusive, and all-around impressive hotels not just in L.A., but in all of California. This opulent early-20th-century castle wins a never-ending stream of praise for its faultless service, luxurious accommodations, and magical ambience. The parklike grounds—rich with ancient trees, fragrant flowers, bubbling fountains, playful statuary, and swan-dotted ponds—are enchanting, and the welcoming, richly traditional public rooms are filled with fine antiques. Rooms, villas, and garden suites are individually decorated but equally stunning; some have Jacuzzis, many have private patios and wood-burning fireplaces, but all feature romantic country French decor.

The hotel is a natural for honeymooners and other celebrants, but families might be put off by the Bel-Air's relative formality, which is geared to the jet set, CEO types, and ladies who lunch. Even if you don't stay here, you might consider a cocktail at the cozy bar; or brunch, lunch, or dinner either inside the highly regarded and ultraromantic restaurant, or on the flower-filled outdoor terrace.

701 Stone Canyon Rd. (north of Sunset Blvd.), Los Angeles, CA 90077. © 800/648-4097 or 310/472-1211. Fax 310/476-5890. www.hotelbelair.com. 91 units. $485–$600 double; $800–$3,700 suite. AE, DC, DISC, MC, V. Parking $20. **Amenities:** Indoor/outdoor restaurant; lounge w/pianist nightly; outdoor heated pool; exercise room; concierge; business center; 24-hr. room service; in-room massage; babysitting; laundry service; dry cleaning; video library. *In room:* A/C, digital TV/VCR w/pay movies, fax, high-speed Internet, minibar, hair dryer, laptop-size safe, CD player.

Hotel Palomar Los Angeles ☆☆   Where else but L.A. would you find a hotel that combines dramatic movie-themed design elements with four-star service and an environment friendly focus? If you just want a bed, don't bother. But if you're looking for the kind of hotel experience that enhances your Hollywood vacation by treating you like a VIP, the new Hotel Palomar in Westwood is now playing. Designed in collaboration with Beverly Hills interior designer Cheryl Rowley, the 19-story Palomar oozes with elements of opulence and exoticism, from the grand rouge marble fireplace in the shimmering lobby to velvet shams and faux snakeskin chests in each guest room. Other high-end perks include L'Occitane bath products, 42" LCD flatscreen TVs, plush terry bathrobes, lighted makeup and full-length mirrors, and Fuji spa tubs in the suites. Sure, it's all a bit over-the-top, but it is fun, and that's what we want on our vacation, eh? So go ahead and book the hotel's personal trainer. Or watch 24-hour in-room yoga and Pilates on the LCD flatscreen TV. Or have James drive you to Spago in the hotel's Lexus Hybrid town car. Or sip Manhattans while sunbathing at the pool with your cockapoo (it's a pet-friendly place). It's your turn to play diva, though I doubt Mariah is sorting her trash at the in-room recycling bins.

10740 Wilshire Blvd., Los Angeles, CA 90024. © 800/472-8556. Fax 310/475-5220. www.hotelpalomar-lawestwood. com. 238 units, 30 suites. $269–$459 double; $369–$559 suite. AE, DC, DISC, MC, V. Valet parking $30. **Amenities:** Blvd 16 Restaurant & Lounge; evening wine reception; heated pool; 24-hr. fitness center; concierge; business center; 24-hr. room service; car service; laundry service; dry cleaning; complimentary overnight shoe shine. *In room:* A/C, TV, minibar, free high-speed Internet, hair dryer, iron, safe, iPod station, in-room spa treatments.

The Hyatt Regency Century Plaza ☆☆   Despite the almost-foreboding scale, I really like this hotel. The spacious lobby lounge is always my first stop for a cocktail and some great people-watching, followed by a walk around the immense pool and garden area behind the hotel (pack swim trunks). The guest rooms are more attractive than you'd expect from a corporate hotel, with contemporary furnishings, gorgeous warm-hued textiles, big closets with terry robes, and almost universally impressive views from the small deck. Hyatt's celestial Grand Bed is a treat, as is the 32-inch LCD flatscreen TV and i-Home radio for iPod connectivity. **Breeze,** the hotel's beautiful 250-seat restaurant and sushi bar designed by architect-of-the-moment Stephen Jacobs, is popular with the L.A. elite (particularly at lunch), and the **X Bar** is handy for that late-night cocktail and appetizers craving. Adjoining the hotel is the tony **Equinox Fitness Club + Spa** (you don't even want to know how much the membership fee is). A $20 daily fee allows guests full access to the state-of-the-art fitness center, fitness classes, and locker room.

2025 Ave. of the Stars (south of Santa Monica Blvd.), Century City, CA 90067. © 800/55-HYATT (800/555-9288) or 310/228-1234. Fax 310/551-3355. www.centuryplaza.hyatt.com. 726 units. $399–$509 double; from $559 suite. Weekend, off-season, and other discounts available. AE, DC, DISC, MC, V. Valet parking $31 with unlimited in-and-out privileges. Pets accepted with $30 deposit. **Amenities:** Restaurant; spa cafe; lobby bar; lounge; outdoor heated pool and Jacuzzi; Spa Mystique health club and sauna; concierge; Hertz car-rental desk; business center; salon; 24-hr. room service; laundry service; dry cleaning; Wi-Fi in lobby. *In room:* A/C, TV w/pay movies, high-speed Internet, minibar, coffeemaker, hair dryer, iron, laptop-size safe.

Le Meridien 🐱🐱   It took deep pockets to hire renowned French architect Pierre Yves Rochon to orchestrate a multimillion-dollar renovation. The result is a visual masterpiece of color, form, and function. Whereas the lobby, bar, and other public areas are replete with futuristic furnishings, busy patterns, and saturated colors, the rooms are given a contemporary European look that's both warm and relaxing. Thanks to amenities such as in-room fax machines, three two-line phones, and large counter/desk space, the rooms function equally well as sleeping quarters and work spaces. All things electrical (lights, TV, climate control) are operated by a bedside remote, and the subdued black marble bathrooms hold elegant Hermès products; after a long day on the job, the huge soaking tubs are perfect for unwinding. Even if you're not staying here, you might want to drop by to admire Pierre's talent.

465 S. La Cienega Blvd., Los Angeles, CA 90048. ② 800/543-4300 or 310/247-0400. Fax 310/247-0315. www. starwoodhotels.com/lemeridien. 300 units. $345–$537 double; from $770 suite. AE, DC, DISC, MC, V. Valet parking $24; free self-parking. Pets accepted with $100 fee (covers 4-night stay). **Amenities:** Restaurant; bar; heated pool; 24-hr. health club; sauna; concierge; business center; 24-hr. room service; massage; same-day laundry and dry cleaning; Wi-Fi in lobby. *In room:* A/C, TV/VCR/DVD w/pay movies, fax and printers, high-speed Internet, minibar, hair dryer, iron, CD player.

Mondrian 🐱🐱   Theatrical, coveted, sophisticated—this is the kind of place super-hotelier Ian Schrager has created from a once-drab apartment building. Working with his regular partner, *enfant terrible* French designer Philippe Starck (as he successfully did at Miami's Delano and Manhattan properties like the Royalton and Hudson), Schrager used the Mondrian's breathtaking views (from every room) as the starting point for his vision of a "hotel in the clouds." Purposely under-lit hallways lead to bright, clean rooms done in shades of white, beige, and pale gray and outfitted with simple furniture casually slipcovered in white; about three-quarters of the rooms and suites have fully outfitted kitchenettes. Truthfully, the accommodations themselves are only secondary—stay here if you want to be part of a superhip, star-studded scene. Set poolside and in a magical treehouse, **Skybar** is still one of L.A.'s hottest watering holes, and booking a room guarantees admission. (Soundproof windows on the entire south side of the building have already dealt with a troublesome noise problem in rooms overlooking the raucous late-night scene.) In addition to its terrific—and ultra-hip—Asian-Latin fusion restaurant **Asia de Cuba,** light meals and sushi are served at a quirky communal table in the lobby. Then there's the elegant **Agua Spa,** offering a full range of spa treatments in a Zen-like atmosphere. The beautiful-people staff isn't strong on service, but so what? They look great.

8440 Sunset Blvd., West Hollywood, CA 90069. ② 800/697-1791 or 323/650-8999. Fax 323/650-5215. www. mondrianhotel.com. 237 units. $330–$580 double; from $405 suite. Weekend rates available. AE, DC, DISC, MC, V. Valet parking $23. **Amenities:** 2 restaurants; bar; outdoor pool; fitness room; Agua Spa; concierge; business center; 24-hr. room service; in-room massage; laundry service; dry cleaning; video, DVD, and CD libraries. *In room:* A/C, TV (DVD player available upon request), Wi-Fi, minibar, coffeemaker, hair dryer, iron, safe, CD player.

Peninsula Beverly Hills 🐱🐱🐱   The Peninsula is one of L.A.'s three finest hotels (a group that includes the Hotel Bel-Air and the Beverly Hills Hotel). This stellar hotel—like its sister Peninsula properties in exotic locales like Hong Kong, Beijing, and Bangkok—has risen above the rest by making ultraservice its hallmark. Set at Beverly Hills's main crossroads, this gardenlike oasis is impeccable in every respect (although laid-back types will surely consider it too formal).

The refined air begins the moment you enter the marbled lobby and continues through the gardenlike grounds. Special features in the large, lavish, European-style guest rooms include controls for everything—lighting, climate, DO NOT DISTURB sign—as well as the luxurious Frette-made bed, an extra-large work desk, an oversize marble bathroom with soaking tub and separate shower, and round-the-clock personal valets; the 16 private villa suites, ensconced within lush gardens, also boast gas fireplaces, kitchens, CD players, and individual security systems. Sure, rooms are ultra-expensive, but a unique 24-hour check-in/checkout policy—which allows you to keep your room for a full 24 hours, no matter what time you check in—means you get your money's worth.

Belvedere is L.A.'s premier hotel dining room; breakfast is a tradition among CAA agents and their thespian clients (insiders order the nowhere-on-the-menu banana-stuffed brioche French toast), and Sunday brunch is the best in town. The mahogany-paneled bar is also popular among the power suits, while the English Garden–style **Living Room** pours L.A.'s best high tea. The newly renovated Peninsula Spa is a day-spa worthy of a visit even if you don't stay at the hotel.

9882 S. Santa Monica Blvd. (at Wilshire Blvd.), Beverly Hills, CA 90212. ✆ **800/462-7899** or 310/551-2888. Fax 310/788-2319. www.peninsula.com. 196 units. $475–$725 double; from $1,000 suite. AE, DC, DISC, MC, V. Parking $28. **Amenities:** Restaurant; bar; rooftop heated lap pool and Jacuzzi; state-of-the-art fitness center; terrific full-service spa; concierge; courtesy Lexus within 5-mile radius; business center; salon; 24-hr. room service; in-room massage; laundry service; dry cleaning; 24-hr. check-in/checkout. *In room:* A/C, TV/VCR w/pay movies and WebTV, fax/copier/scanner, high-speed Internet, minibar, hair dryer, safe.

Raffles L'Ermitage 🐟🐟🐟 If the Beverly Hills Hotel symbolizes Hollywood opulence as it once was, Raffles L'Ermitage epitomizes what it is today. Each enormous (650-sq.-ft.), superbly decorated room is done in a contemporary Asian-meets-Scandinavian style that exudes understatement. The real treat is the in-room technology, which includes a CD/DVD player, Bose speakers, four phones, and "smart" bedside control panels that remember your lighting and climate preferences. The work desk is large, seating is copious and comfortable, carpeting is Berber, fabrics tend to tailored silk, and lighting is soft and on dimmers. The bathrooms feature a soaking tub, a shower for two, and cotton *and* terry robes. The faultless service includes flexible check-in/checkout and a wealth of freebies that include local and 800 calls, all nonalcoholic beverages in your minibar, customized stationery and business cards with your name and direct-dial phone and fax numbers (very slick), and complimentary DVD lending. Room service is reasonable and carries no automatic service charges. The house restaurant, **JAAN,** serves modern French-Indochina cuisine in an über-stylish setting. You'll love the rooftop pool as well. Children are warmly welcomed (rare for an upscale Beverly Hills hotel), as are pets 40 pounds and under.

9291 Burton Way, Beverly Hills, CA 90210. ✆ **800/768-9009** or 310/278-3344. Fax 310/278-8247. www.beverlyhills.raffles.com. 119 units. $445 double; from $608 suite. Ask about corporate rates, specials, and packages. AE, DC, MC, V. Valet parking $26. Pets up to 40 lb. accepted. **Amenities:** Restaurant; bar; tea lounge; heated rooftop pool; Amrita spa and health club; 24-hr. concierge; courtesy car; 24-hr. room service; in-room massage; laundry service; dry cleaning. *In room:* A/C, 40-in. TV w/DVD, fax/printer/copier, free Wi-Fi, high-speed Internet, minibar, hair dryer, safe, in-room movies and Web TV, CD player.

Sofitel LA 🐟🐟 The Sofitel chain has arrived in L.A. with glamour and sophistication to spare. In the heart of L.A.'s Westside, adjacent to Beverly Hills and directly across the street from the Beverly Center, is this upscale, yet comfortable hotel. With the exception of the Euro-beats pumped into the lobby, the Sofitel does everything right. Rooms, though not large, ooze luxury—the thick carpet, high thread-count linens, and contemporary amenities such as 32-inch plasma TVs, sizeable workspaces, and Wi-Fi connections are sure to make anyone comfortable. Bathrooms are big and include an oversize rain shower, Switchlite glass windows, and plush bathrobes. The decor falls somewhere between old Hollywood glamour and Asian-contemporary— look for modern furniture with high-gloss fire-engine reds and candy-apple greens. Suites are even more lavish; they include Bose stereo systems and walk-in closets, as well as flatscreen TVs mounted over soaking tubs in the huge bathrooms. The biggest suite in the house has, in addition to a sizeable bedroom, bathroom, and living area, a full dining space with fireplace, as well as a huge balcony with full bar. We hear rock stars rent the place after playing shows in town. The dimly-lit **Stone Rose** lounge, a Rande Gerber creation, is an über-trendy spot for late-night cocktails and/or canoodling. The on-site **Le Spa** offers an abundance of indulgent skin treatments, massages, baths, and manicure/pedicures.

8555 Beverly Blvd. (at La Cienega), Los Angeles, CA 90048. Ⓒ **800/SOFITEL** (800/763-4835) or 310/278-5444. www. sofitella.com. 295 units. $295–$460 double; from $650 suites. AE, DC, DISC, MC, V. Valet parking $26. Pets welcome. **Amenities:** Restaurant; bar; health club; concierge; room service; laundry service; dry cleaning; nonsmoking floors. *In room:* A/C, TV/DVD, high-speed Internet, Wi-Fi, minibar, hair dryer, iron, laptop-size safe.

EXPENSIVE

Avalon Hotel 🏆🏆 *Finds*   The first style-conscious boutique hotel on the L.A. scene, this mid-20th-century-inspired gem in the heart of Beverly Hills still leads the pack. With a soothing sherbet-hued palette and classic atomic-age furnishings—Eames cabinets, Heywood-Wakefield chairs, Nelson bubble lamps—mixed with smart custom designs, every room looks as if it could star in a *Metropolitan Home* photo spread. But fashion doesn't forsake function at this beautifully designed hotel, which offers enough luxury comforts and amenities to please design-blind travelers, too.

The property is comprised of the former Beverly Carlton (seen on *I Love Lucy* and once home to Marilyn Monroe and Mae West), as well as two neighboring 1950s-era apartment houses. The main building is the hub of a chic but low-key scene, but I prefer the quieter Canon building, where many of the units have kitchenettes and/or furnished terraces. No matter which one you end up in, you'll find a gorgeous, restful cocoon with terry bathrobes and Miscioni linens. You'll also have easy access to the sunny courtyard with its retro-hip amoeba-shape pool, the fitness room, and **blue on blue,** the groovy blue-hued restaurant and bar that shakes a terrific green apple martini. Service is friendlier than you'll find in other style-minded hotels. *Note:* I've received complaints of noisy pool parties that have kept guests up at night—if you're a light sleeper, request a room away from the pool area.

9400 W. Olympic Blvd. (at Beverly Dr.), Beverly Hills, CA 90212. Ⓒ **800/670-6183** or 310/277-5221. Fax 310/277-4928. www.avalonbeverlyhills.com. 86 units. $289–$319 double; from $369–$419 junior or 1-bedroom suite. Extra person $25. AE, DC, MC, V. Valet parking $22. **Amenities:** Restaurant and lounge; courtyard pool; concierge; 24-hr. room service; in-room spa and massage; laundry service; dry cleaning. *In room:* A/C, TV/VCR w/pay movies and video games, fax, dataport, minibar, coffeemaker, hair dryer, iron, safe, CD player.

The Beverly Hilton 🏆   If you're a fan of awards shows you'll probably recognize this hotel as the annual home to the star-studded Golden Globe Awards. Located at the crossroads of Wilshire and Santa Monica boulevards, in the heart of Beverly Hills, this boxlike eight-story hotel has been attracting city business travelers, movie stars, U.S. presidents, royalty, and tourists alike since 1955. It was previously owned by Merv Griffin, who didn't put much into renovations (and it showed), but now the Beverly

Hills–based Hilton Corporation has upgraded the entire interior of the hotel as part of an $80-million renovation. All guest rooms have been completely redesigned with a contemporary casual feel and loads of luxury amenities: Italian linens, L'Occitane bath products, 42-inch plasma TVs, Bose Wave Radios, and even 13-inch flatscreen TVs in the bathroom. Many have balconies that offer views of Century City, Beverly Hills, and the Hollywood Hills. During the summer, the ground-level poolside cabana rooms are a good choice—the alluring pool area alone is worth staying here—thanks to sliding doors that open directly onto the sun deck. For city views, request one of the Wilshire Tower rooms. Among the Beverly Hilton's best advantages are its food and cocktail outlets: It's hard to beat a pupu platter and a rum-spiked Navy Grog at the groovy Polynesian-style **Trader Vic's,** and the new retro-chic **Circa 55** restaurant and lounge on the pool level is a visual stunner. Other new additions include a huge state-of-the-art fitness room, and the serene **Aqua Star Spa** offering treatments for both men and women.

9876 Wilshire Blvd. (at Santa Monica Blvd.), Beverly Hills, CA 90210. ⓒ **800/445-8667** or 310/274-7777. Fax 310/285-1313. www.beverlyhilton.com. 570 units. $189–$370 double; from $395 suite. Ask about discounts, packages, and weekend rates. AE, DC, DISC, MC, V. Valet parking $24; self-parking $21. Pets 20 lb. and under accepted. **Amenities:** 2 restaurants; 3 lounges; heated Olympic-size outdoor pool; state-of-the-art fitness center; full-service spa; 24-hr. concierge; courtesy car within 5-mile radius; business center; salon; 24-hr. room service; laundry service; dry cleaning; gift shop. *In room:* A/C, TV/VCR w/pay movies, dataport, minibar, coffeemaker, hair dryer, iron.

Chateau Marmont ⓖⓖ   Perched secretively in a curve above the Sunset Strip, the château modeled after an elegant Loire Valley castle is a landmark from 1920s-era Hollywood; step inside and you'll expect to find John Barrymore or Errol Flynn holding inebriated court in the baronial living room (in fact, some say it's actually haunted). Greta Garbo regularly checked in as Harriet Brown, and Jim Morrison was one of many celebrities to call this home in later years. This historic landmark built its reputation on exclusivity and privacy, which was shattered when John Belushi overdosed in Bungalow No. 2. Now under the guiding hand of boutique hotelier Andre Balazs (also lord of the Standard [later in this chapter] and New York's temple of SoHo style, the Mercer Hotel), the funky luxury oasis revels in its lore-filled past, yet it's hipper and more exclusive than ever. No two of the antiques-filled accommodations—standard rooms, suites, cottages, and bungalows—are alike: The poolside Spanish-style garden cottages are outfitted in Arts and Crafts style, while suites and bungalows may get a 1950s look or a Gothic style. Many units have fireplaces and CD stereos, and all but 11 have kitchenettes or full kitchens.

The Chateau Marmont is beautifully kept, eternally chic, faultlessly service-oriented, and overflowing with Hollywood and rock-'n'-roll lore (not to mention a look-at-me/don't-look-at-me clientele), but it's not for everybody. This is a place where quirkiness rules, so don't expect traditional luxuries. It's best for those with left-of-center attitudes and a real penchant for Hollywood romanticism. If that's you, don't stay anywhere else—this will be the highlight of your vacation.

8221 Sunset Blvd. (btw. La Cienega and Crescent Heights boulevards), West Hollywood, CA 90046. ⓒ **800/242-8328** or 323/656-1010. Fax 323/655-5311. www.chateaumarmont.com. 63 units. From $335 double; from $425 suite; from $450 cottage; from $1,700 bungalow. AE, DC, MC, V. Valet parking $21. Pets accepted with $100-per-pet fee. **Amenities:** Restaurant (serves in lobby, garden, and dining room); bar; outdoor heated pool w/brick sun deck; exercise room; access to nearby health club; 24-hr. concierge; business center; secretarial services; 24-hr. room service; in-room massage; babysitting; same-day laundry and dry cleaning; CD library. *In room:* A/C, TV/VCR, free Wi-Fi, minibar, fridge, coffeemaker, hair dryer, iron, laptop-size safe, CD player.

Le Montrose Suite Hotel 🌴🌴 *Value*   Nobody pays rack at this terrific all-suite hotel, which offers money-saving specials of every stripe for travelers who want more than a standard room for their accommodations dollars. Nestled on a quiet street just 2 blocks from the red-hot Sunset Strip, cozy Le Montrose features large split-level studio and one-bedroom apartments that feel more like comfortable, upscale condos than hotel rooms. Each contemporary-style suite has a sizable living room with gas fireplace, dining area, comfortable sleeping nook (or dedicated bedroom), and very nice bathroom. Executive and one-bedroom suites have kitchenettes (which can be stocked upon request). The two bedrooms are a great deal for families or sharing friends. You have to go up to the roof for anything resembling a view, but once you're up there, you can swim in the saltwater pool, soak in the Jacuzzi, or brush up on your tennis game. Recent upgrades include a fitness center on the fifth floor and the **Privato** restaurant, lounge, and wine bar. This place is a favorite for long-term stays among the music and film crowd, so don't be surprised if you spot a famous face in the hotel's private restaurant during the breakfast hour (open to hotel guests only).

900 Hammond St., West Hollywood, CA 90069. ✆ **800/776-0666** or 310/855-1115. Fax 310/657-9192. www.le montrose.com. 133 units. $295–$575 suite. Money-saving deals abound; AAA, AARP, seasonal, and weekend rates. AE, DC, DISC, MC, V. Valet and self-parking $18. Pets accepted with a $100-per-pet nonrefundable fee. **Amenities:** Continental restaurant; outdoor heated pool w/whirlpool and sun deck; lighted tennis court; fitness center; exercise room w/sauna; bikes; concierge; car-rental desk; business center; secretarial services; 24-hr. room service; coin-op laundry; laundry service; dry cleaning; executive-level rooms; DVD and CD players. *In room:* A/C, TV/VCR w/pay movies, fax/copier/scanner, high-speed Internet access, minibar, coffeemaker, hair dryer, iron, safe, DVD/CD player, Nintendo.

Le Parc Suite Hotel 🌴🌴   Situated on a quiet, tree-lined residential street, Le Parc is a sophisticated and stylish all-suite hotel that attracts an interesting mix of clientele: Designers stay here because it's a few minutes' walk to the Pacific Design Center; celebrities in the music industry stay because of its low-key neighborhood location; patients and medical consultants check in because it's close to Cedars-Sinai; and tourists enjoy being near the Farmers Market, the Beverly Center, and Museum Row. The newly renovated apartment-like units are extra large—studios are 650 square feet, one-bedrooms 875 to 1,000 square feet—and each has a well-outfitted kitchenette, a dining area, a living room with a fireplace, and a balcony. What the hotel lacks in views it makes up for in value and elbowroom, and the rooftop night-lit tennis court is a rare perk in this area. The hotel's intimate bistro-style restaurant, **Knoll,** is a hidden gem, offering very good contemporary American cuisine and romantic alfresco seating at the rooftop dining area.

733 N. West Knoll Dr., West Hollywood, CA 90069. ✆ **800/578-4837** or 310/855-8888. Fax 310/659-7812. www.le parcsuites.com. 154 units. $215–$500 junior or 1-bedroom suite. Check for theater and bed-and-breakfast packages. AE, DC, DISC, MC, V. Parking $18. Pets accepted for $75 fee. **Amenities:** Restaurant w/full bar; outdoor heated pool and Jacuzzi; rooftop night-lit tennis court; well-equipped exercise room w/sauna; access to nearby health club; concierge; courtesy car; business center; 24-hr. room service; massage; babysitting; coin-op laundry; laundry service; dry cleaning. *In room:* A/C, TV/VCR (w/pay movies, video games, and on-screen Internet access), high-speed Internet, kitchenette, minibar, coffeemaker, microwave, hair dryer, iron, CD player.

Luxe Hotel Sunset Boulevard 🌴   Hidden away on 7 garden acres just a stone's throw from the Getty Center and busy Interstate 405, this low-rise hotel is composed of two levels: The lobby and public areas—plus some rooms—are in the main building, while the most secluded guest rooms (and the Romanesque swimming pool) are uphill on the Garden level. Guest rooms are huge and come with stylish custom furnishings, flatscreen TVs, an iPod base station, and feather comforter; most have a large balcony or patio. This Luxe appeals equally to business clientele, who appreciate the extensive amenities, and to leisure travelers, who can relax in the open, green setting. A free shuttle lets guests avoid the parking hassles at the Getty Center. The hotel is popular for wedding receptions on weekends, and the full-service spa attracts a sizable local clientele, so be prepared for lots of lobby traffic. Still, the overall ambience is very relaxing.

11461 Sunset Blvd. (just east of I-405), Los Angeles, CA 90049. (C) **866/LUXE-411** (866/589-3411) or 310/476-6571. Fax 310/471-6310. www.luxehotelsunsetblvd.com. 161 units. $239–$289 double; $325–$495 suite. Ask about corporate rates as well as bed-and-breakfast and spa packages. Extra person $25. AE, DC, DISC, MC, V. Valet parking $15. **Amenities:** Indoor/outdoor restaurant; cocktail and piano lounge; pool; outdoor tennis court (lit for night play); full-service day spa; concierge; hourly shuttle to the Getty Center; secretarial services; room service (6:30am–10:30pm); laundry service; dry cleaning. *In room:* A/C, TV w/pay movies, fax, Wi-Fi, minibar, coffeemaker, hair dryer.

The Mosaic Hotel Beverly Hills ★★★ (Finds)

I've seen hundreds of hotel renovations in my travels, but none have impressed me as much as this boutique Beverly Hills hotel. The owners pumped $3 million into completely renovating the entire hotel (formerly the Beverly Hills Inn), and the result is spectacular. The lobby is a showcase of functional art, with gleaming tile mosaics; fabrics in deep, rich tones; and a profusion of artfully arranged orchids. Continuing a recent trend that I'm all for, a wall has been removed to allow direct access from the check-in desk to the bar and lounge, where guests are encouraged to sample the house special—a Mosaic sake martini. The guest rooms are equally impressive, all done in soothing earth tones with 300-count linens, goose-down comforters and piles of pillows, windows that open onto the quiet neighborhood street or garden courtyard, minibars stocked with Wolfgang Puck snacks and libations, and sparkling bathrooms with Bulgari bath products and huge rainforest shower heads. Other perks include free high-speed Internet access, poolside cabanas, CD players, DVD players in the suites, late room service from the hotel's small restaurant, a fitness room, and covered parking. *Tip:* The corner deluxe rooms are worth the extra $15.

125 S. Spalding Dr., Beverly Hills, CA 90212. (C) **800/463-4466** or 310/278-0303. Fax 310/278-1728. www.mosaic hotel.com. 49 units. $285–$520 double; from $600 2-bedroom suite. AE, DC, MC, V. Parking $15. Small pets accepted. **Amenities:** Restaurant; full bar; heated outdoor pool; exercise room w/sauna; tour desk; business services; full room-service menu until 10pm; laundry service; dry cleaning. *In room:* A/C, TV, high-speed Internet, fridge, hair dryer, iron, CD player.

Sunset Marquis Hotel & Villas ★★ (Finds)

This sprawling Mediterranean-style all-suite hotel is the ultimate movie-and-music hostelry, regularly hosting the biggest names in rock and film. (The Rolling Stones, Aerosmith, U2, and even Brad Pitt are all repeat customers.) In fact, the hotel even installed a state-of-the-art recording studio and screening room in the basement for its noteworthy guests. After recording sessions, the musicians can then retire to the dark and sexy **Bar 1200** (a favorite refuge of celebs), where their newly recorded session can be piped in directly. Of course, unless you're staying at the hotel, you'll never get in (which, in itself, is reason enough to stay). The hotel is located a short walk from the rowdy Sunset Strip, but it feels a world away, with its four and a half acres of lush gardens, koi ponds, brick paths, and tropical foliage. The only shortcoming used to be the standard suites, outfitted in traditional motel style—until now, that is. After undergoing a $20-million renovation they were remade in a practical but attractive and comfortable modern style, with clean-lined furnishings in mahogany, metal, and nubby textiles; earth-toned fabrics; Noguchi Akari rice-paper lamps; and marble cashmere granite counters. The villas take hospitality to a totally new level—they have private alarm systems and butlers, plus select features like baby grand pianos, flatscreen TVs, and Jacuzzi tubs. Guests who stay in the presidential villa even get the use of an SUV, Bentley, or a limo during their stay. The enhancements to the hotel don't stop there, either. As part of the renovation, the Sunset Marquis has also built two new separate pool areas, an outdoor bar, a spa, and a restaurant with a patio seating.

1200 N. Alta Loma Rd. (just south of Sunset Blvd.), West Hollywood, CA 90069. ✆ **800/858-9758** or 310/657-1333. Fax 310/657-1330. www.sunsetmarquishotel.com. 154 units. $485–$815 junior or 1- or 2-bedroom suite; from $1,000–$3,000 1- or 2-bedroom villa. Ask about corporate rates. AE, DC, DISC, MC, V. Valet parking $24. **Amenities:** Restaurant; bar; 2 outdoor heated pools; exercise room; Jacuzzi; sauna; excellent 24-hr. concierge service; business center; 24-hr. room service; in-room massage; babysitting; laundry service; dry cleaning; state-of-the-art recording studio. *In room:* A/C, TV w/pay movies, Wi-Fi and high-speed Internet, minibar, fridge, iron, laptop-size safe, CD player.

Sunset Tower Hotel 🏵🏵🏵   The Sunset Tower has everything you could hope for in a Los Angeles hotel: a storied history, glamour, elegance, impeccable service, beautiful views, Deco-era decor, Sunset Strip location, full-service spa, romantic restaurant, celebrity clientele, and nary a smidgeon of snobbery from the staff. Standing out like a pearl among the surrounding architectural swine, the 15-story Sunset Tower was built in 1921 as a luxury apartment for Hollywood's top movie stars—Jean Harlow, Clark Gable, Greta Garbo, Errol Flynn, Mae West, Marilyn Monroe, Elizabeth Taylor, Joan Crawford, John Wayne, Frank Sinatra, Howard Hughes, Diana Ross, and Truman Capote are just a few of the celebrities who lived (or housed lovers) here. The building lost its luster in the '60s and was nearly demolished in the '80s, but ever since hotelier Jeff Klein bought and renovated the hotel in 2005 it's been the darling of the Hollywood hotel scene. It's been meticulously restored with fine woods, muted colors of natural brown and beige, and brass fittings. Guest rooms have floor-to-ceiling windows with wonderful city views, as well as oversize tubs, Frette sheets, and a soothing aura of old-Hollywood elegance. What better way to spend a day in L.A. than to have a massage and spa treatments at the hotel's **Argyle Spa,** spend the afternoon sunbathing at the pool while noshing on blinis and rosé from the **Terrace** poolside grill, settle into a Plymouth martini and a lobster cobb at the beautiful **Tower Bar** (the restaurant's debonair maitre d', Dimitri Dimitrov, is from another era as well), then step out the front door and stroll along the famous Sunset Strip?

8358 Sunset Blvd. (on the Sunset Strip), West Hollywood, CA 90069. ✆ **800/225-2637** or 323/654-7100. Fax 323/654-9287. www.sunsettowerhotel.com. 74 units. $345–$445 double; suites from $495; penthouse from $2,500. AE, DC, DISC, MC, V. Valet parking $28. **Amenities:** Restaurant; poolside grill; bar and lounge; heated outdoor pool; full-service spa; in-room spa treatments; 24-hr. fitness center; concierge; 24-hr. room service; laundry service; dry cleaning; pet amenities. *In room:* A/C, TV/DVD, high-speed Internet, minibar, hair dryer, iPod stations.

W Los Angeles 🏵🏵   Design-savvy hipsters looking for cutting-edge style and familiar comforts will enjoy this 15-story, all-suite hotel near UCLA. The former Westwood Marquis underwent a transformation in 2000 under new owners, W Hotels, the "boutique" hotel brand backed by corporate giant Starwood Hotels and Resorts. Hidden behind a severe concrete exterior, this oasis-like property has always had advantages: an all-suite configuration, 2 lush acres of greenery, and eye-catching '60s architectural detailing that's been liberated from its long-standing Sheetrock walls. Rooms range in size from large two-room suites to two-bed, two-bathroom suites, featuring bold, angular furnishings in dark African wenge wood, accented with gray carpeting and soft plum textiles. Luxuries include divinely dressed beds, 27-inch

TVs—plasma screens in some rooms—and DVD and CD players. The bathrooms are spacious but unremarkable, save for inviting waffle-weave robes and exclusive Bliss spa products. W's popular restaurant, **NineThirty,** serves superb American cuisine, while nightlife impresario Rande Gerber's bar, **Whiskey Blue,** pretty much guarantees a celebrity scene on weekend nights. The well-furnished gardenlike pool area has its own outdoor cafe called the **Backyard,** serving Mediterranean "swimwear fare." The 7,000-square-foot **Bliss Spa** offers hip services like movie-while-you-manicure nail stations, and men's and women's lounges that offer snacks to the road-weary.

930 Hilgard Ave., Los Angeles, CA 90024-3033. ℂ **877/W-HOTELS** (877/946-6835) or 310/208-8765. Fax 310/824-0355. www.whotels.com. 258 units. From $329 1- or 2-bedroom suite. AE, DC, DISC, MC, V. Valet parking $31. Pets welcome. **Amenities:** 2 restaurants; cocktail lounge; outdoor heated pool; exercise room; 7,000-sq.-ft. full-service spa, concierge; business center; 24-hr. room service; in-room massage; babysitting; laundry service; dry cleaning; DVD and CD libraries. *In room:* A/C, TV/DVD w/pay movies and on-screen Internet access, dataport, minibar, coffeemaker, hair dryer, iron, laptop-size safe, CD player.

MODERATE

Carlyle Inn ⭐⭐ ⓥalue   Tucked away on an uneventful stretch of Robertson Boulevard just south of Beverly Hills, this four-story inn is one of L.A.'s best midpriced finds. Making the most of a small lot, architects have created an attractive interior courtyard, which almost every room faces, that gives the property a feeling of openness and serenity that most others in this price range lack—not to mention good outdoor space for enjoying the free breakfast or afternoon munchies at umbrella-covered cafe tables on nice days. The well-planned, contemporary guest rooms are fitted with recessed lighting, quality furnishings, firm bedding, and bathrobes. Suites have pull-out sofas but are only slightly larger than standard rooms, so families may be better off in a double/double or connecting rooms. The conscientious manager keeps everything in racing form. The hotel's primary drawback is that it lacks views; curtains must remain drawn at all times to maintain any sense of privacy. Still, it doesn't seem to bother the 90% repeat visitors, who know good value when they find it.

1119 S. Robertson Blvd. (btw. Pico and Olympic boulevards), Los Angeles, CA 90035. ℂ **800/322-7595** or 310/275-4445. Fax 310/859-0496. www.carlyle-inn.com. 32 units. From $199 double; from $209 suite. Rates include full buffet breakfast and weekday-afternoon hors d'oeuvres. Management will deal, so ask for discounts. AE, DC, DISC, MC, V. Parking $11. **Amenities:** Fitness room; Jacuzzi; garden court; sun deck. *In room:* A/C, TV/VCR, complimentary high-speed Internet, dataport, minibar, coffeemaker, hair dryer, iron, safe, daily newspaper.

Chamberlain West Hollywood ⭐   This four-story boutique hotel in a tree-lined residential West Hollywood neighborhood looks and feels much like a high-quality Manhattan apartment building (probably because it used to be an apartment building). The location alone is reason enough to stay here, as it's only 2 blocks from the Sunset Strip and Santa Monica Boulevard. If you're young and hip and have plenty of room on your credit card, you won't need your car once it's parked in the underground garage (hell, you won't even need comfortable shoes). If you've been to the Viceroy in Santa Monica, you'll recognize the English Modern decor—dusky grays, greens, and blues among stark white furnishings. Each guest room is a suite with a separate living and sleeping area, and comes pleasantly equipped with a plush king-size bed with Mascioni 250-count sheets, gas-log fireplace, small balcony, flatscreen TV, DVD/VCR combo, CD player, and large desk with Internet access. The rooftop pool and cabana are ideal for sunbathing, and the roof has a great view of the city. The small restaurant and bar are good for meeting friends for a drink and appetizers before you hit the town (though I suggest you have dinner elsewhere).

1000 Westmount Dr. (1 block west of La Cienega Blvd.), West Hollywood, CA 90069. ℂ 800/201-9652 or 310/657-7400. Fax 310/854-6744. www.chamberlainwesthollywood.com. 112 units. $289–$389 studio to 1-bedroom suites. AE, DC, DISC, MC, V. Valet parking $24 with in/out privileges. **Amenities:** Heated rooftop pool; fitness center; 24-hr. concierge service; room service; coin-op laundry; laundry service; dry cleaning; grocery shopping service. *In room:* A/C, TV/DVD, high-speed Internet, coffeemaker, hair dryer, iron, CD player.

Elan Hotel 🌟🌟 *Finds*   The Elan is truly a find: It's not only one of L.A.'s best boutique-style hotels, it's one of the city's best values as well. Rebuilt and freshly renovated from the bones of a 1969 retirement home, the modern structure blends elements from the original facade with a modern, sophisticated decor. Inside, a mod, loungey lobby leads to handsomely appointed guest rooms done in serene earth tones. The design merges form and function beautifully, resulting in amenity-laden and surprisingly luxurious accommodations, considering the price. The standard rooms aren't huge, but high ceilings and thoughtfully designed custom furnishings create the illusion of space, while plush textured fabrics, beautifully made beds—with cushioned headboards, goose-down comforters, and 350-thread-count Egyptian cotton linens—bathrooms with cotton robes, and the thickest, plushest bath sheets in town elevate comforts well beyond the moderate price point. On the downside, there's no view, no pool, no fitness center (although you can purchase an $8 pass to the nearby health club), and this stretch of Beverly Boulevard isn't exactly the hippest strip in town. But double-paned glass ensures that even boulevard-facing rooms are quiet, and the location in central L.A. is ideal (shoppers will love the walking-distance proximity to the Beverly Center).

8435 Beverly Blvd. (btw. La Cienega Blvd. and Fairfax Ave.), Los Angeles, CA 90048. ℂ 888/611-0398 or 323/658-6663. Fax 323/658-6640. www.elanhotel.com. 49 units. Rooms start at $195. Rates include continental breakfast and managers' wine and cheese reception. Extra person $15. AE, DC, DISC, MC, V. Valet parking $19. **Amenities:** Exercise room; business center; room service from coffee shop across street (5am–2am); laundry service; dry cleaning. *In room:* A/C, HDTV, free Wi-Fi, high-speed Internet, minibar, coffeemaker, hair dryer, iron, safe.

Hotel Angeleno Los Angeles 🌟🌟   This L.A. landmark building is the last of a vanishing breed of circular hotels from the 1960s and 1970s. Formerly a Holiday Inn, it was bought by the Joie de Vivre hotel group that made its name in San Francisco by revamping tired hotels into hip, modern destinations, and this is the company's first L.A. venture. The location alone is a good reason to stay here: It's perched beside the city's busiest freeway, a short hop from the popular Getty Center and centrally located between the beaches, Beverly Hills, and the San Fernando Valley. Each pie-shaped room comes with a private balcony and double-paned glass to keep most of the freeway din at bay—think of it as complimentary white noise—while comfort comes in the form of 300-count Italian linens, feather duvets, and pillow-top mattresses. Little extras like 30-inch plasma TVs, wireless Internet access, ergonomic work stations, and great views add to the panache. Also a hot spot is the 17-story hotel's penthouse-level **West** supper club and cocktail lounge, the city's first Italian steakhouse. Additional perks include an outdoor pool with cabanas and a fire pit, a lobby-level cafe, and complimentary pickup and drop-off service to the Getty Center, UCLA, and Westwood. Be sure to check the hotel's website to see what package deals are being offered.

170 N. Church Lane (at intersection of Sunset Blvd. and I-405), Los Angeles, CA 90049. ℂ 866/ANGELENO (866/264-3536) or 310/476-6411. Fax 310/472-1157. www.hotelangeleno.com. 209 units. $189–$239 double; from $295 suite. AE, DC, DISC, MC, V. Valet parking $18. **Amenities:** Rooftop restaurant and lounge; lobby cafe; heated outdoor pool and fireplace; fitness center; business center; 24-hr. concierge; free shuttle to Getty Center and within a 3-mile

radius; room service; laundry service; dry cleaning; evening wine reception. *In room:* A/C, TV w/pay movies and free HBO, Wi-Fi and high-speed Internet, minibar, coffeemaker, hair dryer, safe, CD player.

Hyatt West Hollywood   This legendary 13-story Sunset Strip hotel is best known for its former debauched life as the rock-'n'-roll "Riot Hyatt." Long gone are the days when John Bonham drove his motorcycle down the halls, Keith Richards dropped a TV out the window, and Jim Morrison hung by his fingertips outside his window. Guest rooms have city or hillside views (about half have balconies) and a massive renovation—to be completed in November 2008—will bring badly needed improvements to this well-worn icon. But the main reason to stay here is to get access to the swank rooftop pool, which offers one the city's best perches for peeping into the luxury homes that dot the hillside behind the hotel.

8401 Sunset Blvd. (at Kings Rd., 2 blocks east of La Cienega Blvd.), West Hollywood, CA 90069. ✆ **800/633-7313** or 323/656-1234. Fax 323/650-7024. www.westhollywood.hyatt.com. 258 units. $185–$300 double; from $3,325 suite. Check for discounted weekend, AAA, and senior rates. Extra person $25; children stay free in parent's room. AE, DC, DISC, MC, V. Valet parking $23; self-parking $18. **Amenities:** Indoor/outdoor restaurant; bar; rooftop heated pool w/chaises and terrific views; state-of-the-art exercise room; concierge; business center; room service; laundry service; dry cleaning; executive-level rooms. *In room:* A/C, TV w/pay movies, high-speed Internet, Wi-Fi, hair dryer, iron, safe.

The Orlando 🍴🍴   If you came to L.A. to shop, you'll definitely want to stay at the Orlando. Not only is it situated between Beverly Hills and West Hollywood in the heart of the Third Street Promenade, it's also within walking distance of the Grove, the Farmers Market, the Beverly Center, and Restaurant Row (is your credit card sweating yet?). Billed as a European-style boutique hotel, the Orlando has a modern, chic look with custom furnishings and cool color schemes of browns, burnt oranges, and light tans. The large guest rooms are comfortably equipped with 32-inch plasma TVs, iPod minibars, and beds with Egyptian cotton sheets, but you'll probably spend most of your time at the rooftop deck, floating beneath sunny blue skies in the saltwater pool. If you're in a splurging mood, request a spacious Executive Garden room with a big ol' king-size bed and private patio. Other hotel perks include a complimentary European breakfast buffet, $10 taxi vouchers per day (smart), and a wonderful Italian restaurant called **La Terza** (I had a parpardelle with oxtail ragout that was superb). Numerous other amenities are available at the Orlando that you would typically only find at a much larger—and far more expensive—luxury hotel, including in-room spa treatments and 24-hour room service. *Tip:* Celebrities like to stay here because of the hotel's low-key location and privacy: Carmen Electra, Jennifer Aniston, Stevie Wonder, Sting, Tori Spelling, and Vince Vaughn have all been guests here.

8384 W. 3rd St. (at Orlando St.), Los Angeles, CA 90048. ✆ **800/62-HOTEL** (800/624-6835) or 323/658-6600. Fax 323/653-4737. www.theorlando.com. 98 units. From $279 standard rooms; from $410 Executive rooms. AE, DC, DISC, MC, V. Valet parking $26. Pets welcome. **Amenities:** Restaurant; bar; outdoor heated pool; 24-hr. fitness center; 2 dry saunas; 24-hr. concierge; business center; room service; in-room massage; free Wi-Fi. *In room:* A/C, TV w/On Demand, dataport, minibar, coffeemaker, hair dryer, iron, laptop-size safe, CD player.

The Standard 🍴🍴   If Andy Warhol had gone into the hotel business (which he no doubt would have, if he had arrived on the scene a few decades later), the Standard would've been the end result. Designed to appeal to the under-35 "it" crowd, André Balazs's swank West Hollywood neo-motel is sometimes absurd, sometimes brilliant, and always provocative (not mention crowded!). It's a scene worthy of its Sunset Strip location: shag carpeting on the lobby ceiling, blue Astroturf around the swimming pool, a DJ spinning ambient sounds while a performance artist showing more skin than talent poses in a display case behind the check-in desk—this place is definitely left of center.

The good news is that the Standard is more than just attitude. Look past the retro clutter and often-raucous party scene, and you'll find a level of service more often associated with hotels costing twice as much. Constructed from the bones of a vintage 1962 motel, it boasts comfortably sized rooms outfitted with cobalt blue indoor-outdoor carpeting, silver beanbag chairs, safety-orange tiles in the bathrooms, and Warhol's poppy-print curtains, plus private balconies, and minibars whose contents include goodies like sake, condoms, and animal crackers. On the downside, the cheapest rooms face noisy Sunset Boulevard, and the relentless scene can get tiring if you're not into it.

Note: The 12-story **Downtown Standard,** 550 S. Flower St. (© **213/892-8080**), opened in mid-2002, brings a similar dose of retro-future style and cool attitude to Downtown. It's worth visiting just to check out the retro-glam rooftop bar with its vibrating waterbed pleasure pods, movies projected onto neighboring buildings, and hot waitresses.

8300 Sunset Blvd. (at Sweetzer Ave.), West Hollywood, CA 90069. © 323/650-9090. Fax 323/650-2820. www. standardhotel.com. 139 units. $160–$295 double; from $500 suite. AE, DC, DISC, MC, V. Valet parking $22. Pets 20 lb. and under accepted for $100-per-pet fee. **Amenities:** 24-hr. coffee shop; poolside cafe; bar/lounge; outdoor heated pool; access to nearby health club; concierge; business center; barbershop; 24-hr. room service; in-room massage; babysitting; laundry service; dry cleaning. *In room:* A/C, large-screen TVs w/DVD, complimentary Wi-Fi, minibar, iPod docking stations.

INEXPENSIVE

Beverly Laurel Motor Hotel (Value)   The Beverly Laurel is a great choice for wallet-watching travelers who want a central location and a room with more style than your average motel. Overlooking the parking lot, the budget-basic but well-kept rooms are smartened up with diamond-print spreads and eye-catching artwork; other features include a minifridge, microwave, and ample closet space, and a large kitchenette for an extra 10-spot. The postage-stamp-size outdoor pool is a little public for carefree sunbathing, but it does the job on hot summer days. Best of all is the motel's own excellent coffee shop, **Swingers** (p. 146)—nobody serves better burgers and malts, and you may even spot your favorite alt-rocker tucking into a 3pm breakfast in the vinyl booth next to yours.

8018 Beverly Blvd. (btw. La Cienega Blvd. and Fairfax Ave.), Los Angeles, CA 90048. © 800/962-3824 or 323/651-2441. Fax 323/651-5225. 52 units. $107–$150 double. AAA and senior discounts may be available. AE, DC, MC, V. Free parking. **Amenities:** Heated outdoor pool; laundry service. *In room:* A/C, TV, dataport, minifridge, microwave, hair dryer.

Farmer's Daughter (Value)   Most people end up at the Farmer's Daughter hotel fortuitously because they're waiting to be the next contestants on *The Price Is Right.* The CBS Studios across the street recommends the budget motel to its game show fans, but I recommend it just because I dig this chic little lodge. It's cheery from the moment you walk in the lobby. Bright yellows and cool blues mix well with the country-kitsch theme: rooster wallpaper, faded barn-wood paneling, denim bedspreads, cow-skin rugs, and a parade of inflatable animals that float around the pool. It's obvious that someone with smart fashion sense and a little money turned a dumpy motel into an oasis of stylish affordability. Money-saving perks include free Internet hookup, free parking, a free DVD library, and across-the-street access to an entire farmers market of inexpensive foodstuffs (p. 158). But now that the hotel opened its own French-country restaurant,

TART, there's little reason to leave. *Tip:* Request a room facing the alley—the view is terrible, but you don't get the 24-hour road noise off Fairfax Avenue.

115 S. Fairfax Ave. (btw. Beverly Dr. and 3rd St.), Los Angeles, CA 90036. (C) **800/334-1658** or 323/937-3930. Fax 323/932-1608. www.farmersdaughterhotel.com. 66 units. $215 double; from $275 suite. AE, DISC, MC, V. Valet parking $12. **Amenities:** Restaurant and bar; morning coffee and tea service; swimming pool; concierge services; daily laundry and dry cleaning. *In room:* A/C, TV/DVD, high-speed Internet, minifridge, coffeemaker, personal safe, CD player, complimentary DVD library, telephone w/voice mail.

4 Hollywood

The geographical area called Hollywood is actually smaller and less glamorous than you might expect. In fact, throughout most of the 1980s and 1990s, Hollywood was pretty much a shambles. But the neighborhood has undergone a major overhaul of late—along the lines of the reinvention of New York City's Times Square—that has turned the seedy area back into tourism central. The re-gentrification is ongoing, but I still don't recommend heading down dark alleys on moonless nights. That said, Hollywood is definitely cleaner and safer than it has been in decades. What's more, the hotels below are great for travelers looking for good midpriced and budget lodging, and families will like the easy freeway access to Universal Studios. Still, those with an aversion for tourist traps should book elsewhere.

EXPENSIVE

Renaissance Hollywood Hotel ♠   Part of the $615-million Hollywood & Highland project to restore Hollywood to the glory of its heyday, the Renaissance Hollywood opened in late 2001. The hotel now serves as Oscar-night headquarters for the frenzy of participants and paparazzi attending the Academy Awards in the Kodak Theater next door. Despite its high profile, the hotel is principally a convention property and not quite as elite or elegant as the media hype might have you believe. Nonetheless, its commitment to the history of the area infuses it with far more personality than most chain hotels. Wood-paneled headboards and Technicolor furniture (think *The Jetsons* meets IKEA) paint guest rooms as swinging '50s bachelor pads. Rooms on the seventh floor and up offer truly impressive views. One-third look toward the Pacific Ocean, one-third face the skyline of Downtown L.A., and one-third take in the lush Hollywood Hills (yes, you can see the sign).

The hotel's location makes getting around on foot unusually easy in a town where most destinations require navigating L.A.'s notorious freeway system. Sightseeing is virtually unavoidable since the hotel shares the same block as two of the city's most famous landmarks—the Hollywood Walk of Fame and Grauman's Chinese Theatre. The Hollywood Bowl is less than a mile away (check with the concierge about shuttle service), and the subway stops under the hotel complex, offering access to Universal Studios and destinations farther afield.

1755 N. Highland Ave., Hollywood, CA 90028. (C) **800/769-4774** or 323/856-1200. Fax 323/856-1205. www.renaissance hollywood.com. 637 units. $299 double; $330 executive bedroom; 1-bedroom suite $329; other suites from $340 and way up. Discount rates and packages available. AE, DC, DISC, MC, V. Valet parking $29. **Amenities:** Restaurant; 2 bars (lobby and poolside); outdoor pool; small fitness room; concierge; business center; shopping complex; 24-hr. room service; dry cleaning. *In room:* A/C, TV w/pay movies, high-speed Internet, 2-line cordless phone, minibar, coffeemaker, hair dryer, iron, safe, robes, CD player.

Roosevelt Hotel, Hollywood ♠♠   After finally completing a $30-million renovation (which took, like, for-EV-er), this venerable 12-story landmark is now *the* place to stay in Hollywood. It's got everything you'd want in a Hollywood Boulevard hotel:

history, style, exclusivity, a steakhouse, models-slash-actresses serving cocktails at the poolside bar, a raucous nightlife scene, and just the right amount of L.A. attitude from the staff. Host to the first Academy Awards in 1929—not to mention a few famous-name ghosts—this national landmark is Hollywood's only historic hotel still in operation today. The renovation has harmoniously melded the Roosevelt's historical highlights with modern hotel luxuries. For example, much of the 1927 Spanish-influenced sunken lobby remains the same—the handcrafted columns and dramatic arches are magnificent—but the guest rooms have been completely (and tastefully) renovated with extra-large bathrooms, dark-wood platform beds with luxurious Frette linens, and all the latest high-tech accessories. Rooms on the upper floors have skyline views, while the individually decorated cabana rooms have a balcony or terrace overlooking the Olympic-size pool (whose mural, by the way, was originally painted by David Hockney). The hotel's main restaurant is an über-hip steakhouse called **Dakota** (the porterhouse is superb), and there's also a popular late-night 1950s-style burger bar called **25 Degrees.** You'll like the location as well: smack-dab in the touristy section of Hollywood Boulevard, across from Grauman's Chinese Theatre and along the Walk of Fame. Long story short, the Roosevelt Hotel has once again become the playground for the young, hot Hollywood set, with antics from the poolside **Tropicana** bar and exclusive **Teddy's** lounge getting as much press as Lindsay Lohan on a bender.

7000 Hollywood Blvd., Hollywood, CA 90028. ✆ **800/950-7667** or 323/466-7000. Fax 323/462-8056. www.hollywood roosevelt.com. 300 units. $285–$360 double; from $425 suite; poolside cabana rooms from $300. AE, DC, DISC, MC, V. Valet parking $18. **Amenities:** 2 restaurants; 3 bars; outdoor pool and Jacuzzi; spa and fitness center; concierge; activities desk; 24-hr. room service; poolside massage service; babysitting; laundry service; dry cleaning; executive-level rooms; complimentary shoe shine. *In room:* A/C, TV w/pay movies, high-speed Internet, minibar, coffeemaker, hair dryer, safe, CD player, video games.

INEXPENSIVE

Best Western Hollywood Hills Hotel ✿   Location is a big selling point for this family-owned (since 1948) member of the reliable Best Western chain: It's just off U.S. 101 (the Hollywood Fwy.); a Metro Line stop just 3 blocks away means easy, car-free access to Universal Studios; and the famed Hollywood and Vine intersection is just a 5-minute walk away. The entire hotel has been recently renovated in a contemporary style, and all the spiffy guest rooms come with a refrigerator, coffeemaker, microwave, and wireless Internet. The rooms in the back building are my favorites, as they sit well back from busy Franklin Avenue, face the gleaming blue-tiled, heated outdoor pool, and have an attractive view of the neighboring hillside. A major convenience is the **101 Hills Coffee Shop** located off the lower lobby.

6141 Franklin Ave. (btw. Vine and Gower sts.), Hollywood, CA 90028. ✆ **800/287-1700** or 323/464-5181. Fax 323/ 962-0536. www.bestwestern.com/hollywoodhillshotel. 86 units. $129–$169 double. AAA and AARP discounts available. AE, DISC, MC, V. Free covered parking. Small pets accepted with $25-per-night fee. **Amenities:** Coffee shop; heated outdoor pool; access to nearby health club; tour desk; coin-op laundry. *In room:* A/C, TV, Wi-Fi, fridge, coffeemaker, microwave, hair dryer, iron.

Days Inn Hollywood   While it's east of the prime Sunset Strip action, this freshly renovated motel is safe and convenient, and extras like free underground parking and continental breakfast make it an especially good value. Doubles are large enough for families. Some rooms have microwaves, fridges, and coffeemakers; if yours doesn't have a hair dryer or an iron, they're available at the front desk. For maximum bang for your buck, ask for a room overlooking the pool.

Where to Stay in the Hollywood Area

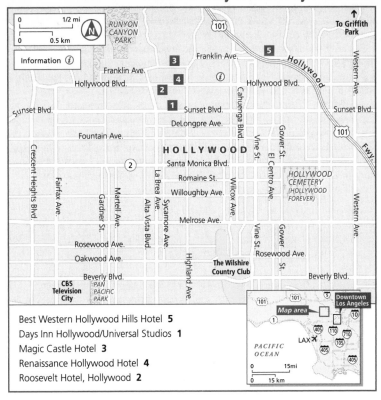

Best Western Hollywood Hills Hotel **5**
Days Inn Hollywood/Universal Studios **1**
Magic Castle Hotel **3**
Renaissance Hollywood Hotel **4**
Roosevelt Hotel, Hollywood **2**

7023 Sunset Blvd. (btw. Highland and La Brea aves.), Hollywood, CA 90028. ✆ **800/329-7466** or 323/464-8344. Fax 323/962-9748. www.daysinn.com. 72 units. $130–$180 double; $145–$220 Jacuzzi suite. Rates include continental breakfast. Ask about AAA, AARP, and other discounted rates (as low as $95 at press time). AE, DC, DISC, MC, V. Free secured parking. **Amenities:** Heated outdoor pool; laundry service. *In room:* A/C, TV.

Magic Castle Hotel ★★ *Kids* *Value*   Located a stone's throw from Hollywood Boulevard's attractions, this garden-style hotel/motel at the base of the Hollywood Hills offers L.A.'s best cheap sleeps and is ideal for wallet-watching families or long-term stays. You won't see the Magic Castle Hotel in *Travel + Leisure* anytime soon but the units are spacious, comfortable, and well kept. Named for the Magic Castle, the illusionist club just uphill, the hotel was once an apartment building; it still feels private and insulated from Franklin Avenue's constant stream of traffic. The units are situated around a central swimming pool. Most are large apartments with fully equipped kitchens complete with a microwave and coffeemaker (grocery-shopping service is available as well).

7025 Franklin Ave. (btw. La Brea and Highland aves.), Hollywood, CA 90028. ✆ **800/741-4915** or 323/851-0800. Fax 323/851-4926. www.magiccastlehotel.com. 40 units. $129 double; $149–$239 suite. Extra person $10. Off-season and other discounts available. Rates include free continental breakfast. AE, DC, DISC, MC, V. Parking $8. **Amenities:** Outdoor heated pool; full-service or coin-op laundry. *In room:* A/C, TV, free Wi-Fi, coffeemaker, hair dryer, iron, safe.

5 Downtown

Traditionally the domain of business folk and convention attendees, Downtown L.A. is becoming increasingly attractive to leisure travelers for several reasons: a Rudy Giuliani–style cleanup in the late 1990s; a growing number of cultural attractions and destination dining; excellent-value weekend packages at luxury hotels that empty out once the workweek ends; and easy, car-free access via the Metro Line to Hollywood and Universal Studios. Every freeway passes through Downtown, so it's a breeze to hop in the car and head off to other neighborhoods (except during weekday rush hour, that is). Consider yourself forewarned, however: Despite the low, low weekend rates, Downtown L.A. can feel like a ghost town compared to Venice Beach or West Hollywood, particularly after sundown. And all that hoopla about an urban revival, well, let's just say that the Downtown area has had more comebacks than Richard Gere.

EXPENSIVE/MODERATE

How much you pay at any of the following hotels largely depends on when you come. All become quite affordable once the business travelers go home; more often than not, rooms go for a relative song over holidays and weekends. Some even offer good-value weekday rates to leisure travelers during periods when rooms would otherwise sit vacant.

Figueroa Hotel *Finds*   With an artistic eye and a heartfelt commitment to creating exotic, whimsical, and oh-so-anti-corporate-style accommodations, charming owner Uno Thimansson has transformed a 1925-vintage former YWCA residence into one of L.A.'s best moderately priced hotels and my top pick for affordable Downtown lodging. This venerable 12-story property sits in an increasingly gentrified corner of Downtown, within shouting distance of the ever-growing L.A. LIVE entertainment complex. The big, airy lobby exudes a romantic Spanish Colonial–Gothic vibe with beamed ceilings and fans, Moroccan chandeliers, soaring columns, tile flooring, and medieval-style furnishings such as big floor pillows made of Kurdish grain sacks, Persian kilims, and exotic fabrics draped from the ceiling. Elevators lead to equally artistic guest rooms that, although poorly lit, are very comfortable. Each comes with a firm, well-made bed with a wrought-iron headboard or canopy and a Georgia O'Keeffe–reminiscent spread, a Mexican-tiled bathroom, and East Asian fabrics that double as blackout drapes. My favorite room is no. 1130, a large double-queen-size with a Spanish terra-cotta print chaise, but you can't go wrong with any room. The Casablanca Suite is a Moroccan pleasure den, ideal for romance. Out back you'll find a desert-garden deck with a mosaic-tiled pool and Jacuzzi, and the Verandah Bar, the poolside place to go on warm Southern California nights for a minty mojito and chat with fellow travelers from around the world.

939 S. Figueroa St. (at Olympic Blvd.), Los Angeles, CA 90015. © **800/421-9092** or 213/627-8971. Fax 213/689-0305. 285 units. $144 double; $245 Casablanca suite; $195–$205 other suites. www.figueroahotel.com. AE, DC, MC, V. Parking $8. **Amenities:** Restaurant; bar; outdoor pool area w/lounge chairs and Jacuzzi; laundry service; dry cleaning. *In room:* A/C, TV, Wi-Fi, minifridge.

Hilton Checkers Los Angeles   The atmosphere at this boutique version of the Biltmore is as removed from "Hollywood" as an L.A. hotel can get, which explains why the stars—Cher, Kevin Costner, Carol Burnett—prefer to stay here when they're in town. Built in 1927, the 12-story hotel is a Historic Cultural Monument. Plenty of polished brass complements the neutral sand-colored decor; both conspire to accentuate the

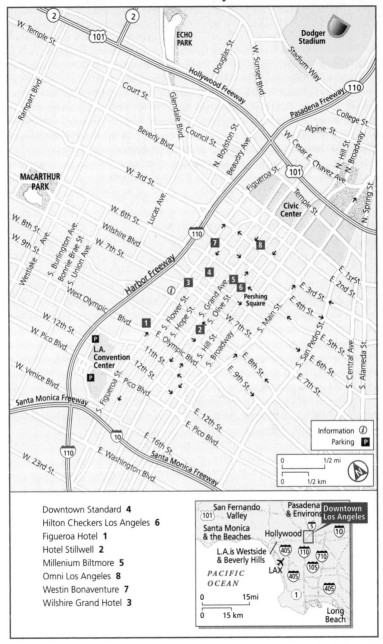

Downtown Standard **4**
Hilton Checkers Los Angeles **6**
Figueroa Hotel **1**
Hotel Stillwell **2**
Millenium Biltmore **5**
Omni Los Angeles **8**
Westin Bonaventure **7**
Wilshire Grand Hotel **3**

impressive architectural features that remained intact during a major renovation in 1989. Checkers is a European-style hotel, without a lot of flashy amenities and possessing an understated luxury. Guest rooms are equipped with 27-inch flatscreen TVs, granite-top desks, and spacious marble bathrooms with plush terry-cloth bathrobes. Public areas include a wood-paneled library, a rooftop lap pool, and serene corridors punctuated with Asian antiques. The spa offers everything from aromatherapy body wraps to couples' massage sessions. **Checkers Restaurant** is one of Downtown's best-kept secrets, serving complex dishes ranging from New American to French in a peaceful setting; the weekend brunch is worth planning for in advance. The warm, intimate bar at Checkers is also a very popular hangout for the Downtown après-work crowd. *Tip:* Be sure to check their website for specials such as $149 weekend rates.

535 S. Grand Ave. (btw. 5th and 6th sts.), Los Angeles, CA 90071. (C) 800/HILTONS (800/445-8667) or 213/624-0000. Fax 213/626-9906. www.hiltoncheckers.com. 188 units. $219–$299 double; from $520 suite. AE, DC, DISC, MC, V. Valet parking $23; self-parking (off-site) $20. **Amenities:** Restaurant; lounge; rooftop heated lap pool and whirlpool; full-service spa; exercise room w/men's and women's saunas; concierge; courtesy car; secretarial services; room service; in-room massage; babysitting; laundry service; dry cleaning; complimentary shoe shine. *In room:* A/C, TV w/pay movies, high-speed Internet, minibar, coffeemaker, hair dryer, iron.

Millennium Biltmore Hotel Los Angeles 𝕲𝕲

The Biltmore is one of those hotels that's worth a visit even if you're not staying here. Built in 1923 and encompassing almost an entire square block, this Italian-Spanish Renaissance landmark is the grande dame of L.A.'s hotels. Chances are you've seen it in many movies, including *The Wedding Crashers, Chinatown, Ghostbusters, Bugsy, Beverly Hills Cop,* and Barbra Streisand's *A Star Is Born.* The hotel lobby—J.F.K.'s campaign headquarters during the 1960 Democratic National Convention—appeared upside-down in *The Poseidon Adventure.* Always in fine shape and host to world leaders and luminaries, the former Regal Biltmore is now under the guiding hand of the Millennium Hotels and Resorts group, and the sense of refinement and graciousness endures. The "wow" factor ends at guest rooms, however, which are a little on the small side (common for older hotels) and aren't quite as eye-popping as the public spaces, but they've recently been redecorated in a style that meshes well with the hotel's vibe. Bathrooms are on the small side as well, but peach-toned marble adds a luxurious edge.

A range of dining and cocktail outlets includes **Sai Sai** for modern Asian cuisine and sushi. Pretty, casual **Smeraldi's** serves homemade pastas and lighter Mediterranean fare. Off the lobby is the stunning **Gallery Bar,** named by *Los Angeles* magazine as one of the sexiest cocktail lounges in L.A. Afternoon tea and cocktails are served in the **Rendezvous Court,** which used to be the hotel's original lobby and resembles the interior of a Spanish cathedral, complete with a Moorish ceiling of carved beams and an altarlike baroque doorway. Spend the few bucks to appreciate the Art Deco health club, with its gorgeous Roman-style pool.

506 S. Grand Ave. (btw. 5th and 6th sts.), Los Angeles, CA 90071. (C) 800/245-8673 or 213/624-1011. Fax 213/612-1545. www.thebiltmore.com. 683 units. $159–$375 double; from $450 suite. Leisure discount packages available. AE, DC, DISC, MC, V. Parking $40. **Amenities:** 3 restaurants; 1 bar; health club w/original 1923 inlaid pool, Jacuzzi, steam, and sauna; concierge; courtesy car; business center; salon; room service; in-room massage; babysitting; laundry service; dry cleaning; executive-level rooms; gift shop. *In room:* A/C, TV w/pay movies, dataport, minibar, coffeemaker, hair dryer.

Omni Los Angeles 𝕲

The Omni chain forsook its old location (now the Wilshire Grand, below) to assume this boxy 17-story tower at the top of Bunker Hill because, as they say, location is everything: It's adjacent to the Museum of Contemporary Art and within walking distance of the L.A. Music Center, Walt Disney Concert Hall, and the Cathedral of Our Lady of the Angels, making the Omni Downtown's best base for culture buffs. Recognizing the geographical appeal, the hotel caters to theatergoers more than any of its peers, with complimentary car service until 11:30pm (great for dinner/show evenings), late-night dining during performances, and good-value theater packages.

An eager-to-please staff runs the property beautifully, and public areas enjoy a graceful air thanks to elegant accents and artworks from the likes of Jim Dine and David Hockney. The spacious, conservatively styled rooms are amenity-packed—25-inch flatscreen TVs, free wireless Internet access for Select Guest members, fluffy robes—and offer floor-to-ceiling views and oversize bathrooms with tubs and showers; larger rooms also have a chaise. Business rooms feature extra-large work desks with halogen task lighting and desk-level inputs (most also have a fax/copier/printer). At $50 extra for two, Club Level rooms are a great value considering the accompanying freebies: continental breakfast, all-day beverages and pastries, evening cocktails and appetizers. Another reason to book a room here is the Omni's flagship restaurant, **Noé,** which has been garnering high praise from the local press for its progressive American cuisine with Japanese influences. *Tip:* Request a room overlooking the Walt Disney Concert Hall.

251 S. Olive St., Los Angeles, CA 90012. (C) 800/444-6664 or 213/617-3300. Fax 213/617-3399. www.omnihotels. com. 453 units. $179–$390 double; from $499 suite. Inquire about weekend rates and packages (as low as $179 at press time), which may include breakfast. AE, DC, DISC, MC, V. Valet parking $30. **Amenities:** Restaurant; lounge; outdoor heated lap pool; updated exercise room; access to nearby health club; Omni Kids program; concierge; courtesy car within 3-mile radius; business center w/secretarial services; room service; babysitting; laundry service; dry cleaning; executive-level rooms. *In room:* A/C, TV w/pay movies, dataport, free Wi-Fi w/Select Guest membership, minibar, hair dryer, iron.

Westin Bonaventure Hotel & Suites (⋆)   This 35-story, 1,354-room monolith is the hotel that locals love to hate. The truth is that the Bonaventure is a terrific hotel. It's certainly not for travelers who want intimacy or personality in their accommodations—but with numerous restaurants and bars, a full-service spa, a monster health club, a business center, and much more on hand, you'll be hard-pressed to want for anything here (except maybe some individualized attention). The hotel's five gleaming glass silos encompass an entire square block and form one of Downtown's most distinctive landmarks. The pie-shaped guest rooms are on the small side, but a wall of windows offering great views, and Westin's unparalleled Heavenly Bed—the ultimate in hotel-bed comfort—make for a very comfortable cocoon. With executive workstation, fax, and wet bar, guest office suites are great for business travelers, while tower suites—with living room, extra half-bathroom, minifridge, microwave, and two TVs—are ideal for families.

404 S. Figueroa St. (btw. 4th and 5th sts.), Los Angeles, CA 90071. (C) 866/716-8132 or 213/624-1000. Fax 213/612-4800. www.westin.com/bonaventure. 1,354 units. $237–$289 double; from $297 suite. Ask about specials and packages. AE, DC, DISC, MC, V. Valet parking $40. **Amenities:** 17 restaurants and fast-food outlets; 5 bars and lounges; outdoor heated lap pool; 15,000-sq.-ft. full-service spa, running track, and access to 4,500-sq.-ft. health club; Westin Kids Club; concierge; Enterprise Rent-a-Car desk; full-service business center; shops; salon; 24-hr. room service; babysitting; laundry service; dry cleaning; valet. *In room:* A/C, TV, high-speed Internet, coffeemaker, hair dryer, iron, laptop-size safe.

Wilshire Grand Los Angeles   This former Omni hotel is now independently operated and dedicated to business travelers, but weekend rates can be stellar for bargain-hunting vacationers. The taupe-toned rooms are business-hotel average; the best ones

Family-Friendly Hotels

Best Western Marina Pacific Hotel & Suites (p. 79) gives families a place to stay just off the carnival-like Venice boardwalk. The suites are a terrific choice for the brood, since each features a full kitchen, a dining area, a pullout sofa, and a connecting door to an adjoining room that lets you form an affordable two-bedroom, two-bathroom suite.

Beverly Garland's Holiday Inn (p. 105) is a terrific choice for wallet-watching families: Rates are low, the North Hollywood location is close to Universal Studios (a free shuttle ride away), kids stay and eat free, and kids even get their own rooms, called KidSuites.

Inn at Venice Beach (p. 80) is ideal for ocean-loving families, thanks to its near-the-beach location. The 3-block walk is lined with snack bars, surf shops, and bike and skate rentals. The 12-and-under set is welcomed free of charge, and everyone starts the day with a complimentary breakfast.

Loews Santa Monica Beach Hotel (p. 73) welcomes kids 10 and under with open arms, gifts, and special menus. And with a great location near the beach and Santa Monica amusement pier, the hotel couldn't be better situated for families in search of surf and sun.

Magic Castle Hotel (p. 99) is a good budget choice, with roomy apartment-style suites; it's close to Hollywood Boulevard's family-friendly attractions.

Sheraton Universal Hotel (p. 106) enjoys a terrifically kid-friendly location, adjacent to Universal Studios and the fun CityWalk mall. Babysitting services are available, and there's a game room on the premises.

have city views or overlook the swimming pool. The executive-level rooms and suites feature extras like fax machines, plush bathrobes, extra towels, and top-floor views—plus access to the Executive Lounge, which offers free continental breakfast, all-day beverages, and hors d'oeuvres at cocktail hour. The 16-story hotel is centrally located in the heart of Downtown shopping, theater, and dining. Five restaurants and bars on-site include an American grill, an upscale Korean barbecue, an Italian trattoria, Japanese cuisine, a tropical lounge in the Trader Vic's vein, and a coffee bar featuring Starbucks brew. I prefer the Omni (above), but this hotel is a fine choice if you can snare a good rate.

930 Wilshire Blvd. (at Figueroa St.), Los Angeles, CA 90071. © **888/773-2888** or 213/688-7777. Fax 213/612-3989. www.wilshiregrand.com. 900 units. $159–$269 double; from $490 suite. Leisure and weekend rates as low as $169 at press time. AE, DC, DISC, MC, V. Valet parking $30. **Amenities:** 4 restaurants; bar; large outdoor heated pool and hydrotherapy pool; fitness room; concierge; Enterprise car-rental desk; courtesy car; business center w/secretarial services; salon; room service; in-room massage; laundry service; dry cleaning; executive-level rooms. *In room:* A/C, TV w/pay movies and video games, dataport, hair dryer, iron.

INEXPENSIVE

Stillwell Hotel   The Stillwell is far from fancy, but its modestly priced rooms are a good option in a generally pricey neighborhood. Built in 1906, this once-elegant 250-room hotel is conveniently located near the STAPLES Center, the Civic Center, and the Museum of Contemporary Art. Rooms are clean, basic, and simply decorated with decent furnishings. The hotel is quiet, though, and hallways feature East Indian artwork. That said, I much prefer the Hotel Figueroa, but this is a less eccentric and perfectly reasonable choice. The lobby-level Indian restaurant is a popular lunch spot for Downtown office workers; other options include a casual Mexican restaurant and the so-old-it's-retro **Hanks Cocktail Lounge.**

838 S. Grand Ave. (btw. 8th and 9th sts.), Los Angeles, CA 90017. ✆ **800/553-4774** or 213/627-1151. Fax 213/622-8940. www.stillwellh.qpg.com. 250 units. $79 double; $85–$115 suite. AE, DC, DISC, MC, V. Parking $4.50. **Amenities:** 2 restaurants; lounge; activities desk; business center; coin-op laundry; laundry service; dry cleaning. *In room:* A/C, TV, fax, fridge, iron.

6 Universal City

If you're planning on visiting the most popular attraction in Los Angeles, Universal Studios Hollywood, you'll save a lot of travel time and hassle by booking a hotel room right next to the park. The hotels listed below are ideally located for quick and easy access to the park; the closest ones are the Hilton Universal City and the Sheraton Universal, which are just a short walk or shuttle ride from the park.

EXPENSIVE

Hilton Universal City & Towers   Although this shiny 24-story hotel sits right outside Universal Studios, there's more of a conservative business-traveler feel here than the raucous family-with-young-children vibe you might expect. Still, free tram service to the theme park and adjacent Universal CityWalk for shopping and dining means that it's hard for families to be better situated. The polished brass and upscale attitude set the businesslike tone, and a light-filled glass lobby leads to a seemingly endless series of conference and banquet rooms, the hotel's bread and butter. The oversize guest rooms are tastefully decorated and constantly refurbished, and have exceptional views (even if the modern, mirror-surfaced windows don't actually open). I prefer the adjacent Sheraton (below) for leisure stays, but go for the best rate.

555 Universal Hollywood Dr., Universal City, CA 91608. ✆ **800/HILTONS** (800/445-8667) or 818/506-2500. Fax 818/509-2058. www.universalcity.hilton.com. 483 units. $199–$299 double; from $350 suite. Weekend and other discounts often available. AE, DC, DISC, MC, V. Valet parking $18; self-parking $14. **Amenities:** Cafe-style restaurant; outdoor heated pool and whirlpool; exercise room; concierge; activities desk; car-rental desk; business center; 24-hr. room service; babysitting; laundry service; dry cleaning; executive-level rooms. *In room:* A/C, TV w/pay movies and video games, high-speed Internet, minibar, coffeemaker, hair dryer, iron, safe.

MODERATE

Beverly Garland's Holiday Inn *Kids*   The "Beverly Garland" in this 258-room hotel's name is the actress who played Fred MacMurray's wife on *My Three Sons.* Grassy areas and greenery abound at this North Hollywood Holiday Inn, a virtual oasis in the concrete jungle. The mission-influenced buildings are a bit dated, but if you grew up with *Brady Bunch* reruns, this only adds to the charm—the spread looks like something Mike Brady would have designed. Southwestern-themed fabrics complement the natural-pine furnishings in the spacious (and soundproof) guest rooms, attracting your attention away from the somewhat unfortunate painted cinder-block walls. On the upside, all of the well-outfitted rooms have balconies overlooking the pleasant grounds, which include a pool and two lighted tennis courts. With Universal Studios just down the street and a free shuttle to the park, the location can't be beat for families. Since proximity to the 101 and 134 freeways also means the constant buzz of traffic, ask for a room facing Vineland Avenue for maximum quiet. *Tip:* If you're bringing the kids along, be sure to inquire about the KidSuites, adjoining rooms designed just for kids.

4222 Vineland Ave., North Hollywood, CA 91602. ℂ **800/238-3759** or 818/980-8000. Fax 818/766-0112. www.beverlygarland.com. 255 units. $139–$189 double; from $220 suite. Ask about AAA, AARP, corporate, military, Great Rates, weekend, and other discounted rates. Children 12 and under stay free in parent's room and eat free. AE, DC, DISC, MC, V. Free parking. **Amenities:** Restaurant; bar; heated outdoor pool; lighted tennis courts; sauna; car-rental desk; complimentary shuttle to Universal Studios. *In room:* A/C, TV, coffeemaker, hair dryer, iron.

Sheraton Universal Hotel 🖈🖈 *Kids*   Despite the addition of the sleekly modern Hilton just uphill, the 21-story Sheraton is still considered "the" Universal City hotel of choice for tourists, businesspeople, and industry folks visiting the studios' production offices. Located on the back lot of Universal Studios, it has a spacious 1960s feel, with updated styling and amenities. Although the Sheraton does its share of convention/event business, the hotel feels more leisure-oriented than the Hilton next door (an outdoor elevator connects the two properties). Choose a Lanai room for balconies that overlook the lushly planted pool area, or a Tower room for stunning views and solitude. The hotel is very close to the Hollywood Bowl, and you can practically roll out of bed and into the theme park (via a continuous complimentary shuttle). An extra $35 per night buys a Club Level room—worth the money for the extra in-room amenities such as concierge service and free continental breakfast and afternoon hors d'oeuvres; business rooms also feature movable workstations and fax/copier/printer.

333 Universal Hollywood Dr., Universal City, CA 91608. ℂ **800/325-3535** or 818/980-1212. Fax 818/985-4980. www.sheraton.com/universal. 436 units. $209–$239 double; from $420 suite. Children stay free in parent's room. Ask about AAA, AARP, and corporate discounts; also inquire about packages that include theme-park admission. AE, DC, DISC, MC, V. Valet parking $21; self-parking $16. **Amenities:** Casual indoor/outdoor restaurant; outdoor pool and whirlpool; health club; game room; concierge; free shuttle to Universal Studios every 15 min.; business center; room service; babysitting; laundry service; dry cleaning; executive Club Level rooms. *In room:* A/C, TV w/pay movies, high-speed Internet, minibar, hair dryer and iron (in Club Level rooms), safe.

INEXPENSIVE

Best Western Mikado Hotel   This Asian-flavored garden hotel has been a Valley fixture for 40-plus years. A 1999 renovation muted but didn't obliterate the kitsch value, which extends from the pagoda-style exterior to the sushi bar (the Valley's oldest) across the driveway. Two-story motel buildings face two well-maintained courtyards, one with a koi pond and wooden footbridge, the other with a shimmering blue-tiled pool and hot tub. The face-lift stripped most of the Asian vibe from guest rooms, which are suitably comfortable and well outfitted. Furnished in 1970s-era chic (leather sofas, earth tones), the one-bedroom apartment is a steal, with enormous rooms and a full-size kitchen. Rates include a full breakfast.

12600 Riverside Dr. (btw. Whitsett and Coldwater Canyon), North Hollywood, CA 91607. ℂ **800/780-7234** or 818/763-9141. Fax 818/752-1045. www.bestwestern.com/mikadohotel. 58 units. $129–$159 double; $250 1-bedroom apartment. Rates include full breakfast. Ask about AAA, senior, and other discounted rates (as low as $98 at press time). Extra person $10. Children 11 and under stay free in parent's room. Rates include full American breakfast. AE, DC, DISC, MC, V. Free parking. **Amenities:** Japanese restaurant and sushi bar; cocktail lounge; outdoor pool and Jacuzzi; fax and copying services at front desk. *In room:* A/C, TV, complimentary high-speed Internet, coffeemaker, hair dryer, iron.

7 Pasadena & Environs

East of Downtown, Pasadena is serene, well-preserved, and architecturally rich. It's close via freeway to both Hollywood and Valley attractions—but forget about basing yourself here if you plan to spend your days at the beach and your nights trolling West Hollywood nightclubs. Those who like a quieter scene will enjoy Pasadena's more bucolic range of accommodations, and the dining and shopping scene stands on its own. Now with the new Metro Gold Line running from Downtown right through Old Town Pasadena and all points east, accessibility to L.A.'s best neighborhoods (without having to deal with traffic) is increasingly easier.

MODERATE

Artists' Inn & Cottage Bed & Breakfast   Pleasantly unpretentious and furnished with wicker throughout, this yellow-shingled Victorian-style inn was built in 1895 as a farmhouse and expanded to include a neighboring 1909 home. Each of the 10 rooms is decorated to reflect the style of a particular artist or period. Among the artistically inspired choices are the country-cozy New England–style Grandma Moses room; the soft, pastel-hued Degas suite; and the bold-lined, primary-hued Expressionist suite, a nod to such artists as Picasso and Dufy. Every room is thoughtfully arranged and features a private bathroom (many with period fixtures, three with Jacuzzi tubs), phone, fresh roses from the front garden, port wine, and chocolates. Most rooms have TVs; if yours doesn't, the innkeeper will provide one if you want it. The quiet residential location is just 5 minutes from the heart of Old Town Pasadena, just a few stops on the Metro Gold Line.

1038 Magnolia St., South Pasadena, CA 91030. (C) **888/799-5668** or 626/799-5668. Fax 626/799-3678. www.artists inns.com. 10 units. $135–$225 double. Rates include full breakfast and afternoon tea. Check for midweek specials. Extra person $20. AE, MC, V. Free parking. *In room:* A/C, TV (upon request), dataport, hair dryer.

Bissell House Bed & Breakfast ⟨+⟩   If you enjoy the true B&B experience, you'll love the Bissell House. Hidden behind hedges that carefully isolate it from busy Orange Grove Avenue, this antiques-filled 1887 gingerbread Victorian—the former home of the vacuum heiress and now owned by the Hoyman family—offers a unique taste of life on what was once Pasadena's "Millionaire's Row." Outfitted in a traditional chintz-and-cabbage-roses style, all individually decorated rooms have private bathrooms (two with an antique claw-foot tub, one with a whirlpool tub, four with showers only), individual heating and air-conditioning (a B&B rarity), Internet access, and very comfortable beds. If you don't mind stairs, request one of the more spacious top-floor rooms. The modern world doesn't interfere with the mood in these romantic sanctuaries, but the downstairs library features a TV with VCR and a telephone/fax machine for guests' use. The beautifully landscaped grounds boast an inviting pool, Jacuzzi, and deck with lounge chairs. Included in the room rate is an elaborately prepared breakfast served in the large dining room, as well as an afternoon tea, cookie, and wine service. A self-serve continental breakfast is also available weekdays for business guests.

201 Orange Grove Ave. (at Columbia St.), South Pasadena, CA 91030. (C) **800/441-3530** or 626/441-3535. Fax 626/441-3671. www.bissellhouse.com. 5 units. $150–$350 double. Rates include full breakfast. AE, MC, V. Free parking. **Amenities:** Outdoor pool and Jacuzzi; CD and video libraries. *In room:* A/C, hair dryer, iron, robes.

INEXPENSIVE

Saga Motor Hotel ⟨Value⟩   This 1950s relic of old Route 66 has far more character than most other motels in its price range. The rooms are small, clean, and simply

Where to Stay in the Pasadena Area

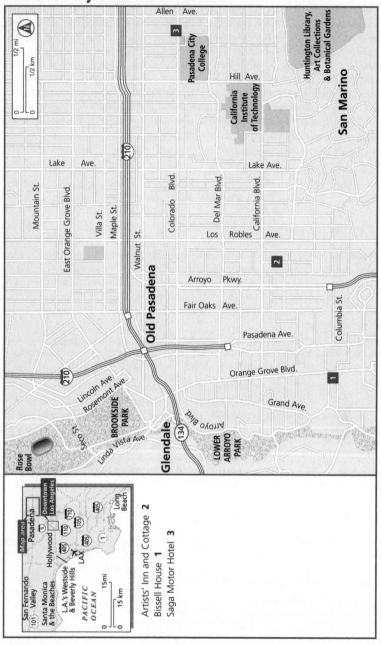

Artists' Inn and Cottage **2**
Bissell House **1**
Saga Motor Hotel **3**

furnished with the basics. The double/doubles are spacious enough for shares, but budget-minded families will prefer the extra-large configuration dedicated to them, which has a king-size bed and two doubles. The best rooms are in the front building surrounding the gated swimming pool, shielded from the street and inviting in warm weather. The grounds are attractive and well kept, if you don't count the Astroturf "lawn" on the pool deck. The location is relatively quiet (considering it's on a busy strip of Colorado Blvd. directly across from the Pasadena Community College) and very convenient, just off the Foothill (210) Freeway about a mile from the Huntington Library and within 10 minutes of both the Rose Bowl and Old Pasadena.

1633 E. Colorado Blvd. (btw. Allen and Sierra Bonita aves.), Pasadena, CA 91106. © **800/793-7242** or 626/795-0431. Fax 626/792-0559. www.thesagamotorhotel.com. 70 units. $76–$92 double; $110–$135 family suite. Rates include continental breakfast. AE, DC, DISC, MC, V. Free parking. **Amenities:** Outdoor heated pool; free self-serve laundromat; laundry service; dry cleaning. *In room:* A/C, TV, dataport.

6

Where to Dine

As one of the world's cultural cross-roads, Los Angeles is a veritable international atlas of exotic cuisines: Afghan, Argentine, Armenian, Burmese, Cajun, Cambodian, Caribbean, Cuban, Ethiopian, Indian, Jewish, Korean, Lebanese, Moroccan, Oaxacan, Peruvian, Persian, Spanish, Thai, Vietnamese . . . well, you get the point. Half the fun of visiting Los Angeles is experiencing worldly dishes that only a major metropolis can provide. Whatever you're in the mood for, this town has it covered, and all you need to join the dinner party is an adventurous palate. And since it's L.A., there's always the bonus of spotting celebrities.

Although it's those famous celebrity chef and celebrity-owned restaurants that attract most of the media limelight, the majority of L.A.'s best dining experiences are at its small neighborhood haunts and minimalls, the kind you'll never find unless someone lets you in on the city's dining secrets—and this chapter is full of them.

While dining in Los Angeles is almost always a hassle-free experience, there are a few things you should keep in mind:

- If you want a table at the restaurants with the best reputations, you should book several weeks in advance for weekends and at least 2 weeks ahead for weekdays.
- If there's a long wait for a table, ask if you can order at the bar, which is often faster and more fun.
- Don't leave anything valuable in your car while dining. Also, it's best to give the parking valet only the key to your car, not to your hotel room or house.
- Remember, it's against the law to smoke in any restaurant in California, even if it has a separate bar or lounge area. You're welcome to smoke outside, however.
- This ain't New York: Plan on dining early. Most restaurants close their kitchens around 10pm.

The restaurants listed below are classified first by area and then by price, using the following categories: Very Expensive, dinner from $75 per person; Expensive, dinner from $50 per person; Moderate, dinner from $35 per person; and Inexpensive, dinner from $20 per person. These categories reflect prices for an appetizer, main course, dessert, and glass of wine.

1 Best Dining Bets

Note: In addition to the Best Dining Bets below, be sure to check out "The Most Unforgettable Dining Experiences" in chapter 1.

- **Best Places for a Power Lunch:** Between 12:30 and 2pm, industry honchos swarm like locusts to a handful of watering holes du jour. Actors, agents, lawyers, and producers flock to perennial favorites the **Ivy** (p. 124), 113 N. Robertson Blvd., West Hollywood (© **310/274-8303**), and to the L.A. branch of New York's venerable the **Palm** (p. 129), 9001 Santa Monica Blvd., West Hollywood (☏ **310/ 550-8811**), a steakhouse where the food is impeccable and the conversations read like dialogue from *Entourage.*

- **Best Old-School Diner:** Stand in line for one of the city's best hamburgers at the **Apple Pan,** 10801 Pico Blvd., West L.A. (☏ **310/475-3585**). Choose from the "steakburger" or the saucy "hickory burger"—though regulars know to get extra hickory sauce on the side (for french-fry dipping). The wallpaper at this beloved family-run cottage on the busy Westside looks like it dates from the opening day in 1947. See p. 136.
- **Best View:** The **Restaurant at the Getty Center,** 1200 Getty Center Dr., West L.A. (☏ **310/440-6810**), has an in-the-clouds locale that makes for postcard views when the L.A. sky is smog-free. Reservations are a must, even for lunch (served Tues–Sun); dinner is served only on Friday and Saturday, when the museum is open late. Make reservations online at www.getty.edu.
- **Best "Old Hollywood" Restaurant:** Haunted by the ghosts of Faulkner, Fitzgerald, and Hemingway—who drank here during their screenwriting days—**Musso & Frank Grill,** 6667 Hollywood Blvd., Hollywood (☏ **323/467-7788**), is virtually unchanged since 1919. The atmosphere urges you to order a martini and chicken potpie. Listen to the longtime waitstaff wax nostalgic about the days when Hollywood Boulevard was still fashionable and Orson Welles held court at Musso's. See p. 142.
- **Best Spot for People-Watching:** Nowhere in L.A. is better for people-watching than Venice's Ocean Front Walk, and no restaurant offers a better seat for the action than the **Sidewalk Cafe,** 1401 Ocean Front Walk, Venice (☏ **310/399-5547**). Unobstructed views of parading skaters, bikers, skateboarders, musclemen, break dancers, street performers, sword swallowers, and other participants in the daily carnival overshadow the food, which is a whole lot better than it needs to be. See p. 122.
- **Best Spots for Celebrity Sighting:** You'll always find well-known faces frequenting Hollywood hot spots, the most sizzling of which is **Katsuya Hollywood** (p. 140), 6300 Hollywood Blvd., Los Angeles (☏ **323/871-8777**), the current fave of Lindsay Lohan, Janet Jackson, Nick Lachey, and so on. The **Hump,** 3221 Donald Douglas Loop Rd., Santa Monica (☏ **310/313-0977**), is a little-known Santa Monica Airport sushi bar where Harrison Ford, Calista Flockhart, Kurt Russell, Goldie Hawn, Dustin Hoffman, Meryl Streep, and Phil Jackson make regular appearances. See p. 117. Other celebrity hangouts include **Pizzeria Mozza** (p. 143), 641 N. Highland Ave., Los Angeles (☏ **323/297-0101**); **Mastro's Steakhouse** (p. 128), 246 N. Canon Dr., Beverly Hills (☏ **310/888-8782**); **Asia de Cuba** at the Mondrian hotel, 8440 Sunset Blvd., West Hollywood (☏ **323/ 848-6000**); the **Ivy** (p. 124), 133 N. Robertson Blvd., West Hollywood (☏ **310/ 274-8303**); and, of course, **Spago Beverly Hills** (p. 130), 176 N. Canon Dr., Beverly Hills (☏ **310/385-0880**).
- **Best Alfresco Dining:** You'll find that more and more Los Angeles restaurants are eager to create appealing outdoor seating, even if it means placing bistro tables along a busy sidewalk. One of my favorites is the garden patio at the **Little Door,** 8164 W. 3rd St. (☏ **323/951-1210**), one of the most romantic restaurants in the city. See p. 141. A more affordable way to enjoy a meal outdoors is to stroll **Sunset**

Boulevard around Sunset Plaza Drive. There are at least a half-dozen sidewalk cafes—and the people-watching is some of the best in the city.

- **Best Wine List:** Year after year, plenty of other restaurants offer thoughtfully chosen vintages, but no one comes close to toppling **Valentino,** 3115 Pico Blvd., Santa Monica (℡ **310/829-4313;** www.welovewine.com), which still boasts L.A.'s best cellar and is continually honored with *Wine Spectator's* highest ratings. See p. 119.

- **Best California Cuisine:** At chef/owner Michael McCarty's eponymous Santa Monica restaurant **Michael's,** 1147 3rd St., Santa Monica (℡ **310/451-0843),** the creative dishes with fresh ingredients at this perennial favorite make it clear why McCarty is considered an originator of California cuisine. See p. 117.

- **Best Italian Cuisine:** I'm going to raise some local eyebrows here and go with **Locanda del Lago,** 231 Arizona Ave., Santa Monica (℡ **310/451-3525),** a heavily touristed restaurant at a Santa Monica shopping mall that specializes in cuisine from Northern Italy's Lombardy region. Until someone serves a better housemade whole-wheat pappardelle tossed in a duck ragout, I'm sticking with the boys from Lombardy. See p. 120.

- **Best Mexican Cuisine:** They may not be Mexican, but *Too Hot Tamales* Mary Sue Milliken and Susan Feniger traveled deep into Mexico to absorb regional tastes and aromas, and returned with secret ingredients and kitchen savvy to pass on to their patrons at the **Border Grill,** 1445 4th St., Santa Monica (℡ **310/451-1655).** See p. 119. I'm also a huge fan of the authentic Mexican cuisine at **Frida,** 236 S. Beverly Dr., Beverly Hills (℡ **310/278-7666).** See p. 132.

- **Best Afternoon Tea:** Surrounded by botanical gardens, the tearoom at the **Huntington Library,** 1151 Oxford Rd., San Marino (℡ **626/683-8131),** is truly an oasis. The Huntington, located in a wealthy residential area near Pasadena, has the added appeal of pre- and post-tea activities, such as strolling the theme gardens, viewing the art gallery or library, and visiting the bookstore/gift shop. The moderately priced tea ($13) is buffet-style, so you can stuff yourself with fresh-baked scones, finger sandwiches, and strawberries with thick Devonshire cream.

- **Best Value:** Former mayor Richard Riordan's the **Original Pantry,** 877 S. Figueroa St., Downtown (℡ **213/972-9279),** stays open 24 hours a day, serving up large plates of traditional American comfort food (meatloaf, coleslaw, ham 'n' eggs) that won't win any culinary awards but offers some of the best values in town (you won't leave hungry, that's for sure). See p. 152. Far more upscale but equally value-oriented is **Joe's Restaurant,** 1023 Abbot Kinney Blvd., Venice (℡ **310/399-5811).** See p. 120.

- **Best Noshing (While Standing):** Open since 1917, **Grand Central Market,** 317 S. Broadway, Downtown (℡ **213/624-2378),** is L.A.'s largest and oldest food hall, selling everything from fresh bread, local and exotic produce, and fresh fruit juice, to smoked meats, Chinese noodles, and chili.

- **Best for Late-Night Dining:** On the theory that later is better, our vote goes to **Toi on Sunset,** 7505½ Sunset Blvd., Los Angeles (℡ **323/874-8062),** and its sister, **Toi on Wilshire,** 1120 Wilshire Blvd., Santa Monica (℡ **310/394-7804).** You'll never feel like the last patron at these places—they're open until 4am and 3am respectively—and the terrific Thai food will give your fading brain a spicy kick. See p. 146.

2 Santa Monica & the Beaches

EXPENSIVE

Boa Steakhouse ★★ STEAKHOUSE   It's a no-brainer: Combine the best-quality steaks with a sexy decor, lively bar, and a key corner location in Santa Monica, and you'll do well. Very well. Cashing in on American's steak craze, the owners of the original Boa in West Hollywood opened this suave steakhouse at the foot of Santa Monica Boulevard. The sophisticated decor eschews the traditional dim steakhouse ambience in favor of a warm, sleek interior highlighted with floor-to-ceiling windows that allow natural light to filter in. Tough decisions abound on the menu: Should you order the bone-in filet mignon, petite filet mignon, Kobe filet mignon, 35-day dry-aged New York strip, bone-in rib-eye, flatiron steak, or porterhouse? Have it prepared with a foie gras butter, tri-peppercorn rub, chef's special J-1 sauce, or creamy horseradish? (Personally I think it's uncouth to flavor a prime cut of dry-aged beef with anything but salt and pepper.) Sides are purchased separately, the most popular being the homemade crispy fries, macaroni and cheese, and roasted garlic whipped potatoes. As for an appetizer, there's a Jumbo Lump crab cake with heart of palm salad and Cajun rémoulade. For a pick-me-up dessert, try the refreshing blackberry crush cocktail, a *mojito*-like mixture made with fresh fruit and top-shelf vodka. *Note:* A second Boa steakhouse is located along the Sunset Strip in West Hollywood (8462 W. Sunset Blvd; ✆ **323/650-8383**).

101 Santa Monica Blvd. (at Ocean Ave.), Santa Monica. ✆ **310/899-4466**. www.boasteak.com. Reservations recommended. Main courses $25–$39. AE, DC, DISC, MC, V. Mon–Sat 11:30am–11:30pm; Sun 11am–11pm. Valet parking $5.

Cafe Del Rey ★★ CALIFORNIA   Cafe Del Rey is one of those lively restaurants where everyone seems to be celebrating something on the company's tab. There's a terrific view of the marina's bobbing sailboats, particularly in the summer when the windows facing the harbor are open, creating an indoor-outdoor dining area. The exhibition kitchen focuses on creative preparations of fresh and seasonal foods, but the choices are so varied that it's impossible to accurately categorize the cafe's cuisine. Sure bets are the Colorado lamb shank prepared *osso buco*–style with creamy polenta, the boar bacon-wrapped filet mignon in cabernet sauce, and the fish de jour. The *Wine Spectator*–award-winning wine list offers more than 340 selections. My advice: Request a table by the window, ask your server what's good today, pair it with a nice bottle of wine, and enjoy a long, leisurely meal.

4451 Admiralty Way (btw. Lincoln and Washington boulevards), Marina del Rey. ✆ **310/823-6395**. www.cafedelrey marina.com. Reservations recommended. Main courses dinner $21–$37, lunch $11–$20. AE, DC, DISC, MC, V. Lunch Mon–Fri 11:30am–3pm, Sat 11:30am–2:30pm; dinner Mon–Thurs 5:30–9:30pm, Fri–Sat 5:30–10pm, Sun 5–9:30pm; Sun brunch 10:30am–2:30pm. Valet parking free for lunch, $4.50 for dinner.

Chinois on Main ★★ FRANCO-CHINESE   Wolfgang Puck's Franco-Chinese eatery bustles nightly with locals and visitors wowed by the restaurant's reputation and rarely disappointed by the food. Groundbreaking in its time, the restaurant still relies on the quirky East-meets-West mélange of ingredients and technique. The menu is almost equally split between Chinois's signature dishes and seasonal creations. The most famous of the former are Cantonese duck in a sweet-tangy plum sauce, and farm-raised whole catfish that's perfectly deep-fried and dramatically presented. Terrific newer dishes include grilled Maine sea scallops on a bed of garlic spinach, and braised short ribs with sweet sake soy glaze served over potato purée. Try the trio of crème brûlées for dessert. The dining room is as visually colorful as it is acoustically

Where to Dine in Santa Monica & the Beaches

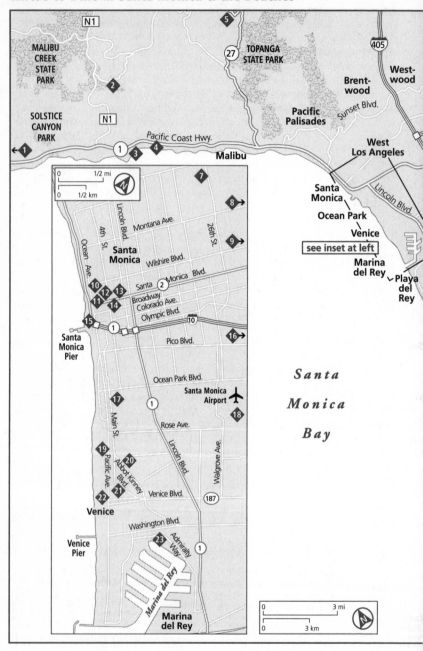

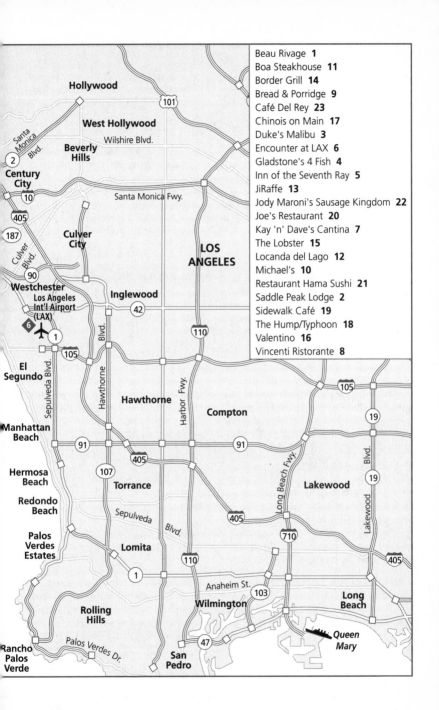

Beau Rivage **1**
Boa Steakhouse **11**
Border Grill **14**
Bread & Porridge **9**
Café Del Rey **23**
Chinois on Main **17**
Duke's Malibu **3**
Encounter at LAX **6**
Gladstone's 4 Fish **4**
Inn of the Seventh Ray **5**
JiRaffe **13**
Jody Maroni's Sausage Kingdom **22**
Joe's Restaurant **20**
Kay 'n' Dave's Cantina **7**
The Lobster **15**
Locanda del Lago **12**
Michael's **10**
Restaurant Hama Sushi **21**
Saddle Peak Lodge **2**
Sidewalk Café **19**
The Hump/Typhoon **18**
Valentino **16**
Vincenti Ristorante **8**

loud. Jackets and ties are requested but not required. *Tip:* If you like fiery cooking demonstrations, ask for a seat at the kitchen counter.

2709 Main St. (south of Pico Blvd.), Santa Monica. ℂ 310/392-9025. www.wolfgangpuck.com. Reservations required. Main courses $23–$43. AE, DC, MC, V. Lunch Wed–Fri 11:30am–2pm; dinner Mon–Thurs 6–10pm, Fri–Sat 6–10:30pm, Sun 5:30–10pm. Valet parking $5.

Encounter at LAX   CALIFORNIA   There has always been a restaurant in the spacey Theme Building (ca. 1961) perched in LAX's midst, but these days it draws as many Angelenos as fly-by travelers (including John Travolta, who had his star-studded birthday party here). The reason? A full makeover transforming the staid Continental dining room (whose best feature was a panoramic view over the runways) into a 1960s *Star Trek* set gone Technicolor. Outer-space lounge music dominates the entire place. The menu features art-food, that L.A. specialty that focuses more on creating sculptural arrangements on the plate than culinary prowess. That said, the food is of the satisfy-all-tastes variety: roast chicken, grilled salmon, New York steak, and so on. If you're stopping at LAX with kids in tow, not to worry—Encounter's party atmosphere ensures they'll enjoy themselves without disrupting the ambience a bit. A travel advisory: At least come up and have a blue cocktail at the lava lamp–festooned bar, because quirky Encounter is worth an encounter.

209 World Way (Theme Building, Los Angeles International Airport). ℂ 310/215-5151. www.encounterrestaurant.com. Reservations recommended for dinner. Main courses dinner $24–$29, lunch $12–$23. AE, DC, DISC, MC, V. Lunch 11am–4pm daily; dinner 4–9:30pm Thurs–Sun only. Valet parking $6.

JiRaffe 𝒜𝒜 NEW AMERICAN/FRENCH   "JiRaffe"—no, it's not named after the long-necked creature, but after a blending of names from the two chefs responsible for this overnight sensation now in its 11th year. Josiah Citrin has since left partner Raphael Lunetta to carry on alone at this crowded, upscale bistro in restaurant-hungry Santa Monica. The deafening din of conversation here is usually praise for JiRaffe's artistic treatment of pepper-crusted ahi tuna, crispy Maine salmon, pancetta-wrapped tiger shrimp, and caramelized pork chops with smoked bacon, apple chutney, and cider sauce. If you're a connoisseur of gnocchi, try the purple Peruvian gnocchi with fresh Florida rock shrimp and roasted purple pearl onions. JiRaffe also wins culinary points for highlighting oft-ignored vegetables such as salsify, Swiss chard, and fennel, as well as complex appetizers that are more like miniature main dishes. For dessert, say hello to a slice of warm chocolate truffle cake and a cup of coffee. *Tip:* Visit JiRaffe's website for Chef Lunetta's special recipes.

501 Santa Monica Blvd. (corner of 5th St.), Santa Monica. ℂ 310/917-6671. www.jirafferestaurant.com. Reservations recommended. Main courses $26–$32. AE, MC, V. Mon 6–9pm; Tues–Thurs 6–10pm; Fri–Sat 6–11pm; Sun 5:30–9pm. Valet parking $4.50.

The Lobster 𝒜𝒜 SEAFOOD   There's been a seafood shack called the Lobster on the Santa Monica Pier since 1923—almost as long as the pier's been standing—but the latest incarnation brings a new sophistication to this perpetually crowded and lively local favorite. The interior is completely rebuilt but still accentuates a seaside ambience and a million-dollar ocean view with its floor-to-ceiling windows. The menu has also been revamped by chef Allyson Thurber, who brings an impressive culinary pedigree (including Downtown's Water Grill) to the kitchen. Although the namesake crustacean from Maine is a great choice, the menu consistently presents a multitude of ultrafresh fish with thoughtful and creative preparation. Specialties range from sautéed tiger prawns "scampi"-style to jumbo lump crab cakes and lobster

Finds L.A.'s Best Sushi & Stir-Fried Crickets

If you want to start a heated argument with L.A.'s foodies, just claim that you know where the best sushi in the city is served. Well, let the tongue-fu begin, because I'm claiming that the **Hump** ✰✰✰ (**(C) 310/313-0977; www.thehump.biz**) at the Santa Monica airport serves L.A.'s best. If I'm ever on death row, I want my last meal to be a giant plate of sushi prepared by these master chefs. Much of the seafood here is flown in daily from Tokyo's Tsukiji and Fukuoka fish markets in oxygen-filled containers and is so fresh that the management had to put a sign at the entrance to warn the faint-of-heart from sitting at the sushi bar. Why? Because much of what they slice is still moving. (When they cut the tails off the feisty giant sweet shrimp, they line up the flailing torsos conga-line style—it's like a macabre death dance.) The specialties here are the *dengaku* (stuffed eggplant and avocado with seafood and miso sauce), live baby squid, live whitefish served in a martini glass with vinegary broth, hairy crab, live red snapper, and the most tender, flavorful baby hamachi I've ever had (and I live for hamachi). If you want to dine Ozzie-style, order the $220 snapping turtle (the blood goes well with a rich cabernet or port), the snake sake (yes, there's a snake in the bottle), and the blowfish (it's to die for). If the menu's all Greek to you, say *"omakase"* and get ready for a chef's choice seven-course seafood adventure.

Directly below the Hump is the much larger **Typhoon** ✰✰ (**(C) 310/390-6565; www.typhoon-restaurant.com**), a very popular and high-energy Pan-Asian restaurant where stir-fried Taiwanese spicy crickets, dried Manchurian ants, and Thai-style crispy white sea worms punctuate a family-style menu filled with less exotic fare from throughout Southeast Asia, most in the $7 to $12 range.

Both restaurants are located on the second and third floors of the airport's administration building at 3221 Donald Douglas Loop Rd. in Santa Monica. Call or visit the websites for direction and hours.

---

grilled, steamed, or pan-roasted. Creative appetizers include ahi carpaccio with tangy tobiko wasabi, steamed mussels and Manila clams with apple-wood bacon, and oysters plain or fancy. For something truly decadent, try the sake-kasu-marinated sea bass accompanied by a bottle of dry chardonnay from the well-stocked cellar. The menu offers a couple of fine steaks for landlubbers, and there's a practiced bar that serves lots of bloody marys garnished with jumbo shrimp to dedicated locals. For dessert, chocolate bread pudding is terrific. *Tip:* Request a table on the deck and enjoy the 180-degree panoramic view of the Pacific.

1602 Ocean Ave. (at Colorado Blvd.), Santa Monica. (C) 310/458-9294. www.thelobster.com. Reservations recommended. Main courses $19–$41. AE, DC, DISC, MC, V. Mon–Thurs 11:30am–10pm; Fri–Sat 11:30am–11pm. Valet parking $4.50.

Michael's ✰✰ CALIFORNIA   Owner Michael McCarty, L.A.'s answer to Alice Waters, is considered by many to be the father of California cuisine. Since Michael's opened in 1979 (when McCarty was only 25), several top L.A. restaurants have caught

Sea Breezes & Sunsets: Oceanview Dining in Malibu

Beau Rivage, 26025 Pacific Coast Hwy. (at Corral Canyon; ⓒ **310/456-5733;** www.beaurivagerestaurant.com). Though it's my only pick located on the *other* side of PCH from the beach, this romantic Mediterranean restaurant (whose name means "beautiful shore") has nearly unobstructed ocean views. The baby-pink villa and its flagstone dining patio are overgrown with flowering vines. The place is prettiest at sunset; romantic lighting takes over after dark. The menu is composed of country French and Italian dishes with plenty of moderately priced pastas, many with seafood. Other main courses are more expensive; they include chicken, duck, rabbit, and lamb, all traditionally prepared. An older, nicely dressed crowd tends to dine at this special-occasion place. It's open Monday through Saturday from 5 to 10pm, and Sunday from 11am to 10pm. Valet parking is $4 (Fri–Sat only; otherwise, free self-parking). *Tip:* Sunday's brunch menu, which isn't limited to breakfast dishes, is a less pricey alternative to dinner.

Duke's Malibu 🐠, 21150 Pacific Coast Hwy. (at Las Flores Canyon; ⓒ **310/ 317-0777;** www.dukesmalibu.com). Lovers of Hawaii and all things Polynesian will thrive in this outpost of the Hawaiian chain. Imagine a South Pacific T.G.I. Friday's where the food is secondary to the decor, then add a rocky perch atop breaking waves, and you have this surfing-themed crowd-pleaser. It's worth a visit for the memorabilia alone—the place is named for Hawaiian surf legend "Duke" Kahanamoku. Duke's offers up pretty good food at inflated but not outrageous prices. You'll find plenty of fresh fish prepared in the Hawaiian regional style, hearty surf and turf, a smattering of chicken and pasta dishes, and plenty of pupus to accompany Duke's Day-Glo tropical cocktails. The Sunday brunch buffet (10am–3pm) is a tasty deal at $22 for adults and $12 for kids. It's open Monday through Friday from 11:30am to 9pm, Saturday from 11:30am to 9:30pm, and Sunday from 11:30am to 10pm. Valet parking is $2 (dinner and weekends only; otherwise, free self-parking).

Gladstone's 4 Fish, 17300 Pacific Coast Hwy. (at Sunset Blvd.; ⓒ **310/454-3474;** www.gladstones.com). A local tradition, Gladstone's is totally immersed in the Malibu scene. It shares a parking lot with a public beach, so the restaurant's wooden deck has a constant view of surfers, bikini-clad sunbathers, and other beachgoers. At busy times, Gladstone's even sets up picnic-style tables on the sand. Prices are moderate, and the atmosphere is casual. The menu offers several pages of fresh fish and seafood, augmented by a few salads and other meals for landlubbers—it's mostly fried tourist food, but the large portions get the job done. Gladstone's is popular for afternoon/evening drinking and offers nearly 20 seafood appetizer platters; it's also known for its decadent chocolate dessert, the Mile High Chocolate Cake, large enough for the whole table. It's open Sunday through Thursday from 8am to 10pm, Friday and Saturday from 8am to 11pm. Parking is $4.50.

up to it, but this fetching Santa Monica venue remains one of the city's best. The dining room is filled with contemporary art by Michael's wife, Kim McCarty, and the restaurant's garden is Santa Monica's most romantic setting for always-inventive menu choices such as grilled Mediterranean loup de mer with chorizo and mussels, oven-roasted Channel spiny lobster with garlic-fennel potato purée, or grilled pork chop with Calvados apple pan sauce. Don't miss Michael's famous warm mushroom salad, tossed with crumbled goat cheese, watercress, caramelized onion, and mustard-sage vinaigrette. The dry-aged New York strip is also fantastic, as are the steak *frites.*

1147 3rd St. (north of Wilshire Blvd.), Santa Monica. © 310/451-0843. www.michaelssantamonica.com. Reservations recommended. Main courses dinner $23–$45, lunch $16–$23. AE, DC, DISC, MC, V. Mon–Fri noon–2:30pm and 6–10:30pm; Sat 6–10:30pm. Valet parking $5.50.

Valentino ★★ NORTHERN ITALIAN   Valentino is a good choice if you're splurging on just one special dinner, particularly if you're passionate about wine. For more than 3 decades the ever-so-charming and world-renowned restaurateur, Piero Selvaggio, has greeted guests and helped guide them through the extensive wine list (and taken a lucky few on a tour of his award-winning wine cellar). Dinners here are typically lengthy, multicourse affairs, often involving several bottles of wine to match the cuisine. You might begin with a crisp pinot Grigio paired with caviar-filled cannoli, or *crespelle*—thin little pancakes with fresh porcini mushrooms and a rich melt of fontina cheese. A rich barolo is the perfect accompaniment to rosemary-infused roasted rabbit; the fantastically fragrant risotto with white truffles is one of the most magnificent dishes I've ever had. If you looking for a more casual dining experience, Piero's new **V-vin wine bar** offers excellent small plates and attractively priced flights of older vintages and rarely seen labels from American and international wineries. Please be aware that jackets are all but required in the elegant dining room.

3115 Pico Blvd. (west of Bundy Dr.), Santa Monica. © 310/829-4313. www.valentinorestaurant.com. Reservations required. Jackets recommended. Main courses $18–$38. AE, DC, MC, V. Mon–Thurs 5–10pm; Fri 11:30am–2:30pm and 5–10:30pm; Sat 5–10:30pm. Valet parking $5.

Vincenti Ristorante ★★ NORTHERN ITALIAN   Despite newer trends sweeping L.A., finely executed northern Italian cuisine is still going strong, as evidenced by this Westside standout. Opened by Maureen Vincenti, widow of Mauro (whose Downtown Rex ruled the scene for years), Vincenti lives up to its promising pedigree. The menu, praised as "authentically Italian," offers creative fare—gnocchi in tomato-squab sauce, sage-enhanced pumpkin-squash ravioli—along with well-prepared classics such as rotisserie-cooked whole fish, game birds, and steak. Economy-minded diners with upwardly mobile palates can easily stick with hearty appetizers and pastas ($14–$18) and still have some room left for one of Vincenti's tempting *dolci,* particularly the vanilla gelato laced with espresso.

11930 San Vicente Blvd. (west of Montana Ave.), Brentwood. © 310/207-0127. www.vincentiristorante.com. Reservations recommended. Main courses $18–$39. AE, MC, V. Mon–Sat 6–10pm; Fri noon–2pm. Valet parking $4.50.

MODERATE

Border Grill ★★ MEXICAN   Before Mary Sue Milliken and Susan Feniger spiced up cable TV with *Too Hot Tamales,* they started this hugely popular haute Mexican restaurant in West Hollywood. Since then the Border Grill has moved to a vibrantly painted, cavernous, and *muy* loud space in Santa Monica that's packed every night with locals and tourists.

Let's get one thing straight: This is not your Combo #7 kind of place. The duck tamale appetizer I ordered the last time I was here was *the* most flavorful and unique Mexican dish I've ever had: freshly made corn masa filled with tender roast duck, *guajillo* chile sauce, and roasted sweet peppers, then topped with an exquisite cranberry salsa (I could have eaten 10). Another favorite are the plantain empanadas with *chipotle* salsa and Mexican *crema,* and the über-tender roasted lamb tacos with strips of poblano chiles and manchego cheese. If it's on the specials menu, you must order the grilled chicken enchiladas verdes simmered in green mole sauce with Oaxacan cheese and hand-rolled corn tortillas. The best meatless dish is the *mulitas,* a layering of portobello mushrooms, roasted peppers, and pickled onions. For dessert, you have to try Tres Leches (a melt-in-your-mouth milk cake with passion fruit and prickly pear sauces) and—what the hell—a slice of the Aztec chocolate cake as well. To join in on the nonstop fiesta, start with one of their superb margaritas or *mojitos.* **Tip:** The happy hour menu (Mon–Fri 4–7pm, Fri–Sat after 10pm) has tasty $3 treats such as tacos, empanadas, and tostadas; and margaritas are only $3.50.

1445 4th St. (btw. Broadway and Santa Monica Blvd.), Santa Monica. ✆ 310/451-1655. www.bordergrill.com. Reservations recommended. Main courses $12–$29. AE, DC, DISC, MC, V. Sun–Thurs 11:30am–10pm; Fri–Sat 11:30am–11pm. Metered parking lots; valet parking $4.

Joe's Restaurant ✶✶ *Value* AMERICAN ECLECTIC   This is one of L.A.'s best dining bargains. Chef/owner Joseph Miller excels in simple New American cuisine, particularly grilled fish and roasted meats accented with piquant herbs. Formerly a tiny, quirky storefront, Joe gutted and completely remodeled the entire place, adding a far more spacious dining room and display wine room (though the best tables are still tucked away on the trellised outdoor patio complete with a gurgling waterfall). But don't let the upscale additions dissuade your budgeted appetite—Joe's remains a hidden treasure for those with a champagne palate but a seltzer pocketbook. Case in point: For lunch, California sand dabs with cherry tomato, arugula, and Maine sweet shrimp goes for a mere $13. And this *includes* a fresh mixed green salad or one of Miller's exquisite soups. Dinner entrees are equally sophisticated: beet risotto with grilled asparagus, fallow deer wrapped in bacon (served in a black currant sauce with a side of roasted root vegetables), monkfish in a saffron broth, wild striped bass with curried cauliflower coulis. A double whammy is Joe's grilled ahi tuna *and* Hudson Valley foie gras appetizer served with rösti potatoes and a red-wine herb sauce, and the desserts are equally fantastic.

1023 Abbot Kinney Blvd., Venice. ✆ 310/399-5811. www.joesrestaurant.com. Reservations required. Main courses dinner $18–$28, lunch $14–$18. AE, MC, V. Tues–Thurs noon–2:30pm and 6–10pm; Fri noon–2:30pm and 6–11pm; Sat 11am–2:30pm and 6–11pm; Sun 11:30am–2:30pm and 6–10pm. Free street parking or valet parking in rear of building.

Locanda del Lago ✶✶ NORTHERN ITALIAN   In a sea of mediocre restaurants along Santa Monica's Third Street Promenade is this corner trattoria that reminds you why Italians are the world's best cooks. Locanda del Lago (Trattoria of the Lake) is the only restaurant in Los Angeles that specializes in cuisine from Northern Italy's Lombardy region. Both the co-owner and executive chef were born in Milan, worked in Bellagio, and share a passion for food that hasn't waned since this warm, friendly restaurant opened more than 14 years ago. I dined there with my chef friend recently, and we both agreed that the house-made whole-wheat pappardelle tossed in a duck ragout was the best pasta dish we've ever had. (Unfortunately it's not on the regular menu, but I'm lobbying for it.) On sunny days there's no better place in L.A. to people-watch than at the trattoria's outdoor patio, savoring a glass of chianti while tucking into the house spe-cialty—*osso buco alla Milanese,* a veal shank slow-cooked in white wine and vegetables, topped with traditional *gremolata* (a parsley, garlic, and lemon zest mixture) and served with saffron risotto. Other outstanding dishes include the butternut squash risotto with seared scallops, and *tagliatelle Lago,* house-made tagliolini tossed with pink trout and escarole in a thyme-infused white-wine sauce. After a hard day's shopping there's no better place on the Promenade to relax than Lago.

231 Arizona Ave. (at 3rd St.), Santa Monica. ⒸⒸ 310/451-3525. www.lagosantamonica.com. Reservations recom-mended. Main courses $14–$30. AE, DC, DISC, MC, V. Mon–Thurs and Sun 11:30am–10pm; Fri–Sat 11am–11pm. Valet parking $5.

Restaurant Hama (Hama Sushi) 𝒦𝒦 *(Finds)* SUSHI   It's called a sushi "bar" for a reason—a place where people gather to socialize, drink, and have a good time. Most California sushi bars focus more on presentation than salutation, so imagine my sur-prise when I walked into Hama Sushi for the first time and was greeted with a chorus of "Heeeyyy!!!" from the six jolly chefs behind the bar (along with a few well-juiced regulars). Because everybody's a somebody at Hama Sushi, it's only a matter of time before you, too, are cheering newcomers and buying those madcap chefs another round of Sapporos. Located in Venice at the town's only roundabout, the restaurant is usually packed each night with regulars, so expect to wait a bit before diving into Hama's melt-in-your-mouth (literally) yellowtail, albacore, unagi, and specialty rolls. Standard Japanese hot plates such as chicken teriyaki and grilled Chilean sea bass are available as well (the grilled marinated squid is excellent), along with a wide selection of premium, chilled sake. Pass on the outside patio dining area and request a stool at the sushi bar to get the full Hama effect. *Tip:* Stay long enough to close the place down, and you'll be in for a singing surprise.

213 Windward Ave. (at Main St.), Venice. ⒸⒸ 310/396-8783. www.hamasushi.com. Main courses $6–$25. AE, DC, DISC, MC, V. Mon–Sat 6–11pm; Sun 5:30–10:30pm. Valet parking $4.

INEXPENSIVE

Bread & Porridge 𝒦𝒦 *(Value)* AMERICAN/BREAKFAST   A dozen tables are all that comprise this neighborhood cafe, but steady streams of locals mill outside, read-ing their newspapers and waiting for a vacant seat. Once inside, surrounded by the vintage fruit-crate labels adorning the walls and tabletops, you can sample the deli-cious breakfasts, fresh salads and sandwiches, and super-affordable entrees. There's a vaguely international twist to the menu, which leaps from breakfast quesadillas and omelets—all served with black beans and salsa—to the Southern comfort of Cajun crab cakes and coleslaw and typical Italian pastas adorned with Roma tomatoes and plenty of garlic. All menu items are cheap—truck-stop cheap—but with an inventive elegance that truly makes this a best-kept secret. This place thoughtfully serves break-fast all day; get a short stack of one of five varieties of pancakes with any meal.

2315 Wilshire Blvd. (3 blocks west of 26th St.), Santa Monica. ⒸⒸ 310/453-4941. Main courses $6–$9. AE, MC, V. Daily 7am–9pm. Metered street parking.

Jody Maroni's Sausage Kingdom 𝒦𝒦 *(Finds)* SANDWICHES   Your cardiologist might not approve, but Jody Maroni's all-natural, preservative-free "haute dogs" are some of the best wieners served anywhere. The grungy walk-up (or in-line skate-up) counter looks fairly foreboding—you wouldn't know there was gourmet fare behind that aging hot dog stand facade, from which at least 14 different grilled-sausage sand-wiches are served up. Bypass the traditional hot Italian and try the Toulouse garlic,

Bombay curried lamb, all-chicken apple, or orange-garlic-cumin. Each is served on a freshly baked onion roll and smothered with onions and peppers. Burgers, BLTs, and rotisserie chicken are also served, but why bother?

Other locations include the Valley's Universal CityWalk (*C* **818/622-5639**), and inside LAX Terminals 3, 4, and 6, where you can pick up some last-minute vacuum-packed sausages for home. Having elevated sausage worship to an art form, Jody's now boasts a helpful and humorous cookbook, plus its own website offering franchising opportunities.

2011 Ocean Front Walk (north of Venice Blvd.), Venice. *C* 310/822-5639. www.jodymaroni.com. Sandwiches $4–$8. No credit cards. Daily 10am–sunset.

Kay 'n Dave's Cantina *Kids* BREAKFAST/MEXICAN A beach community favorite since 1991, Kay 'n Dave's is well known for serving big portions of healthy (cooked lard-free) Mexican food at low prices. Come early—and be prepared to wait—for breakfast, as local devotees line up for five kinds of fluffy pancakes (my favorite is the cinnamon swirl), zesty omelets, or one of the best breakfast burritos in town. Spinach and chicken enchiladas in tomatillo salsa, seafood fajitas tostada, vegetable-filled corn tamales, and other Mexican specialties are served in huge portions, making this mostly locals minichain a great choice to energize for (or reenergize after) an action-packed day of sightseeing. Bring the family—there's a kids' menu and plenty of crayon artwork.

262 26th St. (south of San Vicente Blvd.), Santa Monica. *C* 310/260-1355. www.kayndaves.com. Reservations not accepted. Main courses $5–$15. AE, MC, V. Mon–Thurs 11am–9:30pm; Fri 11am–10pm; Sat 8:30am–10pm; Sun 8:30am–9:30pm. Metered street parking.

Sidewalk Cafe AMERICAN/BREAKFAST Nowhere in L.A. is the people-watching better than along Ocean Front Walk. The constantly bustling Sidewalk Cafe is ensconced in one of Venice's few remaining early-20th-century buildings. The best seats, of course, are out front, around overcrowded open-air tables, all with perfect views of the crowd, which provides nonstop entertainment. The menu is extensive, and the food is a whole lot better than it has to be at a location like this. Choose from the seriously overstuffed sandwiches or other oversize American favorites: omelets, salads, and burgers.

1401 Ocean Front Walk (btw. Horizon Ave. and Market St.), Venice. *C* 310/399-5547. www.thesidewalkcafe.com. Main courses $8–$13. MC, V. Daily 8am–11pm. Free parking with validation.

IN MALIBU

Inn of the Seventh Ray *★★* HEALTH FOOD/VEGETARIAN This former church in the beautiful (some say spiritual) Topanga Canyon oozes "aura" and is the perfect setting for a romantic dining experience, far from the bright lights of the city. About half of the seating is outdoors, at tables overlooking a creek and endless tangles of untamed vines and shrubs. Inside, the dining room is rustic, with a sloped roof and a glass wall offering mountain views. Everything is prepared from scratch, and foods are organic and chemical- and preservative-free, with a large vegan menu. The fish are caught in deep water far offshore and served the same day; you can even order unpasteurized wines that are quite good. Ten main dishes from the seasonally changing menu are available daily, and all are served with hors d'oeuvres, soup or salad, and vegetables. Light dishes, such as Five Secret Rays, consist of lightly steamed vegetables served with lemon-tahini and caraway-cheese sauces, but you'll also find a New York steak cut from naturally fed beef. Other dishes range from vegan duck with roasted chestnuts to grilled salmon served with French lentils and artichoke hearts; they also have a varied "raw food" menu.

128 Old Topanga Canyon Rd. (on Calif. 27), Topanga Canyon. (© 310/455-1311. www.innoftheseventhray.com. Reservations preferred. Main courses $16–$25. AE, DC, DISC, MC, V. Mon–Fri 11:30am–3pm; Sat 10:30am–3pm; Sun 9:30am–3pm; daily 5:30–10pm. Free parking.

Saddle Peak Lodge ⋒⋒   When you've had it with the L.A. noise and traffic, it's time to hop in the car for a leisurely drive high in the hills above Malibu to Saddle Peak Lodge, an old hunting lodge that has been converted into one of L.A.'s most popular restaurants. It looks exactly like a hunting lodge should—a rustic, weathered ol' three-story building made of massive timbers and native rock that's been gussied up with Teddy-era antiques, a crackling fireplace, and a heady collection of stuffed game. Vegetarians beware; the menu is custom-made for meat lovers: Grilled lamb loin and braised lamb shank; crispy skin wild Scottish salmon; and the house specialty—roasted elk tenderloin that's so tender you can cut it with a fork. You'll need a strong selection of rich reds to pair with this genre of cuisine, hence the lengthy *Wine Spectator*–award-winning wine list. Service is friendly and attentive, and the ambience is so romantic (no cellphone coverage to ruin the mood) that even a few ghosts have refused to leave. The restaurant also hosts a very popular Sunday brunch on the garden terrace, serving equally adventurous dishes such as thick buffalo burgers and the wild game trio.

419 Cold Canyon Rd. (call for directions), Calabasas. (© 818/222-3888. www.saddlepeaklodge.com. Main courses $24–$45. AE, DC, MC, V. Wed–Sun 5–10pm; brunch Sat–Sun 11am–3pm. Valet parking $4.

3 L.A.'s Westside & Beverly Hills
EXPENSIVE
Crustacean ⋒⋒ SEAFOOD/VIETNAMESE   It's an amazing story how this Beverly Hills restaurant came to be. Helene An, matriarch and executive chef of the An family restaurants, is by title a Vietnamese princess, great-granddaughter of the vice king of Vietnam. When she and her family fled from Saigon penniless in 1975, they relocated to San Francisco, purchased a small deli, and introduced the city to their now-legendary recipe: An Family's Famous Roast Crab and Garlic Noodles. This single dish spawned a Horatio Alger story and a family restaurant dynasty. The Beverly Hills location is pure drama from the moment you walk in: You're immediately scrutinized by the patrons to see 1) if you're a somebody and 2) what you're wearing. However, you're too busy admiring the Indochina-themed decor—a curvaceous copper bar, balcony seating, a bamboo garden, a waterfall, and an 80-foot-long "stream" topped with glass and filled with exotic koi—to notice. What you won't see is the Secret Kitchen (literally, it's off-limits to most of the staff), where the An family's signature dishes such as tiger prawns with garlic noodles, roasted lobster in tamarind sauce, and roast Dungeness crab are prepared. Although all these dishes are quite good, they're also heavy on the butter—I prefer the lighter sea bass dish with ginger and garlic-black bean sauce. On weekend nights, Helene (a real sweetheart and timeless beauty) often holds court, making sure your dining experience is faultless.

9646 Little Santa Monica Blvd. (at Bedford St.), Beverly Hills. (© 310/205-8990. www.anfamily.com. Reservations recommended. Main courses $19–$45. AE, DC, DISC, MC, V. Mon–Thurs 11:30am–2:30pm and 5:30–10:30pm; Fri 11:30am–2:30pm and 5:30–11:30pm; Sat 5:30–11:30pm. Valet parking $4.50.

Tips The Sturgeon King, Take 2

New Yorkers suffering L.A. culture shock can seek comfort food on the fifth floor of the Barneys New York department store in Beverly Hills. The elevator doors open and *voilà*—a **Barney Greengrass** on the Left Coast. This authentic— and expensive—New York deli not only air-delivers their renowned smoked sturgeon and Nova Scotia salmon direct from the Big Apple, but it has even bejeweled the swanky lunch spot with subway-style tiles. You'll have to move quickly to get a coveted table on the outdoor terrace—all those power lunchers from the entertainment industry won't hesitate. The raison d'être dishes here are the Nova Scotia salmon (or sturgeon) scrambled with eggs and onion, cheese blintzes, and chopped chicken liver sandwiches—all washed down with New York–style seltzer water on tap. It's open Monday, Tuesday, Wednesday and Friday from 10am to 7pm; Thursday from 10am to 8pm; Saturday from 10am to 7pm; Sunday from noon to 6pm. 9570 Wilshire Blvd. (at Camden Dr.), Beverly Hills. ✆ **310/276-4400.**

Fogo de Chao ★★ BRAZILIAN STEAKHOUSE   What was started long ago by four brothers in São Paulo, Brazil, has finally made its way to California—Beverly Hills, even—and is now one of the most popular restaurants in the city. Pronounced *fogo dee SHOWN,* this enormous Southern Brazilian–style steakhouse is packed nightly with fans of the *churrasco* style of cooking carne—large cuts of meat slow-roasted over an open wood flame, then deftly sliced and continuously served onto your plate until you give in and flip your disk to red (you'll see). It's a prix-fixe system where everything on the menu except alcohol is available for a flat fee, and the superb waitstaff are always hovering nearby with meat-laden platters in the off-chance that you actually clear your plate. Truly, it's bacchanalia revisited as you wander wide-eyed around what must be the most dazzling salad bar ever conceived (be careful not to ruin your appetite). The gluttony continues with mountains of freshly roasted meats and endless side dishes, all washed down with rich red wines from among the 10,000 bottles that surround you in two-story temperature-controlled towers of glass and steel. Dessert? *Si, por favor.*

133 N. La Cienega Blvd. (btw. W. 3rd St. and Beverly Blvd.), Los Angeles. ✆ **310/289-7755.** www.fogodechao.com. Reservations recommended. Fixed-price menu $53. AE, DC, DISC, MC, V. Mon–Thurs 5–10pm; Fri 5–10:30pm; Sat 4:30–10:30pm; Sun 4–9:30pm. Valet parking $5.50.

The Ivy ★★ NEW AMERICAN   If you're willing to endure the cold shoulder to ogle L.A.'s celebrities and pay lots for a perfect meal, the Ivy can be enjoyable. This snobby place attracts one of the most industry-heavy crowds in the city and treats celebrities and nobodies as differently as Brahmins and untouchables. Just past the cool reception lie two disarmingly countrified dining rooms filled with rustic antiques, comfortably worn chintz, and hanging baskets of fragrant flowers. Huge roses bloom everywhere, including out on the charming brick patio (where the highest-profile patrons are seated and dutifully ignore the stares). The food is excellent, by the way. The Ivy's Caesar salad is perfect, as are the plump and crispy crab cakes. Recommended dishes include spinach linguine with a peppery tomato-basil sauce, prime rib dusted with Cajun spices, and tender lime-marinated grilled chicken. There's even

Where to Dine in L.A.'s Westside & Beverly Hills

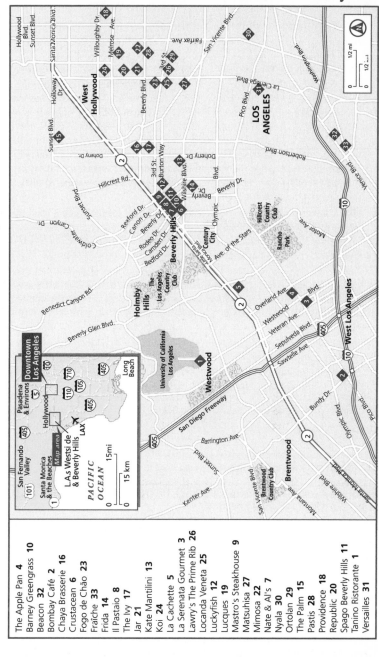

The Apple Pan **4**
Barney Greengrass **10**
Beacon **32**
Bombay Café **2**
Chaya Brasserie **16**
Crustacean **6**
Fogo de Chão **23**
Fraîche **33**
Frida **14**
Il Pastaio **8**
The Ivy **17**
Jar **21**
Kate Mantilini **13**
Koi **24**
La Cachette **5**
La Serenata Gourmet **3**
Lawry's The Prime Rib **26**
Locanda Veneta **25**
Luckyfish **12**
Lucques **19**
Mastro's Steakhouse **9**
Matsuhisa **27**
Mimosa **22**
Nate & Al's **7**
Nyala **30**
Ortolan **29**
The Palm **15**
Pastis **28**
Providence **18**
Republic **20**
Spago Beverly Hills **11**
Tanino Ristorante **1**
Versailles **31**

(Kids) Family-Friendly Restaurants

Cafe Pinot (p. 148) and **Pinot Bistro** (p. 153) are upscale offshoots of chic Patina that don't often come to mind when you're searching for family eats, and many kids are certainly too antsy to behave during an entire bistro meal. But the Pinot dynasty welcomes little ones with a special child-friendly menu, and kids 10 and under can order anything from the menu free of charge. It's a great way to enjoy L.A.'s finest and stay close to your budget, too.

On the other end of the scale is **Pink's Hot Dogs** (p. 145) in Hollywood, an institution that has been serving politically incorrect franks for what seems like forever. Everyone loves Pink's chili dogs, but you may never get the orange grease stains out of your kids' clothes.

The Mexican minichain **Kay 'n Dave's Cantina** is a great spot to fuel up with the kids at the start of a long day. They serve five kinds of fluffy pancakes, a killer breakfast burrito, enchiladas, fajitas, and more—all cooked lard-free—plus there's a kids' menu and crayons at every table. See p. 122.

Miceli's (p. 153), in Universal City, is a cavernous Italian restaurant that the whole family is sure to love. The gimmick? The waitstaff sings show tunes or opera favorites while serving (and sometimes instead of). Kids will love the boisterous atmosphere, which might even drown them out.

Jerry's Famous Deli (p. 153), in Studio City, is frequented mostly by industry types who populate this Valley community; their kids often sport baseball caps or production T-shirts from Mom's or Dad's latest project. Jerry's has the most extensive deli menu in town and a casual, coffee-shop atmosphere. Families flock here for lunch, early dinner, and (crowded) weekend breakfast.

---

a great burger and kick-ass fried chicken. The wine list is notable, and there's always a terrific variety of desserts (pink boxes are on hand for chocolate-chip cookies to go).

113 N. Robertson Blvd. (btw. 3rd St. and Beverly Blvd.), West Hollywood. © **310/274-8303.** Reservations recommended on weekends. Main courses dinner $22–$38, lunch $10–$25. AE, DC, DISC, MC, V. Mon–Sat 11:30am–10:30pm; Sun 10:30am–10:30pm. Valet parking $4.

Jar 🐾🐾🐾 MODERN CHOPHOUSE   Jar offers everything you could hope for in a restaurant: a warm and relaxed setting, excellent service, and generous servings of reliably fantastic food. During my last visit I devoured not one but two of the most flavorful meat dishes I've ever tasted: the braised Kurobuta pork shank and a Kobe-style filet of beef—both perfectly cooked, simply seasoned, and divinely flavorful. It was always Chef Suzanne Tracht's dream to open a contemporary version of a 1940s-era chophouse, and you can tell that she's putting her best into every plate that leaves the kitchen (it's no surprise that Tracht was named one of "America's Best New Chefs of 2002" by *Food & Wine* magazine). Everything she makes is a lesson in quality and simplicity. Among her most popular dishes are the Niman Ranch char sui pork chops and her coup de grâce—a sensational pot roast with caramelized onions and carrots (if you've had a better one let me know). An extensive wine list and martini menu are two good reasons to arrive early and stay for a nightcap at the beautiful Parisian-style bar. *Tip:* Suzanne's Sunday brunch is one of the best in the city.

8225 Beverly Blvd (at Harper Ave.), Los Angeles. ⓒ 323/655-6566. www.thejar.com. Reservations recommended. Main courses $21–$48. AE, DC, DISC, MC, V. Mon–Thurs 5:30–10pm; Fri–Sat 5:30–11pm; Sun 10am–2pm and 5:30–9:30pm. Valet parking $6.

La Cachette 🦀🦀🦀 FRENCH   Widely considered one of the most influential French chefs in America, Jean François Meteigner literally wrote the book on this cuisine—*Cuisine Naturelle*—a revolutionary approach to fine French cuisine that eschews heavy creams, butter, and complex recipes in favor of dishes that are simple, light, full of flavor, and 90% free of cream and butter. Meteigner began his career as a chef in France, moved to Los Angeles in 1980 to serve as executive chef at L'Orangerie, and then opened La Cachette ("the Hideaway") in 1994. Situated on the edge of a residential neighborhood in Century City, the elegant, romantic, white-on-white dining room is a bit hard to find—you have to access it from an alley off Little Santa Monica Boulevard—but it only adds to the restaurant's charm. As a fan of rich lobster bisque, I found Meteigner's dairy-free crab and lobster bisque to be intensely flavorful but lacking the richness that only heavy cream can provide (cream is an option, however), and the escargot was bland, but all was forgiven as I devoured my entree: braised Kurobuta black pork shank with braised baby back ribs and Banyul vinegar sauce, served with a side of roasted apples and Yukon mashed potatoes (it took effort not to lick the plate). Matching the right wine isn't a problem, as the wine list has earned the *Wine Spectator* Award of Excellence. The warm fruit tart is a fitting finale—light and flavorful.

10506 Santa Monica Blvd. (btw. Beverly Glen Blvd. and Overland Ave.), Century City. ⓒ 310/470-4992. www.la cachetterestaurant.com. Reservations recommended. Main courses dinner $26–$35, lunch $15–$32. AE, DC, MC, V. Lunch Mon–Fri noon–2pm; dinner Mon–Thurs 6–9:30pm, Fri–Sat 5:30–10:30pm, Sun 6–9pm. Valet parking $3.50.

Lawry's The Prime Rib 🦀🦀 STEAKS/SEAFOOD   Most Americans know Lawry's only as a brand of seasoned salt (which was invented here). Going to this family-run institution is an old-world event, where the main menu offerings are four cuts of prime rib that vary in thickness from two fingers to an entire hand. Every standing rib roast is dry-aged for 2 to 3 weeks, sprinkled with Lawry's famous seasoning, and then roasted on a bed of rock salt. A carver wheels the cooked beef tableside, then slices it properly, rare to well-done. All dinners come with creamy whipped horseradish, Yorkshire pudding, and the Original Spinning Bowl Salad (drenched in Lawry's signature sherry French dressing). Lawry's moved across the street from its original location several years ago but retained its throwback-to-the-1930s clubroom atmosphere, complete with Persian-carpeted oak floors, high-backed chairs, and European oil paintings.

100 N. La Cienega Blvd. (north of Wilshire Blvd.), Beverly Hills. ⓒ 310/652-2827. www.lawrysonline.com. Reservations recommended. Main courses $20–$30. AE, DC, DISC, MC, V. Mon–Fri 5–10pm; Sat 4:30–11pm; Sun 4–9:30pm. Valet parking $5.50.

Lucques 🦀🦀 FRANCO-MEDITERRANEAN   Once Los Angeles became accustomed to this restaurant's unusual name—"Lucques" is a variety of French olive, pronounced "Luke"—local foodies fell hard for this quietly and comfortably sophisticated home of former Campanile chef Suzanne Goin. The old brick building, once silent star Harold Lloyd's carriage house, is decorated in muted, clubby colors with subdued lighting that extends to the handsome enclosed patio. Goin cooks with bold flavors, fresh-from-the-farm produce, and an instinctive feel for the food of the Mediterranean. The short and oft-changed menu makes the most of unusual ingredients such as salt cod and oxtails. Standout dishes include Tuscan bean soup with tangy greens and pistou, grilled duck breast served alongside braised red cabbage with chanterelle mushrooms and chestnuts, braised beef short ribs with potato purée and horseradish cream, and a perfect vanilla *pòt de crème* for dessert. Lucques's bar menu, featuring steak frites béarnaise, omelets, and tantalizing hors d'oeuvres (olives, warm almonds, sea salt, chewy bread), is a godsend for late-night diners, and the bartenders make a mean vodka Collins. *Tip:* On Sundays, Lucques offers a bargain $40 prix-fixe three-course dinner from a weekly changing menu.

8474 Melrose Ave. (east of La Cienega Blvd.), West Hollywood. © 323/655-6277. www.lucques.com. Reservations recommended. Main courses $18–$30. AE, DC, MC, V. Mon 6–10pm; Tues–Sat noon–2:30pm and 6–11pm; Sun 5–10pm. Metered street parking or valet ($5.50).

Mastro's Steakhouse ★★★ STEAKS/SEAFOOD   Located down the street from Spago—so you know it's expensive—is one of the best steakhouses in Southern California: Mastro's. Typical of an upscale steakhouse, the dimly lit dining room on the first floor has a dark, leathery, serious men's club feel to it, so be sure to request a table on the second floor, where the bar, live music, and cool vibe are located. Slide into a plush black leather booth, order a Mastro Dry Ice Martini (which comes with the shaker, so it takes only one to get a groove on), and start off the feast with an Iced Seafood Tower—a massive pyramid of crab legs, lobster, shrimp, clams, and oysters the size of your palm. Oh, and I've found the beef: Fred Flintstone–size slabs of hand-cut USDA beef served on sizzling plates heated to 400°F (204°C) so your steak stays warm and juicy throughout the meal. Forget the greens—the only side you need is the Mastro Mash, a big bowl of creamy mashed potatoes mixed with sour cream, chives, bacon, and butter. ("I'll have a Diet Coke with that.") The bad news is that a bone-in rib-eye runs about $50; the good news is that one will feed three normal-size people. The white-jacketed waiters are friendly and attentive; be sure to say hello to the manager, Jin Yu—he's got some great stories to tell about this celebrity-filled joint.

246 N. Canon Dr. (btw. Dayton Way and Wilshire Blvd.), Beverly Hills. © 310/888-8782. www.mastrossteakhouse.com. Reservations recommended. Main courses dinner $26–$84. AE, DC, MC, V. Daily 5pm–2am. Valet parking $7.

Matsuhisa ★★ JAPANESE/PERUVIAN   Japanese chef/owner Nobuyuki Matsuhisa arrived in Los Angeles via Peru in 1987 and opened what may be the most creative restaurant in the city. A true master of fish cookery, Matsuhisa creates unusual dishes by combining Japanese flavors with South American spices and salsas (he was the first to introduce Americans to yellowtail sashimi with sliced jalapeños). Broiled sea bass with black truffles, miso-flavored black cod, sautéed squid with garlic and soy, tempura sea urchin in a shiso leaf, and Dungeness crab tossed with chiles and cream are just a few examples of the masterfully prepared dishes available, in addition to thickly sliced nigiri and creative sushi rolls. Matsuhisa is perennially popular with celebrities and hard-core foodies, so reserve well in advance for those hard-to-get tables. The small, crowded main dining room suffers from poor lighting and precious lack of privacy; many big names are ushered through to private dining rooms. Expect a bit of attitude from the staff as well. *Tip:* If you're feeling adventurous, ask for *omakase,* and the chef will personally compose a selection of eccentric dishes.

129 N. La Cienega Blvd. (north of Wilshire Blvd.), Beverly Hills. © 310/659-9639. www.nobumatsuhisa.com. Reservations recommended. Main courses $15–$50; sushi $4–$13 per order; full *omakase* dinner from $75. AE, DC, MC, V. Mon–Fri 11:45am–2:15pm; daily 5:45–10:15pm. Valet parking $5.

Ortolan ✦✦ FRENCH   Named after a small bird that's been savored to near extinction by French gourmands (and now an outlawed delicacy), this wonderful restaurant is a partnership between former L'Orangerie chef Christophe Emé and Jeri Ryan, the stunning *Boston Public* actress. The restaurant is cleverly designed into four separate sections to match your mood: a glamorous main dining room with creamy leather booths, matching velvet curtains, and crystal chandeliers; a smaller, more rustic dining room with Pennsylvania barn-plank flooring and a long communal table where patrons dine family style; a small, dimly lit bar replete with dark woods, potted herbs, and a zinc top; and a cozy fireplace lounge for small dinner parties or romancing couples. Emé's sophisticated French cuisine is cleverly arranged as well: bread dippings arrive in a trio of test tubes; John Dory is served on a hot river stone; dessert arrives in baby ice-cream cones. His most popular dishes include crispy langoustines with a shot of minestrone, a superb lamb *pastilla* wrapped in phyllo and served in thick slices, and the most tender squab I've ever tasted. For dessert, try the melting chocolate cake with pralines. *Tip:* If you don't have a reservation, join the dinner party at the enormous communal table or find a spot in the fireside lounge.

8338 W. 3rd St. (at N. Kings Rd.), Los Angeles. ✆ **323/653-3300**. www.ortolanrestaurant.com. Reservations recommended. Main courses $19–$43. AE, DISC, MC, V. Tues–Thurs 6–10pm; Fri–Sat 6–10:30pm. Bar open until midnight. Valet parking $4.

The Palm ✦✦ STEAKS/LOBSTER   Every major American city has a renowned steakhouse; in Los Angeles it's the Palm. The child of the famous New York restaurant of the same name, the Palm is widely regarded by local foodies as one of the best traditional American eateries in the city. The glitterati seem to agree, as stars and their handlers are regularly in attendance. In both food and ambience, this West Coast apple hasn't fallen far from the proverbial tree. The restaurant is brightly lit, bustling with energy, and playfully decorated with dozens of celebrity caricatures on the walls. Live Nova Scotia lobsters are flown in almost daily and then broiled over charcoal and served with big bowls of melted butter. Most are enormous (3–7 lb.), and, although they're obscenely expensive, can be shared. The steaks and swordfish are similarly sized, perfectly grilled to order, and served a la carte by cheeky white-jacketed waiters who have been around since the Nixon administration. Diners also swear by the creamed spinach and celebrated Gigi Salad—a mixture of lettuce, shrimp, bacon, green beans, pimento, and avocado. For dessert, stick with the Palm's perfect New York cheesecake, flown in straight from the Bronx.

9001 Santa Monica Blvd. (btw. Doheny Dr. and Robertson Blvd.), West Hollywood. ✆ **310/550-8811**. www.the palm.com. Reservations recommended. Main courses dinner $17–$41, lobsters $18 per pound; lunch $10–$19. AE, DC, MC, V. Mon–Fri noon–10:30pm; Sat 5–10:30pm; Sun 5–9:30pm. Valet parking $5.

Providence ✦✦✦ MODERN AMERICAN SEAFOOD   The city's best seafood chef and the city's best maitre d' have combined their talents to create, well, the city's best seafood restaurant—Providence. After 6 years at Water Grill—long regarded as one of L.A.'s finest seafood restaurants—Chef Michael Cimarusti and his quadrilingual Italian compatriot, Donato Poto, fulfilled their dream to create the city's preeminent seafood experience. It's a pleasure to just relax at this sleek, modern space and converse with Donato at the bar, so be sure to arrive a bit early. Because Cimarusti visits the fish market daily for the choicest seafood available, I recommend asking the waiter which are the evening's best dishes or, better yet, inquire if Michael has time to make a brief visit to your table and offer his advice (he's a wonderful guy). Because his philosophy is to let the divine flavors of wild fish prevail, sauces are never overpowering—striped sea bass in a pea tendril broth, wild king salmon with a truffle vinaigrette, kelp-marinated fluke. If you're in a mood to splurge, go with the $140 Market Menu: nine memorable courses paired with superb wines (the young sommelier here is a wizard). Lastly, be sure to order anything Cimarusti makes with sea urchin, especially if you don't like sea urchin. Trust me, he'll convert you.

5855 Melrose Ave. (at N. Cahuenga Blvd.), Los Angeles. ℂ 323/460-4170. www.providencela.com. Reservations recommended. Main courses $32–$49. AE, MC, V. Lunch Fri noon–2:30pm; dinner Mon–Fri 6–10pm, Sat 5:30–10pm, Sun 5:30–9pm. Valet parking $6.

Republic ⭑⭑ CONTEMPORARY AMERICAN   If you like a lot of pomp with your pulled pork, you'll want to make a reservation at Republic, where the scene is as important as the cuisine (if not more). The show starts right at the entrance, where a door of falling water automatically parts as you enter the patio—very cool. Artistic elements prevail throughout the multilevel restaurant—giant parchment paper light fixtures, glass-beaded wall finishes, python upholstery, Brazilian walnut trim, chain mail draping—but the coup de grâce is certainly the 20-foot tall "Tower of Wine" featuring "wine fairies" that float trapeze-style to retrieve the bottles. Following the city's latest trend toward hefty servings of meaty comfort food, the Southern-enhanced menu offers dishes ranging from a mesquite-grilled veal porterhouse to a venison chop. Naturally there's a mac and cheese on the sides menu, though I prefer the sweet-potato gratin and truffle grits. After dinner you'll want to waddle over to the lounge's leather sofa for a *digestif* and to watch L.A.'s pretty people in their element.

650 N. La Cienega Blvd. (just north of Melrose Place), Los Angeles. ℂ 310/360-7070. www.therepublicla.com. Reservations recommended. Main courses $23–$44. AE, DC, DISC, MC, V. Daily 6–11pm. Bar is open until 2am. Valet parking $7.

Spago Beverly Hills ⭑⭑⭑ CALIFORNIA   Wolfgang Puck is more than a great chef; he's also a masterful businessman and publicist who has made Spago one of the best-known restaurants in the United States. Despite all the hoopla—and years of stiff competition—Spago remains one of L.A.'s top-rated restaurants and continues to live up to the hype. Talented Puck henchman Lee Hefter presides over the kitchen, delivering the culinary sophistication demanded by an upscale Beverly Hills crowd. This high-style indoor/outdoor space glows with the aura of big bucks, celebrities, and the perfectly honed California cuisine that can honestly take credit for setting the standard. Spago is also one of the last places in L.A. where men will feel most comfortable in jacket and tie (suggested, but not required). All eyes may be on the romantically twinkle-lit outdoor patio (the most coveted tables), but the food takes center stage. You simply can't choose wrong—highlights include the appetizer of foie gras "three ways"; crawfish salad; savory duck either honey-lacquered and topped with foie gras or Cantonese-style with a citrus tang; slow-roasted Sonoma lamb with braised greens; and rich Austrian dishes from "Wolfie's" childhood, such as spicy beef goulash and perfect veal schnitzel.

176 N. Canon Dr. (north of Wilshire Blvd.), Beverly Hills. ℂ 310/385-0880. www.wolfgangpuck.com. Reservations required. Jacket and tie advised for men. Main courses $17–$42; tasting menu $125. AE, DC, DISC, MC, V. Lunch Mon–Fri 11:30am–2:15pm, Sat noon–2:30pm; dinner Sun–Thurs 5:30–10:30pm, Fri–Sat 5:30–11pm. Valet parking $4.50.

MODERATE

Beacon ⭑⭑ *Value* ASIAN FUSION   Ranked number one in a recent "Top 25 Restaurants" article in *Los Angeles Magazine,* Beacon is the best thing to happen to the Culver City dining scene in years. For more than a decade, Chef Kazuto Matsusaka has worked in the kitchen of some of L.A.'s top restaurants (Spago, Chinois on Main), mastering the art of fusion cooking. Along with his wife Vicki Fan (she's the GM), the duo recently opened this small, minimally decorated cafe within the Helms Bakery complex, and it's been packed ever since. On most nights you'll see a stern-faced Kazuto in the open kitchen (he's actually a hilarious guy) while Vicki oversees the L-shaped dining room. The reasonably priced cuisine is simple yet superb, combining fresh California ingredients with traditional Asian cooking styles and a dash of Vicki's family recipes. If available, you must start with the outstanding Kaki Fry appetizer—warm crispy oysters set in cool lettuce cups and topped with *yuzu* tartar sauce (a steal at $6.25)—and the stir-fried mushroom salad, a heavenly mix of organic mushrooms, mixed greens, manchego cheese, and tangy *yuzu* dressing. Other fantastic dishes I devoured were the miso-marinated black cod with sesame-tossed green beans, the ever-so-tender grilled hangar steak spiced with wasabi relish, and a savory bowl of *kakuni udon*—thick wheat-flour noodles flavored with a generous cut of braised pork belly, bamboo shoots, baby bok choy, and warm broth. For dessert, try the Rice Krispy sundae with chocolate and caramel sauces. *Tip:* On sunny days request a table at the back patio.

3280 Helms Ave. (at Washington Blvd.), Culver City. ℂ 310/838-7500. www.beacon-la.com. Reservations recommended. Main courses $13–$20. AE, DISC, MC, V. Lunch Mon–Sat 11:30am–2pm; dinner Sun and Tues–Wed 5:30–9pm, Thurs–Sat 5:30–10pm. Free lot parking.

Bombay Café ★★ INDIAN   This friendly sleeper may be L.A.'s best Indian spot, serving excellent curries and kormas typical of South Indian street food. Once seated, immediately order *sev puri* for the table; these crispy little chips topped with chopped potatoes, onions, cilantro, and chutneys are the perfect accompaniment to what's sure to be an extended menu-reading session. Also recommended are the burrito-like "frankies," juicy little bread rolls stuffed with lamb, chicken, or cauliflower. The best dishes come from the tandoor and include spicy yogurt-marinated swordfish, lamb, and chicken. While some dishes are authentically spicy, plenty of others have a mellow flavor for less incendiary palates. This restaurant is phenomenally popular and gets its share of celebrities.

12021 W. Pico Blvd. (at Bundy Dr.), Los Angeles. ℂ 310/473-3388. Reservations recommended for dinner. Main courses $9–$17. MC, V. Mon–Fri 11:30am–3pm and 5–10pm; Sat–Sun 5–10pm. Metered street parking (lunch); valet parking $3.50 (dinner).

Chaya Brasserie ★★ FRANCO-JAPANESE   Open for more than 2 decades, Chaya has a strong reputation as one of Los Angeles's most reliable restaurants. This Continental bistro with Asian overtones is popular with film agents during lunch and a particularly beautiful assembly of stars at night (George Clooney, Mark Wahlberg, the Baldwin brothers). The place is loved for its exceptionally good East/West dishes, unpretentious atmosphere, and flawless martinis—try their award-winning Pineapple Infusion. Despite a high noise level, the stage-lit dining room feels sensuous and swoony. On warm afternoons and evenings, the best tables are on the outside terrace, overlooking the busy street. Chaya is best known for superb grilled fish and meats, such as miso-marinated white sea bass with wasabi tamari beurre blanc. Chef Shigefumi Tachibe's lobster ravioli with basil pesto cream sauce is both stylish and superb, as is tangy wood-grilled chicken Dijon, a house specialty. Excellent sushi is available as well. Chaya is also a hot late-night rendezvous with a short but choice late-dinner menu served Tuesday through Saturday. *Note:* There's also a Chaya near the beach: **Chaya Venice,** located at 110 Navy St. (at Main St.) in Venice (ℂ 310/396-1179).

8741 Alden Dr. (east of Robertson Blvd.), Los Angeles. (C) **310/859-8833.** www.thechaya.com. Reservations recommended. Main courses dinner $15–$27, lunch $10–$16. AE, MC, V. Lunch Mon–Fri 11am–2:30pm; dinner Mon–Thurs 6–10:30pm, Fri–Sat 6–11pm, Sun 6–10pm; brunch Sat 11am–2:30pm, Sun 11am–3pm. Valet parking $5.50.

Fraîche ★★★ MEDITERRANEAN   Like many of L.A.'s rising star chefs, Jason Travi cut his chops as a sous chef at Spago, cranking out 400 plates a night in that pressure cooker of a kitchen. Dues paid, he's now at the helm of one on the most talked-about new restaurants in Southern California, a tribute to the ingredient-driven dishes that make eating your way through the Mediterranean such a joy. His mornings are spent at the farmers' market—annoying other shoppers as he buys up the best produce—and evenings within his impressive open kitchen with his trusty crew of pirate-like line cooks, whipping up plate after plate of rustic French and Italian dishes such as tortelli with braised rabbit or lamb *spezzatino* atop celery root gnocchi. His standout dish, however, is the branzino (European sea bass) served en papillote with fennel, roasted peppers, and fingerling potatoes. You'll enjoy the decor as well, as it's reminiscent of a country estate with earthy Tuscan colors and textures, walls clad in farmhouse stone, distressed walnut flooring, and an lively indoor-outdoor terrace overlooking Culver and Main streets. *Tip:* The bar menu is served every night until 1am.

9411 Culver Blvd. (at Main St.), Culver City. (C) **310/839-6800.** www.fraicherestaurantla.com. Reservations recommended. Main courses dinner $16–$26, lunch $10–$22. AE, DC, DISC, MC, V. Lunch Mon–Fri 11:30am–2:30pm; dinner daily 5:30–10:30pm.

Frida ★★ *Finds* MEXICAN   The last time I had Mexican food this good I was living on the shores of Lake Chapala near Guadalajara. Made from recipes handed down by the owner's ancestors, the Mexican cuisine at Frida is as traditional and authentic as it gets on this side of the border. It's the kind of food you find when you're so far south of Tijuana that the culture appears more Maya than Mexican. Both the friendly owner and waiters are justly proud of the dishes they present as patrons eagerly tuck into handmade soft tacos brimming with sautéed shrimp bathed in a dark, tangy pasilla-orange sauce (fantastic), or generous portions of carnitas in an annatto-seed sauce topped with onion-habanero relish and served over fresh corn tortillas. And we've only started. Seviches, *sopas, ensaladas,* moles, *pescados, carnes*—there are so many choices of dishes you've probably never heard of that it helps to enlist the advice of the waitstaff. Trust me on a couple, though: the dark, rich chicken mole simmered in ground pumpkin-seed sauce; and the Filete Tentacion, charbroiled filet mignon on a bed of dry chile and Mexican truffle sauce *(cuitlacoche),* topped with goat cheese and jalapeño sauce, and served with a side of grilled chayote squash. The wide selection of superb margaritas is the perfect accompaniment to the spicy dishes. Even the velvety refried beans were the best I've ever had. If you like authentic Mexican cuisine, *Achiwawa!* will you love Frida's. *Tip:* There's another location at the Brentwood Country Mart, 225 26th St., Santa Monica ((C) **310/394-9440).**

236 S. Beverly Dr. (btw. Charleville Blvd. and Gregory Way), Beverly Hills. (C) **310/278-7666.** Fax 310/278-9699. www.fridarestaurant.com. Reservations recommended. Main courses dinner $10–$29, lunch $7–$20. AE, DC, MC, V. Mon–Sat 11am–10pm; Sun 4–9pm. Valet parking $7.

Il Pastaio ★★ NORTHERN REGIONAL ITALIAN   Sicilian-born chef/owner Giacomino Drago (scion of L.A.'s well-known Drago restaurateur family) hit the jackpot with this hugely successful, value-priced trattoria, located on a busy corner in the shopping district of Beverly Hills. All day long, Giacomino's fans take a break from work or shopping and converse over glasses of chianti and plates of oh-so-authentic pasta. With 57 menu items to choose from, I haven't come close to trying everything, but I can tell you with certainty that you will swoon over the *arancini,* breaded rice cones that are filled with mozzarella cheese and peas, then fried crispy brown (highly addictive); the pumpkin tortelloni in a light sage-and-cream sauce; the *arrabbiata,* a simple penne pasta dish in a fantastic spicy tomato-and-garlic sauce; and for dessert, the panna cotta (the silkiest in Southern California). There's almost always a wait— and not much room to wait in—but by meal's end it always seems worth it.

400 N. Canon Dr. (at Brighton Way), Beverly Hills. ✆ 310/205-5444. www.giacominodrago.com. Main courses dinner $16–$30, lunch $10–$27. AE, DC, MC, V. Mon–Sat 11:30am–11pm; Sun 11:30am–10pm.

Kate Mantilini ★★ AMERICAN/TRADITIONAL/BREAKFAST   It's rare to find a restaurant that feels comfortably familiar yet cutting-edge trendy at the same time— and also happens to be one of L.A.'s few late-night eateries. Kate Mantilini fits the bill perfectly. One of the first to bring meatloaf back into fashion, Kate's offers a huge menu of upscale truck-stop favorites such as "white" chili (made with chicken, white beans, and Jack cheese); grilled steaks, chicken, and fish; a few token pastas; and just about anything you might crave. At 2am, nothing quite beats a steaming bowl of lentil-vegetable soup and some garlic-cheese toast, unless your taste runs to fresh oysters, a candy bar–ice-cream pie, and a dry martini—yep, Kate's has it all. The huge mural of the Hagler-Hearns boxing match that dominates the stark, open interior provides the only clue to the namesake's identity: Mantilini was an early female boxing promoter in the late 1940s.

9101 Wilshire Blvd. (at Doheny Dr.), Beverly Hills. ✆ 310/278-3699. Reservations accepted only for parties of 6 or more. Main courses $7–$16. AE, MC, V. Mon–Thurs 11:30am–midnight; Fri 11:30am–1am; Sat 11am–1am; Sun 10am–midnight. Validated valet parking.

Koi ★★ ASIAN-FUSION   If your goal is to spot Hollywood's A-list of celebrities, make a reservation at Koi, the current fave of L.A.'s glam scene: George Clooney, Jennifer Garner, Demi and Ashton, Liv Tyler, J.Lo, Jessica Simpson, Nick Lachey, Martin Lawrence—they've all been patrons. Or just make a reservation because the food is so wonderful (overpriced, but wonderful). Either way, you won't be disappointed. Incorporating feng shui elements of trickling water, votive candles, open-air patios, and soft lighting, the minimalist earthen-hued interior has a calming ambience that is a welcome relief from the hectic Melrose scene just outside the ornately carved gates. The chef's brilliant fusions of Japanese and Californian cuisine account for the repeat clientele. Start with the refreshing cucumber *sunomono* tower flavored with sweet vinegar and edible flowers, followed by a baked crab roll with edible rice paper (fantastic), the tuna tartare and avocado on crispy wontons, the yellowtail carpaccio delicately flavored with grape-seed oil, and the house specialty of black cod bronzed with miso that's warm-butter soft and exploding with sweet flavor. *Tip:* Request one of the horseshoe booths on the back patio amid Buddha statues and candlelight.

730 N. La Cienega Blvd. (btw. Melrose Ave. and Santa Monica Blvd.), West Hollywood. ✆ 310/659-9449. www. koirestaurant.com. Reservations recommended. Main courses $13–$27. AE, DC, DISC, MC, V. Sun–Thurs 6–10pm; Fri–Sat 6pm–midnight. Valet parking $5.

La Serenata Gourmet ★★ MEXICAN   Westsiders rejoiced when this branch of Boyle Heights's award-winning La Serenata de Girabaldi began serving its authentic, but innovative, Mexican cuisine just a block away from the Westside Pavilion shopping center. This place is casual, fun, and intensely delicious. Local favorites are the Mexican shrimp with rich *mojo de ajo* sauce, fish tacos, shrimp enchiladas, pork *gorditas,* and the garlicky beef tongue in tomatillo sauce. All dishes are accented with hand-patted corn tortillas, fresh chips dusted with *añejo* cheese, and flavorful fresh salsas. It's always packed to capacity, so try to avoid the prime lunch and dinner hours.

10924 W. Pico Blvd. (at Westwood Blvd.), West L.A. ℭ **310/441-9667**. Main courses $8–$13. DISC, MC, V. Mon–Thurs 11am–3pm and 5–10pm; Fri 11am–3pm and 5–10:30pm; Sat 9am–10:30pm; Sun 9am–10pm. Metered street parking.

Locanda Veneta ✿✿ NORTHERN ITALIAN   Locanda Veneta's citywide renown belies its tiny size and unpretentious setting. Its location, across from the unsightly monolith that is Cedars-Sinai Hospital, is a far cry from Venice's Grand Canal, and the single, loud, tightly packed dining room can sometimes feel like Piazza San Marco at the height of tourist season. But the sensible prices reflect the restaurant's efficient decor. While the dining room is decidedly unfancy, the kitchen is dead serious, making this restaurant a kind of temple for knowledgeable foodies. The soups are excellent, seafood dishes extraordinary, and pastas as good as they get. Signature dishes include pasta-and-bean soup, veal chops, lobster ravioli, shrimp risotto, and perfectly grilled vegetables. Though the dessert menu is long and tempting, I usually go for the *crema de vaniglia,* a dense, silky custard topped with caramel and chocolate sauces.

8638 W. 3rd St. (btw. San Vicente and Robertson boulevards), Los Angeles. ℭ **310/274-1893**. Reservations required. Main courses $31–$50. AE, MC, V. Mon–Fri 11:30am–2:30pm and 5:30–11pm; Sat 5:30–11pm; Sun 5–10pm. Valet parking $3.50.

Luckyfish ✿ SUSHI   Yes, another sushi restaurant in L.A., but this time with a clever twist. It's called *kaiten-zushi* style of dining, where sushi and sashimi wind through the restaurant on little covered plates via a conveyor belt (the term *kaiten* literally means "going in circles"). It's a common way to speedily dine on sushi in big, fast-paced cities like London and Tokyo, and if you've never tried it I think you'll find it highly entertaining. Everything about Luckyfish exudes modernity, from the gleaming white leather booths and nickel-plated chairs, to the ultra-modern 38-foot conveyer belt lined with little high-tech sushi plates—each with a radio frequency chip embedded in it so that, after 45 minutes, an unloved dish is automatically whisked off the belt and replaced with a fresh item. The chefs prepare about 100 different types of Japanese dishes—including entree items from the menu such as miso-marinated cod—and there's a little cheat-sheet on each table to help you identify the wide variety of nigiri sushi and rolls (it's a great way for the novice to learn about sushi). While it's not the best sushi in L.A., it's relatively inexpensive, you get to eye before you try, and it's fun. You'll like the location as well, in the heart of Beverly Hills amid all those ritzy boutiques. *Tip:* When you're sated on sushi, walk across the street to Nic's Martini Lounge and order their superb pear martini (yum).

338 N. Cañon Dr. (btw. Brighton and Dayton ways), Beverly Hills. ℭ **310/274-9800**. www.luckyfishsushi.com. Reservations not accepted. Main courses $9–$14. AE, DC, DISC, MC, V. Daily 11:30am–10:30pm. Valet parking $7.

Mimosa ✿✿ FRENCH PROVENÇAL   Decked out in traditional bistro garb (butter-yellow walls, artistic photos, French posters), this modest storefront restaurant attracts plenty of French expatriates and Euro-style denizens with a truly authentic menu. You won't get the classic French of caviar and truffles, but rather regional specialties such as rich veal *daube, andouillette* (tripe sausage), perfect steak fries, and a slow-cooked pork roast with horseradish lentils. The appetizer list usually includes a fantastic terrine, and bowls of house-cured *cornichons* (gherkins) and spicy Dijon mustard accompany bread to every table. Despite the occasional tinge of trendy attitude—usually precipitated by the presence of habitués like Tom Cruise and Jennifer Aniston dining on the house favorite, macaroni and cheese with prosciutto—you'll appreciate Mimosa for its casual, comforting bistro fare.

8009 Beverly Blvd. (west of Fairfax Ave.), Los Angeles. ℂ 323/655-8895. www.mimosarestaurant.com. Reservations recommended. Main courses $11–$26. AE, DC, MC, V. Tues–Sat 6–11pm. Metered street parking.

Nyala Ethiopian Cuisine 🗲🗲 *Value* ETHIOPIAN   There are no fewer than four Ethiopian eateries along two compact blocks of Fairfax, but our favorite is Nyala; it's one of the largest and still the most popular. In a mellow setting—all earthen colors, tribal prints, and African music—an ethnically mixed crowd finds common ground in the expertly spiced (smoldering rather than fiery) cuisine. For the uninitiated, Ethiopian food is a mosaic of chopped salads, chunky stews, and saucy vegetables, all served on a colorful enamel platter for communal enjoyment. There are no utensils, merely a basket of *injera*, the thick, sour, plate-size pancake that triples as utensil, plate, and bread. Choices range from hearty chicken or lamb chunks stewed with tomatoes and onions to a parade of vegetarian choices (lentils, chickpeas, greens), each with a distinctive marinade. African beers and honey wine are perfect accompaniments. *Tip:* The daily lunch buffet is a great deal.

1076 S. Fairfax Ave. (south of Olympic Blvd.), Los Angeles. ℂ 323/936-5918. www.nyala-la.com. Reservations suggested. Main courses $7–$12. AE, DC, MC, V. Daily 11:30am–11:30pm. Street parking.

Pastis 🗲🗲 FRENCH PROVENÇAL   Of the country French bistros in town, Pastis usually takes a back seat to the ultrahip, celebrity-frequented Mimosa (p. 134), which happens to be just a block away. But locals and regulars often prefer this rustic yet civilized spot, named for the licorice-flavored liqueur. Intimate and friendly, with sidewalk tables and a warmly ocher-toned dining room, Pastis manages to be both elegant and the kind of place where you can scrape your chair, raise your voice, or drink a little too much wine. Distinctive menu selections include wild striped bass papillote, the sautéed skate, Moroccan chicken tajine, and the Pastis bouillabaisse. Dessert lovers will swoon over the lavender crème brûlée.

8114 Beverly Blvd. (west of Crescent Heights Blvd.), Los Angeles. ℂ 323/655-8822. Reservations recommended. Main courses $15–$28. AE, MC, V. Sun–Thurs 6–10pm; Fri–Sat 6–11pm. Metered street parking or valet parking ($3.50).

Tanino Ristorante and Bar 🗲🗲 SOUTHERN ITALIAN   It's worth visiting Tanino just to marvel at the 1929 Italianate Renaissance–style building, one of only 12 remaining since Westwood's founding days. Designed by renowned Southern California architect Paul Revere Williams, the decor consists of magnificent original ceiling frescoes, carvings, murals, and artisan plaster that blends well with the checkerboard terrazzo marble flooring, dark hardwoods, sumptuous booths, wrought-iron chandeliers, and candlelit tables—an ideal setting for a romantic evening. Chef/owner Tanino Drago (scion of L.A.'s well-known Drago restaurateur family) has created a menu based on regional dishes from his native home of Sicily; most dishes are cooked *cartoccio*-style (in their own juices), such as lamb shank *osso buco* atop soft polenta, roasted rabbit in green Mediterranean olive sauce, and striped bass baked in papillote with white wine. Be sure to start with the pumpkin tortelloni in a light sage-and-cream sauce. A wide array of pasta and risotti is available as well. The charming Italian-accented servers add to the faux-Mediterranean atmosphere. *Tip:* Arrive a little early to enjoy a glass of grappa by the fireplace.

⌐Tips **Star Search: The Ivy League**

If you're searching for incognito celebrities dining among us common folk, casually stroll past the elevated sidewalk patio at the **Ivy** (p. 124), 113 N. Robertson Blvd. (btw. 3rd St. and Beverly Blvd.), West Hollywood, around 1pm. On a sunny day the odds are good (though the goods may be odd). If that doesn't pan out, walk over to the **Palm** (p. 129), 9001 Santa Monica Blvd. (btw. Doheny Dr. and Robertson Blvd.), West Hollywood, and order a Coca-Cola at the bar followed by a long, leisurely trip to the risqué bathroom.

1043 Westwood Blvd. (btw. Kinross and Weyburn sts.), Westwood. ✆ 310/208-0444. www.tanino.com. Reservations recommended. Main courses $11–$36. AE, DC, MC, V. Mon–Fri 11am–3pm and 5–11pm; Sat 5–11pm; Sun 4:30–10pm. Valet parking $5.

INEXPENSIVE

The Apple Pan ✪✪ SANDWICHES/AMERICAN   There are no tables, just a U-shape counter, at this classic American burger shack and hugely popular L.A. landmark. Open since 1947, the Apple Pan is a diner that looks—and acts—the part. It's famous for juicy burgers, grumpy service, and an authentic frills-free atmosphere. The hickory burger is best, though the tuna sandwich also has its share of fans. Ham, egg-salad, and Swiss-cheese sandwiches round out the menu. Definitely order fries, and if you're in the mood, the house-baked apple pie. Expect to wait a bit during the lunch rush (don't worry, the line moves pretty fast).

10801 Pico Blvd. (east of Westwood Blvd.), Los Angeles. ✆ 310/475-3585. Most menu items under $6. No credit cards. Tues–Thurs and Sun 11am–midnight; Fri–Sat 11am–1am. Free parking.

Nate 'n Al Delicatessen ✪✪ DELICATESSEN/BREAKFAST   If you want to know where old-money rich-and-famous types go for comfort food, look no further. Despite its location in the center of Beverly Hills's "Golden Triangle," Nate 'n Al has remained unchanged since 1945, from the Naugahyde booths to the motherly wait-resses, who treat you the same whether you're a house-account celebrity regular or just a visitor stopping in for an overstuffed pastrami on rye, beef brisket, or short ribs. The too-salty chicken soup keeps Nate 'n Al from being the best L.A. deli (actually, I'd be hard-pressed to choose any one deli as the city's best), but staples such as chopped liver, dense potato pancakes, blintzes, borscht, and well-dilled pickles more than make up for it. *Tip:* This is a little-known and low-rent hot spot for celebrity spying.

414 N. Beverly Dr. (at Brighton Way), Beverly Hills. ✆ 310/274-0101. Main courses $8–$16. AE, DISC, MC, V. Daily 7am–9pm. Free parking with validation.

Versailles ✪✪ *Value* CARIBBEAN/CUBAN   Outfitted with Formica tabletops and looking something like an ethnic IHOP, Versailles feels much like any number of restaurants in Miami that cater to the Cuban community. The menu reads like a veritable survey of Havana-style cookery and includes specialties such as "Moors and Christians" (flavorful black beans with white rice), *ropa vieja* (a stringy beef stew), and fried whole fish (usually sea bass). Anybody who's eaten here will tell you the same thing: "Order the shredded roast pork." Tossed with the restaurant's trademark garlic-citrus sauce, it's highly addictive. Equally fetching is the garlic chicken—succulent, slow roasted, and smothered in onions and garlic-citrus sauce. Almost everything is served with black beans and rice; wine and beer are available. Because meals are good, bountiful, and cheap, there's often a wait.

1415 S. La Cienega Blvd. (south of Pico Blvd.), Los Angeles. ② **310/289-0392.** Main courses $5–$13. AE, MC, V. Daily 11am–10pm. Free parking.

4 Hollywood & West Hollywood
EXPENSIVE

Campanile ✮✮✮ BRUNCH/CALIFORNIA-MEDITERRANEAN   Built as Charlie Chaplin's private offices in 1928, this Tuscan-style building has a multilevel layout with flower-bedecked interior balconies, a bubbling fountain, and a skylight through which diners can see the campanile (bell tower). Consistently ranked as one of L.A.'s finest restaurants, a meal here might begin with fried zucchini flowers drizzled with melted mozzarella or lamb carpaccio surrounded by artichoke leaves—a dish that arrives looking like one of van Gogh's sunflowers. Spago alumnus chef/owner Mark Peel heads up the kitchen and is particularly known for his grills and roasts. Try the wood-grilled prime rib smeared with black-olive tapenade; pappardelle with braised rabbit, roasted tomato, and collard greens; or the rosemary-charred lamb with artichokes and fava beans. The weekend brunch is a surprising crowd-pleaser and a terrific way to appreciate this beautiful space on a budget. One of the most popular nights is still Grilled Cheese night on Thursdays, when the bar fills up with regular fans of haute versions of the childhood treat. *Tip:* On Monday nights chef Peel offers a $40 three-course family-style themed menu that's been voted Best Monday Night Dinner by *Los Angeles Magazine.*

624 S. La Brea Ave. (north of Wilshire Blvd.), ② **323/938-1447.** www.campanilerestaurant.com. Reservations required. Main courses $26–$38. AE, DC, DISC, MC, V. Mon–Wed 11:30am–2:30pm and 6–10pm; Thurs–Fri 11:30am–2:30pm and 5:30–11pm; Sat 9:30am–1:30pm and 5:30–11pm; Sun 9:30am–1:30pm. Valet parking $5.50.

Citizen Smith ✮✮ MODERN AMERICAN   Hip Hollywood restaurants geared toward the club scene tend to open and close faster than I can finish this review, but I'm hoping that Citizen Smith will be an exception. Unlike most of the dig-me diners in this area, the model/actor waitstaff here—and beautiful they are—actually care that you have an enjoyable dining experience. And because the menu is all about upscale comfort food (which is pretty hard to screw up), the cuisine is pleasing as well, both in quality and quantity. The dimly lit, high-ceiling interior is replete with avant-garde appointments, the coup de grâce being the giant tubular chandeliers lined with translucent prints of women's faces. The meaty menu, however, will bring you back on familiar ground: Angus half-pound burgers, aged cuts of prime beef, center-cut pork chops, plump fried chicken breasts, and the requisite bowel-bursting sides such as mac and cheese, whipped potatoes, and onion rings. If you prefer dining alfresco, the back alley has been converted into a patio, but chances are good you'll be sitting next to young smokers. The restaurant converts into a club at around 11pm, so unless

---

Grilled Cheese Night

Every Thursday evening Campanile (see review above) hosts a hugely popular Grilled Cheese Night. The menu offers 12 different gourmet sandwiches along with appetizers.

you want people dancing next to your table as you're starting on dessert (which is what happened to me), I suggest you arrive before 8pm.

1600 N. Cahuenga Blvd., Hollywood. © 323/461-5001. www.citizensmith.com. Reservations recommended. Main courses $10–$42. AE, MC, V. Mon–Fri 11am–3pm and 6pm–2am; Sat–Sun 11am–2am. Valet parking $7.

Dar Maghreb 🌶🌶 MOROCCAN   If you're a lone diner in search of a quick bite, this isn't the place for you. Dinner at Dar Maghreb is an entertaining dining experience that improves exponentially the larger your party and the longer you linger. Enter an exotic Arab world of genie waitresses who wash your hands with warm water and belly dancers who shimmy around an exquisite fountain in the center of a patio. You'll feel like a guest in an ornately tiled palace as you dine at traditional tables on either low sofas or goatskin cushions.

Nothing is available a la carte here. The fixed-price meal is a multicourse feast, starting with bread and traditional Moroccan salads, followed by *b'stilla,* an appetizer of shredded chicken, eggs, almonds, and spices wrapped in a flaky pastry shell and topped with powdered sugar and cinnamon. The main courses—your choice of lamb, quail, chicken, and more—are each sublimely seasoned and delectable. Perhaps it's the atmosphere that makes everyone eat more than they expected, but you'll be thankful that dessert is a simple fruit-and-nut basket, accompanied by warm mint tea poured into traditional glasses. All is eaten with your hands—a sensual experience that grows on you as the night progresses.

7651 Sunset Blvd. (corner of Stanley Ave.). © 323/876-7651. www.darmaghrebrestaurant.com. Reservations recommended. Fixed-price dinner $37. DC, MC, V. Mon–Fri 6–11pm; Sat 5:30–11pm; Sun 5:30–10:30pm. Valet parking $4.50.

Grace 🌶🌶🌶 NEW AMERICAN   I'm going to start an argument here by stating that Grace is the best restaurant in Los Angeles. I dined here with two friends, and everything was flawless: the service, the cuisine, the wine, the decor—even the patrons were well dressed, well-behaved, and unpretentious (a rarity in this town). High ceilings, well-spaced tables, and soothing earth tones of orange, green, brown, and rose evoke a relaxed atmosphere at Grace, which is fortuitous because you'll want to slowly savor each dish created by executive chef and co-owner Neal Fraser, a culinary scion of Wolfgang Puck, Thomas Keller, and Joachim Splichal, an Iron Chef veteran. Our memorable dinner started with plump Kumamoto oysters with a trio of superb dipping sauces, a roast beet salad with grilled radicchio and onion marmalade, pumpkin risotto with sea urchin and sweet Maine shrimp, a carpaccio of tuna with fried green olives and pepper vinaigrette, and the most beautiful plate of foie gras I've ever seen (and I live for foie gras), served both as a pâté and sautéed with pistachio-cocoa nib crust and a dab of huckleberry compote. Entrees included generous servings of wildboar tenderloin with violet mustard sauce, and slow-braised pork shank with smoked shallots and cider-sage sauce—both paired with an excellent pinot noir by the glass. The coup de grâce of our unrivaled meal was a sublime warm Cajeta bread pudding topped with pumpkin-seed ice cream. Yes, it's expensive, but if you're going to splurge on a meal in L.A., Grace is where I'd go.

7360 Beverly Blvd. (at N. Fuller Ave.), Los Angeles. © 323/934-4400. www.gracerestaurant.com. Reservations recommended. Main courses $26–$38. AE, DC, DISC, MC, V. Tues–Thurs 6–10:30pm; Fri–Sat 6–11pm; Sun 6–10pm. Valet parking $5.50.

Katana Robata & Sushi Bar 🌶🌶 JAPANESE ROBATA   In the City of Sushi you need to stand out from the crowd if you want to run a successful Japanese restaurant. And that's just what they did at Katana. They hired red-hot designer Dodd Mitchell

Where to Dine in the Hollywood Area

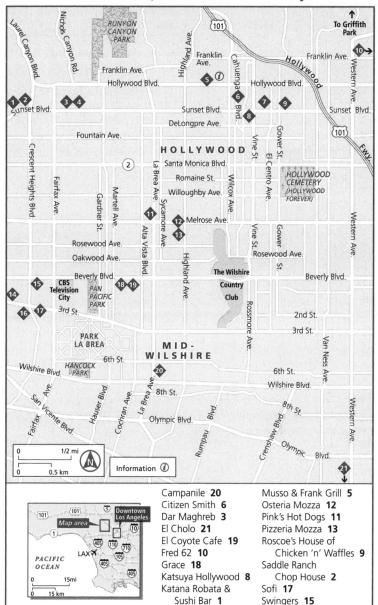

Campanile **20**
Citizen Smith **6**
Dar Maghreb **3**
El Cholo **21**
El Coyote Cafe **19**
Fred 62 **10**
Grace **18**
Katsuya Hollywood **8**
Katana Robata &
    Sushi Bar **1**
Kings Road Cafe **14**
The Little Door **16**

Musso & Frank Grill **5**
Osteria Mozza **12**
Pink's Hot Dogs **11**
Pizzeria Mozza **13**
Roscoe's House of
    Chicken 'n' Waffles **9**
Saddle Ranch
    Chop House **2**
Sofi **17**
Swingers **15**
Toi on Sunset **4**
The Waffle **7**

Dining in the Dark

Imagine dining at a restaurant where your entire meal—bread, salad, entree, dessert, wine—is served in complete darkness. The pitch kind, where you can't see the person you're talking to you or your hand in front of your face. It's called Dining in the Dark, a nouveau European dining trend where specially trained blind or sight-impaired waitstaff serve **three-course meals in a pitch-black dining room.** Brought to the U.S. for the first time by German entrepreneur Ben Uphues, this highly entertaining event starts in a lighted lobby at the Hyatt West Hollywood, where you select your dinner and drinks from a set menu, then you're introduced and escorted by your waiter to the darkened dining room. It's a bit eerie and awkward at first (I buttered my hand more than once), but we were surprised at how quickly our other senses kicked into overdrive to make up for our loss of vision. Granted, the first few attempts at getting my Moroccan-barbecued salmon from fork to mouth were comical, but once I got my bearings I was pouring wine and sharing bites with aplomb. From the laughter emanating throughout the darkened dining room it appeared everyone else was enjoying their sightless experience as well. The evening isn't cheap—$99 per person, not including gratuity and drinks—but I guarantee this will be a dining experience that you'll never forget. It takes places most Friday and Saturday nights; for more information, log onto www.darkdining.com, or call ℰ **800/710-1270.**

to give the restaurant sex appeal by using aesthetically pleasing accents such as steel beams, perforated metallic screens, exotic woods, and worn brick. Next they introduced robata-yaki to mainstream L.A.—a traditional Japanese style of cooking where meats, fish, and vegetables are cooked on small bamboo skewers over imported *bincho tan* coal that imparts a unique smoky essence to the food. Lastly, they trained their waitstaff well (a rarity in L.A.), hired a sake sommelier to create the city's best sake list, and converted the patio above Sunset Boulevard into a coveted alfresco dining area. The result? Well, make a reservation at least a week in advance, because the only walk-in seating you'll find is at the sushi and robata bars. Yes, the sushi is very good, but it's the incredibly flavorful skewers that you'll want to sample: foie gras and asparagus wrapped with filet mignon, fresh lobster with a peppercorn-miso glaze, giant seared scallops with shiitake mushrooms, Kurobuta pork and pineapple drizzled with plum sauce (okay, now I'm hungry). Each comes with a trio of dipping sauces, adding yet more complexity to the mingling of flavors. Sushi, tempura, steak, and noodles are available as well. Be sure to start the adventure with a $15 Sake Sampler and a glass of their house-special Red Sun beer, brewed exclusively for the restaurant.

8439 W Sunset Blvd. (near La Cienega Blvd.), West Hollywood. ℰ **323/650-8585.** www.katanarobata.com. Reservations recommended. Main courses $11–$44. AE, DC, DISC, MC, V. Dinner Sun–Mon 6–11pm; Tues–Wed 6–11:30pm; Thurs–Sat 6pm–12:30am. Valet parking $7.

Katsuya Hollywood ✿✿✿ JAPANESE   Every year somebody opens an über-hip new restaurant that has all the L.A. foodies and snooties agog, and this time it's the opening of Katsuya Hollywood. Capitalizing on their raging success of the original Katsuya in Brentwood, the SBE Restaurant & Nightlife Group spent a small fortune hiring celebrated designer Philippe Starck to collaborate with Master Sushi Chef Katsuya Uechi and create a shrine to sushi and design (at Hollywood and Vine!). Looking more like a scene from a David Lynch movie than a restaurant, the decor is an intriguing mix of gleaming white leather and chrome furniture, overblown images of a geisha's facial parts, and a sinister black banner bearing the *kanji* symbol for Katsuya, who is one of only four Master Sushi Chefs in Los Angeles. Katsuya's must-try signature dishes include the crispy rice with spicy tuna, the Kobe filet with foie gras and plum soy sauce, and the baked white fish with truffle in a shell of salt. But if you really want the true Katsuya experience, throw down a Franklin and order *omakase*—a chef's choice selection of the freshest fish available. Reservations may be difficult to get, particularly on a weekend night, so be sure to call as far in advance as possible.

6300 Hollywood Blvd. (at Vine St.), Hollywood. (C) **323/871-8777.** www.sbe.com/katsuya. Reservations recommended. Main courses $12–$28. AE, DC, DISC, MC, V. Mon–Fri 11am–3pm and 5pm–midnight; Sat–Sun 11am–1am. Valet parking $6.

The Little Door ★★ FRENCH MEDITERRANEAN   For more than a decade this provincial hideaway off 3rd Street has been voted one of L.A.'s most romantic restaurants. From the street all you see is a high fence and two carved little wooden doors, but pass through them and *voilà!*—a bastion of quaint French countryside in the midst of the bustling city. The Little Door consists of four dining areas situated throughout a converted cottage-style house, the most popular being the "Patio" with its tile fountain, koi pond, wrought-iron candelabras, and lush greenery. If you can't get a table here, ask for one in the back room by the fireplace, which is both quieter and roomier. Fittingly, the cuisine is French/Mediterranean, ranging from a terrine of duck foie gras with strawberries to pistachio-encrusted scallops with Moroccan greens to rosemary-encrusted rack of lamb in a parsnip purée. Because the chef shops at the local farmer's market daily, the menu changes often—ergo, be sure to ask your waiter for recommendations. All wines on the list are also served by the glass, which makes for some fun wine paring with the medley of menu choices. Caveats? It's pricey ($30 for fettuccine?), the tables are a tad too close together, and the attitude from the servers can be a bit . . . er . . . French as well. But when it all comes together perfectly—the candlelit table you requested, an attentive waiter, a warm summer night, you looking marvelous in the candlelight, a nice glass of wine, a soupçon of foie gras melting on your tongue—it's easy to see why the Little Door is where the locals go when they're in the mood for romance.

8164 W. 3rd St. (btw. Crescent Heights and La Jolla sts.), Los Angeles. (C) **323/951-1210.** www.thelittledoor.com. Reservations recommended. Main courses $30–$48. AE, MC, V. Mon–Thurs 6–10:30pm; Fri–Sat 6–11:30pm. Valet parking $5.50.

MODERATE

El Coyote Cafe ★★ *Value* MEXICAN   Everyone from 20-something hipsters to slick showbiz player-types, rockers, movie stars, and regular folk like yourself can be found at this family-owned cantina that has been around since 1931. The rowdy bar scene alone is a great reason to hang out at this highly popular (yet eminently affordable) Mexican restaurant. During prime dining hours, the restaurant's bustling atmosphere spills over into the bar, which is frequently crowded to capacity. Settle in by sampling from the *grande*-size menu of appetizers such as taquitos, quesadillas, and nachos, and be sure to wash them down with a couple of World Famous House Margaritas (a bargain at $4.50). The fare is traditional Mexican and well prepared; recommended plates include the enchilada Howard smothered with chile con carne, ostrich tacos (yes, ostrich), and sizzling fajita platters.

7312 Beverly Blvd. (at N. Poinsettia Place), Los Angeles. (© 323/939-2255. www.elcoyotecafe.com. Main courses $8–$10. AE, MC, V. Mon–Thurs and Sun 11am–10pm; Fri–Sat 11am–11pm.

Kings Road Cafe ♠♠ AMERICAN   This is the cafe you wish was down the street from your place instead of that Starbucks. The Kings Road Cafe has the perfect combo of everything you'd want in a neighborhood cafe—sunny sidewalk seating along bustling Beverly Boulevard, excellent coffee served in big bowl-like cups, great people-watching, attitude-free service, the occasional celebrity sighting, a huge magazine stand right next door, and fresh, healthy, inexpensive food served in large portions. It's open from morning until night, so you can drop by anytime for such local favorites as their banana-pecan buttermilk pancakes, fluffy French toast, spinach and shiitake mushroom omelet, chipotle chicken salad, Baja fish tacos, blackened ahi with sweet mashed potatoes, and their signature panini-style sandwiches (the chicken breast with garlic aioli is my favorite). You can pretty much count on waiting for an outside table on weekends, but it gives you time to do a bit of inconspicuous star searching, pick up a few magazines, and check out the Kings Road Cafe Bakery next door (the black currant scones are wonderful).

8361 Beverly Blvd. (at Kings Rd.), Los Angeles. (© 323/655-9044. www.kingsroadcafe.com. Reservations not accepted. Main courses lunch/dinner $8–$14, breakfast $6–$11. MC, V. Mon–Sat 7:30am–10pm; Sun 7:30am–7pm. Metered street parking.

Musso & Frank Grill ♠♠ AMERICAN/CONTINENTAL   A survey of Hollywood restaurants that leaves out Musso & Frank is like a study of Las Vegas singers that fails to mention Wayne Newton. As Hollywood's oldest eatery (since 1919), Musso & Frank is the paragon of Old Hollywood grillrooms. This is where Faulkner and Hemingway drank during their screenwriting days and where Orson Welles used to hold court. The restaurant is still known for its bone-dry martinis and perfectly seasoned bloody marys. The setting is what you'd expect: oak-beamed ceilings, gruff red-coated waiters, red-leather booths and banquettes, mahogany room dividers, and chandeliers with tiny shades. The extensive old-school menu is a veritable survey of American/Continental cookery. Hearty dinners include veal scaloppini Marsala, roast spring lamb with mint jelly, and broiled lobster. Grilled meats (particularly the Welsh rabbit) are a specialty, as is the Thursday-only chicken potpie. Regulars also flock in for Musso's trademark flannel cakes, crepe-thin pancakes flipped to order. *Tip:* Sit at either the counter for the full M&F effect, or request table no. 1 in the west room, which was Charlie Chaplin's regular table.

6667 Hollywood Blvd. (at Cherokee Ave.), Los Angeles. (© 323/467-7788. Reservations recommended. Main courses $13–$32. AE, DC, MC, V. Tues–Sat 11am–11pm. Self-parking $2.25 with validation.

Osteria Mozza ♠♠♠ ITALIAN   When's the last time you had a dining experience that was so wonderful you kept thinking about for days afterward? If it's been too long, come here. If you've read my review of Pizzeria Mozza (see below), then you already know what a fan I am of Nancy Silverton and Mario Batali. Well, nothing succeeds like success, and they've opened yet another restaurant together, right next to their original—an airy, lively, Italianesque space with a central free-standing mozzarella bar of dark wood and marble (Nancy's helm), a full bar along the south wall with beautiful millwork, and an indoor/outdoor dining area that opens onto Melrose Avenue. Osteria Mozza continues the Silverton-Batali formula of using only the finest and freshest ingredients to create dishes gleaned from their culinary adventures in New York and Bologna. The result is small-dish heaven for the adventurous epicurean, and of the dozen or so dishes we ordered—all praiseworthy—these were the stand-outs: the fresh ricotta and egg ravioli with browned butter, the monkfish *alla diavolo,* the bufala mozzarella with caperberry relish (sigh), and for dessert the *bombolini,* a huckleberry compote with vanilla gelato. Reservations can be tough, so make them as far in advance as possible, and take me with you.

6602 Melrose Ave. (at N. Highland Ave.), Los Angeles. (C) **323/297-0100.** www.mozza-la.com. Reservations recommended. Main courses $17–$29. AE, MC, V. Mon–Fri 5:30–11pm; Sat 5–11pm; Sun 5–10pm. Valet parking $6.

Pizzeria Mozza ★★ ITALIAN   One of the hardest reservations to get in town is at this little pizza place on the corner of Melrose and Highland. Locals are calling up to a month in advance for an opportunity to experience celeb-chef Nancy Silverton's arti-sanal pies. Nancy's passion for all things Italian and bread-related—she founded the famed La Brea Bakery—has culminated in her quest for baking the perfect Italian-style pizza (which, according to her, is all in the crust). So when she and chef/restau-rateur Mario Batali partnered in an attempt to create the best pizza outside of Italy, L.A.'s foodies swooned and surged. I had to call a friend of Nancy's just to reserve a table, and I still had to wait 20 minutes (then again, so did Scarlet Johansson and Paul Reiser, which made me feel a little better). In contrast to the restaurant's celebrity sta-tus, the ambience and decor are entirely unpretentious. The interior consists of a box-like space with a high ceiling, a small wine bar, about a dozen tables, some counter seating, and an open kitchen where Nancy can usually be spotted most evenings ensuring quality control. The menu is modest as well—about 15 styles of pizza, a spe-cial entree each day of the week, and several small plates of antipasti, panini, bruschette, insalate, and salami. The pizzas are small and inexpensive enough for everyone to order their own. Favorites are the house-made fennel sausage with panna and red onion; the Gorgonzola dolce with fingerling potatoes, radicchio, and rose-mary; and the rapini with black olives, cherry tomatoes, and anchovies. But the top-pings are secondary to Nancy's complex crust—in true Italian style each is wafer thin in the middle, yet impossibly puffy, crunchy, and flavorful on the edges (I dare you to replicate it in your kitchen). Fittingly, the wines are all Italian, and moderately priced between $25 and $50. The only common complaint I've heard so far is the noise level—with so many people packed into such a small space, you'll need to speak up to be heard. Oh, and make that reservation now.

641 N. Highland Ave. (at Melrose Ave.), Los Angeles. (C) **323/297-0101.** www.mozza-la.com. Reservations recommended. Main courses $11–$20. AE, MC, V. Daily noon–midnight. Valet parking $6.

Saddle Ranch Chop House AMERICAN   Let's say you wake up one morning in L.A. and you say to yourself, "Hey, I'm really in a mood to ride a mechanical bull today." Well, pardner, you're in luck. Smack-dab on the Sunset Strip is the Saddle Ranch Chop House, a sort of wild-west Hard Rock Cafe where everything is done Texas-style—the drinks are tall and stiff, the platters of fried chicken and ribs are ginormous, and when a buxom cowgirl is riding the bull like a rodeo pro, the fellers tend to get a bit loco. The huge pinewood building—fashioned after an Old Western saloon complete with dummy prostitutes perched on the lanai—is impossible to miss. If the weather's warm you'll want a table on the large patio fronting Sunset Boulevard,

---

Tips Hallelujah!: A Brunch Worth Singing About

Have mercy and say "Hallelujah!" for the Gospel Brunch at the **House of Blues** (8430 Sunset Blvd., West Hollywood; www.hob.com). For more than a decade, it's been a Sunday tradition at the HOB to feed both the body and soul with inspiring gospel performances and heaping plates of all-you-can-eat Southern home cookin'. Every week different gospel groups from around the region perform uplifting and energetic music that invariably gets the crowd on its feet and raising the roof. Seatings are every Sunday at 10am and 1pm. Tickets are $40, including tax and gratuity, and are available only through the HOB Sunset Strip box office; call ℂ **323/848-5100.**

---

and after dinner you can roast s'mores at the stone campfire pits. Then mosey up to the circular bar inside to get your drink on (if y'all are beer drinkers, ask about the Beer Tower) and watch the tourists flail around on the mechanical bull. Yes, they lay on the cheesy Western theme a bit thick, and no local would ever admit going to such a blatant tourist trap, but after a couple of Texas Tea Party cocktails, you can't help but loosen up and get into the hoedown spirit. And after your third Texas Tea Party, you'll even ponder a go at riding the bull (you'll chicken out, of course, but you'll ponder it). *Note:* There's a second Saddle Ranch location at the Universal Studio's CityWalk (ℂ **818/760-9680**), near the entrance to the park.

8371 Sunset Blvd. (at La Cienega Blvd.), West Hollywood. ℂ 323/656-2007. www.srrestaurants.com. Reservations recommended for dinner. Main courses dinner $10–$35, lunch $6–$23, breakfast $9–$16. AE, DC, DISC, MC, V. Daily 8am–2am. Valet parking free before 4pm, $4 with validation.

Sofi ⭐⭐ *Finds* GREEK   Look for the simple black awning over the narrow passageway that leads from the street to this hidden Aegean treasure. Be sure to ask for a table on the romantic patio amid twinkling lights, and immediately order a plate of their thick, satisfying *tsatziki* (yogurt-cucumber-garlic spread) accompanied by a basket of warm pita for dipping. Other hearty tavern favorites (recipes courtesy of Sofi's old-world grandmother) include herbed rack of lamb with rice, fried calamari salad, and *saganaki* (kasseri cheese flamed with ouzo). Sofi's odd, off-street setting, near the Farmers Market in a popular part of town, has made it an insiders' secret.

8030¾ W. 3rd St. (btw. Fairfax Ave. and Crescent Heights Blvd.), Los Angeles. ℂ 323/651-0346. Reservations recommended. Main courses $7–$14. AE, DC, MC, V. Mon–Sat 11:30am–2:30pm and 5:30–11pm; Sun 5:30–11pm. Metered street parking or valet parking $3.

INEXPENSIVE

El Cholo ⭐⭐ MEXICAN   L.A.'s oldest Mexican restaurant (Gary Cooper and Bing Crosby were regulars, and Jack Nicholson and Warren Beatty still are), El Cholo has been serving up authentic Mexican cuisine in this pink adobe hacienda since 1925, even though the once-outlying mid-Wilshire neighborhood around it has since turned into Koreatown. El Cholo *muy* strong margaritas, invitingly messy nachos—the first served in the U.S.—and classic combination dinners don't break new culinary ground, but the kitchen has perfected these standards over 80 years (I wish they bottled their rich enchilada sauce). Other specialties include seasonally available green-corn tamales and creative sizzling vegetarian fajitas that go way beyond just eliminating the meat. The atmosphere is festive, as people from all parts of town dine happily in the many rambling rooms that compose the restaurant. There's valet parking as well as a free self-parking lot directly across the street. Westsiders head to El Cholo's Santa Monica branch at 1025 Wilshire Blvd. (at 11th St.; © **310/899-1106**). *Note:* Be prepared for a long wait on weekends.

1121 S. Western Ave. (south of Olympic Blvd.), Los Angeles. © **323/734-2773**. www.elcholo.com. Reservations suggested. Main courses $8–$15. AE, DC, DISC, MC, V. Mon–Sat 11am–10pm; Sun 11am–9pm. Free self-parking or valet parking $5.

Fred 62 AMERICAN/BREAKFAST   Opened in the heart of trendy Los Feliz by chef Fred Eric, this slightly skewed 24-hour coffee shop comes by its retro kitsch honestly. Eric remodeled the tiny corner diner with spiffy 1950s car-culture icons, including hood-ornament sconces and blue service-station smocks for the waitstaff. He then named it after himself (and his birth year, 1962) and peppered the menu with puns and inside jokes. There's a daily "cream of what Fred wants" soup, plus sandwiches (the smoked salmon is great), burgers, salads, tofu scrambles, and a handful of Asian noodle bowls, including "SEOUL-FULL NOO*DEL–I," a cryptic name for Korean potato-starch noodles, vegetables, and sesame dressing in hot broth. You might feel like you've stepped into a Route 66 beatnik diner in TV land, but the clientele is very real and the food is comforting (slow service, though). Don't miss the house-made potato chips, "punk tarts," and fresh lemonade dispensed from a churning tank on the counter.

1850 N. Vermont Ave., at Russell Ave., Los Feliz. © **323/667-0062**. www.fred62.com. Main courses $4–$14. MC, V. Daily 24 hr. Metered street parking.

Pink's Hot Dogs *(Kids* SANDWICHES/BURGERS/HOT DOGS   Pink's isn't your usual guidebook recommendation, but then again, this corner stand isn't your typical hot dog shack. Name another hot dog stand that has its own valet who deftly parks the stream of Rolls-Royces and Mercedes that pull up regularly. This L.A. icon grew around the late Paul and Betty Pink, who opened for business in 1939 selling 10¢ wieners from a used hot dog cart. Now 2,000 of them are served every day on Pink's soft steamed rolls. There are 24 varieties of dogs available, many of them coined by the celebrities who order them. Martha Stewart once stopped her caravan to order a 10-incher with mustard, relish, onions, chopped tomatoes, sauerkraut, bacon, and sour cream, and now you too can order a "Martha Stewart" dog. The heartburn-inducing chili dogs (made from Betty's chili formula that's still a secret) are craved by even the most upstanding, health-conscious Angelenos. There's lots of folklore emanating from this wiener shack as well: Bruce Willis reportedly proposed to Demi Moore in the parking lot, and Orson Welles holds the record for the most hot dogs consumed in one sitting (18). Even though the dogs are churned out every 30 seconds, expect to wait in line even at midnight—you'll invariably meet a true crossroads of Los Angeles cultures. Pray that greedy developers spare this little nugget of Americana.

709 N. La Brea Ave. (at Melrose Ave.), Los Angeles. © **323/931-4223**. www.pinkshollywood.com. Chili dog $2.85. No credit cards. Sun–Thurs 9:30am–2am; Fri–Sat 9:30am–3am.

Roscoe's House of Chicken 'n' Waffles BREAKFAST/SOUTHERN   It sounds like a bad joke—fried chicken and waffles on the same plate. But Roscoe's is one of those places that you have to visit at least once to see how it works (and judging by the wait, it definitely works). This Hollywood institution's proximity to CBS Television City has turned this Harlem-inspired restaurant into a kind of de facto commissary for the network. A chicken-and-cheese omelet isn't everyone's ideal way to begin the day, but it's de rigueur at Roscoe's. At lunch, few calorie-unconscious diners can resist the juicy fried chicken smothered in gravy and onions, a house specialty that's served with waffles or grits and biscuits. Large chicken-salad bowls and chicken sandwiches also provide plenty of cluck for the buck. Homemade corn bread, sweet-potato pie, homemade potato salad, and corn on the cob are available as side orders. Granted, the waffles are of Eggo quality and come with enough whipped butter to stop your heart, but the Southern-fried chicken is addictive. *Tip:* The waffles tend to come a bit undercooked, so ask for them crispy.

1514 N. Gower St. (at Sunset Blvd.), Los Angeles. (🕿) **323/466-7453.** www.roscoeschickenandwaffles.com. Main courses $4–$15. No credit cards. Sun–Thurs 9am–midnight; Fri–Sat 8:30am–4am. Metered street parking.

Swingers AMERICAN/TRADITIONAL/BREAKFAST   Resurrected from a motel coffee shop, Swingers was transformed by a couple of L.A. hipster nightclub owners into a 1990s version of comfy Americana. The interior seems like a slice of the 1950s until you notice the plaid upholstery and Warhol-esque graphics, which contrast nicely with the retro red-white-and-blue Swingers logo adorning *everything.* Guests at the attached Beverly Laurel Motor Hotel chow down alongside body-pierced industry hounds from nearby record companies, while a soundtrack that runs the gamut from punk rock to *Schoolhouse Rock* plays in the background. It's not all attitude, though—you'll enjoy a menu of high-quality diner favorites with trendy crowd-pleasers: Steel-cut Irish oatmeal, challah French toast, grilled Jamaican jerk chicken, and a selection of tofu-enhanced vegetarian dishes are just a few of the eclectic offerings. Sometimes I just swing by for a malt or milkshake to go—they're among the best in town. *Note:* There's a second location in Santa Monica at 802 Broadway (at Lincoln Ave.; (🕿) **310/393-9793**).

8020 Beverly Blvd. (west of Fairfax Ave.), Los Angeles. (🕿) **323/653-5858.** www.swingersdiner.com. Most items less than $8. AE, DISC, MC, V. Daily 6am–4am. Metered street parking.

Toi on Sunset 🌟🌟 *(Value)* THAI   Because it's open *really* late, Toi has become an instant fave of Hollywood hipsters such as Sean Penn and Woody Harrelson, who make postclubbing excursions to this rock-'n'-roll eatery a few blocks from the Sunset Strip. After all the hype, I was surprised to find possibly L.A.'s best bargain Thai food, authentically prepared and served in portions so generous the word *enormous* seems inadequate. Menu highlights include hot-and-sour chicken, coconut soup, and the house specialty: chicken curry *somen,* a spicy dish with green curry and mint sauce spooned over thin Japanese rice noodles. Vegetarians will be pleased with the vast selection of meat-free items such as *pad kee mao,* rice noodles served spicy with tofu, mint, onions, peppers, and chili. The interior is a noisy amalgam of cultish movie posters, rock-'n'-roll memorabilia, and haphazardly placed industrial-issue dinette sets; and the plates, flatware, and drinking glasses are cheap coffee-shop issue. In other words, it's all about the food and the scene—neither will disappoint.

   Westsiders can opt for Toi on Wilshire, 1120 Wilshire Blvd., Santa Monica ((🕿) **310/ 394-7804**), open daily from 11am to 3am.

7505½ Sunset Blvd. (at Gardner St.), Los Angeles. (🕿) **323/874-8062.** www.toirockinthaifood.com. Reservations accepted only for parties of 6 or more. Main courses $6–$11. AE, DISC, MC, V. Daily 11am–4am.

The Waffle 🌟🌟 NOUVEAU AMERICAN   This is another one of those restaurants that you wish was right down the street from where you lived. It's got everything on the menu a country girl needs to survive, and then some. The Waffle is the brainchild of Chef Scooter Kanfer-Cartmill, a protégé of Wolfgang Puck and one of the most well-respected chefs in L.A. Her philosophy is that "you can have plenty of fun, even with serious food," and that's exactly what she serves up at her neo-classic American coffee shop. Plop your bum in a booth, rest your elbows on the Formica table, and ponder her enticingly eclectic menu while sipping good coffee from a plain ol' white mug: cornmeal jalapeno waffles, French toast soaked in vanilla bean custard, chicken potpie with flakey buttermilk biscuit crust. Oy vey! This being no ordinary diner, the Waffle also has a full bar and even a signature cocktail—the Maple Syrup Martini. And this being L.A., there's also a fair selection of vegan and vegetarian items, such as Scooter's vegan Ruben with tofurkey and soy cheese. Friendly service too. Trust me, you'll wish the Waffle was near your home too.

6255 W. Sunset Blvd. (at Vine St.), Los Angeles. ℭ 323/465-6901. www.thewaffle.us. Reservations not accepted. Main courses $8–$12. AE, DC, DISC, MC, V. Sun–Thurs 6:30am–2:30am; Fri–Sat 6:30am–4:30am.

5 Downtown

EXPENSIVE

Arnie Morton's Steakhouse ★★ STEAK/SEAFOOD   The best steakhouse in Downtown is Arnie Morton's, the legendary steakhouse chain with branches as far flung as Hong Kong. You'll often see both movie and sports celebrities here, knocking down the cocktails and trying their best to polish off a porterhouse. Located below street level, the windowless restaurant has that old-fashioned Midwestern steakhouse feel to it: dark mahogany woods, brass fittings, high-backed leather booths, white table linens, and a tuxedoed maitre d' who warmly greets you as he escorts you to your table. There's no menu to peruse; rather, the waiter pushes a cart to your table and does a well-rehearsed show-and-tell presentation of the Saran-wrapped meats, vegetables, and seafood available (including a giant live lobster that looks mighty forlorn). House specialties are the double filet mignon, the 48-ounce porterhouse for two, and the rib-eye, with a baked Idaho on the side and a slice of Key lime pie for dessert. Lamb chops, chicken, and swordfish steaks are available as well, but it's the cuts of Chicago grain-fed cow that have made Morton's the godfather of American steakhouses.

735 S. Figueroa (at 7th St.), Los Angeles. ℭ 213/553-4566. www.mortons.com. Reservations recommended. Main courses dinner $26–$84, lunch $13–$27. AE, DC, MC, V. Mon–Fri 11:30am–11pm; Sat 5:30–11pm; Sun 5–10pm. Valet parking $6.

Patina ★★ FRENCH   When celebrity L.A. restaurateur Joachim Splichal moved his flagship Patina restaurant from Melrose Avenue to the new Walt Disney Concert Hall, it raised one pertinent question: "Is it as good as the old Patina?" If you arrived after a performance ended, you wouldn't hear the answer anyway. Billowing walls of laser-cut walnut and floor-to-ceiling glass panels only augment the hubbub as droves of smartly clad fans of the performing arts dine on Splichal's signature dishes of wild game and the de rigueur ahi tuna appetizer. The après-show performances continue with a trio of carts—mounds of caviar, giant rib-eye steaks for two, and expensive cheeses—crisscross the dining room. My dinner started with soft, thin slices of hamachi matched with green-apple granite and mango, met its match with the seared foie gras atop caramel-poached apples, and segued into an entree of crispy skinned yellowtail snapper served on a bed of fava bean purée. Dishes I reluctantly passed on included a puff pastry–encrusted grouse with caramelized endive-and-black-olive reduction sauce, sautéed black-truffled Brussels sprouts with a sweet-potato purée, and roasted venison loin with porcini–foie gras polenta. Vegetarian dishes and wine pairings are also available, as are prix-fixe theater menus. Jackets are suggested but not required for dinner, and valet service is recommended as it's a bit of a hike from the nearest pay lot. *Tip:* If you want a quiet, romantic dinner, ask the hostess to schedule it at the *start* of a performance.

141 S. Grand Ave. (near 1st St.), Los Angeles. (②) 213/972-3331. www.patinagroup.com. Reservations recommended. Main courses dinner $31–$45, lunch $15–$30. AE, DC, MC, V. Lunch Tues–Fri 11:30am–1:30pm; dinner Tues–Sat 5–9:30pm, Sun 4–9:30pm (on L.A. Philharmonic performance evenings, dinner Tues–Sat 5–11pm, Sun 4–10:30pm). Valet parking $8.

Water Grill 😄😄 SEAFOOD   Widely considered by L.A. foodies to be the best seafood house in the city, Water Grill is popular with the suit-and-tie crowd at lunch and with concertgoers en route to the Music Center at night. The dining room is a stylish and sophisticated fusion of wood, leather, and brass, but it gets a lighthearted lift from cavorting papier-mâché fish that play against an aquamarine ceiling painted with bubbles. The restaurant is known for its shellfish; among the appetizers are a dozen different oysters, Nantucket Bay scallops with Queensland blue pumpkin, and crispy sweetbreads with crayfish, chanterelles, and roasted asparagus. Main courses are imaginative dishes influenced by the cuisines of Hawaii, the Pacific Northwest, New Orleans, and New England. A good start to the feast is the appetizer seafood platter, a mouthwatering assortment served with well-made aioli. Other selections from the menu may range from Santa Barbara spot prawns paired with fingerling potato salad to line-caught pan-roasted Alaskan halibut with Niman Ranch bacon and sweet pea tendril juice. For dessert, try the mascarpone with figs and cherries, or the chocolate bread pudding. Better yet, splurge on the $95 seven-course tasting menu.

544 S. Grand Ave. (btw. 5th and 6th sts.), Los Angeles. (②) 213/891-0900. www.watergrill.com. Reservations recommended. Main courses $19–$49. AE, DC, DISC, MC, V. Mon–Fri 11:30am–9:30pm; Sat 5–9:30pm; Sun 4:30–8:30pm. Valet parking $5.

MODERATE

Cafe Pinot 😄😄 *Kids* CALIFORNIA-FRENCH   A member of superstar-chef Joachim Splichal's L.A. restaurant empire, Cafe Pinot is less formal and lighter on the palate—and the pocketbook—than his Patina restaurant at the Walt Disney Concert Hall. The restaurant's location, in the front garden of the L.A. Public Library, makes it a natural for Downtown business folk; at night there's a free shuttle to the Music Center. Be sure to request a table on the patio, shaded by umbrellas and the well-landscaped library courtyard.

Splichal has installed a giant rotisserie in the kitchen, and this is where the best meals come from. The moist, tender, mustard-crusted roast chicken is your best bet. A kids' menu is offered, and (even better) kids 10 and under eat free.

700 W. 5th St. (btw. Grand and Flower sts., next to the L.A. Public Library), Los Angeles. (②) 213/239-6500. www.patinagroup.com. Reservations recommended. Main courses $15–$35. AE, DC, DISC, MC, V. Lunch Mon–Fri 11:30am–2:30pm; dinner Mon–Tues 5–9pm, Wed–Thurs 5–9:30pm, Fri–Sat 5–10pm, Sun 4:30–9pm. Self-parking free–$3.

Cha Cha Cha 😄😄 BREAKFAST/CARIBBEAN/CUBAN   Cha Cha Cha serves the West Coast's best Caribbean food in a fun and funky space on the seedy fringe of Downtown. The restaurant is a festival of flavors and colors both upbeat and offbeat. It's impossible to feel down when you're part of this eclectic hodgepodge of pulsating Caribbean music, wild decor, and kaleidoscopic clutter; still, the intimate dining rooms cater to lively romantics, not the obnoxious types. Claustrophobes should choose seats in the airy covered courtyard. The very spicy black-pepper jumbo shrimp gets top marks, as does the paella, a generous mixture of chicken, sausage, and seafood

Where to Dine in the Downtown Area

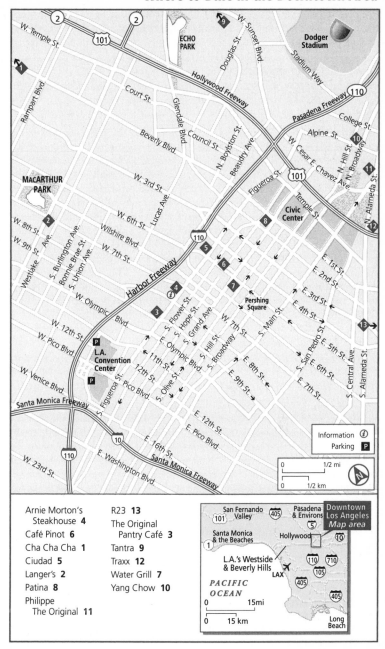

Arnie Morton's
  Steakhouse **4**
Café Pinot **6**
Cha Cha Cha **1**
Ciudad **5**
Langer's **2**
Patina **8**
Philippe
  The Original **11**

R23 **13**
The Original
  Pantry Café **3**
Tantra **9**
Traxx **12**
Water Grill **7**
Yang Chow **10**

blended with saffron rice. Other Jamaican-, Haitian-, Cuban-, and Puerto Rican–inspired recommendations include jerk pork and mambo gumbo, a zesty soup of okra, shredded chicken, and spices. Hard-core fans of Caribbean cuisine might visit for breakfast, when the fare ranges from plantain, yucca, onion, and herb omelets to scrambled eggs with fresh tomatillos served on hot grilled tortillas.

656 N. Virgil Ave. (at Melrose Ave.), Silver Lake. © 323/664-7723. www.theoriginalchachacha.com. Reservations recommended. Main courses $12–$22. AE, DC, DISC, MC, V. Mon–Thurs 8am–10pm; Fri–Sat 8am–11pm. Valet parking $3.50.

Ciudad ✿✿ LATIN   The latest L.A. venture of celebrity chefs Susan Feniger and Mary Sue Milliken is this intriguing restaurant in the heart of Downtown. *Ciudad* means "city" in Spanish and is a nod to the partners' long-ago venture, City Restaurant. Here, amid juicy sherbet pastel walls and Miró-esque abstract designs, exuberant crowds gather to revel in a menu that brings together cuisines from the world's great Latin urban centers: Havana, Rio de Janeiro, Barcelona, and so on. Standout dishes include the tortilla soup, Argentine empanadas, Swiss chard with tomatillo sauce, citrus-roasted Cuban-style chicken (served with Puerto Rican rice and fried plantains), and a Brazilian *moqueca*—shrimp, mussels, and other seafood in a coconut-lime broth over coconut rice. Between 4 and 9pm on Sundays, Ciudad presents happy hour tapas served at the bar; it's easy to make a meal of several, choosing from carnitas tacos, goat cheese fritters with sherry-soaked cherries, lamb meatballs with chimichurri, and more. As with the pair's superb Border Grill (p. 119), desserts are worth saving room for and are large enough to share. *Tip:* From Tuesday through Saturday Ciudad provides free shuttle service to the Music Center, the Walt Disney Concert Hall, and select STAPLES Center events.

445 S. Figueroa St. (at 5th St.), Los Angeles. © 213/486-5171. www.ciudad-la.com. Reservations recommended. Main courses $16–$29; tapas $4–$6. AE, MC, V. Mon–Tues 11:30am–9pm; Wed–Thurs 11:30am–10pm; Fri 11:30am–11pm; Sat 5–11pm; Sun 5–9pm. Day parking $3 with validation; valet parking (after 5pm) $5.

R23 ✿✿ *Finds* JAPANESE/SUSHI   This gallery-like space in Downtown's out-of-the-way warehouse/artist loft district has been the secret of sushi connoisseurs since 1991 and has consistently ranked as one of the city's top sushi restaurants. At the back of R23's single, large exposed-brick dining room, the 12-seat sushi bar shines like a beacon; what appear at first to be ceramic wall ornaments are really stylish sushi platters hanging in wait for large orders. More functional art reveals itself in the corrugated cardboard chairs designed by renowned architect Frank Gehry—they're funky yet far more comfortable than wood. Genial sushi wizards stand in wait, cases of the finest fish before them. Salmon, yellowtail, shrimp, tuna, and scallops are among the always-fresh selections; an excellent and unusual offering is seared *toro*, in which the rich belly tuna absorbs a faint and delectable smoky flavor from the grill. Though R23's sublimely perfect sushi is the star, the short but inventive menu includes pungent miso based soup with mixed seafood, sautéed scallops with shiitake mushrooms, deep-fried sawa crab, and several other choices. Browse a wide selection of premium wines and sakes (try the addictively sweet *nigori*).

923 E. 2nd St. (btw. Alameda St. and Santa Fe Ave.), Los Angeles. © 213/687-7178. www.r23.com. Reservations recommended. Main courses $12–$20; sushi $4–$12. AE, DC, DISC, MC, V. Mon–Fri 11:30am–2pm and 5:30–10pm; Sat 5:30–10pm. Free parking.

Tantra ✿✿ INDIAN   In typical L.A. over-the-top fashion, Tantra owner Navraj Singh hired a studio design company to create an Indian restaurant unlike any you've ever seen. Hammered copper doors, iron-and-silk light fixtures, curtains of oxidized metals, murals of gender-fused beings, and black-and-white Bollywood movies shown on a giant plasma screen are just a few of the unorthodox props that vie for your attention. Part restaurant and part nightclub, Tantra is one of L.A.'s current "in" destinations, both for its scene and the cuisine. The gym-size building is equally divided: Veer right at the foyer and join the eclectic Silver Lake hipsters sipping too-cool cocktails such as Tears of Ganesha and Shiva's Revenge while the DJ spins vinyl; veer left and behold Lord Ganesha, god of prosperity, perched high above the temple-style dining room. Just about all of the curries, stir-fries, masalas, and kabobs are expertly prepared, but two are standout dishes: coconut curry shrimp flavored with *ajwain* (caraway seeds) and stir-fried with palm vinegar, red onions, and peppers, and then finished with tomato coconut broth; and the *Mumbai* crepes—chickpea-and-corn crepes with a tangy cream-cheese filling and topped with mango sauce.

3705 W. Sunset Blvd., Silver Lake. (C) 323/663-8268. www.tantrasunset.com. Reservations for parties of 6 or more. Main courses $11–$16. AE, MC, V. Tues–Wed and Sun 5–11pm; Thurs 5pm–midnight; Fri–Sat 5pm–1am. Valet parking $3.50.

Traxx ★★ *Finds* CALIFORNIA   There's always been a restaurant—of some sort—inside the Union Station passenger concourse, but Traxx is the first to do justice to its grand, historic setting. Showcasing a stylish mix of retro-evocative Art Deco character with sleek contemporary touches, the interior blends seamlessly with the station's architecture, a unique fusion of Spanish colonial revival and Streamline Moderne. Elegant enough for a romantic dinner, yet welcoming to the casual commuter in search of a stylish lunch or sit-down snack, Traxx features a menu with the same cosmopolitan flavor as the station itself. Samples range from "small plates" of red chile–crusted shrimp, and "really good" (and they are) crab cakes with a chipotle kick to main dishes such as pork chops with mission fig polenta and the much-talked-about Gorgonzola-crusted beef tenderloin presented atop crispy and mashed potatoes surrounded by a pool of demi glace/herb reduction. The top dessert is the crunchy chocolate truffle cake with crème anglaise.

In Union Station, 800 N. Alameda St. (at Cesar E. Chavez Ave.), Los Angeles. (C) 213/625-1999. www.traxxrestaurant.com. Reservations suggested for dinner. Main courses $19–$28. AE, DC, MC, V. Mon–Fri 11:30am–9:30pm; Sat 5–9:30pm. Free valet parking with validation.

Yang Chow Restaurant ★★ CHINESE   Open for more than 30 years, family-operated Yang Chow is one of Downtown's most popular Chinese restaurants. It's not the dining room's bland and functional decor that accrues accolades; what makes Yang Chow so popular is an interesting menu of seafood specialties complementing well-done Chinese standards. After covering the Mandarin and Szechuan basics—sweet-and-sour pork, shrimp with broccoli, moo shu chicken—the kitchen leaps into high gear, concocting zesty dishes such as sautéed pork shreds with spicy garlic sauce, hot and spicy whole fish, and spicy Hunan beef. The key to having a terrific meal is to first order the house specialties—Slippery Shrimp and plump steamed pork dumplings—and then ask for recommendations from your server.

819 N. Broadway (at Alpine St.), Chinatown. (C) 213/625-0811. www.yangchow.com. Reservations recommended on weekends. Main courses $8–$14. AE, DC, MC, V. Sun–Thurs 11:30am–9:45pm; Fri–Sat 11:30am–10:45pm. Free parking.

INEXPENSIVE
Langer's Deli BREAKFAST/DELICATESSEN   A leader in L.A.'s long-running deli war—Al Langer and his son Norm have been serving the business community

and displaced New Yorkers since 1947—this deli-institution makes some of the best kishka and matzo-ball soup this side of the Hudson. For many, however, it's the fresh chopped liver, lean, spicy hot pastrami sandwiches on crispy rye, and melt-in-your-mouth corned beef that make Langer's L.A.'s best deli. After the riots, when things got dicey around this MacArthur Park neighborhood, the restaurant began a curbside pickup service: Phone in your order with an ETA, and they'll wait for you at the curb—with change.

704 S. Alvarado St. (at 7th St.), Los Angeles. ✆ 213/483-8050. www.langersdeli.com. Main courses $6–$17. MC, V. Mon–Sat 8am–4pm. Free parking with validation.

The Original Pantry AMERICAN/BREAKFAST   An L.A. institution in a city that thrives on change, this bastion of blue-collar cooking has been serving huge portions of comfort food round-the-clock since 1924. In fact, there isn't even a key to the front door. Owned by former L.A. mayor and botched governor contender Richard Riordan, the cash-only Pantry is popular with politicos, who come here for weekday lunches, and with conferencegoers en route to the nearby L.A. Convention Center. The well-worn restaurant is also a welcoming beacon to clubbers after-hours, when Downtown becomes a virtual ghost town. A bowl of celery stalks, carrot sticks, and whole radishes greets you at your Formica table, and creamy coleslaw and sourdough bread come free with every meal. The menu? It's a chalkboard hanging on the wall. Famous for quantity rather than quality, the Pantry serves huge T-bone steaks, densely packed hamburger loaf, macaroni and cheese, and other American favorites to an already overfed crowd. A typical breakfast—served all day—consists of a huge stack of hotcakes, a big slab of sweet cured ham, home fries, and coffee.

877 S. Figueroa St. (at 9th St.), Los Angeles. ✆ 213/972-9279. www.pantrycafe.com. Main courses $6–$14. No credit cards. Daily 24 hr. Free parking across the street with validation.

Philippe The Original *Value* BREAKFAST/SANDWICHES   Good old-fashioned value is what this legendary landmark cafeteria is all about. Popular with both South Central project residents and Beverly Hills elite, Philippe's unspectacular dining room with sawdust floors is one of the few places in L.A. where everyone can get along. Philippe's claims to have invented the French-dipped sandwich at this location in 1908; it remains the most popular menu item. Patrons push trays along the counter and watch while their choice of beef, pork, ham, turkey, or lamb is sliced and layered onto crusty French bread that's been dipped in meat juices. Other menu items include house-made beef stew, navy bean soup, chili, and pickled pigs' feet. A hearty breakfast, served daily from 6 to 10:30am, is worthwhile if only for Philippe's uncommonly good cinnamon-dipped French toast. Beer and wine are available. For added entertainment, request a booth in the Train Room, which houses the nifty Model Train Museum.

Tip: A regular coffee at Philippe The Original is the same price it was when the diner opened in 1924: 9¢. That explains why they serve more than 20,000 cups per week.

1001 N. Alameda St. (at Ord St.), Los Angeles. ✆ 213/628-3781. www.philippes.com. Most menu items under $7. No credit cards. Daily 6am–10pm. Free parking.

6 Universal City

There are more than three dozen dining choices at Universal Studios, including those in Universal CityWalk. But just in case you need respite from the frenzied theme-park atmosphere, we've also included some of our favorite San Fernando Valley restaurants, which are within easy driving distance of Universal Studios.

EXPENSIVE

Pinot Bistro ★★ *Kids* CALIFORNIA/FRENCH   When the Valley crowd doesn't want to make the drive to Patina, they pack into Pinot Bistro, one of Joachim Splichal's cadre of successful restaurants. The Valley's only great bistro is designed with dark woods, etched glass, and cream-colored walls that scream "trendy French" almost as loudly as the rich, straightforward cooking. The menu, a symphony of California and Continental elements, includes a beautiful warm goat cheese tart with arugula, shaved fennel and olives, and baby lobster tails with creamy polenta—both studies in culinary perfection. The generously portioned main dishes continue the gourmet theme: crispy whitefish with potatoes, Parmesan risotto with English peas, braised lamb with green olives, and roast duck. The service is good, attentive, and unobtrusive. Many regulars prefer Pinot Bistro at lunch, when a less expensive menu is served to a more easygoing crowd. You might not normally bring your kids to a bistro—which is why they let kids 9 and under eat free.

12969 Ventura Blvd. (west of Coldwater Canyon Ave.), Studio City. ℂ **818/990-0500**. www.patinagroup.com. Reservations suggested. Main courses dinner $16–$25, lunch $7–$13. AE, DC, DISC, MC, V. Lunch Mon–Fri noon–2pm; dinner Mon 5:30–9pm, Tues–Thurs 5:30–9:30pm, Fri–Sat 5:30–10pm, Sun 5:30–9pm. Valet parking $3.50.

MODERATE

Casa Vega ★★ *Value* MEXICAN   Every neighborhood needs a friendly dive that's open until 2am, and Casa Vega has been the local favorite for nearly half a century. A faux-weathered adobe exterior conceals red Naugahyde booths lurking among fake potted plants and 1960s amateur oil paintings of dark-eyed Mexican children and cape-waving bullfighters. (The decor achieves critical mass at Christmas, when everything drips with tinsel.) Locals and celebs love this family-owned and -operated place for its strong, cheap margaritas, bottomless baskets of hot and salty chips, and traditional combination dinners, which all come with Casa Vega's patented tostada-style dinner salad. Street parking is so plentiful here you should use the valet only as a last resort. On warm days ask for a table on the patio, and be prepared to wait for a table on weekends.

13301 Ventura Blvd. (at Fulton Ave.), Sherman Oaks. ℂ **818/788-4868**. Main courses $5–$11. AE, DC, DISC, MC, V. Daily 11:30am–2am. Metered street parking or valet $2.50.

Jerry's Famous Deli ★★ *Kids* BREAKFAST/DELICATESSEN   Here's a simple yet sizable deli where all the Valley's hipsters go to relieve their late-night munchies. This place probably has one of the largest menus in America—a tome that spans cultures and continents, from Central America to China to New York. From salads to sandwiches to steak-and-seafood platters, everything—including breakfast—is served all day. Jerry's is consistently good at lox and eggs, pastrami sandwiches, potato pancakes, and all the deli staples. It's also an integral part of L.A.'s cultural landscape and a favorite of the show-business types—and their kids; Jerry's is a popular spot for families who populate the adjacent foothill neighborhoods. It even has a full bar.

12655 Ventura Blvd. (just east of Coldwater Canyon Ave.), Studio City. ℂ **818/980-4245**. www.jerrysfamousdeli.com. Main courses dinner $9–$14, sandwiches and salads $4–$12, breakfast $2–$11. AE, MC, V. Daily 24 hr. Free parking.

Miceli's *Kids* TRADITIONAL ITALIAN   Mostaccioli marinara, lasagna, thin-crust pizza, and eggplant parmigiana are indicative of the Sicilian-style fare at this cavernous, stained-glass-windowed Italian restaurant adjacent to Universal City. The waitstaff sings show tunes or opera favorites in between serving dinner (and sometimes instead of); make sure you have enough chianti to get into the spirit of it all. This is a great place for kids but is too rollicking for romance.

3655 Cahuenga Blvd. (east of Lankershim Blvd.), Los Angeles. © **323/851-3344.** www.micelisrestaurant.com. Main courses $7–$15; pizza $9–$19. AE, DC, MC, V. Mon–Thurs 11:30am–midnight; Fri 11:30am–1am; Sat 4pm–1am; Sun 4–11pm. Parking $2.50.

INEXPENSIVE

Du-par's Restaurant & Bakery ✦✦ AMERICAN/TRADITIONAL/BREAK-FAST   It's been called a "culinary wax museum," the last of a dying breed, the kind of coffee shop Donna Reed took the family to for blue-plate specials. This isn't a trendy new theme place, it's the real deal—and that motherly waitress who calls everyone under 60 "hon" has probably been slinging hash here for 20 or 30 years. Du-par's is popular among old-timers who made it part of their daily routine decades ago, show business denizens who eschew the industry watering holes, a new generation that appreciates a tasty, cheap meal . . . well, everyone, really. It's common knowledge that Du-par's makes the best buttermilk pancakes in town, though some prefer the eggy, perfect French toast (extra crispy around the edges, please). Mouthwatering pies (blueberry cream cheese, coconut cream, and more) line the front display case and can be had for a song.

12036 Ventura Blvd. (1 block east of Laurel Canyon Blvd.), Studio City. © **818/766-4437.** www.dupars.com. All items under $11. AE, DC, DISC, MC, V. Sun–Thurs 6am–1am; Fri–Sat 6am–4am. Free parking.

7 Pasadena & Environs

EXPENSIVE

Bistro 45 ✦✦ CALIFORNIA-FRENCH   All class, yet never stuffy, Bistro 45 is a favorite among Pasadena's old guard and nouvelle riche. The restaurant's warm, light ambience and gallery-like decor are an unexpected surprise after the ornately historic Art Deco exterior (the building is a former bank), and provide a romantic backdrop for owner Robert Simon's award-winning cuisine. The seasonally inspired menu changes frequently; dishes might include braised veal short ribs with Asian five spice, rock shrimp risotto with saffron, pan-roasted monkfish with garlic polenta, roasted veal loin filled with Roquefort, Fanny Bay oyster salad, and Nebraska pork with figs. For dessert, try the "chocolate soup," a creamy soufflé served with chocolate-kirsch sauce and vanilla ice cream. The knowledgeable waitstaff can answer questions about the excellent wine list; Bistro 45 appears regularly on *Wine Spectator*'s Best Of lists, and hosts special-event wine dinners.

45 S. Mentor Ave. (btw. Colorado Blvd. and Green St.), Pasadena. © **626/795-2478.** www.bistro45.com. Reservations recommended. Main courses dinner $17–$36, lunch $13–$33. AE, DC, MC, V. Tues–Thurs 11:30am–2pm and 6–9pm; Fri 11:30am–2pm and 6–9:30pm; Sat 6–9:30pm; Sun 5–9pm. Valet parking $4.50.

Parkway Grill ✦✦ CALIFORNIA   This vibrant, quintessentially Southern California restaurant has been one of the L.A. area's top-rated spots since 1985, quickly gaining a reputation for avant-garde flavor combinations and gourmet signature pizzas to rival Spago's. Although some critics find many dishes too fussy, others thrill to appetizer innovations such as lobster-stuffed cocoa crepes or Dungeness crab cakes with ginger cream and two salsas. Take my advice and start with the hot cheese-pear-walnut flatbread and the roasted beet salad, followed by any main dish from the iron mesquite grill. The richly sweet and substantial desserts can easily satiate two

Where to Dine in the Pasadena Area

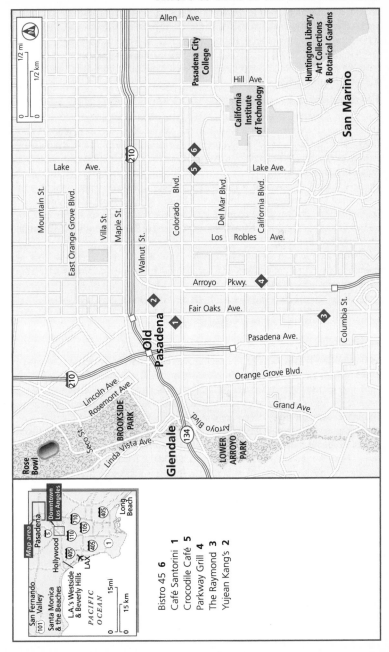

Allen Ave.

Pasadena City College

Huntington Library, Art Collections & Botanical Gardens

Hill Ave.

California Institute of Technology

San Marino

210

Lake Ave.

Mountain St.

East Orange Grove Blvd.

Villa St.

Maple St.

Lake Ave.

Colorado Blvd.

Del Mar Blvd.

California Blvd.

Walnut St.

Los Robles Ave.

Arroyo Pkwy.

Fair Oaks Ave.

Old Pasadena

Columbia St.

Pasadena Ave.

210

Orange Grove Blvd.

Lincoln Ave.

Rosemont Ave.

BROOKSIDE PARK

Seco St.

Linda Vista Ave.

Glendale

134

Arroyo Blvd.

Grand Ave.

LOWER ARROYO PARK

Rose Bowl

1/2 mi

1/2 km

Map area

San Fernando Valley

101

Santa Monica & the Beaches

PACIFIC OCEAN

L.A.'s Westside & Beverly Hills

Hollywood

405

LAX

405

5

110

210

Pasadena

Downtown Los Angeles

710

105

405

Long Beach

1

15mi

15 km

Bistro 45 **6**
Café Santorini **1**
Crocodile Café **5**
Parkway Grill **4**
The Raymond **3**
Yujean Kang's **2**

155

appetites. Located where the old Arroyo Seco Parkway glides into an ordinary city street, the Parkway Grill is within a couple of minutes' drive from Old Pasadena and thoughtfully offers free valet parking.

510 S. Arroyo Pkwy. (at California Blvd.), Pasadena. © **626/795-1001.** www.theparkwaygrill.com. Reservations recommended. Main courses $8–$27. AE, DC, MC, V. Mon–Fri 11:30am–2:30pm and 5–10pm; Sat 5:30–11pm; Sun 5:30–10pm. Free valet parking.

The Raymond ★★ NEW AMERICAN/CONTINENTAL With its easy-to-miss setting in a sleepy part of Pasadena, the Raymond is a jewel even few locals know about. This Craftsman cottage was once the caretaker's house for a grand Victorian hotel called the Raymond. Though the city has grown to surround it, the place maintains an enchanting air of seclusion, romance, and serenity. In 2005, the classic restaurant got a face-lift, as did the haute American- and European-inspired menu, which changes seasonally. A typical dinner may start with a pancetta-wrapped shrimp appetizer tossed in an orange reduction sauce, followed by roast Long Island duckling with raspberry port sauce and the coup de grâce—chocolate Moelleux soufflé cake with a melted chocolate center served with vanilla ice cream. Tables are scattered throughout the house and in the lush English garden, and there's plenty of free, nonvalet parking (you won't find *that* on the Westside). *Note:* If you're a fan of finger sandwiches, afternoon tea (a great excuse to drink champagne under the sun) is offered Friday through Sunday from 1:30 to 3pm.

1250 S. Fair Oaks Ave. (at Columbia St.), Pasadena. © **626/441-3136.** www.theraymond.com. Reservations required. Main courses dinner $16–$36, lunch $9–$24. AE, DC, DISC, MC, V. Tues–Fri 11:30am–2:30pm and 5:30–10pm; Sat 10am–2:30pm and 5:30–10pm; Sun 10am–2:30pm and 5–9pm. Free parking.

MODERATE

Café Santorini ★★ GREEK Located at ground zero of Pasadena's crowded Old Town shopping mecca, this second-story gem has a secluded Mediterranean ambience, due in part to its historic brick building with patio tables overlooking, but insulated from, the plaza below. In the evening, lighting is subdued and romantic, but ambience is casual; many diners are coming from or going to an adjacent movie-theater complex. The food is terrific and affordable, featuring grilled meats and kabobs, pizzas, fresh and tangy hummus, plenty of warm pita, and other staples of Greek cuisine. The menu includes regional flavors such as lamb, feta cheese, spinach, or Armenian sausage; the vegetarian baked butternut squash is filled with fluffy rice and smoky roasted vegetables.

64 W. Union St. (main entrance at the shopping plaza at the corner of Fair Oaks Ave. and Colorado Blvd.), Pasadena. © **626/564-4201.** www.cafesantorini.com. Reservations recommended on weekends. Main courses $9–$29. AE, DC, DISC, MC, V. Mon–Thurs 11:30am–10pm; Fri–Sat 11:30am–midnight; Sun 11am–10pm. Valet or self-parking $7.

Yujean Kang's Gourmet Chinese Cuisine ★★ CHINESE Many Chinese restaurants put the word *gourmet* in their name, but few really mean it—or deserve it. Not so at Yujean Kang's, where Chinese cuisine is taken to an entirely new level. A master of fusion cuisine, the eponymous chef/owner snatches bits of techniques and flavors from both China and the West, merging them in an entirely fresh way. Can you resist such provocative dishes as "Ants on Tree" (beef sautéed with glass noodles in chili and black sesame seeds), lobster with caviar and fava beans, or Chilean sea bass in passion-fruit sauce? Kang is also a wine aficionado and has assembled a magnificent cellar of California, French, and particularly German wines. Try pairing a German

Spätlese with tea-smoked duck salad. The red-wrapped dining room is less subtle than the food, but just as elegant.

67 N. Raymond Ave. (btw. Walnut St. and Colorado Blvd.), Pasadena. ✆ **626/585-0855.** Reservations recommended. Main courses $8–$19. AE, MC, V. Sun–Thurs 11:30am–2:30pm and 5–9:30pm; Fri–Sat 11:30am–2:30pm and 5–10pm. Street parking.

INEXPENSIVE
Crocodile Cafe AMERICAN/TRADITIONAL/INTERNATIONAL   Casual and colorful, this offshoot of Pasadena's groundbreaking Parkway Grill builds a menu around simple crowd-pleasers (pizza, pasta, burgers, salads) prepared with fresh ingredients and jazzed up with creative marinades, vinaigrettes, and salsas. It's a formula that works; this Lake Avenue branch is the original location, but siblings have sprung up throughout the San Fernando and San Gabriel Valleys—even as far away as San Diego. Popular selections include the oakwood-grilled burger with curly french fries, the Croc's signature blue-corn chicken tostada with warm black beans and fresh guacamole, wood-grilled gourmet pizzas in the California Pizza Kitchen style, excellent chili, zesty tortilla soup, and ooey-gooey desserts.

140 S. Lake Ave., Pasadena. ✆ **626/449-9900.** www.crocodilecafe.com. Main courses $8–$18. AE, MC, V. Sun–Thurs 11am–10pm; Fri–Sat 11am–midnight. Free self-parking.

7

What to See & Do in Los Angeles

You'll need to make a lot of tough decisions if you're touring L.A. for the first time: surfing lessons or a jogging tour? Join the live studio audience at the *Tonight Show* or *Jeopardy!*? Go to Disneyland or Universal Studios Hollywood? You get the point; it would take you months to do *all* the things listed in this chapter. For some help in narrowing down the options, read chapter 1, "The Best of Los Angeles," and chapter 4, "Suggested Los Angeles Itineraries."

To find out what's going on while you're in town, pick up a copy of the free *L.A. Weekly,* the monthly magazine *Los Angeles,* or the Sunday *Los Angeles Times* "Calendar" section; each has detailed listings covering events and entertainment around town, often accompanied by helpful commentary on which activities might be worth your while. Better yet, plan ahead via the Web (see "Website-Seeing: The Best of L.A. Online" in chapter 3) and score those hard-to-get tickets in advance.

Also, note that you usually have to drive everywhere in L.A. Be sure you have a map handy and try to plan your itinerary with as little time on the freeways as possible, *especially* during rush hour.

1 L.A.'s Top Attractions

Farmers Market and The Grove ★★ *Kids*   Now entering its 8th decade, the original market was little more than an empty lot with wooden stands set up by farmers during the Depression so they could sell directly to city dwellers. Eventually, permanent buildings grew up, including the trademark shingled 10-story clock tower. Today the place has evolved into a sprawling marketplace with a carnival atmosphere, a kind of "turf" version of San Francisco's Fisherman's Wharf. About 70 restaurants, shops, and grocers cater to a mix of workers from the CBS Television City complex, locals, and tourists brought here by the busload. Retailers sell greeting cards, kitchen implements, candles, and souvenirs, but everyone comes for the food stands, which offer oysters, hot doughnuts, Cajun gumbo, fresh-squeezed orange juice, corned beef sandwiches, fresh-pressed peanut butter, and all kinds of international fast foods. You can still buy produce here—it's no longer a farm-fresh bargain, but the selection's better than at the grocery store. Don't miss **Kokomo** (© 323/933-0773), a "gourmet" outdoor coffee shop that has become a power breakfast spot for showbiz types. Red turkey hash and sweet-potato fries are the dishes that keep them coming back. The seafood gumbo and gumbo ya ya at the **Gumbo Pot** (© 323/933-0358) are also very popular.

At the eastern end of the Farmers Market is the **Grove,** a massive 575,000-square-foot Vegas-style retail complex composed of various architectural styles ranging from Art Deco to Italian Renaissance. Miniature streets link the Grove to the Market via a

(Value) Money-Saving Tourist Passes

If you're the type who loves to cram as many tourist attractions as possible in one trip, then you might want to consider purchasing a **Hollywood CityPass** or **GO Los Angeles Card.** The CityPass (© **888/330-5008;** www.citypass.com) book-let includes tickets to four attractions, all within 2 blocks of each other: the **Hol-lywood Wax Museum, Star Line Tour of Hollywood, Redline Tours,** and the **Kodak Theatre Guided Tour** or the **Hollywood Museum.** Purchase the pass at any of the above attractions, or visit the CityPass website to buy advance passes online. The pass costs $50 for adults ($39 for kids 4–11) and will expire 9 days from the first use. Is it a good deal? If you use all the tickets, you end up sav-ing about 45% over individual, full-price admission.

I think the better deal, however, is the **GO Los Angeles Card** (© **800/887-9103;** www.golosangelescard.com). It offers free or discounted admission to more than 45 of L.A.'s most popular attractions, activities, and tours; has far more flexibility (available in 1-, 2-, 3-, 5-, and 7-day increments over a 14-day period); and comes with a nifty little full-color guidebook that fits in your back pocket. The 2-day card costs $89 for adults ($69 for kids 3–13), and doesn't need to be used on consecutive days. The 3-, 5-, and 7-day cards include admission to Universal Studios Hollywood (a great bargain). You can purchase the GO Cards via their website or at the Hollywood Visitor Information Center (6801 Holly-wood Blvd. at Highland Ave.; © **323/467-6412**).

---

double-deck electric trolley. Granted, it's all a bit Disney-gaudy, but the locals love it. Where else can you power-shop until noon, check all your bags at a drop-off station, get a spa treatment at **Amadeus Aveda Spa** (© **323/297-0311;** www.amadeusspa.com), see a movie at the 14-screen **Grove Theatre** (© **323/692-0829;** www.thegrovela. com), have an early dinner at **Maggiano's Little Italy** (© **323/965-9665;** www. maggianos.com), and be home by 7pm?

6333 W. 3rd St. (at Fairfax Ave.), Hollywood. © **888/315-8883** or 323/900-8080. www.thegrovela.com. Mon–Thurs 10am–9pm; Fri–Sat 10am–10pm; Sun 11am–8pm.

The Getty Center Los Angeles ★★ (Kids) Since opening in 1997, the Richard Meier–designed Getty Center has quickly assumed its place in the L.A. landscape (lit-erally and figuratively) as the city's cultural acropolis and international mecca. Head-quarters for the Getty Trust's research, education, philanthropic, and conservation concerns, the postmodernist complex—perched on a hillside in the Santa Monica Mountains and swathed in Italian travertine marble—is most frequently visited for the museum galleries displaying the Getty's enormous collection of Impressionist paintings, truckloads of glimmering French furniture and decorative arts, fine illumi-nated manuscripts, contemporary photography, and European drawings. The area that's open to the public consists of five two-story pavilions set around an open court-yard, and each gallery within is specially designed to complement the works on dis-play. A sophisticated system of programmable window louvers allows many works (particularly paintings) to be displayed in the natural light in which they were created for the first time in the modern era. One of these is van Gogh's *Irises,* one of the museum's finest and most popular holdings. Trivia buffs will enjoy knowing that the

L.A.'s Attractions at a Glance

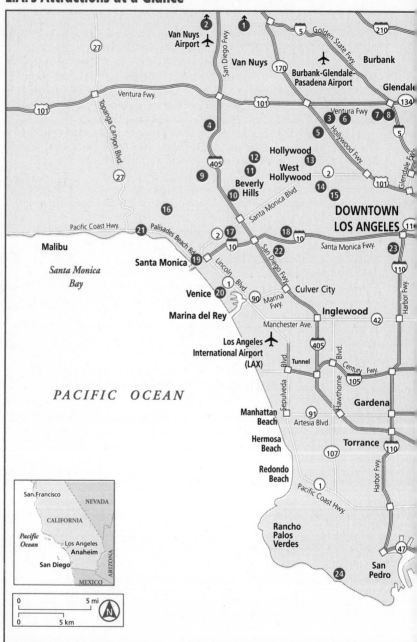

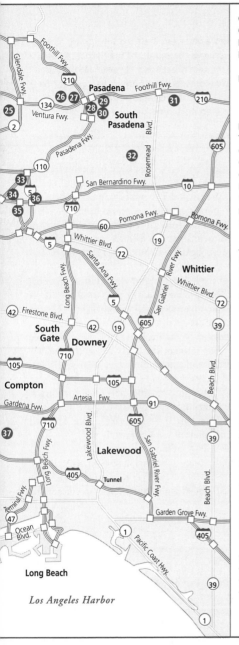

(*Moments* **Marina Oasis**

One of my favorite places in L.A. to get away from it all is a tiny, quiet, little-known park in Marina del Rey that overlooks the mouth of the harbor. All day long you can sit on a bench and enjoy the cool breeze as a never-ending parade of beautiful yachts and sailboats slowly works its way to the ocean or back to the marina. To reach this relaxing oasis, from Venice Beach drive to the south end of Pacific Avenue, turn left on Via Marina, and park in one of the metered spaces (bring quarters and binoculars).

museum spent $53.9 million to acquire this painting; it's displayed in a complex that cost roughly $1 *billion* to construct.

A new addition to the Getty Center is the Fran and Ray Stark Sculpture Collection. This collection of 28 modern and contemporary outdoor sculptures from the collection of the late legendary film producer Ray Stark and his wife Fran was donated to the Getty Museum by the Ray Stark Revocable Trust and features many of the 20th century's greatest sculptors, including works by Roy Lichtenstein, Joan Miró, and Isamu Noguchi.

Visitors to the center park at the base of the hill and ascend via a cable-driven electric tram. On clear days, the sensation is of being in the clouds, gazing across Los Angeles and the Pacific Ocean (and into a few chic Brentwood backyards). If you're like me and don't remember a thing from your college art-appreciation class (like I even went), get one of the new GettyGuide Audio Guides at the information desk. The nifty device allows visitors to take their own guided tour through the Getty Museum. The 45-minute human-led architectural tours, offered throughout the day, are also worth looking into. Dining options include several espresso/snack carts, a cafeteria, a self-service cafe, and the elegant (though informal) "Restaurant" offering table service for lunch (Tues–Sun) and dinner (Fri–Sat), with breathtaking views overlooking the ocean and mountains (restaurant reservations are recommended, though walk-ins are accepted; call ✆ **310/440-6810** or make reservations online at www.getty.edu).

Realizing that fine-art museums can be boring for kids, the center provides several clever programs for kids, including a family room filled with hands-on activities for families; weekend family workshops; Art Detective cards to help parents and kids explore the grounds and galleries; and self-guided audio tours made specifically for families.

Entrance to the Getty Center is free and no reservations are required. Cameras and video cams are permitted, but only if you use existing light (flash units are *verboten*).

1200 Getty Center Dr., Los Angeles. ✆ **310/440-7300**. www.getty.edu. Free admission. Tues–Thurs and Sun 10am–6pm; Fri–Sat 10am–9pm. Closed major holidays. Parking $8.

The Getty Villa Malibu ✸✸ *Kids*   After 8 years and $275 million in renovations, the magnificent Getty Villa is receiving guests again. As the Getty Center was the cultural coup of 1997, a ticket to the newly renovated Villa is still one of the most sought-after items in the city. This former residence of oil tycoon J. Paul Getty, built in 1974 on the edge of a Malibu bluff with dazzling views of the ocean, was modeled after a first-century Roman country house buried by the eruption of Mount Vesuvius in A.D. 79—the Villa dei Papiri in Herculaneum, Italy. In fact, as you enter the sun-filled inner courtyard, it's not hard to imagine toga-clad senators wandering the gardens where fountains and bronze busts occupy the same spots as the original villa.

The museum's permanent collection of Greek, Roman, and Etruscan artifacts—dating from 6500 B.C. to A.D. 400—consists of more than 1,200 works in 23 galleries arranged by theme, and five additional galleries for changing exhibitions. Exhibits on display range from everyday items such as coins, jewelry, and sculpture to modern interactive exhibits that illustrate key moments in the history of the ancient Mediterranean. Highlights include *Statue of a Victorious Youth,* a large-scale bronze discovered in an Adriatic shipwreck that is kept in a special climate-controlled room to preserve the metal (it's one of the few life-size Greek bronzes to have survived to modern times), as well as a beautiful 450-seat open-air theater where visitors are encouraged to take a break. And for keeping the kids entertained, the Villa's education team created a hands-on space called the Family Forum where children can partake in art-related activities.

For a more enlightening museum experience, I strongly suggest you rent a $3 Getty-Guide Audio Player, which features commentary from curators and conservators on over 150 works (it's available at the Pick-Up Desk on Floor 1). Admission to the Getty Villa is free but, unlike the Getty Center, advance tickets are required and can be obtained online or by phone.

17985 Pacific Coast Hwy. (1 mile north of Sunset Blvd.), Malibu. © 310/440-7300. www.getty.edu. Free admission, but tickets required. Thurs–Mon 10am–5pm. Closed major holidays. Parking $8.

Grauman's Chinese Theatre ★ *Kids*   This is one of the world's great movie palaces and one of Hollywood's finest landmarks. The theater was opened in 1927 by impresario Sid Grauman, a brilliant promoter who's credited with originating the idea of the paparazzi-packed movie "premiere." Outrageously conceived, with both authentic and simulated Chinese embellishments, Grauman's theater was designed to impress. Original Chinese heavenly doves top the facade, and two of the theater's columns once propped up a Ming dynasty temple.

Visitors by the millions flock to the theater for its famous entry court, where stars like Elizabeth Taylor, Paul Newman, Ginger Rogers, Humphrey Bogart, Frank Sinatra, Marilyn Monroe, and about 160 others set their signatures and hand-/footprints in concrete (a tradition started when actress Norma Talmadge "accidentally" stepped in wet cement during the premiere of Cecil B. DeMille's *King of Kings*). It's not always hands and feet: Betty Grable's shapely leg; the hoofprints of Gene Autry's horse, Champion; Jimmy Durante's and Bob Hope's trademark noses; Whoopi Goldberg's dreadlocks; George Burns's cigar; and even R2D2's wheels are all captured in cement.

6925 Hollywood Blvd. (btw. Highland and La Brea aves.). © 323/464-8111. www.manntheaters.com/chinese. Movie tickets $11. Call for showtimes.

Griffith Observatory ★★   Made world-famous in the film *Rebel Without a Cause,* Griffith Observatory's bronze domes have been Hollywood Hills landmarks since

---

(Tips) Parking: Better Secure than Sorry

If you're driving to Venice Beach, pay the $5 to $7 fee for a secured lot, hide your valuables, and walk to the beach—car break-ins aren't uncommon.

Fun Fact **Body Double**

Here's a really cheap and easy way to get a great seat at a fancy Hollywood award ceremony: Log on to Seatfiller.com and sign up to be one of those people who make sure all the front seats are occupied.

1935. Closed for renovation for what seemed like forever, it finally reopened in November of 2006 after a $93-million overhaul. The central dome houses the 300-seat **Samuel Oschin Planetarium,** where hourly screenings of a narrated half-hour projection show called "Centered in the Universe" reveal the stars and planets that are hidden from the naked eye by the city's ubiquitous lights and smog.

The observatory also features 60 space-related exhibits designed to "sparkle your imagination," the highlight being the largest astronomically accurate image ever produced—a 20×152-foot porcelain enamel dazzler that's cleverly called "The Big Picture." It supposedly encompasses a million galaxies, but I lost count after 11. There's also a new 200-seat Leonard Nimoy Event Horizon Theater (go Spock!), a Wolfgang Puck "Café at the End of the Universe," and several Zeiss and solar telescopes for public use both day and night.

Truth be told, most locals never actually go inside the observatory; they come to this spot on the south slope of Mount Hollywood for the unparalleled city views. On warm nights, with the lights twinkling below, this is one of the most romantic places in L.A.

2800 E. Observatory Rd. (in Griffith Park, at the end of Vermont Ave.). ℭ **213/473-0800.** www.griffithobservatory. org. Planetarium tickets $7 adults, $5 seniors 60 or older and students with ID, $3 children ages 5–12. Tues–Fri noon–10pm; Sat–Sun 10am–10pm. Call or check website for planetarium showtimes.

The HOLLYWOOD Sign ℭ These famous 50-foot-high white sheet-metal letters have come to symbolize the movie industry and the city itself. The sign was erected on Mount Lee in 1923 as an advertisement for a real-estate development. The full text originally read HOLLYWOODLAND and was lined with thousands of 20-watt bulbs around the letters (changed periodically by a caretaker who lived in a small house behind the sign). The sign gained dubious notoriety when actress Peg Entwistle leapt to her death from the "H" in 1932. The LAND section was damaged by a landslide, and the entire sign fell into major disrepair until the Hollywood Chamber of Commerce spearheaded a campaign to repair it (Hugh Hefner, Alice Cooper, Gene Autry, and Andy Williams were all major contributors). Officially completed in 1978, the 450-foot-long installation is now protected by a fence and motion detectors. The best view is from down below, at the corner of Sunset Boulevard and Bronson Avenue. *Tip:* It may look like it on a map, but Beachwood Drive does not lead to the sign. If you want to reach the sign on foot, it requires a rather arduous 5-mile round-trip hike on the Brush Canyon Trail in Griffith Park—the trail head is at the end of Canyon Drive. For more information call the Griffith Park headquarters at ℭ **323/913-4688.**

Hollywood Walk of Fame ℭℭ *Kids* When the Hollywood honchos realized how limited the footprint space was at Grauman's Chinese Theatre, they came up with another way to pay tribute to the stars. Since 1960, more than 2,200 celebrities have been honored along the world's most famous sidewalk. Each bronze medallion, set into the center of a terrazzo star, pays homage to a famous television, film, radio, theater, or recording personality. Although about a third of them are just about as obscure as Michael Jackson's sexual preference—their fame simply hasn't withstood the test of time—millions of visitors are thrilled by the sight of famous names like **James Dean** (1719 Vine St.), **John Lennon** (1750 Vine St.), **Marlon Brando** (1765 Vine St.), **Rudolph Valentino** (6164 Hollywood Blvd.), **Marilyn Monroe** (6744 Hollywood Blvd.), **Elvis Presley** (6777 Hollywood Blvd.), **Greta Garbo** (6901 Hollywood Blvd.), **Louis Armstrong** (7000 Hollywood Blvd.), **Barbra Streisand** (6925 Hollywood Blvd.), and **Eddie Murphy** (7000 Hollywood Blvd.). **Gene Autry** is all over the place: The singing cowboy earned five different stars (a sidewalk record), one in each category.

The sight of bikers, metalheads, homeless wanderers, and hordes of disoriented tourists all treading on memorials to Hollywood's greats makes for a bizarre and somewhat tacky tribute. But the Hollywood Chamber of Commerce has been doing a terrific job sprucing up the pedestrian experience with filmstrip crosswalks, swaying palms, and more. And at least 1 weekend a month, a group of fans calling themselves Star Polishers busy themselves scrubbing tarnished medallions.

The legendary sidewalk is continually adding new names, such as Muhammad Ali in front of the Kodak Theatre. The public is invited to attend dedication ceremonies; the honoree—who pays a whopping $15,000 for the eternal upkeep—is usually in attendance. Contact the **Hollywood Chamber of Commerce,** 6255 Sunset Blvd., Ste. 911, Hollywood, CA 90028 (© **323/469-8311**), for information on who's being honored this week.

Hollywood Blvd., btw. Gower St. and La Brea Ave.; and Vine St., btw. Yucca St. and Sunset Blvd. © **323/469-8311.** www.hollywoodchamber.net.

La Brea Tar Pits & Page Museum ★★ *Kids*   An odorous swamp of gooey asphalt oozes to the earth's surface in the middle of Los Angeles. No, it's not a low-budget horror-movie set—it's La Brea Tar Pits, a truly bizarre primal pool on Museum Row where hot tar has been bubbling from the earth for more than 40,000 years. The bubbling pools may look like a fake Disney set, but they're the real thing and have enticed thirsty animals throughout history. Nearly 400 species of mammals, birds, amphibians, and fish—many of which are now extinct—walked, crawled, landed, swam, or

---

Moments **Sunset Margarita Horse Rides**

This is so cool. Every Friday night, the Sunset Ranch Hollywood Stables company hosts the **Friday Night Dinner Ride.** They saddle you up on a big ol' horse, and then y'all take a scenic 1½-hour ride through Griffith Park—with the city lights shining far below—to the Viva Fresh Mexican restaurant in Burbank. After dinner and a few tasty margaritas, you mount up and ride back to the ranch, arriving at about 11pm. Anyone under 250 pounds can go, and no reservations are required—it's strictly first-come, first-served. The ride costs $60, not including dinner, drinks, and tipping the guide. Sign up begins at 4:30pm and the ride leaves at 5:30pm. Consider yourself warned, however: Many a sore derriere has wished it hadn't been subjected to 180 minutes in the saddle. The ranch is located at the very end of Beachwood Drive off Franklin Avenue, just under the HOLLYWOOD sign. For more information, call © **323/469-5450** or log on to www.sunsetranchhollywood.com.

Fun Fact **The Tar-nished Prince**

One of the L.A. sights Prince Charles asked to visit during his trip to Los Angeles was La Brea Tar Pits.

---

slithered into the sticky sludge, got stuck in the worst way, and stayed forever. In 1906, scientists began a systematic removal and classification of entombed specimens, including ground sloths, giant vultures, mastodons, camels, bears, lizards, and even prehistoric relatives of today's super-rats. Today it's one of the world's richest excavation sites for Ice Age fossils. The best finds are on display in the adjacent **Page Museum at the La Brea Tar Pits,** which houses the largest and most diverse collection of Ice Age plants and tar-stained skeletons in the world. Archaeological work is ongoing; you can watch as scientists clean, identify, and catalog new finds in the Paleontology Laboratory. An entertaining 15-minute film documenting the recoveries is also shown.

5801 Wilshire Blvd. (east of Fairfax Ave.), Los Angeles. (C) **323/934-7243.** www.tarpits.org. Museum admission $7 adults, $4.50 seniors 62 and older and students with ID, $2 children ages 5–12, free for kids 4 and under; free for everyone the 1st Tues of every month. Mon–Fri 9:30am–5pm; Sat–Sun 10am–5pm (museum). Parking $6 with validation.

L.A. LIVE   If you watched the Grammys last year you probably already know about the new L.A. LIVE "entertainment campus" that is the keystone of L.A.'s Downtown gentrification project. This being Los Angeles, the envy-me capital of the world, L.A. LIVE will eventually become one of the largest and flashiest mixed-used entertainment complexes in the world, costing $2.5 billion to build and covering more than 6 city blocks (hence its nickname—Times Square West). It's anchored by the **NOKIA Theatre,** the **STAPLES Center** (where the Lakers and Clippers play their home games), and the **Los Angeles Convention Center,** and is crammed with a dozen trendy restaurants and cafes, two huge nightclubs, the **GRAMMY Museum,** a bowling center, and **ESPN's West Coast broadcast headquarters.** Future plans include JW Marriott and Ritz-Carlton hotels (both within a 54-story tower), luxury condominiums, a 40,000-square-foot outdoor plaza, and a 14-screen movie complex. Whether it's worth the trip from Hollywood or the beaches depends on your interest in mega-size sports and entertainment complexes, but I do recommend logging on to the L.A. LIVE website to see who's playing or performing while you're in town.

Figueroa St. btw. Venice and Olympic boulevards, Los Angeles. (C) **866/548-3452** or 213/763-5483. www.lalive.com.

Santa Monica Pier *★★ (Moments (Kids*   Piers have been a tradition in Southern California since the area's 19th-century seaside resort days. Many have long since disappeared (like Pacific Ocean Park, an entire amusement park perched on offshore pilings), and others have been shortened by battering storms and are now mere shadows (or stumps) of their former selves, but you can still experience those halcyon days of yesteryear at world-famous Santa Monica Pier.

Built in 1908 for passenger and cargo ships, the Santa Monica Pier does a pretty good job of recapturing the glory days of Southern California. The wooden wharf is now home to seafood restaurants and snack shacks, a touristy Mexican cantina, a gaily colored turn-of-the-20th-century indoor wooden **carousel** (which Paul Newman operated in *The Sting*), and an **aquarium** filled with sharks, rays, octopus, eels, and other local sea life. Summer evening concerts, which are free and range from big band to

Secrets of Santa Monica

If you're the type of traveler who eschews crowded tourist attractions, here are a few of my favorite places in Santa Monica that only the locals know about:

Camera Obscura   It's well named, because even most Santa Monicans don't know about this truly obscure attraction though they've passed right by it countless times. Located within the Senior Recreation Center in Palisades Park, the Camera Obscura (which is Latin for "dark room"), is, well, a dark room that's round and has a white circular table in the middle. Turn the old boat steering wheel, which turns the overhead periscope thingy, and a reverse projection of the park, ocean, and avenue is reflected onto the table (that's your car getting a parking ticket). It's an ancient invention that offers a few minutes of mindless voyeuristic amusement in a modern world. To see it you have to go into the Senior Center (mmmm, smell that Salisbury steak!), give the person at the desk your driver's license, and get the key to the Camera Obscura door located up the stairs to your right. The whole experience is a bit surreal, but fun (and free). It's open Monday to Friday 9am to 2pm and Saturday 11am to 4pm. 1450 Ocean Ave., between Broadway and Santa Monica Boulevard, Santa Monica (✆ **310/458-8644**).

Father's Office   If you just want to tuck into a great burger and a beer without having to endure the Santa Monica tourist scene, join the young and beautiful at Father's Office, a small, unpretentious beer bar and grill that offers 40 beers on tap and one of the best burgers in L.A.—dry-aged sirloin with a composite of apple wood–smoked bacon, caramelized onion, arugula, Gruyère, and Maytag blue cheese on a French roll. Addictive french fries are piled into toy shopping carts (you'll see). It's usually standing room only on most evenings so come early if you want a table. 1018 Montana Ave., at 10th Street, Santa Monica (✆ **310/393-2337;** www.fathersoffice.com).

Chez Jay's   It may look like a dumpy bar (okay, it is a dumpy bar), but it's *my* kind of dumpy bar. Located on a multimillion-dollar plot of land near the Santa Monica Pier, this creaky classic is owned and run by Jay "Peanuts" Fiondella, a gray-bearded old-timer who won't sell out to developers at any price. Marlon Brando, Frank Sinatra, Peter Sellers, Kevin Spacey, Madonna, George Clooney—they've all been regulars at one time or another during the past 45 years. Rumor has it astronaut Alan Shepard took a peanut from Jay's to the moon and back (and Steve McQueen tried to eat it). Naturally, there's a jukebox in the corner, a marlin mounted on the wall, peanut shells on the floor, and well-worn red vinyl booths. I hear they serve a great steak but I've never seen the menu. The place is a bit hard to find—look for the little neon sign on the east side of Ocean Avenue, ½ block south of the pier. No cover. 1657 Ocean Ave., between Pico Boulevard and Colorado Avenue, Santa Monica (✆ **310/395-1741;** www.chezjays.com).

(Tips Seeing the Getty Without the Crowd

Avoid the masses at the Getty Center by visiting in the late afternoon or evening; the center is open until 9pm Friday and Saturday. The nighttime view is breathtaking, and you can finish with a late dinner on the Westside.

Miami-style Latin, draw crowds, as does the small amusement area perched halfway down. Its name, **Pacific Park** (© 310/260-8744; www.pacpark.com), hearkens back to the granddaddy pier amusement park in California, Pacific Ocean Park; this updated version has a **solar-powered Ferris wheel,** a mild-mannered **roller coaster,** and 10 other rides, plus a high-tech **arcade** shootout. But anglers still head to the end to fish, and nostalgia buffs to view the photographic display of the pier's history. This is the last of the great pleasure piers, offering rides, romance, and perfect panoramic views of the bay and mountains.

The pier is about a mile up Ocean Front Walk from Venice; it's a great round-trip stroll. Parking is available for $6 to $8 on both the pier deck and the beachfront nearby. Limited short-term parking is also available. For information on twilight concerts (generally held Thurs btw. mid-June and the end of Aug), call © **310/458-8900** or visit www.santamonicapier.org.

Ocean Ave. at the end of Colorado Blvd., Santa Monica.

Six Flags California (Magic Mountain and Hurricane Harbor) ★★ *Kids* What started as a countrified little amusement park with a couple of relatively tame roller coasters in 1971 has been transformed by Six Flags into a thrill-a-minute daredevil's paradise called The Xtreme Park. Located about 20 to 30 minutes north of Universal Studios, Six Flags Magic Mountain is one of the only ones out of the 38 Six Flags parks that is open year-round. The 17 world-class roller coasters (more than any other place in the world) make it enormously popular with teenagers and young adults, and the children's playland—Bugs Bunny World—creates excitement for the pint-size set (kids under 48 in. tall.) Bring an iron constitution; rides with names like Goliath, Déjà Vu, Ninja, Viper, Colossus, and Psyclone will have your cheeks flapping with the G-force, and queasy expressions are common at the exit. Some rides are themed to action-film characters (such as Superman The Escape and the Riddler's Revenge); others are loosely tied to their themed surroundings, such as a Far East pagoda or gold rush mining town. The newest thrill rides are TATSU, a "flying beast" that's the tallest, fastest, and longest flying coaster in the world; Scream!, where riders are strapped into a "flying chair" and raced upside down seven times at 65 mph; and X, the world's first and only roller coaster where riders rotate 360 degrees forward and backward. Arcade games and summer-only entertainment (stunt shows, animal shows, and parades) round out the park's attractions.

Hurricane Harbor is Six Flags's tropical paradise. It's located right next door to Magic Mountain and is open May through September. You really can't see both in 1 day—combo tickets allow you to return sometime before the end of the season. Bring your own swimsuit; the park has changing rooms with showers and lockers. Like Magic Mountain, areas have themes like a tropical lagoon or an African river (complete with ancient temple ruins). The primary activities are swimming, going down the 23 water slides, rafting, playing volleyball, and lounging; many areas are designed especially for the little "buccaneer."

Note: Be sure to check their website for money-saving discounts on admission tickets—you could save up to $25 per ticket by buying online.

Magic Mountain Pkwy. (off Golden State Fwy. [I-5 N.]), Valencia. © **661/255-4100** or 818/367-5965. www.sixflags. com. Magic Mountain $60 adults, $30 children under 48 in. high, free for kids 2 and under; Hurricane Harbor $30 adults, $21 children under 48 in. high, free for kids 2 and under; 2-park combo ticket $70. Magic Mountain daily Apr to Labor Day, and weekends and holidays the rest of the year; Hurricane Harbor daily Memorial Day to Labor Day, weekends May and Sept, closed Oct–Apr. Both parks open at 10:30am, and closing hours vary btw. 6pm and midnight. Parking $15. All prices and hours are subject to change without notice, so please call before you arrive.

Sunset Boulevard & The Sunset Strip ★★   Unless you were raised in a cave,

you've undoubtedly heard of L.A.'s Sunset Boulevard. The most famous of the city's many legendary boulevards, it winds dozens of miles over prime real estate as it travels from Downtown to the beach, taking its travelers on both a historical and microcosmic journey that defines Los Angeles as a whole—from tacky strip malls and historic movie studios to infamous strip clubs and some of the most coveted zip codes on earth. In fact, driving the stretch from Hollywood to the Pacific should be required for all first-time visitors because it is such a good example of what L.A. is all about: instant gratification.

Bam! From the start, you'll see the **Saharan Motor Hotel,** of many a movie shoot; the Guitar Center's **Hollywood RockWalk,** where superstars like Chuck Berry, Little Richard, Santana, and the Van Halen brothers left handprints or signatures; the **"Riot Hyatt,"** where the Doors, Led Zeppelin, and Guns N' Roses crashed and smashed from the '60s through the '80s; and **Chateau Marmont,** where Greta Garbo lived and John Belushi died.

Phew! And you've barely even started. Once you pass the Chateau Marmont, you're officially cruising the **Sunset Strip**—a 1¾-mile stretch of Sunset Boulevard from Crescent Heights Boulevard to Doheny Drive. The tour continues with the **Comedy Store,** where Roseanne, Robin Williams, and David Letterman rose to stardom; Dan Aykroyd's ramshackle **House of Blues,** where the rock stars still show up for an impromptu show; the **Sunset Tower Hotel,** where Clark Gable, Marilyn Monroe, and John Wayne once lived; the ultraexclusive **Skybar** within the Mondrian hotel; Johnny Depp's **Viper Room,** where River Phoenix overdosed in 1993; **Whisky A Go-Go,** where the Doors were once a house band; and the **Rainbow Bar & Grill,** where Jimi Hendrix, Bruce Springsteen, and Bob Marley became legends.

Once you emerge from the strip, things calm down considerably as you drive through the tony neighborhoods of **Beverly Hills, Bel Air, Brentwood,** and **Pacific Palisades.** By the time you've reached **Malibu** and the beach where *Baywatch* was filmed, you'll have seen a vivid cross section of the city and have a pretty good idea of what L.A. is all about.

Universal Studios Hollywood & CityWalk ★★ *(Kids)*   Believing that filmmaking

itself is a bona fide attraction, Universal Studios began offering tours to the public in 1964. The concept worked: Today Universal is more than just one of the largest movie

---

Fun Fact **Tune Time**

The organ within the Walt Disney Concert Hall is so complex that it took a full year to tune.

Moments   **A Great Day in Downtown L.A.**

If you haven't heard the news, it's hip to hang out in Downtown L.A. these days. What used to be a ghost town after 5pm is speedily becoming a trendy destination as chic hotels (the Standard), bars (Edison), and venues (Walt Disney Concert Hall) sprout up like weeds between all those tall buildings. Start the day early with a 9¢ cup of coffee and cinnamon-dipped French toast at **Philippe The Original** (p. 152). At 10am, join the gaggle for a highly entertaining **Inside Historic Downtown L.A. Walking Tour** hosted by Red Line Tours (p. 187), followed by a self-guided audio tour of the spectacular new **Walt Disney Concert Hall** (bring a camera).

Time for lunch, so spend a few hours noshing your way through the dozens of ethnic food stalls at the **Grand Central Market** (p. 250). After lunch, the options abound: Wander the **Jewelry District** (a must-do is the beautiful open-air **St. Vincent's Jewelry Center,** the largest jewelry complex in the world) for great finds on cheap costume jewelry, or tour the poignant **Japanese American National Museum** (p. 180) or **Museum of Contemporary Art** (p. 180). If you did your homework, you already made reservations for a play or performance at the **Dorothy Chandler Pavilion** or **Walt Disney Concert Hall** (see chapter 10). After the show, it's time for a late-night bite at the suave **Noé** restaurant at the Omni hotel (p. 102), which stays open until midnight during performances. Cap off this grand day with a martini at the revolving **BonaVista cocktail lounge** high atop the Westin Bonaventure Hotel (p. 103). *Tip:* Be sure to get a DASH shuttle map (p. 39) so you can get around Downtown quickly and easily; rides are only 25¢.

studios in the world—it's one of the largest theme parks as well. By integrating shows and rides with behind-the-scenes presentations on moviemaking, Universal created a new genre of theme park, stimulating a number of clone and competitor parks.

The main attraction continues to be the **Studio Tour,** a nearly 1-hour guided tram ride around the company's 420 acres that's "hosted" (via video screen) by Whoopi Goldberg. En route you pass stars' dressing rooms and production offices before visiting famous back-lot sets that include a clean New York City street, the famous town square from the *Back to the Future* films, and newer sets such as *Curse of the Mummy's Tomb, Jurassic Park III, The Grinch,* and the airplane crash site from *War of the Worlds.* Along the way, the tram encounters several staged "disasters," which I won't divulge here lest I ruin the surprise (they're all very tame), and a staged street race "accident" echoing the action in Universal's "Fast and Furious" movie series. Though the wait to board might appear long, don't be discouraged—each tram carries several hundred people and departures are frequent, so the line moves quickly.

Other attractions are more typical of high-tech theme-park fare, but all have a film or TV-oriented slant. The **Simpsons Ride** allows guests to join Homer, Marge, Bart, Lisa, and Maggie as they soar high above the fictional "Krustyland" theme park in a "virtual roller coaster," creating the sensation of thrilling drops and turns and a full 360-degree loop. **Revenge of the Mummy** is a high-tech indoor roller coaster that whips you backward and forward through a dark Egyptian tomb filled with creepy Warrior Mummies (and ends a bit too soon). **Jurassic Park—The Ride** is short in duration as well but long on dinosaur animatronics; riders in jungle boats float through a world of five-story-tall T-rexes and airborne raptors that culminates in a pitch-dark vertical drop with a splash ending. **Terminator 2: 3D** is a high-tech cyberwar show that combines live action along with triple-screen 3-D technology, explosions, spraying mists, and laser fire (Arnold prevails, of course). **Shrek 4D** is one of the park's best attractions, a multisensory animated show that combines 3-D effects, a humorous story line, and "surprise" special effects—the flying dragon chase is wild.

There are also several live shows performing daily. At the **Fear Factor Live** show—based upon the NBC hit—park guests compete against each other in a progression of extreme stunts. **Waterworld** is a fast-paced outdoor theater presentation (and far better than the film that inspired it) featuring stunts and special effects performed on and around a small man-made lagoon (most performances are sold out, so arrive at the theater at least 15 min. before the showtime listed in the handout park map). In **Backdraft,** guests move from theater to theater amid realistic ruptured fuel lines, melting metal, and scorching warehouse scenes. On the **Animal Actors Stage** trained monkeys, pigs, hawks, and other animals perform various entertaining tricks (well, most of the time). Also be sure to check out the **Wardrobe Dept.,** a retail store offering an eclectic array of men's and women's clothing from popular television and movie productions all accompanied by a certificate of authenticity, documenting the television or movie production on which the item was originally worn.

Straight ahead of the park's main entrance on Main Street is the **Hollywood Ticket Office,** where you can obtain free tickets (subject to availability) for any TV shows that are taping during your visit—including the *Tonight Show with Jay Leno*—as well as tickets and passes to other local museums, sporting events, and entertainment attractions.

Universal Studios is an exciting place for kids and teens, but just as in any theme park, lines can be brutally long; the wait for a 5-minute ride can sometimes last more than an hour. In summer, the stifling Valley heat can dog you all day. To avoid the crowds, try not to visit on weekends, school vacations, and Japanese holidays. If you're willing to pay extra money to skip the hassle of standing in line, the park offers a **"Front of Line" pass** with—obviously—front-of-the-line privileges, as well as VIP passes (essentially private tours). You can also save time standing in line by purchasing and printing your tickets online. Log on to www.universalstudioshollywood.com for more information. Another ticket option is the **"All You Can Eat"** pass, which allows guests to dine all day at selected in-park restaurants for one price.

Fun Fact **Glaring Mistake**

The only people who weren't applauding the new Walt Disney Concert Hall were the condominium owners across the street. To them the stainless-steel building was a giant Easy-Bake oven—every time the sunlight reflected off the Concert Hall and into the condos, it increased daytime room temperatures up to 15%. The final solution was to dull the finish on certain sections of the Concert Hall.

For the freeway-phobic or those car-less at Disneyland, Universal offers an **Anaheim Shuttle Service** available to guests who purchase a full-price admission ticket to Universal Studios online via Print@Home ticketing at www.universalstudioshollywood. com. The shuttle bus departs from various Anaheim-area hotels twice daily. Additionally, the **Southern California CityPass** (p. 159) offers admission to five SoCal attractions including Universal Studios Hollywood and the Disneyland Resort.

Located just outside the gate of Universal Studios Hollywood is **Universal City-Walk** (© 818/622-4455; www.citywalkhollywood.com). If you have any money left from the amusement park, you can spend it at this 3-block-long pedestrian promenade crammed thick with flashy name-brand stores (Billabong, Fossil, Skechers, Abercrombie & Fitch), nightclubs (Blues at B. B. King's, Howl at the Moon dueling piano bar, Rumba Room Latin dance club), restaurants (Hard Rock Cafe, Daily Grill, Bubba Gumps, Saddle Ranch), a six-story 3-D IMAX theater, the 18-screen **City-Walk Cinemas**, a 6,200-seat amphitheater, an indoor sky-diving wind tunnel, NASCAR virtual racing, and even a bowling alley (Take *that,* Disney!). Be sure to stop into the **Zen Zone** (© 818/487-7889) where you can get an inexpensive 20-minute "aqua massage." You lay down fully clothed in what looks like a tanning bed, and strong rotating jets of water massage your backside from neck-to-toe (a blue rubber sheet keeps you dry). Entrance to CityWalk is free; it's open until 9pm on weekdays and until midnight Friday and Saturday. *Tip:* The sushi at the Wasabi at CityWalk restaurant (© 818/622-7224) was surprisingly good and very reasonably priced.

Hollywood Fwy. (Universal Center Dr. or Lankershim Blvd. exits), Universal City. © **800-UNIVERSAL** (800/864-8377) or 818/622-3801. www.universalstudioshollywood.com. Admission $65 adults, $55 children under 48 in. tall, free for kids 2 and under. Parking $10. Winter hours 10am–6pm; summer hours 9am–7pm. Hours are subject to change.

Venice Beach's Ocean Front Walk ★★★ *(Kids)*   This has long been one of L.A.'s most colorful areas and a must-visit for any first-time tourist. Founded at the turn of the last century, Venice was a development inspired by its Italian namesake. Authentic gondolas plied miles of inland waterways lined with rococo palaces. In the 1950s, Venice became the stamping grounds of Jack Kerouac, Allen Ginsberg, William S. Burroughs, and other Beats. In the 1960s, this was the epicenter of L.A.'s hippie scene.

Today, Venice is still one of the world's most engaging bohemian locales. It's not an exaggeration to say that no visit to L.A. would be complete without a stroll along the famous paved beach path, an almost surreal assemblage of every L.A. stereotype—and then some. Among stalls and stands selling cheap sunglasses, Mexican blankets, and "herbal ecstasy" pills swirls a carnival of humanity that includes bikini-clad in-line skaters, tattooed bikers, tan hunks pumping iron at Muscle Beach, panhandling vets, beautiful wannabes, and plenty of tourists and gawkers. On any given day, you're bound to come across all kinds of performers: mimes, break-dancers, stoned drummers, chain-saw jugglers, talking parrots, and the occasional apocalyptic evangelist.

On the beach, btw. Venice Blvd. and Rose Ave., Venice. www.venicebeach.com.

Walt Disney Concert Hall ★★★   The strikingly beautiful Walt Disney Concert Hall isn't just the new home of the Los Angeles Philharmonic; it's a key element in an urban revitalization effort now underway Downtown. The Walt Disney family insisted on the best and, with an initial gift of $50 million to build a world-class performance venue, that's what they got: A masterpiece of design by world-renowned architect Frank Gehry, and an acoustical quality that equals or surpasses those of the best concert halls in the world. Similar to Gehry's most famous architectural masterpiece, the Guggenheim

Overrated L.A.'s Top Tourist Traps

Some things are better left unspoken and, in some circumstances, unseen as well. Such is the case with the following schlock-shock attractions, the kind of money-sucking businesses that do a very, very poor job at attracting repeat clientele. Not surprisingly, they're all located in the heart of Hollywood on cheese-laden Hollywood Boulevard.

Hollywood Guinness World Records Museum Scale models, photographs, and push-button displays of the world's fattest man, biggest plant, smallest woman, fastest animal, and other superlatives don't make for a superlative experience. 6764 Hollywood Blvd., Hollywood. *(C)* **323/463-6433.** www.guinnessattractions.com. Admission $13 adults, $6.95 children ages 6 to 13. Daily 10am to midnight.

The Hollywood Wax Museum Cast in the Madame Tussaud mold, the Hollywood Wax Museum features more than 120 lifelike figures of movie stars, many of whom are still kicking. A wax replica of Marilyn Monroe I can understand, but Ben Affleck? Eeew. Yes, it's pretty cheesy and overpriced for what it offers, but it can still be good for a corny laugh or two. 6767 Hollywood Blvd., Hollywood. *(C)* **323/462-8860.** www.hollywoodwax.com. Admission $16 adults, $14 seniors, $6.95 children ages 6 to 12, free for kids age 5 and under. Daily 10am to midnight.

Ripley's "Believe It Or Not!" Museum Believe it or not, this tired dog of a "museum" is still open. Its bizarre collection of 300 wax figures, photos, and models depicts unnatural oddities from Robert Leroy Ripley's infamous arsenal. My favorite oddities include the skeleton of a two-headed baby, a statue of Marilyn Monroe sculpted with shredded money, and a portrait of John Wayne made from laundry lint. Right. 6780 Hollywood Blvd. *(C)* **323/466-6335.** www.ripleys.com. Admission $13 adults, $9 children ages 5 to 12, free for children ages 4 and under. Sunday through Thursday 10am to 10pm; Friday and Saturday 10am until midnight.

Museum in Bilbao, the concert hall's dramatic stainless-steel exterior consists of a series of undulating curved surfaces that partially envelop the entire building, presenting multiple glimmering facades to the surrounding neighborhood. Within is a dazzling 2,273-seat auditorium replete with curved woods and a dazzling array of organ pipes (also designed by Gehry), as well as Joachim Splichal's Patina restaurant, the hip Concert Hall Cafe, a bookstore, and a gift shop.

The 3½-acre Concert Hall is open to the public for viewing, but to witness it in its full glory, do whatever it takes to attend a concert by the world-class Los Angeles Philharmonic (p. 278). Also highly recommended are the $12 audio tours, which lead visitors through the Concert Hall's history from conception to creation. The 45-minute self-guided tour is narrated by actor John Lithgow and includes interviews with Frank Gehry, Los Angeles Philharmonic music director Esa-Pekka Salonen, and acoustician Yasuhisa Toyota, among others. One big caveat is that you see just about everything except the auditorium: There's almost always a rehearsal in progress and the acoustics are so good that there's no discreet way to sneak a peek. The audio tours are available on most non-matinee days from 10am to 2pm (be sure to check their website for the monthly tour schedule).

111 S. Grand Ave. (at 1st St). © 323/850-2000 or 213/972-4399. www.disneyhall.com or www.musiccenter.org.

2 Museums & Galleries

See p. 159 for the **J. Paul Getty collection** at the Getty Center Los Angeles.

L.A.'S WESTSIDE & BEVERLY HILLS

Hammer Museum ⚘   Created by the former chairman and CEO of Occidental Petroleum, the Hammer Museum is ensconced in a two-story Carrara marble building attached to the oil company's offices. It's better known for its high-profile and often provocative visiting exhibits. With a reputation for championing contemporary political and experimental art, the Hammer continues to present often daring and usually popular special exhibits, and it's definitely worth calling ahead to find out what will be there during your visit to L.A. The permanent collection (Armand Hammer's personal collection) consists mostly of traditional western European and Anglo-American art, and contains noteworthy paintings by Toulouse-Lautrec, Rembrandt, Degas, and van Gogh.

10899 Wilshire Blvd. (at Westwood Blvd.). © 310/443-7000. www.hammer.ucla.edu. Admission $5 adults, $3 seniors 65 and over, free for kids ages 17 and under; free for everyone Thurs. Tues–Wed and Fri–Sat 11am–7pm; Thurs 11am–9pm; Sun 11am–5pm. Parking $3 for 1st 3 hr. with validation.

Museum of Tolerance ⚘   The Museum of Tolerance is designed to expose prejudices, bigotry, and inhumanity while teaching racial and cultural tolerance. Since its opening in 1993, it's hosted 4 million visitors from around the world, including King Hussein of Jordan and the Dalai Lama. It's located in the Simon Wiesenthal Center, an institute founded by the legendary Nazi hunter. While the Holocaust figures prominently here, this is not a Jewish museum—it's an academy that broadly campaigns for a live-and-let-live world. Tolerance is an abstract idea that's hard to display, so most of this $50-million museum's exhibits are high-tech and conceptual in nature. Fast-paced interactive displays are designed to touch the heart as well as the mind, and engage everyone from heads of state to the MTV generation.

9786 W. Pico Blvd. (at Roxbury Dr.). © 310/553-8403. www.museumoftolerance.com. Admission $13 adults, $11 seniors 62 and above, $10 students with ID and youth 5–18, free for children ages 4 and under. Advance purchase recommended; photo ID required for admission. Mon–Fri 10am–5pm; Sun 11am–5pm. Closed Sat and many Jewish and secular holidays; call for schedule.

The Paley Center for Media ⚘   Want to see the Beatles on *The Ed Sullivan Show* (1964), or Edward R. Murrow's examination of Joseph McCarthy (1954), or Arnold Palmer's victory in the 1958 Masters Tournament; or want to listen to radio excerpts like FDR's first "Fireside Chat" (1933) and Orson Welles's famous *War of the Worlds* UFO hoax (1938)? All these, plus a gazillion episodes of *The Twilight Zone, I Love Lucy,* and other beloved series (including numerous pilots never aired on national television), can be viewed within the starkly white walls of architect Richard Meier's neutral, contemporary building. Like the ritzy Beverly Hills shopping district that surrounds it, the Center (formerly the Museum of Television and Radio) is more flash than substance. Once you gawk at the celebrity and industry-honcho names adorning every hall, room, and miscellaneous area, it becomes quickly apparent that "library"

⌒Value Free Culture

To beef up attendance and give indigent folk like us travel writers a break, almost all of L.A.'s art galleries and museums are open free to the public 1 day of the week or month (or both), and several charge no admission. Use the following list to plan your week around the museums' free-day schedules; refer to the individual attractions listings in this chapter for more information on each museum.

Free Every Day
- J. Paul Getty Museum at the Getty Center
- The Getty Villa Malibu
- Paley Center for Media (donation suggested)
- Los Angeles County Museum of Art, *after* 5pm
- California African American Museum
- California Science Center
- Bergamot Arts Station & Santa Monica Museum of Art

Free Every Thursday
- Museum of Contemporary Art (MOCA), from 5 to 8pm
- Museum of the American West, from 4 to 8pm
- UCLA Hammer Museum, from 11am to 9pm
- Japanese American National Museum, from 5 to 8pm
- Skirball Cultural Center, from noon to 9pm
- Geffen Contemporary at MOCA, from 5 to 8pm

Free Every Friday
- Schindler House, from 4 to 6pm

Free Every First Tuesday
- Natural History Museum of Los Angeles County, from 9:30am to 5pm
- Page Museum at La Brea Tar Pits, from 9:30am to 5pm

Free Every First Wednesday
- Craft & Folk Art Museum, from 11am to 5pm

Free Every First Thursday
- Huntington Library, Art Collections & Botanical Gardens, from noon to 4:30pm

Free Every First Friday
- Norton Simon Museum of Art, from 6 to 9pm

Free Every Second Tuesday
- Museum of the American West, from 10am to 5pm
- Los Angeles County Museum of Art, from noon to 8pm

Free Every Third Tuesday
- Los Angeles County Arboretum and Botanic Garden, from 9am to 4:30pm
- Japanese American National Museum, from 10am to 8pm

Free Every Fourth Friday
- Pacific Asia Museum, from 10am to 8pm

Moments **Greystone Mansion**

If you've seen *The Witches of Eastwick* or *War and Remembrance,* then you already know how beautiful and opulent the Greystone Mansion and surrounding gardens are. Situated on a gentle slope overlooking Beverly Hills, the 19-acre park is a prime filming location where dozens of TV episodes, movies (*Spiderman, X-Men, Batman, Ghostbusters, The Bodyguard*), commercials, and music videos are filmed annually. It's worth a visit just to admire the matriarch of Beverly Hills mansions and the meticulously groomed gardens. A self-guided tour takes you through the Formal Gardens, Mansion Gardens, and Lower Ground Estate. Picnics are welcome in designated areas (as are dogs), and **Afternoon Tea on the Terrace** is offered one Saturday per month from May through August at 4pm. The price is $43 for nonresidents and includes musical entertainment and a tour of the Mansion's first floor. Tickets must be purchased in advance by calling ✆ **310/550-4654.** The park is located at 905 Loma Vista Dr., just off Doheny Drive, and is open daily from 10am to sunset. Admission is free. For more information, log on to www.beverlyhills.org.

would be a more fitting name for this collection, since the main attractions—120,000 television and radio programs and commercials—are requested via sophisticated computer catalogs and viewed in private consoles. Although no one sets out to spend a vacation watching TV, it can be tempting once you start browsing the archives. This West Coast branch of the venerable New York facility succeeds in treating our culture's favorite pastime as a legitimate art form of historical significance.

465 N. Beverly Dr. (at Santa Monica Blvd.), Beverly Hills. ✆ 310/786-1000. www.mtr.org. Suggested contribution $10 adults, $8 students and seniors, $5 kids ages 12 and under. Wed–Sun noon–5pm. Closed New Year's Day, July 4, Thanksgiving Day, and Christmas Day. Parking free for 2 hr. with validation.

Skirball Cultural Center ✦ This strikingly modern museum/cultural center is quick to remind us that Jewish history is about more than the Holocaust. Nestled in the Sepulveda Pass uphill from the Getty Center, the Skirball explores American Jewish life, American democratic values, and the pursuit of the American dream—a theme shared by many immigrant groups. The Skirball's core exhibit, "Visions and Values: Jewish Life from Antiquity to America," chronicles the experiences and accomplishments of the Jewish people over 4,000 years. Related events are held here throughout the year; one recent highlight was a rollicking festival of klezmer music (a traditional Jewish folk-music style). Call for free docent-led tour times.

2701 N. Sepulveda Blvd. (at Mulholland Dr.). ✆ 310/440-4500. www.skirball.org. Admission $10 adults, $7 students and seniors 65 and over, $5 children 2–12, free for kids 1 and under; free for everyone Thurs. Tues–Fri noon–5pm (Thurs to 9pm); Sat–Sun 10am–5pm. Closed on Mon. Free parking. From I-405, exit at Skirball Center Dr./Mulholland Dr.

HOLLYWOOD

Craft & Folk Art Museum This gallery, housed in a prominent Museum Row building, has grown into one of the city's largest. "Craft and folk art" encompasses everything from clothing, tools, religious artifacts, and other everyday objects to woodcarvings, papier-mâché, weaving, and metalwork. The museum displays folk objects from around the world, but its strongest collection is masks from India, America, Mexico, Japan, and

Hollywood Area Attractions

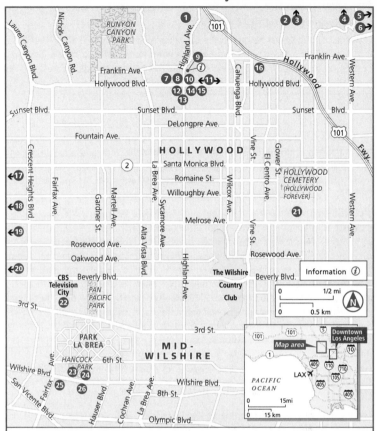

Capitol Records Building **16**
Craft & Folk Art Museum **26**
Egyptian Theater **14**
Freeman House **1**
Grauman's Chinese Theatre **7**
Griffith Park & Observatory **4**
The Grove at the Farmers Market **22**
Hollywood & Highland **8**
Hollywood Guinness
  World of Records **15**
Hollywood Museum **13**
HOLLYWOOD Sign **3**
Hollywood Walk of Fame **11**
Hollywood Wax Museum **10**
La Brea Tar Pits / Page Museum **24**

Los Angeles County Museum
  of Art **23**
Los Angeles Zoo **6**
Museum of Television & Radio **17**
Museum of the American West **5**
Pacific Design Center **19**
Paramount Pictures Studios **21**
Petersen AutomotiveMuseum **25**
Ripley's "Believe It Or Not" Museum **12**
Schindler House **18**
Sunset Ranch Hollywood Stables **2**
Tail o' the Pup **20**
Visitor Information Center Hollywood **9**

Fun Fact **L.A.-Style XXX-ercise**

Actress Sheila Kelley has taken the L.A. exercise craze in an X-citing new direction with "the S Factor," a workout regimen inspired by striptease and pole dancing. A 2-hour intro course is only $40, but be sure to sign up early as they fill up fast (sorry guys, it's for women only). Check it out at www.sfactor.com.

China. The museum is also known for its annual International Festival of Masks, held each October in Hancock Park, across the street. Be sure to stop in the funky, eclectic Museum Shop to peruse the wearable art, folk-art books, and various handmade crafts.

5814 Wilshire Blvd. (btw. Fairfax and La Brea aves.). © 323/937-4230. www.cafam.org. Admission $5 adults, $3 seniors and students, free for children 11 and under; free to all 1st Wed each month. Tues–Wed and Fri 11am–5pm; Thurs 11am–7pm; Sat–Sun noon–6pm.

The Hollywood Museum   The historic Max Factor Building—Max Factor was the patriarch of the Hollywood makeup industry—has finally been restored to its original 1935 Art Deco splendor and is now the home of the Hollywood Museum, which features four floors of famous and rare props (including Hannibal Lecter's cell), costumes (Nicole Kidman's from *Moulin Rouge*), scripts, cameras, awards, and numerous vintage photos and posters from the television, stage, and recording industries. It's arranged for the visitor to experience Hollywood chronologically—from the Silent Era and Golden Era to current production technology and a glimpse into the future of the industry. The museum, located across from the Hollywood & Highland entertainment complex, also houses a library, a screening room, an education center, and a museum-studio gift shop. Private guided tours are available upon request.

1660 N. Highland Ave. (at Hollywood Blvd.), Hollywood. © 323/464-7776. www.thehollywoodmuseum.com. Admission and tour $15 adults, $12 seniors and children 11 and under. Thurs–Sun 10am–5pm. Parking $2 with validation.

Los Angeles County Museum of Art (LACMA) ★★   For more than 50 years LACMA has been one of the finest art museums in the nation, housing a 110,000-piece collection that includes works by Degas, Rembrandt, Hockney, and Monet. The huge 20-acre complex—it's the largest visual arts museum west of Chicago—has been expanded even more with the recent opening of the $56-million, three-story **Broad Contemporary Art Museum** (also known as BCAM). Boasting 60,000 square feet of exhibition space, it's the first new art museum built in L.A. since the Getty Center opened in 1997. BCAM is one of the largest column-free art spaces in the U.S., and opening installations include works by such contemporary artists as Richard Serra, Jeff Koons, Jasper Johns, Andy Warhol, and Roy Lichtenstein.

Other highlights include LACMA's **Pavilion for Japanese Art,** which has exterior walls made of Kalwall, a translucent material that, like shoji screens, permits the entry of soft natural light. Inside is a collection of Japanese Edo paintings that's rivaled only by the holdings of the emperor of Japan. The **Ahmanson Building** houses the majority of the museum's permanent collections—everything from 2,000-year-old pre-Columbian Mexican ceramics to 19th-century portraiture, to a unique glass collection spanning the centuries. Other displays include one of the nation's largest holdings of costumes and textiles, and an important Indian and Southeast Asian art collection. Free 50-minute guided tours of many of LACMA's special exhibitions are offered weekly—check the museum's online calendar for times and locations.

5905 Wilshire Blvd. ℂ **323/857-6000.** www.lacma.org. Admission $12 adults, $8 students and seniors ages 62 and over, free for children 17 and under; regular exhibitions free for everyone after 5pm and all day the 2nd Tues of each month. Mon–Tues and Thurs noon–8pm; Fri noon–9pm; Sat–Sun 11am–8pm. Parking $5.

Museum of the American West ★★

Located north of Downtown in Griffith Park, this is one of the country's finest and most comprehensive museums of the American West. More than 78,000 artifacts showcasing the history of the region west of the Mississippi River are intelligently displayed. Evocative exhibits illustrate the everyday lives of early pioneers, not only with antique firearms, tools, saddles, and the like, but with many hands-on displays that successfully stir the imagination and the heart. You'll find footage from Buffalo Bill's Wild West Show, movie clips from the silent days, contemporary films, the works of Wild West artists, and plenty of memorabilia from Gene "the Singing Cowboy" Autry's film and TV projects. The Hall of Merchandising displays Roy Rogers bedspreads, Hopalong Cassidy radios, and other items from the collective consciousness—and material collections—of baby boomers. Provocative visiting exhibits usually focus on cultural or domestic regional history. Docent-led tours are generally scheduled on Saturdays at 11am and noon. Admission is free every second Tuesday of the month.

4700 Western Heritage Way (in Griffith Park). ℂ **323/667-2000.** www.autrynationalcenter.org. Admission $9 adults, $5 seniors 60 and over and students ages 13–18, $3 children ages 2–12, free for children 1 and under; free to all Thurs after 4pm. Tues–Sun 10am–5pm (Thurs until 8pm). Free parking.

Petersen Automotive Museum ★★ *Kids*

When the Petersen opened in 1994, many locals were surprised that it had taken this long for the city of freeways to salute its most important shaper. Indeed, this museum says more about the city than probably any other in L.A. Named for Robert Petersen, the publisher responsible for *Hot Rod* and *Motor Trend* magazines, the four-story, 300,000-square-foot museum displays more than 200 cars and motorcycles, from the historic to the futuristic. Cars on the first floor are exhibited chronologically in period settings. Other floors are devoted to frequently changing shows of race cars, early motorcycles, famous movie vehicles, and celebrity wheels such as Jack Benny's old Chrysler Imperial. On the third floor is the Discovery Center, a 6,500-square-foot interactive "hands-on" learning center that teaches adults and kids the basic scientific principles of how a car works. Past shows have included a comprehensive exhibit of "woodies" and surf culture, Hollywood "star cars," and the world's fastest and most valuable cars.

6060 Wilshire Blvd. (at Fairfax Ave.). ℂ **323/930-CARS** (323/930-2277). www.petersen.org. Admission $10 adults, $5 seniors and students, $3 children ages 5–12, free for kids ages 4 and under. Tues–Sun 10am–6pm. Parking $6.

DOWNTOWN

California African American Museum

This small museum is both a celebration of individual African Americans and a living showplace of contemporary culture. The best exhibits are temporary and touch on themes as varied as the human experience. Previous shows have included a sculpture exhibit examining interpretations of home, a survey of African puppetry, and a look at black music in Los Angeles in the 1960s. In the gift shop you'll find sub-Saharan wooden masks and woven baskets, as well as hand-embroidered Ethiopian pillows. There are also posters, children's books, and calendars. The museum offers a full calendar of lectures, concerts, and special events; call for the latest.

600 State Dr., Exposition Park. ℂ **213/744-7432.** www.caamuseum.org. Free admission; donation requested. Tues–Sat 10am–5pm and 1st Sun of each month 11am–5pm. Closed Thanksgiving, Christmas, and New Year's Day. Parking $6.

California Science Center ★★ (Kids) A $130-million renovation—reinvention, actually—has turned the former Museum of Science and Industry into Exposition Park's most popular attraction. Using high-tech sleight of hand, the center stimulates kids of all ages with questions, answers, and lessons about the world. The museum is organized into themed worlds, and one of the museum's highlights is Tess, a 50-foot animatronic woman whose muscles, bones, organs, and blood vessels are revealed, demonstrating how the body reacts to a variety of external conditions and activities. (Appropriate for children of all ages, Tess doesn't possess reproductive organs.) Another highlight is the **Air and Space Gallery,** a seven-story space where real air- and spacecraft are suspended overhead.

There are nominal fees, ranging from $2 to $5, to enjoy the science center's more thrilling attractions. You can pedal a bicycle across a high-wire suspended 43 feet above the ground (demonstrating the principle of gravity and counterweights) or get strapped into the Space Docking Simulator for a virtual-reality taste of zero gravity. There's plenty more, and plans for expansion are always in the works. The IMAX theater screen is seven stories high and 90 feet wide, with state-of-the-art surround-sound and 3-D technology. Films are screened throughout the day until 9pm and are nearly always breathtaking, even the two-dimensional ones.

700 State Dr., Exposition Park. ℂ 323/724-3623; IMAX theater ℂ 213/744-7400. www.casciencectr.org. Free admission to the museum; IMAX theater $8 adults, $5.75 seniors 59 and over and children ages 13–17, $4.75 ages 4–12. Multishow discounts available. Daily 10am–5pm. Closed Thanksgiving, Christmas, and New Year's Day. Parking $6.

Japanese American National Museum ★★ (Finds) Located in an architecturally acclaimed modern building in Little Tokyo, this soaring 85,000-square-foot pavilion—designed by renowned architect Gyo Obata—is a private nonprofit institute created to document and celebrate the history of the Japanese in America. The permanent and rotating exhibits chronicle Japanese life in the United States, highlighting distinctive aspects of Japanese-American culture ranging from the internment camp experience during the early years of World War II to the lives of Japanese Americans in Hawaii. The experience is made even more poignant by the personal accounts of the docents, many of whom are elderly Japanese-American citizens who were interred in these camps during the war. It's a very popular museum, attracting more than 150,000 annual visitors. *Tip:* Don't miss the museum store, which carries excellent gift items ranging from hand-fired sake sets to mini Zen gardening kits.

369 E. 1st St. (at Central Ave.). ℂ 213/625-0414. www.janm.org. Admission $8 adults, $5 seniors, $4 students and kids 6–17, free for kids ages 5 and under; free to all the 3rd Thurs of each month and every Thurs after 5pm. Tues–Sun 11am–5pm (Thurs until 8pm).

The Museum of Contemporary Art, Los Angeles (MOCA) MOCA is Los Angeles's only institution devoted to art from 1940 to the present. Displaying one of the country's finest collections of American and European art, the MOCA holds roughly 5,000 objects of various visual mediums—ranging from masterpieces of abstract expressionism and pop art to recent works by young and emerging artists—housed in three distant buildings. The Grand Avenue main building (250 S. Grand Ave.), which has received numerous design accolades, is a contemporary red sandstone structure by renowned Japanese architect Arata Isozaki. Also at the Grand Avenue location is the museum's popular restaurant, **Patinette** (Mon and Fri 11am–5pm, Wed 11am–2pm, Thurs 11am–8pm, Sat–Sun 11am–6pm; ℂ 213/626-1178), the casual-dining creation of celebrity chef Joachim Splichal (Patina, p. 147).

Downtown Area Attractions

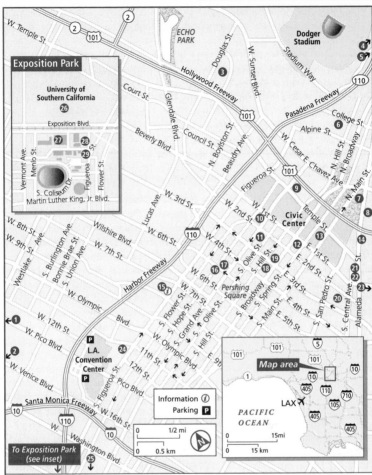

Exposition Park

University of Southern California 26

Exposition Blvd.

27 28 29

S. Coliseum Dr.
Martin Luther King, Jr. Blvd.

ECHO PARK

Dodger Stadium

To Exposition Park (see inset)

Information ⓘ
Parking Ⓟ

0   1/2 mi
0   0.5 km

Map area

LAX ✈

PACIFIC OCEAN

0   15mi
0   15 km

Angelino Heights **3**	Geffen Contemporary at MOCA **21**	Natural History Museum of Los Angeles County **27**
Boyle Heights **14**	Grand Central Market **18**	The Southwest Museum **5**
Bradbury Building **19**	Japanese American National Museum **22**	STAPLES Center/ L.A. Live **24**
California African American Museum **29**	Leimert Park Village **2**	Union Station **8**
California Science Center **28**	Little Tokyo **20**	University of Southern California (USC) **26**
Cathedral of Our Lady of the Angels **9**	The Los Angeles Times Building **12**	US Bank Tower **17**
Central Library **16**	Mariachi Plaza **23**	Visitors Information Center **15**
Chinatown **6**	Museum of Contemporary Art **11**	Walt Disney Concert Hall **10**
City Hall **13**	Museum of Tolerance **1**	Watts Towers **25**
El Alisal **4**		
El Pueblo de Los Angeles Historic District **7**		

The museum's second space, on Central Avenue in Little Tokyo (152 N. Central Ave.), was the "temporary" Contemporary while the Grand structure was being built and now presents rotating exhibits in a warehouse-type space that's been renamed the **Geffen Contemporary at MOCA** for entertainment mogul and art collector David Geffen. Unless there's a visiting exhibit of great interest at the main museum, I recommend that you start at the Geffen building, where it's also easier to park.

The third gallery is the **MOCA Pacific Design Center** (8687 Melrose Ave., West Hollywood)—it's the compact building next to the Pacific Design Center. Unlike the other two, admission to this gallery is free, and emphasis is on contemporary architecture and design, as well as new work by emerging and established artists.

Main MOCA information line: ☎ **213/626-6222**. www.moca.org. Admission (to all 3 galleries) $8 adults, $5 seniors 65 and over and students, free for children ages 11 and under. Free admission to all MOCA galleries every Thurs 5–8pm. Mon and Fri 11am–5pm; Thurs 11am–8pm; Sat–Sun 11am–6pm.

Natural History Museum of Los Angeles County ★★ *Kids*

The "Fighting Dinosaurs" are not a high school football team, but the trademark symbol of this massive museum: *Tyrannosaurus rex* and triceratops skeletons poised in a stance so realistic that every kid feels inspired to imitate their *Jurassic Park* bellows (think *Calvin & Hobbes*). Opened in 1913 in a beautiful domed Spanish Renaissance building, this massive museum—it's the largest natural and historical museum in the western United States—is a 35-hall warehouse of earth's history, chronicling the planet and its inhabitants from 600 million years ago to the present day, and housing more than 33 million specimens and artifacts. There's a mind-numbing array of exhibits of prehistoric fossils, bird and marine life, gems and minerals, and North American mammals. The kid-friendly **Discovery Center** entertains children via hands-on, interactive exhibits: Kids can make fossil rubbings, dig for fossils, and view live animals such as snakes and lizards. **Thomas the T. rex Lab** is a specially designed workroom where visitors can watch the actual work of paleontologists as they prepare and assemble the fossils of a 66-million-year-old *Tyrannosaurus rex* nicknamed "Thomas." The best permanent displays include the world's rarest shark, a walk-through vault of priceless gems (including the largest collection of gold in the United States), and an Insect Zoo.

The **Dinosaur Shop** sells ant farms and exploding volcano and model kits, the **Ethnic Arts Shop** has one-of-a-kind folk art and jewelry from around the world, and the bookstore has an extensive selection of scientific titles and hobbyists' field guides.

900 Exposition Blvd., Exposition Park. ☎ **213/763-DINO** (213/763-3466). www.nhm.org. Admission $9 adults; $6.50 children ages 13–17, seniors, and students with ID; $2 children ages 5–12; free for kids 4 and under; free for everyone 1st Tues of month. Mon–Fri 9:30am–5pm; Sat–Sun 10am–5pm.

SANTA MONICA

Santa Monica Museum of Art at Bergamot Station ★★

One of Santa Monica's primary cultural destinations is this campuslike art complex located just off the I-10 freeway. The location dates from 1875 when it was a stop for the Red Line trolley, and it retains a quasi-industrial look. Filled with more than 20 galleries, the unique installations on display here range from photography and sculpture to interactive pieces that are both eclectic and cutting edge. Its central location allows visitors to park in the free lot and spend the day seeing art rather than drive from one gallery to the next. Most pieces are available for purchase.

2525 Michigan Ave. (off Cloverfield Blvd.), Santa Monica. ☎ **310/586-6488**. www.smmoa.org. Free admission. Tues–Sat 11am–6pm; Sat 11am–8pm.

(Kids) Kid-Cool Attractions in L.A.

Much of larger-than-life L.A. is as appealing to kids as it is to adults. Many of the city's best attractions, like Venice Beach's **Ocean Front Walk** (p. 172), Hollywood's **Farmers Market** (p. 158), and Downtown's **Olvera Street** (part of El Pueblo de Los Angeles Historic Monument; p. 185) have a kid-friendly, carnival-like atmosphere. The novelty of sights such as the **Walk of Fame** (p. 164) and **Grauman's Chinese Theatre** (p. 163) appeals to kids as well. Older kids in particular love to go on **studio tours** (p. 199) and to **TV tapings** (p. 202).

Then there's the kid-centric museums. Kids who are into dinosaurs will dig **La Brea Tar Pits** (p. 165) and the cool prehistoric creatures on display at the adjoining **Page Museum** (really, you have to drag your kids out of here; p. 165). The **California Science Center** (p. 180) will entertain, stimulate, and even teach (sshhhh) kids about science, technology, biology, and the world around them. The **Natural History Museum** (p. 182), the Science Center's neighbor in Exposition Park, has giant dinosaur skeletons, an insect zoo, and a museum shop packed with terrifically fun model kits and other irresistible toys. The **Petersen Automotive Museum** (p. 179) is packed with cool-looking cars and motorcycles, as well as a science-themed Discovery Center designed just for kids.

Thanks to the **Winnick Family Children's Zoo** (p. 198), the Los Angeles Zoo is an all-day adventure for the kids. This excellent children's zoo has a top-notch petting zoo, exhibition animal-care center, Adventure Theater, and other kid-cool attractions. Or how about an afternoon of **horseback riding** (p. 214) on the trails through the Hollywood hills? Here's one you haven't thought of: the **J. Paul Getty Museum** at the Getty Center (p. 159). Deceptively educational programs for kids include exploratory games such as *The Getty Art Detective* and *Perplexing Paintings*. There's also a family room filled with picture books and games, storytelling sessions, weekend family workshops, and self-guided audio tours made specifically for families.

But wait, there's more. Young tourists will also like the surreal **Universal CityWalk** shopping mall (p. 254), the carousel and arcade at **Santa Monica Pier** (p. 166), and the miniature train ride at the **Travel Town Transportation Museum** in Griffith Park (p. 194). If they're sports fans there's sure to be a few tickets available for a pro **baseball, basketball,** or **soccer** game in town (p. 216). And if all this isn't enough, there's always **Universal Studios Hollywood** (p. 169), **Disneyland** (p. 219), **Knott's Berry Farm** (p. 234), and **Six Flags California** (p. 168) amusement parks. Or heck, just get the kids a toy bucket and shovel and spend the day at **Santa Monica State Beach** (p. 207).

PASADENA

Norton Simon Museum of Art ✦✦✦ (Finds)   Named for a food-packing king and financier who reorganized the failing Pasadena Museum of Modern Art, the Norton Simon displays one of the finest private collections of European, American, and Asian art in the world (and yet another feather in the cap of architect Frank Gehry, who redesigned the interior space). Comprehensive collections of masterpieces by Degas, Picasso, Rembrandt, and Goya are augmented by sculptures by Henry Moore and Auguste Rodin, including *The Burghers of Calais,* which greets you at the gates. The "Blue Four" collection of works by Kandinsky, Jawlensky, Klee, and Feininger is impressive, as is a superb collection of Southeast Asian sculpture. *Still Life with Lemons, Oranges, and a Rose* (1633), an oil by Francisco de Zurbarán, is one of the museum's most important holdings. Perhaps the most popular piece is *The Flower Vendor/Girl with Lilies,* by Diego Rivera, followed by Goya's *Disasters of War.* The collection of paintings, sculptures, pastels, and prints by French Impressionist Edgar Degas is among the best in the world. *Tip:* Unless you're an art expert, you'll probably want to take the "Acoustiguide" audio tour—it's $3 well spent.

411 W. Colorado Blvd., Pasadena. (✆) 626/449-6840. www.nortonsimon.org. Admission $8 adults, $4 seniors, free for students and kids 17 and under; free for everyone the 1st Fri of each month 6–9pm. Wed–Mon noon–6pm (Fri until 9pm). Free parking.

Pacific Asia Museum The most striking aspect of this museum is the building itself. Designed in the 1920s in Chinese Imperial Palace style, it's rivaled in flamboyance only by Grauman's Chinese Theatre in Hollywood (see "L.A.'s Top Attractions," earlier in this chapter). Rotating exhibits of 14,000 rare Asian and Pacific Islands art and artifacts span the centuries, from 100 B.C. to the current day. This manageable-size museum is worth a visit, particularly if you're an adherent of Buddhism.

46 N. Los Robles Ave., Pasadena. (✆) 626/449-2742, ext. 10. www.pacificasiamuseum.org. Admission $7 adults, $5 students and seniors, free for children 11 and under; free for everyone the 4th Fri of each month. Wed–Sun 10am–6pm. Free parking.

3 L.A.'s Ethnic Neighborhoods

Los Angeles has the highest concentration of Mexicans outside Mexico, Koreans outside Korea, and even Samoans outside Samoa. Tiny Russian, Ethiopian, Armenian, and even British enclaves also coexist throughout L.A. But to call the city a "melting pot" wouldn't be quite accurate; to paraphrase Alex Haley, it's really more of a tossed salad, composed of distinct, albeit overlapping, cultures.

The following neighborhoods all fall under the "Downtown" label, as we've defined it in "Orientation" in chapter 4.

Boyle Heights In the first decades of the 20th century, Boyle Heights was inhabited by Jewish immigrants, who have since migrated west to the Fairfax district and beyond. They left behind the oldest orthodox synagogue in Los Angeles, and Brooklyn Avenue, which has since been renamed Cesar E. Chavez Avenue. Boyle Heights is now the heart of the Latino barrio.

Westsiders come here for cheap Mexican food, but many miss my favorite Boyle Heights sight: Near the corner of Boyle Avenue and 1st Street is **Mariachi Plaza,** a colorful street corner where three-, four-, and five-man mariachi bands stand ready to entertain each afternoon and evening. Resplendent in matching ruffled shirts and tailored bolero jackets with a rainbow of embroidery, the mariachis loiter beneath three-story murals of their forebears with guitars at the ready. It's not unusual to see someone drive up in a minivan, offer a price for a night's entertainment, and carry off an ensemble to play a private party or other gathering.

East of Downtown; bounded by U.S. 101, I-10, Calif. 60, and Indiana St.

Chinatown   Many Chinese settled in this once-rural area during the second half of the 19th century. Today, most Angelenos of Chinese descent are well integrated into the city's suburbs; few can be found living in this rough pocket of Downtown. But though the neighborhood hardly compares in quality or size to the Chinese quarters of London, San Francisco, or New York, Chinatown's bustling little mom-and-pop shops and profusion of ethnic restaurants provide an interesting Downtown diversion.

Chinatown centers on a mall, **Mandarin Plaza,** 970 N. Broadway, reconstructed in 1938 a few blocks from its original site just south of Dodger Stadium. Go on a Sunday morning for dim sum at **Empress Pavilion,** 988 N. Hill St. (© **213/617-9898**), and then browse through the collection of shops jammed with Chinese slippers, cheap jewelry, and china. You'll also find some upscale stores specializing in inlaid furniture, Asian art, fine silks, and other imports.

Chinatown is especially worth going out of your way for during **Chinese New Year,** a month-long celebration that usually begins in late January. The neighborhood explodes into a colorful fantasy of sights and sounds with the Golden Dragon Parade, a beauty pageant, and a 5K/10K run. There are plenty of firecrackers and all the Lin Go New Year's cakes you can eat. For more information about Chinatown, log on to www.chinatownla.com.

Downtown; bounded by N. Broadway, N. Hill St., Bernard St., and Sunset Blvd.

El Pueblo de Los Angeles Historic Monument ☆ (Kids)   This historic district was built in the 1930s on the site where the city was founded, as an alternative to the razing of a particularly unsightly slum. The result is a contrived nostalgic fantasy of the city's beginnings, a kitschy theme park portraying Latino culture in a Disney-esque fashion. Nevertheless, El Pueblo has proven wildly successful, as L.A.'s Latinos have adopted it as an important cultural monument.

El Pueblo is not without authenticity. Some of L.A.'s oldest buildings are here, and the area really does exude the ambience of Old Mexico. At its core is a Mexican-style marketplace on old brick-paved **Olvera Street.** On weekends the carnival of sights and sounds is heightened by mariachis, piñatas, and more-than-occasional folkloric dancing. Olvera Street, the district's primary pedestrian street, and adjacent Main Street are home to about two dozen 19th-century buildings. Free 1-hour walking tours are given Tuesday through Saturday; for tour times contact **El Pueblo Visitor Center** (622 N. Main St.; © **213/628-1274;** www.lasangelitas.org). Also, don't miss the **Avila Adobe,** at E-10 Olvera St. (Mon–Sat 10am–5pm; free admission); built in 1818, it's the oldest building in the city.

Enter El Pueblo Historic Monument via Alameda St. across from Union Station.

Koreatown   Here's something you probably didn't know: There are more Koreans in Los Angeles than anywhere else in the world outside of Korea—some 100,000. If you drive down Western Avenue between Olympic and Wilshire boulevards it won't take much imagination to believe that you're suddenly in a section of Seoul. Hundreds of signs in Korean script are bolted onto dozens of minimalls and office buildings within this vibrant commercial district. Park the car and spend a few hours browsing the elixir shops, bargain stores, malls, and authentic Korean barbecue joints. You might also want to visit the museum within the **Korean Cultural Center,** 5505 Wilshire Blvd. (Mon–Fri 9am–5pm, Sat 10am–1pm; © **323/936-7141;** www.kccla. org), which houses historical photographs, Korean antiques, and rotating exhibits.

West of Downtown; bounded by Wilshire Ave., Crenshaw Blvd., Olympic Blvd., and Vermont Ave.

Leimert Park Village The neighborhood around tiny Leimert Park is becoming a center of African-American artistic life and historical focus. It features galleries, restaurants, and shops filled with local crafts and African imports. Folks flock here to jazz clubs that evoke the heyday of L.A.'s Central Avenue jazz scene, when greats like Ella Fitzgerald mesmerized audiences. In December, Kwanzaa celebrations enliven Leimert Park further.

Southwest of Downtown; bounded by Crenshaw Blvd., Vernon Ave., Leimert Blvd., and 43rd Place.

Little Tokyo Like nearby Chinatown, this redeveloped ethnic neighborhood isn't home to the majority of Angelenos of Japanese ancestry; suburban Gardena has that distinction. But Little Tokyo functions as the community's cultural focal point and is home to several malls filled with bakeries, bookshops, restaurants, and boutiques, as well as the occasional Buddhist temple. The **Japanese American National Museum** (p. 180) is here, as is the **Japanese American Cultural and Community Center,** 244 S. San Pedro St. (© **213/628-2725;** www.jaccc.org), which regularly offers traditional Kabuki dramas and modern music concerts.

Unfortunately Little Tokyo is shabbier than almost any district in the Japanese capital, and it has difficulty holding a visitor's attention for much longer than the time it takes to eat lunch. Exceptions to this rule come twice yearly, during the **Cherry Blossom Festival** in spring and **Nisei Week** in late summer. Both heritage festivals celebrate Japanese culture with parades, traditional Ondo street dancing, a carnival, and an arts fair. The Japanese American Network provides a community calendar, a map of Little Tokyo points of interest, and useful Web links online at www.janet.org/janet_little_tokyo/ja_little_tokyo.html.

Downtown, southeast of the Civic Center; bounded by 1st, 2nd, San Pedro, and Los Angeles sts.

4 Architectural Highlights

Because it's more receptive to experimentation than some other American cities, Los Angeles is a veritable Disneyland of architecture. The city is home to an amalgam of distinctive styles, from Art Deco to Spanish Revival, to coffee-shop kitsch, to suburban ranch, to postmodern—and much more.

The movie industry, more than anything else, has defined Los Angeles. The process of moviemaking has never been confined to studio offices and back lots; it spills into the city's streets and other public spaces. The city itself is an extension of the movie set, and Angelenos have always seen it that way. All of Los Angeles has an air of Hollywood surreality (or disposability), even in its architecture. The whole city seems a bit larger than life. Cutting-edge, over-the-top styles that would be out of place in other cities are perfectly at home in L.A. The world's top architects, from Frank Lloyd Wright to Frank Gehry, have flocked to L.A., reveling in the artistic freedom here. Between 1945 and 1966, *Arts & Architecture* magazine focused the design world's attention on L.A. with its series of "Case Study Houses," prototypes for postwar living, many of which were designed by prominent émigrés like Pierre Koenig, Richard Neutra, and Eero Saarinen. Los Angeles has taken some criticism for not being a "serious" architectural center, but in terms of innovation and style, the city gets high marks.

Although much of it is gone, you can still find some prime examples of the kitschy roadside art that defined L.A. in earlier days. The famous Brown Derby is no more, but you can still find a neon-lit **1950s gas station/spaceship** (at the corner of Little

L.A.'s Top Architectural Tours

The **L.A. Conservancy** (© 213/623-2489; www.laconservancy.org) conducts a dozen information-packed walking tours of historic **Downtown L.A.,** seed of today's sprawling metropolis. The most popular is Broadway Theaters, a look at movie palaces. Other intriguing tours include Marble Masterpieces, Art Deco, Little Tokyo, and tours of the Biltmore Hotel and City Hall. Most tours take place on Saturday mornings at 10am and last about 2½ hours. Call Monday through Friday between 9am and 5pm for information or, better yet, click on the "Walking Tours" link on the website.

Red Line Tours (© 323/402-1074, ext. 11; www.redlinetours.com) offers two 90-minute walking tours of Downtown L.A.: the **Inside Historic Downtown L.A.** Tour, focusing on the city's historic sites, such as the Grand Central Market, the Bradbury Building, Central Library, and Palace Theatre; and the **Inside Contemporary Downtown L.A. Tour,** which includes the Walt Disney Concert Hall and Music Center. Wireless "live audio" headphones are provided to enhance the tour experience (the guide wears a microphone and wireless radio transmitter).

In **Pasadena,** various tours spotlighting Old Pasadena or the surrounding neighborhoods are intriguing, given this area's history of wealthy estates and ardent preservation. Call **Pasadena Heritage** (© 626/441-6333; www.pasadenaheritage.org) for a schedule of guided tours, or pick up one of the self-guided walking or driving maps available at the **Pasadena Convention and Visitors Bureau,** 171 S. Los Robles Ave. (© 626/795-9311; www.pasadena cal.com).

Santa Monica Blvd. and Crescent Dr. in Beverly Hills), in addition to some newer structures carrying on the tradition, such as the **Chiat/Day offices** in Venice (see below).

SANTA MONICA & THE BEACHES

When you're strolling the historic canals and streets of Venice, be sure to check out the **Chiat/Day** offices at 340 Main St. What would otherwise be an unspectacular contemporary office building is made fantastic by a **three-story pair of binoculars** that frames the entrance. The sculpture is modeled after a design created by Claes Oldenburg and Coosje van Bruggen.

When you're on your way in or out of LAX, be sure to stop for a moment to admire the **Control Tower** and **Theme Building.** The spacey *Jetsons*-style Theme Building, which has always loomed over LAX, has been joined by a more recent silhouette. The main control tower, designed by local architect Kate Diamond to evoke a stylized palm tree, is tailored to present Southern California in its best light. You can go inside to enjoy the view from the Theme Building's observation deck, or have a space-age cocktail at the Technicolor bachelor pad that is the **Encounter at LAX** restaurant (p. 116).

Constructed on a broad cliff with a steep face, the **Wayfarers Chapel** in Rancho Palos Verdes enjoys a fantastic spot overlooking the waves of the Pacific. It was designed by Lloyd Wright, son of celebrated architect Frank Lloyd Wright. Known locally as the "glass church," Wayfarers is a memorial to Emanuel Swedenborg, an 18th-century Swedish philosopher who claimed to have visions of spirits and heavenly hosts. The church is constructed of glass, redwood, and native stone. Rare plants, some of which are native to Israel, surround the building. The church is open daily from 8am to 5pm and is located at 5755 Palos Verdes Dr. S. Call ℭ **310/377-1650** (www.wayfarerschapel.org) in advance to arrange a free escorted tour.

L.A.'S WESTSIDE & BEVERLY HILLS

In addition to the sights below, don't miss the **Beverly Hills Hotel** (p. 82), and be sure to wind your way through the wide rural streets of Beverly Hills between Sunset and Santa Monica boulevards.

Church of the Good Shepherd   Built in 1924, this is Beverly Hills's oldest house of worship. In 1950, Elizabeth Taylor and her first husband, Nicky Hilton, were married here. The funerals of Alfred Hitchcock, Gary Cooper, Eva Gabor, and Frank Sinatra were all held here as well.

505 N. Bedford Dr., Beverly Hills. ℭ 310/285-5424. www.shepherd.catholicweb.com.

Pacific Design Center   The bold architecture and overwhelming scale of the Pacific Design Center, designed by Argentine architect Cesar Pelli, aroused controversy when it was erected in 1975. Sheathed in gently curving cobalt-blue glass, the seven-story building houses more than 750,000 square feet of wholesale interior-design showrooms and is known to locals as "the Blue Whale." When the property for the design center was acquired in the 1970s, almost all of the small businesses that lined this stretch of Melrose Avenue were demolished. Only Hugo's Plating, which still stands in front of the center, successfully resisted the wrecking ball. In 1988, a second boxlike structure, dressed in equally dramatic Kelly green, was added to the design center and surrounded by a protected outdoor plaza.

8687 Melrose Ave., West Hollywood. ℭ 310/657-0800. www.pacificdesigncenter.com.

Schindler House ⓖ   A protégé of Frank Lloyd Wright and contemporary of Richard Neutra, Austrian architect Rudolph Schindler designed this innovative modern house for himself in 1921 and 1922. It's now home to the Los Angeles arm of Austria's Museum of Applied Arts (MAK). The house is noted for its complicated interlocking spaces; the interpenetration of indoors and out; simple, unadorned materials; and technological innovations. Docent-guided tours are conducted at no additional charge on weekends only.

The MAK Center offers guides to L.A.-area buildings by Schindler and other Austrian architects, and presents visiting related exhibitions and creative arts programming. Call for schedules.

835 N. Kings Rd. (north of Melrose Ave.), West Hollywood. ℭ 323/651-1510. www.makcenter.com. Admission $7 adults, $6 students and seniors, free to children ages 12 and under; free to all every Fri after 4pm, Sept 10 (Schindler's birthday), May 24 (International Museum Day), and Dec 1. Wed–Sun 11am–6pm.

HOLLYWOOD

In addition to the buildings listed below, don't miss the **Griffith Observatory** and **Grauman's Chinese Theatre** (see "L.A.'s Top Attractions" earlier in this chapter), and the **Roosevelt Hotel, Hollywood** (p. 97).

Fun Fact **Not Quite SOS, but . . .**

The light on the rooftop spire of the Capitol Records building flashes "H-O-L-L-Y-W-O-O-D" in Morse code. Really, it does.

Capitol Records Building   Opened in 1956, this 13-story tower, just north of the legendary intersection of Hollywood and Vine, is one of the city's most recognizable buildings. The world's first circular office building is often, but incorrectly, said to have been made to resemble a stack of 45s under a turntable stylus (it kinda does, though). Nat "King" Cole, songwriter Johnny Mercer, and other 1950s Capitol artists populate a giant exterior mural. Look down and you'll see the sidewalk stars of Capitol's recording artists (including John Lennon). In the lobby, numerous gold albums are on display.

1750 Vine St. © 323/462-6252.

The Egyptian Theatre   Conceived by grandiose impresario Sid Grauman, the Egyptian Theatre is just down the street from his better-known Chinese Theatre, but it remains less altered from its original design, which was based on the then-headline-news discovery of hidden treasures in Pharaohs' tombs—hence the hieroglyphic murals and enormous scarab decoration above the stage. Hollywood's first movie premiere, *Robin Hood,* starring Douglas Fairbanks, was shown here in 1922, followed by the premiere of *The Ten Commandments* in 1923. The building recently underwent a sensitive restoration by American Cinematheque, which now screens rare, classic, and independent films (see chapter 10 for details). *Tip:* Check the website schedule for screenings hosted by celebrity guest speakers and directors such as Ron Howard and George Clooney.

6712 Hollywood Blvd. © 323/466-FILM (323/466-3456). www.egyptiantheatre.com.

Freeman House   Frank Lloyd Wright's Freeman House, built in 1924, was designed as an experimental prototype of mass-produced affordable housing. The home's richly patterned "textile-block" exterior was Wright's invention and is the most famous aspect of the home's design. Situated on a dramatic site overlooking Hollywood, Freeman House is built with the world's first glass-to-glass corner windows. Dancer Martha Graham, bandleader Xavier Cugat, art collector Galka Sheye, photographer Edward Weston, and architects Philip Johnson and Richard Neutra all lived or spent significant time at this house, which became known as an avant-garde salon. The house is currently closed for restoration; call ahead to see if it's open.

1962 Glencoe Way (off Hillcrest Rd., near Highland and Franklin aves.). © 323/851-0671.

DOWNTOWN

For a taste of what Downtown's Bunker Hill was like before the bulldozers, visit the residential neighborhood of **Angelino Heights,** near Echo Park. Entire streets are still filled with stately gingerbread Victorian homes; most still enjoy the beautiful views that led early L.A.'s elite to build here. The 1300 block of Carroll Avenue is the best preserved. Don't be surprised if a film crew is scouting locations while you're there—these blocks appear often on the silver screen.

Moments Divine Vibrations

Every Wednesday from 12:45 to 1:15pm, the Cathedral of Our Lady of the Angels—the city's $163-million architectural jewel—hosts an **organ recital** that is open to the public and free of charge. The power of the 42-ton organ's 6,019 pipes makes the cathedral vibrate, enabling you to not only hear the music, but also feel it, making the experience physically poignant as well as emotionally moving. Be sure to call © **213/680-5200** to confirm the Wednesday recital.

The Bradbury Building　This National Historic Landmark, built in 1893 and designed by George Wyman, is Los Angeles's oldest commercial building and one of the city's most revered architectural achievements. Legend has it that an inexperienced draftsman named George Wyman accepted the $125,000 commission after communicating with his dead brother through a Ouija board. Capped by a magical five-story skylight, Bradbury's courtyard combines glazed brick, ornate Mexican tile floors, rich Belgian marble, Art Nouveau grillwork, handsome oak paneling, and lacelike wrought-iron railings—it's one of the great interior spaces of the 19th century. The glass-topped atrium is often used as a movie and TV set; you've probably seen it before in *Chinatown* and *Blade Runner*.

304 S. Broadway (at 3rd St.). © **213/626-1893.** Mon–Fri 9am–6pm; Sat–Sun 9am–5pm.

Cathedral of Our Lady of the Angels ⟨★⟩　Completed in September 2002 at a cost of $163 million and built to last 500 years, this ultracontemporary cathedral is one of L.A.'s newest architectural treasures and the third-largest cathedral in the world. It was designed by award-winning Spanish architect Jose Rafael Moneo and features a 20,000-square-foot plaza with a meditation garden, more than 6,000 crypts and niches (making it the largest crypt mausoleum in the U.S.), mission-style colonnades, biblically inspired gardens, and numerous artworks created by world-acclaimed artists. While most Angelinos admit that the exterior of this austere, sand-colored structure is rather uninspiring and uninviting (the church doors don't face the street, but rather a private plaza in back surrounded by fortresslike walls), the view from the inside is breathtaking: Soaring heights, 12,000 panes of translucent alabaster, and larger-than-life tapestries lining the walls create an awe-inspiring sense of magnificence and serenity. The 25,000-pound bronze doors, created by sculptor Robert Graham, pay homage to Ghiberti's bronze baptistery door in Florence. Free self-guided tours are available, and there's a small cafe and gift shop as well.

555 W. Temple St. (at Grand Ave.), Los Angeles. © **213/680-5200.** www.olacathedral.org. Mon–Fri 6:30am–6pm; Sat 9am–6pm; Sun 7am–6pm.

City Hall　Built in 1928, the 27-story Los Angeles City Hall was the tallest building in the city for more than 30 years. The structure's distinctive ziggurat tower was designed to resemble the Mausoleum at Halicarnassus, one of the seven wonders of the ancient world. The building has been featured in numerous films and television shows, but it is probably best known as the headquarters of the *Daily Planet* in the *Superman* TV series (or from *Beverly Hills Cop*, depending on your birth date). When it was built, City Hall was the sole exception to an ordinance outlawing buildings taller than 150 feet. While you're here, be sure to take the elevator to the rarely used

27th-floor Observation Deck—on a clear day (yeah, right), you can see to Mount Wilson 15 miles away. Free docent-led tours are available at 10 and 11am Monday through Friday, and self-guided tours are available at other times. Call ℂ **213/978-1995** for tour information.

200 N. Spring St. ℂ **213/485-2121**. www.lacityhall.org. Mon–Fri 8am–5pm.

El Alisal ⟨★ El Alisal is a small, rugged, two-story "castle," built between 1889 and 1910 from large rocks and telephone poles purchased from the Santa Fe Railroad. The architect and creator was Charles F. Lummis, a Harvard graduate, archaeologist, and writer, who walked from Ohio to California and coined the slogan "See America First." A fan of Native American culture, Lummis is credited with popularizing the concept of the "Southwest," referring to New Mexico and Arizona. He often lived the lifestyle of the Indians, and he founded the Southwest Museum (234 Museum Dr.; ℂ **323/667-2000**), a repository of Indian artifacts. Lummis held fabulous parties for the theatrical, political, and artistic elite; his guest list often included Will Rogers and Theodore Roosevelt. The outstanding feature of his house is the fireplace, which was carved by Mount Rushmore creator Gutzon Borglum. The lawn has been turned into an experimental garden of water-conserving plants.

200 E. Ave. 43, Highland Park. ℂ **323/222-0546**. www.socalhistory.org. Free admission. Fri–Sun noon–4pm.

L.A. Central Library ⟨★★ This is one of L.A.'s early architectural achievements and the third-largest library in the United States. The city rallied to save the library when arson nearly destroyed it in 1986; the triumphant restoration has returned much of its original splendor. Working in the early 1920s, architect Bertram G. Goodhue employed the Egyptian motifs and materials popularized by the discovery of King Tut's tomb, and combined them with a more modern use of concrete block to great effect. Walking tours are the best way to explore this old beauty; they're led Monday through Friday at 12:30pm, Saturday at 11am and 2pm, and Sunday at 2pm. *Warning:* Parking in this area can involve a heroic effort. Try visiting on the weekend and using the Flower Street parking entrance; the library will validate your ticket, and you can escape for only $2.

630 W. 5th St. (btw. Flower St. and Grand Ave.). ℂ **213/228-7168**. www.lapl.org/central.

Union Station ⟨★ Union Station, completed in 1939, is one of the finest examples of California mission-style architecture and one of the last of America's great rail stations. It was built with the opulence and attention to detail that characterize 1930s WPA projects, such as its cathedral-like size and richly paneled ticket lobby and waiting area. When you're strolling through these grand historic halls, it's easy to imagine the glamorous movie stars who once boarded *The City of Los Angeles* and *The Super Chief* to journey back East during the glory days of rail travel; it's also easy to picture the many heartfelt reunions between returning soldiers and loved ones following the victorious end to World War II, in the station's heyday. Movies shot here include *Bugsy, The Way We Were,* and *Blade Runner.* There's always been a restaurant in the station; the latest to occupy this unusually beautiful setting is **Traxx** (p. 151).

800 N. Alameda St. (at Cesar E. Chavez Ave.).

US Bank Tower (also known as Library Tower) Designed by renowned architect I. M. Pei, L.A.'s most distinctive skyscraper (it's the round one) is the tallest building between Chicago and Singapore. Built in 1989 at a cost of $450 million, the

76-story monolith is both square and rectangular, rising from its 5th Street base in a series of overlapping spirals and cubes. The Bunker Hill Steps wrapping around the west side of the building were inspired by Rome's Spanish Steps. *Gee whiz fact:* The glass crown at the top—illuminated at night—is the highest building helipad in the world.

633 W. 5th St. (at S. Grand Ave.).

Walt Disney Concert Hall ★★★   See "L.A.'s Top Attractions," earlier in this chapter.

Watts Towers & Art Center   Watts became notorious as the site of riots in the summer of 1965, during which 34 people were killed and more than 1,000 were injured. Today, a visit to Watts is a lesson in inner-city life. It's a high-density land of gray strip malls, well-guarded check-cashing shops, and fast-food restaurants; but it's also a neighborhood of hardworking families struggling to survive in the midst of gangland. Although there's not much for the casual tourist here, the Watts Towers are truly a unique attraction, and the adjoining art gallery illustrates the fierce determination of area residents to maintain cultural integrity.

The Towers—the largest piece of folk art created by a single person—are colorful, 99-foot-tall cement and steel sculptures ornamented with mosaics of bottles, seashells, cups, plates, pottery, and ceramic tiles. They were completed in 1955 by folk artist Simon Rodia, an immigrant Italian tile-setter who worked on them for 33 years in his spare time. True fans of decorative ceramics will enjoy the fact that Rodia's day job was at the legendary Malibu Potteries (are those fragments of valuable Malibu tile encrusting the Towers?). Closed in 1994 due to earthquake damage, the towers were triumphantly reopened in 2001 and now attract more than 20,000 visitors annually. Tours are by request.

Note: Next to these designated Cultural Landmarks is the Art Center, which has an interesting collection of ethnic musical instruments as well as several visiting art exhibits throughout the year.

1727 E. 107th St., Los Angeles. ✆ 213/847-4646. www.trywatts.com. Art Center Tues–Sat 10am–4pm; Sun noon–4pm. Free admission. Towers Fri–Sat 11am–3pm; Sun 12:30–3pm. Admission $7 adults, $3 seniors 55 and over and teens 13–17, free for children 12 and under.

PASADENA & ENVIRONS

See "L.A.'s Top Architectural Tours" box, earlier, and "Sightseeing Tours," later in this chapter, for more information on touring the many well-preserved historic neighborhoods in Pasadena. For a quick but profound architectural fix, stroll past Pasadena's grandiose and baroque **City Hall,** 100 N. Garfield Ave., 2 blocks north of Colorado Boulevard; closer inspection will reveal its classical colonnaded courtyard, formal gardens, and spectacular tiled dome.

The Gamble House ★★   The huge two-story Gamble House, built in 1908 as a California vacation home for the wealthy family of Procter and Gamble fame, is a sublime example of Arts and Crafts architecture. The interior, designed by the famous Pasadena-based Greene & Greene architectural team, abounds with handcraftsmanship, including intricately carved teak cornices, custom-designed furnishings, elaborate carpets, and a fantastic Tiffany glass door. No detail was overlooked. Every oak wedge, downspout, air vent, and switch plate contributes to the unified design. Admission is by 1-hour guided tour only, which departs every 15 minutes. Tickets go on sale on tour

---

(*Fun Fact* **House Hygiene**

The restoration of the Gamble House was so meticulous that workers used dental picks to scrape gunk from the home's 262 rafters.

---

days in the bookstore at 10am Thursday through Saturday, and at 11:30am on Sunday. No reservations are necessary, but tours are often sold out, especially on weekends by 2pm. And don't wear high heels or they'll make you put on slippers.

If you can't fit the tour into your schedule but have an affection for Craftsman design, visit the well-stocked bookstore and museum shop located in the former garage (you can also see the exterior and grounds of the house this way). The bookstore is open Tuesday through Saturday 10am to 5pm, and Sunday 11:30am to 5pm.

Additional elegant Greene & Greene creations (still privately owned) abound 2 blocks away along **Arroyo Terrace,** including nos. **368, 370, 400, 408, 424,** and **440.** The Gamble House bookstore can give you a walking-tour map and also conducts guided neighborhood tours by appointment.

4 Westmoreland Place (in the 300 block of N. Orange Grove Blvd.), Pasadena. (C) 626/793-3334. www.gamble house.org. Tours $10 adults, $7 students and seniors 65 and over, free for children 11 and under. Tours Thurs–Sun noon–3pm. Closed holidays.

Mission San Fernando   In the late 18th century, Franciscan missionaries established 21 missions up the California coast, from San Diego to Sonoma. Each uniquely beautiful mission was built 1 day's trek from the next, along a path known as El Camino Real ("the Royal Road"), remnants of which still exist. The missions' construction marked the beginning of European settlement of California and the displacement of the Native American population. The two L.A.-area missions are located in the valleys that took their names: the San Fernando Valley and the San Gabriel Valley (see below). A third mission, San Juan Capistrano, is located in Orange County (see chapter 11).

Established in 1797, Mission San Fernando once controlled more than 1½ million acres, employed 1,500 Native Americans, and boasted more than 22,000 head of cattle and extensive orchards. The fragile adobe mission complex was destroyed several times but was always faithfully rebuilt with low buildings surrounding grassy courtyards. The aging church was replaced in the 1940s and again in the 1970s after an earthquake. The **Convento,** a 250-foot-long colonnaded structure dating from 1810, is the compound's oldest remaining building. Some of the mission's rooms, including the old library and the private salon of the first bishop of California, have been restored to their late-18th-century appearance. A half-dozen padres and many hundreds of Shoshone Indians are buried in the adjacent cemetery.

15151 San Fernando Mission Blvd., Mission Hills. (C) 818/361-0186. www.missionscalifornia.com. Admission $4 adults, $3 seniors and children 7–15, free for kids 6 and under. Daily 9am–4:30pm. From I-5, exit at San Fernando Mission Blvd. E and drive 5 blocks to the mission.

Mission San Gabriel Arcangel   Founded in 1771, Mission San Gabriel Arcangel retains its original facade, notable for its high oblong windows and large capped buttresses said to have been influenced by the cathedral in Cordova, Spain. The mission's self-contained compound encompasses an aqueduct, a cemetery, a tannery, and a working winery. Within the church stands a copper font with the distinction of being the first one used to baptize a Native Californian. The most notable contents of the mission's museum are Native American paintings depicting the Stations of the Cross, done on sailcloth, with colors made from crushed desert flower petals.

428 S. Mission Dr., San Gabriel (15 min. south of Pasadena). ℂ **626/457-3048.** www.sangabrielmission.org. Admission $5 adults, $4 seniors and students, $3 children ages 6–17, free for kids ages 5 and under. Daily 9am–4:30pm. Closed holidays.

5 L.A. Parks, Gardens, Views & Zoos
PARKS
In addition to the two excellent examples of urban parkland below, check out **Pan Pacific Park,** a hilly retreat near the Farmers Market and CBS Studios, named for the Art Deco auditorium that, unfortunately, no longer stands at its edge.

Griffith Park ⊛★★ *Kids*   Mining tycoon Col. Griffith J. Griffith donated these 4,107 acres to the city in 1896 as a Christmas gift. Today Griffith Park is the largest urban park in America. There's a lot to do here, including 53 miles of hiking trails (the prettiest is the Fern Dell trail near the Western Ave. entrance, a shady hideaway cooled by waterfalls and ferns), horseback riding, golfing, swimming, biking, and picnicking (see "Golf, Hiking & Other Fun in the Warm California Sun," later in this chapter). For a general overview of the park, drive the mountainous loop road that winds from the top of Western Avenue, past Griffith Observatory, and down to Vermont Avenue. For a more extensive foray, turn north at the loop road's midsection, onto Mount Hollywood Drive. To reach the golf courses, the **Museum of the American West** (p. 179), or **Los Angeles Zoo** (p. 198), take Los Feliz Boulevard to Riverside Drive, which runs along the park's western edge.

Near the zoo, in a particularly dusty corner of the park, you can find the **Travel Town Transportation Museum,** 5200 Zoo Dr. (ℂ **323/662-5874**), a little-known outdoor museum with a small collection of vintage locomotives and old airplanes. Kids love the miniature train ride that circles the perimeter of the museum. The museum is open Monday through Friday from 10am to 4pm, and Saturday and Sunday from 10am to 5pm; admission is free.

Hollywood; entrances are along Los Feliz Blvd., at Riverside Dr., Vermont Ave., and Western Ave. ℂ **323/913-4688.** Free admission.

Will Rogers State Historic Park   Will Rogers State Historic Park was once Will Rogers's private ranch and grounds. Willed to the state of California in 1944, the 168-acre estate is now both a park and a historic site, supervised by the Department of Parks and Recreation. Visitors may explore the grounds, the former stables, and the 31-room house filled with the original furnishings, including a porch swing in the living room and many Native American rugs and baskets. Charles Lindbergh and his wife, Anne Morrow Lindbergh, hid out here in the 1930s during part of the craze that followed the kidnapping and murder of their first son. There are picnic tables, but no food is sold. Guided Ranch House tours are available as well.

Who's Will Rogers, you ask? He was born in Oklahoma in 1879 and became a cowboy in the Texas Panhandle before drifting into a Wild West show as a folksy, speechifying roper. The "cracker-barrel philosopher" performed lariat tricks while carrying on a humorous deadpan monologue on current events. The showman moved to Los Angeles in 1919, where he become a movie actor as well as the author of numerous books detailing his down-home "cowboy philosophy."

1501 Will Rogers State Park Rd., Pacific Palisades (btw. Santa Monica and Malibu). ⓒ 310/454-8212. Park entrance $7 per vehicle. Daily 8am–sunset. House daily 10am–5pm; guided Ranch House tours offered Tues–Sun at 11am, 1pm, and 2pm. From Santa Monica, take the Pacific Coast Hwy. (Calif. 1) north, turn right onto Sunset Blvd., and continue to the park entrance.

BOTANICAL GARDENS

Descanso Gardens 🌟   Camellias—evergreen flowering shrubs from China and Japan—were the passion of amateur gardener E. Manchester Boddy, who began planting them here in 1941. Today his 160-acre Descanso Gardens contain more than 100,000 camellias in more than 600 varieties, blooming under a canopy of California oak trees. The shrubs now share the limelight with a 9-acre International Rosarium, home to hundreds of varieties. This is a very relaxing place, with paths and streams that wind through the towering forest, bordering a lake, bird sanctuary, Japanese Garden & Tea House, and Boddy House art museum. Each season features different plants: daffodils, azaleas, tulips, and lilacs in the spring; chrysanthemums in the fall; and so on. Monthly art exhibits are held in the garden's hospitality house, and the Courtyard Café offers light meals daily from 10am to 3pm. Guided tram tours, which cost $3, run Tuesday through Friday at 1, 2, and 3pm, and Saturday and Sunday at 11am and 1, 2, and 3pm. Picnicking is allowed in specified areas.

1418 Descanso Dr., La Cañada (about 20 min. from Downtown L.A.). ⓒ 818/949-4200. www.descansogardens.org. Admission $7 adults, $5 students and seniors 62 and over, $2 children ages 5–12, free for kids ages 4 and under. Daily 9am–5pm. Closed Christmas Day. Free parking.

Huntington Library, Art Collections & Botanical Gardens 🌟🌟 *Kids*   The Huntington Library is the jewel in Pasadena's crown. The 207-acre hilltop estate was once home to industrialist and railroad magnate Henry E. Huntington (1850–1927), who bought books on the same massive scale on which he acquired businesses. The continually expanding collection includes dozens of Shakespeare's first editions, Benjamin Franklin's handwritten autobiography, a Gutenberg Bible from the 1450s, and the earliest known manuscript of Chaucer's *Canterbury Tales.* Although some rare works are available only to visiting scholars, the library has a regularly changing (and always excellent) exhibit showcasing different items in the collection.

If you prefer canvas to parchment, Huntington also put together a terrific 18th-century British and French art collection. The most celebrated paintings are Gainsborough's *The Blue Boy* and *Pinkie,* a companion piece by Sir Thomas Lawrence depicting the youthful aunt of Elizabeth Barrett Browning. These and other works are displayed in the stately Italianate mansion on the crest of this hillside estate, so you can also get a glimpse of its splendid furnishings. American art and Renaissance paintings are exhibited in two additional galleries.

But it's the vast **botanical gardens** featuring more than 14,000 different species of plants that draw most locals to the Huntington. The Japanese Garden comes complete with a traditional open-air Japanese house, koi-filled stream, and serene Zen garden. There's also an exotic **Desert Garden,** intriguing **Jungle Garden, Bing Children's Garden** (designed specifically for kids ages 2–7), and the glass-and-steel **Conservatory for Botanical Science** where visitors learn some of the fundamentals of botany via state-of-the-art science stations. The latest addition is a new 12-acre **Chinese Garden,** the largest classical garden outside mainland China and one of the largest of the Huntington's 14 specialized gardens. Highlights include a lake, teahouse, pavilions, and bridges within a landscape of plants native to China.

Stargazing in L.A.: Top Spots for Sighting Celebrities

Celebrities pop up everywhere in L.A. If you spend enough time here, you'll surely bump into a few of them. I recently had a random encounter with Roseanne Barr at the St. Regis Hotel, in which a polite exchange at the bar turned into a 2-hour tête-à-tête about politics and the nature of humankind. (Ah, a typically unpredictable day in L.A.) If you're in the city for only a short time, however, it's best to go on the offensive.

Restaurants are your surest bet. Dining out is such a popular recreation among Hollywood's elite that you sometimes wonder whether frequently sighted folks like Nicole, Kobe, and Harrison ever actually eat at home. Places like **Matsuhisa,** the **Ivy,** the **Palm, Koi, Pizzeria Mozza, CUT, Eleven,** the **Prime Grill,** and **Spago Beverly Hills** can almost guarantee sightings most nights of the week. The city's stylish hotels can also be good bets—the poolside cabanas at the **Viceroy** in Santa Monica are a good bet; **Mondrian** draws stars galore to its dining room **Asia de Cuba,** 8440 W. Sunset Blvd. (© **323/848-6000**), as well as the elite **Skybar; Shutters'** lobby lounge is the rendezvous of choice for famous faces heading to dinner at the hotel's **One Pico** restaurant; and spotting stars at the **Beverly Hills Hotel** is almost too easy. The trendiest clubs and bars—**Whiskey Bar, Viper Room, Skybar**—are good for star sighting, but cover charges can be astronomical and the velvet rope gauntlet oppressive. And it's not always Mick and Quentin and Madonna; a recent night on the town turned up only Yanni, Ralph Macchio, and Judge Judy.

Because the Huntington surprises many with its size and wealth of activities to choose from, first-timers might want to start with a tour. One-hour garden tours are offered daily; no reservations or additional fees are required. Times vary, so check at the information desk upon arrival. I also recommend that you tailor your visit to include the popular **English high tea** served Tuesday through Friday from noon to 4:30pm, and Saturday and Sunday from 10:45am to 4:30pm (last seating at 3:30pm). The tearoom overlooks the Rose Garden (home to 1,000 varieties displayed in chronological order of their breeding), and since the finger sandwiches and desserts are served buffet-style, it's a genteel bargain even for hearty appetites at $20 per person (please note that museum admission is a separate required cost). Phone © **626/ 683-8131** for tearoom reservations, which are required and should be made at least 2 weeks in advance.

1151 Oxford Rd., San Marino. © 626/405-2100. www.huntington.org. Admission $15 adults, $12 seniors 65 and over, $10 students and children ages 12–18, $6 children ages 5–11, free for children 4 and under; free to all the 1st Thurs of each month. Sept–May Mon and Wed–Fri noon–4:30pm, Sat–Sun 10:30am–4:30pm; June–Aug Wed–Mon 10:30am–4:30pm. Closed major holidays. Free parking.

The Los Angeles County Arboretum and Botanic Garden ♣

Tucked into the hillsides of the San Gabriel Mountains, this sprawling horticultural and botanical center was formerly the estate of silver magnate "Lucky" Baldwin—the man responsible

Often the best places to see members of the A-list aren't as obvious as a back-alley stage door or the front room of Spago. Shops along Sunset Boulevard are often star-heavy, as are chichi shops within the **Beverly Center** mall. **Book Soup,** that browser's paradise across the street from Tower, is usually good for a star or two. A midafternoon stroll along **Melrose Avenue** might also produce a familiar face (particularly at **Fred Segal**); likewise for the chic European-style shops of **Sunset Plaza** or the **Beverly Center.**

Or you can seek out the celebrities on the job. It's not uncommon for star-studded movie productions to use L.A.'s diverse cultural landscape for **location shots;** in fact, it's such a regular occurrence that locals are usually less impressed with an A-list presence than perturbed about the precious parking spaces lost to all those equipment trucks and dressing-room trailers. On-the-street movie shoots are part of what makes L.A. unique, and onlookers gather wherever hastily scrawled production signs point to a hot site. For the inside track on where the action is, check the **Daily Shoot Sheet** at www. eidc.com. This isn't some word-of-mouth groupie posting—it's a strictly legit online listing of every filming permit applied for within the city limits. Entries are classified by type (commercial advertisement, feature film, student film, TV program) and working title, and the site lists production hours and exact street addresses.

If you're really intent on seeing as many stars as possible, log on to **www.seeing-stars.com**, a website that keeps tabs on where all the stars shop, eat, stay, and play in L.A.

for bringing horse racing to Southern California—who lived until 1909 on these lushly planted 127 acres overlooking the Santa Anita racetrack. You might recognize Baldwin's red-and-white Queen Anne cottage from the opening sequence of *Fantasy Island* ("de plane, de plane"); the gardens are also a favorite location for movie filming and local weddings. In addition to spectacular flora (every continent is represented here), the Arboretum boasts a bevy of resident peafowl who seem unafraid of humans—one of the best treats here is being up close when the peacocks, attempting to impress passing hens, unfold their brilliant rainbow plumage. Avid gardeners will want to visit the nursery-like gift shop on the way out. Admission is free every third Tuesday from 9am to 4:30pm.

301 N. Baldwin Ave., Arcadia. (℃) **626/821-3222.** www.arboretum.org. Admission $7 adults, $5 students and seniors 62 and over, $2.50 children ages 5–12, free for kids ages 4 and under. Daily 9am–5pm. Admission closes at 4:30pm. Closed Christmas Day. Free parking.

VIEWS

It's not always easy to get a good city view in Los Angeles. Even if you find the right vantage, the smog may keep you from having any kind of panorama. But, as they say, on a clear day, you can see forever. One of the best views of the city can be had from **Griffith Observatory** (see "L.A.'s Top Attractions," earlier in this chapter). The view of Santa Monica Bay from the end of **Santa Monica Pier** is also impressive.

Mulholland Drive *&* Los Angeles is the only major city in the world divided by a mountain range, and the road on top of this range is the famous Mulholland Drive. It travels 21 miles along the peaks and canyons of Hollywood Hills and the Santa Monica Mountains, separating the Los Angeles basin from the San Fernando Valley. The winding road provides amazing views of the city (particularly at night) and offers many opportunities to pull over and enjoy the view 1,400 feet above sea level.

Completed in 1924, it's named after William Mulholland, the engineer of the aqueduct connecting L.A. and the Valley. Yes, there are celebrities up in them thar hills—Leonardo DiCaprio, Kevin Costner—but you'll never find them, as most of the mansions are well hidden. You don't need to drive the whole road to get the full effect. From Cahuenga Boulevard (near the Hollywood Bowl), take the Mulholland Drive turnoff heading west. After about a mile, you'll see the scenic view area on your left (look for the black iron fence). Park at the small paved parking lot (which closes at sunset), ooh and aah over the view of the L.A. basin, and then drive a few miles farther west until you spot the other scenic view area on your right (dirt this time) overlooking the San Fernando Valley. The whole trip should take you less than an hour. *Tip:* Don't drive here after 3pm on the weekdays—the rush hour traffic in this area is horrible. Also, no matter what your map says, there is no Mulholland Drive exit off U.S. 101; you have to get on at Cahuenga Boulevard.

Btw. Coldwater Canyon Dr. and U.S. 101.

ZOOS

Los Angeles Zoo *& & Kids* The L.A. Zoo has been welcoming visitors and busloads of school kids since 1966. In 1982, the zoo inaugurated a display of cuddly koalas, still one of its biggest attractions among 1,200 animals from around the world. Although it's smaller than the world-famous San Diego Zoo, the L.A. Zoo is far more easy to fully explore. As much an arboretum as a zoo, the grounds are thick with mature shade trees from around the world that help cool the once-barren grounds, and new habitats are light-years ahead of the cruel concrete roundhouses originally used to exhibit animals (though you can't help feeling that, despite the fancy digs, all the creatures would rather be in their natural habitat).

The zoo's latest attraction is new $19-million **Campo Gorilla Reserve,** a habitat for six African lowland gorillas that closely resembles their native West African homeland. Visitors partake in a pseudo-African-jungle experience as they journey along a misty, forested pathway with glassed viewing areas for close-up views of the gorillas living in two separate habitats: one for a family troop of gorillas, led by a silverback male; and a separate habitat for two bachelors. Other highlights include the **Sea Lion Cliffs** habitat, home to the zoo's five sea lions where visitors can view the saltwater habitat from an underwater glass viewing area; the **Chimpanzees of the Mahale Mountains** habitat, where visitors can see plenty of primate activity; the **Red Ape Rainforest,** a natural orangutan habitat; the entertaining **World of Birds** show; the **Pachyderm Forest** (climate-controlled digs for the elephants and hippos, complete with an underwater viewing area); and the **Mandrills Exhibit** (the world's largest and most colorful baboons). The gargantuan Andean condor had me enthralled as well (the facility is renowned in zoological circles for the successful breeding and releasing of California condors, and occasionally some of these majestic and endangered birds are on exhibit). Kids will also enjoy the **Winnick Family Children's Zoo,** which contains a petting area, exhibition animal-care center, Adventure Theater storytelling and puppet show, and other kid-hip exhibits and activities. *Tip:* To avoid the busloads of rambunctious school kids, arrive after noon.

5333 Zoo Dr., Griffith Park. ℂ 323/644-4200. www.lazoo.org. Admission $10 adults, $7 seniors 62 and over, $5 kids ages 2–12, free for children 1 and under. Daily 10am–5pm (until 6pm July 1 to Labor Day). Closed Christmas Day. Free parking.

6 Studio & Sightseeing Tours

STUDIO TOURS

NBC Studios *(Kids)*   According to a security guard, John Wayne and Redd Foxx once got into a fight here after Wayne refused to ride in the same limo as Foxx, who called the movie star a "redneck." Well, your NBC tour will probably be a bit more docile than that. The guided indoor walking tour includes a behind-the-scenes unstaged look at *The Tonight Show with Jay Leno* set (p. 171 on how to get free Jay Leno tickets); wardrobe, makeup, and set-building departments; and several sound studios. In fact, NBC is the only TV studio that offers the public a behind-the-scenes look at the inner workings of its television operation, and it's a lot less expensive than the competition's studio tours. Granted, it doesn't have the cachet of a major motion picture studio tour, but it's entertaining nonetheless.

Tours depart at the top of the hour Monday through Friday from 9am to 3pm, and tickets are sold at the Guest Relations Department (bring cash—they don't take credit cards). Also, this is one of the few studio tours that doesn't have a minimum age requirement. *Note:* Before you make the drive to Burbank be sure to call the studio and make sure tours are being offered that day and aren't already sold out.

3000 W. Alameda Ave. (off California St.), Burbank. ℂ 818/840-3537. Tours $8.50 adults, $7.50 seniors 60 and over, $5 children ages 5–12, free for children 4 and under. Mon–Fri 9am–3pm.

Paramount Pictures *(★★)*   Paramount is the only major studio still located in Hollywood, which makes the 2-hour "cart tour" around its Hollywood headquarters far more historically enriching than the modern studios in Burbank (even the wrought-iron gates Gloria Swanson motored through in *Sunset Boulevard* are still there). The tour is both a historical ode to filmmaking and a real-life, behind-the-scenes look at a working movie and television facilities in day-to-day operation; ergo, no two tours are alike, and chances of spotting a celebrity are pretty good. Visits typically include a walk-through of the soundstages of TV shows or feature films, though you can't enter while taping is taking place. The $35 tours depart Monday through Friday *by advance reservations only.* You need to be 12 or older to take the tour, and cameras and recording equipment are *verboten. Tip:* After the tour, have lunch at the Paramount Studio's world-famous commissary; you never know who might drop in for a bite, and the food's pretty darn good.

5555 Melrose Ave. ℂ 323/956-1777. www.paramount.com. Tours $35 per person by advance reservation only. Mon–Fri 10am–2pm.

Sony Pictures Studio Tour   Although it doesn't have quite the same historical cachet as Warner Brothers or Paramount, a lot of movie history was made at this Culver City lot. The 2-hour walking tour includes stops at classic stage scenes such as the Yellow Brick Road winding through Munchkinland, sets from modern thrillers like *Spiderman,* and an opportunity to drop in on the *Jeopardy!* or *Wheel of Fortune* sets. But the main reason for the tour is the chance to catch a glimpse at the stars who work here (it's one of the busiest studio lots in the world). Tours depart from the Sony Pictures Plaza near the parking lot; be sure to call ahead and make a reservation.

Sony Picture Studios, 10202 W. Washington Blvd., Culver City. ⓒ 323/520-8687. www.sonypicturesstudios.com. Reservations highly recommended; children 11 and under not admitted. Tours $28 per person, departing Mon–Fri at 9:30am, 10:30am, 1:30pm, and 2:30pm. Photo ID required. Free parking.

Universal Studios ⚡   Universal offers daily 1-hour tram tours of its studio lot as part of the general admission price to the amusement park, which is open from 9am to 7pm in the summer and from 10am to 6pm in the winter. See p. 169 for more information.

Warner Bros. Studios ⚡   The Warner Brothers' "VIP Tour" takes visitors on a 2¼-hour jaunt around the world's busiest movie and TV studio. After a brief introductory film about the history of WB, groups of 12 pile into stretch golf carts for an intimate view of the inner workings of a motion picture and television studio: back-lot streets, sound stages, sets, and craft shops. Because nothing is staged there's no telling what or who you might encounter, and no two tours are the same. The tour ends with a visit to the Warner Bros. Museum, which contains original costumes, props, sets, scripts, and correspondence from classic WB films and television shows. Advance tickets are recommended and available online via their website, or by calling ⓒ **866/777-8932;** otherwise, tickets are sold the day of the tour on a first-come, first-served basis, but they recommended arriving at the ticket office early to make sure they don't sell out. Children 7 and under are not admitted, you must bring valid photo ID, and they recommend you show up about 30 minutes before the tour starts.

3400 Riverside Dr., Burbank. ⓒ **818/972-8687.** www.wbstudiotour.com. Advance reservations recommended. Tours $45 per person, departing Mon–Fri every half-hour btw. 8:20am–3:20pm (extended hours during spring and summer).

SIGHTSEEING TOURS
BUS/VAN TOURS

L.A. Tours (ⓒ **323/460-6490;** www.latours.net) operates regularly scheduled tours of the city. Plush shuttle buses pick up riders from major hotels for morning or afternoon tours of Sunset Strip, the movie studios, the Farmers Market, Hollywood, homes of the stars, and other attractions. Different itineraries are available, from Downtown and the Music Center to Disneyland, Universal Studios, or Six Flags Magic Mountain. Tours vary in length from a half-day Beaches & Shopping tour to a full-day Grand City tour. Advance reservations are required.

The other major tour company in L.A. is **Starline Tours** ⚡⚡ (ⓒ **800/959-3131;** www.starlinetours.com)—you'll see their air-conditioned minibuses, double-decker Big Red buses, and open-air trolleys all over the city. Since 1935, Starline has been offering a wide selection of L.A. tours, including the first-ever Movie Stars' Homes tour. Its most popular tour, the 2-hour neighborhood jaunt, departs every half-hour from the front of Grauman's Chinese Theatre between 9:30am and 4pm (you'll see the Starline kiosk to the right of the theater entrance at 6925 Hollywood Blvd.). If you really like driving tours, sign up for the piece d' resistance: the 5½-hour Grand Tour of L.A. Check out their website for more tour information.

WALKING TOURS

If you want the classic Hollywood walking tour, **Red Line Tours** (ⓒ **323/402-1074;** www.redlinetours.com) offers daily sightseeing expeditions to all the famous (and infamous) landmarks in Hollywood. Its unique "live-audio" system allows customers to hear the tour guide even over the city noise. Customers wear an audio headset

Plane Spotting at LAX

You've undoubtedly heard of train spotters—those supergeeks sporting a pair of binoculars in one hand and a journal in the other—but what about plane spotters? The hobby of maintaining meticulous records of every type of commercial aircraft spotted has become so popular that the city of El Segundo recently invested $150,000 into a "hilltop aircraft observation area" near LAX, complete with benches, tables, and telescopes. It's located at the end of the southern runways on West Imperial Avenue between Sepulveda Boulevard and Main Street. For more information, log on to www.planespotting.com.

receiver while the tour guide wears a headset microphone transmitter (pretty clever, actually). Trips depart from the Stella Adler Academy & Theatres (6773 Hollywood Blvd.) at 10am, noon, 2pm, and 4pm, 7 days a week. Rates are $20 for adults, $18 for students and seniors, and $15 for children ages 9 to 15. Tours of Downtown L.A. are offered as well (see "L.A.'s Top Architectural Tours," p. 187). Log on to the Red Line Tour website for more information.

The **L.A. Conservancy** (✆ **213/623-2489;** www.laconservancy.org) conducts about a dozen entertaining walking tours of historic Downtown L.A. In Pasadena, **Pasadena Heritage** (✆ **626/441-6333;** www.pasadenaheritage.org) offers a walking tour of Old Pasadena. (For both tours, see the box "L.A.'s Top Architectural Tours," on p. 187.)

BICYCLE TOURS

Perry's Beach Café & Rentals in Santa Monica offers 1½-hour bicycle tours of the Santa Monica and Venice beach communities. It's a great way to explore the area while learning about its history and landmark architecture. The package costs $30 per person and includes a tour guide, a 3-hour bike rental with protective gear, water, a bike lock, and goody bag. *Note:* A minimum of three people are required for the tour. For more information or to make a reservation, call ✆ **310/372-3138.**

HELICOPTER TOURS

Touring L.A. from above is certainly a unique perspective. Just the thrill of riding in a helicopter is worth the price. **Celebrity Helicopters** (✆ **877/999-2099;** www.celeb heli.com) offers a wide array of themed trips, ranging from a 35-minute Celebrity Home Tour ($169) to a 25-minute fly-by of the L.A. coastline ($99). Other tour packages are available as well: Check their website for more information.

JOGGING TOUR

Off 'N Running Tours (✆ **310/246-1418;** www.offnrunningtours.com) combines sporting with sightseeing, taking joggers on guided runs through Los Angeles. The themed tours such as "Running from the Paparazzi" are customized to take in the most entertaining areas around the city and can accommodate any skill level for 4 to 12 miles. One of the most popular routes is up to Holmby Hills, past the Playboy Mansion and other massive estates. It's a fun way to get the most out of your morning jog. Tours cost about $60 and include a T-shirt, a light breakfast, snacks, and plenty of water.

BEVERLY HILLS TROLLEY TOURS

The city of Beverly Hills offers inexpensive trolley tours that detail the city's history as well as little-known facts and celebrity tidbits. The tour takes visitors on a 40-minute docent-led tour through the tony avenues of Beverly Hills, including Rodeo Avenue and the Golden Triangle. It runs every Saturday on the hour from 11am to 4pm. The fare is a mere $5 for adults and $1 for kids 12 and under. The trolley departs at the "Trolley Stop" at the intersection of Rodeo Drive and Dayton Way. For more information, call ℂ **310/285-2438** or log on to www.beverlyhills.org.

7 Live-Audience TV Tapings

Being part of the audience for the taping of a television show might be the quintessential L.A. experience. This is a great way to see Hollywood at work, to find out how your favorite sitcom or talk show is made, and to catch a glimpse of your favorite TV personalities. Timing is important—remember that most series go on hiatus between March and July. And tickets to the top shows are in greater demand than others, so getting your hands on them takes advance planning—and possibly some waiting in line.

Request tickets as far in advance as possible. Several episodes may be shot on a single day, so you may be required to remain in the theater for up to 4 hours (in addition to the recommended 1-hr. early check-in). If you phone at the last moment, you may luck into tickets for your top choice. More likely, however, you'll be given a list of shows that are currently filming, and you won't recognize many of the titles; studios are always taping pilots, few of which end up on the air. But you never know who may be starring in them—look at all the famous faces that have launched new sitcoms in the past couple of years. Tickets are always free, are usually limited to two per person, and are distributed on a first-come, first-served basis. Many shows don't admit children under the age of 10; in some cases, no one under the age of 18 is admitted.

Tickets are sometimes given away to the public outside popular tourist sites like Grauman's Chinese Theatre in Hollywood and Universal Studios in the Valley; L.A.'s visitor information centers in Downtown and Hollywood often have tickets as well (see "Orientation" in chapter 4). But if you're determined to see a particular show, contact the following suppliers:

Audiences Unlimited, Inc. (ℂ **818/753-3470;** www.tvtickets.com) is a good place to start. It distributes tickets for most of the top sitcoms, including *Two And A Half Men, Rules of Engagement,* and more. This service is organized and informative (as is its website), and fully sanctioned by production companies and networks. ABC, for example, no longer handles ticket distribution directly, but refers all inquiries to Audiences Unlimited, Inc. **TVTIX.COM** (ℂ **323/653-4105;** www.tvtix.com) also distributes tickets for numerous talk and game shows, including *The Tonight Show with Jay Leno* and *Jeopardy!*

⌐Tips The Cold Truth About Talk Shows

The sets of most talk shows are kept at a cool temperature (the hot lights raise the temperature on stage), so be sure to bring a sweater or jacket. And if you dress well—no T-shirts or shorts—your chances of getting a front-row seat increase dramatically.

How to Be a Game Show Contestant

So you've been thinking of taking a chance on fame and fortune the next time you're in L.A., eh? Well, both are more attainable than you might think—actress Markie Post's career began with her audition for a game show; and as far as fortune goes, *somebody* has to win the big money.

If you're serious about trying to get on a show, be sure you have some flexibility in your schedule; although most production companies go out of their way to give priority to out-of-town contestants, you should be prepared to return to Los Angeles one or more times for a final audition and/or taping. Here are some tips that might help you prepare:

The Bubblier, the Better: Be friendly, cheerful, and bright at your audition and during taping. Be good-natured when you lose or make mistakes, and above all, be exuberant if you win the "big money." When you're onstage, nothing feels quite real.

Dress for Success: Contestant coordinators look for players who won't alienate viewers. It's awfully hard for a granny in the heartland to relate to a trendy big-city type. So dress as conservatively as possible for your auditions, and avoid the fashion no-nos—white, black, stripes, metallics—that would require lighting and camera adjustments.

Most Unglamorous Advice: Remember income taxes. Should you be lucky enough to win big, bear in mind that all cash winnings, as well as the retail value of all your prizes, will be reported to the IRS as earnings.

Some Game Shows Currently in Production:

Jeopardy! Trivia quiz not for the fainthearted (the contestant, that is; watching isn't nearly as difficult!). Call © **310/244-5367** or log on to www. sonypictures.com/tv/shows/jeopardy.

Wheel of Fortune Less about your skill with the "hangman"-style puzzles than your luck spinning the carnival wheel. Call © **213/520-5555** or log on to www.wheeloffortune.com.

The Price Is Right Contestants are chosen from the studio audience to test their shopping expertise. Call © **323/575-2449** or log on to www.cbs.com/daytime/price/tickets.

You also may want to contact the networks for information on a specific show, including some whose tickets are not available at the above agencies. At **ABC,** all ticket inquiries are referred to Audiences Unlimited (see above), but you may want to check out ABC's website at **www.abc.com** for a colorful look at their lineup and links to specific show sites.

For **CBS Television City,** 7800 Beverly Blvd., Los Angeles, CA 90036, call © **323/575-2458** between Monday and Friday from 9am to 5pm to see what's being filmed while you're in town. Tickets for CBS tapings are distributed on a first-come, first-served basis; you can write in advance to reserve them or pick them up at the studio up to an hour before taping. Tickets for many CBS sitcoms are also available from

Stargazing in L.A., Part II: The Less-Than-Lively Set

Almost everybody who visits L.A. hopes to see a celebrity—they are, after all, the city's most common export. But celebrities usually don't cooperate, failing to gather in readily viewable herds. There is, however, an absolutely guaranteed method to approach within 6 feet of many famous stars. Cemeteries are *the* place for star (or at least headstone) gazing: The star is always available, and you're going to get a lot more up close and personal than you probably would to anyone who's actually alive. Here is a guide to the most fruitful cemeteries, listed in order of their friendliness to stargazers. If you're looking for someone in particular, log on to www.findagrave.com. (There's a website for *everything*.)

Weathered Victorian and Art Deco memorials add to the decaying charm of **Hollywood Forever** ★★ (formerly Hollywood Memorial Park), 6000 Santa Monica Blvd., Hollywood (© **323/469-1181**; www.hollywoodforever.com). Fittingly, there's a terrific view of the HOLLYWOOD sign over the graves, as many of the founders of the community rest here. The most notable tenant is Rudolph Valentino, who rests in an interior crypt. Outside are Tyrone Power, Jr.; Douglas Fairbanks, Sr.; Cecil B. DeMille (facing Paramount, his old studio); Carl "Alfalfa" Spritzer from *The Little Rascals* (the dog on his grave is not Petey); Hearst mistress Marion Davies; John Huston; and a headstone for Jayne Mansfield (she's really buried in Pennsylvania with her family). In 2000, Douglas Fairbanks, Jr., joined his dad at Hollywood Forever. The best epitaph is Mel Blanc's "That's all, Folks." Grab a map at the entrance for a self-guided tour.

The Catholic **Holy Cross Cemetery**, 5835 W. Slauson Ave., Culver City (© **310/836-5500**), founded in 1939, hands out maps to the stars' graves. In one area, within mere feet of each other, lie Bing Crosby, Bela Lugosi (buried in his Dracula cape), and Sharon Tate; not far away are Rita Hayworth and Jimmy Durante. Also here are "Tin Man" Jack Haley and "Scarecrow" Ray Bolger, Mary Astor, John Ford, and Gloria Morgan Vanderbilt. More recent arrivals include John Candy and Audrey Meadows.

The front office at **Hillside Memorial Park**, 6001 Centinela Ave., Baldwin Hills (© **800/576-1994**; www.hillsidememorial.com), can provide a guide to this Jewish cemetery, which has an L.A. landmark: the behemoth tomb of Al Jolson. His rotunda, complete with a bronze reproduction of Jolson and cascading fountain, is visible from I-405. Also on hand are Jack Benny, Eddie Cantor, Vic Morrow, and Michael Landon.

You just know developers get stomachaches looking at **Westwood Village Memorial Park**, 1218 Glendon Ave., Westwood (© **310/474-1579**; the staff

Audiences Unlimited (see above). For tickets to *The Price Is Right*, call the 24-hour ticket hot line at © **323/575-2449** or log on to www.cbs.com/daytime/price/tickets.

For **NBC**, 3000 W. Alameda Ave., Burbank, CA 91523 (© **818/840-3537**), call to see what's on while you're in L.A. Tickets for NBC tapings, including *The Tonight Show with Jay Leno* (minimum age to attend this show is 16), can be obtained three can direct you around), smack-dab in the middle of some of L.A.'s priciest real estate (behind the AVCO office building south of Wilshire Blvd.). But it's not going anywhere, especially when you consider its most famous resident: Marilyn Monroe (entombed in a simple wall crypt, number 24). It's also got Truman Capote, Roy Orbison, John Cassavetes, Armand Hammer, Donna Reed, and Natalie Wood. Walter Matthau and Jack Lemmon are buried here as well, a fitting ending for the Odd Couple.

Forest Lawn Glendale, 1712 S. Glendale Ave. (© **800/204-3131;** www.forestlawn.com), likes to pretend it has no celebrities. The most prominent of L.A. cemeteries, it's also the most humorless. The place is full of bad art, all part of the continuing vision of founder Huburt Eaton, who thought cemeteries should be happy places. So he banished those gloomy upright tombstones and monuments in favor of flat, pleasant, character-free, flush-to-the-ground slabs. Contrary to urban legend, Walt Disney was *not* frozen and placed under Cinderella's castle at Disneyland. His cremated remains are in a little garden to the left of the Freedom Mausoleum. Turn around, and just behind you are Errol Flynn and Spencer Tracy. In the Freedom Mausoleum itself are Nat "King" Cole, Chico Marx, Gummo Marx, and Gracie Allen—finally joined by George Burns. In a columbarium near the Mystery of Life is Humphrey Bogart. Unfortunately, some of the best celebs—such as Clark Gable, Carole Lombard, and Jean Harlow—are in the Great Mausoleum, which you often can't get into unless you're visiting a relative.

You'd think a place that encourages people to visit for fun would understand what the attraction is. But no—Forest Lawn Glendale won't tell you where any of their illustrious guests are, so don't ask. This place is immense—and, frankly, dull in comparison to the previously listed cemeteries, unless you appreciate the kitsch value of the Forest Lawn approach to art.

Forest Lawn Hollywood Hills, 6300 Forest Lawn Dr. (© **800/204-3131;** www.forestlawn.com), is slightly less anal than the Glendale branch, but the same basic attitude prevails. On the right lawn, near the statue of George Washington, is Buster Keaton. In the Courts of Remembrance are Lucille Ball, Charles Laughton, and the not-quite-gaudy-enough tomb of Liberace. Outside, in a vault on the Ascension Road side, is Andy Gibb. Bette Davis's sarcophagus is in front of the wall, to the left of the entrance to the Courts. Gene Autry is also buried here, almost within earshot of the museum that bears his name.

ways: 1) Pick them up at the NBC ticket counter on the day of the show—two tickets per person are distributed on a first-come, first-served basis at the ticket counter off California Avenue starting at 8am (be sure to get there early); 2) at least 6 weeks before your visit, send a self-addressed, stamped envelope with your ticket request to the address above; 3) go to the Audiences Unlimited ticket booth at Universal Studios

Hollywood (p. 206). Be sure to include show name, number of tickets (four per request), and dates desired. All the NBC shows are represented online at either www.nbc.com or www.tvtickets.com.

Paramount Studios also offers free tickets to their live audience shows. All you need to do is call one of the friendly employees at Paramount Guest Relations (© **323/956-1777**) between 9am and 6pm on weekdays and make a reservation. For seating reservations for *Dr. Phil,* call © **323/461-7445. Universal Studios** (© **800/ UNIVERSAL** [800/864-8377]; www.universalstudios.com) also offers free tickets to their live audience shows. At the amusement park's **Audiences Unlimited ticket booth,** you can obtain free tickets to join the audience for any TV shows that are taping during your visit (subject to availability).

8 Beaches

Los Angeles County's 72-mile coastline sports more than 30 miles of beaches, most of which are operated by the **Department of Beaches & Harbors,** 13837 Fiji Way, Marina del Rey (© **310/305-9503**). County-run beaches usually charge for parking ($4–$8). Alcohol, bonfires, and pets are prohibited. For recorded **surf conditions** (and coastal weather forecast), call © **310/457-9701.** The following are the county's best beaches, listed from north to south.

EL PESCADOR, L.A. PIEDRA & EL MATADOR BEACHES   These rugged and isolated beaches (real finds) front a 2-mile stretch of the Pacific Coast Highway (Calif. 1) between Broad Beach and Decker Canyon roads, a 10-minute drive from the Malibu Pier. Picturesque coves with unusual rock formations are great for sunbathing and picnicking, but swim with caution as there are no lifeguards. The beaches can be difficult to find; only small signs on the highway mark them. There are a limited number of parking spots atop the bluffs. Descend to the beach via stairs that cling to the cliffs.

ZUMA BEACH COUNTY PARK 😊   Jampacked on warm weekends, L.A. County's largest beach park is located off the Pacific Coast Highway (Calif. 1), a mile past Kanan Dume Road. While it can't claim to be the most scenic beach in the Southland, Zuma has the most comprehensive facilities: plenty of restrooms, lifeguards, playgrounds, volleyball courts, and snack bars. The southern stretch, toward Point Dume, is Westward Beach, separated from the noisy highway by sandstone cliffs. A trail leads over the point's headlands to Pirate's Cove, once a popular nude beach.

PARADISE COVE   This private beach in the 28000 block of the Pacific Coast Highway (Calif. 1) charges $25 to park and $5 per person if you walk in. Changing rooms and showers are included in the price. The beach is often full by noon on weekends.

MALIBU LAGOON STATE BEACH 😊😊   Not just a pretty white-sand beach, but an estuary and wetlands area as well, Malibu Lagoon is the historic home of the Chumash Indians. The entrance is on the Pacific Coast Highway (Calif. 1) south of Cross Creek Road, and there's a small admission charge. Marine life and shorebirds teem where the creek empties into the sea, and the waves are always mild. The historic **Adamson House** is here, a showplace of Malibu tile now operating as a museum.

SURFRIDER BEACH   Without a doubt, L.A.'s best waves roll ashore here. One of the city's most popular surfing spots, this beach is located between the Malibu Pier and the lagoon. In surf lingo, few "locals-only" wave wars are ever fought here—surfing is not as territorial here as it can be in other areas, where out-of-towners can be

Good Day, Marina del Rey

There are several new reasons to spend a day at Marina del Rey. Chief among them are the surf and harbor **kayaking excursions** now offered by the county. Lifeguards will give you all the instruction you need and then send you off to explore the calm marina's wildlife-filled basins for the day (at $30 for all the equipment, it's a real bargain). There's also a new **Bird-Watching Experience** within Burton Chace Park. The 2-hour walks explore the fresh and saltwater marshes, nesting sites of the great blue and black crowned night herons (for reservations for kayaking and bird-watching, call the park at (✆ 310/305-9595). Kayaks, power boats, jet skis, sailboats, and pedal boats are also available at the **Marina Boat Rentals** ((✆ 310/574-2822).

After an alfresco lunch on the elevated deck overlooking the harbor at **Cafe Del Rey** (p. 113), head over to the **Fisherman's Village,** rent a bicycle at **Daniel's Bicycle Rentals** ((✆ 310/980-4045), and spend the afternoon cruising alongside the docks on the South Bay Bicycle Trail. If it's a Thursday or Saturday during the summer, arrive early for a good seat at the **free classical, jazz, and pop concerts** held at 7pm at Burton Chace Park. After the show, end your fun-filled day with a romantic dinner overlooking the harbor at the **Jer-nē** restaurant within the Ritz-Carlton, Marina del Rey (p. 74). For more information about Marina del Rey activities, call the **Marina del Rey Convention & Visitors Bureau** at (✆ 310/305-9545 or log on to www. visitmarina.com.

made to feel unwelcome. Surfrider is surrounded by all of Malibu's hustle and bustle; don't come here for peace and quiet as the surf is always crowded.

TOPANGA STATE BEACH   Highway noise prevents solitude at this short, narrow strip of sand located where Topanga Canyon Boulevard emerges from the mountains. Why go? Ask the surfers who wait in line to catch Topanga's excellent right point breaks. There are restrooms and lifeguard services here, and across the street you'll find one of the best fresh fish restaurants around, the **Reel Inn,** 18661 Pacific Coast Hwy., Malibu ((✆ 310/456-8221).

WILL ROGERS STATE BEACH   Three miles along the Pacific Coast Highway (Calif. 1), between Sunset Boulevard and the Santa Monica border, are named for the American humorist whose ranch-turned-state-historic-park (see "L.A. Parks, Gardens, Views & Zoos," earlier in this chapter) is nestled above the palisades that provide the backdrop for this popular beach. A pay parking lot extends the entire length of the beach, and facilities include restrooms, lifeguards, and a snack hut in season. While the surfing is not the best, the waves are friendly for swimmers, and there are always competitive volleyball games to be found.

SANTA MONICA STATE BEACH   The family-friendly beaches on either side of the Santa Monica Pier (see "L.A.'s Top Attractions," earlier in this chapter) are popular for their white sands and accessibility. There are big parking lots, cafes, and well-maintained restrooms. A paved beach path runs along here, allowing you to walk, bike, or skate to Venice and points south. Colorado Boulevard leads to the pier; turn

Los Angeles Beaches & Coastal Attractions

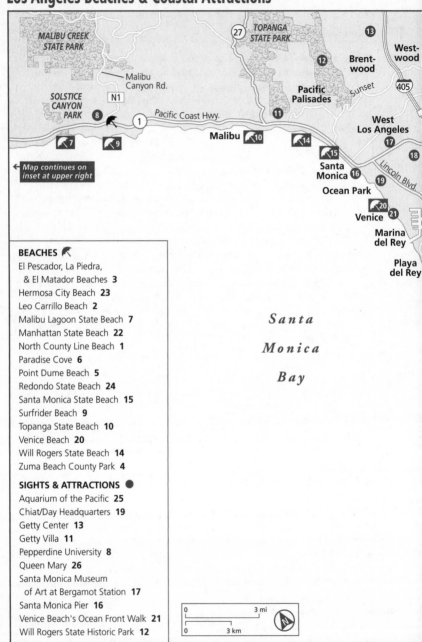

BEACHES

El Pescador, La Piedra,
  & El Matador Beaches **3**
Hermosa City Beach **23**
Leo Carrillo Beach **2**
Malibu Lagoon State Beach **7**
Manhattan State Beach **22**
North County Line Beach **1**
Paradise Cove **6**
Point Dume Beach **5**
Redondo State Beach **24**
Santa Monica State Beach **15**
Surfrider Beach **9**
Topanga State Beach **10**
Venice Beach **20**
Will Rogers State Beach **14**
Zuma Beach County Park **4**

SIGHTS & ATTRACTIONS ●

Aquarium of the Pacific **25**
Chiat/Day Headquarters **19**
Getty Center **13**
Getty Villa **11**
Pepperdine University **8**
Queen Mary **26**
Santa Monica Museum
  of Art at Bergamot Station **17**
Santa Monica Pier **16**
Venice Beach's Ocean Front Walk **21**
Will Rogers State Historic Park **12**

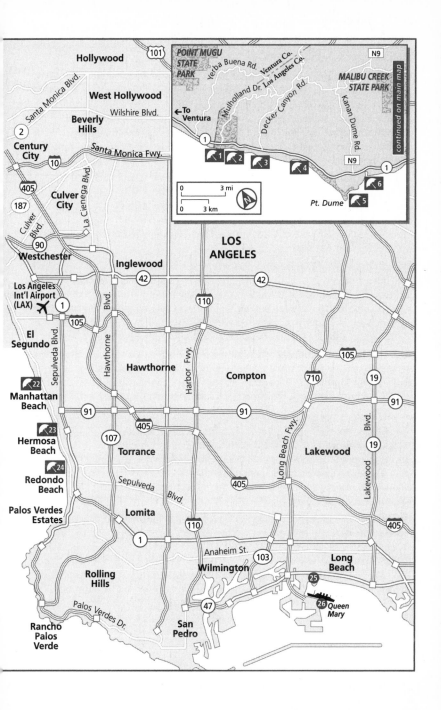

Hollywood

West Hollywood

Wilshire Blvd.

Beverly Hills

Santa Monica Blvd.

101

2

Century City

10

Santa Monica Fwy.

405

187

Culver City

Culver Blvd.

La Cienega Blvd.

90

Westchester

Inglewood

42

LOS ANGELES

Los Angeles Int'l Airport (LAX)

1

42

110

105

El Segundo

Sepulveda Blvd.

Hawthorne Blvd.

Hawthorne

Harbor Fwy.

Compton

105

710

19

91

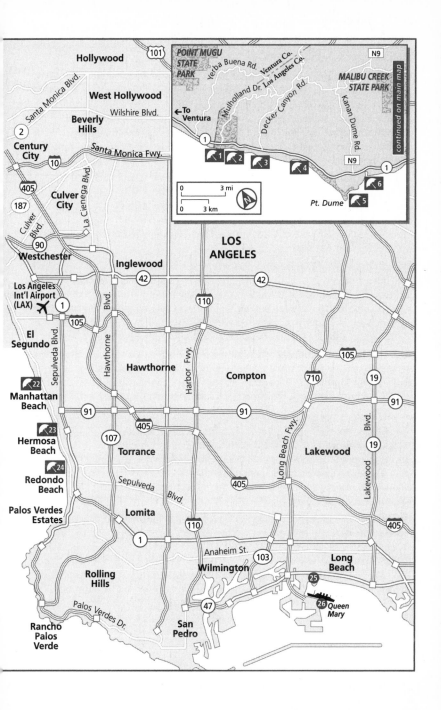22

Manhattan Beach

91

405

91

91

19

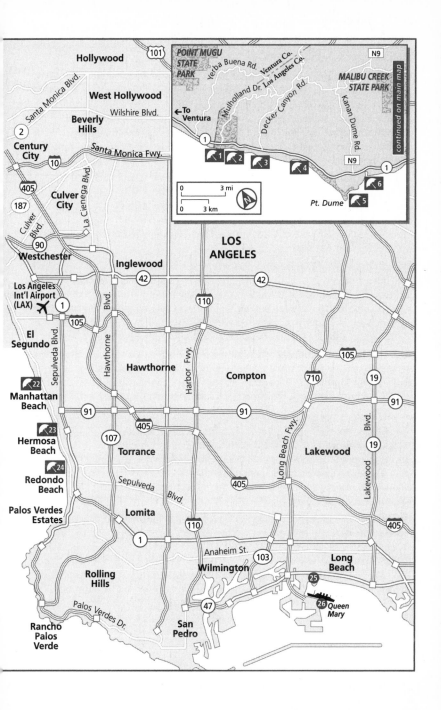23

Hermosa Beach

107

Lakewood Blvd.

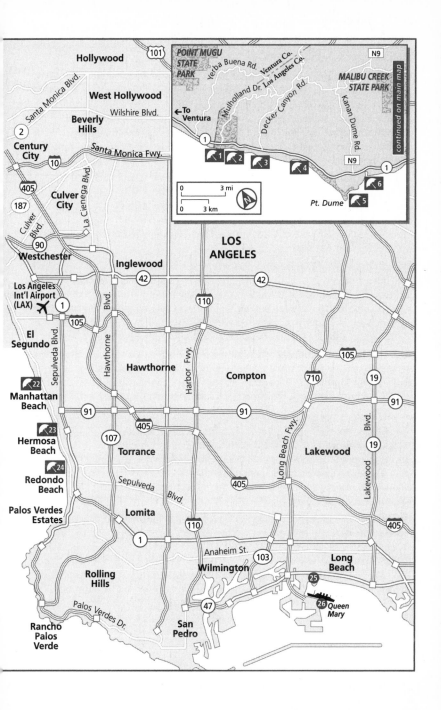24

Redondo Beach

Torrance

Lakewood

19

Palos Verdes Estates

Sepulveda Blvd.

405

405

Lomita

110

1

Anaheim St.

103

Long Beach

Rolling Hills

Palos Verdes Dr.

47

Wilmington

25

26 Queen Mary

Rancho Palos Verde

San Pedro

POINT MUGU STATE PARK

Yerba Buena Rd.

Ventura Co.

Los Angeles Co.

Mulholland Dr.

Decker Canyon Rd.

Kanan Dume Rd.

MALIBU CREEK STATE PARK

N9

continued on main map

←To Ventura

1

1

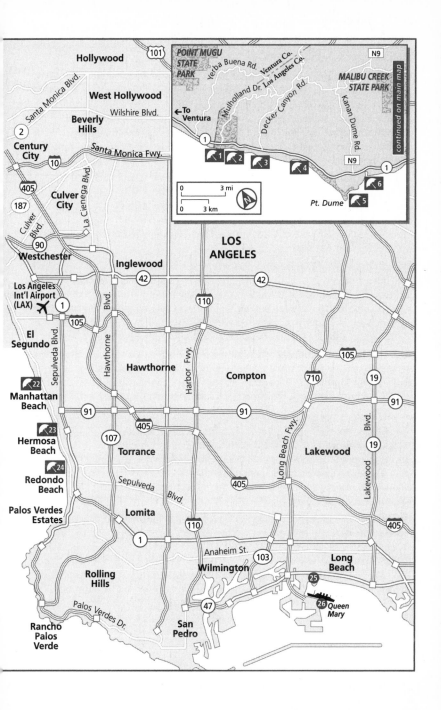1

2

3

4

N9

1

6

Pt. Dume

5

0   3 mi

0   3 km

N

north on the Pacific Coast Highway (Calif. 1) below the coastline's bluffs, or south along Ocean Avenue; you can find parking in both directions.

VENICE BEACH ⚜⚜ Moving south from the city of Santa Monica, the paved pedestrian Promenade becomes Ocean Front Walk and gets progressively weirder until it reaches an apex at Washington Boulevard and the Venice fishing pier. Although there are people who swim and sunbathe, Venice Beach's character is defined by the sea of humanity on the Ocean Front Walk, plus the bevy of boardwalk vendors and old-fashioned pedestrian streets a block away (see "L.A.'s Top Attractions," earlier in this chapter). Park on the side streets or in the plentiful lots west of Pacific Avenue.

MANHATTAN STATE BEACH The Beach Boys used to hang out at this wide, friendly beach backed by beautiful oceanview homes. Plenty of parking on 36 blocks of side streets (btw. Rosecrans Ave. and the Hermosa Beach border) draws weekend crowds from the L.A. area. Manhattan has some of the best surfing around, restrooms, lifeguards, and volleyball courts. Manhattan Beach Boulevard leads west to the fishing pier and adjacent seafood restaurants.

HERMOSA CITY BEACH ⚜⚜ This very wide white-sand beach is one of the best in Southern California and my favorite. Hermosa extends to either side of the pier and includes The Strand, a wide, smooth pedestrian lane that runs its entire length. Main access is at the foot of Pier Avenue, which is lined with interesting shops and cafes with outdoor seating. There's plenty of street parking, as well as restrooms, lifeguards, volleyball courts, a fishing pier, playgrounds, and good surfing.

REDONDO STATE BEACH Popular with surfers, bicyclists, and joggers, Redondo's white sand and ice-plant-carpeted dunes are just south of tiny King Harbor, along the Esplanade (S. Esplanade Dr.). Get there via the Pacific Coast Highway (Calif. 1) or Torrance Boulevard. Facilities include restrooms, lifeguards, and volleyball courts.

9 Golf, Hiking & Other Fun in the Warm California Sun

Bisected by the Santa Monica Mountains and fronted by long stretches of beach, Los Angeles is one of the best cities in the world for nature and sports lovers. Where else can you hike in the mountains, in-line skate along the beach, swim in the ocean, and enjoy a gourmet meal, and then take in a pro basketball, soccer, hockey, or baseball game—all in the same day?

BICYCLING Los Angeles, being mostly flat, is great for biking. If you're into distance pedaling, you can do no better than the flat, paved bicycle trail that follows about 22 miles of state beaches, harbors, LAX, and laid-back beach towns such as Venice, Manhattan Beach, Hermosa Beach, and Redondo Beach. The first stretch starts at Will Rogers State Beach in Pacific Palisades and runs south through Santa Monica and Venice to Marina del Rey—about 8 miles. The second stretch—called the South Bay Bike Trail—starts at the south end of Marina del Rey and takes you all the way to Torrance Beach. If you want to ride the entire path you'll have to detour around Marina del Rey, which only takes about 15 minutes. The bike path attracts all levels of riders and gets pretty busy on weekends, so ixnay the time trials. Don't worry about packing food and water—there's plenty of fountains, snack stands, and public restrooms along the trail. For information on this and other city bike routes, log on to www.labikepaths.com. For **guided bicycle tours** of the Santa Monica and Venice beach communities, see "Bicycle Tours" on p. 201

Topanga Canyon: Nature's Solution to L.A.'s Noise Pollution

When you've had enough of cellphones, cement, and Mercedes, then it's time to take the short drive from L.A. to Topanga Canyon to bargain shop, drink margaritas, and play cowgirl for a day. Here's the game plan: Call **Los Angeles Horseback Riding** (© **818/591-2032;** www.losangeleshorseback riding.com) and make a reservation for a guided horseback ride in the late afternoon. Next, take the winding drive up Topanga Canyon Boulevard to tiny **Topanga**, one of the last art communities left in Southern California— it was the former haunt of Fleetwood Mac, Neil Young, and other music legends of the '60s and '70s—and the perfect antidote to the dig-me L.A. scene. Spend an hour or so picking though the treasure-trove of vintage clothes, accessories, and antiques at **Hidden Treasures** (154 S. Topanga Canyon Blvd.; © **310/455-2998**), one of the funkiest little shops I've ever seen (the custom-made sea-theme toilet seat lids are mesmerizing). After the scenic horseback ride through the boulder-strewn Topanga canyons lined with oaks, sycamores, chaparral, and sage, finish off your relaxing day with a leisurely dinner in Topanga at **Abuelitas** (137 S. Topanga Canyon Blvd.; © **310/455-8688;** www.abuelitastopanga.com), a popular Mexican restaurant; or try the romantic **Inn of the Seventh Ray** (p. 122).

The best place to mountain bike in the L.A. region is along the trails of **Malibu Creek State Park** (© 818/880-0367), in the Santa Monica Mountains between Malibu and the San Fernando Valley in Calabasas. Fifteen miles of trails rise to a maximum of 3,000 feet and are appropriate for intermediate to advanced bikers. Pick up a trail map at the park entrance, 4 miles south of U.S. 101 off Las Virgenes Road, just north of Mulholland Highway. Park admission is $5 per car. For more information on mountain-bike trails in the L.A. region, log on to **www.latrails.com**.

Spokes 'N Stuff Bike Rental has four locations, one of which is located at 4175 Admiralty Way, Marina del Rey (© 310/306-3332), which is only open on weekends, and another located at 1715 Ocean Front Walk, behind Loews Hotel, Santa Monica (© 310/395-4748), which is open every day. They rent 10-speed cruisers for about $7 per hour and $16 per day; 15-speed mountain bikes rent for about $8 per hour and $20 per day. Another good Santa Monica rental shop is **Blazing Saddles Bike Rentals** (Santa Monica Pier; © 310/393-9778). The rates are about the same as those at Spokes 'N Stuff. Be sure to ask for a free **self-guided tour map** (it's really handy).

In Hollywood, **Hollywood Pro Bicycles** (6731 Hollywood Blvd., Hollywood; © 323/466-5890; www.hollywoodprobicycles.com) rents mountain bikes at $30 for a 24-hour period and $20 for each additional day. Every rental comes with a free tour map, a safety helmet, a bike lock, and a handlebar bag for storage.

In the South Bay, bike rentals—including tandem bikes—are available 1 block from The Strand at **Hermosa Cyclery,** 20 13th St. (© 310/374-7816; www.hermosa cyclery.com). Cruisers are $7 per hour; tandems are $13 per hour. FYI, The Strand is an excellent car-free path that's tailor-made for a leisurely bike ride.

FISHING   Del Rey Sport Fishing, 13759 Fiji Way, Marina del Rey (© **800/ 822-3625;** www.marinadelreysportfishing.com), has three deep-sea boats departing daily on half- and full-day ocean fishing trips. Of course, it depends on what's running when you're out, but bass, barracuda, halibut, and yellowtail are the most common catches on these party boats. Excursions start at $35 for half-day trips; tackle rental is available as well. Phone for reservations.

No permit is required to cast from shore or drop a line from a pier. Local anglers will hate me for giving away their secret spot, but the **best saltwater fishing spot** in all of L.A. is at the foot of Torrance Boulevard in Redondo Beach.

GOLF   The greater Los Angeles area has more than 100 golf courses, which vary in quality from abysmal to superb. Most of the city's public courses are administered by the Department of Recreation and Parks, which follows a complicated registration/reservation system for tee times. While visitors cannot reserve start times in advance, you're welcome to play any of the courses by showing up and getting on the call sheet. Expect to wait for the most popular tee times, but try to use your flexible vacationer status to your advantage by avoiding the early morning rush.

Of the city's seven 18-hole and three 9-hole courses, you can't get more central than the **Rancho Park Golf Course,** 10460 W. Pico Blvd. (© **310/838-7373;** www.rpgc. org), located smack-dab in the middle of L.A.'s Westside. The par-71 course has lots of tall trees, but not enough to blot out the towering Century City buildings next door. For the money it's a real bargain (heck, even Bill Clinton golfed here). Rancho also has a 9-hole, par-3 course, as well as a driving range.

For a genuinely woodsy experience, try one of the three courses inside Griffith Park, northeast of Hollywood (see "L.A. Parks, Gardens, Views & Zoos," earlier in this chapter). The courses are extremely well maintained, challenging without being frustrating, and (despite some holes alongside I-5) a great way to leave the city behind. Bucolic pleasures abound, particularly on the 9-hole **Roosevelt,** on Vermont Avenue across from the Greek Theatre; early morning wildlife often includes deer, rabbits, raccoons, and skunks (fore!). **Wilson** and **Harding** are each 18 holes and start from the main clubhouse off Riverside Drive, the park's main entrance.

Greens fees on all city courses are $24 Monday through Friday, and $31 on weekends and holidays; 9-hole courses cost $15 on weekdays and $19 on weekends and holidays. For details on other city courses, or to contact the starter directly by phone, call the Department of Recreation and Parks at © **888/527-2757** or log on to the city's parks website at www.laparks.org.

If you're not a fan of crowded city courses, it's well worth the 20-minute drive north to play **Robinson Ranch,** 27734 Sand Canyon Rd., Santa Clarita (© **661/252-8484;** www.robinsonranchgolf.com), one of the best and least-crowded public courses in the L.A. region (my golfing buddy loves this place). Golfers can choose between two Troon-managed courses, Mountain or Valley, both of which offer challenging, hilly terrain—bring extra balls—and great views of the Santa Clarita Valley. The striking 25,000-square-foot clubhouse makes a nice view as well, and houses a well-stocked pro shop and full-service restaurant. Greens fees for both courses are $87 Monday through Thursday, $117 Friday through Sunday. Carts and practice balls are included.

The **Trump National Golf Club,** 1 Ocean Trails Dr. (© **310/265-5000;** www. trumpgolf.com/trumplosangeles), recently opened in Rancho Palos Verdes. Perched on a bluff overlooking the Pacific Ocean, the course provides a spectacular view from every hole. Originally designed by Pete Dye as the Ocean Trails Golf Course, the

---

Fun Fact **The Big Sprawl**

How crowded is L.A.? If the five-county area was a state, it would surpass all states in total population size, with the exception of California, New York, and Texas.

---

property was purchased by developer Donald Trump, who spent more than $250 million to redesign it with elements such as lakes and waterfalls. Located on the Palos Verdes Peninsula, 30 minutes south of Downtown Los Angeles, the course also offers a 45,000-square-foot clubhouse with locker rooms, a pro shop, three dining options, conference rooms, and a grand ballroom. Greens fees at the public course are $275 Monday through Thursday, $375 Friday through Sunday.

Industry Hills Golf Club, 1 Industry Hills Pkwy., City of Industry (© **626/810-4653;** www.ihgolfclub.com), has two 18-hole courses designed by William Bell. Together they encompass eight lakes, 160 bunkers, and many long fairways. The Eisenhower Course, consistently ranked among *Golf Digest*'s top 25 public courses, has extra-large undulating greens and the challenge of thick *Kikuyu* grass. (*Kikuyu,* even coarser than Bermuda's broad-leaf terrain, is often called Bermuda on steroids.) An adjacent driving range is lit for night use. Greens fees are $85 Monday through Friday and $120 Saturday and Sunday, including a cart; call in advance for tee times.

For more information on regional golf courses, log on to www.golfcalifornia.com.

HANG GLIDING   Up and down the California coast, it's not uncommon to see people poised on the crests of hills, hanging from enormous colorful kites. You can, too. **Windsports Soaring Center,** 12623 Gridley St., Sylmar (© **818/367-2430;** www.windsports.com), offers instruction and rentals for both novices and experts. A 1-day lesson in a solo hang glider on a bunny hill costs $120. If it's more of a thrill you're looking for, choose the 3,000-foot-high tandem flight for $199, where you fly with an instructor. Beginner lessons are waterside at Dockweiler State Beach Training Flight Park (near LAX), while tandem flights take off from a San Fernando Valley hilltop. Phone for reservations.

HIKING   The **Santa Monica Mountains,** a small range that runs only 50 miles from Griffith Park to Point Mugu, on the coast north of Malibu, makes Los Angeles a great place for hiking. The mountains, which peak at 3,111 feet, are part of the Santa Monica Mountains National Recreation Area, a contiguous conglomeration of 350 public parks and 65,000 acres. Many animals live in this area, including deer, coyote, rabbit, skunk, rattlesnake, fox, hawk, and quail. The hills are also home to almost 1,000 drought-resistant plant species, including live oak and coastal sage.

Hiking is best after spring rains, when the hills are green, flowers are in bloom, and the air is clear. Summers can be very hot; hikers should always carry fresh water. Beware of poison oak, a hearty shrub that's common on the West Coast. Usually found among oak trees, poison oak has leaves in groups of three, with waxy surfaces and prominent veins. If you come into contact with this itch-producing plant, you'll end up with a California souvenir that you'll soon regret.

Santa Ynez Canyon, in Pacific Palisades, is a long and difficult climb that rises steadily for about 3 miles. At the top, hikers are rewarded with fantastic views over the Pacific. At the top is **Trippet Ranch,** a public facility providing water, restrooms, and picnic tables. From Santa Monica, take Pacific Coast Highway (Calif. 1) north. Turn

> (*Tips* **Segway Rentals in Santa Monica**
>
> Those weird-looking upright electronic scooters zipping around the Santa Monica beach scene are coming from the **Segway Los Angeles** rental shop near the Santa Monica Pier. Riding these Human Transporters is a hoot: lean forward, go forward; lean back, go back; stand straight up, stop. Simple. After the free 25-minute lesson it becomes intuitive, then you're on your own to scoot around the paved shoreline path around Venice Beach and the Santa Monica Pier (*everyone* checks you out). It's the closest you'll come to being a celebrity. A 2-hour rental with lesson is $75. Guided tours are available as well. *Note:* You have be at least 21 to rent one. 1660 Ocean Ave., 1 block south of the pier, Santa Monica; (*©* **310/395-1395;** www.segway.la.

right onto Sunset Boulevard and then left onto Palisades Drive. Then continue for 2½ miles, turn left onto Verenda de la Montura, and park at the cul-de-sac at the end of the street, where you can find the trail head.

Temescal Canyon, in Pacific Palisades, is far easier than the Santa Ynez trail and far more popular, especially among locals. This is one of the quickest routes into the wilderness. Hikes here are anywhere from 1 to 5 miles. From Santa Monica, take Pacific Coast Highway (Calif. 1) north; turn right onto Temescal Canyon Road, and follow it to the end. Sign in with the gatekeeper, who can also answer your questions.

Will Rogers State Historic Park, Pacific Palisades, is also a terrific place for hiking. An intermediate-level hike from the park's entrance ends at Inspiration Point, a plateau from which you can see a good portion of L.A.'s Westside. See "L.A. Parks, Gardens, Views & Zoos" earlier in this chapter, for complete information.

For more information on hiking in the L.A. region, log on to **www.latrails.com**.

HORSEBACK RIDING   **Griffith Park Horse Rental,** 480 Riverside Dr. (in the Los Angeles Equestrian Center), Burbank (*©* **818/840-8401**), rents horses by the hour for guided rides through Griffith Park's hills; no experience is necessary. Horse rental costs $25 for 1 hour, cash only. The stables are open daily from 8am to 5pm ('til 6pm in the summer), and you must be at least 6 years old to ride. If you have a rider 5 or younger, you can either opt for the pony rides in Griffith Park (p. 194), or arrange for a private 1-hour lesson by calling *©* **818/569-3666.**

Another popular horseback-riding outfit is **Sunset Ranch,** located at 3400 Beachwood Dr. off of Franklin Avenue, just under the HOLLYWOOD sign. Horse rentals are offered daily from 9am to 5pm for all levels of riders. The ranch is on the edge of Griffith Park with access to 52 miles of trails. Also available are private night rides (very romantic), dinner rides (see the "Sunset Margarita Horse Rides" box, earlier in this chapter), and riding lessons. Rates are $25 for a 1-hour ride, $40 for 2 hours, not including tip. No reservations are required. For more information, call *©* **323/469-5450** or log on to www.sunsetranchhollywood.com.

Closer to the ocean in Topanga Canyon is **Los Angeles Horseback Riding** (2623 Old Topanga Canyon Rd., Topanga; *©* **818/591-2032;** www.lahorsebackriding.com), a small, friendly outfit that offers guided Western-style trail rides for beginners to advanced riders. It's situated at the top of a 1,800-foot ridgeline—about a 25-minute drive from Santa Monica—with panoramic views of the ocean and San Fernando Valley (best seen on one of the sunset or full-moon rides). What I like about this outfit is that, if the guide feels that the group is experienced enough, she'll pick up the pace to a canter. Although same-day reservations are sometimes possible, try to book at least 3 days in advance. Kids 6 and older are welcome, and kids 17 and under must wear helmets (bring a bike helmet, if possible). Prices start at about $60 for a guided 70-minute ride, plus tip; 2-hour canyon rides and full-moon trips are available as well.

SAILING   Marina del Rey, the largest man-made marina in the world, is the launching point for L.A.'s sailboat charters such as **Free Spirit Sailing Adventures,** which offers trips ranging from a 2-hour harbor tour ($96 per person) to full-day outings along the coast and even 4-day voyages to the Channel Islands. Your host is Captain Larry, and the boat is the *Carmina Mare,* a 46-foot cutter-rigged motorsailor. You can either bring your own food and drinks or have Captain Larry prepare lunch and dinner for you. Bring your own rods and tackle and you can even go fishing. For more information call Captain Larry's cellphone number, © **310/780-3432,** or log on to www.captlarry.com.

SEA KAYAKING   Sea kayaking is all the rage in Southern California, a simple and serene way to explore the southern coastline. **Southwind Kayak Center** (17855 Skypark Circle, Irvine; © **800/768-8494** or 949/261-0200; www.southwindkayaks.com) rents sit-on-top sea kayaks for use in the bay or open ocean at their Newport Beach and Dana Point rental bases. Rates are $50 per day; instructional classes are available on weekends only. The center also conducts several easygoing guided outings, including a $55 Back to Nature trip that highlights the marine life around Dana Point. Visit their website for more details.

SKATING   The 22-mile-long South Beach Trail that runs from Pacific Palisades to Torrance is one of the premier skating spots in the country. In-line skating is especially popular, but conventional skates are often seen here, too. Skating is allowed just about everywhere bicycling is, but be advised that cyclists have the right of way. **Spokes 'N Stuff,** 4175 Admiralty Way, Marina del Rey (© **310/306-3332;** weekends only), is just one of many places to rent wheels near the Venice portion of Ocean Front Walk. In the South Bay, in-line skate rentals are available 1 block from The Strand at **Hermosa Cyclery,** 20 13th St. (© **310/374-7816;** www.hermosacyclery.com). Skates cost $6 per hour ($18 for the day); kneepads and wrist guards come with every rental.

SURFING   George Freeth (1883–1918), who first surfed Redondo Beach in 1907, is widely credited with introducing the sport to California. But surfing didn't catch on until the 1950s, when CalTech graduate Bob Simmons invented a more maneuverable lightweight fiberglass board. The Beach Boys and other surf-music groups popularized Southern California in the minds of beach-babes and -dudes everywhere, and the rest, as they say, is history.

If you're a first-timer eager to learn the sport, contact **Learn to Surf L.A.** (© **310/663-2479;** www.learntosurfla.com). This highly respected school features a team of experienced instructors that will supply all necessary equipment and get you up and riding a foam board on your first day (trust me, it's a blast). Private lessons are $120, and group lessons are $75. Another great source for learning to surf is Malibu Longboards (© **310/467-6898** or 818/990-7633; www.malibulongboards.com), the official surf instruction for Santa Monica College (don't you wish you'd spent a semester here?). The company offers private lessons for $60 per hour, as well as group lessons and 5-day surf camps.

Fun Fact **The Surfing Rabbi**

This is *so* only-in-L.A.: Surfing instructor and orthodox rabbi Nachum Shifren hosts "Surf and Soul" sermons on the sand in Santa Monica. Not only will the rabbi teach you how to surf, his wise words will empower you to succeed in this competitive world we live in. Yes, even gentiles are welcome (© 310/877-1482; www.surfingrabbi.com).

If you want to try it on your own, surfboards are available for rent at shops near all top surfing beaches in the L.A. area. **Zuma Jay Surfboards,** 22775 Pacific Coast Hwy., Malibu (© 310/456-8044; www.zumajays.com), Malibu's oldest surf shop, is about a quarter-mile south of Malibu Pier. Rentals are about $20 per day, plus $10 for wet suits in winter. For more information about surfing in Southern California, log on to www.surfline.com.

TENNIS   While soft-surface courts are more popular on the East Coast, hard surfaces are most common in California. If your hotel doesn't have a court and can't suggest any courts nearby, try the well-maintained, well-lit **Griffith Park Tennis Courts,** on Commonwealth Road, just east of Vermont Avenue (© 323/662-7772). Call or log on to the website of the **City of Los Angeles Department of Recreation and Parks** (© 888/527-2757; www.laparks.org) to see a long list of free tennis courts or make a reservation at a municipal court near you. *Tip:* Spectators can watch free collegiate matches at the UCLA campus's L.A. Tennis Center from October through May. For a schedule of tournaments, call © 310/206-6831.

WINDSURFING   Invented and patented by Hoyle Schweitzer of Torrance in 1968, windsurfing, or sail-boarding, is a fun sport that's much more difficult than it looks. **Long Beach Windsurf & Kayak Center,** 3850 E. Ocean Ave., Long Beach (© 562/433-1014; www.windsurfcenter.com), offers lessons and rentals in Alamitos Bay. A $180 learner's package includes instruction from 8am to noon, and use of board and wet suit. Kayak and in-line skate rentals are also available.

10 Spectator Sports

BASEBALL   The **Los Angeles Dodgers** (© 866/DODGERS [866/363-4377]; www.dodgers.com), winner of eight National League championships and five World Series titles, play at Dodger Stadium, located at 1000 Elysian Park near Sunset Boulevard. Watching a game at this old-school ballpark is a great way to spend the day, chomping on Dodger Dogs and basking in the sunshine. Tickets are reasonably priced, too. And even if you can't score tickets, you can still take a 90-minute **"Championship Tour" of Dodger Stadium,** including access to the field, the Dodger Dugout, the Dugout Club, the press box, and the Tommy Lasorda Training Center. Tours are offered Tuesday, Thursday, Saturday, and Sunday at 10 and 11:30am through October. The cost is $15 for adults, $10 for seniors (55 and up), and children 14 and under. You can reserve and purchase tour tickets online at www.dodgers.com (click on "Dodger Stadium," then scroll down to "Stadium Tours").

The 2002 World Series champion **Los Angeles Angels of Anaheim** (© 888/796-HALO [888/796-4256]; http://losangeles.angels.mlb.com) play American League ball at Anaheim Stadium, at 2000 Gene Autry Way, in Anaheim, about 30 minutes

---

Tips Another Kind of Spectator Sport

Attention, sports fans: If you want to see your favorite **NBA or NHL players** up close in their civvies, find out when they're playing the L.A. Lakers, Clippers, or Kings, and then dress up nice and drive over to the Ritz-Carlton Hotel in Marina del Rey. This is where all the pro teams stay whenever they're playing in L.A. You don't have to rent a room—just order a drink in the lounge and keep an eye on the lobby (you can't miss the huge basketball players). On game nights, they typically check out around 3pm.

---

from Downtown L.A. The regular Major League baseball season runs from April to October. Log on to either team's website for ticket information.

BASKETBALL   Los Angeles has two NBA franchises: the **L.A. Lakers** (www. lakers.com), who have won 14 NBA titles, and the **L.A. Clippers** (www.clippers. com), who haven't. Both teams play in the **STAPLES Center** in Downtown L.A., 1111 S. Figueroa St. Celebrity fans like Jack Nicholson, Leonardo DiCaprio, Heather Locklear, and Dyan Cannon have the best tickets, but this 20,000-seater should have room for you—that is, if you have the big bucks for a Lakers ticket or the interest in watching a Clippers game. The season runs from October to April, with 2 months of playoffs following. For tickets to see either team, call © **213/742-7340** or log on to www.staplescenter.com.

FOOTBALL   Los Angeles suffers from an absence of major-league football, but it gets by just fine with two popular college teams and an Arena League team. The college season runs September through November; if you're interested in checking out a game, contact **UCLA Bruins Football** (© **310/825-2101;** www.uclabruins.com) or **USC Trojan Football** (© **213/740-2311;** www.usctrojans.com). Described as "fun, fast, and furious," Arena League football tends to be action-packed and exciting, and it sure costs a lot less than its NFL counterpart. The local team is the **L.A. Avengers** (© **888/AVENGER** [888/283-6437]; www.laavengers.com); games run April through July and are played Downtown at the STAPLES Center (see "Basketball," above).

HORSE RACING   One of the most beautiful tracks in the country, **Santa Anita Racetrack,** 285 W. Huntington Dr., Arcadia (© **626/574-7223;** www.santaanita. com), offers racing from late December through late April (a separate racing event called the Oak Tree Meeting runs early Oct through early Nov). Set against the majestic San Gabriel Mountains, the track was featured in the Marx Brothers' film *A Day at the Races* and in the 1954 version of *A Star Is Born.* On weekdays during the season, the public is invited to watch morning workouts from 5 to 9:30am at Clockers' Corner. Admission is free; be sure to call or check the website for exact post times. *Tip:* The infield is ideal for picnics, as well as getting an up-close look at the horses and jockeys in action—it even has a children's playground.

Located just down the road from LAX, the scenic **Hollywood Park Racetrack,** 1050 S. Prairie Ave., in Inglewood (© **310/419-1500;** www.hollywoodpark.com), with its lakes and flowers, features thoroughbred racing from mid-April to July, as well as from mid-November through mid-December. Opened in 1938, it had shareholders that included movie mogul Harry Warner, Walt Disney, and Bing Crosby.

Polo, Anyone?

Way back in 1930 cowboy humorist Will Rogers got a hankerin' to play some polo, so he cleared the field in front of his Pacific Palisades home for a friendly match with his ponies and celebrity pals. Shortly after, he started his famed **Will Rogers Polo Club,** and of the 25 polo organizations that existed at the time, his polo field is the only one that remains. Matches are still held on weekends from mid-April through early October, and the bucolic setting of wide green fields, whitewashed fences, and majestic oaks is ideal for a leisurely picnic lunch and a bit of respite from the city. The polo field is located at 1501 Will Rogers State Park Rd. in Pacific Palisades, off West Sunset Boulevard. For more information, call the club at © 310/573-5000 or log on to its website at www.willrogerspolo.org (there's a great feature on "How to Watch a Polo Game").

Well-placed monitors project views of the backstretch as well as stop-action replays of photo finishes. Races are usually held Thursday through Monday. Post times are 1pm in summer (7pm on Fri) and 12:30pm on weekends and holidays. General admission is $7; admission to the clubhouse is $10.

ICE HOCKEY   The **L.A. Kings** (© 888/546-4752; www.lakings.com) hold court at their STAPLES Center home (see above); and down the road in Orange County, the **Mighty Ducks** (© 714/940-2900; www.mightyducks.com) play at the Arrowhead Pond in Anaheim. The hockey season typically runs from October through mid-April, with playoffs following. Tickets are available at either arena or through Ticketmaster.

SOCCER   Since its inaugural season in 1996, the **Los Angeles Galaxy** (© 877/3-GALAXY [877/342-5299]; www.lagalaxy.com) has already won the Major League Soccer Cup and earned a reputation as a major force in MLS. But the big draw these days is soccer superstar David Beckham, who joined the roster in 2007. He and his pop star wife, Victoria Beckham, have made international headlines by making Los Angeles their home. In fact, within the first hour following the announcement, the L.A. Galaxy sold more than 500 home game tickets. Visitors can catch a game at the Home Depot Center stadium at 18400 Avalon Blvd. in Carson. Tickets for individual games are available through the Galaxy box office and Ticketmaster.

8

The Disneyland Resort & Knott's Berry Farm

There are newer and sometimes larger Disney parks in Florida, Tokyo, France, and Hong Kong, but the original and the inspiration for all of them still opens its gates in Anaheim every day, proudly proclaiming itself "The Happiest Place on Earth." Smaller than Walt Disney World, Disneyland—which opened in 1955 on a 107-acre tract surrounded almost exclusively by orange groves—has always capitalized on being the world's first family-oriented mega–theme park. Nostalgia is a big part of the original park's appeal, and despite many advancements, changes, and expansions over the years, Disneyland remains true to the vision of founder Walt Disney.

In 2001, Disney unveiled a new theme park (Disney's California Adventure), a shopping/dining/entertainment district (Downtown Disney), and a third on-site hotel (Disney's Grand Californian Hotel). I'll give you the lowdown on the best of what's new, as well as on the classic Disneyland experience.

While the Disneyland Resort is the undisputed front-runner in family-friendly vacation destinations in Southern California, I've included another appealing amusement park that's a short drive away from Disneyland: Knott's Berry Farm. Hosting a far better selection of high-speed roller coasters, it's hugely popular with teens who crave thrill rides.

1 The Disneyland Resort

33 miles S of Los Angeles

ESSENTIALS

GETTING THERE   To reach the Disneyland Resort by car from LAX, take I-105 east to I-605 north, then I-5 south. From Los Angeles, take I-5 south until you see signs for Disneyland. Dedicated offramps from I-5 lead to the attraction's parking lots and surrounding streets (follow signs leading to THEME PARKS). The drive from LAX takes approximately 40 minutes with no traffic. (Right!)

If Anaheim is your first—or only—destination and you want to avoid L.A. altogether, consider flying directly into **John Wayne Airport** in Santa Ana (© 949/ 252-5200; www.ocair.com), Orange County's largest airport. It's about 15 miles from Disneyland at the intersection of I-405 and California 55. Check to see if your hotel has a free shuttle to and from either airport (some will pick you up at LAX), or call one of the following commercial shuttle services: **Disneyland Resort Express** (© 714/978-8855; http://anaheim.coachusa.us; fares are adults $15 one-way, $25 round-trip, children $13 one-way, $17 round-trip); **Xpress** (© 800/427-7483; www. xpressshuttle.com); **Prime Time** (© 800/733-8267; primetimeshuttle.com); or **SuperShuttle** (© 800/258-3826; www.supershuttle.com). Car-rental agencies located at the John Wayne Airport include **Budget** (© **800/527-0700;** www.budget. com) and **Hertz** (© **800/654-3131;** www.hertz.com). To reach Anaheim from LAX, take California 55 north to I-5 north, and then take the Harbor Boulevard exit and follow signs to THEME PARKS. You can also catch a ride with **American Taxi** (© **888/482-9466**), whose cabs queue up at the Ground Transportation Center on the lower level; reservations are not necessary. Expect the fare to Disneyland to cost about $30.

VISITOR INFORMATION   For information on the **Disneyland Resort,** including show schedules and ride closures that apply to the specific day(s) of your visit, call © **714/781-4565** for automated information or © **714/781-7290** to speak to Guest Relations (but expect a long wait). Better yet, log on to the Disneyland Resort's official website at **www.disneyland.com**.

For general information on the entire Anaheim region, contact the **Anaheim/Orange County Visitor and Convention Bureau,** 800 W. Katella Ave., inside the Anaheim Convention Center (© **714/765-8888;** www.anaheimoc.org). It's open Monday to Friday from 8:30am to 5:30pm. Staffers can fill you in on area activities and shopping, as well as send you their *Official Visitors Guide* and the AdventureCard, which offers discounts at dozens of local attractions, hotels, restaurants, and shops.

You can find out everything you need to know about the Disneyland Resort online, beginning with the official site, **www.disneyland.com**, which contains the latest information on park improvements and additions, plus special offers (sometimes on airfare or reduced admission) and an interactive trip planner that lets you build a custom Disney vacation package. If you prefer human interaction, contact a Walt Disney Travel Company specialist at © **866/60-DISNEY** (866/603-4763) and ask about money-saving package deals.

There are numerous unofficial Disney websites as well, which provide very detailed—and often judgmental—information about the Disneyland Resort. The best I've found are: **Disneyland: Inside & Out** (www.intercotwest.com), an active and friendly website filled with detailed information on every corner of the Disneyland Resort; **LaughingPlace.com** and **MouseInfo.com**, which both feature daily updated headlines and columns on all things Disney; **Mouseplanet.com**, a comprehensive Disneyland information resource that offers features and reviews by guest writers; and **MouseSavers.com**, which offers in-depth information on Disney theme parks and helps users save money on lodging and admissions.

ADMISSION, HOURS & INFORMATION   As of press time, admission to *either* Disneyland or Disney's California Adventure, including unlimited rides and all festivities and entertainment, is $66 for adults and children 10 and over, $56 for children

---

Tips CityPass Savings

If your vacation includes a visit to San Diego, look into purchasing a Southern California CityPass (www.citypass.com). It includes a 3-Day Park Hopper ticket to Disneyland and Disney's California Adventure, plus a 1-day admission to Universal Studios Hollywood, SeaWorld Adventure Park, and the San Diego Zoo or Wild Animal Park. It costs $247 for adults and $199 for children, and if you visit all these attractions you'll save more than $90.

Value **The Art of the (Package) Deal**

If you intend to spend 2 or more nights in Disney territory, it pays to investigate the bevy of packaged vacation options. Start by logging onto www.disneyland.com to peruse their standard package offers, take a virtual tour of Disney hotel properties, and get online price quotes for customized, date-specific packages—including airline tickets. The packages are value-packed time-savers with abundant flexibility. Rates are highly competitive, considering that each package includes multiday and multipark admission, plus keepsake souvenirs, preferred seating at Disney shows, Disney pocket guides, and coupon books. If you're staying in a non-Disney hotel (even those in Los Angeles or San Diego), ask whether they sell Disneyland admission packages; many hotels offer inclusive vacation packages that include Disneyland and Disney's California Adventure (and other attractions). To make sure you're getting the absolute best deal, call the official Disney travel planners at **Walt Disney Travel Co.** (© **866/60-DISNEY** [866/603-4763] or 714/520-5050) and compare their package deals with the ones you've already been quoted.

---

3 to 9, and free for children 2 and under. Parking is $11. A 1-Day Park Hopper ticket, which allows you to go back and forth as much as you'd like, is $91 for adults and $81 for children. A 2-day Park Hopper ticket is $132 for adults and children 10 and over, and $112 for children 3 to 9. Other multiday, multipark combination passes are available as well. In addition, many area accommodations offer lodging packages that include admission for 1 or more days. Be sure to check the Disney website, www.disneyland.com, for seasonal ticket specials.

If you plan on arriving during a busy time (when the gates open in the morning, or btw. 11am and 2pm), purchase your tickets in advance and get a jump on the crowds at the ticket counters. Advance tickets may be purchased through Disneyland's website (www.disneyland.com), at Disney stores in the United States, by calling the ticket mail-order line (© **714/781-4043**), at any nearby Disneyland Resort Good Neighbor Hotel, or as part of your travel package.

Disneyland and Disney's California Adventure are open every day of the year, but operating hours vary, so be sure to call for information that applies to the specific day(s) of your visit (© **714/781-7290**). The same information, including ride closures and show schedules, can also be found online at **www.disneyland.com**. Generally speaking, the parks are open from 9 or 10am to 6 or 7pm on weekdays, fall to spring; and from 8 or 9am to midnight or 1am on weekends, holidays, and during winter, spring, or summer vacation periods. *Tip:* The park's operating hours can give you some idea of what kinds of crowds Disney planners are expecting: The later the parks close, the more people will be there.

WHEN TO GO   The Disneyland Resort is busiest in summer (btw. Memorial Day and Labor Day), on holidays (Thanksgiving week, Christmas week, Presidents' Day weekend, and Easter week), plus weekends year-round. All other periods are considered off season. Peak hours are from noon to 5pm; visit the most popular rides before and after these hours, and you'll cut your waiting times substantially. If you plan to arrive during a busy time, buy your tickets in advance and get a jump on the crowds at the ticket booths. For information on purchasing advance tickets, see the "Admission, Hours & Information" section above.

Attendance falls dramatically during the winter, so the park offers discounted or two-for-one admission to Southern California residents, who may buy up to five tickets per zip code verification. If you'll be visiting the park with someone who lives here, be sure to take advantage of this promotion.

Another secret time-saving tip is to enter Disneyland from the turnstile at the Monorail Station in Downtown Disney. The line is usually shorter and the Monorail will take you straight into Tomorrowland (but it doesn't stop in Disney's California Adventure). Another time-saver is booking your vacation through the Walt Disney Travel Company—those package guests can enter Mickey's Toontown and Fantasyland 1 hour before the general public.

Once in the park, many visitors tackle Disneyland (or Disney's California Adventure) systematically, beginning at the entrance and working their way clockwise around the park. My advice: Arrive early and run to the most popular rides—the Indiana Jones Adventure, Star Tours, Big Thunder Mountain Railroad, Splash Mountain, the Haunted Mansion, and Pirates of the Caribbean, all in Disneyland; and Twilight Zone Tower of Terror, Soarin' Over California, California Screamin', Grizzly River Run, and It's Tough to Be a Bug rides in Disney's California Adventure. Waits for these rides can last an hour or more in the middle of the day.

This time-honored plan of attack may eventually become obsolete, thanks to Disney's complimentary **FASTPASS** system. Here's how it works: Say you want to ride Space Mountain, but the line is long—*so* long the current wait sign indicates a 75-minute standby. Instead, you can head to the automated FASTPASS ticket dispenser, where you pop in your park ticket to receive a free voucher listing a computer-assigned boarding time later that day. When you return at the assigned time, you enter through the FAST-PASS gate and only have to wait about 10 minutes (to the envy of everyone in the slow-poke line). The hottest features at Disney's California Adventure had FASTPASS built in from the start; for a complete list for each park, check your official map/guide when you enter and look for the red FP symbol. *Note:* You can obtain a FASTPASS for only one attraction at a time. Also, the FASTPASS system doesn't eliminate the need to arrive at the theme park early because there's only a limited supply of FASTPASSes available for each attraction on a given day. So, if you don't show up until the middle of the afternoon, you might find that all the FASTPASSes have been distributed to other guests.

DISNEYLAND ๑๑๑

Disneyland is divided into eight sub-areas or "lands" arranged around a central hub, each of which has a number of rides and attractions that are, more or less, related to that land's theme. Be sure to pick up a free park map on the way in, or you'll probably get lost almost immediately.

MAIN STREET U.S.A.   Located at the park's entrance, Main Street U.S.A. is an idealized version of a turn-of-the-20th-century American small-town street inspired by Marceline, Missouri (Walt Disney's childhood home), and built on a ⅞ scale. Attention to detail here is exceptional—interiors, furnishings, and fixtures conform to the period. As with any real Main Street, the Disney version is essentially a collection of shops and eating places, with a city hall, a fire station, and an old-time silent cinema. Live performances include piano playing at the Carnation ice-cream parlor and Dapper Dan's barbershop quartet along the street. A mixed-media attraction combines a presentation on the life of Walt Disney (The Walt Disney Story) with a patriotic remembrance of Abraham Lincoln. Horse-drawn trolleys, fire engines, and horseless carriages give rides along Main Street and transport visitors to the central hub (properly known as the Central Plaza).

Because there are no major rides, it's best to tour Main Street during the middle of the afternoon, when lines for rides are longest, and in the evening, when walkways can be packed with visitors viewing Disneyland's parades and shows. There's always something happening on Main Street; stop in at the information booth to the left of the Main Entrance for a schedule of the day's events.

ADVENTURELAND   Inspired by the most exotic regions of Asia, Africa, India, and the South Pacific, Adventureland is home to several popular rides. Here's where you can cavort inside **Tarzan's Treehouse,** a climb-around attraction based on the animated film. Its neighbor is the **Jungle Cruise,** where passengers board a large, authentic-looking Mississippi River paddleboat and float along an Amazon-like river; a spear's throw away is the **Enchanted Tiki Room,** one of the most sedate attractions in Adventureland. Inside, you can sit down and watch a 20-minute musical comedy featuring electronically animated tropical birds, flowers, and "Tiki gods."

The **Indiana Jones Adventure** is Adventureland's star ride. Based on the Steven Spielberg films, this ride takes adventurers into the Temple of the Forbidden Eye in joltingly realistic all-terrain vehicles. Riders follow Indy and experience the perils of bubbling lava pits, whizzing arrows, fire-breathing serpents, collapsing bridges, and the familiar tumbling boulder (an effect that's very realistic to riders in the front seats).

NEW ORLEANS SQUARE   A large, grassy green dotted with gas lamps, New Orleans Square is home to the **Haunted Mansion,** where the dated effects are more funny than scary. One of Disneyland's most popular rides, **Pirates of the Caribbean,** has a whole new look. Visitors still float on boats through mock underground caves, but now the plot is Captain Jack Sparrow and his cohorts from the hit film franchise doing battle with Davy Jones. Even in the middle of the afternoon you can dine by the cool moonlight and to the sound of crickets in the **Blue Bayou** restaurant, situated in the middle of the ride itself.

CRITTER COUNTRY   An ode to the backwoods, Critter Country is a sort of Frontierland without those pesky settlers. Older kids and grown-ups head straight for **Splash Mountain,** one of the largest water flume rides in the world. Loosely based on the Disney movie *Song of the South,* the ride is lined with about 100 characters that won't stop singing "Zip-A-Dee-Doo-Dah." Be prepared to get wet, especially if someone sizable is in the front seat of your log-shaped boat. The **Many Adventures of Winnie the Pooh** is a children's attraction based on Winnie the Pooh and his friends from the Hundred-acre Wood—Tigger, Eeyore, Piglet, and the gang. The attraction is of the kindler, gentler sort, where you board "hunny bee-hives" and take a slow-moving journey through the Hundred-acre Wood in endless pursuit of "hunny." The high-tech gadgetry and illusions are spellbinding for kids and mildly entertaining for adults. (*Tip:* It's a very popular attraction, so be sure to arrive early or make use of FASTPASS.) While it may not be the fastest ride in the park, **Davy Crockett's Explorer Canoes** allow folks to row around Tom Sawyer Island. It's the only ride where you actively control your boat (no underwater rails!). Hop into replica canoes, grab a paddle, and away you go.

FRONTIERLAND   Inspired by 19th-century America, Frontierland features a raft to **Pirate's Lair at Tom Sawyer's Island,** a do-it-yourself play area with live pirates, island caverns, and rope bridges leading to buried treasure. You'll also find the **Big Thunder Mountain Railroad,** a runaway roller coaster that races through a deserted 1870s gold mine. Children will dig the petting zoo, and there's an Abe Lincoln–style log cabin; both are great for exploring with the little ones. This is also where you board one of two riverboats—*Mark Twain* and the *Sailing Ship Columbia*—that navigate the waters around Tom Sawyer Island and Fort Wilderness. Beautiful crafts, the riverboats provide lofty perches from which to see Frontierland and New Orleans Square. The *Sailing Ship Columbia,* however, has far more historic and aesthetic appeal. As with the other river craft, the riverboats suspend operations at dusk.

When it's showing (it's a seasonal presentation), head to Frontierland's **Rivers of America** after dark to see the *FANTASMIC!* show. It mixes magic, music, 50 live performers, floats, and sensational special effects. Just as he did in *The Sorcerer's Apprentice,* Mickey Mouse battles evil and conjures good, using his magical powers to create giant water fountains, enormous flowers, and fantasy creatures. There are plenty of pyrotechnics, lasers, and fog, as well as a 45-foot-tall dragon that breathes fire and sets the water of the Rivers of America aflame.

MICKEY'S TOONTOWN   This is a colorful, whimsical world inspired by the film *Who Framed Roger Rabbit?*—a wacky, gag-filled land populated by 'toons. It even looks like a cartoon come to life, a trippy, smile-inducing world without a straight line or right angle in sight. In addition to serving as a place where guests can be certain of finding Disney characters at any time during the day, Mickey's Toontown also serves as an elaborate interactive playground where it's okay for the kids to run, climb, and let off steam. There are several rides and play areas, including **Roger Rabbit's Car-ToonSpin, Donald's Boat, Chip 'n' Dale's Treehouse, Gadget's Go Coaster,** and **Mickey's House & Minnie's House.** *Tip:* Because of its popularity with families, Toontown is most crowded during the day but often deserted after dinnertime.

FANTASYLAND   With a storybook theme, this is the catchall "land" for stuff that doesn't quite fit anywhere else. Most of the rides are geared to the under-6 set, including the **King Arthur Carousel, Mad Tea Party, Dumbo the Flying Elephant ride,** and **Casey Jr. Circus Train.** Some, like **Mr. Toad's Wild Ride** and **Peter Pan's Flight,** appeal to grown-ups as well, and are original attractions from opening day in 1955. You'll also find **Alice in Wonderland, Snow White's Scary Adventures, Pinocchio's Daring Journey,** and more.

The most lauded attraction is **It's a Small World,** a slow-moving indoor river ride through a saccharine scenario of all the world's children singing the song everybody loves to hate. (Perhaps the ride would be more entertaining if each person got four softballs on the way in?) For a different kind of thrill, try the **Matterhorn Bobsleds,** a zippy roller coaster through chilled caverns and drifting fog banks. It's one of the park's most popular rides and the world's first steel tubular track roller coaster.

TOMORROWLAND   Conceived as an optimistic look at the future, Tomorrowland employs an angular, metallic look popularized by futurists like Jules Verne. Longtime Tomorrowland favorites include the newly revamped **Space Mountain** (a pitch-black indoor roller coaster that assaults your equilibrium and ears), and **Star Tours,** the original Disney–George Lucas joint venture. It's a 40-passenger Star-Speeder that encounters a spaceload of misadventures on the way to the Moon of Endor, achieved with wired seats and video effects—not for the queasy.

Other Tomorrowland attractions include: **Buzz Lightyear Astro Blasters,** where guests pilot their own Star Cruiser through a comical interactive space mission to conquer the Evil Emperor Zurg; *Honey, I Shrunk the Audience,* an interactive 3-D movie based on the popular movie series featuring Rick Moranis in the role of Wayne Szalinski; the **Disneyland Monorail,** a "futuristic" elevated monorail that takes you to Downtown Disney and back again (and offers the only practical opportunity for escaping the park during the crowded lunch period and early afternoon); and **Innoventions,** a huge, busy collection of industry-sponsored hands-on exhibits such as the **Dream Home,** a 5,000+ sq. ft. home belonging to the fictional Elias family that provides a glimpse of the emerging digital advances for future high-tech homes. Exhibits, many of which change each year, demonstrate such products as virtual-reality games, voice-activated appliances, and various digital applications, among others.

DISNEY'S CALIFORNIA ADVENTURE 🍎🍎

With a grand entrance designed to resemble one of those "Wish you were here" scenic postcards, the 55-acre Disney's California Adventure starts out with a bang. You walk beneath the scale model of the Golden Gate Bridge (keep watching—the monorail will pass overhead) into **Sunshine Plaza,** which is anchored by a perpetual wave fountain and an enormous gold titanium "sun" that shines all day (it's illuminated by six computerized heliostats that follow the real sun's path). From this point, visitors can head into four themed "districts," each containing rides, interactive attractions, live-action shows, and plenty of dining, snacking, and shopping opportunities.

THE GOLDEN STATE This multidimensional area represents California's history, heritage, and physical attributes. Sound boring? Actually, the park's splashiest attractions are here. **Condor Flats** is a tribute to daring aviators; inside a weathered corrugated test-pilots' hangar is **Soarin' Over California,** the simulated hang-glider ride that immediately rose to the top on everyone's "ride first" list (it's equipped with FASTPASS, and I highly recommend using it). It uses cutting-edge technology to combine elevated seats with a spectacular IMAX-style surround-movie—riders literally "soar" over California's scenic lands, feeling the Malibu ocean breeze and smelling the Central Valley orange groves and Yosemite pines.

Nearby, California Adventure's iconic Grizzly Peak towers over the **Grizzly River Run,** a splashy gold-country ride through caverns, mine shafts, and water slides; it culminates with a wet plunge into a spouting geyser. Kids can cavort nearby on the **Redwood Creek Challenge Trail,** a forest playground with smoke-jumper cable slides, net climbing, and swaying bridges.

Pacific Wharf was inspired by Monterey's Cannery Row and features mouthwatering demonstration attractions by **Boudin Sourdough Bakery** and **Mission Tortillas.** If you get hungry, each has a food counter where you can enjoy soup in a sourdough bowl or tacos, burritos, and enchiladas.

PARADISE PIER Journey back to the glory days of California's beachfront amusement piers—remember Santa Monica, Santa Cruz, and Belmont Park?—on this fantasy boardwalk. Highlights include **California Screamin',** a classic roller coaster that replicates the whitewashed wooden white-knucklers of the past—but with state-of-the-art steel construction and a smooth, computerized ride that catapults you from zero to 55 mph in less than 5 seconds, then takes a loop-de-loop through a silhouette of Mickey Mouse's ears. There's also the **Maliboomer,** a trio of towers (giant strongman sledgehammer tests) that catapult riders to the tiptop bell and then let them down bungee-style with dangling feet; the **Orange Stinger,** a whooshing swing ride inside an enormous orange, complete with orange scent piped in; **Mulholland Madness,** a wacky, wild trip along L.A.'s precarious hilltop street that is way scarier than it looks; and the **Sun Wheel Carousel,** featuring unique zigzagging cars that bring a new twist to the familiar ride. In 2008 the **Toy Story Mania** ride debuted. Guests donning 3-D glasses are "shrunk" to the size of a toy and hop into fanciful ride vehicles that travel and twist along a midway-themed route. Upon arriving at each game booth you aim for animated targets using your onboard "toy cannon."

Paradise Pier also has all the familiar boardwalk games (complete with stuffed prizes); guilty-pleasure fast foods like pizza, corn dogs, and burritos; plus a full-service over-water restaurant called **Ariel's Grotto.**

HOLLYWOOD PICTURES BACKLOT   If you've visited Disney in Florida, you might recognize many elements of this *trompe l'oeil* re-creation of a Hollywood movie studio lot. Pass through a classic studio archway flanked by gigantic golden elephants and you'll find yourself on a surprisingly realistic Hollywood Boulevard. The resort's hottest attraction is the **Twilight Zone Tower of Terror.** This truly scary ride has been a huge hit since its debut at Walt Disney World. Legend has it that during a violent storm on Halloween night 1939, lightning struck the Hollywood Tower Hotel, causing an entire wing and an elevator full of people to disappear, and you're about to retrace their steps from that fateful night as you become the star in a special Disney episode of . . . *The Twilight Zone.* In this once glamorous but now eerily vacant hotel, you tour the lobby, library, and boiler room, and ultimately board the elevator to plunge 13 stories to the fifth dimension and beyond.

The Backlot's other main attraction is **Playhouse Disney—Live on Stage!,** starring the characters from the popular *Playhouse Disney* kids' program on the Disney Channel. It's a hugely popular high-energy show where Bear in the Big Blue House, Jo Jo, Stanley, and other television characters entertain kids with songs, music, and stories of friendship. Other popular shows include **Monsters, Inc. Mike & Sully to the Rescue!,** where guests ride taxis through Monstropolis on a mission to safely return "Boo" to her bedroom; and *Jim Henson's MuppetVision 3D,* an on-screen comedy romp featuring Kermit, Miss Piggy, Gonzo, Fozzie Bear—and even hecklers Waldorf and Statler. Although it's not nearly as entertaining as *It's Tough to Be a Bug* (see below), it has its moments and won't scare the bejesus out of little kids.

At the end of the street, the replica movie palace **Hyperion Theater** presents Broadway-caliber live-action shows of classic Disney films such as *Aladdin—A Musical Spectacular.* In the **Disney Animation** building, visitors can participate in different interactive galleries and learn how stories become animated features as told by Disney artists in the Drawn to Animation studio.

A BUG'S LAND   This bug-themed land encompasses *It's Tough to Be a Bug,* **Flik's Fun Fair,** and **Bountiful Valley Farm.** Inspired by the movie *A Bug's Life, It's Tough to Be a Bug* uses 3-D technology to lead the audience on an underground romp in the insect kingdom with bees, termites, grasshoppers, stink bugs, spiders, and a few surprises that keep everyone hopping, ducking, and laughing along. (I could see how little kids might find the show rather terrifying, however.) The **Flik's Fun Fair** area features bug-themed rides and a water playground designed especially for little ones ages 4 to 7—but sized so their parents can ride along, too. **Bountiful Farm** pays tribute to California's agriculture. Exhibits include a demonstration vineyard, mission-style "aging room" (with *Seasons of the Vine,* a film presented by Robert Mondavi on the art of winemaking), wine bars, and the park's most upscale eatery, the **Vineyard Room,** a great place to sip champagne and watch Disney's Electrical Parade.

DOWNTOWN DISNEY DISTRICT ✦

Borrowing a page from central Florida's successful Disney compound, the **Downtown Disney District** is a colorful (and very sanitized) "street scene" filled with restaurants, shops, and entertainment for all ages. Options abound: Window-shop with kids in tow, have an upscale dinner for two, or party into the night. The promenade begins at the amusement park gates and stretches toward the Disneyland Hotel; there are nearly 20 shops and boutiques, and a dozen-plus restaurants, live music venues, and entertainment options.

Highlights include **House of Blues,** the blues-jazz restaurant/club that features Delta-inspired cuisine, big-name musicians, and the hand-clapping Sunday Gospel Brunch; **Ralph Brennan's Jazz Kitchen,** a spicy mix of New Orleans traditional foods and live jazz; **ESPN Zone,** the ultimate sports, dining, and entertainment experience, including an interactive game room with a rock-climbing wall; and **World of Disney,** one of the biggest Disney shopping experiences anywhere, with a vast and diverse range of toys, souvenirs, and collectibles. There is also an AMC Theatres 12-screen multiplex, the LEGO Imagination Center, a Sephora cosmetics store, and more.

WHERE TO STAY
VERY EXPENSIVE
Disney's Grand Californian Hotel ✦✦✦ *Kids*   Disney didn't miss the details when constructing this enormous version of an Arts and Crafts–era lodge (think Yosemite's Ahwahnee and Pasadena's Gamble House), hiring craftspeople throughout the state to contribute one-of-a-kind tiles, furniture, sculptures, and artwork. Taking inspiration from California's redwood forests, mission pioneers, and plein-air painters, designers created a nostalgic yet state-of-the-art high-rise hotel that has its own private entrance into Disney's California Adventure park and Downtown Disney District.

Enter through subtle (where's the door?) stained-glass sliding panels to the hotel's centerpiece, a six-story "living room" with a William Morris–designed marble "carpet," an angled skylight seen through exposed support beams, display cases of Craftsman treasures, and a three-story walk-in "hearth" whose fire warms Stickley-style rockers and plush leather armchairs.

Guest rooms are spacious and smartly designed, carrying through the Arts and Crafts theme surprisingly well considering the hotel's grand scale. The best ones overlook the park, but you'll pay for that view. Despite the sophisticated air of the Grand Californian, this is a hotel that truly caters to families, with a bevy of room configurations including one with a double bed plus bunk beds with a trundle. Since the hotel provides sleeping bags (rather than rollaways) for kids, this standard-size room will sleep a family of six—but you have to share the bathroom. *Tip:* Ask for a free upgrade to a room with a view of the park when you check in—they're pretty generous about this.

The hotel's two main restaurants are the upscale **Napa Rose** and the **Storytellers Cafe,** a "character dining" restaurant that's always bustling with excited kids who pay more attention to Chip and Dale than their eggs and bacon (be sure to make a breakfast reservation). Also on the property is **Mandara Spa,** offering a complete array of spa services for men and women.

1600 S. Disneyland Dr., Anaheim, CA 92802. ⓒ **714/956-MICKEY** (714/956-6425) (central reservations), or 714/635-2300. For vacation packages, call the Walt Disney Travel Company at **866/60-DISNEY** (866/603-7639). Fax 714/956-6099. www.disneyland.com. 745 units. $215–$345 double; from $355 suite. AE, DC, DISC, MC, V. Free self-parking; valet $6. **Amenities:** 3 restaurants; lounge; 2 outdoor pools; whirlpool; full-service spa; children's center; game room/arcade; concierge; business center; 24-hr. room service; laundry service; dry cleaning; concierge-level rooms. *In room:* A/C, TV, dataport, minibar, coffeemaker, hair dryer, iron, safe, robes, portable crib.

EXPENSIVE

The Disneyland Hotel *★★ (Kids)*   The Holy Grail of Disney-goers has always been this, the "Official Hotel of the Magic Kingdom." A monorail connection via Downtown Disney means you'll be able to return to your room anytime, whether to take a much-needed nap or to change your soaked shorts after riding Splash Mountain. The theme hotel is an attraction unto itself and is the best choice for families with small children. The rooms aren't fancy, but they're comfortably furnished and all have balconies. In-room amenities include movie channels (with free Disney Channel, naturally) and even Disneyland-themed toiletries and accessories such as Sneezy on the tissue box. When you turn out the lights in the guest rooms, the wallpaper glows with Tinker Bell's pixie dust. This all-inclusive resort offers several restaurants (see below for a full review of **Goofy's Kitchen**), snack bars, and cocktail lounges; every kind of service desk imaginable; a video-game center; and the Never Land Pool Complex with a white-sand beach and separate adult pool nearby.

1150 W. Magic Way, Anaheim, CA 92802. © **714/956-MICKEY** (714/956-6425). For vacation packages, call the Walt Disney Travel Company at **866/60-DISNEY** (866/603-4763). Reservations fax 714/956-6582. www.disneyland.com. 990 units. $80–$320 double; from $275 suite. AE, MC, V. Parking $10. **Amenities:** 4 restaurants; 3 lounges; 3 outdoor pools; health club; whirlpool; children's programs; game room; concierge; shopping arcade; room service; babysitting; laundry service; dry cleaning. *In room:* A/C, TV, dataport, minibar, hair dryer, safe.

Paradise Pier Hotel *★★ (Kids)*   The whimsical beach boardwalk theme of this 15-story hotel ties in with the Paradise Pier section of Disney's California Adventure park across the street. The surfer theme salutes the heyday of seaside amusement parks with nautical and beach decor in the guest rooms, nostalgic California artwork, and a water slide modeled after the wooden roller coasters of yesteryear. Book a room at this smallest Disney property only if the other two are full—it's not as "magical" as the original Disneyland Hotel and is soundly trounced by the superlative Grand Californian. It's also not as centrally located as the other two hotels, which could be a problem if you're not fond of walking. It does, however, offer "family suites" that comfortably accommodate families of six or more, as well as Lilo & Stich's Aloha Breakfast featuring island songs and tableside visits at the hotel's **PCH Grill.** Kids even get to make their own pizzas (pseudo breakfast pizzas with peanut butter and gummy bears and such, or, for lunch/dinner, traditional pizzas baked in the kitchen oven). *Tip:* Request a room that either overlooks the Paradise Pier section of California Adventure or has direct access to the poolside cabanas.

1717 S. Disneyland Dr., Anaheim, CA 92802. © **714/956-MICKEY** (714/956-6425). For vacation packages, call the Walt Disney Travel Company at 866/60-DISNEY (866/603-7639). Reservations fax 714/956-6582. www.disneyland. com. 489 units. $180–$320 double; from $275 suite. AE, MC, V. Parking $10. **Amenities:** 2 restaurants; lounge; outdoor pool; fitness center; whirlpool; children's programs; game room; concierge; shopping arcade; room service; babysitting; laundry service; dry cleaning. *In room:* A/C, TV w/pay movies, dataport, minibar, coffeemaker, hair dryer, safe.

Sheraton Anaheim Hotel *★*   This hotel rises to the festive theme-park occasion with its fanciful English Tudor architecture; it's a castle that lures business conventions, Disney-bound families, and local high school proms. The public areas are quiet and elegant—intimate gardens with fountains and koi ponds, and a plush lobby and lounges—which can be a pleasing touch after a frantic day at the amusement park. The rooms are modern and unusually spacious, but otherwise not distinctive. A large swimming pool sits in the center of the complex, surrounded by attractive landscaping. Don't be put off by the high rack rates; rooms commonly go for $100 to $130, even on busy summer weekends.

900 S. Disneyland Dr. (at I-5), Anaheim, CA 92802. (C) **800/325-3535** or 714/778-1700 in the U.S. Fax 714/535-3889. www.sheraton.com. 489 units. $210–$245 double; $300–$370 suite. AE, DC, MC, V. Parking $10; free Disneyland shuttle. **Amenities:** 2 restaurants; lounge; outdoor pool; fitness center; whirlpool; concierge; 24-hr. room service; coin-op laundry; laundry service; dry cleaning. *In room:* A/C, TV w/pay movies, dataport, minibar, coffeemaker, hair dryer, iron.

MODERATE

The Anabella Hotel ✦   Uniting several formerly independent low-rise hotels across the street from Disney's California Adventure, the developers behind the Anabella started from scratch, gutting each building to create carefully planned rooms for park-bound families and business travelers alike. The complex features a vaguely mission-style facade of whitewashed walls and red-tiled roofs, though guest room interiors are strictly contemporary in style and modern in appointments. Bathrooms are generously sized and outfitted in honey-toned granite; most have a tub/shower combo—just a few are shower only. Though parking areas dot the grounds, you'll also find a pleasant garden around the central swimming pool and whirlpool; a separate adult pool hides out next to the street-side fitness room. Business travelers will appreciate the in-room executive desks with high-speed Internet access, while families can take advantage of "kids' suites" complete with bunk beds and separate bedrooms. There's a pleasant indoor-outdoor all-day restaurant, and the hotel is a stop on both the Disney and Convention Center shuttle routes. *Note:* Rooms and rates vary wildly in terms of room size, layout, and occupancy limits; extra time spent at the hotel's website and with the reservationist will pay off in the most comfortable room for your needs.

1030 W. Katella Ave., Anaheim, CA 92802. (C) **800/863-4888** or 714/905-1050. Fax 714/905-1054. www.anabella hotel.com. 360 units. $99–$319 double. AE, DC, DISC, MC, V. Free parking. **Amenities:** Restaurant; lounge; 2 outdoor heated pools; exercise room; whirlpool; concierge; activities desk; business center; room service; self-service laundromat; laundry service; dry cleaning; nail salon. *In room:* A/C, TV w/pay movies, dataport, high-speed Internet, fridge, coffeemaker, hair dryer, iron, safe, Web TV, PlayStation.

Anaheim Plaza Hotel & Suites ✦✦ *Value*   Although it's located across the street from the Disneyland Resort's main gate, you'll appreciate the way this hotel's clever design shuts out the noisy world. In fact, the seven two-story garden buildings remind me more of 1960s Waikiki than busy Anaheim (maybe it's the palm trees). A key feature is the Olympic-size heated outdoor pool and whirlpool. The furnishings are motel-bland but you won't spend much time here anyway. On the plus side, little has changed about the friendly rates, which often drop as low as $59.

1700 S. Harbor Blvd., Anaheim, CA 92802. (C) **800/631-4144** or 714/772-5900. Fax 714/772-8386. www.anaheim plazahotel.com. 300 units. $99–$170 double; from $205 suite. Rates include continental breakfast. AE, DC, DISC, MC, V. Free parking and Disneyland shuttle. **Amenities:** Restaurant; lounge; outdoor pool; whirlpool; room service; coin-op laundry; laundry service; dry cleaning. *In room:* A/C, TV, coffeemaker, hair dryer.

Portofino Inn & Suites ✦✦ *Kids*   Emerging from the rubble of the former Jolly Roger Hotel renovation, this complex of low- and high-rise all-suite buildings sports a cheery yellow exterior and family-friendly interior. The location couldn't be better—directly across the street from California Adventure's back side. You can either walk or take the ART (Anaheim Resort Transit) to the front gate. Designed to work as well for business travelers from the nearby Convention Center as for Disney-bound families, the Portofino offers contemporary, stylish furnishings as well as vacation-friendly rates and suites for any family configuration. Families will want a Kids' Suite, which features bunk beds and a sleeper sofa, plus a TV, fridge, and microwave—and that's just in the kids' room; Mom and Dad have a separate bedroom with grown-up comforts like a double vanity, shower massage, and their own TV. There's even a Kids Eat Free program at the inn's cafe.

1831 S. Harbor Blvd. (at Katella Ave.), Anaheim, CA 92802. © 800/398-3963 or 714/782-7600. Fax 714/782-7619. www.portofinoinnanaheim.com. 190 units. $104–$169 double; $119–$229 suite. Midweek, off-season, and other discounts available. AE, DC, DISC, MC, V. Free parking and Disneyland shuttle. **Amenities:** Restaurant; outdoor pool; fitness center; whirlpool; game room; tour desk; coin-op laundry; laundry service; dry cleaning; Wi-Fi. *In room:* A/C, TV, dataport, coffeemaker, hair dryer, iron.

INEXPENSIVE

Candy Cane Inn *(★★) (Value)*   Take your standard U-shaped motel court with outdoor corridors, spruce it up with cobblestone drives and walkways along with old-time streetlamps, add flowering vines engulfing room balconies, and you have the Candy Cane. The face-lift worked, making this gem near Disneyland's main gate a treat for the stylish bargain hunter. The rooms are decorated in bright floral motifs with comfortable furnishings, including queen-size beds and a separate dressing and vanity area. Breakfast is served in the courtyard, where you can also splash around in a heated pool, spa, or kids' wading pool. If you feel like splurging, request one of the Premium Rooms with extended checkout and nightly turndown service.

1747 S. Harbor Blvd., Anaheim, CA 92802. © 800/345-7057 or 714/774-5284. Fax 714/772-1305. www.candycane inn.net. 172 units. $82–$159 double. Rates include expanded continental breakfast. AAA discount available. AE, DC, DISC, MC, V. Free parking and Disneyland shuttle. **Amenities:** Outdoor pool; whirlpool; coin-op laundry; laundry service; dry cleaning. *In room:* A/C, TV, fridge, coffeemaker, hair dryer.

Travelodge Anaheim   Located on the back side of Disneyland, this modest hotel appeals to the budget-conscious traveler who's looking for plenty of free perks such as wireless Internet and continental breakfast. All rooms have a refrigerator and microwave, and you can relax by the large outdoor heated pool and spa while using the laundry room. The extra-large family rooms accommodate virtually any brood, and shuttles run regularly to the park.

1057 W. Ball Rd., Anaheim, CA 92802. © 800/578-7878 or 714/774-7600. Fax 714/535-6953. www.travelodge. com. 95 units. $90–$110 double; $115 family room. Rates include full breakfast. AE, DC, DISC, MC, V. Free parking and Disneyland shuttle. **Amenities:** Restaurant; outdoor pool; whirlpool; self-service laundry; Wi-Fi. *In room:* A/C, TV, fridge, coffeemaker, microwave, hair dryer, iron.

WHERE TO DINE

There's nothing quite like an energetic family vacation to build an appetite, and sooner or later you'll have to make the inevitable Disney dining decisions: Where, when, and for how much? The expanded Disneyland Resort has something for everyone, a respectable lineup that can easily meet your needs for the duration of the typical visit. Until recently, dining options were pretty sparse, limited to those inside Disneyland and some old standbys at the Disneyland Hotel. But Disney's big expansion upped the ante with national theme/concept restaurants along Downtown Disney and competitive dining options at the resort hotels. The best of the bunch are reviewed below. For dining reservations at any place throughout the Disneyland Resort, call © **714/781-DINE** (714/781-3463).

EXPENSIVE

Napa Rose *(★★★)* CALIFORNIA   Situated inside the upscale Grand Californian Hotel, Napa Rose is the first really serious (read: on "foodie" radar) restaurant at the Disneyland Resort. Its warm and light dining room mirrors the Arts and Crafts style of the hotel, down to Frank Lloyd Wright stained-glass windows and Craftsman-inspired

---

Tips Standard Fruit

As a welcome relief to those ubiquitous salty, sugary junk-food stands, both the Disneyland and California Adventure parks offer several bastions of healthful snacking: rustic wooden **fruit stands** teeming with a variety of quality seasonal fresh fruit and juices that sell for a fraction of the price you'd pay for a hot dog, fries, and a Coke. Ask a Disney "Cast Member" (any employee) for the nearest stand.

---

seating throughout the restaurant and adjoining lounge. Executive chef Andrew Sutton was lured away from the Napa Valley's chic Auberge du Soleil, bringing with him a wine-country sensibility and passion for fresh California ingredients and inventive preparations. You can see him busy in the impressive open exhibition kitchen, show-casing specialty items like Sierra golden trout, artisan cheeses from Humboldt County and the Gold Country, and the Sonoma rabbit in Sutton's signature braised mush-room-rabbit tart. The tantalizing Seven Sparkling Sins starter platter (for two) features jewel-like portions of foie gras, caviar, oysters, lobster, and other exotic delicacies; the same attention to detail is evident in seasonally composed main-course standouts like grilled yellowtail with tangerine-basil fruit salsa atop savory couscous, or free-range veal *osso buco* in rich bacon–forest mushroom ragout. Leave room for dessert, to at least share one of pastry chef Jorge Sotelo's creative treats; our favorites are Sonoma goat cheese flan with Riesling-soaked tropical fruit, and chocolate crepes with house-made caramelized banana ice cream. Napa Rose boasts an impressive and balanced wine list, with 60 by-the-glass choices (and 40-plus sommeliers, the most of any restaurant in the world); and outdoor seating is arranged around a rustic fire pit, facing a landscaped arroyo toward California Adventure's distinctive Grizzly Peak. *Tip:* My favorite place to sit is at the counter facing the exhibition kitchen. Also, you can skip all the pomp and circumstance of a full sit-down meal by dining at the restaurant's lounge, which offers full menu service.

1600 S. Disneyland Dr. (in Disney's Grand Californian Hotel). ℂ **714/300-7170.** www.disneyland.com. Reservations strongly recommended. Main courses $19–$30. AE, DC, DISC, MC, V. Daily 11:30am–2pm and 5:30–10pm.

Yamabuki ✹✹ JAPANESE   Often ignored by all but their thriving clientele of Asian tourists and business folk, the low-profile Yamabuki restaurant has been tucked away in Paradise Pier Hotel for years. With a casual yet quietly traditional Japanese aesthetic, Yamabuki—the name of a Japanese rose—imparts a very un-Disney ambi-ence. Lunch fare includes casual bento boxes, lunch specials, and sushi/sashimi selec-tions (try the Crunchy Roll). At dinner, tradition demands a languorous procession of courses, from refreshing seafood starters and steaming noodle bowls to grilled teriyaki meats or table-cooked specialties like sukiyaki or *shabu shabu.*

1717 S. Disneyland Dr. (in Disney's Paradise Pier Hotel). ℂ **714/239-5683,** or reservations 714/956-6755. www. disneyland.com. Reservations recommended at dinner. Main courses dinner $20–$30, lunch $7.50–$11. AE, DC, DISC, MC, V. Mon–Fri 11:30am–2pm; daily 5:30–10pm.

MODERATE

Catal Restaurant/Uva Bar ✹✹ MEDITERRANEAN/TAPAS   Branching out from the acclaimed Patina restaurant in Los Angeles, high-priest-of-cuisine Joachim Splichal brings us this Spanish-inspired Mediterranean concept duo at the heart of Downtown

Disney. The main restaurant, Catal, features a series of intimate second-floor rooms that combine rustic Mediterranean charm with fine dining. Complemented by an international wine list, the menu is a collage of flavors that borrow from France, Spain, Italy, Greece, Morocco, and the Middle East—all united in selections that manage to be intriguing but not overwhelming. Though the menu will vary seasonally, expect to find selections that range from seared sea scallops over saffron risotto or chorizo-spiked Spanish paella to herb-marinated rotisserie chicken or Sicilian rigatoni with ricotta cheese.

The Uva Bar (*uva* means "grape" in Spanish) is a casual tapas bar located at an outdoor courtyard right in the middle of the Downtown Disney walkway. Martinis are a standout here; there are also 40 different wines by the glass. The affordable menu features the same pan-Mediterranean influence, even offering many items from the Catal menu; standouts include cabernet-braised short ribs atop horseradish mashed potatoes, marinated olives, and cured Spanish ham; and Andalusian gazpacho with rock shrimp.

1580 Disneyland Dr. (at Downtown Disney). © 714/774-4442. Reservations recommended Sun–Thurs, not accepted Fri–Sat for Catal; not accepted for Uva Bar. Main courses $14–$24; tapas $5–$8. AE, DC, DISC, MC, V. Mon–Thurs 11am–11pm; Fri–Sun 11am–midnight.

Goofy's Kitchen *Kids* AMERICAN   Your younger kids will never forgive you if they miss an opportunity to dine with their favorite Disney characters at this colorful, lively restaurant inside the Disneyland Hotel. Known for its entertainment and wacky and off-center Toontown-esque decor, Goofy's Kitchen features tableside visits by Disney characters (Goofy, Alice, Geppetto, Pocahontas, Aladdin, the Beast) who thrill the youngsters with dancing, autograph signing, and up-close-and-personal encounters. Meals are buffet-style and offer an adequate selection of crowd pleasers and reliable standbys, from bacon and eggs at breakfast to fried chicken, Caesar salad, deli sandwiches, and Italian pastas at lunch and dinner. The most popular kid food is the peanut butter and jelly pizza (even for breakfast), the buffet of gummy worms, Mickey Mouse–shaped waffles, and Mickey ear–shaped chicken nuggets. This place isn't really about the food, though, and is definitely *not* for kidless grown-ups (unless you're trying to make up for a deprived childhood). Bring a camera and Disney autograph book for capturing the family's "candid" encounters. *Tip:* Make reservations for an early or late breakfast or dinner to avoid the mayhem.

1150 Magic Way (inside the Disneyland Hotel). © 714/956-6755 or 714/781-DINE (714/781-3463). www.disneyland. com. Reservations recommended. Buffet prices (child/adult): dinner $10–$27, breakfast/lunch $10–$18. AE, DC, DISC, MC, V. Daily 7am–9pm.

House of Blues AMERICAN/SOUTHERN   For years, fans have been comparing the House of Blues to Disneyland, so this celeb-backed restaurant/nightclub fits right into the Disney compound. Locations in Las Vegas, L.A., Orlando, and so forth all sport a calculated backwoods-bayou-meets-Country-Bear-Jamboree appearance that fits right into the Disney-fied world. The Anaheim HOB follows the formula, filled with made-to-look-old found objects, amateur paintings, uneven wood floors, seemingly decayed chandeliers, and a country-casual attitude. The restaurant features Delta-inspired stick-to-your-ribs cuisine like Louisiana crawfish cakes, Creole seafood jambalaya, cornmeal-crusted catfish, baby back ribs glazed with Jack Daniel's sauce, and spicy Cajun meatloaf—plus some out-of-place Cal-lite stragglers like seared ahi and pesto pasta. Sunday's Gospel Brunch is an advance-ticket event of hand-clapping, foot-stomping proportions. The adjacent Company Store offers logo ware interspersed with selected pieces of folk art. HOB's state-of-the-art Music Hall is a welcome addition to the local music scene (advance tickets are highly recommended for big-name bookings).

> ### *Tips* For Sports Lovers
>
> Sports fans may prefer to dine at the **ESPN Zone** in Downtown Disney, 1545 Disneyland Dr. (© **714/300-ESPN** [714/300-3776]; www.espnzone.com). More than 175 TV monitors allow you to watch just about every current sporting event in the U.S. while dining on American grill food and pub fare.

1530 S. Disneyland Dr. (at Downtown Disney). © 714/778-2583. www.hob.com. Reservations not accepted for restaurant (tickets required for performances). Main courses $8–$17. AE, DC, DISC, MC, V. Mon–Sat 11am–midnight; Sun 10am–midnight.

Rainforest Cafe *Kids* INTERNATIONAL   Designed to suggest ancient temple ruins in an overgrown Central American jungle, this national chain favorite successfully combines entertainment, retail, and family-friendly dining in one fantasy setting. There are cascading waterfalls inside and out, a canopy of lush vegetation, simulated tropical mists, and even a troupe of colorful parrots beckoning shoppers into the Retail Village. Once seated, diners choose from an amalgam of wildly flavored dishes inspired by Caribbean, Polynesian, Latin, Asian, and Mediterranean cuisines. Masquerading under exotic-sounding names like Jungle Safari Soup (a meaty version of minestrone) and Mojo Bones (barbecued pork ribs), the food is really fairly familiar: A translated sampling includes Cobb salad, pita sandwiches, pot stickers, shrimp-studded pasta, and charbroiled chicken. Fresh-fruit smoothies and tropical specialty cocktails are offered, as is a best-shared dessert called the Giant Chocolate Volcano. After your meal, you can browse through logo items, environmentally educational toys and games, stuffed jungle animals and puppets, straw safari hats, and other themed souvenirs in the lobby store. There's a children's menu, and the Rainforest Cafe is one of the few Downtown Disney eateries to have full breakfast service.

1515 S. Disneyland Dr. (at Downtown Disney). © 714/772-0413. www.rainforestcafe.com. Reservations recommended for peak mealtimes. Main courses $9–$21. AE, DC, DISC, MC, V. Sun–Thurs 7am–11pm; Fri–Sat 7am–midnight.

Ralph Brennan's Jazz Kitchen *Kids* CAJUN-CREOLE   If you always thought Disneyland's New Orleans Square was just like the real thing, wait until you see this authentically Southern concept restaurant at Downtown Disney. Ralph Brennan, of the New Orleans food dynasty responsible for NOLA landmarks like Commander's Palace and a trio of Big Easy hot spots, commissioned a handful of New Orleans artists to create the handcrafted furnishings that give the Jazz Kitchen its believable French Quarter ambience. Lacy wrought-iron grillwork, cascading ferns, and trickling stone fountains enhance three separate dining choices: The upstairs Carnival Club is an elegant dining salon with silk-draped chandeliers and terrace dining that overlooks the "street scene" below; casual Flambeaux is downstairs, where a bead-encrusted grand piano hints at the nightly live jazz that sizzles in this room; and the Creole Cafe is a quick stop for necessities like muffulettas or beignets. Expect traditional Cajun-Creole fare with heavy-handed seasonings and rich, heart-stopping sauces—now *that's* authentically New Orleans.

1590 S. Disneyland Dr. (at Downtown Disney). © 714/776-5200. www.rbjazzkitchen.com. Reservations strongly recommended. Main courses $16–$25; cafe items $4–$8. AE, DC, DISC, MC, V. Daily 11am–3pm and 5–11pm.

INEXPENSIVE
La Brea Bakery Express & Cafe BAKERY/MEDITERRANEAN   Fresh from the ovens of L.A.'s now nationally known artisan bakery, this La Brea Bakery duo occupies

a coveted position at the beginning of Downtown Disney, right across from the theme parks' ticket kiosks. Each morning, still-groggy early-bird parkgoers stumble from the parking-lot tram and head straight to La Brea's cafeteria-style Express for a caffeinated pick-me-up or a meal to start the day. Light breakfast items are served in addition to creator Nancy Silverton's irresistible breads and pastries. The outdoor patio is comfortably outfitted with woven bistro chairs (plus heat lamps for brisk mornings) and provides a relaxing setting before you brave the Disney throngs. Throughout the day, folks stop in for a lunch of sandwiches, filled brioche, or herb-laden focaccia. The kids' menu offers less-grown-up choices like grilled cheese and PB&J.

1556 Disneyland Dr. (at Downtown Disney). © 714/490-0233. www.labreabakery.com. Reservations recommended for Cafe. Light fare under $5 (Express); main courses $10–$20 (Cafe). AE, DISC, MC, V. Express daily 8am–11pm. Cafe daily 11am–11pm.

2 Knott's Berry Farm

30 miles SE of Downtown Los Angeles

Although destined to forever be in the shadow of Mickey's megaresort, the reality is that Knott's doesn't even attempt to compete with the Disney empire: Instead, it targets Southern California thrill-seekers (droves of them) by offering a far better selection of scream-inducing thrill rides.

Like Disneyland, Knott's Berry Farm is not without historical background. In 1920, Walter Knott began farming 20 acres of leased land on Hwy. 39 (now Beach Blvd.). When things got tough during the Depression, Mrs. Knott began selling pies, preserves, and home-cooked chicken dinners. Within a year, she was selling 90 meals a day. Lines became so long that Walter decided to create an Old West Ghost Town—America's first theme park—in 1940 as a diversion for waiting customers.

Today Knott's amusement park offers a whopping 165 shows, attractions, and state-of-the-art rides that are far more intense than most of the rides at the Disneyland Resort. Granted, it's less than half the size of the Disney Resort and doesn't have quite the same magical appeal, but if you're more into fast-paced amusement rides than swirling teacups, spend your money here.

ESSENTIALS
GETTING THERE
Knott's Berry Farm is at 8039 Beach Blvd. in Buena Park. It's about a 10-minute ride north on I-5 from Disneyland. From I-5 or California 91, exit south onto Beach Boulevard. The park is about half a mile south of California 91.

VISITOR INFORMATION
The **Buena Park Convention and Visitors Office,** 6601 Beach Blvd., Ste. 200, Buena Park (© **714/562-3560;** www.buenapark.com), provides specialized information on the area, including Knott's Berry Farm. To learn more about the amusement park before you arrive, call © **714/220-5200** or log on to **www.knotts.com.**

ADMISSION PRICES & OPERATING HOURS
Admission to the park, including unlimited access to all rides, shows, and attractions, is $49 for adults and children 12 and over; $20 for kids 3 to 11 and seniors 62 and older; and free for children 2 and under. Admission after 4pm (on any day the park is open past 6pm) is $25 for adults and $18 for kids 3 to 11. Parking is $10. Tickets can

also be purchased at many Southern California hotels, where discount coupons are sometimes available.

Like Disneyland, Knott's offers discounted admission—$36 for adults—for Southern California residents with zip codes 90000 through 93599, so if you're bringing local friends or family members along, try to take advantage of the bargain. Also like Disneyland, Knott's Berry Farm's hours vary from week to week, so call ahead. The park generally opens daily at 10am and closes at 6 or 7pm, except Saturdays, when it stays open until 10pm. Operating hours and prices often change with seasonal promotions, so it's always a good idea to call Knott's Info at © 714/220-5200 for specific hours on the day you plan to visit. Stage shows and special activities are scheduled throughout the day; pick up a schedule at the ticket booth.

TOURING THE PARK

Despite all the high-tech multimillion-dollar rides, Knott's Berry Farm maintains much of its original Old West motif and also features the Peanuts gang: Snoopy, Charlie Brown, Woodstock, and pals are the official costumed characters of Knott's. The park is divided into six themed areas, each one of which features at least one of the thrill roller coasters that are the Knott's claim to fame. The California MarketPlace is located adjacent to, but outside of, the theme park, and features 14 unique shops and restaurants, including the original favorite, Mrs. Knott's Chicken Dinner Restaurant and a TGI Friday's.

GHOST TOWN

The park's original attraction is a collection of authentic 19th-century buildings relocated from deserted Old West towns in Arizona and California. You can pan for gold, ride an authentic stagecoach, take rickety train cars through the Calico Mine, and get held up aboard the Calico Railroad. If you love wooden roller coasters, don't miss the clackity GhostRider.

Calico Railroad   Board this 1881 narrow-gauge steam-engine train—once part of the Denver and Rio Grande Southern Line—for a round-trip tour of half the theme park, interrupted by "bandit" holdups.

Ghost Town Artisans 🎯🎯 *Finds*   An entertaining holdover from the earliest days of the park, these living-history booths present old-time crafts and tall tales presented by costumed blacksmiths, woodcarvers, a spinner, and storytellers who help bring Ghost Town to life for curious kids and history buffs.

GhostRider 🎯🎯🎯   Looming 118 feet high, this coaster is the park's single largest attraction and one of the longest and tallest wooden roller coasters in the world. Riders enter through a replica mine and are strapped into gold, silver, or copper mining cars for an adventure that twists and careens through sudden dips, banked turns, and cheek-flattening G-forces. The ride isn't nearly as smooth and quiet as the steel roller coasters, and that's part of the thrill. Coaster enthusiasts worldwide worship this classic.

Silver Bullet 🎯🎯   This inverted coaster dangles riders from the steel track that weaves its way through the center of the park. Flying over Reflection Lake from the edge of the stagecoach stop to the top of the Log Ride mountain at a height of 146 feet, this high-speed thriller sends riders head over heels six times with cobra rolls, spirals, corkscrews, and other whacked-out whirls.

Timber Mountain Log Ride 🎯   Riders emerge from a dark and twisting "sawmill" waterway and plummet down a 42-foot flume for the grand splash. Compared to the other water rides in the park, this one leaves you only slightly sprinkled.

Wild West Stunt Show   This wild and woolly stunt spectacular is a raucous salute to the Old West presented throughout the day in the open-air Wagon Camp Theater.

FIESTA VILLAGE

Here you'll find a south-of-the-border theme—festive markets and an ambience that suggests old Spanish California. A cluster of carnival-style rides (in addition to the roller coasters listed below) includes a 100-year-old merry-go-round, plus Knott's version of Disneyland's Tea Cups, where you can sit-and-spin in your own sombrero. You can stroll the paths of Fiesta Village, which are lined with old-time carnival games and state-of-the-art electric arcades.

Jaguar! ✸✸   Loosely themed around a tropical jungle setting, this wild roller coaster includes two heart-in-the-mouth drops and a view of Fiesta Village from high above. It's a good family roller coaster for first-timers or the easily frightened.

La Revolución ✸   A real stomach-churner, this ride spins you in circles while swinging back and forth more than 65 feet in the air. It's like being in the rinse cycle of a washing machine that's swinging from a rope.

Montezooma's Revenge ✸   Blasting from 0 to 60 mph in 5 seconds, this not-for-the-fainthearted thriller then propels riders through a giant 360-degree loop both forward and backward.

THE BOARDWALK

The park's Boardwalk area is a salute to Southern California's beach culture, where colorful architecture and palm trees are the backdrop for a trio of thrill rides. Other amusements include arcade and boardwalk games, and the **Charles M. Schulz Theatre,** where seasonal productions include a *Snoopy* ice show or holiday pageant (check the marquee or park entertainment schedule for showtimes).

Boomerang ✸   This corkscrew scream machine sends you twisting through three head-over-heels loops in less than a minute—but it doesn't end there, since you're sent through the track again . . . backward.

Lazer Invaders *(Kids*   In this adaptation of the classic Lazer Runner, participants equipped with lasers and fiber-optic vests battle for supremacy in a richly evocative atmosphere. Each combatant must make use of protective walls and laser power to vanquish opponents.

Perilous Plunge ✸✸   Just 34 feet shorter than Niagara Falls, this wet adventure sends riders to a height of 127 feet and then drops them down a 115-foot water chute at a 75-degree angle—15 degrees from a sheer vertical. Prepare for a thorough soaking (a boon on hot days, but best experienced before nightfall, when it can get chilly).

Sky Cabin ✸   Just when you were thinking all the rides were for hard-core adrenaline-seekers (most are, actually), this quiet ride offers the same spectacular views at a calmer pace. The slowly rotating "cabin" ascends Knott's vertical tower, providing panoramic views of the park and surrounding area.

Supreme Scream ✸✸   They could've called this one the Evil Elevator: Seated and fully exposed riders are hoisted straight up a 30-story tower with their feet dangling in the air, then held at the top just long enough to rattle the nerves before plunging downward faster than gravity at more than 60 mph. The whole descent takes only a bowel-shaking 3 seconds. It's one of the tallest (and most unnerving) thrill rides in the world.

Xcelerator (★★★) It's scary just looking at this super-high-tech 1950s-themed roller coaster, which launches you from 0 to 82 mph in 2⅓ seconds, then whips you straight up 20 stories (with a half-twist thrown in for added addling) and almost straight back down again. It's like riding on the outer edge of a gigantic paper clip.

CAMP SNOOPY (Kids

This will probably be the youngsters' favorite area. The first-ever theme park area dedicated solely for kids, it's meant to re-create a wilderness camp in the High Sierras. Six rustic acres are the playgrounds of Charles Schulz's beagle and his pals, Charlie Brown and Lucy, who greet guests and pose for pictures. There are over a dozen rides in the camp; several kid-size rides are made especially for the younger set, while the entire family can enjoy others. Scaled-down stock cars, locomotives, steamboats, 18-wheeler semis, hot-air balloons, and even the Peanuts gang's school bus give kids a playland of their own. There's also a child-size version of Supreme Scream, called Woodstock's Airmail, and Joe Cool's GR8 SK8, a mini–thrill ride for the whole family. Interactive attractions include the **Camp Snoopy Theatre** starring the Peanuts gang (little kids are transfixed by this show).

WILD WATER WILDERNESS

This $10-million, 3½-acre area is styled like a turn-of-the-20th-century California wilderness park with a raging white-water river, cascading waterfalls, soaring geysers, and old-style ranger stations.

Bigfoot Rapids (★★) The centerpiece of Wild Water Wilderness is this outdoor white-water river raft ride, the longest of its kind in the world. Climb aboard a six-seat circular raft, and prepare to be bounced, buffeted, tossed, spun, and splashed along fast-moving currents, under cascading waterfalls, and around soaring geysers. Let there be no doubt: You will get *extremely* wet on this one.

Mystery Lodge (★★) This amazing high-tech, trick-of-the-eye tribute to the magic of Native American storytelling is a theater attraction for the whole family. The Old Storyteller takes the audience on a mystical, multisensory journey into the culture of local tribes by employing centuries-old legends passed down through oral history.

INDIAN TRAILS

Explore the ride-free Indian Trails cultural area, which offers demonstrations of Native dance and music by authentically costumed Native American and Aztec dancers, singers, and musicians performed in the round on the Indian Trails stage. In addition, the compound showcases a variety of traditional Native American structures from the Pacific Northwest, Great Plains, and Southwest. The area includes four towering totem poles, standing from 15 to 27 feet high; three authentic tepees, representing the Arapaho, Blackfoot, and Nez Perce tribes; and more. The arts and crafts of Native American tribes from the western part of North America are also demonstrated and displayed. While exploring Indian Trails, visitors can enjoy a sampling of Native American foods, including Navajo tacos, Indian fry bread, and fresh-roasted ears of corn.

WHERE TO STAY

Knott's Berry Farm Resort Hotel (★★ (Kids) Within easy walking distance of Knott's Berry Farm, this nine-story hotel offers the only accommodations near the amusement park. Despite the hotel's lengthy moniker, the exterior and lobby have the look of a business hotel. There are two things I like best about this hotel: the Peanuts-themed rooms

---

Tips **Getting Soaked at Knott's**

Surf's up at **Knott's Soak City Water Park,** a 13-acre water park next door to Knott's Berry Farm, with a theme of surf woodies and longboards of the 1950s Southern California coast. The fun includes the **Pacific Spin,** a multiperson raft ride that drops riders 75 feet into a six-story funnel tube, as well as body slides, speed slides, an artificial wave lagoon, and an area for youngsters with their own pool and beach-shack fun house. The park is located at 8039 Buena Park (② **714/220-5200;** www.soakcityusa.com). Admission prices are $29 for adults, $18 for kids 3 to 11, and free for children 2 and under; parking is $9. After 3pm, tickets for all ages are $18. Ask about special promotions and discount coupons (or check the website). The park is open daily May 24 to September 3 and weekends September 8 to September 30. Soak City Water Park opens at 10am and closes between 5 and 7pm, based on the season.

---

complete with Snoopy tuck-in service and Camp Kids bedtime stories (told via the in-room phone by the bed), and free shuttle service to Disneyland, 7 miles away. There's also a large family pool with a children's water play structure, and an arcade. Be sure to inquire about special rates and Knott's multiday vacation package deals.

7675 Crescent Ave. (at Grand Ave.), Buena Park, CA 90620. ② **866/752-2444** or 714/995-1111. Fax 714/828-8590. www.knottshotel.com. 320 units. $179 standard room; $224 Snoopy room. Prices vary depending on date of visit and room availability. Discount packages available. AE, DC, DISC, MC, V. Parking $10 per night. **Amenities:** Restaurant; lounge; outdoor pool; 2 outdoor tennis and basketball courts (lit for night play); fitness center; whirlpool; video arcade; concierge; free Disneyland shuttle; room service; self-service laundry; laundry service; dry cleaning; Wi-Fi (fee). *In room:* A/C, TV w/pay movies, fax, dataport, high-speed Internet (fee), coffeemaker, hair dryer, iron, safe, video games.

WHERE TO DINE

Mrs. Knott's Chicken Dinner Restaurant *Kids* AMERICAN   Knott's Berry Farm got its start as a roadside diner in 1934, and you can still get a filling—albeit unhealthful—all-American meal without even entering the theme park. Cordelia Knott's down-home cooking was so popular that her husband created a few humble attractions to amuse patrons as they waited to be served. Today more than 1.5 million annual patrons line up around the building to experience Cordelia's original recipe (very similar to the Colonel's, I must admit). Looking just as you'd expect—country cute, with window shutters, old black-and-white photos of the original diner, and calico prints aplenty—the restaurant serves up its featured attraction of the original fried chicken dinner, complete with soup, salad, warm buttermilk biscuits, mashed potatoes and chicken gravy, and a slice of famous pie (the boysenberry pie is fantastic). Country-fried steak, pot roast, roast turkey, and pork ribs are options, as are sandwiches, salads, and a terrific chicken potpie. Boysenberries abound, from breakfast jam to traditional double-crust pies, and there's even an adjacent takeout shop that's always crowded. If you're not visiting the amusement park, park in the lot that offers 3 free hours.

8039 Beach Blvd. (near La Palma Ave.), Buena Park. ② **714/220-5080.** Reservations not accepted. Main courses $7–$10; complete dinners $14. DC, DISC, MC, V. Open daily at 7am; closing times vary.

9

Shops & Spas

Whether you're looking for trendsetting fashions or just some tourist schlock mementos, Los Angeles has your shopping needs covered like no other place in the world. Heck, Los Angeles practically *invented* the shopping mall.

But to really shop L.A.-style, you need to combine your outing with a trip to a day spa and make it an all-day event. For example, if you're planning an outing to the Grove, an outdoor mall (highly recommended), you should first make an appointment at the **Amadeus Aveda** spa (© **323/297-0311;** www.amadeusaveda.com); make a lunch reservation at **Maggiano's Little Italy** (© **323/965-9665;** www.maggianos.com); and then go online to buy movie tickets to the **Grove Theatres** (© **323/692-0829;** www.thegrovela.com). When the big day arrives, you meet your friends for coffee in the morning, hit the shops, check your packages with the

Grove concierge, have lunch, enjoy your spa treatments, see a matinee, pick up your purchases, and call it a day. Nicely done.

A note on shopping hours: Street shops are generally open Monday through Saturday from 10 or 11am to 5 or 6pm. Many are open Sunday, particularly those near the beaches, movie theaters, or clusters of other stores. In addition, quite a few offer extended evening hours 1 night a week, often Wednesday or Thursday. Mall shops take their cue from the anchor department stores and generally open from 10am to 8 or 9pm. On Sunday, shave an hour or two off each side, while holiday periods increase mall hours substantially.

Sales tax in Los Angeles is 8.25%; savvy out-of-state shoppers know to have larger items shipped directly home to save the tax.

1 Shops & Spas: L.A.'s Top Streets & Neighborhoods

Here's a rundown of L.A.'s top shopping areas and spas—from chic to cheap—along with some highlights of each neighborhood to give you an idea of what you'll find there. If addresses and phone numbers are *not* given, refer to the store's expanded listing by category in "Shopping A to Z," later in this chapter.

L.A.'S WESTSIDE & BEVERLY HILLS

BEVERLY BOULEVARD (from Robertson Blvd. to La Brea Ave.) ⋆ Beverly is L.A.'s premier boulevard for mid-20th-century furnishings. Expensive showrooms line the street, but the shop that started it all is **Modernica,** 7366 Beverly Blvd. (© **323/933-0383;** www.modernica.net). You can still find vintage Stickley and Noguchi pieces, but Modernica has become best known for the authentic—and more affordable—replicas they offer (Eames storage units are one popular item). **Scent Bar,** 8327 Beverly Blvd. (© **323/782-8300**), the sleek retail shop from the wildly popular fragrance website www.luckyscent.com, is the place to go for exclusive fragrances from Monyette Paris and Parfums de Nicolai.

Urban Shopping Adventures

Shopping may be a casual pastime in other cities, but in the urban jungle of Los Angeles it's a competitive sport. If you're a shopping rookie at best, you might consider an outing with **Urban Shopping Adventures,** which offers custom guided shopping tours to the L.A. Fashion District—90 sprawling blocks loaded with wholesale and retail venues—and the trendy Melrose Heights Shopping District, L.A.'s Westside destination for celebrity-frequented boutiques. Hosted by shopping expert Christine Silvestri, the 3-hour walking tours start at just $36 per person, and merchants are often willing to provide deep discounts to her tour guests. All shopping excursions include an ample-size shopping bag, district map, bottled water, snack, and plenty of time to browse at your own pace. She also offers round-trip transportation options such as shuttle, bus, or limousine service from your hotel to either district for an additional cost. Advance reservations are required for all tours, and additional shopping districts are also available upon request. Call ℂ **213/683-9715** or log onto www.urbanshoppingadventures.com.

British designer and rock royalty **Stella McCartney** (8823 Beverly Blvd.; ℂ **310/273-7051;** www.stellamccartney.com) opened her eponymous digs in an ivy-covered 1920s cottage. Here you'll find the entire collection, from ready-to-wear and fragrance to footwear and handbags. If you complain that they just don't make 'em like they used to . . . well, they do at **Re-Mix,** 7605½ Beverly Blvd. (btw. Fairfax and La Brea aves.; ℂ **323/936-6210;** www.remixvintageshoes.com). This shop sells only vintage (1940s–1970s)—but brand-new (as in unworn)—shoes for men and women, such as wingtips, Hush Puppies, Joan Crawford pumps, and 1970s platforms. It's more like a shoe-store museum. A rack of unworn vintage socks all display their original tags and stickers, and the prices are downright reasonable. Celebrity hipsters and hepcats from Madonna to Roseanne are often spotted here.

Other vintage wares are found at **Second Time Around Watch Co.,** 8840 Beverly Blvd. (west of Robertson Blvd.; ℂ **310/271-6615;** www.secondtimearoundwatchco.com). The city's best selection of collectible timepieces includes dozens of classic Tiffanys, Cartiers, Piagets, and Rolexes, plus rare pocket watches. Priced for collectors, but a fascinating browse for the Swatch crowd, too.

When it's time to unwind and beautify, hit **Ona Spa** (see review later in this chapter) for a tension-relieving massage. The attached **Privé Salon** is one of the city's trendiest salons where celebrity-sighting is common. One of the best-kept-secret spas in the neighborhood is **Skin Haven Spa Studio,** 300 N. Crescent Heights Blvd. (at Beverly Blvd.; ℂ **323/658-7546**), where owner Sharon Ronen's customized facials will leave you glowing for weeks.

LA BREA AVENUE (north of Wilshire Blvd.) ⊀   This is L.A.'s artiest shopping strip. La Brea is anchored by the giant **American Rag, Cie** alterna-complex, and is also home to lots of great urban antiques stores dealing in Art Deco, Arts and Crafts, 1950s modern, and the like. You'll also find vintage clothiers, furniture galleries, and other warehouse-size stores, as well as some of the city's hippest restaurants, such as Campanile (p. 137).

Bargain hunters find flea-market furnishings at **Nick Metropolis,** 100 S. La Brea Ave. (© **323/934-3700**), while more upscale seekers of home decor head to **Mortise & Tenon,** 446 S. La Brea Ave. (© **323/937-7654**), where handcrafted heavy wood pieces sit next to overstuffed velvet-upholstered sofas and even vintage steel desks. The best place for a snack is Nancy Silverton's **La Brea Bakery,** 624 S. La Brea Ave. (© **323/939-6813;** www.labreabakery.com), which foodies know from gourmet markets and the attached Campanile restaurant.

Stuffed to the rafters with hardware and fixtures of the past 100 years, **Liz's Antique Hardware,** 453 S. La Brea Ave. (© **323/939-4403;** www.lahardware.com), thoughtfully keeps a canister of wet wipes at the register—believe us, you'll need one after sifting through bags and crates of doorknobs, latches, finials, and any other home hardware you can imagine. Perfect sets of Bakelite drawer pulls and antique ceramic bathroom fixtures are some of the more intriguing items. Be prepared to browse for hours, whether you're redecorating or not. There's a respectable collection of coordinating trendy clothing for men and women, too.

ROBERTSON BOULEVARD (btw. Wilshire and Beverly boulevards) ✦ If you're a fan of celeb magazines like *US Weekly*, you simply must pay a visit to one of L.A.'s most popular shopping streets. It's common to see the likes of Jessica Simpson, Lindsey Lohan, and Paris Hilton shopping at trend-obsessed boutiques like **Kitson,** 115 S. Robertson Blvd. (© **310/859-2652**); and **Lisa Kline,** 136 S. Robertson Blvd. (© **310/ 246-0907**). At nearby **Erica Courtney,** 117 N. Robertson Blvd. (© **310/858-6700**), guys can watch ESPN on the flatscreen while gals browse drop-dead gorgeous diamonds. Julia Roberts, Sandra Bullock, and Eva Longoria Parker are all fans of Courtney's creations. After shopping like a celebrity, dine among them at the **Ivy** (p. 124).

Just up the street, two of L.A.'s most unique day spas beckon the tired, the stressed, and the famous. **L.A. Vie L'Orange,** 638½ N. Robertson Blvd. (© **310/289-2501;** www.lavielorange.com), specializes in manicures and pedicures that use yummy ingredients like milk, honey, oatmeal, and orange-scented oils. Two doors away, you can spend an entire afternoon at the **Kinara Spa & Café,** 656 N. Robertson Blvd. (© **310/ 657-9188;** www.kinaraspa.com), just like faithful fans Halle Berry, Naomi Watts, and Jennifer Garner.

RODEO DRIVE & BEVERLY HILLS' GOLDEN TRIANGLE (btw. Santa Monica Blvd., Wilshire Blvd., and Crescent Dr., Beverly Hills) ✦✦ Everyone knows about Rodeo Drive, the city's most famous shopping street. Couture shops from high fashion's Old Guard are located along these 3 hallowed blocks, along with plenty of newer high-end labels. And there are two examples of the Beverly Hills version of minimalls, albeit more insular and attractive: the **Rodeo Collection,** 421 N. Rodeo Dr., a con-

---

Tips **Window-Shopping—L.A. Style**

The gorgeous Bulgari jewelry store at the corner of Rodeo Drive and Wilshire Boulevard—former home of the Brown Derby restaurant—displays many of the priceless (literally) jewels worn by the stars at the big awards ceremonies. Look wealthy and they might even invite you upstairs for an espresso.

Tips **A Little Bit o' Country**

With its red barn facade and easygoing neighborhood vibe, the **Brentwood Country Mart,** which was built in 1948, has recovered rather nicely from a major face-lift in 2006. It's one of the easiest places to shop in L.A. because so many chic stores are in one spot, and parking is free. Be sure to visit the menswear outpost Apartment Number 9, the upscale beauty shop Marie Mason Apothecary, and the first City Bakery west of Manhattan (a great place for an inexpensive lunch). The Mart is located at 225 26th St., just off San Vicente Boulevard in Brentwood ((C) **310/451-9877;** www.brentwoodcountrymart.com).

---

temporary center with towering palms; and **2 Rodeo,** a cobblestoned Italianate piazza at Wilshire Boulevard. The 16-square-block area surrounding Rodeo Drive is known as the Golden Triangle. Shops off Rodeo are generally not as name-conscious as those on the strip (and you might actually be able to afford something), but they're nevertheless plenty upscale. Little Santa Monica Boulevard has a particularly colorful line of specialty stores, and Brighton Way is as young and hip as relatively staid Beverly Hills gets. Parking is a bargain, with nine city-run lots offering 2 hours of free parking and a flat fee of $2 after 2pm.

The big names to look for here are **Prada,** 343 N. Rodeo Dr. ((C) **310/278-8661**); **Chanel,** 400 N. Rodeo Dr. ((C) **310/278-5500**); **Bulgari,** 201 N. Rodeo Dr. ((C) **310/ 858-9216**); **Gucci,** 347 N. Rodeo Dr. ((C) **310/278-3451**); **Hermès,** 434 N. Rodeo Dr. ((C) **310/278-6440**); **Louis Vuitton,** 295 N. Rodeo Dr. ((C) **310/859-0457**); **Polo/ Ralph Lauren,** 444 N. Rodeo Dr. ((C) **310/281-1500**); and a three-story **Tiffany & Co.** that's one of the largest Tiffany stores in the world, 210 N. Rodeo Dr. ((C) **310/ 273-8880**). There's also the ultrachic clothiers **Dolce & Gabbana,** 312 N. Rodeo Dr. ((C) **310/888-8701**); British plaid palace **Burberry Limited,** 9560 Wilshire Blvd. ((C) **310/550-4500**); and **NikeTown,** on the corner of Wilshire Boulevard and Rodeo Drive ((C) **310/275-9998**), a behemoth shrine to the reigning athletic-gear king.

Wilshire Boulevard is also home to New York–style department stores (each in spectacular landmark buildings), like **Saks Fifth Avenue,** 9600 Wilshire Blvd. ((C) **310/ 275-4211**); **Barneys New York,** 9570 Wilshire Blvd. ((C) **310/276-4400**); and **Neiman Marcus,** 9700 Wilshire Blvd. ((C) **310/550-5900**).

When all that walking and gawking tires you out, do what all the Beverly Hills beauties do: Hit a spa. Aida Thibiant has been offering classic treatments at **Thibiant Beverly Hills Day Spa,** 449 N. Canon Dr. ((C) **310/278-7565;** www.thibiantspa. com), since the 1970s. Guys have a place of their own at the new high-end barbershop, the **Shave,** 230 S. Beverly Dr. ((C) **310/888-2898;** www.theshavebeverlyhills. com). You don't need to stay in one of the fabulously luxurious Beverly Hills hotels to get all the pampering services. At the **Spa at the Four Seasons** (p. 262), California-flavored treatments use everything from tequila to caviar in decadent massages and facials. The **Spa at the Peninsula Beverly Hills** (p. 262) uses diamonds, emeralds, rubies, and sapphires in some of their signature treatments. At the **Beverly Hills Hotel Spa by La Prairie** (p. 82), the facials and massages are some of the most expensive in town, but it's a great reason to spend a decadent day at the "Pink Palace" without having to drop $1,000 a night on a room.

THE SUNSET STRIP (btw. La Cienega Blvd. and Doheny Dr., West Hollywood) The monster-size billboards advertising the latest rock god make it clear this is rock-'n'-roll territory. The Strip is lined with trendy restaurants, industry-oriented hotels, and dozens of shops offering outrageous fashions and stage accessories. One anomaly is Sunset Plaza, an upscale cluster of Georgian-style shops resembling Beverly Hills at its snootiest. You'll find **Billy Martin's,** 8605 Sunset Blvd. (© **310/289-5000**), founded by the legendary Yankees manager in 1978. This chic men's Western shop—complete with fireplace and leather sofa—stocks hand-forged silver and gold belt buckles, Lucchese and Liberty boots, and stable staples like flannel shirts. **Book Soup,** 8818 Sunset Blvd. (© **310/659-3110;** www.booksoup.com), has long been one of L.A.'s most celebrated bookshops, selling mainstream and small-press books and hosting book signings and readings.

The Sunset Strip's trendiest hotels have in-house spas and spa services—like **Agua at the Mondrian,** 8440 Sunset Blvd. (© **323/848-6070;** www.mondrianhotel.com)—which offer great added amenities for hotel guests. But to feel like a real super star on the Strip, go to the "facialist of the stars": **Ole Henriksen Face/Body,** 8622 W. Sunset Blvd. (© **310/854-7700;** www.olehenriksen.com/spa), is where stunners like Ashley Judd and Charlize Theron go for glowing skin.

WEST 3RD STREET (btw. Fairfax and Robertson boulevards) ☆ You can shop until you drop on this trendy strip, anchored on the east end by the **Farmers Market and The Grove** (p. 158). Many of Melrose Avenue's shops have relocated here, along with terrific up-and-comers, several cafes, and the much-lauded restaurant **Locanda Veneta** (p. 134). *Fun* is more the catchword here than *funky,* and the shops (including the vintage-clothing stores) are a bit more refined than those along Melrose. The **Cook's Library,** 8373 W. 3rd St. (© **323/655-3141;** www.cookslibrary.com), is where the city's top chefs find classic and offbeat cookbooks, wine guides, and other food-oriented tomes. Browsing is welcomed, even encouraged, with tea, tasty treats, and rocking chairs. **Traveler's Bookcase,** 8375 W. 3rd St. (© **323/655-0575;** www. travelbooks.com), is one of the best travel bookshops in the West, stocking a huge selection of guidebooks and travel literature, as well as maps and travel accessories.

A Very Beverly Hills Bookstore

If you're a connoisseur of small bookstores, you'll definitely want to pay a visit to the **TASCHEN** bookstore at 354 N. Beverly Dr., in Beverly Hills (© **310/274-4300;** www.taschen.com). It's the German-based publishing house's first American store (the other two are in Cologne and Paris) and a fitting monument to the company's beautiful high-quality books. French designer *célèbre* Philippe Starck was commissioned to create the long, narrow store's dramatic interiors—glossy walnut woods, shimmering bronze bookshelves, purple mirrors, and handmade glass walls. Befitting the world's leading art publisher, the artwork alone is worth the trip: Artist Albert Oehlen created 20 computer-generated collages for the walls and ceiling, inspired from the wide selection of TASCHEN's art, design, and erotic books. Prices range from a few dollars to several thousand for Helmut Newton's *SUMO,* the biggest and most expensive book produced in the 20th century. Truly, TASCHEN is unlike any other bookstore you've browsed. Open Monday through Saturday 10am to 7pm, Sunday noon to 5pm.

There's lots more to see along this always-growing street. Refuel at **Chado Tea Room,** 8422 W. 3rd St. (© **323/655-2056**), a temple for tea lovers. Chado is designed with a nod to Paris's renowned Mariage Frères tea purveyor; one wall is lined with nooks whose recognizable brown tins are filled with more than 250 different varieties of tea from around the world. Among the choices are 15 kinds of Darjeeling, Indian teas blended with rose petals, and ceremonial Chinese and Japanese blends. You can also get tea meals here, featuring delightful sandwiches and individual pots of any loose tea in the store.

HOLLYWOOD

HOLLYWOOD BOULEVARD (btw. Gower St. and La Brea Ave.)   One of Los Angeles's most famous streets is, for the most part, a cheesy tourist strip. But along the Walk of Fame, between the T-shirt shops and greasy pizza parlors, you'll find some excellent poster shops, souvenir stores, and Hollywood-memorabilia dealers worth getting out of your car for—especially if there's a chance of getting your hands on that long-sought-after Ethel Merman autograph or *200 Motels* poster.

Some long-standing purveyors of memorabilia include **Hollywood Book and Poster Company,** 6562 Hollywood Blvd. (© **323/465-8764;** www.hollywoodbook andposter.com), which has an excellent collection of posters (from about $15 each), strong in horror and exploitation flicks. Photocopies of around 5,000 movie and television scripts are sold for $10 to $15 each—*Pulp Fiction* is just as good in print, by the way—and the store carries music posters and photos.

The legendary **Fredericks of Hollywood,** 6751 Hollywood Blvd. (© **323/957-5953;** www.fredericks.com), located just a block east of Hollywood & Highland, is worth a stop if you're looking for devilish dainties. The flagship store features lingerie worn by celebrities like Sharon Stone, Julianne Moore, and Halle Berry.

LARCHMONT BOULEVARD (btw. Beverly Blvd. and 2nd St.)   Neighbors congregate on this old-fashioned street just east of busy Vine Avenue. As the surrounding Hancock Park homes become increasingly popular with artists and young industry types, the shops and cafes lining Larchmont get more stylish. Sure, chains like Jamba Juice and the Coffee Bean are infiltrating this formerly mom-and-pop terrain, but plenty of unique shopping awaits amid charming elements like diagonal parking, shady trees, and sidewalk bistro tables.

One of L.A.'s landmark independent bookstores is **Chevalier's Books,** 126 N. Larchmont Blvd. (© **323/465-1334**), a 60-year Larchmont tradition. If your walking shoes are letting you down, stop into **Village Footwear,** 248 N. Larchmont Blvd. (© **323/461-3619**), which specializes in comfort lines like Josef Siebel. Or even better,

---

Tips **Celebrity Cloned Clothing**

If your dream is to dress like your favorite celebrity who may have stepped right off the red carpet at one of Hollywood's numerous award shows, then a visit to **A.B.S. by Allen Schwartz** should be on your to-do list. As soon as one of these high-profile events is over (think Golden Globes, SAG Awards, Oscars), A.B.S. has already produced a knockoff version that is every bit as lovely, but much more affordable. 1533 Montana Ave. (at 15th St.); © **310/393-8770.**

GR8 Finds in West L.A.'s J-Town

What started off as a magazine has spawned two of L.A.'s most talked-about stores—**Giant Robot**, 2015 Sawtelle Blvd. (℃ 310/478-1819); and **GR2**, 2062 Sawtelle Blvd. (℃ 310/445-9276)—and **gr/eats** restaurant, 2050 Sawtelle Blvd. (℃ 310/478-3242; www.gr-eats.com). Located across the street from each other in West L.A.'s Japantown (at Sawtelle and Olympic boulevards), both shops specialize in a wide range of Asian-American pop-culture items, including T-shirts, books, music, stationery, toys (you *must* get a Kubrick doll), art, and accessories (check out the Tadashi Murakami pins and felt pins by Saejean Oh). There are several other cool shops and restaurants along this 1½-block stretch as well. One of my favorite stores is **Happy Six**, 2115 Sawtelle Blvd. (℃ 310/479-5363), which looks like Hello Kitty on acid and sells playful apparel and accessories for men and women. If you're hungry, my favorites along Sawtelle are **Manpuku**, 2125 Sawtelle Blvd. (℃ 310/473-0580); **Sawtelle Kitchen**, 2024 Sawtelle Blvd. (℃ 310/445-9288); and **Hurry Curry**, 2131 Sawtelle Blvd. (℃ 310/473-1640). Or you can pop into **Nijiya Market**, 2130 Sawtelle Blvd. (℃ 310/575-3300), and grab a *bento* (Japanese boxed lunch) to go.

stop in for a foot—or full body—massage at **Healing Hands Wellness Center**, 414 N. Larchmont Blvd. (℃ **323/461-7876**; www.healinghandswc.com), which offers afford-able 1-hour massages starting at $55. An entire afternoon of pampering can be had at **Le Petite Retreat Day Spa**, 331 N. Larchmont Blvd. (℃ **323/466-1028**; www.lpr dayspa.com), which offers great packages for couples or a girls' day out.

MELROSE AVENUE (btw. Fairfax and La Brea aves.) ⟨✹✹ It's showing some wear—some stretches have become downright ugly—but this is still one of the most exciting shopping streets in the country for cutting-edge fashions (and some eye-popping people-watching, to boot). Melrose is always an entertaining stroll, dotted with plenty of hip restaurants and funky shops selling the latest in clothes, gifts, jewelry, and accessories that are sure to shock. Where else could you find green patent-leather cowboy boots, a 19th-century pocket watch, an inflatable girlfriend, and glow-in-the-dark condoms on the same block? From east to west, here are some highlights:

l.a. Eyeworks, 7407 Melrose Ave. (℃ **323/653-8255**), revolutionized eyeglass designs from medical supply to stylish accessory, and now their brand is nationwide. **Off the Wall** is filled with neon-flashing, bells-and-whistles kitsch collectibles, from vintage Wurlitzer jukeboxes to life-size fiberglass cows. The L.A. branch of a Bay Area hipster hangout, **Wasteland** has an enormous steel-sculpted facade. There's a lot of leather and denim, and some classic vintage—but mostly funky 1970s-style garb, both vintage and contemporary. More racks of vintage treasures (and trash) are found at **Aardvark's Odd Ark,** which stocks everything from suits and dresses to neckties, hats, handbags, and jewelry. This place also manages to anticipate some of the hottest new street fashions. An outpost of the edgy **Floyd's Barbershops**, 7300 Melrose Ave. (℃ **323/965-7600**), keeps the street's style-for-less theme by charging around $24 for men's and women's cuts. It's like a salon, music store, and Internet cafe rolled into one.

MELROSE HEIGHTS (btw. La Cienega Blvd. and Fairfax Ave.) ☆☆   This posh section of Melrose, anchored by the venerable favorite **Fred Segal,** 8100 Melrose Ave. (℃ **323/655-3734**), houses designer boutiques such as **Diane Von Furstenberg,** 8407 Melrose Ave. (℃ **323/951-1947**); and **Paul Smith,** 8221 Melrose Ave. (℃ **323/ 951-4800**). L.A. jewelry designer **Suzanne Felsen,** 8332 Melrose Ave. (℃ **323/653-5400**), is a celebrity favorite—she transformed a 1920s Spanish home to house her gold and platinum baubles lined with Peruvian opals and Mandarin garnets. Perennial fashion favorite **Marc Jacobs** has three stores at 8400, 8409, and 8410 Melrose Ave., featuring ready-to-wear, accessories, menswear, and the less expensive Marc by Marc Jacobs collection.

SANTA MONICA & THE BEACHES

MAIN STREET (btw. Pacific St. and Rose Ave., and Santa Monica and Venice boulevards) ☆   An excellent street for strolling, Main Street is crammed with a combination of mall standards and upscale, left-of-center individual boutiques. You can also find plenty of casually hip cafes and restaurants. The primary strip connecting Santa Monica and Venice, Main Street has a relaxed, beach-community vibe that sets it apart from similar strips. The stores here straddle the fashion fence between upscale trendy and beach-bum edgy. Highlights include **Obsolete,** 222 Main St. (near Rose Ave; ℃ **310/399-0024**), the most hip antiques store I've ever seen. Collectibles range from antique carnival curios to 19th-century anatomical charts from Belgium (you'd be amazed at how much some of that junk in your attic is worth). **CP Shades,** 2937 Main St. (btw. Ashland and Pier sts.; ℃ **310/392-0949**), is a San Francisco ladies' clothier whose loose and comfy cotton and linen line is carried by many department stores and boutiques. **Horizons West,** 2011 Main St. (south of Pico Blvd.; ℃ **310/ 392-1122**), sells brand-name surfboards, wet suits, leashes, magazines, waxes, lotions, and everything else you need to catch the perfect wave. If you're looking for some truly sophisticated, finely crafted eyewear, the friendly **Optical Shop of Aspen,** 2904 Main St. (btw. Ashland and Pier sts.; ℃ **310/392-0633**), is for you. Ask for frames by cutting-edge L.A. designers Bada and Koh Sakai. For aromatherapy nirvana, it's **Cloud's,** 2719 Main St. (℃ **310/399-2059**), where Jill Cloud (happily assisted by her lovely mom) carries the most heavenly scented candles. Then there's **Arts & Letters,** 2665 Main St. (℃ **310/314-7345**), a stationery haven that includes invitations by the

---

A Mecca For High-End Vintage

If your style is more Hepburn than Hilton, you won't want to miss the treasure-trove of high-end vintage shopping L.A. has to offer. Doris Raymond's the **Way We Wore,** 334 S. La Brea Ave. (℃ **323/937-0878**), is a favorite among celebs and stylists for vintage Chanel, Balenciaga, and Fortuny. Cameron Silver's **Decades,** 8214½ Melrose Ave. (℃ **323/655-0223**), is an L.A. institution, where you'll find frocks from Halston, Gucci, Lilly Pulitzer, and Missoni. **Lily et Cie,** 9044 Burton Way (℃ **310/724-5757**), supplies many of the glamour gowns you see on the red carpet. Owner and vintage maven Rita Watnick has an impeccable collection of pieces from important designers like Yves Saint Laurent, Givenchy, and Trigere.

Abbot Kinney Boulevard: L.A.'s Antithesis to Rodeo Drive

When you're finally fed up with the Rodeo Drive attitude and megamall conformity, it's time to drive to Venice and stroll the eclectic shops along **Abbot Kinney Boulevard.** This refreshingly anti-establishment stretch of street has the most diverse array of shops, galleries, and restaurants in Los Angeles. (Locals still cheer that there are no franchises in the neighborhood.) You can easily spend the entire afternoon here poring over vintage clothing, antique furniture, vintage Vespas, local art, and amusing gifts. For one-of-a-kind designed jewelry, check out **Nagual,** 1142 Abbott Kinney Blvd. (© **310/396-8500**), whose "metals with an edge" designs have caught the eye of many a celebrity. Or if you're looking for a unique gift, you'll want to try **Strange Invisible Perfumes,** 1138 Abbot Kinney Blvd. (© **310/314-1505**), where they can custom-make a scent to match your musk. Then there's **Firefly,** 1413 Abbot Kinney Blvd. (© **310/450-6288**), a local favorite. It's that one store you can go into and find everything from great baby gifts, stationery, and books to quirky handbags and cool clothing. **DNA Clothing Co.,** 411 Rose Ave. (© **310/399-0341**), is the mother lode for those in search of the coolest, most current styles for men and women at great prices (stylists and costumers often use DNA as their resource for sitcoms to feature films). You'll find all your major brands as well as their own private label wear, and fresh stock arrives weekly. Take a break to eat at one of the boulevard's many restaurants, including **Joe's** (the best California cuisine in L.A.; p. 120), **Primitivo, Axe, Lilly's, Massimo's, Jin's Patisserie, French Market Café,** and, of course, **Hal's Bar & Grill,** with its live jazz music. Heck, there are even 2 hours of free street parking.

owner herself, Marilyn Golin. Outdoors types will get lost in 5,600-square-foot **Patagonia,** 2936 Main St. (© **310/314-1776;** www.patagonia.com), where climbers, surfers, skiers, and hikers can gear up in the functional, colorful duds that put this environmentally friendly firm on the map. For a dose of beachy pampering, check out the **Bey's Garden,** 2919 Main St. (© **310/399-5420;** www.beysgarden.com). Part aromatherapy apothecary, part gift shop, part day spa, you'll find everything from waxing to "energy work" available.

MONTANA AVENUE (btw. 17th and 7th sts., Santa Monica; www.montanaave.com) This breezy stretch of slow-traffic Montana has gotten a lot more pricey than in the late 1970s, when tailors and laundromats ruled the roost, but the specialty shops still outnumber the chains. Look around and you can see upscale moms with strollers and cellphones shopping for designer fashions, country home decor, and gourmet takeout.

Montana is still original enough for residents from across town to make a special trip here, seeking out distinctive shops like **Shabby Chic,** 1013 Montana Ave. (© **310/394-1975**), a much-copied purveyor of slipcovered sofas and flea-market furnishings, while clotheshorses shop for designer wear at minimalist **Savannah,** 706 Montana Ave. (© **310/458-2095**); ultrahip **Jill Roberts,** 920 Montana Ave. (© **310/260-1966**); and sleekly professional **Weathervane,** 1209 Montana Ave. (© **310/393-5344**).

Leona Edmiston, 1007 Montana Ave. (📞 **310/587-1100**), houses the Aussie designer's famed frocks. For more grown-up style, head to **Ponte Vecchio,** 702 Montana Ave. (📞 **310/394-0989**), which sells Italian hand-painted dishes and urns. If Valentine's Day is approaching, duck into **Only Hearts,** 1407 Montana Ave. (📞 **310/ 393-3088**), for heart-themed gifts and seductively comfortable intimate apparel. And don't forget the one-of-a-kind shops such as **Sun Precautions,** 1600 Montana Ave. (📞 **310/451-5858**), specializing in 100% UV protection apparel, and the second-largest **Kiehl's** store outside of New York City, 1516 Montana Ave. (📞 **310/255-0055**). Skin is taken incredibly seriously at the flagship store and spa, **Dermalogica on Montana,** 1022 Montana Ave. (📞 **310/260-8682**), where "touch therapies" and "skin mapping" are just the beginning of the dynamite facials. Enjoy a meal at the local favorite, **Café Montana,** 1534 Montana Ave. (📞 **310/829-3990**), for great people-watching through its floor-to-ceiling glass windows.

THIRD STREET PROMENADE (3rd St. btw. Wilshire Blvd. and Broadway; www.downtownsm.com) 🎀 Packed with those ubiquitous corporate chain stores, restaurants, and cafes (gee, another Starbucks), Santa Monica's pedestrians-only section of 3rd Street is one of the most popular shopping areas in the city. The Promenade bustles all day and well into the evening with a seemingly endless assortment of street performers among the shoppers, bored teens, and home-challenged. There are, however, a few shopping gems squeezed between Gap, Abercrombie & Fitch, and Old Navy. You can easily browse for hours at **Hennessey & Ingalls,** 214 Wilshire Blvd. (📞 **310/458-9074**), a bookstore devoted to art and architecture. **Restoration Hardware,** 1221 Third Street Promenade (📞 **310/458-7992**), is still the retro-current leader for reproduction home furnishings and accessories. **Puzzle Zoo,** 1413 Third Street Promenade (📞 **310/393-9201**), voted "Best in L.A." by *Los Angeles* magazine, is where you'll find the double-sided World's Most Difficult Puzzle, the Puzzle in a Bottle, and many other brain-teasing challenges.

Music lovers can get CDs and vinyl at **Hear Music** while sipping a latte from the Starbucks located inside the record store. **Exhale** is perfect for those seeking quiet time and relief from the crowds. There's yoga and Core Fusion classes, the Healing Waters sanctuary with eucalyptus steam rooms, relaxing spa services, and the simply titled "Quiet Room" for rejuvenation. Stores stay open late (often until 1 or 2am on the weekends) for the moviegoing crowds, and there's plenty of public parking in six structures along 2nd and 4th streets between Broadway and Wilshire Boulevard.

SILVER LAKE & LOS FELIZ

Located at the eastern end of Hollywood and technically part of Los Angeles, these two communities have been rising steadily on the hipness meter. Silver Lake, named for the man-made Silver Lake reservoir at its center, is a bohemian community of artists and ethnic families that's popular for nightclubbing and barhopping. Los Feliz is northwest of Silver Lake, centered on Vermont and Hillhurst avenues between Sunset and Los Feliz boulevards; it's slightly tamer and filled with 1920s and 1930s buildings. You'll find tons of unique businesses of all sorts, including artsy boutiques, music stores, and furniture dealers.

Because so many alternative bands call Silver Lake home, it's not surprising to find cutting-edge music stores around every corner. A neighborhood mainstay with lots of used CDs, collectible disks, and new releases is **Rockaway Records,** 2395 Glendale Blvd. (south of Silver Lake Blvd.; 📞 **323/664-3232;** www.rockaway.com).

Tips **Lingerie Insider**

Panty Raid, a very charming boutique, carries brands for the serious lingerie collector such as Cosabella, Mary Green, and Felina, as well as Hanky Panky (cute lace tank tops and boy short sets), Betsey Johnson, T & C California, Eberjey, and Only Hearts. A selection of hosiery, socks, yoga outfits, loungewear, and gift items—including candles, and bath and body products—is also available. 2378½ Glendale Blvd., Los Angeles. ⓒ **323/668-1888.**

Vintage clothing is another big draw in these parts. The most reliable yet eclectic selections to browse through are at **Ozzie Dots,** 4637 Hollywood Blvd. (west of Hillhurst Ave.; ⓒ **323/663-2867**); **Pull My Daisy,** 3908 Sunset Blvd. (at Griffith Park Blvd.; ⓒ **323/663-0608**); and **Squaresville,** 1800 N. Vermont Ave. (south of Franklin Ave.; ⓒ **323/669-8464**).

For those in the know, the **Circle** is that hidden jewel of a place where samples and overstock items including designer tops, pants, skirts and, on occasion, accessories can be found. You'll score items from independent designers including Rachel Pally, Magpie Rita, Harvey's, Mon Petit Oiseau, Alicia Lawhon, and Lockets at unbelievable prices. It's located at 2395 Glendale Blvd. in Silver Lake, within a minimall between Silver Lake Boulevard and Dean Street (ⓒ **323/665-5336**). It's open 7 days a week from noon to 7pm.

Although the art of millinery often seems to have gone the way of white afternoon gloves for ladies, inventive **Drea Kadilak** bucks the trend with her specialty shop **Clover,** 2756 Rowena Ave. (at Glendale Blvd.; ⓒ **323/661-4142**). Drea designs in straw, cotton duck, wool felt, and a number of more unusual fabrics. Handmade furniture, men's and women's clothing, and unique gift items are available as well.

Edna Hart, 2941 Rowena Ave. (south of Hyperion Ave.; ⓒ **323/661-4070**), is a prime spot for jewelry, knitting supplies, and gifts, while **Rubbish,** 1630 Silver Lake Blvd. (north of Sunset Blvd.; ⓒ **323/661-5575**), specializes in vintage furnishings. One not-to-be-missed highlight is the wacky and eclectic **Soap Plant/Wacko/La Luz de Jesus Art Gallery,** 4633 Hollywood Blvd. (west of Hillhurst Ave.; ⓒ **323/666-7667**), a three-in-one business with candles, art books, erotic toys, soap and bathing items, and a large selection of lava lamps. Local fixture **Y-Que,** 1770 N. Vermont Ave. (ⓒ **323/664-0021**), almost defies description, selling a variety of stuff ranging from a knockoff *Austin Powers* penis pump to psychedelic lava lamps.

With a focus on small production, high quality, affordable wine from around the world, and a large selection of microbrew beer and sake, **Silverlake Wine,** 2395 Glendale Blvd. (ⓒ **323/662-9024;** www.silverlakewine.com), is a great place to visit. Get your friends together and check out any one of their weekly tastings: Sunday at 3pm, Blue Monday from 5 to 9pm, and Thursday Night Flights from 5 to 9pm (call ahead to confirm times). Also in the neighborhood is the **Cheese Store of Silverlake,** 3926–28 W. Sunset Blvd. (ⓒ **323/644-7511;** www.cheesestoresl.com), a purveyor of fine cheeses, wines, and gourmet products such as Revival confections, Latini pastas, Agrumato flavored oils, and McQuade's chutneys. It's located in Sunset Junction at the southeast corner of Sanborn Avenue and Sunset Boulevard.

DOWNTOWN

Since the late lamented Bullock's department store closed in 1993 (its Art Deco masterpiece salons were rescued to house the Southwestern Law School's library), Downtown has become less of a shopping destination than ever. Although many of the once-splendid streets are lined with cut-rate luggage and electronics stores, shopping here can be a rewarding—albeit gritty—experience for the adventuresome.

Savvy Angelenos still go for bargains in the garment and fabric districts (see "Discount" under "Fashions," later in this chapter); florists and bargain hunters arrive at the vast **Los Angeles Flower District,** 766 Wall St. (btw. E. 8th and E. 7th sts.; *©* **213/622-1966;** www.laflowerdistrict.com), before dawn for the city's best selection of fresh blooms; and families of all ethnicities stroll the **Grand Central Market** ✹✹, 317 S. Broadway (btw. 3rd and 4th sts.; *©* **213/624-2378;** www.grandcentralsquare.com). Opened in 1917, this bustling market has watched the face of Downtown L.A. change while changing little. Today its sawdust-covered aisles serve Latino families, enterprising restaurateurs, and cooks in search of unusual ingredients—stuffed goat heads, mole, plantains, deep-fried smelt, Mexican cane alcohol—and bargain-priced produce. On weekends you'll be greeted by a mariachi band at the Hill Street entrance, near my favorite market feature, the fruit-juice counter, which dispenses 20 fresh varieties from wall spigots and blends the tastiest, healthiest "shakes" in town. Farther into the market you'll find produce and prepared foods, spice vendors who seem straight out of a Turkish bazaar, and a grain-and-bean seller who'll scoop out dozens of exotic rices and dried legumes. It's open 9am to 6pm daily.

Another of my favorite Downtown shopping zones is **Olvera Street** ✹✹✹ (*©* **213/628-1274;** www.olvera-street.com), a lively brick pedestrian lane near Union Station that's been lined with stalls selling Mexican wares since the 1930s. Everything that's sold south of the border is available here, including custom leather accessories, huarache sandals, maracas, and—but of course—freshly baked churros. On weekends, you're bound to see strolling bolero musicians, mariachis, folk dancers, and performances by Aztec Indians. It's open daily from 10am to about 8pm.

If you're looking to find *the* best shopping deals in handbags, luggage, shoes, costume jewelry, and trendy fashions, then find a parking meter or park in one of the parking structures from Olympic Boulevard to 12th Street and explore **Santee Alley,** located in the alley between Santee Street and Maple Avenue. Often referred to as the heart of the fashion district, this is where you'll find everything you've ever wanted at bargain prices. Go early on Saturday mornings if you want to blend in with the locals.

Okay, so you have to wake up a little early to experience the **Southern California Flower Mart,** 742 Maple Ave. between 7th and 8th streets (*©* **213/627-2482**), but if you do it right—wear comfortable shoes, bring cash, and pick up a cup o' joe—you'll

---

Tips **Downtown Deals**

At the base of the Fashion Institute of Design & Merchandising's Downtown campus, you'll find the **FIDM Scholarship Store,** where donated new merchandise is sold at bargain prices. All sales go toward scholarships for FIDM students, so you can shop with the karmic awareness that you're helping the fashion industry's next generation of designers with their tuition. It's located at 919 S. Grand Ave. (at W. 9th St.) (*©* **213/624-1200**).

find walking through the myriad of flower stalls a very tranquil experience. Besides the usual buds and stems that you see in *Sunset Magazine,* you'll be surprised to find tropicals such as torch ginger, protea, and bird of paradise. You can purchase flowers by the bundles at amazingly low prices.

THE SAN FERNANDO VALLEY

STUDIO CITY (Ventura Blvd. btw. Laurel Canyon Blvd. and Fulton Ave.) Long beloved by Valley residents, Studio City is where you'll find small boutiques and antiques stores, quirky little businesses (many dating from the 1940s and 1950s), and less congested branches of popular chains like Gap, Pier 1 Imports, and Blockbuster. Melanie Shatner, daughter of William, stocks Marc Jacobs and Joie at her chic boutique **Dari,** 12184 Ventura Blvd. (© **818/762-3274**). Fashionistas flock to TV personality Lisa Rinna's **Belle Gray,** 13812 Ventura Blvd. (© **818/789-4021**). Actress Kirsten Dunst's mother has a day spa, **Belle Visage,** 13207 Ventura Blvd. (© **818/ 907-0502;** www.bellevisage.com), that caters to the young and the beautiful—or at least those in search of youth and beauty. Parking is a cinch on the street except during holiday season, when stores team up to decorate these blocks and often observe extended evening hours. The 4 blocks of Ventura Boulevard between Laurel Canyon Boulevard and Whitsett Avenue are the most concentrated.

PASADENA & ENVIRONS

Compared to L.A.'s behemoth shopping malls, the streets of pretty, compact Pasadena are a breeze to stroll. As a general rule, stores are open daily from about 10am, and while some close at the standard 5 or 6pm, many stay open until 8 or 9pm to accommodate the before- and after-dinner/movie crowd.

OLD PASADENA (centered on the intersection of Colorado Blvd. and Fair Oaks Ave.) 🎔🎔 Dating back to the 1880s, the 22-block-long Old Pasadena district (© **626/744-4005;** www.oldpasadena.com) offers some of the best shopping in L.A.—*if* it retains the mom-and-pop businesses currently being pushed out by the likes of Banana Republic and Crate & Barrel. Going through its own sort of renaissance, more upscale shopping has been added to the strip, including a **Tiffany & Co.,** 68 W. Colorado Blvd. (© **626/793-7424;** www.tiffany.com), which has become somewhat of an attraction more than a store, and the new (and hugely popular) **H&M** fashion store, 60 W. Colorado Blvd. (© **626/793-8974;** www.hm.com), which now is an anchor to the neighborhood. As you move eastward, the mix of businesses begins to include more eclectic shops and galleries commingling with dusty, pre-yuppie relics, but it's a good segue between Old Pasadena and the Paseo Colorado mall.

Travelers also seem to find something they need at **Distant Lands Bookstore and Outfitters,** 56 S. Raymond Ave. © **800/310-3220** or 626/449-3220; www.distant lands.com), a pair of related stores. The bookstore has a terrific selection of maps, guides, and travel-related literature, while the outfitter two doors away offers everything from luggage and pith helmets to space-saving travel accessories.

OTHER PASADENA SHOPPING

In addition to Old Pasadena, there are numerous good hunting grounds in the surrounding area. Antiques hounds might want to head to the **Green Street Antique Row,** 985–1005 E. Green St. (east of Lake Ave.), or the **Pasadena Antique Center,** on South Fair Oaks Boulevard (south of Del Mar Blvd.). Each has a rich concentration of collectibles that can captivate for hours.

You never know what you might find at the **Rose Bowl Flea Market**(★), at the Rose Bowl, 1001 Rose Bowl Dr., Pasadena (© **323/560-SHOW** [323/560-7469]; www.rgcshows.com). The horseshoe-shaped Rose Bowl, built in 1922, is one of the world's most famous stadiums, home to UCLA's Bruins, the annual Rose Bowl Game, and an occasional Super Bowl. **California's largest monthly swap meet,** held here on the second Sunday of every month from 9am to 3pm rain or shine, is a favorite of Los Angeles antiques hounds (who know to arrive as early as 7am for the best finds). Antique furnishings, clothing, jewelry, and other collectibles are assembled in the parking area to the left of the entrance, while the rest of the flea market surrounds the exterior of the Bowl. Expect everything from used surfboards and car stereos to one-of-a-kind lawn statuary and bargain athletic shoes. Admission is $8 after 9am. (Early bird admission is $10 at 8am and $15 at 7am.) Kids 12 and under are free.

Anglophiles will enjoy **Rose Tree Cottage,** 828 E. California Blvd. (just west of Lake Ave.; © **626/793-3337;** www.rosetreecottage.com), and its charming array of all things British. This cluster of historic Tudor cottages surrounded by traditional English gardens holds three gift shops and a tearoom, where a superb $33 high tea is served thrice daily among the knickknacks (and supervised by the resident cat, Miss Moffett). In addition to imported teas, linens, and silver trinkets, Rose Tree Cottage sells English delicacies like steak-and-kidney pies, hot cross buns, and shortbread. It's also the local representative of the British Tourist Authority and offers a comprehensive array of travel publications.

2 Shopping Malls

L.A.'S WESTSIDE & BEVERLY HILLS

The Beverly Center   When the eight-story Beverly Center opened on L.A.'s Westside, there was more than a bit of concern about the impending "mallification" of Los Angeles. Loved for its convenience and disdained for its penitentiary-style architecture (and the "no validations" parking fee), Beverly Center contains about 160 standard mall shops, including the wildly popular **H&M,** and even a few boutiques that are open by advance reservation only (*so* L.A.). It's anchored on opposite sides by Macy's and Bloomingdale's department stores. You can see it from blocks away, looking like a gigantic climbing wall. 8500 Beverly Blvd. (at La Cienega Blvd.), Los Angeles. © **310/854-0071.** www.beverlycenter.com.

The Grove (★)   Located at the eastern end of the Farmers Market, this massive 575,000-square-foot Vegas-style retail complex is one of L.A.'s most popular megamalls. See "L.A.'s Top Attractions" in chapter 7 for more information. 189 The Grove Dr. (W. 3rd St. at Fairfax Ave.), Hollywood. © **888/315-8883** or 323/900-8000. www.thegrovela.com.

Tips **All American Girls**

Filled to the brim with all the things young girls love, the **American Girl Place** at the Grove shopping mall at 189 The Grove Dr. (© **877/AG-PLACE** [877/247-5223]; www.americangirlplace.com) features the flagship line of historical dolls and books. Find the contemporary Just Like You dolls, accessories, and girl-size clothing. For a real treat, girls can take in a performance at the American Girl Theater, dine with their dollies at the American Girl Café, and treat their doll to a new coif at the Doll Hair Salon.

> **Tips** **Stellar Shopping**
>
> If you want to mix in some celebrity sightings along with your shopping spree, head to the Beverly Center. A handful of high-end shops here cater to the famous and wealthy, particularly **Jacqueline Jarrot** and **Jennifer Kaufman** (jewelry), **Hugo Boss, D&G,** and **Just Cavalli.**

Pacific Design Center   Something of an architectural and cultural landmark, the Pacific Design Center is the West Coast's largest facility for interior design goods and fine furnishings. It houses 200 showrooms filled with furniture, fabrics, flooring, wall-coverings, kitchen and bath fixtures, lighting, art, and accessories. Locals refer to the PDC as the Blue Whale in reference to its exterior, composed entirely of brilliant blue glass. Technically, businesses here sell to the trade only, and their wholesale prices reflect that. *Tip:* For a small fee the center will provide a decorator-for-the-day to serve as official broker for your purchases. 8687 Melrose Ave., West Hollywood, CA. ℂ **310/657-0800.** www.pacificdesigncenter.com.

Westfield Century City   Since Westfield acquired this open-air shopping center in 2002, it's undergone a massive $150-million renovation in an attempt to revitalize this lackluster location into the area's premier shopping, dining, and entertainment destination. Along with a sorely needed face-lift, Westfield added 30 new shops, 7 new restaurants, a new flagship 15-screen AMC movie theater, and 260 luxury condominiums. Anchored by **Macy's** and **Bloomingdale's** department stores, it's located on what was once a 20th Century Fox back lot, just west of Beverly Hills. Among the nearly 200 offerings are **Ann Taylor, J. Crew, bebe,** and **Crocs.** 10250 Santa Monica Blvd. (at Ave. of the Stars), Century City. ℂ **310/277-3898.** www.westfield.com/centurycity.

Westside Pavilion   Located at the intersection of Westwood and Pico boulevards on the Westside of Los Angeles, this shopping center has the only **Nordstrom** in the area and attracts a very style-conscious crowd with a taste for the finest in women's fashions, handbags, and shoes. It's within easy access of the I-405 and I-10 freeways, major arterials to the L.A. area. It boasts a roster of over 160 specialty shops, such as **BCBG, Aeropostale, Guess, Aldo, Banana Republic,** and **Nine West** as well as a food court and its own **Westside Pavilion Cinemas.** This mall is big on community and kids' events, and is host of the annual Night of Delight, a wine and food sampling. 10800 W. Pico Blvd., Los Angeles. ℂ **310/474-6255.** www.westsidepavilion.com.

HOLLYWOOD

Hollywood & Highland   A sure sign that this formerly seedy section of the city is on the fast track to recovery is the massive $615-million "entertainment complex" at the corner of Hollywood Boulevard and Highland Street (hence the name). Surrounded by souvenir shops and tattoo parlors, the gleaming 8¾-acre center contains all the top-end merchants—Ann Taylor, Louis Vuitton, bebe—as well as studio broadcast facilities and the gorgeous **Kodak Theatre,** home of the Academy Awards (really, you'll want to take a peek at this theater). The mall's other centerpiece is Babylon Court; designed after a set from the 1916 film *Intolerance,* the open-air space attempts to re-create an over-the-top golden-age movie set, complete with giant pillars topped with 13,500-pound elephants and a colossal arch that frames the HOLLYWOOD sign in the distance. Parking isn't a problem, as the six-level underground lot can cram in 3,000 cars. 6834 Hollywood Blvd., Hollywood. © 323/467-6412. www.hollywoodandhighland.com.

PASADENA

Paseo Colorado This open-air mall in the heart of Pasadena is ground zero for local shopaholics. Anchored by Macy's, the two-level 3-block monolith houses about 140 retailers and restaurants (but few men's fashions), a Gelson's market, a fitness center, a full-service day spa, and a 14-screen multiplex theater. What's unique about the Paseo is the dozens of offices, apartments, and studios built atop the mall, which allows residents easy access to all the daily necessities a city dweller needs to survive. 280 E. Colorado Blvd. (at Marengo Ave.), Pasadena. © 626/795-8891.

THE SAN FERNANDO VALLEY

Universal Citywalk *(Kids* Designed to resemble an almost-cartoonish depiction of an urban street, Universal CityWalk gets a mention because it's unique. Situated next door to Universal Studios—you must walk through it if you use Universal City's main parking structure—CityWalk is dominated by brightly colored, oversize storefronts. The heavily touristed faux street is home to a number of restaurants, including **B. B. King's Blues Club** and the **Saddle Ranch Chop House.** In terms of shopping, CityWalk is not worth a special visit—it's got the ubiquitous Abercrombie & Fitch, Guess, Sunglass Hut, and the like. Still, kids will love the carnival atmosphere and the **Warner Brothers store.** Universal Center Dr., Universal City. © 818/622-9841. www.citywalkhollywood.com.

3 Shopping A to Z

ADULT TOYS

WEST HOLLYWOOD

Hustler Hollywood Here's a bit of shopping trivia for you: Teresa Flynt, daughter of *Hustler Magazine* maven Larry Flynt, is the manager of Hustler Hollywood, the largest erotica store in the country. Although the magazine is pretty raunchy, this boutique-style store is surprisingly chic and not the least bit intimidating. Whereas most sex shops are small, cramped, and poorly lit (from what I hear, of course), Hustler Hollywood's entire facade is floor-to-ceiling windows, and merchandise is artfully arranged on well-lit displays throughout the store. Sure, a spot-lit vibrator is still a vibrator, but it's the packaging that makes all the difference. 8920 Sunset Blvd., West Hollywood. © 310/860-9009. www.hustlerhollywood.com.

ANTIQUES

L.A.'S WESTSIDE & BEVERLY HILLS

Del Mano   It's worth a visit to this contemporary crafts gallery to see the cool creations—some whimsical, some exquisite—of American artists working with glass, wood, ceramics, and jewelry. 11981 San Vicente Blvd., Brentwood. ✆ 310/476-8508.

HOLLYWOOD

Off The Wall   This collection of oversize antiques includes kitschy statues, Art Deco furnishings, carved wall reliefs, Wurlitzer jukeboxes, giant restaurant and gas-station signs, pinball machines, and lots and lots of neon. 7325 Melrose Ave., Los Angeles. ✆ 323/930-1185.

THE SAN FERNANDO VALLEY

Arte de Mexico   Seven warehouses full of carved furniture and wrought iron once sold only to moviemakers and restaurants are now open to the public. This is one of the most fascinating places in North Hollywood. 5356 Riverton Ave., North Hollywood. ✆ 818/769-5090. www.arteshowrooms.com.

ART

SANTA MONICA & THE BEACHES

Bergamot Station ★★★ *Finds*   Once a station for the Red Car trolley line, this industrial space is now home to the Santa Monica Museum of Art, plus two dozen art galleries, a cafe, a bookstore, and offices. Most of the galleries are closed Monday. The train yard is located at the terminus of Michigan Avenue, west of Cloverfield Boulevard.

The wide variety of exhibits changes often: Julius Shulman's black-and-white photo retrospective of L.A.'s Case Study Houses; a provocative exhibit of Vietnam War propaganda posters from the United States and Vietnam; whimsical furniture constructed entirely of corrugated cardboard. A sampling of offerings includes the **Gallery of Functional Art** (✆ 310/829-6990), which features one-of-a-kind and limited-edition furniture, lighting, bathroom fixtures, and other functional art pieces, as well as smaller items like jewelry, flatware, ceramics, and glass. The **Rosamund Felsen Gallery** (✆ 310/828-8488) is well known for showcasing L.A.-based contemporary artists; this is a good place to get a taste of current trends. **Track 16 Gallery** (✆ 310/264-4678) has exhibitions that range from pop art to avant-garde inventiveness. 2525 Michigan Ave. (east of Cloverfield Blvd.), Santa Monica. ✆ 310/829-5854.

Every Picture Tells A Story ★★★ *Kids*   This gallery, devoted to the art of children's literature, is frequented by young-at-heart art aficionados as well as parents introducing their kids to the concept of an art gallery. Works by Maurice Sendak *(Where the Wild Things Are)*, Tim Burton *(The Nightmare Before Christmas)*, and original lithos of *Curious George* and *Charlotte's Web* are featured. Call for events; the store usually combines exhibitions of illustrators with story readings and interactive workshops. 1311-C Montana Ave., Santa Monica. ✆ 310/451-2700.

⸨Tips⸩ L.A. Souvenirs on the Cheap

Ocean Front Walk in Venice Beach is one of the best places in L.A. to shop for inexpensive souvenirs.

Getting Artsy

If you're in an artsy mood, then a trip to Robertson Boulevard should be on your agenda. A gem is the **Koplin del Rio Gallery,** 6031 Washington Blvd., Culver City (© 310/836-9055; www.koplindelrio.com), which focuses on contemporary painting, drawing, and sculpture of established internationally known artists, as well as emerging California artists. The gallery's main emphasis is representational, figurative, landscape, and still-life works. If you haven't had your artistic fill, stop in at **Gallery 825/Los Angeles Art Association (LAAA),** 825 N. La Cienega Blvd., Los Angeles (© 310/652-8272; www.laaa.org). It's one of the oldest surviving visual arts organizations (nonprofit) in town and supports Southern California artists with an emphasis on emerging talent.

BOOKS

SANTA MONICA & THE BEACHES

Hennessey + Ingalls   This bookstore is devoted to art and architecture, from magnificent coffee-table photography books to graphic arts titles and obscure biographies of artists and histories of art movements. 214 Wilshire Blvd., Santa Monica. © 310/458-9074. www.hennesseyingalls.com.

Small World Books 🅐   This sunny little shop is located right on the Venice boardwalk, with a friendly and dedicated staff whose mission is helping customers locate that hard-to-find book. Along with a wide selection of titles published by major presses, Small World carries titles published by smaller presses. 1407 Ocean Front Walk, Venice. © 310/399-2360. www.smallworldbooks.com.

L.A.'S WESTSIDE & BEVERLY HILLS

Barnes & Noble   This national chain is represented throughout the city. B&N offers discounts on bestsellers and also comfy chairs to shoppers who like to read a bit before they buy. The Westwood branch is one of their largest stores and is conveniently attached to the vast Westside Pavilion shopping mall; there's plenty of free parking downstairs. Other branches: Santa Monica (1201 Third Street Promenade; © 310/260-9110) and Pasadena (111 W. Colorado Blvd.; © 626/585-0362). 10850 W. Pico Blvd. (Westside Pavilion), Los Angeles. © 310/475-3138. www.bn.com.

Book Soup 🅐🅐   This is one of L.A.'s most celebrated bookshops, selling mainstream and small-press books and hosting regular book signings and author nights. Book Soup is a great browsing shop; it has a large selection of showbiz books and an extensive outdoor news and magazine stand. The owners annexed an adjacent cafe space so they can better cater to hungry intellectuals. The **Book Soup Bistro** has a bar, a great outdoor patio, and a classical bistro menu. 8818 Sunset Blvd., West Hollywood. © 310/659-3110. www.booksoup.com.

Borders   Borders offers one-stop shopping for books, CDs, greeting cards, and even cappuccino. This La Cienega branch is a block away from the Beverly Center. 330 S. La Cienega Blvd. (at 3rd St.), Los Angeles. © 310/659-4045. www.borders.com.

C. G. Jung Bookstore & Library   This bookshop specializes in analytical psychology, folklore, fairy tales, alchemy, dream studies, myths, symbolism, and other related topics. Tapes and videocassettes are also sold. 10349 W. Pico Blvd. (east of Beverly Glen Blvd.), Los Angeles. (C) 310/556-1196.

The Cook's Library (C)   There's a specialty bookshop for everyone in L.A.; this is where the city's top chefs find both classic and offbeat cookbooks and other food-oriented tomes. Browsing is welcomed, even encouraged, with tea, tasty treats, and rocking chairs. 8373 W. 3rd St., Los Angeles. (C) 323/655-3141.

Dutton's Brentwood Books   This huge bookshop is well known not only for an extensive selection of new books, but also for its good children's section and an eclectic collection of used and rare books. There are more than 120,000 titles in stock at any one time. Dutton's hosts regular author readings and signings, and sells cards, stationery, prints, CDs, and select software. Rumors are floating around that it might be closing (alas, along with many other independent bookstores in America), so be sure to call ahead before visiting. 11975 San Vicente Blvd. (west of Montana Ave.), Los Angeles. (C) 310/476-6263. www.duttonsbrentwood.com.

Los Angeles Audubon Society Bookstore   A terrific selection of books on nature, adventure travel, and ecology is augmented by bird-watching equipment and accessories. Phone for information on L.A. nature walks. Closed Monday. 7377 Santa Monica Blvd., West Hollywood. (C) 323/876-0202. www.LAAudubon.org.

The Mystery Bookstore   An enormous collection of used, rare, and out-of-print titles make this the city's best mystery, espionage, detective, and thriller bookshop. Author appearances and other special events are regularly scheduled. There's even 2 hours of free parking before 6pm in the adjacent structure just north of the store entrance. 1036-C Broxton Ave. (just south of UCLA campus), Los Angeles. (C) 800/821-9017 or 310/209-0415. www.mystery-bookstore.com.

Traveler's Bookcase (C)   This store, one of the best travel bookshops in the West, stocks a huge selection of guidebooks and travel literature, as well as maps and travel accessories. A quarterly newsletter chronicles the travel adventures of the genial owners, who know firsthand the most helpful items to carry. Look for regular readings by well-known travel writers. 8375 W. 3rd St., Los Angeles. (C) 323/655-0575. www.travelbooks.com.

HOLLYWOOD

Samuel French Book Store   This is L.A.'s biggest theater and movie bookstore. Plays, screenplays, and film books are all sold here, as well as scripts for Broadway and Hollywood blockbusters. 7623 Sunset Blvd. (btw. Fairfax and La Brea aves.), Hollywood. (C) 323/876-0570. www.samuelfrench.com.

PASADENA

Vroman's Bookstore   Open for more than 110 years, this is Southern California's oldest and largest independent bookstore. Don't expect dusty shelves and musty smells; it's clean, up-to-date, and chock-full of everything a book lover would want or need. The visiting-author series is one of the best in the area. Vroman's Fine Writing, Gifts, and Stationary store is right next door. 695 E. Colorado Blvd. (btw. Oak Knoll and El Molino aves.), Pasadena. (C) 626/449-5320. www.vromansbookstore.com.

CDS & MUSIC

SANTA MONICA & THE BEACHES

Hear Music   At the first L.A. branch of Boston's Hear Music chain, albums are grouped by genre, theme, and mood. Headphones are everywhere, so you can test a brand-new disc before you buy. 1429 Third Street Promenade, Santa Monica. ℂ **310/319-9527.**

L.A.'S WESTSIDE & BEVERLY HILLS

Rhino Records ⟨★   This is L.A.'s premier alternative shop, specializing in new artists and independent-label releases. In addition to new releases, there's a terrific used selection; music-industry types come here to trade in the records they don't want for the records they do, so you'll be able to find never-played promotional copies of brand-new releases at half the retail price. You'll also find the definitive collection of records on the Rhino label, as well as used CDs, DVDs, books, and more. The "Blow It" outlet has everything for $5 and under. 2028 Westwood Blvd., Westwood. ℂ **310/474-8685.** www.rhinorecords.com.

HOLLYWOOD

Amoeba Music ⟨★   Just as movie fans must walk the Hollywood Walk of Fame, fans of music must walk the aisles of Amoeba. With nearly 1 million new and used CDs, LPs, 45s, and 78s, as well as DVDs and other video formats, Amoeba prides itself on its breadth and depth with music of every genre from hip-hop, pop, rock, jazz, and country, to R&B, folk, classical, blues, reggae, dance, and so on. With the largest collection of vinyl albums in one location anywhere on the planet, they also stock a huge assortment of new and vintage music and film-oriented posters. 6400 Sunset Blvd., Los Angeles. ℂ **323/245-6400.** www.amoebamusic.com.

FASHIONS

FOR MEN & WOMEN

Santa Monica & the Beaches

Fred Segal ⟨★★   They've become an L.A. institution, these breezy collections of ultrahip boutiques linked like departments of a single-story fashion maze. Shops include the latest apparel for men, women, and toddlers, plus lingerie, shoes, hats, luggage, cosmetics, workout/lounge wear, and a cafe. Fred Segal also has major star-spotting potential (Matt Damon, Cameron Diaz, Sandra Bullock, and Kate Hudson are regulars; David Duchovny reportedly met his wife here when he asked her to help him pick out a suit). The original Fred Segal complex (opened in 1960) is at 8118 Melrose Ave. in West Hollywood (ℂ **323/655-3734**), but either is a rewarding shopping foray. 500 Broadway, Santa Monica. ℂ **310/458-9940.**

L.A.'s Westside & Beverly Hills

American Rag Cie   First to draw shoppers back to industrial La Brea in the early '80s, American Rag has grown from a small vintage clothing store to include trendy new fashions on its own label, as well as adjacent boutiques selling shoes and children's clothes; there's even a kitchen and housewares shop with a small cafe. Once a best-kept secret of hip teenagers, the American Rag dynasty today draws more tourists than trendsetters. 150 S. La Brea Ave., Los Angeles. ℂ **323/935-3154.**

H&M ⟨★★   If you haven't heard of H&M then you obviously don't know a thing about affordably priced fashion. So popular among the city's shopping elite, it created a frenzy when Southern California's first Swedish-brand H&M store opened in September 2006 at Old Pasadena. (People were lined up around the block and even camping out.) The Pasadena location only carries women's fashions while the larger Beverly Center location has a men's section and a better selection of accessories. Pasadena, 60 W. Colorado Blvd. ((ℱ) 626/793-8974). Beverly Center, 8500 Beverly Blvd. (at La Cienega Blvd.), Los Angeles. ℱ 310/855-1009. www.hm.com.

Maxfield ℱ Here you'll find some of L.A.'s best-quality avant-garde designs, including men's and women's fashions by Yamamoto, Comme des Garçons, Dolce & Gabbana, Jil Sander, and the like. Furniture and home accessories are also sold. The store's provocative window displays have ranged from sharp political statements to a Jerry Garcia tribute. 8825 Melrose Ave., West Hollywood. ℱ 310/274-8800.

FOR WOMEN & CHILDREN
Santa Monica & the Beaches

CP Shades CP Shades is a San Francisco ladies' clothier whose line is carried by many department stores and boutiques. Fans will love this store, devoted solely to loose, casual cotton and linen separates. CP Shades's trademark monochromatic neutrals are meticulously arranged within an airy, well-lit interior. 2937 Main St., Santa Monica. ℱ 310/392-0949.

L.A.'s Westside & Beverly Hills

Oilily _Kids_ This colorful line of kids' play clothes came from the Netherlands like a storm, and now kids around town are all sporting candy-bright colors and retro-bold florals. Moms get into the action, too, with a coordinating line of sun wear. 9520 Brighton Way, Beverly Hills. ℱ 310/859-9145. www.oilily-world.com.

Polkadots & Moonbeams This is actually two stores several doors apart, one carrying (slightly overpriced) hip young fashions for women, and the other a vintage store with clothing, accessories, and fabrics from the 1920s to the 1960s, all in remarkable condition. Vintage store, 8367 W. 3rd St.; modern store, 8381 W. 3rd St., Los Angeles. ℱ 323/651-1746.

Hollywood

Betsey Johnson Boutique The New York–based designer has brought to L.A. her brand of fashion—trendy, cutesy, body-conscious women's wear in colorful prints and faddish fabrics. 8050 Melrose Ave., Los Angeles. ℱ 323/852-1534. www.betseyjohnson.com.

DISCOUNT

Loehmann's Loehmann's is huge and packed to the rafters with clothes, shoes, and accessories. Most of its stock is name-brand and designer labels, though nothing ultra-trendy is represented. The store is popular for business attire, conservative leisure wear, and bargains on fancy dress wear. Known for years as a women's enclave, Loehmann's also has a men's department offering the same great deals. Serious shoppers should check out the Back Room, where heavyweight designers like Donna Karan and Calvin Klein are represented alongside beaded and formal evening gowns. 333 S. La Cienega Blvd. (south of 3rd St.), Los Angeles. ℱ 310/659-0674.

Los Angeles Fashion District Reminiscent of the New York garment district, but not quite as frenetic, L.A.'s 90-block Fashion District, bordered by 7th, Spring, and San Pedro streets and the Santa Monica Freeway, has dozens of small shops selling designer and name-brand apparel at heavily discounted prices. A concentration of retail women's wear bargains—many by name-brand designers—can be found at the Cooper Building, 860 S. Los Angeles St. (at 9th St.). Men should have some luck

Tips Where to Find Hollywood's Hand-Me-Downs

Admit it: You've dreamed of being a glamorous movie or TV star—everyone has. Well, don't expect to be "discovered" during your L.A. vacation, but you can live out your fantasy by dressing the part. Costumes from famous movies, TV show wardrobes, cast-offs from celebrity closets—they're easier to find (and more affordable to own) than you might think.

For sheer volume, you can't beat **It's A Wrap,** 3315 W. Magnolia Blvd., Burbank (© 818/567-7366; www.movieclothes.com). Every item here is marked with its place of origin, and the list is staggering: *Beverly Hills, 90210; Melrose Place; Seinfeld; Baywatch; Seventh Heaven; Sabrina the Teenage Witch; American Beauty; The Truman Show;* and so on. Many of these wardrobes (which include shoes and accessories) aren't outstanding except for their Hollywood origins: Jerry Seinfeld's trademark Polo shirts, for instance, are standard mall-issue. Some collectible pieces, like Sylvester Stallone's *Rocky* stars-and-stripes boxers, are framed and on display. Open Monday through Saturday from 11am to 6pm, and Sunday from 11am to 4pm.

When you're done at It's A Wrap, stop in across the street at **Junk For Joy,** 3314 W. Magnolia Blvd., Burbank (© 818/569-4903; www.junkforjoy.com). A Hollywood wardrobe coordinator or two will probably be hunting through the racks right beside you at this wacky little store. The emphasis here is on funky items more suitable as costumes than everyday wear (the store is mobbed each year around Halloween). When I visited, the shop was loaded with 1970s polyester shirts and tacky slacks, but you never know what you'll find. Open Tuesday through Friday from 10am to 6pm, and Saturday from 11am to 6pm.

The grande dame of all wardrobe and costume outlets is **Western Costume,** 11041 Vanowen St., North Hollywood (© 818/760-0900; www.western costume.com). In business since 1912, Western Costume still designs and executes wardrobes for major motion pictures; when filming is finished, the garments are added to their staggering rental inventory. This place is perhaps best known for outfitting Vivien Leigh in *Gone With the Wind.* Several of Scarlett O'Hara's memorable gowns were available for rent until they were auctioned off at a charity event. Western also maintains an outlet store, where damaged garments are sold at rock-bottom (nothing over $15) prices. If you're willing to do some rescue work, there are definitely hidden treasures here. Open for rentals Monday through Friday from 8am to 6pm, and for sales Monday through Friday from 8:30am to 6pm.

Finally, don't miss **Golyester** (p. 261). This shop is almost a museum of finely preserved (but reasonably priced) vintage clothing and fabrics. The staff will gladly flip through stacks of *Vogue* magazines from the 1930s, 1940s, and 1950s with you, pointing out the lavish, star-studded original advertisements for various outfits in their stock. Open every day 11am to 6pm.

along the upper blocks of Los Angeles Street, where mostly business attire is displayed, with deep discounts on Hugo Boss, Armani, and other current suits (mainly Italian), plus similar savings on sport coats and shirts. Ties and vests are usually less stylish. Los Angeles Street btw. 7th Street and Washington Boulevard. www.fashiondistrict.org.

VINTAGE
Santa Monica & the Beaches
Aardvark's Odd Ark This large storefront near the Venice Beach Walk is crammed with racks of antique and used clothes from the 1960s, 1970s, and 1980s. It stocks vintage everything, from suits and dresses to neckties, hats, handbags, and jewelry—and it manages to anticipate some of the hottest new street fashions. 7579 Melrose Ave. ((C 323/655-6769) and 85 Market St. (corner of Pacific Ave.), Venice. (C 310/392-2996.

L.A.'s Westside & Beverly Hills
Golyester Before she opened this ladies' boutique, the owner's friends would take one look at her collection of vintage fabrics and clothes and gasp, "Golly, Esther!" Hence the whimsical name. You pay a little extra for the pristine condition of hard-to-find garments like unusual embroidered sweaters from the 1940s and 1950s, Joan Crawford–style suits from the 1940s, and vintage lingerie, but it's worth every penny. 136 S. La Brea Ave., Los Angeles. (C 323/931-1339.

Hollywood
Wasteland An enormous steel-sculpted facade fronts this L.A. branch of the Berkeley/Haight-Ashbury hipster hangout, which sells vintage and contemporary clothes for men and women. You'll find leathers and denim as well as some classic vintage but mostly funky 1970s garb. This trendy store is packed with colorful polyester halters and bell-bottoms from the decade I'd rather forget. 7248 Melrose Ave., Los Angeles. (C 323/653-3028.

The San Fernando Valley
Playclothes Men and women alike will marvel at the pristine selection of vintage clothes housed in this boutique, tucked into a burgeoning antiques row west of Coldwater Canyon Avenue. Playclothes approaches its stock with a sense of humor and knows exactly how each item was worn and accessorized in its heyday. 11422 Moorpark St. (1 block west of Laurel Canyon Ave.), Studio City. (C 818/755-9559.

4 L.A.'s Top Day Spas

L.A.'S WESTSIDE & BEVERLY HILLS
Bliss Los Angeles 𝄃𝄃 Located at the W Hotel, this outpost of a popular New York spa is part of a new breed of day spas that are more about sass than Zen. You won't find classical or wave-simulated music here; instead, it's rhythm and blues. Forget the lemon water in the women's lounge, and look for the brownie bar. The men get sports magazines, heated shaving cream, and a flatscreen TV in their lounge. There's a retail boutique, three movie-while-you-manicure nail stations, and 10 treatment rooms in the second-floor, 7,000-square-feet space. And just like the vibe, the menu offers up something a little bit different, like the hot milk and almond pedicure ($65 for 60 min.); carrot and sesame-seed body buff ($165); the "hangover herbie" detoxifying package ($215); and the ultra-relaxing Blissage 75 massage ($125), what they call a "virtual countdown to 'butter'." 930 Hilgard Ave. (at the W Hotel), Westwood. (C 323/930-0330. www.blissworld.com.

Kinara Spa & Café ★★   Whether you're a Hollywood starlet primping for a big night or just pretending to be, Kinara is a one-stop location for everything you'll need. The multifaceted space—a day spa, boutique, cafe, and salon—is subtle, but not bare; calm but not Zen; natural but not serious. Spa services range in price from $35 to $110, with multi-treatment packages starting at $215. Not bad for a place that attracts the toned and the beautiful Halle Berry, Naomi Watts, and Jennifer Garner. But you don't even need to be a star to get star-treatment: The Red Carpet facial, one of the most popular treatments, is a custom-blended procedure that exfoliates, brightens, and smoothes the face. The cafe features seasonal menus of healthful, delicious cuisine prepared by co-owner Christine Splichal (wife of Joachim, whose Patina Restaurant Group changed the L.A. dining scene forever). The boutique, Kinara Cadeaux, features a range of exclusive luxury clothing, gifts, and beauty products. 656 N. Robertson Blvd. (btw. Melrose Ave. and Santa Monica Blvd.), West Hollywood. ☏ 310/657-9188. www.kinaraspa.com.

Ona Spa & Privé Salon ★   Ona means "all things good" in the French Basque dialect, and that's certainly the treatment you'll receive in the hands of Ona's Daniel Krasofski, one of the top massage therapists around. This small, full-service day spa specializes in custom treatments using both ancient and traditional techniques, particularly Ayurveda. The massages here run the gamut, from the $95 tension-relieving Ona Quick Fix to the $220 Onaaah, a choreographed four-handed tandem Balinese massage. Body and facial enhancements such as laser hair removal, Botox, filler, and chemical peels are also available, as is acupuncture therapy. On the bottom floor of the same building is the **Privé Salon,** one of the city's trendiest salons where celebrity-sighting is common. 7373 Beverly Blvd. (at N. Fuller Ave.), Los Angeles. Ona: ☏ 323/931-4442. Privé: ☏ 323/931-5559. www.onaspa.com.

Peninsula Spa ★★★   *Condé Nast Traveler* recently rated the 4,600-square-foot Peninsula Spa number one in Service and number two in Treatments for Urban Spas, and indeed, this is one of the top spots in the U.S. for pampering. Sure, it's pricey, but what would you expect from the only hotel in Southern California to earn both the AAA Five Diamond and Mobil Five Star awards for 13 straight years? Bonus: The spa just had a $7-million revamp, adding an extra 1,000 square feet of space, with mosaic tile work in serene shades of blue and pure white Calacatta marble. The spa is the first in North America to offer Shiffa precious gem oil treatments, which contain rubies, emeralds, sapphires, and diamonds, and are said to bring healing powers. In addition to the seven treatment rooms, you can opt to have some services in one of the Peninsula's famed cabanas overlooking the 60-foot lap pool. They even offer a good selection of services geared toward the guys, such as the 50-minute Men's Foot Recovery and 60-minute Gentlemen's Facial Rejuvenation. The Roof Garden restaurant is the perfect spot for a pre- or post-treatment lunch or tonic. And don't be surprised if you spot an A-lister, as the Peninsula is a perennial celeb favorite. 9882 S. Santa Monica Blvd. (near Wilshire Blvd.), Beverly Hills. ☏ 310/551-2888. http://beverlyhills.peninsula.com.

Spa at the Four Seasons Hotel ★★   There's already something so indulgent about the Four Seasons in Beverly Hills, that a caviar facial in the spa seems positively pedestrian. The 4,000-square-foot spa has eight treatment rooms, men's and women's locker rooms, and a menu full of rejuvenating services. The wildly popular Punta Mita Massage uses tequila and sage oil; combined with the Margarita Salt Scrub, it's like a happy hour for your skin. One of the signature treatments—a California Sunset Massage at a private, candlelit poolside cabana—is oh-so-very L.A. Along with the full-service spa,

For Bored Non-Shoppers: A Lamborghini Test-Drive

So, your better half has planned a full day of shopping and spa treatments and, after you drop her off at the mall, she won't need your services for a while. Since you're in L.A.—where everyone's judged by the car they drive—this is the perfect time to call Shawn Williams, a very down-to-earth car enthusiast who co-owns an exotic car dealership called **Exclusive Motorcars.** Even if you have no intention of buying or leasing a Ferrari or Lamborghini, he'll be happy to talk cars, take you on a tour of his showroom, and perhaps test drive a new or slightly used Bentley Continental GT, Mercedes SL600, or Porsche Carrera GT. If you're the type that has to have it *now,* you can drive your new baby while vacationing in L.A. (Shawn can arrange financing and insurance while you wait), then either take the car home or have it shipped. He'll be happy to arrange a short-term rental as well (me, I'd go with the black Ferrari F430 Spider F-1). If you want to make an appointment, call Shawn at © **310/558-3300,** or just drop by the showroom at 10534 W. Pico Blvd. near Overland Avenue. (Tell him Matthew from Frommer's says hello.) It's open Monday through Friday 9am to 6pm, and Saturday 10am to 5pm. Log onto www.emcars.com.

the view-endowed fourth-floor deck features a lap pool, poolside cafe, and glass-walled fitness center, all of which guests are welcome to use before or after a spa treatment. 300 S. Doheny Dr. (at W. 3rd St.), Beverly Hills. © **310/273-2222.** www.fourseasons.com/losangeles.

SANTA MONICA

Exhale 🐾🐾   Escape the crowds at the Third Street Promenade at this luxury retreat that hails from New York but is so fittingly SoCal, with a yoga studio, well-being workshops, "healing waters" room, eucalyptus saunas, and Core Fusion Pilates classes. You'll find 15,000 square feet of Ohm here, all with a tranquil design and natural aesthetic. The signature Fusion Massage uses therapeutic massage practices from around the world, like rhythmic movements and potent herbal and aromatherapy oils. Before any treatment, you're encouraged to arrive early to sit in the "quiet room" where teas are ceremoniously blended for each individual guest. Remember . . . just breathe. 1422 2nd St. (btw. Santa Monica Blvd. and Broadway), Santa Monica. © **310/899-6222.** www.exhalespa.com.

ONE Spa 🐾🐾   This beach-themed spa—it's designed to resemble a ship—is owned by the tony Shutters on the Beach Hotel but located in a separate building, giving it a little more privacy than the typical hotel spa. Featuring Ole Henriksen's (the "facialist to the stars") all-natural products and services, ONE has a great selection of treatments and day packages with cheeky seaside names like the Beach Baby, an eight-step customized facial and re-texturizing sea mineral body scrub ($185 for 80 min.) or the Surf's Up pedicure ($85). When they suggest you Get Stoned, it's not what you think: They're talking 110 minutes of hot stone therapeutic massage that's designed to restore balance to the body ($230). 1 Pico Blvd., Santa Monica. © **310/587-1712.** www.shutters onthebeach.com.

Spa at Le Merigot 🐾🐾   Le Merigot is a low-key luxury hotel that doesn't try to be anything other than a comfortable place to spend your seaside vacation, and its spa is the perfect place to unwind after a busy day of shopping and sightseeing. The 5,500-square-foot space offers a full range of services, everything from waxing to couples massage. The aestheticians have such a wonderful touch that a 60-minute facial seems to heal more than your skin: You walk out feeling beautified *and* blissed-out. Non-hotel guests can go in for any treatment (including brow waxes) and still use all the state-of-the-art fitness equipment, pool, saunas, and other hotel amenities before or afterward. 1740 Ocean Ave., Santa Monica. © 310/395-9700. www.lemerigothotel.com.

DOWNTOWN

Pho-Siam Thai Spa *★★ Finds*   I used to live in Thailand, and there's nothing I miss more than a traditional Thai massage, an ancient healing art that combines yogalike stretching, deep-tissue massage, and therapeutic balms. You walk in tense and stiff and walk out a happy noodle. The family-run Pho-Siam Thai Spa is located near Downtown L.A. at the south end of Echo Park and staffed by a group of Thai women who are well-trained in the art of Thai massage. For a mere $40 your body will undergo 60 minutes of such indulgence that you'll be planning a vacation to Thailand by the time you're done. Foot massages, waxes, facials, and couples massages are offered as well, but for the ultimate indulgence request the 3-hour mega-massage, a bargain at $120. Walk-ins are welcome, but it's better to call and make an appointment, and be sure to tell the owner, Mr. Chao (the sweetest man you'll ever meet), that Matthew from Frommer's says hello. Free parking. 1525 Pizarro St. (at Glendale Blvd. 1 block west of Temple St.), Los Angeles. © 213/484-8484. www.phosiam.com.

Los Angeles After Dark

L.A. didn't invent the word *hip,* but it certainly holds the patent on it. The City of Angels has some of the most cutting-edge clubs and bars in the world and is the polestar for the best and brightest in the music scene. Entertainment of all types—from Hollywood Bowl picnic performances to cool jazz venues, retro chic bars, and rock-'n'-roll clubs—can be found in the following pages.

Of course, first you need to find out who's performing while you're in town. Your best bet for current entertainment info is the ***L.A. Weekly*** (www.laweekly. com), a free weekly paper available at sidewalk stands, shops, and restaurants. It has all the most up-to-date news on what's happening in Los Angeles's playhouses, cinemas, museums, and live-music venues. The Sunday **"Calendar"** and Thursday **"Weekend"** sections of the *Los Angeles*

Times (www.theguide.latimes.com) are also a good source of information for what's going on throughout the city. For more online info on L.A.'s entertainment scene, see "Website-Seeing: The Best of L.A. Online" on p. 22.

To purchase tickets in advance, first try buying them directly from the venue to avoid paying a surcharge. If that doesn't work, log on to **Good Time Tickets'** website at www.goodtime-tickets.com or call © **800/464-7383.** Based in Hollywood for more than 30 years, the privately owned company specializes in selling tickets to sporting, theater, concerts, and other entertainment events throughout Los Angeles—at a markup, of course. If all else fails, take out a loan and call **Ticketmaster** (© **213/480-3232;** www.ticketmaster.com), but beware of their absurdly high processing fees.

1 The Live Music Scene

Los Angeles's music scene is extremely diverse, to say the least, a daunting and dizzying beast. But on any given night, finding something to satisfy any musical taste is easy because this city is at the center of the entertainment industry. Every day, countless national and international acts are drawn here. From acoustic rock to jazz-fusion, heavy metal to Latin funk, and up-and-coming to put-to-pasture, L.A.'s got it all.

But there's a rub. The big events are easy to find, but by the time you get to town, odds are the good tickets will be gone. The best advice is to plan ahead. On the Internet, both **Ticketmaster** (see above) and concert business trade publication *Pollstar* (www.pollstar.com) have websites that include tour itineraries of acts that are on—or will be going on—the road. Just start your search in advance. For a listing of smaller shows closer to the date of your arrival, both the *L.A. Weekly* and the *Los Angeles Times* "Calendar" section have websites (see above). Sometimes tickets may become available at the box office before shows, or when all else fails, try "negotiating" with some of the locals in front of the venue.

Tips **A Note on Smoking**

In 1998, California enacted legislation that banned smoking in all restaurants and bars. Despite repeated efforts by opponents to repeal the law—and willful disregard by some proprietors—it's more widely enforced every year. If you're looking to light up in clubs, lounges, and other nightspots, better check to see what the locals are doing first.

LARGE CONCERT VENUES

Mostly gone are the days of the behemoth stadium shows, excepting, of course, the occasional U2 or Rolling Stones tour. Still, major national and international acts tend to be attracted to some of the city's larger venues.

The crown of Downtown and home to the Lakers and Clippers pro basketball teams is the **STAPLES Center,** 1111 S. Figueroa St. (© **213/742-7340;** www.staples center.com). Along with the new 7,200-seat **Nokia Theatre** (www.nokiatheatre.com), this combination sports/event stadium is the city's primary concert venue. Part of the $4.5-billion, 4-million-square-foot "L.A. LIVE" complex being built over the next 5 years to complement the STAPLES Center and the Los Angeles Convention Center, the Nokia Theatre is expected to host star-studded award ceremonies and more than 150 live annual performances.

Amphitheaters are the staple of national rock and pop concert tours. Los Angeles's two main warriors are the outdoor **Greek Theatre** in Griffith Park, 2700 N. Vermont Ave., Los Angeles (© **323/665-1927**) and the indoor **Gibson Amphitheatre** (formerly Universal Amphitheatre), Universal City Drive, Universal City (© **818/622-4440**), each seating about 6,000. Both are among the most accommodating and comfortable facilities for big-name acts. Nearly as beautiful as the Hollywood Bowl, the Greek books a full season of national acts ranging from The White Stripes and Robert Plant to Al Green and Melissa Etheridge. After a recent multimillion-dollar renovation project, the Greek is nicer than ever. Be advised that getting out afterward can still be a problem, as cars are stacked in packed lots, making exiting a painfully slow process.

Gibson Amphitheatre has one advantage over the Greek: It has a roof, so it can book year-round. It's not as aesthetically pleasing, but it is quite comfortable and none of its seats are too far from the stage. For some events, the "Party in the Pit" offers a general admission section next to the stage. In addition to pop stars from The Strokes to Kid Rock, the Universal has booked such theater events as *The Who's Tommy.* While the neon jungle of Universal's CityWalk doesn't appeal to everyone, it does offer plenty of pregig dining and drinking options.

Orange County's **Verizon Wireless Amphitheatre** (formerly Irvine Meadows), 8800 Irvine Center Dr., Laguna Hills (© **949/855-8096;** www.vwatx.com), which holds 15,000 (including a general-admission lawn *way* in the back), hosts KROQ's often-spectacular summertime "Weenie Roast" and KIIS FM's "Summer Jam" each year, as well as a plethora of touring rock acts, including recent shows from Dave Matthews Band and John Mayer. If you're going from L.A. on a weekday, get an early start, because Irvine is located at one of the most heavily traveled freeway junctions in the country.

Another popular venue is the **Honda Center** (formerly Arrowhead Pond of Anaheim), 2695 E. Katella Ave. (1 mile east of I-5), Anaheim (© **714/704-2500;** www.hondacenter.com), a combination sports/event stadium that's gaining momentum as a primary concert venue. It's about an hour from Los Angeles via the always-crowded I-5 freeway, but it's convenient to Disneyland-goers (about 8 min. away).

MIDSIZE CONCERT VENUES

The Avalon Hollywood   Formerly known as the Palace, this 1,200-capacity theater and nightclub—just across Vine from the famed Capitol Records tower—was the site of numerous significant alternative-rock shows throughout the late '90s and has been given a much-needed makeover. Club nights feature famous DJs like Moby and Paul Oakenfold. 1735 N. Vine St., Hollywood. © 323/462-8900. www.avalonhollywood.com.

El Rey Theatre   Another restored relic of L.A.'s old Art Deco movie theaters, this small venue holds about 1,500 for such performers as Lucinda Williams and The Aquabats. It offers upstairs and downstairs views of the stage, but plan on standing all night as there are usually no seats available. 5515 Wilshire Blvd. © 323/936-6400. www.theelrey.com.

House of Blues ⊛   With three great bars, cutting-edge Southern art, and a key Sunset Strip location, there are plenty of reasons music fans and industry types keep coming back to House of Blues. Night after night, audiences are dazzled by performances from nationally and internationally acclaimed acts as diverse as Jeff Beck, The Black Eyed Peas, and Motorhead. The food in the upstairs restaurant can be great (reservations are a must), and the Sunday Gospel Brunch, though a bit pricey, puts a mean raise on the roof. 8430 Sunset Blvd., West Hollywood. © 323/848-5100. www.hob.com.

The Mayan Theatre   Perhaps the strangest yet coolest concert venue in town, with an elaborate decor in the mode of a Mayan temple (or something), this former movie house is a fine relic of L.A.'s glorious past. It seats about 1,000 for such performers as PJ Harvey and morphs into Club Mixx with hip-hop DJs on Friday nights. The place is in a part of Downtown that most people don't usually visit, but there's plenty of parking and the interior makes it seem like another dimension. 1038 S. Hill St., Downtown. © 213/746-4674. www.clubmayan.com.

The Wiltern ⊛⊛   Saved from the wrecking ball in the mid-1980s, this 1930s-era Art Deco showcase is perhaps the most beautiful theater in town. Countless national and international acts such as Beck and Audioslave have played here. In addition, plenty of non-pop music events such as Penn & Teller and Cedric the Entertainer complement the schedule. 3790 Wilshire Blvd., Los Angeles. © 213/388-1400. www.wiltern.com.

THE CLUB SCENE

With more small clubs than you can swing a Stratocaster at, Los Angeles is *the* place for live music. Check the *L.A. Weekly* (www.laweekly.com) to see who's in town during your visit. Unless otherwise noted, listed clubs admit only patrons 21 and over.

MOSTLY ROCK

The Dragonfly   Not one to miss a trend, the Dragonfly went from being a dance club that offered live music to becoming a live stage that offers dancing. From "surprise" shows by top-notch local acts to national acts like Jane's Addiction, the Dragonfly is soaring. Great DJs and dancing rock the joint, while smokers and the overheated enjoy its cool outdoor patio. 6510 Santa Monica Blvd., Hollywood. © 323/466-6111. www.thedragonfly.com.

Jon Brion Live

When it comes to real musical talent, few L.A. music lovers will argue that there's a better all-around musician than **Jon Brion**. At a Los Angeles supper club called Largo (see review above), Brion performs an amazing one-man show that always leaves his audience in awe. Producer, songwriter, and multi-instrumentalist, he has an amazing ability to play multiple instruments simultaneously. (He *is* the house band at Largo.) Brion is famous for making up songs on the spot, usually from titles shouted from the audience. He's also well known for his on-stage antics and idiosyncratic takes on famous classics such as the Beatles and Cheap Trick. Brion on Brion: "It's like spraying musical Raid on the classics, until each dying song flips on its back and wiggles its little musical legs in surrender." His shows tend to start pretty late (for Californians, that is), but it's worth the wait; check the schedule at Largo's website to see when he's playing. And don't be surprised if Elvis Costello or Beck makes a guest appearance. (Kanye West made a cameo rap the last time I was here.)

King King 𝒦 I'm not normally keen on Hollywood clubs (too much über-hip dig-me crap), but King King is a refreshing change of venue. The warehouse-size venue feels more SoHo than L.A.: exposed brick walls and ceilings, dark lighting, black velvet curtains, and a square bar on wheels that's moved to accommodate whatever's going on. The last time I was there I watched a rather disturbing play followed by a sensational rockabilly band. 6555 Hollywood Blvd. btw. Hudson and Whitley aves., Hollywood. 𝒞 323/960-5765. www.kingkinghollywood.com. Cover $5–$10.

The Knitting Factory Straight from the New York City legend, a West Coast branch of the famous Knitting Factory has arrived in the redeveloping Hollywood Boulevard nightlife district. The Main Stage was inaugurated by a Posies performance and sees such diverse bookings as Kristin Hersh, Pere Ubu, and Jonathan Richman; a secondary AlterKnit stage has sporadic shows. The Knitting Factory is totally wired for digital, including interactive online computer stations throughout the club. 7021 Hollywood Blvd., Hollywood. 𝒞 323/463-0204. www.knittingfactory.com.

Largo 𝒦 There's always an eclectic array of performances going on at this dinner and music venue, ranging from the plugged-in folk set to vibrant trip hoppers. Since 1997, pop-music archaeologist Jon Brion has been putting forth some amazing Friday-night shows, and there have been regular appearances by the Eels and Grant Lee Phillips—and some not-so-regular drop-in appearances from national acts like Fiona Apple and Kanye West. This is an all-ages club. 432 N. Fairfax Ave., Los Angeles. 𝒞 323/852-1073 or 323/852-1851. www.largo-la.com. Cover $5–$15.

McCabe's Guitar Shop 𝒦𝒦 *Finds* Since 1958 this funky, cluttered music shop has opened its backroom for some memorable acoustic sets from the likes of Doc Watson, Jackson Browne, John Hammond, Aimee Mann, John Lee Hooker, Bill Frisell, and Ann Wilson. With just 150 seats, McCabe's is intimate in the extreme; the gig would have to be in your living room to get any cozier. A guitar shop first and music venue second, McCabe's doesn't serve alcohol and tickets are always reasonably priced (if hard to get). All ages are admitted. 3101 Pico Blvd., Santa Monica. ℂ 310/828-4497. www. mccabes.com. Cover $10–$25.

The Roxy Theatre   Veteran record producer/executive Lou Adler opened this Sunset Strip club in the mid-1970s with concerts by Neil Young and a lengthy run of the pre-movie *Rocky Horror Show.* Since then, it's remained among the top showcase venues in Hollywood. Although the revitalized Troubadour and such new entries as the House of Blues challenge its preeminence among cozy clubs, you can still find national acts like the Black Crowes that will pop in and great local bands. 9009 W. Sunset Blvd. ℂ 310/278-9457. www.theroxyonsunset.com.

Spaceland 🖈   The wall-to-wall mirrors and shiny brass posts decorating the interior create the feeling that, in a past life, Spaceland must've been a seedy strip joint, but the club's current personality offers something entirely different. Having hosted countless performances by artists such as Pavement, Mary Lou Lord, Elliot Smith, and Beck, this hot spot on the fringe of east Hollywood has become one of the most important clubs on the L.A. circuit. 1717 Silver Lake Blvd., Silver Lake. ℂ 323/661-4380. www. clubspaceland.com.

The Troubadour   This West Hollywood mainstay radiates rock history—from the 1960s to the 1990s, the Troub really has seen 'em all. Audiences are consistently treated to memorable shows from the already-established or young-and-promising acts that take the Troubadour's stage. But bring your earplugs—this beer- and sweat-soaked club likes it loud. All ages are accepted. 9081 Santa Monica Blvd., West Hollywood. ℂ 310/276-6168. www.troubadour.com.

Viper Room   This world-famous club on the Strip has been king of the hill since it was first opened by actor Johnny Depp and co-owner Sal Jenco back in 1993. With an intensely electric and often star-filled scene, the intimate club is also known for unforgettable late-night surprise performances from such powerhouses as the late Johnny Cash, Iggy Pop, Tom Petty, Slash, and Trapt (to name but a few) after headline gigs elsewhere in town. 8852 Sunset Blvd., West Hollywood. ℂ 310/358-1880. www.viperroom.com.

Whisky A Go-Go 🖈   This legendary bi-level venue personifies L.A. rock 'n' roll, from Jim Morrison and X to Guns N' Roses and Beck. Every trend has passed through this club, and it continues to be the most vital venue of its kind. With the hiring of an in-house booker a few years ago, the Whisky began showcasing local talent on free-admission Monday nights. All ages are welcome. 8901 Sunset Blvd., West Hollywood. ℂ 310/ 652-4202, ext. 15. www.whiskyagogo.com.

The Woods   The interior of this small bar and performance space, located in a *très* ugly strip mall, is very inventive. The lovely owner, a former set decorator, calls the motif "Vegas in hell." Think trailer tacky coupled with big-city chic. Live music includes mostly surf-a-billy with an occasional polyester disco cover band, and regulars include Quentin Tarantino. 1533 La Brea Ave., Hollywood. ℂ 323/876-6612. Cover $2–$5.

BLUES & JAZZ

Babe's & Ricky's Inn 🖈🖈 *Finds*   Located in South Central L.A.'s up-and-coming Leimert Park, this blues club stands out as an original, a place where you can imagine B. B. King himself would have played before he became famous. Mama Laura Gross is the cultivator of the fabulous, endangered sound and the house goddess of this intimate bar. Great guitarists are the rule, not the exception here. 4339 Leimert Blvd., Leimert Park. ℂ 323/295-9112. www.bluesbar.com.

Finds All That Free Jazz

Art, jazz, beer, and free—baby, that's for me. That's why I always mark my calendar for the free jazz concerts hosted Friday evenings at the **Los Angeles County Museum of Art**, 5905 Wilshire Blvd., Los Angeles (© **323/857-6000; www.lacma.org**). The museum hosts free concerts in its open central courtyard every Friday night from 6 to 8pm, April through Thanksgiving. It's a great way to listen to good music with a glass of wine on a warm Los Angeles evening.

The Baked Potato   This restaurant/nightspot offers missile-size spuds while hosting a steady roster of jazz performances by local and visiting acts. Guitarist Andy Summers (of Police fame) does gigs now and again. The valley location is a few blocks from Universal City. 3787 Cahuenga Blvd., North Hollywood. © 818/980-1615. www.thebakedpotato.com.

B. B. King's Blues Club   Nestled away in Universal CityWalk's commercial plaza, this three-level club/restaurant—the ribs alone are worth the trip—hosts plenty of great local and touring national blues acts and is a testament to the establishment's venerable namesake. There's no shortage of good seating, but if you find yourself on the top two levels, it's best to grab a table adjacent to the railing to get an ideal view of the stage. CityWalk, Universal City. © 818/622-5464. www.bbkingclubs.com.

Catalina Bar & Grill   This clubby old-timer represents the very best of downtown Hollywood's golden era. Though the neighborhood has become rough around the edges, this premier supper club manages to book some of the biggest names in contemporary jazz for multi-night stints. The acoustics are great and there really are no bad seats. All ages are welcome. 6725 W. Sunset Blvd., Hollywood. © 323/466-2210. www.catalina jazzclub.com. Cover $20.

Fais Do-Do 🕏   Most nights of the week, this architecturally unique New Orleans–style nightspot hosts jazz, blues, and the occasional rock combo. It's located in a once-upscale suburb west of Downtown, but the surrounding neighborhood has become somewhat sketchy. Originally built as a bank, the building has gone through several jazz-club incarnations. It's even rumored that Miles Davis once graced the stage. The club offers great music in a memorable atmosphere, as well as good Cajun and soul food from the busy kitchen. 5257 W. Adams Blvd., Los Angeles. © 323/931-4636. www.fais-dodo.com.

Harvelles Blues Club 🕏   Open since 1931, this Santa Monica bastion of blues claims to be the oldest blues club in Los Angeles. Dark and sexy like a blues club should be, you can always rely on a good local band playing here; many famous musicians have passed through as well, including Albert King and Bonnie Raitt. The mostly 30-and-up crowd usually needs a few cocktails before hitting the dance floor. Great website. 1432 4th St., Santa Monica. © 310/395-1676. www.harvelles.com. Cover $10–$20.

Jazz Bakery *Finds*   Ruth Price's nonprofit venue is renowned for attracting some of the most important names in jazz—and for the restored Helms bakery factory that houses the club and inspires its name. Hers is a no-frills, volunteer-run, all-about-the-music, 7-nights-a-week nonprofit venue where iconic musicians turn up regularly to the delight of serious jazz fans. There's a no-food policy for the theater, but the lobby cafe sells beer, wine, and champagne that you can bring in. 3233 Helms Ave., Culver City. © 310/271-9039. www.jazzbakery.org.

2 Dance Clubs

The momentous popularity of Latin dance and swing has resulted in the opening of new clubs dedicated to both, taking some of the pressure off the old standbys. DJ club culture is also on the rise locally, featuring noteworthy shows at some enjoyable clubs; such dance clubs, however, can come and go as quickly as you can say "jungle rave." Mere whispers of a happening thing elsewhere can practically relegate a club to a been-there-done-that status. Check the *L.A. Weekly* for updates on specific club information.

The Derby This class-A east-of-Hollywood club has been at ground zero of the swing revival since the very beginning. Located at a former Brown Derby site, the club was restored to its original luster and detailed with a heavy 1940s edge. With Big Bad Voodoo Daddy as the one-time house band and regular visits from Royal Crown Revue, hep guys and dolls knew that the Derby was money even before *Swingers* transformed it into one of the city's most happenin' hangs. But if you come on the weekends, expect a wait to get in, and once you're inside, dance space is at a premium. 4500 Los Feliz Blvd., Los Feliz. ✆ 323/663-8979. www.clubderby.com. Cover $7–$10.

El Floridita *(Finds* This tiny Cuban restaurant-and-salsa club is hot, hot, hot. Despite its modest strip-lot locale, it draws the likes of Jennifer Lopez, Sandra Bullock, Jimmy Smits, and Jack Nicholson, in addition to a festive crowd of Latin-dance devotees who groove well into the night. The hippest nights continue to be Mondays, when Johnny Polanco and his swinging New York–flavored salsa band get the dance floor jumpin'. 1253 N. Vine St., Hollywood. ✆ 323/871-8612. www.elfloridita.com. Cover $10.

Nacional ✮ At what is quickly becoming Hollywood's most desirable dance floor, you'll find a hip and gorgeous crowd engaging in an orgiastic celebration of youth. It also has a well-designed balcony where you can watch all the flirting in a lively outdoor smoking area. So grab a *mojito* and mingle among the young, beautiful, and unshakably self-assured, and remember, even the rest of us can have fun here. 1645 Wilcox Ave., Hollywood. ✆ 323/962-7712. www.nacional.cc.

Viper Room ✮ Every Tuesday night, this live-music hot spot (see "The Live Music Scene," earlier) hosts Atmosphere, featuring the sounds of trance, drum and bass, garage, techno, and hip-hop spun by an eclectic assemblage of DJs, MCs, and mix masters. On Mondays, a head-banging tribute to '80s metal/hard rock shakes the walls. 8852 Sunset Blvd., West Hollywood. ✆ 310/358-1880. www.viperroom.com. Cover $10.

Dinner & a Movie & DJs & Dancing

If your big night on the town involves dinner, a movie, DJs, and dancing, **Cine-Space** has got it all covered. Every Thursday through Saturday this stylish, intimate Hollywood supper club serves contemporary American cuisine—and stiff cocktails—while screening recent hits, indies, classics, and shorts. When the (free) film's over, the DJ party starts at around 10pm and goes until 2am. Check the CineSpace event calendar online to see what's playing, then call to make a reservation. It's located in the heart of Hollywood at 6356 Hollywood Blvd. at Ivar Street on the second level; ✆ 323/817-3456; www.cine-space.com.

Out & About: L.A.'s Gay & Lesbian Nightlife Scene

Like San Francisco to the north, Los Angeles has a vibrant and politically powerful gay and lesbian community. Every year in June, this active community comes out (pun intended) in full force for one of the city's most popular events: the Gay Pride parade, which all but takes over West Hollywood in the spirit of activism and audacity. If you're in town, this is one party you don't want to miss (see "Los Angeles–Area Calendar of Events" in chapter 3).

Although **West Hollywood (WeHo)**, often referred to as Boys Town, is the best-known gay neighborhood in Los Angeles, there are several other noteworthy enclaves. **Silver Lake** has a long-standing gay community that's worked hard to preserve the area's beautiful homes once occupied by the likes of Charlie Chaplin and Cecil B. DeMille. To the west of WeHo, **Santa Monica** and **Venice** also have a strong gay and lesbian presence.

If you're looking for specific info on gay culture in L.A., check out *Frontiers* (✆ 323/857-0578), one of the most prominent free biweekly gay mags, available in coffeehouses and at newsstands citywide. For this and other GLBT magazines, call or visit **A Different Light Bookstore**, 8853 Santa Monica, West Hollywood (✆ 310/854-6601). The *L.A. Weekly* and *New Times Los Angeles* also have lesbian and gay articles and listings.

The Abbey This is *the* social spot for WeHo's gay scene. It's part coffeehouse, bar, and restaurant, so you can start with lattes in the morning and switch to cocktails in the afternoon. In fact, most of West Hollywood seems to end up here on Saturday nights. 692 N. Robertson Blvd., West Hollywood. ✆ 310/289-8410. www.abbeyfoodandbar.com.

Akbar See "Bars & Cocktail Lounges" below.

Apache Territory The small dance floor fills on weekends with Valley boys bored by the snootier WeHo scene. This is a major pickup scene and is especially popular on Thursday nights. 11608 Ventura Blvd., Studio City. ✆ 818/506-0404.

Club 7969 Fashionable of late, Club 7969 features male and female strippers baring it all while mingling with the gay, lesbian, and straight crowd. Each night has a different theme, ranging from drag burlesques to techno parties. On Tuesdays, Michelle's CC revue—with its legion of topless female

3 Bars & Cocktail Lounges

Akbar *Finds* On the outside, Akbar isn't much to look at with its brown stucco facade and simple (almost imperceptible) sign. Step inside, though, and you'll find one of the city's more moody and elegant rooms. Friendly barkeeps ply the patrons with cocktails from behind the arabesque mirrored bar, and an astonishingly diverse CD jukebox is filled to capacity with tunes old and new. This is a mixed bar that's predominantly gay, but always comfortable for straights. 4356 W. Sunset Blvd. (at Fountain Ave.), Los Angeles. ✆ 323/665-6810. www.akbarsilverlake.com.

dancers—attracts a largely lesbian crowd. 7969 Santa Monica Blvd., West Hollywood. ✆ 323/654-0280.

Dragstrip 66 Note the cover disparity: If you ain't in drag, prepare to pay for it (and wait in line a bit longer than the more fashionably hip). This great drag night, held at Safari Sam's, offers up every type of music—except disco and Liza. That's entertainment. Dragstrip 66 is now held four times a year, so check the website for upcoming dates. 5214 Sunset Blvd., Hollywood ✆ 323/969-2596. www.dragstrip66.com. Cover $10–$20.

Eleven Hormones and hot bods abound throughout this WeHo club's lower bar/lounge and upstairs dining area. It's called Eleven because at that appointed time there's a sort of Cirque du Soleil–style performance involving a high-wire setup. 8811 Santa Monica Blvd. (at Larrabee St.), West Hollywood. ✆ 310/855-0800. No cover.

Jewel's Catch One Open until 3am most nights and 4am on weekends, Catch One pulls in an ethnically diverse gay, lesbian, and straight crowd. Thursday nights see a mostly female crowd. 4067 W. Pico Blvd., Los Angeles. ✆ 323/734-8849.

Micky's A diverse, outgoing, and mostly older crowd cruises back and forth between the front-room bar and the dance floor in back. More women—probably looking to party with the friendly crowd and enjoy the great drink specials—are drawn to Micky's than to some of the neighboring bars. 8857 Santa Monica Blvd., West Hollywood. ✆ 310/657-1176. www.mickys.com.

The Other Side This amiable place reputedly serves the best martini in Silver Lake. It's a handsome and intimate piano bar with plenty of friendly patrons, and the ideal place to meet people if you're new in town. 2538 Hyperion Ave., Silver Lake. ✆ 323/661-0618.

Rage For almost 20 years, this high-energy, high-attitude disco has been the preferred mainstay on WeHo's gay dance club circuit. Between turns around the dance floor, shirtless muscle boys self-consciously strut about—like peacocks flashing their plumes—looking to exchange vital statistics. 8911 Santa Monica Blvd., West Hollywood. ✆ 310/652-2814.

Bar NINETEEN12 I'll take any excuse to walk through the front doors of the luscious Beverly Hills Hotel and rub shoulders with the celebs who love to hang out here and be seen. Suck on an apple martini popsicle while striking a pose on the golden-toned velvet sofas and high-backed leather chairs. Me, I'm out on the veranda nursing a $14 Manhattan while pretending not to notice Pamela's cleavage. *Tip:* Thursdays are the hot night, but arrive before 9pm or you might not make it in. 9641 Sunset Blvd., Beverly Hills; ✆ 310/273-1912; www.barnineteen12.com.

Beauty Bar It's a proven concept in New York, Las Vegas, and San Francisco: a cocktail lounge/beauty salon. Decorated with vintage salon gear and sporting a hip-retro vibe, the Beauty Bar is both campy and trendy. Where else can you actually get a manicure while sipping cocktails with names like Blue Rinse (made with blue Curaçao) or Prell (their version of a grasshopper)? 1638 N Cahuenga Blvd., Hollywood. (C) 323/464-7676. www.beautybar.com.

Bob's Frolic Room | This classic L.A. dive bar is located next door to the Pantages Theatre on Hollywood and Vine. Pumping too-loud music from one of the best CD jukeboxes in Los Angeles, Hollywood vampires hang out with rough-around-the-edges hipsters and old coots getting their fill of stiff, cheap drinks amid the Art Deco decor. Look for Hedy Lamarr's star out front on the Hollywood Walk of Fame ("That's HEDLEY!"). 6245 Hollywood Blvd. Hollywood. (C) 323/462-5890.

The Brig   This ultrahip bar, located at the end of the Abbot Kinney strip in Venice, attracts an eclectic crowd of young clubgoers from all over L.A. The spacious main room pumps house beats, creating an atmosphere in which the scantily clad women and well-dressed men vie for attention from the opposite sex. If you're just rolling off the beach, however, don't be worried about being underdressed because at the Brig, less is more. If you are lucky enough to get on the lone pool table, you can show off your skills and perhaps attract some of that sought-after attention to yourself. 1515 Abbot Kinney Blvd., Venice. (C) 310/399-7537.

Circle Bar   This hip spot is particularly popular with the post-college crowd. A place to see and be seen, the Circle Bar packs them in nightly. Although it's located in Santa Monica, the scene is often more reminiscent of Hollywood. Its namesake, a large circular bar, gets very crowded on the weekends, but the bartenders pour a stiff drink that normally makes the wait worthwhile. The DJ spins everything from '80s to more progressive beats as the crowd dictates. Students, locals, and struggling actors all dance the night away and get their groove on while looking for that special someone. 2926 Main St., Santa Monica. (C) 310/450-0508.

The Dresden Room ✦   Hugely popular with L.A. hipsters because of its longevity, location, often-overlooked cuisine, and elegant ambience, "the Den" was pushed into the mainstream of L.A. nightlife thanks to its inclusion in the movie *Swingers.* But it's the timeless lounge act of Marty and Elayne (the couple has been performing there up to 5 nights a week since 1982) that has proven that, fad or no fad, this place is always cool. Sidle up to the bar for a blue glass of the house classic, Blood and Sand—a space-age margarita of sorts. 1760 N. Vermont Ave., Hollywood. (C) 323/665-4294.

El Carmen   Opened by L.A. restaurant-and-bar impresario Sean Macpherson, the man with the mescal touch, El Carmen conjures the feel of a back-alley Mexican cantina of a bygone era. Vintage Mexican movie posters, vibrant Latin American colors, and oil paintings of masked Mexican wrestlers decorate the Quonset-hut interior, while an eclectic jukebox offers an array of tunes from Tito Puente to the Foo Fighters. The busy bar boasts a gargantuan list of more than 100 tequilas and a small menu of tacos and light fare. 8138 W. 3rd St., Los Angeles. (C) 323/852-1552.

Firefly ✦   Opened by Jeffery Best, a veteran of the Hollywood club scene, this dream of a bar and restaurant is the meeting place of choice for Hollywood clubbers and those hipsters who live in Silver Lake and Los Feliz. Flavored by '40s noir (think Bogie in *The Big Sleep*), this is a sexy and simple nightspot where visitors can recline on comfy cushions, warm up by the fire pit in the middle of the restaurant, or relax at the patio with its cabana-like tables enclosed by drapes. DJs offer up a pumping mix of soul and ambient sounds, and who knows what could happen in those coed bathrooms? 11720 Ventura Blvd., Studio City. (C) 818/762-1833.

Glow *(Finds)* Yes, it's at the Marriott Hotel in Marina del Rey, but I know what you're thinking and you're wrong—this place is swank. How swank you ask? Playboy.com recently ranked it as one of the top 10 lounges in the U.S., joining the ranks of notable nightlife hot spots such as the Tropicana Bar at the Roosevelt Hotel in Hollywood, and the Palms Pool and Bungalows in Las Vegas. It's an outdoor venue that literally glows in shades of deep amber as young L.A. hipsters and surprised hotel guests lounge in semi-private booths and order bottle service from the lithe staff. Check the website and you get it. 4100 Admiralty Way, Marina del Rey. ✆ **310/578-4152.** www. glow-bar.com.

Good Luck Bar Until they installed a flashing neon sign outside, only locals and hipsters knew about this kung fu–themed room in the Los Feliz/Silver Lake area. The dark-red windowless interior boasts Asian ceiling tiles, fringed Chinese paper lanterns, sweet-but-deadly drinks like the Yee Mee Loo (translated as "blue drink"), and a juke-box with selections ranging from Thelonius Monk to Cher's "Half Breed." The spacious sitting room, furnished with mismatched sofas, armchairs, and banquettes, provides a great atmosphere for conversation or romance. Arrive early to avoid the throngs of L.A. scenesters. 1514 Hillhurst Ave. (btw. Hollywood and Sunset boulevards), Los Angeles. ✆ **323/666-3524.**

Green Door Unless you're in your twenties, live in L.A., and go clubbing a lot, you've probably never heard Johnny Zander and Chris Breed, two key players in the resurgence of Hollywood's nightlife scene. The Green Door is their latest creation, a quasi nightclub, lounge, and salon that's been elaborately made over to resemble an old-world French saloon complete with regal couches, antique mirrors, and a massive chandelier hanging from the high ceiling. It's divided into three areas depending on your mood: smoke, drink, or dance. I suggest arriving early (around 9pm) or you might get turned away at the door for reasons only the egomaniacal bouncers can fathom. 1439 Ivar Ave., Hollywood. ✆ **323/463-0008.**

Hank's Bar Although the original grand old man behind the bar, Henry "Hank" Holzer, is no longer with us, his legacy endures at this classic Downtown watering hole on the ground floor of the Stillwell Hotel. Its battered booths and well-liquored patrons, who have been elbowing up to the bar here for a decade, mingle nicely with the drop-in customers currently infusing the new surge in Downtown L.A.'s nightlife. 840 S. Grand Ave., Los Angeles. ✆ **213/623-7718.**

Ivan Kane's Forty Deuce Owner Ivan Kane reopened this suave nightclub, formerly known as Kane. Designed as a "back-alley, striptease lounge," the low bar, lounge chair seating, vintage brass registers, and cocktail tables with chic lamps all chip in to create a sexy, burlesque vibe. Models use the bar as a runway, so watch your cocktail. 5574 Melrose Ave., Hollywood. ✆ **323/465-4242.** www.fortydeuce.com.

Lola's The swimming pool–size martinis are enough reason to trek over to Lola's. From the classic gin or vodka martini for the purist to the chocolate- or apple-flavored concoctions for the adventurous, Lola's has a little something for everyone. Two bars, a billiard table, and plush couches hidden in dark, romantic corners make for an enjoyable setting and plenty of celeb spotting. 945 N. Fairfax Ave. (south of Santa Monica Blvd.), Los Angeles. ✆ **213/736-5652.**

Lounge 217 A lounge in the true sense of the word, these plush Art Deco surroundings just scream "martini"—and the bartenders stand ready to shake or stir up your favorite. Comfortable seating lends itself well to intimate socializing. On Monday, the

Lounge hosts classical guitarists, and Thursday it welcomes the torch singer and cigar bar set. Come early on the weekends for a more raucous late-night crowd. 217 Broadway (btw. 2nd and 3rd sts.), Santa Monica. ✆ 310/394-6336.

Nic's Beverly Hills ⭐⭐   There's nothing like a really good martini to take the edge off, and some of the best martinis I've ever had are poured at Nic's (the pear martini with Grey Goose La Poire vodka and Parmesan cheese garnish is sublime). Unlike the surrounding Beverly Hills establishments, there's no attitude here, just lots of retro-groovy slippery white leather, bold colorful stripes, and laid-back locals noshing on cocktail cuisine while listening to good jazz bands and big-band trios. Owner Larry Nicola—a really fun guy to hang out with by the way—takes pride in his self-anointed title as Vodkateur™, which means he's an expert regarding all things vodka. In fact, he built a walk-in freezer called a VODBOX just so he could have a proper tasting room so his guests can sample the best vodkas from around the world. Give Larry a call and ask him to give you the VODBOX experience when you arrive. 453 N. Canon Dr., Beverly Hills. ✆ 310/550-5707. www.nicsbeverlyhills.com.

O'Brien's Pub   O'Brien's offers everything it takes to make a great pub, including more beers on tap than you could possibly attempt to drink at one sitting. The food is far better than pub grub, so come hungry. Three levels and a patio allow you to either post up inside listening to live bands 6 nights a week or grab some sun outside during the day. The clientele is mostly on the young side, but everyone seems to be treated like family. 2941 Main St., Santa Monica. ✆ 310/396-4725.

Red Lion Tavern   A hidden veteran of the Silver Lake circuit, this kitschy, over-the-top German tavern—complete with dirndl-clad waitresses—is where neighborhood hipsters mingle with cranky, working-class German expats. The place serves hearty half-liters of Warsteiner, Becks, and Bitburger, but braver souls—with bottomless bladders—can take on a 1.5-liter boot. The astonishingly good food offerings include schnitzel, bratwurst, and potato pancakes. 2366 Glendale Blvd., Silver Lake. ✆ 323/662-5337.

Skybar *Overrated*   Since its opening in hotelier Ian Schraeger's refurbished Sunset Strip hotel, Skybar has been a favorite among L.A.'s most fashionable of the fashionable set. This place was at one time so hot that even the agents to the stars needed agents to get in. (Rumor has it that one agent was so desperate to gain entrance that he promised one of the servers a contract.) Nevertheless, a little image consulting—effect the right look, strike the right pose, and look properly disinterested—might get you in to rub elbows with some of the faces that regularly appear on the cover of *People* (but please don't stare). 8440 W. Sunset Blvd., West Hollywood. ✆ 323/848-6025.

The Standard Downtown ⭐⭐   This rooftop bar, located atop the Standard Hotel in Downtown L.A. (formerly Superior Oil headquarters), is surrounded by high office towers and helipads, and the view is magnificent. The skyscrapers act like strangely glowing lava lamps in the night sky as exotic ladies sip exotic cocktails amid waterbeds and bent-plastic loungers. 550 S. Flower St., Downtown. ✆ 213/892-8080. www.standardhotel.com.

Star Shoes ⭐   From the same club gurus who run Beauty Bar around the corner, Star Shoes is a combo shoe store and dance club. It's usually packed with a trendy young crowd who bump around the narrow dance floor while a projectionist plasters the walls with vintage celluloid (a stony effect). The scene here is far more energetic than that at the Beauty Bar, and the DJs are among the best in town. 6364 Hollywood Blvd., Hollywood. ✆ 323/462-7827.

Three Clubs *(Finds* In the tradition of Hollywood hipster hangouts trying to maintain a low profile, Three Clubs (like the playing card) is absent of any signage indicating where you are. (Look for the BARGAIN CLOWN MART sign on the facade.) Inside this dark and cavernous lounge, you'll find a youthful, hoping-to-become-a-star-soon set mingling into the night. Even with two rooms, plenty of cushiony sofas, two long bars, and lots of spacious tables, this place is always loud and packed. 1123 N. Vine St., Hollywood. ✆ 323/462-6441. www.threeclubs.com.

Trader Vic's Opened in 1955, this trendy but fun bar and lounge is Polynesian Tiki-kitsch deluxe, especially if you are in the mood for strong exotic drinks. A favorite watering hole for some Hollywood heavies, this is part of Victor Bergron's famous chain of Tahitian-themed restaurants where the mai tai originated. Vic's has a huge menu of specialty drinks, like the mind-melting Scorpion bowl and Navy Grog, and features great appetizers (also known as pupu platters) like the Beef Cho Cho, do-it-yourself skewers of teriyaki beef roasted over a flaming hibachi. 9876 Wilshire Blvd., Beverly Hills. ✆ 310/285-1300.

Voda *(★* Upscale and elegant, Voda uses natural elements such as candlelight and a waterfall that runs along the entire wall behind a huge backlit bar to create an atmosphere that pulses with a vibrant, hip undercurrent. Besides many star sightings, such as Robert De Niro and Quentin Tarantino, you'll find excellent food and generous martinis. 1449 2nd St., Santa Monica. ✆ 310/394-9774. www.vodabar.com.

Whiskey Blue When ascending the dramatic backlit staircase and entering the dimly lit, seductive interior, it's hard to believe Whiskey Blue in the W Hotel is situated on UCLA's Sorority Row. The atmosphere is as chic as the decor, which features high screen partitions, low cushioned couches, sleek private rooms, and a row of carved stumps of wood where manicured martinis may be set. Patrons are encouraged to dress their best, especially on the weekends when the Westside's glitterati come out to this scene to be seen. Hotel guests are given priority entrance. 930 Hilgard Ave., Westwood. ✆ 310/443-8232.

Winston's The lack of a sign gives you a pretty good indication of the type of crowd you'll encounter at this tiny West Hollywood bar opened by überhip owners Andy Fiscella (of "Dime" fame) and *GQ* editor Chris Huvane. The decor is pure 1920s Tinseltown with DJs spinning vintage '80s and '90s for young starlets like Lindsay Lohan, Mary Kate Olsen, and Jessica Alba. Plan on snotty service, strong drinks, and attitude in abundance. Oh, and good luck getting in on a weekend night if you don't have the right look. 7746 Santa Monica Blvd., West Hollywood. ✆ 323/654-0105.

World Café Its excellent restaurant, top-notch appetizer menu, low-key jazz bands, unique artwork, and frequent drink specials make this a perfect place to begin any Santa Monica evening adventure. A refreshing venue with spacious and comfortable seating, warm patios, and a buzz of activity, the World acts as a reflection of the beehive of activity that flows around this part of the city. 2820 Main St., Santa Monica. ✆ 310/392-1661. www.worldcafela.com.

Yamashiro *(★* Enjoy the view of the city from this pagoda-and-garden perch in the Hollywood Hills. Though the place has long been considered a "special-occasion" Japanese restaurant, I prefer to sit in the lounge—mai tai in hand—and watch Hollywood's dancing searchlights dot the night sky. Great sushi and even better specialty drinks. There's no cover, but there's also no way around the $6 valet parking fee. 1999 N. Sycamore Ave., Hollywood. ✆ 323/466-5125.

4 Performing Arts

CLASSICAL MUSIC & OPERA

While L.A. is best known for its pop realms (see earlier in this chapter), other types of music here consist of top-flight orchestras and companies—both local and visiting—to fulfill the most demanding classical music appetites; scan the papers to find out who's performing while you're in the city.

The world-class **Los Angeles Philharmonic** (© 323/850-2000; www.laphil.org) is the only major classical music company in Los Angeles, and it just got a whole lot more popular with the completion of its incredible home: the **Walt Disney Concert Hall** (p. 172), located at the intersection of 1st Street and Grand Avenue in the historic Bunker Hill area. Designed by world-renowned architect Frank Gehry, this exciting addition to the Music Center of L.A. includes a breathtaking 2,265-seat concert hall, outdoor park, restaurant, cafe, bookstore, and gift shop.

The Philharmonic's Finnish-born music director, Esa-Pekka Salonen, concentrates on contemporary compositions; despite complaints from traditionalists, he does an excellent job attracting younger audiences. Tickets can be hard to come by when celebrity players like Itzhak Perlman, Emanuel Ax, and Yo Yo Ma are in town. In addition to performances at the Walt Disney Concert Hall, the Philharmonic plays a summer season at the **Hollywood Bowl** (see "Concerts Under the Stars" below) and a chamber music series at the **Skirball Cultural Center** (p. 176).

Slowly but surely, the **Los Angeles Opera** (© 213/972-8001; www.losangeles opera.com), which performs at the **Dorothy Chandler Pavilion,** is gaining respect and popularity with inventive stagings of classic pieces, modern operas, visiting divas, and the contributions from high-profile artistic director Plácido Domingo. The 120-voice **Los Angeles Master Chorale** sings a varied repertoire that includes classical and pop compositions. Concerts are held at the **Walt Disney Concert Hall** (© 213/972-7200) October through June.

The **UCLA Center for the Performing Arts** (© 310/825-2101; www.uclalive. org) has presented music, dance, and theatrical performances of unparalleled quality for more than 60 years and continues to be a major presence in the local and national cultural landscape. Presentations occur at several different theaters around Los Angeles, both on and off campus. UCLA's **Royce Hall** is the Center's pride; it has even been compared to New York's Carnegie Hall. Recent standouts from the Center's busy calendar included the famous Gyuto Monks Tibetan Tantric Choir and the Cinderella story *Cendrillon,* with an original score by Sergei Prokofiev.

CONCERTS UNDER THE STARS

Also see "The Live Music Scene" earlier in this chapter.

Hollywood Bowl ☆☆☆ *Moments*   Built in the early 1920s, the Hollywood Bowl has just undergone a major overhaul. The elegant Greek-style natural outdoor amphitheater,

---

Fun Fact **Fun with Festivals**

The L.A. Philharmonic's summer concert series at the Hollywood Bowl is the world's largest outdoor music festival.

Half-Price Theater Tickets

There's a convenient new source for purchasing half-price theater tickets in L.A. The new **Hollywood Visitor Information Center,** located at the Hollywood & Highland Center at 6801 Hollywood Blvd., has three staffers on duty from 10am to 11pm daily who will sell you half-price theater tickets for up to 100 venues throughout the city. Tickets are released on Tuesdays for shows that week, so visitors can select not only the production but the specific day they would like to attend (you'll get a printout of your reservation, and the tickets are held at the theater until the night of the performance).

cradled in a small mountain canyon, is the summer home of the Los Angeles Philharmonic and Hollywood Bowl orchestras, and often hosts internationally known conductors and soloists on Tuesday and Thursday nights. Friday and Saturday concerts typically feature orchestral swing or pops concerts. The summer season also includes a jazz series; past performers have included Natalie Cole, Dionne Warwick, and Chick Corea. Other events, from standard rock-'n'-roll acts like Radiohead to Garrison Keillor programs, summer fireworks galas, and the annual Mariachi Festival, are often on the season's schedule.

To round out an evening at the Bowl, many concertgoers use the occasion to enjoy a picnic dinner and a bottle of wine—it's one of L.A.'s grandest traditions. You can prepare your own or order a picnic basket with a choice of hot and cold dishes and a selection of wines and desserts from Patina's on-site catering department, which also provides delivery to box seats: Call © **323/850-1885** by 4pm the day before you go to place your food order. Arrive a couple of hours before the show starts, in order to dine while listening to the orchestra or band tune up. 2301 N. Highland Ave. (at Pat Moore Way), Hollywood. © **323/850-2000.** www.hollywoodbowl.org.

THEATER
MAJOR THEATERS & COMPANIES

Tickets for most plays cost $10 to $35, although big-name shows at the major theaters can fetch up to $75 for the best seats. **LA Stage Alliance** (© **213/614-0556**), a nonprofit association of live theaters and producers in Los Angeles, offers full- and half-price tickets to more than 100 venues via their Internet-only service at **www. LAStageTIX.com**. This handy site features a frequently updated list of shows and availability. Tickets can be purchased online with a credit card and they'll be waiting for you at the box office; a service fee is applied depending on the cost of the ticket. *Note:* One caveat of the half-price bargain is that the seating assignments are solely at the discretion of the theater—there's no guarantee you'll be sitting next to your partner—and you must bring a printed or faxed copy of your e-mail confirmation to the box office.

The all-purpose **Music Center of Los Angeles County,** 135 N. Grand Ave., Downtown, houses the city's top two playhouses: the **Ahmanson Theatre** and **Mark Taper Forum.** They're both home to the Center Theater Group (www.taperahmanson. com), as well as traveling productions (often Broadway or London bred). Each season, the Ahmanson Theatre (© **213/628-2772**) hosts a handful of high-profile shows, such as the Tony Award–winning *Jersey Boys,* Andrew Lloyd Webber's *Phantom of the*

Opera, and Oprah Winfrey's musical *The Color Purple.* **Tip:** The best seats in the theater are in the mezzanine section.

The **Mark Taper Forum** (② 213/628-2772; www.centertheatregroup.com) is a more intimate theater with a thrust stage—where the audience is seated on three sides of the acting area—that hosts contemporary works by international and local playwrights. Neil Simon's humorous and poignant *The Dinner Party* and Tom Stoppard's witty and eclectic *Arcadia,* which has won 3 Pulitzer Prizes and 18 Tony Awards, are among the more popular productions performed on this internationally recognized stage.

One of L.A.'s most venerable landmarks, the **Orpheum Theatre,** 842 S. Broadway at 9th Street (② 213/749-5171; www.laorpheum.com), recently reopened after a 75-year hiatus. Built in 1926, this renowned venue has hosted an array of theatrical productions, concerts, film festivals, and television and movie shoots—from Judy Garland's 1933 vaudeville performance to a taping of *Ally McBeal.* The 2,000-seat theater is home to the Mighty Wurlitzer, one of three original theater organs still existing in Southern California theaters.

Across town, the moderate-size **Geffen Playhouse,** 10886 Le Conte Ave., Westwood (② 310/208-5454; www.geffenplayhouse.com), presents dramatic and comedic work by prominent and emerging writers. UCLA purchased the theater—which was originally built as a Masonic temple in 1929, and later served as the Westwood Playhouse—back in 1995 with a little help from philanthropic entertainment mogul David Geffen. This striking venue is often the West Coast choice of many acclaimed off-Broadway shows, and also attracts locally based TV and movie actors eager for the immediacy of stage work. One recent production featured the world premiere of *Wishful Drinking,* a poignant comedy written and performed by Carrie Fisher. Always audience-friendly, the Playhouse prices tickets in the $28 to $43 range.

You've probably already heard of the **Kodak Theatre,** 6834 Hollywood Blvd. (② 323/308-6300; www.kodaktheatre.com), home of the Academy Awards. The crown jewel of the Hollywood & Highland entertainment complex, this modern beauty hosts a wide range of international performances, musicals, and concerts ranging from Alicia Keys and David Gilmour to the Moscow Stanislavsky Ballet and Sesame Street Live. Guided tours are given 7 days a week from 10:30am to 2:30pm.

The recently restored **Pantages Theatre,** 6233 Hollywood Blvd. between Vine St. and Argyle Ave. (② 323/468-1770; www.pantages-theater.com), reflects the full Art Deco glory of L.A.'s theater scene. Opened in 1930, this historical and cultural landmark was the first Art Deco movie palace in the U.S. and site of the Academy Awards from 1949 to 1959. The theater recently presented *Cats, Les Miserables,* and *Wicked.*

Located at the foot of the Hollywood Hills, the 1,245-seat outdoor **John Anson Ford Amphitheatre** (② 323/461-3673; www.fordamphitheatre.org) is located in a county regional park and is set against a backdrop of cypress trees and chaparral. It is

---

⸢Tips⸥ Great Theater, Cheap Tickets

Two hours before curtain time, the Ahmanson Theatre and Mark Taper Forum offer specially priced $12 tickets that must be purchased in person at the box office with cash. All performances are subject to availability, with restrictions.

> **Finds Free Morning Music at Hollywood Bowl**
>
> It's not widely known, but the Bowl's summer morning rehearsals are open to the public and absolutely free. On Tuesday, Thursday, and Friday from 9:30am to 12:30pm, you can see the program scheduled for that evening. So bring some coffee and doughnuts (the concession stands aren't open) and enjoy the best seats in the house (© **323/850-2000; www.hollywoodbowl.org**).

an intimate setting, with no patron more than 96 feet away from the stage. Music, dance, film, theater, and family events run May through September. The indoor theater space, a cozy 87-seat space that was extensively renovated in 1998 and renamed **[Inside] The Ford,** features live music and theater year-round.

One of the most highly acclaimed professional theaters in L.A., the **Pasadena Playhouse,** 39 S. El Molino Ave., near Colorado Boulevard, Pasadena (© **626/356-7529; www.pasadenaplayhouse.org**), is a registered historic landmark that has served as the training ground for many theatrical, film, and TV stars, including William Holden and Gene Hackman.

For a schedule at any of the above theaters, check the listings in *Los Angeles* magazine (www.lamag.com), available at most area newsstands, or the "Calendar" section of the Sunday *Los Angeles Times* (www.theguide.latimes.com); or call the box offices at the numbers listed above.

SMALLER PLAYHOUSES & COMPANIES

On any given night, there's more live theater to choose from in Los Angeles than in New York City, due in part to the surfeit of ready actors and writers chomping at the bit to make it in Tinseltown. Many of today's familiar faces from film and TV spent plenty of time cutting their teeth on L.A.'s busy theater circuit, which is home to nearly 200 small and medium-size theaters and theater companies, ranging from the 'round-the-corner, neighborhood variety to high-profile, polished troupes of veteran actors. With so many options, navigating the scene to find the best work can be a monumental task. A good bet is to choose one of the theaters listed below, which have established excellent reputations for their consistently high-quality productions; otherwise, consult the *L.A. Weekly* (www.laweekly.com), which advertises most current productions, or call **Theatre L.A.** (© **213/614-0556;** www.theatrela.org) for up-to-date performance listings.

Housed in the same complex as Walt Disney Concert Hall, **REDCAT** (an acronym for the Roy and Edna Disney/CalArts Theater) is a relatively new multiuse forum for cutting-edge performance and media arts. Befitting its ultramodern location, the REDCAT is one of the most versatile and technologically advanced presentation spaces in the world. Be sure to arrive a bit early so you can visit the REDCAT lounge and bookstore for a pre-performance espresso or cocktail—wrapped in signature Frank Gehry plywood, it's one of the best-kept secret bars in the city. The REDCAT is located at 631 W. 2nd St. at the southwest corner of the Walt Disney Concert Hall; © **213/237-2800;** www.redcat.org.

The **Colony Studio Theatre,** 555 N. 3rd St., Burbank (© **818/558-7000;** www.colonytheatre.org), was formed in 1975 and has developed from a part-time ensemble of TV actors longing for their theatrical roots into a nationally recognized company.

The company produces plays in all genres at the 276-seat Burbank Center Stage, which is shared with other performing arts groups.

Actors Circle Theater, 7313 Santa Monica Blvd., West Hollywood (✆ **323/882-6805;** www.actorscircle.net), is a 47-seater that's as acclaimed as it's tiny. Look for original contemporary works throughout the year.

Founded in 1965, **East West Players,** 120 N. Judge John Aiso St., Los Angeles (✆ **213/625-7000;** www.eastwestplayers.org), is the oldest Asian-American theater company in the United States. It's been so successful that the company moved from a 99-seat venue to the 200-seat David Henry Hwang Theater in Downtown L.A.'s Little Tokyo (p. 186).

The **L.A. Theatre Works** (✆ **310/827-0808**) is renowned for its marriage of media and theater and has performed more than 200 plays and logged more than 350 hours of on-air programming. Performances are held at the Skirball Cultural Center (see "Museums & Galleries" in chapter 7), nestled in the Sepulveda Pass near the Getty Center. In the past, personalities such as Richard Dreyfuss, Julia Louis-Dreyfus, Jason Robards, Annette Bening, and John Lithgow have given award-winning performances of plays by Arthur Miller, Neil Simon, Joyce Carol Oates, and more. For nearly a decade, the group has performed simultaneously for viewing and listening audiences in its radio theater series. Tickets are usually around $35; a full performance schedule can be found online at www.latw.org.

5 Comedy

L.A.'s comedy clubs have launched the careers of many comics who are now household names. In addition to the clubs below, check out the alternative comedy featured Monday nights at **Largo** (see "Mostly Rock," earlier in this chapter), 432 N. Fairfax Ave., Los Angeles (✆ **323/852-1073**).

Acme Comedy Theater   The Acme players provide a barrage of laughs with their improv and sketch comedy acts—a veritable grab bag of funnies. 135 N. La Brea Ave., Hollywood. ✆ 323/525-0202. www.acmecomedy.com. Cover $8–$15.

Comedy Store 🖈   You can't go wrong here: New comics develop their material, and established ones work out their kinks at this landmark owned by Mitzi Shore (Pauly's mom). The **Best of the Comedy Store Room,** which seats 400, features professional stand-ups continuously on Friday and Saturday nights. Several comedians are always featured, each doing about a 15-minute stint. The talent is always first-rate and includes comics who regularly appear on the *Tonight Show* and other shows. The **Original Room** features a dozen or so comedians back-to-back nightly. Sunday night is amateur night: Anyone with enough guts can take the stage for 3 minutes—Lord only knows what you'll get. 8433 Sunset Blvd., West Hollywood. ✆ 323/650-6268. www.comedystore.com. Cover $10–$20, plus 2 drink minimum.

Groundling Theater 🖈   L.A.'s answer to Chicago's Second City has been around for more than 25 years, yet it remains the most innovative and funny group in town. The skits change every year or so, but they take new improvisational twists every night and the satire is often savage. The Groundlings were the springboard to fame for Pee-Wee Herman, Elvira, and former *Saturday Night Live* stars Jon Lovitz, Phil Hartman, and Julia "It's Pat" Sweeney. Phone for showtimes and reservations. 7307 Melrose Ave., Los Angeles. ✆ 323/934-4747. www.groundlings.com. Tickets $11–$21.

The Improv   A showcase for top stand-ups since 1975, the Improv offers something different each night. Although it used to have a fairly active music schedule, the place is now mostly doing what it does best—showcasing comedy. Owner Budd Freedman's buddies—like Jay Leno, Billy Crystal, and Robin Williams—hone their skills here more often than you would expect. But even if the comedians on the bill are all unknowns, they won't be for long. Shows are at 8pm Sunday and Thursday, and at 8:30 and 10:30pm Friday and Saturday. 8162 Melrose Ave., West Hollywood. (C) 323/651-2583. www.improvclubs.com. Tickets $5–$12, plus 2 drink minimum.

Laugh Factory ⟨ₖ   Yes, this is where Michael Richards made his infamous racist comments toward two black men who were heckling him (and where Mr. Richards is no longer welcome). In fact, just about every comedian you've seen on TV—living or dead—has been a regular at the Laugh Factory: Rodney Dangerfield, Dave Chappelle, Robin Williams, Richard Pryor, Jim Carrey, Jerry Seinfeld, and others. The best night to attend is the Friday All Star Comedy show, because you never know when a celebrity guest is going to sneak onstage and try out a new routine. 8001 Sunset Blvd., Hollywood. (C) 323/656-1336. www.laughfactory.com. Tickets $18–$30, plus 2 drink minimum.

6 Movies: Play It Again, Sam

This being L.A., the city is saturated with megaplexes catering to high-budget, high-profile flicks featuring the usual big-ticket lures such as Hanks, Willis, and DiCaprio. But there are times when those polished Hollywood-studio stories just won't do. Below are some nonmainstream options that play movies from bygone eras or those with an indie bent. Consult the *L.A. Weekly* (www.laweekly.com) to see what's playing when you're in town.

Film festivals are another great way to explore the other side of contemporary movies. In addition to the American Film Institute's yearly November fete (see the "Los Angeles–Area Calendar of Events," in chapter 3), the **Film Independent's Los Angeles Film Festival** ((C) 866/345-6337 or 310/432-1240; www.lafilmfest.com) looks at what's new in American indies, short films, and music videos during a week-long event in late June. Each July since 1982, the **Gay and Lesbian Film Festival** ((C) 213/480-7088; www.outfest.org), also known as Outfest, has aimed to bring high-quality gay, lesbian, bi, and transgender films to a wider public awareness. In

Cinema at the Cemetery

If you prefer your movie settings to be slightly macabre, boy are you in luck. Every other Saturday in the summer, the **Hollywood Forever Cemetery** hosts civilized screenings of rarely seen movie classics, which are projected against the cemetery's massive mausoleum wall. Guests are encouraged to arrive early for a picnic on the lush lawn while listening to DJs spin records (Grateful Dead, mostly). A $10 donation admission is suggested, and parking is free within the cemetery. Bring a sweater, a flashlight, and—if you're having a picnic—bring a trash bag as well. Hollywood Forever Cemetery is located at 6000 Santa Monica Blvd., between Gower Street and Van Ness Avenue. For more information, log on to www.cinespia.org.

The World's Most Private Public Theater

Part of the culture of L.A. is to always avoid standing in line because you're far too important and busy. So it was only a matter of time before someone came up with the idea of treating everyone like a VIP at the movie theater. **ArcLight Cinemas** (② ② **323/464-4226;** www.arclightcinemas.com) is specifically designed for anyone who abhors rude patrons (ushers keep it quiet), late arrivals (forbidden), searching for seats (reserved in advance by customer preference), uncomfortable chairs (think Lay-Z-Boy), neck strain (the first rows start 25 ft. from the screen), pimply teenage employees (most of the staff are struggling actors or film students), crappy popcorn (real butter and freshly made caramel popcorn), and paying for parking (4 free hours are included in the ticket price). And it only gets better: There's a full bar and a groovy lounge where themed cocktails such as the Mordor are served with appetizers.

The ArcLight shows a mix of indie and Hollywood films, and ticket prices—as you would expect—are higher than the industry average: $11 for an afternoon show and $14 on weekend nights. But the rewards are worth the occasional splurge. The sound and picture quality are so good that filmmakers come here to host Q & A sessions, and celebrities such as Brad Pitt and Leonardo DiCaprio prefer the ArcLight's reserved seating system. Be sure to review the "Now Playing" and "Coming Soon" sections at the ArcLight's website to see what movies and Q & A sessions are scheduled. It's located at 6360 W. Sunset Blvd., between Vine and Ivar streets.

1998, the festival became Los Angeles's largest, with more than 32,000 audience members.

Promoting moving pictures as this country's great art form, the **American Cinematheque** in Hollywood (② **323/466-3456;** www.egyptiantheatre.com) presents not-readily-seen videos and films, ranging from the wildly arty to old classics. Since relocating to the historic and beautifully refurbished 1923 **Egyptian Theatre,** 6712 Hollywood Blvd. in Hollywood, American Cinematheque has hosted several film events, including a celebration of contemporary flicks from Spain, a tribute to the femme fatales of film noir, and a retrospective of the films of William Friedkin. Events highlighting a specific individual are usually accompanied by at least one in-theater audience Q and A session with the honoree.

The **Leo S. Bing Theater** at the **L.A. County Museum of Art,** 5905 Wilshire Blvd., Los Angeles (② **323/857-6010;** www.lacma.org), presents a themed film series each month. Past subjects have ranged from 1930s blonde bombshell films to Cold War propaganda flicks to contemporary British satire (complete with a 3-day *Monty Python's Flying Circus* marathon).

Despite being a multiplex in a bright outdoor mall, **Laemmle's Sunset 5,** 8000 Sunset Blvd., West Hollywood (② **323/848-3500;** www.laemmle.com), features films that most theaters of its ilk won't even touch. This is the place to come to see interesting independent art films. There's often a selection of gay-themed movies.

The Nuart Theater, 11272 Santa Monica Blvd., Los Angeles (*©* **310/281-8223**), digs deep into its archives for real classics, ranging from campy to cool. They also feature frequent in-person appearances and Q and A sessions from stars and filmmakers, and screen *The Rocky Horror Picture Show* (yes, still!) every Saturday at midnight.

Although it's only open for social events and once-a-month movies when the new owner fancies, fans of silent-movie classics will enjoy the **Silent Movie Theatre,** 611 N. Fairfax Ave. (½ block south of Melrose Ave.), near the Miracle Mile (*©* **323/ 655-2520** for recorded program information, or 323/655-2510 for main office; www. silentmovietheatre.com). Tickets are $10.

If TV's more your thing, the **Paley Center for Media,** 465 N. Beverly Dr., Beverly Hills (*©* **310/786-1025;** www.mtr.org), celebrates this country's long relationship with the tube. The museum often features a movie of the month, and it also shows free selections from past television programs (p. 174).

7 Late-Night Bites

Finding places to dine in the wee hours is getting easier in L.A., as each year sees more 24-hour and after-midnight eateries staking a place in the culinary landscape.

The Apple Pan *☆☆*   This classic American burger shack, an L.A. landmark, hasn't changed much since 1947—and its burgers and pies continue to hit the spot. Open until 1am Friday and Saturday, and until midnight other nights; closed Monday. See p. 136 for a full review. 10801 W. Pico Blvd., West L.A. *©* **310/475-3585.**

Canter's Fairfax Restaurant, Delicatessen & Bakery   This 24-hour Jewish deli has been a winner with late-nighters since it opened more than 66 years ago. If you show up after the clubs close, you're sure to spot a bleary-eyed celebrity or two alongside the rest of the after-hours crowd, chowing down on a giant pastrami sandwich, matzo-ball soup, potato pancakes, or other deli favorites. Try a potato knish with a side of brown gravy—trust me, you'll love it. 419 N. Fairfax Ave., West Hollywood. *©* **323/651-2030.**

Dolores's   One of L.A.'s oldest surviving coffee shops, Dolores's offers just what you might expect: Naugahyde, laminated counters, lots of linoleum, and comforting predictability. Expect the usual coffee-shop fare of pancakes, burgers, and eggs at this 24-hour joint. 11407 Santa Monica Blvd., Los Angeles. *©* **310/477-1061.**

Du-par's Restaurant & Bakery *☆*   During the week, this popular Valley coffee shop serves up blue-plate specials until 1am; come the weekend, they're slingin' hash until 5:30am. See p. 154 for a full review. 12036 Ventura Blvd. (1 block east of Laurel Canyon), Studio City. *©* **818/766-4437.**

Fred 62   Silver Lake/Los Feliz hipsters hankering for a slightly demented take on classic American comfort grub skulk into Fred round-the-clock. See p. 145 for a full review. 1850 N. Vermont, Los Feliz. *©* **323/667-0062.**

Jerry's Famous Deli *☆*   Valley hipsters head to 24-hour Jerry's to satiate the late-night munchies. See p. 153 for a full review. 12655 Ventura Blvd. (east of Coldwater Canyon Ave.), Studio City. *©* **818/980-4245.**

Kate Mantilini *☆*   Kate's serves stylish nouveau comfort food in a striking setting. It's open until midnight Sunday and Monday, Tuesday through Thursday until 1am, and Friday and Saturday until 2am. See p. 133 for a full review. 9101 Wilshire Blvd. (at Doheny Dr.), Beverly Hills. ℂ **310/278-3699.**

Mel's Drive-In   Straight from an episode of *Happy Days,* this 24-hour 1950s diner on the Sunset Strip attracts customers ranging from chic shoppers during the day to rock 'n' rollers at night. The fries and shakes here are among the best in town. 8585 Sunset Blvd. (west of La Cienega Blvd.), West Hollywood. ℂ **310/854-7200.**

101 Coffee Shop   A retro coffee shop right out of the early '60s with rock walls, funky colored tiles, comfy booths, and cool light fixtures, all pulled together nicely in a hip yet subdued fashion. Count on tasty grinds until 3am (try the breakfast burritos). 6145 Franklin Ave., Hollywood. ℂ **323/467-1175.**

The Original Pantry   Owned by former Los Angeles mayor Richard Riordan, this Downtown diner has been serving huge portions of comfort food round-the-clock for more than 60 years; in fact, they don't even have a key to the front door. See p. 152 for a full review. 877 S. Figueroa St. (at 9th St.), Downtown. ℂ **213/972-9279.**

Pink's Hot Dogs   Many a woozy hipster has awakened with the telltale signs of a post-cocktailing trip to this greasy street-side hot-dog stand—the oniony morning-after breath and chili stains on your shirt are dead giveaways. Open Friday and Saturday until 3am, and all other nights until 2am. See p. 145 for a full review. 709 N. La Brea Ave., Los Angeles. ℂ **323/931-4223.**

Swingers ✦   This hip coffee shop keeps L.A. scene-stealers happy with its retro comfort food. Open daily until 4am. See p. 146 for a full review. There's a second location at 802 Broadway (at Lincoln Ave.; ℂ **310/393-9793**) in Santa Monica. 8020 Beverly Blvd. (west of Fairfax Ave.), Hollywood. ℂ **323/653-5858.**

Toi on Sunset ✦   Those requiring a little more *oomph* from their late-night snack should come here. At this colorful and *loud* hangout, garbled pop-culture metaphors mingle with the tastes and aromas of "rockin' Thai" cuisine in delicious ways until 4am nightly. See p. 146 for a full review. 7505½ Sunset Blvd. (at Gardner St.), Hollywood. ℂ **323/874-8062.**

Side Trips from Los Angeles

Los Angeles may be one of the world's most stimulating cities, but don't let it monopolize your time to the point of ignoring its scenic side trips—from famous resort communities such as Santa Barbara to sun-filled South Coast beach towns (Long Beach, Newport Beach, Huntington Beach, Laguna Beach) and the island oasis of Catalina.

From L.A., you can reach any of these points in 1 to 2 hours by car or boat, and accommodations and dining are available at all these destinations.

1 Long Beach & the *Queen Mary*

21 miles S of Downtown L.A.

The fifth-largest city in California, Long Beach is best known as the permanent home of the former cruise liner *Queen Mary* and the Long Beach Grand Prix, whose star-studded warm-up race sends hipster Jason Priestly and perennial racer Paul Newman burning rubber through the streets of the city in mid-April. Please see the beginning of this guide for a color map of the Long Beach area.

ESSENTIALS

GETTING THERE See chapter 3 for airport and airline information. Driving from Los Angeles, take either I-5 or I-405 to I-710 south, which leads directly to both downtown Long Beach and the *Queen Mary* seaport.

ORIENTATION Downtown Long Beach is at the eastern end of the vast Port of Los Angeles; Pine Avenue is the central restaurant and shopping street, which extends south to Shoreline Park and the Aquarium. The *Queen Mary* is docked just across the waterway, gazing south toward tiny Long Beach marina and Naples Island.

VISITOR INFORMATION Contact the **Long Beach Area Convention & Visitors Bureau,** One World Trade Center, Ste. 300 (© **800/452-7829** or 562/436-3645; www.visitlongbeach.com). For information on the **Long Beach Grand Prix,** call © **562/981-2600** or check out www.longbeachgp.com.

THE MAJOR ATTRACTIONS

Aquarium of the Pacific 🐾 *Kids* This enormous aquarium—one of the largest in the U.S.—is the cornerstone of Long Beach's ever-changing waterfront. Figuring that what stimulated flagging economies in Monterey and Baltimore would work in Long Beach, planners gave their all to this project, creating a crowd-pleasing attraction just across the harbor from Long Beach's other mainstay, the *Queen Mary.* The vast facility—it has enough exhibit space to fill three football fields—re-creates three areas of the Pacific: the warm Baja and Southern California regions, the Bering Sea and chilly northern Pacific, and faraway tropical climes, including impressive re-creations of a

---

Tips Save Some Cash

If you plan on visiting the *Queen Mary* and the Aquarium the same day, you can purchase a combined ticket package at either venue for $34 ($19 for kids 3–11). You'll save about $10 (hey, that's a free lunch).

---

lagoon and barrier reef. There are more than 12,500 creatures in all, from 150 sharks (some you can touch, some you can't) prowling a 90,000-gallon habitat to delicate sea horses, moon jellies, and gaggles of tropical birds within the Lorikeet Forest. Learn little-known aquatic facts at the many educational exhibits, or come nose-to-nose with sea lions, moray eels, and other inhabitants of giant, three-story-high tanks.

100 Aquarium Way, off Shoreline Dr., Long Beach. © **562/590-3100**. www.aquariumofpacific.org. Admission $21 adults, $18 seniors ages 62 and over, $12 ages 3–11, free for kids 2 and under. Daily 9am–6pm. Closed Christmas Day and Toyota Grand Prix weekend (mid-Apr). Parking $6.

The *Queen Mary* ★   It's easy to dismiss this old cruise ship/museum as a barnacle-laden tourist trap, but it's the only surviving example of this particular kind of 20th-century elegance and excess. From the staterooms paneled lavishly in now-extinct tropical hardwoods to the perfectly preserved crew quarters and the miles of hallway handrails made of once-pedestrian Bakelite, wonders never cease aboard this 81,237-ton Art Deco luxury liner. Stroll the teakwood decks with just a bit of imagination and you're back in 1936 on the maiden voyage from Southampton, England. Don't miss the streamlined modern observation lounge, featured often in period motion pictures; have drinks and listen to some live jazz. Kiosk displays of photographs and memorabilia are everywhere—following the success of the movie *Titanic,* the *Queen Mary* even hosted an exhibit of artifacts from its less fortunate cousin. The Cold War–era Soviet submarine *Scorpion* resides alongside; separate admission is required to tour the sub. *Tip:* Buy a First Class Passage ticket to both the sub and the ship and you'll also get a behind-the-scenes guided tour, peppered with worthwhile anecdotes and details—well worth the extra $7.

1126 Queen's Hwy. (end of I-710), Long Beach. © **562/435-3511**. www.queenmary.com. Admission $23 adults, $20 seniors ages 55 and over and military, $12 children ages 5–11, free for kids 4 and under. First Class Passage admission $30 adults, $27 seniors ages 55 and over and military, $19 children ages 5–11, free for kids 4 and under. Daily 10am–6pm. Parking $10.

WHERE TO STAY

Hotel Queen Mary ★ *Finds*   The *Queen Mary* isn't only a piece of maritime history; it's also a hotel. But although the historic ocean liner is considered the most luxurious vessel ever to sail the Atlantic, with some of the largest rooms built aboard a ship, the quarters aren't exceptional when compared to those on terra firma today, nor are the amenities. The idea is to enjoy the novelty and charm of features like the original bathtub watercocks ("cold salt," "cold fresh," "hot salt," "hot fresh"). The beautifully carved interior is a feast for the eye and fun to explore, and the weekday rates are hard to beat. Three onboard restaurants are overpriced but convenient, and the shopping arcade has a decidedly British feel (one shop sells great *Queen Mary* souvenirs). An elegant Sunday champagne brunch—complete with ice sculpture and harpist—is served in the ship's Grand Salon, and it's always worthwhile to have a cocktail in the Art Deco Observation Bar. If you're too young to have traveled on the old luxury liners, this is the perfect opportunity to experience the romance of an Atlantic crossing—with no seasickness or cabin fever.

1126 Queen's Hwy. (end of I-710), Long Beach, CA 90802-6390. ℂ 562/437-3511. www.queenmary.com. 365 units. Inside cabin from $119; deluxe cabin from $179; suite from $360. Many packages available. AE, DC, MC, V. Valet parking $20; self-parking $12. **Amenities:** 3 restaurants; spa; shopping arcade. *In room:* A/C, TV.

WHERE TO DINE

The Sky Room ★★ CALIFORNIAN/FRENCH   It takes a 40-minute drive from Los Angeles to Long Beach to get a sense of what fine dining must have been like during Hollywood's Golden Age. Built in 1926 and meticulously restored by proprietor Bernard Rosenson, the restaurant's Art Deco–period design inspires oohs and aahs among first-time guests. Awash in brilliant white, the interior's massive pillars, curvaceous ramps, glimmering brass, elevated maple-and-ebony dance floor, and classic jazz band playing enticing dance tunes all combine to create the illusion of dining on a luxury ocean liner (the beautiful view of the stately *Queen Mary* certainly enhances the effect). Opulence continues with white Frette linens, custom black-rimmed china, Villeroy and Boch tableware, and a *Wine Spectator*–award-winning wine list. The Californian/French menu offers a pleasing presentation of the classics: grilled chicken breast in a chanterelle au jus, line-caught salmon with goat-cheese pesto, New York steak on a grilled onion brioche. Menu-wise there's nothing groundbreaking here, but that's not what the Sky Room is about. I highly recommend that you take the advice of the experienced waitstaff and sommelier; our duo handled the task flawlessly. A night of dinner, drinking, dancing, and romance—what's not to like?

40 S. Locust Ave. (at Ocean Blvd.), Long Beach, CA 90802. ℂ 562/983-2703. www.theskyroom.com. Reservations recommended. Dinner main courses $24–$41. AE, DC, DISC, MC, V. Mon–Thurs 5:30–10:30pm; Fri–Sat 5:30pm–midnight. Valet parking $6.

Yard House ★ AMERICAN ECLECTIC   Not only does it have one of the best outdoor dining venues in Long Beach, the Yard House also features one of the *world's* largest selection of draft beers. The keg room houses more than 1,000 gallons of beer, all visible through a glass door where you can see the golden liquids transported to a signature oval bar via miles of nylon tubing to the dozens of taps. The restaurant takes its name from the early Colonial tradition of serving beer in 36-inch-tall glasses—or yards—to weary stagecoach drivers. Customers are encouraged to partake in this tradition and can drink from the glass yards, as well as half-yards and traditional pint glasses. Signature dishes range from the tortelike California roll to the crab cake hoagie and an impressive selection of steaks and chops. There's also an extensive list of appetizers—perfect for a tapas-style meal—salads, pasta, and rice dishes, as well as sandwiches and individual pizzas (the Thai chicken pizza is excellent, as are the crab cakes and coconut-encrusted shrimp). On sunny days, be sure to request a table on the deck overlooking the picturesque harbor.

401 Shoreline Village Dr., Long Beach. ℂ 562/628-0455. www.yardhouse.com. Reservations not accepted. Main courses $10–$30. AE, DC, MC, V. Sun–Thurs 11am–11pm; Fri–Sat 11am–1am.

2 The South Coast ★

Seal Beach is 36 miles S of Los Angeles; Newport Beach, 49 miles; Dana Point, 65 miles

Whatever you do, don't say "Orange County" here. The mere name evokes images of smoggy industrial parks, cookie-cutter housing developments, and the staunch Republicanism that prevails behind the so-called "orange curtain." We're talking instead about the Orange Coast, one of Southern California's best-kept secrets—a string of seaside jewels that have been compared with the French Riviera or the Costa del Sol. Forty-two miles of beaches offer pristine stretches of sand, tide pools teeming with marine life, ecological preserves, secluded coves, picturesque pleasure-boat harbors, and legendary surf breaks. My advice? Make it a day trip from L.A.—hit the road early for a scenic cruise down the Pacific Coast Highway starting at Seal Beach, stop for lunch at Laguna Beach (the prettiest of all the SoCal beach towns), continue south to Dana Point where the *really* expensive resorts reside, then take the freeway back to L.A. (I-5 to the I-405).

ESSENTIALS

GETTING THERE   See "Getting There & Getting Around" in chapter 3 for airport and airline information. By car from Los Angeles, take I-5 or I-405 south. The scenic, shore-hugging Pacific Coast Highway (Calif. 1, or just PCH to the locals) links the Orange Coast communities from Seal Beach in the north to Capistrano Beach just south of Dana Point, where it merges with I-5. To reach the beach communities directly, take the following freeway exits: **Seal Beach,** Seal Beach Boulevard from I-405; **Huntington Beach,** Beach Boulevard/California 39 from either I-405 or I-5; **Newport Beach,** California 55 from either I-405 or I-5; **Laguna Beach,** California 133 from I-5; **San Juan Capistrano,** Ortega Highway/California 74 from I-5; and **Dana Point,** Pacific Coast Highway/California 1 from I-5.

VISITOR INFORMATION   The **Seal Beach Chamber of Commerce,** 201 8th St., Ste. 120, next to City Hall (② **562/799-0179;** www.sealbeachchamber.com), is open Monday through Friday from 10am to 4pm.

The **Huntington Beach Conference & Visitors Bureau,** 301 Main St., Ste. 208 (② **800/729-6232** or 714/969-3492; www.surfcityusa.com), enthusiastically offers tons of information and personal anecdotes. Open Monday through Friday from 9am to 5pm.

The **Newport Beach Conference & Visitors Bureau,** 110 Newport Center Dr., Ste. 120 (② **800/94-COAST** [800/942-6278] or 949/719-6100; www.newportbeach-cvb.com), distributes brochures, sample menus, a calendar of events, and the free *Visitor's Guide.* Call or stop in Monday through Friday from 8am to 5pm (plus weekends in summer).

The **Laguna Beach Visitors Bureau,** 252 Broadway (② **800/877-1115** or 949/497-9229; www.lagunabeachinfo.org), is in the heart of town and distributes lodging, dining, and art gallery guides. It's open Monday through Friday from 9am to 5pm, and Saturday from 10am to 4pm (plus Sun in summer).

The **San Juan Capistrano Chamber of Commerce,** Franciscan Plaza, 31781 Camino Capistrano, Ste. 306 (② **949/493-4700;** www.sanjuancapistrano.com), is

---

Tips **A Special Arts Festival**

A tradition for 60-plus years in arts-friendly Laguna, the **Festival of Arts & Pageant of the Masters** is held each summer throughout July and August. It's pretty large now, and it includes the formerly "alternative" Sawdust Festival across the street. See the "Los Angeles–Area Calendar of Events" in chapter 3 for details, or log on to www.foapom.com.

The South Coast

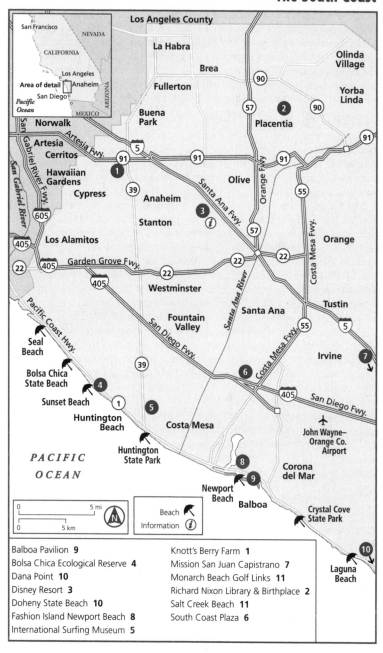

Balboa Pavilion **9**
Bolsa Chica Ecological Reserve **4**
Dana Point **10**
Disney Resort **3**
Doheny State Beach **10**
Fashion Island Newport Beach **8**
International Surfing Museum **5**

Knott's Berry Farm **1**
Mission San Juan Capistrano **7**
Monarch Beach Golf Links **11**
Richard Nixon Library & Birthplace **2**
Salt Creek Beach **11**
South Coast Plaza **6**

within walking distance of the mission and offers a walking tour guide to historic sites. Open Monday through Friday from 9am to 5pm.

The **Dana Point Chamber of Commerce Visitor Center,** located in the Clocktower Building at LaPlaza Center (© **800/290-DANA** [800/290-3262] or 949/496-1555; www.danapoint-chamber.com), is open Monday through Friday from 9am to 5pm (closed noon–1pm for lunch) and carries some restaurant and lodging information, as well as a comprehensive recreation brochure.

DRIVING THE ORANGE COAST

You'll most likely be exploring the coast by car, so the beach communities are covered in order, from north to south. And keep in mind that if you're traveling between Los Angeles and San Diego, the Pacific Coast Highway (Calif. 1) is a breezy, scenic detour that adds less than an hour to the commute—so pick out a couple of seaside destinations and take your time.

Seal Beach, on the border between Los Angeles and Orange counties, and a neighbor to Long Beach's Naples Harbor, is geographically isolated by both the adjacent U.S. Naval Weapons Station and the self-contained Leisure World retirement community. As a result, the beach town appears untouched by modern development—it's Orange County's version of small-town America. Take a stroll down Main Street for a walk back in time, culminating in the Seal Beach Pier. Although the clusters of sunbathing, squawking seals that gave the town its name aren't around any more, old-timers still fish, lovers still stroll, and families still cavort by the seaside, enjoying great food and retail shops or having a cold drink at Hennessey's tavern.

Huntington Beach—or Surf City, as it's known—is the largest Orange Coast city; it stretches quite a way inland and has seen the most urbanization. To some extent, this has changed the old boardwalk and pier to a modern outdoor mall where cliques of teens coexist with families and the surfers who continue to flock here, drawn by Huntington's legendary place in surf lore. Hawaiian-born George Freeth is credited with bringing the sport here in 1907, and some say the breaks around the pier and Bolsa Chica are the best in California. The world's top wave riders flock to Huntington each August for the rowdy but professional **U.S. Open of Surfing.** If you're around at Christmastime, try to see the gaily decorated marina homes and boats in Huntington Harbor by taking the **Cruise of Lights,** a 45-minute narrated sail through and around the harbor islands. The festivities generally last from mid-December until Christmas; call © **714/840-7542** for schedules and ticket information.

The name **Newport Beach** conjures comparisons to Rhode Island's Newport, where the well-to-do enjoy seaside living with all the creature comforts. That's the way it is here, too, but on a less grandiose scale. From the million-dollar Cape Cod–style cottages on sunny Balboa Island to elegant shopping complexes like Fashion Island and South Coast Plaza (an über-mall with valet parking, car detailing, limo service, and concierge), this is where fashionable socialites, right-wing celebrities, and business mavens can all be found. Alternatively, you could explore **Balboa Peninsula's** historic Pavilion and old-fashioned pier, or board a passenger ferry to Catalina Island.

Laguna Beach, whose breathtaking geography is marked by bold elevated headlands, coastal bluffs, pocket coves, and a very inviting beach, is known as an artists' enclave, but the truth is that Laguna has became so "in" (read: expensive) that it's driven most of the true bohemians out. Their legacy remains with the annual **Festival of Arts & Pageant of the Masters** (see "A Special Arts Festival," above), as well as a proliferation of art galleries mingling with high-priced boutiques along the town's cozy streets. In warm weather, Laguna Beach has an overwhelming Mediterranean-island ambience, which makes *everyone* feel beautifully, idly rich.

San Juan Capistrano, in the verdant headlands inland from Dana Point, is defined by Spanish missions and by its loyal swallows. The mission architecture is authentic, and history abounds. Think of San Juan Capistrano as a compact, life-size diorama illustrating the evolution of a small Western town—from Spanish-mission era to secular rancho period, statehood, and into the 21st century. Surprisingly, Mission San Juan Capistrano (see "Seeing the Sights," below) is once again the center of the community, just as the founding friars intended 200 years ago.

Dana Point, the last town south, has been called a "marina development in search of a soul." Overlooking the harbor stands a monument to 19th-century author Richard Henry Dana, who gave his name to the area and described it in *Two Years Before the Mast.* Activities generally center on yachting and Dana Point's beautiful harbor. Nautical themes are everywhere, particularly the streets named for old-fashioned shipboard lights—a hodgepodge that includes Street of the Amber Lantern, Street of the Violet Lantern, Street of the Golden Lantern, and so on. Bordering the harbor is Doheny State Beach (see "Beaches & Nature Preserves," below), one of the very best for its seaside park and camping facilities.

ENJOYING THE OUTDOORS

BEACHES & NATURE PRESERVES   The **Bolsa Chica Ecological Reserve,** in Huntington Beach (© **714/846-1114;** www.bolsachica.org), is a 900-acre restored urban salt marsh that's a haven to more than 200 bird species, as well as a wide variety of protected plants and animals. Naturalists come to spot herons and egrets as well as California horn snails, jackknife clams, sea sponges, common jellyfish, and shore crabs. An easy 1.5-mile loop trail begins from a parking lot on the Pacific Coast Highway (Calif. 1) a mile south of Warner Boulevard; docents lead a narrated walk the first Saturday of every month. The trail heads inland, over Inner Bolsa Bay and up Bolsa Chica bluffs. It then loops back toward the ocean over a dike that separates the Inner and Outer Bolsa bays and traverses a coastal sand-dune system. This beautiful hike is a terrific afternoon adventure. The Bolsa Chica Conservancy has been working since 1978 on reclaiming the wetlands from oil companies that began drilling here more than 70 years ago. It's an ongoing process, and you can still see those "seesaw" drills dotting the outer areas of the reserve.

Huntington City Beach, adjacent to Huntington Pier, is a haven for volleyball players and surfers; dense crowds abound, but so do amenities like outdoor showers, beach rentals, and restrooms. Just south of the city beach is 3-mile-long **Huntington State Beach.** Both popular beaches have lifeguards and concession stands seasonally. The state beach also has restrooms, showers, barbecue pits, and a waterfront bike path. The main entrance is on Beach Boulevard, and there are access points all along the Pacific Coast Highway (Calif. 1).

Newport Beach runs for about 5 miles and includes both Newport and Balboa piers. It has outdoor showers, restrooms, volleyball nets, and a vintage boardwalk that just may make you feel as though you've stepped 50 years back in time. **Balboa Bike and Beach Stuff** (© **949/723-1516**), at the corner of Balboa and Palm near the pier, rents a variety of items, from pier fishing poles to bikes, beach umbrellas, and body boards. The **Southwind Kayak Center,** 17855 Sky Park Circle, Irvine (© **800/768-8494** or 949/261-0200; www.southwindkayaks.com), rents sea kayaks for use in the bay or open ocean at rates starting at $70 per day; instructional classes are available on weekends, with some midweek classes in summer. The center also conducts several easygoing guided outings, including a $55 Back to Nature trip that highlights the marine life around Dana Point.

Crystal Cove State Park, which covers 3 miles of coastline between Corona del Mar and Laguna Beach and extends into the hills around El Moro Canyon, is a good alternative to the more popular beaches for seekers of solitude. (There are, however, lifeguards and restrooms.) The beach is a winding, sandy strip, backed with grassy terraces; high tide sometimes sections it into coves. The entire area offshore is an underwater nature preserve. There are four entrances, including Pelican Point and El Moro Canyon. For information, call © **949/494-3539** or log onto www.crystalcovestate park.com.

Salt Creek Beach Park lies below the palatial Ritz-Carlton Laguna Niguel; guests who tire of the pristine swimming pool can venture down the staircase on Ritz-Carlton Drive to wiggle their toes in the sand. The setting is spectacular, with wide white-sand beaches looking out toward Catalina Island (which explains why the Ritz-Carlton was built here). The park has lifeguards, restrooms, a snack bar, and convenient parking near the hotel.

Doheny State Beach in Dana Point, just south of Dana Point Marina (enter off Del Abispo St.), has long been known as a premier surfing spot and camping site. Doheny has the friendly vibe of beach parties in days gone by: Tree-shaded lawns give way to wide beaches, and picnicking and beach camping are encouraged. There are 121 sites that can be used for either tents or RVs, plus a state-run visitor center featuring several small aquariums of sea and tide-pool life. For more information and camping availability, call © **949/492-0802.**

BICYCLING   Biking is the most popular beach activity up and down the coast. A slower-paced alternative to driving, it allows you to enjoy the clean, fresh air and notice smaller details of these laid-back beach towns and harbors. The Newport Beach visitor center (see "Visitor Information," above) offers a free *Bike Ways* map of trails throughout the city and harbor. Bikes and equipment can be rented at **Balboa Bike & Beach Stuff,** 601 Balboa Blvd., Newport Beach (© **949/723-1516**), and at **Laguna Beach Cyclery,** 240 Thalia St. (© **949/494-1522;** www.lagunacyclery.net).

GOLF   Many golf-course architects have used the geography of the Orange Coast to its full advantage, molding challenging and scenic courses from the rolling bluffs. Most courses are private, but a few outstanding ones are open to the public. The **Links at Monarch Beach,** 50 Monarch Beach Resort N., Dana Point (© **877/635-8792** or 949/240-8247; www.monarchbeachgolf.com), is particularly impressive. This hilly, challenging course, designed by Robert Trent Jones, Jr., offers great ocean views. Afternoon winds can sneak up, so accuracy is essential. Weekend greens fees are $210 ($170 weekdays). The rates after 1pm drop to $135 weekends and $110 weekdays.

SEEING THE SIGHTS

Beyond the sights listed below, one of the most popular Orange Coast attractions is **Balboa Island** (www.balboaisland.com). The charm of this pretty little neighborhood isn't diminished by knowing that the island was man-made—and it certainly hasn't affected the price of real estate (it's hard to believe that the original property lots sold for $250). Tiny clapboard cottages in the island's center and modern houses with two-story windows and private docks along the perimeter make a colorful and romantic picture. You can drive onto the island on Jamboree Road to the north or take the

Biplane, Air Combat & Warbird Adventures: The Thrill of a Lifetime

For anyone with a thirst for adrenaline-pumping excitement, boy have I got a recommendation for you. At a small airport in the coastal town of Carlsbad, about 30 miles north of San Diego, is a company called Biplane, Air Combat & Warbird Adventures, run by husband-and-wife team Kate and Tom. Turning a passion for old planes into a thriving business, this cheerful duo offers a knockout package of nostalgia, romance, fun, and—for the truly adventurous—a mind-blowing chance to fly a World War II fighter plane, an open-cockpit biplane, or a modern combat aircraft (or all three!).

For the mild-mannered, the 1920s-era biplane ride is pure romance: Couples wearing soft leather headgear and goggles (think Snoopy vs. The Red Baron) sit side-by-side at the front of the open cockpit while the pilot—seated in the back—flies a leisurely route along the sunny coast. At your request, the pilot will perform a few dips and lazy eights to add a touch of excitement, but nothing compares to the loops and rolls you'll perform (yes, you who's never flown a plane in your life) in their big blue AT-6 Texan, a 600-horsepower fighter aircraft equipped with machine-gun barrels that looks like a killer and flies like a pussycat. "Okay, it's your plane," are four words you'll remember forever as the pilot, seated in front, calmly talks you through the aerobatic procedures, which are surprisingly easy to perform. (It's one of the most incredible things I've ever done.)

Other toys on the tarmac include a pair of modern prop-driven dogfighters. Real fighter pilots from the nearby marine base will give you a preflight lesson on aerial combat maneuvers, then get you airborne and let you fly the plane as you try to blast your partner—flying the "enemy" plane—out of the sky (figuratively, of course). For more information about Biplane, Air Combat & Warbird Adventures, call ✆ **800/SKY-LOOP** (800/759-5667) or 760/930-0903. And be sure to visit their website—www.barnstorming.com—for special Internet rates and package deals.

three-car ferry from Balboa Peninsula (www.balboaislandferry.com). It's generally more fun to park and take the 30-minute ferry ride as a pedestrian, since the island is crowded and lacks parking, and the tiny alleys they call streets are more suitable for strolling. **Marine Avenue,** the main commercial street, is lined with small shops and cafes that evoke a New England fishing village. Shaved ices sold by sidewalk vendors will relieve the heat of summer.

Balboa Pavilion & Fun Zone 🐸 🦩*Kids* This historic cupola-topped structure, a California Historical Landmark, was built in 1906 as a bathhouse for swimmers in their ankle-length bathing costumes. Later, during the Big Band era, dancers rocked the Pavilion doing the Balboa Hop. Now it serves as the terminal for Catalina Island passenger service, harbor and whale-watching cruises, and fishing charters. The surrounding boardwalk is called the Balboa Fun Zone (✆ **949/673-0408;** www.thebalboafun zone.com), a collection of carnival rides, game arcades, and vendors of hot dogs and cotton candy. For Newport Harbor or Catalina cruise information, call © **949/673-5245;** for sport fishing and whale-watching, call © **949/673-1434.**

600 E. Bay Ave., Balboa, Newport Beach. © **949/675-1905.** www.balboapavilion.com. From Calif. 1, turn south onto Newport Blvd. (which becomes Balboa Blvd. on the peninsula); turn left at Main St.

International Surfing Museum Nostalgic Gidgets and Moondoggies shouldn't miss this monument to the laid-back sport that has become synonymous with California beaches. You'll find gargantuan longboards from the sport's early days, memorabilia of Duke Kahanamoku and the other surfing greats represented on the Walk of Fame near Huntington Pier, and a gift shop where a copy of the *Surfin'ary* can help you bone up on your surfer slang even if you don't know which foot is goofy.

411 Olive Ave., Huntington Beach. © **714/960-3483.** www.surfingmuseum.org. Admission $2 adults, $1 students, free for kids ages 6 and under. Mid-June to late Sept daily noon–5pm; rest of the year Wed–Sun noon–5pm (hours tend to vary, so call ahead).

Laguna Art Museum This beloved local institution is working hard to position itself as the artistic cornerstone of the community. In addition to a small but interesting permanent collection, the museum presents installations of regional works that are definitely worth a detour. Past examples include a display of surf photography from the coast's 1930s and 1940s golden era, and dozens of plein-air Impressionist paintings (ca. 1900–30) by the founding artists of the original colony. The museum is also open during Laguna Beach Artwalk, the first Thursday each month, when admission is free.

307 Cliff Dr., Laguna Beach. © **949/494-8971.** www.lagunaartmuseum.org. Admission $10 adults, $8 students and seniors, free for kids 11 and under. Daily 11am–5pm.

Mission San Juan Capistrano The 7th of California 's 21 coastal missions, Mission San Juan Capistrano is continually being restored. The mix of old ruins and working buildings is home to small museum collections and various adobe rooms that are as quaint as they are interesting. The intimate mission chapel with its ornate baroque altar is still used for religious services, and the mission complex is the center of the community, hosting performing arts, children's programs, and other cultural events year-round.

This mission is best known for its **swallows,** which are said to return to nest each year at their favorite sanctuary. According to legend, the birds wing their way back to the mission annually on March 19, St. Joseph's Day, arriving at dawn; they are said to take flight again on October 23, after bidding the mission farewell. In reality, you'll probably see the well-fed birds here any day of the week, winter or summer.

Ortega Hwy. (Calif. 74), San Juan Capistrano. © **949/234-1300.** www.missionsjc.com. Admission $9 adults, $8 seniors, $5 children. Daily 8:30am–5pm.

WHERE TO STAY
VERY EXPENSIVE
Montage Resort & Spa ★★★ The rich have it good when it comes to vacationing. Spend a few minutes walking around the new 30-acre Montage resort in Laguna Beach and you'll see why. Unfazed by the two luxury resorts—the St. Regis and the Ritz-Carlton Laguna Niguel—just down the road, the investors behind this Arts and Crafts beauty have created yet another reason for big spenders to unwind along the Orange Coast. You can barely see it from the PCH, and the front entrance is rather understated, but as you walk through the lobby and onto the balcony overlooking

the . . . oh my. The change of scenery is so breathtakingly abrupt that it takes composure not to sprint down to the gorgeous mosaic-tiled pool or run barefoot along the sun-kissed beach. It's the same view from the balcony of every room, and you never tire of it.

The Montage Resort is all about style. You don't even check in at the front desk—as soon as you arrive you're warmly greeted and given a well-rehearsed tour of the resort by attractive khaki-clad employees wearing tailored jackets. The tour ends at the neo-Craftsman-style guest rooms, which are spacious, immaculate, and tastefully decorated with muted color schemes, museum-quality plein-air artwork, huge marble bathrooms with oversize tubs and plush robes, 27-inch flatscreen TVs with DVD players, quality dark-wood furnishings, feather-top beds with goose-down pillows, and very inviting balconies. But don't get too attached: You'll be spending very little time here as you lounge by the infinity-edged pool sipping a lemonade, spend hours exploring the tide pools, stroll through the hotel's impeccably manicured park and pristine beaches, spoil yourself rotten with skin treatments and massages at the oceanfront Spa Montage, and then feast on chef James Boyce's superb Mediterranean-style cuisine at the resort's signature restaurant, **Studio.** There's plenty for kids to do as well: They have their own pool and several fun-filled programs to keep them entertained (and, of course, there's the beach).

30801 S. Coast Hwy., Laguna Beach, CA 92651. (*) **866/271-6953** or 949/715-6000. Fax 949/715-6100. www.montage lagunabeach.com. 262 units. $475–$735 double; from $1,100 suite. AE, DISC, MC, V. Valet parking $25. **Amenities:** 3 restaurants and lobby lounge w/live entertainment; oceanfront fitness facilities and spa; concierge and business services; 24-hr. in-room dining; daily laundry/valet service; newspaper delivery. *In room:* A/C, flatscreen TV and DVD/CD player, high-speed Internet, minibar, hair dryer, iron, personal safe, 3 multiline phones w/voice mail.

Ritz-Carlton Laguna Niguel ☆☆☆
After a sorely needed $40-million renovation to keep up with neighboring resorts such as the Montage and St. Regis, this Dana Point grande dame has recaptured its status as one of the top resorts on the Orange Coast. From its location on the edge of a 150-foot-high bluff overlooking an idyllic 2-mile-long beach, the view from most every window is spectacular (truly, you can spend hours on your balcony admiring the ocean). The most welcome change is that every guest room and public space has been completely remodeled with a much more chic and contemporary look (gone are those frumpy prints of English fox hunts). The spacious rooms are now outfitted with 42-inch plasma TVs with DVD players, sumptuous furnishings and fabrics, an Italian marble bathroom equipped with a double vanity, and the most comfortable feather beds I've ever slept in. The resort's new **Restaurant 162'** is a dramatic improvement as well, with gorgeous ocean views and superb cuisine (the Ocean Curry dish is fantastic). Other welcome improvements include a new luxury spa and oceanfront fitness center. As always, lush terraces and colorful flower gardens abound throughout the well-tended property, and service—in typical Ritz-Carlton style—is unassuming and impeccable. Garden tours, beach shuttles, surf lessons, and excellent kids' programs are available as well.

1 Ritz-Carlton Dr., Dana Point, CA 92629. (*) **800/241-3333** or 949/240-2000. Fax 949/240-0829. www.ritzcarlton. com. 393 units. From $475 gardenview/poolview double; $775 oceanview double; from $875 suite. Children age 17 and under stay free in parent's room. Midweek and special packages available. AE, DC, DISC, MC, V. Parking $35. **Amenities:** 2 restaurants; 1 lounge; 4 outdoor tennis courts; health club; spa; children's programs; concierge; regular shuttle to/from the beach and the golf course; business center; 24-hr. room service; in-room massage; babysitting; laundry service; dry cleaning; executive-level rooms; free Wi-Fi. *In room:* A/C, TV w/pay movies, minibar, hair dryer, iron, safe, robes.

St. Regis Monarch Beach Resort & Spa ✸✸✸

Let's cut to the chase: The St. Regis Monarch Beach Resort is one of the finest luxury hotels I have ever had the pleasure of reviewing—and I've reviewed a *lot* of luxury hotels. They nailed it with this one, setting a standard for all other resort hotels to follow. Everything oozes with indulgence here, from the stellar service to the striking artwork, high-tech electronics, absurdly comfortable beds, stellar restaurants, and a 30,000-square-foot spa that will blow your mind. The $240-million, 172-acre resort opened on July 30, 2001, with a massive star-studded gala, and has since been wooing the wealthy with its gorgeous Tuscan-inspired architecture and soothing ocean views.

Perfection is all in the details, and the St. Regis is full of them: a three-lane lap pool with an underwater sound system; a yoga, spinning, and "movement" studio; a full-service Vogue salon; private poolside cabanas; fantastic Modern American cuisine at Michael Mina's popular **Stonehill Tavern** restaurant ✸✸✸; couples' spa treatment rooms with whirlpool baths and fireplaces; an 18-hole Robert Trent Jones, Jr., golf course; and even a private beach club. Then there are the guest rooms, loaded with beautiful custom-designed furniture, 32-inch Sony Vega flatscreen TVs with CD/DVD audio systems and a 300-DVD library, huge marble-laden bathrooms with glass shower doors that must weigh 100 pounds, and the most comfortable bathrobe I've ever worn.

The resort's only caveat is that it's near the beach, but unlike the Ritz-Carlton Laguna Niguel, and Montage (see reviews above), it's not on it. The view of the terraced pool area, golf course, and shimmering ocean beyond is fantastic, however, and the hotel offers complimentary shuttle service to the 2-mile-long beach, as well as exclusive access to the **St. Regis Beach Club,** where beach attendants set up beach chairs, towels, and umbrellas, and also take food and beverage (including alcohol) orders. You can even hire a "Surf Butler," who will take your measurements for a wet suit, bring out a longboard, and give you surfing lessons.

1 Monarch Beach Rd., Dana Point, CA 92629. © **800/722-1543** or 949/234-3200. Fax 949/234-3201. www.stregis mb.com. 400 units. From $475 resort-view double; from $585 oceanview double; from $895 suite. Golf and spa packages available. AE, DC, DISC, MC, V. Valet parking $28. **Amenities:** 6 restaurants; lounge; 3 pools; 18-hole golf course; 3 tennis courts (lit for night play); Spa Gaucin and a fitness center; 2 hot tubs; kids' club; concierge; complimentary local shuttle; 24-hr. business center; retail shops; 24-hr. room service; in-room massage; babysitting; laundry service; dry cleaning; executive-level rooms; morning paper; 24-hr. butler service, wine cellar tasting room. *In room:* A/C, TV w/DVD library, high-speed Internet, minibar, hair dryer, safe, robes, CD/DVD player, 3 phones.

Surf and Sand Resort ✸✸

Perhaps the most beloved hotel on the Orange Coast, the nine-story Surf and Sand Resort has come a long way since it started in 1948 as a beachside motor lodge with 13 units. Still occupying the same fantastic oceanside location, it now features 152 guest rooms that, despite their simplicity and standard size, feel enormously decadent. They're all very bright and beachy; each has a private balcony with a dreamy ocean view, a marble bathroom accented handsomely with granite, and plush cotton terry robes. *Tip:* Try getting one of the deluxe corner rooms, affording an expanded 90-degree view of the California coastline—it's well worth the additional dollars. Also, be sure to check their website for special package deals. Opened in early 2002, the hotel's Mediterranean-style **Aquaterra Spa** offers a tantalizing array of personalized massage, skin-care, and body treatments. You'll find the requisite ocean-inspired treatments, but personal choice is the rule here: The menu features eight different specialty massages, each with your choice of four aromatherapy oils. The spa's four Couples Rituals offer themed body treatments followed by a bubble bath for two (the tub has an ocean view) and a massage to finish. **Splashes** restaurant serves breakfast, lunch, and dinner daily in a beautiful oceanfront setting; the rich Mediterranean cuisine is perfect against a backdrop of sunlight and crashing waves.

1555 S. Coast Hwy. (south of Laguna Canyon Rd.), Laguna Beach, CA 92651. (C) **888/869-7569** or 949/497-4477. Fax 949/494-2897. www.surfandsandresort.com. 152 units, 13 suites. Jan 3–Mar 28 $290–$485 double, $475–$780 suite; Mar 29–June 27 $295–$375 double, $395–$1,085 suite; June 28–Oct 5 $385–$485 double, $475–$1,125 suite; Oct 6–Jan 2 $285–$465 double, $425–$725 suite. AE, DC, DISC, MC, V. **Amenities:** Restaurant; bar; outdoor heated pool; fitness room; full-service spa; whirlpool; summer children's programs; concierge; business center; room service (6:30am–10pm); in-room massage; babysitting; laundry service; dry cleaning; concierge-level rooms. *In room:* TV w/pay movies, minibar, hair dryer, iron, safe, robes, video games, CD player.

MODERATE

Blue Lantern Inn 🏅🏅   A three-story New England–style gray clapboard inn, the Blue Lantern is a pleasant cross between romantic B&B and modern, sophisticated small hotel. Almost all the rooms, which are decorated with reproduction traditional furniture and plush bedding, have a balcony or deck overlooking the harbor. All have a fireplace and whirlpool tub. You can have your breakfast here in private (clad in the fluffy robe provided), or go downstairs to the sunny dining room that also serves complimentary afternoon tea. There's also an exercise room and a cozy lounge with menus for many area restaurants. The friendly staff welcomes you with home-baked cookies at the front desk.

34343 St. of the Blue Lantern, Dana Point, CA 92629. (C) **800/950-1236** or 949/661-1304. Fax 949/496-1483. www. bluelanterninn.com. 29 units. $175–$500 double. Rates include full breakfast and afternoon wine and hors d'oeuvres. AE, DC, MC, V. **Amenities:** Exercise room; whirlpool; complimentary bikes; laundry service; dry cleaning. *In room:* A/C, TV/VCR, minibar, coffeemaker, hair dryer.

Casa Laguna Inn & Spa 🏅   Once you see this romantic terraced complex of Spanish-style cottages amid lush gardens and secluded patios—which offers all the amenities of a B&B *and* affordable prices—you might wonder, what's the catch? Well, the noise of busy PCH wafts easily into Casa Laguna, which might prove disturbing to sensitive ears and light sleepers. Still, the Casa has been a favorite hideaway since Laguna's early days and now glows under the watchful eye of a terrific owner, who has upped the comfort ante by adding a spa. Some rooms—especially the suites—are downright luxurious, with fireplace, kitchen, bathrobes, CD player, VCR, and other in-room goodies. Throughout the property, Catalina tile adorns fountains, and bougainvillea spills into paths; each room has an individual charm. Breakfast is served in the sunny morning room of the Craftsman-style Mission House, where a cozy living room also invites relaxation and conversation.

2510 S. Coast Hwy., Laguna Beach, CA 92651. (C) **800/233-0449** or 949/494-2996. Fax 949/494-5009. www.casa laguna.com. 21 units. $150–$330 double; from $260 suite. Rates include breakfast, afternoon wine, and hors d'oeuvres. Off-season and midweek discounts available. AE, DISC, MC, V. **Amenities:** Heated outdoor pool; spa; whirlpool. *In room:* TV.

WHERE TO DINE

Options in Seal Beach are limited, but a good choice for seafood is **Walt's Wharf,** 201 Main St. ((C) **562/598-4433**), a bustling, polished restaurant featuring market-fresh selections either plain or with Pacific Rim accents.

EXPENSIVE

Five Feet 🏅🏅 CALIFORNIA/ASIAN   While Five Feet may no longer break culinary ground, the kitchen still combines the best in California cuisine with Asian

Tips **The Ramos House Café**

If you're anywhere near San Juan Capistrano you *have* to stop for breakfast or lunch at the Ramos House Cafe, a petite restaurant within an adorable little old house in the historic Los Rios district of San Juan Capistrano. Chef John Humphreys' swoon-inducing menu changes daily and everything—from his roast turkey hash scramble with apple cider gravy to his corn & buttermilk crab cakes and Southern fried chicken salad—is made from scratch (even the ice cream is turned by hand). And if that's not the best Soju bloody mary you'll ever have, send me a better recipe. The cafe is located at 31752 Los Rios St.—the oldest remaining residential street in California—near the train depot and is open for breakfast and lunch Tuesday through Sunday from 8:30am to 3pm (© **949/ 443-1342;** www.ramoshouse.com).

technique and ingredients. The restaurant has a minimalist, almost-industrial decor that's brightened by a friendly staff and splendid cuisine. Menu selections run the gamut from tea-smoked filet mignon topped with Roquefort cheese and candied walnuts to a hot Thai-style mixed grill of veal, beef, lamb, and chicken stir-fried with sweet peppers, onions, and mushrooms in curry-mint sauce. The menu changes daily, but you can always find the house specialty, whole braised catfish.

328 Glenneyre St., Laguna Beach. © 949/497-4955. www.fivefeetrestaurants.com. Reservations recommended. Main courses $18–$49. AE, DC, DISC, MC, V. Sun–Thurs 5–10pm; Fri–Sat 5–11pm.

Roy's of Newport Beach ✿✿ HAWAIIAN REGIONAL/PACIFIC RIM Any foodie who's been to Hawaii in the past decade knows the name Roy Yamaguchi, father of Hawaiian Regional Cuisine (HRC) and the islands' answer to Wolfgang Puck. Roy's empire expanded to Southern California in 1999 with the opening of this dinner-only restaurant on the fringe of Fashion Island shopping center. Yamaguchi developed a menu that represents his groundbreaking East/West/Polynesian cuisine but can be reliably executed by chefs in far-flung kitchens. Most of each night's specials are fresh Pacific fish, given the patented HRC touch with Japanese, Thai, and even Latin accents. Signature dishes include island-style *ahi poke,* spicy Mongolian-glazed rack of lamb, and blackened yellowfin tuna in soy-mustard-butter sauce. The bar whips up "vacation" cocktails in tropical colors, and there's a to-die-for chocolate soufflé dessert.

453 Newport Center Dr., Fashion Island. © 949/640-7697. www.roysrestaurant.com. Reservations suggested. Main courses $18–$32. AE, DC, DISC, MC, V. Sun–Thurs 5–10pm; Fri–Sat 5–11pm.

MODERATE

Crab Cooker SEAFOOD Since 1951, folks in search of fresh, well-prepared seafood have headed to this bright-red former bank building. Also a fish market, the Crab Cooker has a casual atmosphere of humble wooden tables, uncomplicated smoked and grilled preparations, and meticulously selected fresh fare. The place is especially proud of its Maryland crab cakes; clams and oysters are also part of the repertoire.

2200 Newport Blvd., Newport Beach. © 949/673-0100. www.crabcooker.com. Main courses dinner $10–$25, lunch $8–$19. AE, MC, V. Sun–Thurs 11am–9pm; Fri–Sat 11am–10pm.

Harbor Grill SEAFOOD/STEAK   Located in a business/commercial mall right in the center of the Dana Point Marina, the Harbor Grill is enthusiastically recommended by locals for mesquite-broiled ocean-fresh seafood. Hawaiian mahimahi with a mango-chutney baste is on the menu, along with Pacific swordfish, crab cakes, and beefsteaks.

34499 St. of the Golden Lantern, Dana Point. ℂ **949/240-1416.** www.harborgrill.com. Reservations recommended. Main courses $10–$27. AE, DC, DISC, MC, V. Daily 11:30am–10pm; Sun brunch 9am–2pm.

Las Brisas *Moments* MEXICAN/SEAFOOD   Las Brisas's breathtaking view of the Pacific (particularly at sunset) and potent margaritas are a surefire combination for a *muy romantico* evening. In fact, it's so popular that it can get pretty crowded during the summer months, so be sure to make a reservation. Affordable during lunch but pricey at dinner, the menu consists mostly of seafood recipes from the Mexican Riviera. Even the standard enchiladas and tacos get a zesty update with crab or lobster meat and fresh herbs. Calamari steak is sautéed with bell peppers, capers, and herbs in a garlic-butter sauce, and king salmon is mesquite-broiled and served with a creamy lime sauce. Although a bit on the touristy side, Las Brisas can be a fun part of the Laguna Beach experience.

361 Cliff Dr. (off the PCH north of Laguna Canyon), Laguna Beach. ℂ **949/497-5434.** www.lasbrisaslagunabeach. Reservations recommended. Main courses $10–$27. AE, DC, DISC, MC, V. Mon–Thurs 8am–10pm; Fri–Sat 8am–11pm; Sun 9am–10pm. Valet parking $4 lunch, $5 dinner.

3 Santa Catalina Island

22 miles W of mainland Los Angeles

After an unhealthy dose of the mainland's soupy smog and freeway gridlock, you'll appreciate an excursion to Santa Catalina Island, with its clean air, crystal-clear water, and the blissful absence of traffic. In fact, there isn't a single traffic light on "the Island of Romance." Conditions like these can fool you into thinking that you're miles away from the hustle and bustle of the city, but the reality is that you're only 22 miles off the Southern California coast and *still* in L.A. County.

Because of its relative isolation, out-of-state tourists tend to ignore Santa Catalina—which everyone calls simply Catalina—but those who do make the crossing have plenty of elbowroom to boat, fish, swim, scuba, and snorkel. There are also miles of hiking and biking trails, plus golf, tennis, and horseback riding, but the main sport here seems to be barhopping.

Catalina is so different from the mainland that it almost seems like a different country, remote and unspoiled. In 1919, the island was purchased by William Wrigley, Jr., the chewing-gum magnate, who had plans to develop it into a fashionable pleasure resort. To publicize the new vacationland, Wrigley brought big-name bands to the Avalon Ballroom and moved the Chicago Cubs, which he owned, to the island for spring training. His marketing efforts succeeded and Catalina soon became a world-renowned playground, luring such celebrities as Laurel and Hardy, Cecil B. DeMille, John Wayne, and even Winston Churchill.

In 1975, the Santa Catalina Island Conservancy—a nonprofit operating foundation organized to preserve and protect the island's nature habitat—acquired about 88% of Catalina Island, protecting virtually all of the hilly acreage and rugged coastline that make up what is known as the interior. In fact, some of the most spectacular outlying areas can only be reached by arranged tour (see "Exploring the Island," below).

Fun Fact **Cart Culture**

One of the first things you'll notice when you arrive in Avalon, the only city on the island, is the abundance of golf carts in a comical array of styles and colors. Since Avalon is the only city in California authorized by the state legislature to regulate the number of vehicles allowed to drive on city streets, there are no rental cars and only a handful of privately owned vehicles.

ESSENTIALS

GETTING THERE   The most common way to get to and from the island is on the **Catalina Express** ferryboat (*©* **800/481-3470;** www.catalinaexpress.com), which operates up to 30 daily departures year-round from Long Beach, San Pedro, and Dana Point. High-speed catamarans make the trip in about an hour. Captain's and Commodore Lunge upgrades are available. Round-trip fares are $60 for adults, $54 for seniors 55 and over, $47 for children ages 2 to 11, and $4 for infants. Fares for Dana Point are $2 more, except for infants. In San Pedro, the Catalina Express departs from the **Sea/Air Terminal,** Berth 95; take the Harbor Freeway (I-110) south to the Harbor Boulevard exit, and then follow signs to the terminal. In Long Beach, boats leave from the **Catalina Landing;** take the 710 Freeway south into Long Beach. Stay to the left, follow signs to downtown, and exit Golden Shore. Turn right at the stop sign and follow around to the terminal on the right. Parking is in the parking structure on the left. In Dana Point, boats depart from Dana Wharf Sportfishing. From San Diego, take I-5 North and exit at Beach Cities Hwy. 1, left at Dana Point Harbor Drive, then left at Golden Lantern. Call ahead for reservations. *Note:* Check-in at the ticket window is required and begins 1 hour prior to each departure. Passengers must be checked in, holding tickets, and ready to board 15 minutes prior to departure, or the reservation will be canceled and the credit card will be charged for the full amount of the round-trip fare. Luggage is limited to 70 pounds per person; reservations are necessary for bicycles, surfboards, and dive tanks; and there are restrictions on transporting pets. You can leave your car at designated lots at each departure terminal; the parking fee is around $10 per 24-hour period.

The **Catalina Flyer,** 400 Main St., Balboa (*©* **949/673-5245;** www.catalinainfo. com), the largest passenger-carrying catamaran on the West Coast, departs daily from Newport Beach's historic Balboa Pavilion. The boat leaves once a day at 9am and returns to Newport at 4:30pm daily. Travel time is about 75 minutes each way. Round-trip fares are $61 for adults, $56 for seniors, $46 for children 3 to 12, and $4 for infants. Pets are not allowed.

Island Express Helicopter Service, 1175 Queens Way Dr., Long Beach (*©* **800/ 2-AVALON** [800/228-2566] or 310/510-2525; www.islandexpress.com), flies from Long Beach or San Pedro to Avalon in about 15 minutes. The expense is definitely worth the thrill and convenience, particularly if you're prone to seasickness. It flies on demand between 8am and sunset year-round, charging $84 plus tax each way, or $162 round-trip. The weight limit for luggage, however, is a mere 25 pounds. It also offers brief air tours over the island; prices vary. In Long Beach, the heliport is located a few hundred yards southwest of the *Queen Mary.*

Catalina Marina del Rey Flyer, 13737 Fiji Way, Ste. C, Marina del Rey, CA 90292 (*©* **310/305-7250;** www.catalinaferries.com), departs from Fisherman's Village at

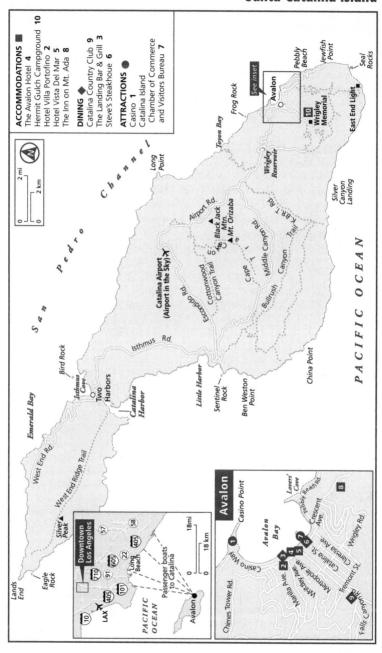

Santa Catalina Island

ACCOMMODATIONS ■
The Avalon Hotel **4**
Hermit Gulch Campground **10**
Hotel Villa Portofino **2**
Hotel Vista Del Mar **5**
The Inn on Mt. Ada **8**

DINING ◆
Catalina Country Club **9**
The Landing Bar & Grill **3**
Steve's Steakhoue **6**

ATTRACTIONS ●
Casino **1**
Catalina Island
Chamber of Commerce
and Visitors Bureau **7**

Pebbly Beach
Jewfish Point
Seal Rocks
East End Light
Wrigley Memorial
Avalon
See inset
Silver Canyon Landing
Toyon Bay
Frog Rock
Wrigley Reservoir

PACIFIC OCEAN

San Pedro Channel

Long Point
Bird Rock
Isthmus Cove
Two Harbors
Catalina Harbor
Emerald Bay
West End Rd.
West End Ridge Trail
Lands End
Eagle Rock
Silver Peak

Airport Rd.
Black Jack Mtn.
Mt. Orizaba
Catalina Airport (Airport in the Sky)
Cottonwood Canyon Trail
Escondido Rd.
Cape Canyon Trail
Middle Canyon Rd.
Bullrush Canyon
K-Brr Rd.
Isthmus Rd.
Little Harbor
Sentinel Rock
Ben Weston Point
China Point

0 2 mi
0 2 km

Avalon

Casino Point
Lovers' Cove
Pebbly Beach Rd.
Avalon Bay
Crescent Ave.
Wrigley Rd.
Clarissa Ave.
Catalina St.
Metropole Ave.
Whittley Ave.
Marilla Ave.
Tremont St.
Chimes Tower Rd.
Falls Canyon
Casino Way

1
2 3 4
5 6 7
8
9

Downtown Los Angeles

57
58
405
605
22
91
710
405
101
10
LAX
405
101

Long Beach
Passenger boats to Catalina
Avalon

0 18 mi
0 18 km

PACIFIC OCEAN

Marina del Rey. Schedule varies. Travel time to Avalon is 1¾ hours. Round-trip fare is $62 for adults, $64 for seniors, $53 for children 2 to 11 years old, $6 for infants.

VISITOR INFORMATION   The **Catalina Island Chamber of Commerce and Visitors Bureau,** P.O. Box 217, Avalon, CA 90704 (© **310/510-1520;** fax 310/510-7606; www.catalinachamber.com), located on the Green Pleasure Pier, distributes brochures and information on island activities, hotels, and transportation. Call for a free 75-page visitors' guide. Its colorful website, **www.catalinachamber.com**, offers hotel availability and local weather, in addition to updated activities, events, and general information.

ORIENTATION   The picturesque town of **Avalon** is both the port of entry for the island and the island's only city. From the ferry dock, you can wander along Crescent Avenue, the main road along the beachfront, and easily explore adjacent side streets.

Northwest of Avalon is the village of **Two Harbors,** accessible by boat or shuttle bus. Its twin bays are favored by pleasure yachts from L.A.'s various marinas, so there's more camaraderie and a less touristy ambience overall.

GETTING AROUND   Once in Avalon, take a taxi from the **Catalina Cab Company** (© **310/510-0025**) from the heliport or dock to your hotel, and enjoy the quick and colorful trip through town (don't blink or you'll miss it). Only a limited number of cars are permitted on the island; visitors are not allowed to drive cars on the island, and most residents motor around in golf carts (many of the homes only have golf cart–size driveways). Don't worry, though—you'll be able to get everywhere you want to go by renting a cart yourself or just hoofing it, which is what most visitors do.

If you want to explore the area around Avalon beyond where your feet can comfortably carry you, rent a mountain bike or tandem from **Brown's Bikes,** 107 Pebbly Beach Rd. (© **310/510-0986**). If you'll be exploring, you'll want to rent a gas-powered golf cart from **Cartopia Golf Cart Rentals** on Crescent Avenue at Pebbly Beach Road (© **310/510-2493**), or **Island Rentals** (© **310/510-1456**), across from the boat terminal. Both companies offer a map of town for a self-guided tour. Rates are about $45 per hour plus a deposit. You must be 25 or older to drive.

EXPLORING THE ISLAND

ORGANIZED TOURS   The Santa Catalina Island Company's **Discovery Tours** (© **800/626-1496** or 310/510-TOUR [310/510-8687]; www.visitcatalinaisland.com) has a ticket and information office on Crescent Avenue across from the Green Pier. It offers the greatest variety of excursions from Avalon; many last just a couple of hours and don't monopolize your whole day. Tours are available in money-saving combo packs; inquire when you call.

Noteworthy excursions include the new **Cape Canyon,** which takes you into the heart of Catalina's "outback" in an open-air four-wheel-drive Mercedes Benz Unimog Vehicle. The tour's rugged route includes the American Bald Eagle and Catalina Island Fox habitats at Middle Ranch, lunch at Airport-in-the-Sky, and plenty of photo stops ($99 per adults, $89 for seniors and children over the age of 6 years, includes lunch). You can also try the **Undersea Tour,** a leisurely 45-minute cruise of Lover's Cove Marine Preserve in a semi-submersible vessel that allows you to sit 5 feet under the water in a climate-controlled cabin where you comfortably observe Catalina's kelp forests by day or night ($36 adults, $18 kids, $32 seniors). The **Casino Tour** is a fascinating 1-hour look at the style and inventive engineering of this elegant ballroom (see "Catalina's Grand Casino" box, below; $16 adults, $15 seniors, $8 kids). The

Catalina's Grand Casino

No trip to Catalina is complete without taking the **Casino Tour** (see "Organized Tours," above). The Casino Building, Avalon's world-famous Art Deco landmark, is not—and never was—a place to gamble your vacation money away (*casino* is an Italian word for a place of entertainment or gathering). Rather, the incredibly ornate structure (the craftsmanship inside and out is spectacular) is home to the island's only movie theater and the world's largest circular ballroom. Virtually every big band of the '30s and '40s played in the 158-foot-diameter ballroom, carried over CBS radio beginning with its grand opening in May 1929. Today it's a coveted venue for elaborate weddings, dances, gala dinners, and the Catalina Jazz Festival. The 3-week **JazzTrax Festival** (© 866/872-9849; www.jazztrax.com) takes place every October. To experience the festival, be sure to book your tickets and accommodations as far in advance as possible.

nighttime **Flying Fish Boat Trips (seasonal)** are a 50-minute Catalina tradition in searchlight-equipped open boats ($20 adults, $18 seniors, $10 kids). And the new **Classic Inland Motor Tour** is a 31-mile, 4-hour jaunt through the island's rugged interior. The journey follows the 1800s stagecoach trail though Middle Ranch, where you will enjoy the Native Plant Nursery and the Catalina Island Fox habitat. Continue on to the beautiful windward shoreline and up to **El Rancho Escondido,** a working ranch where some of America's finest Arabian horses are raised and trained. Returning to Avalon, you'll visit the famous Airport-in-the-Sky ($69 adults, $62 seniors, $35 kids).

VISITING TWO HARBORS   If you want to get a better look at the rugged natural beauty of Catalina and escape the throngs of beachgoers, head over to Two Harbors, the quarter-mile "neck" at the island's northwest end that gets its name from the "twin harbors" on each side, known as the Isthmus and Catalina Harbor. An excellent starting point for campers and hikers, Two Harbors also offers just enough civilization for the less-intrepid traveler.

The **Banning House Lodge** (© 800/626-1496; www.VisitTwoHarbors.com) is an 11-room bed-and-breakfast overlooking the Isthmus. The clapboard house was built in 1910 for Catalina's pre-Wrigley owners and has seen duty as on-location lodging for movie stars like Errol Flynn and Dorothy Lamour. Peaceful and isolated, the simply furnished but comfortable lodge has spectacular views of both harbors. Rates range from $199 to $299 including deluxe continental breakfast (June–Sept), and they'll even give you a lift from the pier.

Everyone eats at the **Harbor Reef Restaurant** (© 310/510-4215) on the beach. This nautical, tropical-themed saloon/restaurant serves breakfast, lunch, and dinner, the latter consisting of hearty steaks, ribs, swordfish, chicken teriyaki, and buffalo burgers in summer. The house drink is sweet "buffalo milk," a potent concoction of vodka, crème de cacao, banana liqueur, milk, whipped cream, and nutmeg.

WHAT TO SEE & DO IN AVALON   Walk along horseshoe-shaped Crescent Avenue, past private yachting and fishing clubs, toward the landmark **Casino** building. You can see the Art Deco **theater** for the price of a movie ticket any night. Also

---

Tips **Instant Massaging**

After a full day of island activity, why not pamper yourself with a relaxing professional massage in the privacy and comfort of your hotel room? Make a reservation with **Massage by Michelle** (© 310/510-8920; www.catalinamassageby michelle.com) and she'll tote her table and oils to you. Michelle specializes in sports, deep tissue, Swedish, Thai, Swede-Thai combo, and pregnancy massage. Other treatments include heavenly aromatherapy wraps, sugar glow, body polishing, foot scrubs, peppermint scalp massage, couples massages, and lavender or honey facial massages. Michelle works in 50- to 80-minute increments, offers packages, and caters to groups. If you're just visiting for the day, Michelle offers her own pampering facility for you to visit. Prices range from $75 to $125.

---

on the ground floor is the **Catalina Island Museum** (© 310/510-2414; www.catalina museum.org), which explores 7,000 years of island history including fascinating exhibits of archaeology, steamships, big bands, and natural history. The museum has a contour relief map of the island that's helpful to hikers. Open daily. Admission is $5 for adults, $4 for seniors, and $2 for kids; it's included in the price of Discovery's Casino Tour (see above).

Around the point from the Casino lies **Descanso Beach Club** (© 310/510-7410), a mini–Club Med in a private cove. While you can get on the beach year-round, the club's facilities (including showers, restaurant/bar, sandy beach, volleyball lawns, dance area, and thatched beach umbrellas) are only open from Easter to September 30. Admission is $1.50.

About 1½ miles from downtown Avalon is **Wrigley Memorial and Botanical Garden** (© 310/510-2595). The specialized gardens, a project of Ada Wrigley, showcase plants endemic to California's coastal islands. It's open daily from 8am to 5pm; admission is $5 for adults, free for children 11 and under.

DIVING, SNORKELING & SEA KAYAKING ⚓

Snorkeling, scuba diving, and sea kayaking are among the main reasons mainlanders head to Catalina. Catalina Island's naturally clean water and giant kelp forests teeming with marine life have made it a renowned diving destination that attracts experts and beginning divers alike. **Casino Point Marine Park,** Southern California's first city-designated underwater park, was established in 1965 and is located behind the Casino. Due to its convenient location, it can get outrageously crowded in the summer (just like everything else at that time of year).

Catalina Divers Supply (© 800/353-0330 or 310/510-0330; www.catalinadivers-supply.com) runs two full-service dive shops: one from a large trailer behind the Casino at the edge of Avalon's underwater park, where they offer guided snorkeling tours and introductory scuba dives; and another at the Green Pier, where they launch boat dives aboard the *Scuba Cat.* The three best locations for snorkeling are **Lover's Cove Marine Preserve, Casino Point Marine Park,** and **Descanso Beach Club. Catalina Snorkeling Adventures,** at Lover's Cove (© 877/SNORKEL [877/766-7535]), offers snorkel-gear rental. Snorkeling trips that take you outside of Avalon depart from **Joe's Rent-a-Boat** (© 310/510-0455), on the Green Pier.

At Two Harbors, stop by **West End Dive Center** (© **310/510-4272**). Excursions range from half-day introductory dives to complete certification courses and multiday dive packages. It also rents snorkel gear and offers kayak rental, instruction, and tours.

HIKING & BIKING

When the summer crowds become overwhelming, it's time to head on foot for the peacefulness of the interior, where secluded coves and barren, rolling hills soothe frayed nerves. Visitors can obtain a free **hiking permit** at the Conservancy Office (125 Claressa Ave.; © **310/510-2595;** www.catalinaconservancy.org), where you'll find maps, wildlife information, and friendly assistance from Conservancy staffers who love to share their knowledge of the interior. It's open daily from 9am to 5pm, and closed for lunch on weekends. Among the sights you may see are the many giant buffalo roaming the hills, scions of movie extras that were left behind in 1929 and have since flourished.

Mountain biking is allowed on the island's designated dirt roads, but requires a $20 permit (valid for 2 consecutive days) or a $60-per-person annual permit ($85 per family) that must be purchased in person at the Conservancy Office.

BEACHES

Unfortunately, Avalon's beaches leave much to be desired. The town's central beach, located off Crescent Avenue, is small and completely congested in the busy season. Be sure to claim your spot early in the morning before it's full. **Descanso Beach Club** offers the best beach in town but also gets crowded very quickly. Your best bet is to kayak out to a secluded cove where you have the beach virtually to yourself.

WHERE TO STAY

If you plan to stay overnight, be sure to reserve a room in advance because most places fill up quickly during the summer and holiday seasons. There are only a handful of hotels whose accommodations and amenities actually justify the rates that they charge. Some are downright scary, so book as far in advance as possible to get a room that makes the trip worthwhile. Don't stress too much over your accommodations, as you'll probably spend most of your time outdoors. Keep in mind that the best time to visit is in September or October when the water is warm, the crowds have somewhat subsided, and hotel occupancy is easier to come by. If you're having trouble finding a vacancy, try calling the Catalina Chamber of Commerce & Visitors Bureau (© **310/510-1520**); they keep daily tabs on last-minute cancellations.

VERY EXPENSIVE

The Inn on Mt. Ada ✦✦   When William Wrigley, Jr., purchased Catalina Island in 1921, he built this ornate hilltop Georgian Colonial mansion as his summer vacation home; it's now one of the finest small hotels in California. The opulent inn—considered to be the best in town for its luxury accommodations and views—has several ground-floor salons, a club room with a fireplace, a formal library, and a sunroom where tea, cookies, and fruit are always available. The best guest room is the Grand Suite, fitted with a fireplace and a large private patio. Amenities include bathrobes and the use of a golf cart during your stay. TVs are in the rooms, but there are no phones. A hearty full breakfast, a light deli-style lunch, appetizers, fresh fruit, freshly baked cookies, soft drinks, beers, wines, and champagne are included in the rate. *Tip:* Even if you find that they're sold out or too pricey to fit your budget, make a lunch reservation and enjoy amazing views from the Inn's spectacular balcony.

398 Wrigley Rd. (P.O. Box 2560), Avalon, CA 90704. 𝒞 **800/608-7669** or 310/510-2030. Fax 310/510-2237. www. innonmtada.com. 6 units. Nov–April Mon–Thurs $350–$520 double, $605 suite; Fri–Sun $390–$605 double, $730 suite. May–Oct $390–$605 double; $730 suite. Rates include 2 meals daily. AE, MC, V. **Amenities:** Courtesy car; complimentary golf cart. *In room:* TV, hair dryer, iron, no phone.

EXPENSIVE

The Avalon Hotel   Catalina's newest boutique hotel is all about the details. The lot was originally developed at the turn of the last century as the Pilgrim Club, a gentleman's club that vanished in the great fire of 1915. After many incarnations, the dilapidated property was acquired in 2003 by locals Rock and Kathleen Gosselin and partner Carl Lambert, who have transformed it into one of the island's most luxurious hideaways. The cozy Craftsman-style hotel is decked out in rich, hand-carved mahogany and imported slate tastefully accented with handmade tile and local artwork. Catalina's silhouette is artfully etched into the slate, stained glass, and light fixtures, while shadow boxes showcase island memorabilia throughout the hotel's homey public space. Guest rooms, which come in a variety of sizes, feature garden or ocean views (some with balconies), gleaming white bathrooms with natural skin-care products, and an incredibly comfy queen- or king-size Supple-Pedic memory foam bed.

124 Whittley Ave. (P.O. Box 706), Avalon, CA 90704. 𝒞 **310/510-7070.** www.theavalonhotel.com. 15 units. Mid-Nov to mid-Mar $195–$395 double; mid-June to mid-Sept $295–$495 double. Rates include continental breakfast, complimentary taxi pickup from the boat or helicopter, nightly turndown, wine and cheese service. AE, MC, V. **Amenities:** Rooftop deck w/360-degree views; beautifully furnished garden patio w/fountain; laptops and DVDs to borrow at front desk. *In room:* Flatscreen TV w/DVD, high-speed Internet, fridge w/refreshments, coffeemaker, microwave, hair dryer, nature-based bath products, Supple-Pedic memory foam mattresses, fresh flowers, local artwork.

MODERATE

Hotel Villa Portofino ⚔   Enjoy European elegance on the oceanfront from your courtyard room or deluxe suite after a warm welcome from the hotel's efficient and friendly staff. The hotel boasts recently renovated rooms and a spacious rooftop deck overlooking the bay that is perfect for people-watching, sunbathing, cocktail sipping, or just enjoying the fantastic view. Some rooms have luxurious touches like fireplaces, balconies, deep soaking tubs, and separate showers. The hotel is just steps away from the beach, shops, and sights.

111 Crescent Ave. (P.O. Box 127), Avalon, CA 90704. 𝒞 **888/510-0555** or 310/510-0555. Fax 310/510-0839. www. hotelvillaportofino.com. 35 units. May–Oct $187–$249 double, from $335 suite; winter $95–$160 double, from $235 suite. Rates include continental breakfast, beach towels, and chairs. AE, DC, MC, V. **Amenities:** Award-winning restaurant; adjacent art gallery. *In room:* A/C, TV, fridge, coffeemaker, hair dryer, iron.

Hotel Vista Del Mar   The hotel's location smack-dab in the middle of town, lush, open-aired atrium garden courtyard, gigantic fish tank, freshly baked cookies and milk each evening, and friendly staff make it an island favorite for families and couples alike. The oceanview suites with double-Jacuzzi tubs are fantastic but hard to secure, as the only two are booked by regulars almost year-round.

417 Crescent Ave. (P.O. Box 1979), Avalon, CA 90704. 𝒞 **310/510-1452.** www.hotel-vistadelmar.com. 15 units. May–Oct $125–$350 double; Nov–Apr $105–$300 double. Winter discounts and midweek rates available. Rates include continental breakfast, and freshly baked cookies and milk in the evening. AE, DISC, MC, V. **Amenities:** Garden atrium courtyard w/sitting area and balcony w/huge fish tank and views of the harbor; baggage storage facility; free Wi-Fi. *In room:* A/C, cable TV w/VCR, wet bar w/fridge, coffeemaker, Jacuzzi, fireplace.

INEXPENSIVE

Our recommended choices for inexpensive lodgings are **Pavilion Lodge** (𝒞 **800/414-2754** or 310/510-2500; www.visitcatalinaisland.com), which recently completed an

---

Tips For Travelers Who Use Wheelchairs

Visitors who use wheelchairs should request a room at **Hotel Metropole** (© **800/300-8528** or 310/510-1884). One of the most modern properties in Avalon, it has an elevator, a large sun deck that overlooks Avalon Bay, a shopping complex, and a very convenient location in the heart of Avalon.

---

extensive renovation on all guest rooms, which are basic but affordable and clean (a great alternative when budgets and availability are tight); **Hotel Catalina** (© **800/ 540-0184** or 310/510-0027; www.hotelcatalina.com), a well-maintained Victorian-style hotel just a half-block from the beach, with tons of charm, family cottages, a courtyard with beautiful stained glass, and large verandas with bay views; **Zane Grey** (© **310/510-0966;** www.zanegreypueblohotel.com), a Hopi-style pueblo built in 1926 and former home of American author Zane Grey, situated above town and equipped with a cozy living room with fireplace and piano, free shuttle service, and a swimming pool; and **Hermit Gulch Campground** (© **310/510-8368;** www.visit catalinaisland.com), Avalon's only campground, which can be crowded and noisy in peak season. Campsites can be tough to secure, especially when hotels are booked, so it's a good idea to make reservations in advance. The walk to town and back can be draining, so hop on the red trolley that runs you back and forth to town for a couple dollars each way.

WHERE TO DINE

Along with the choices below, recommended Avalon options include the **Busy Bee** on Crescent Avenue (© **310/510-1983**), an always-crowded waterfront diner with a heated and wind-protected patio. On the Two Harbors side of the island, the **Harbor Reef Restaurant** is the place to eat; see "Exploring the Island," above.

EXPENSIVE

Catalina Country Club ⓕ CALIFORNIA   You'll find some of Avalon's most elegant meals at this landmark Catalina Country Club, whose stylish Spanish-Mediterranean clubhouse was built by William Wrigley, Jr., during the 1920s. Recently restored, it exudes a chic and historical atmosphere; the menu is peppered with archival photos and vintage celebrity anecdotes. Sit outdoors in an elegant tiled Fountain Terrace courtyard, or inside the intimate, exquisite dining room. The executive chef infuses new American cuisine with creative influences from around the world, using only the finest free-range, organic meats, fresh produce, and seafood from environmentally sensitive fisheries. The Club is only a few minutes from the waterfront but uphill, so shuttle service is available from Island Plaza (on Sumner Ave.) on weekends.

1 Country Club Dr. (above Sumner Ave.). © **310/510-7404.** Reservations recommended. Main courses $9–$18 lunch, $26–$35 dinner. AE, DISC, MC, V. Daily 11:30am–2:30pm and 5–9pm. (Closing hours vary seasonally.)

MODERATE

The Landing Bar and Grill AMERICAN   With a secluded heated deck overlooking the harbor, the Landing is one of the most romantic dining spots in Avalon. It boasts beautiful Spanish-style architecture located in the historic El Encanto Center that manages to attract as many jeans-clad vacationers as dressed-up islanders. The menu is enticing, with local seafood offerings, pasta, Mexican cuisine, and gourmet pizzas that can be delivered to your hotel room if you wish.

Intersection of Crescent and Marilla aves. ✆ 310/510-1474. Reservations recommended. Main courses $11–$22. AE, DISC, MC, V. Daily 11am–3pm and 4–10pm (subject to changes in winter).

Steve's Steakhouse AMERICAN   Step up above the busy bayside promenade into a fantastic collage of museum-quality photos capturing the Avalon of old. This setting overlooking Avalon Bay feels just right for the hearty menu of steaks, seafood, and pasta—all of which can be ordered at the full bar as well as in the dining room. Catalina swordfish is their specialty, along with excellent cuts of meat. You can also make a respectable repast from the many appetizer selections, especially the fresh oysters and sashimi.

417 Crescent Ave. (directly across from the Green Pier, upstairs). ✆ 310/510-0333. Reservations recommended on weekends. Main courses $7–$15 lunch, $15–$32 dinner. AE, DISC, MC, V. Daily 11am–3pm and 5–10pm.

INEXPENSIVE

Note: Street addresses are useless in a town as small as Avalon, but all these restaurants are near each other on the main strip. My three favorites for a low-bucks meal are **Rosie's Fish and Chips** (✆ 310/510-0197), on the Green Pier, which serves fresh seafood favorites like fish and chips and seafood cocktails; **Casino Dock Café** (✆ 310/ 510-2755), with live summertime entertainment, marina views from the sun-drenched deck, breakfast burritos loaded with homemade salsa, and kicking bloody marys; and **Lori's Good Stuff** (✆ 310/510-2489), a tiny spot with fresh, healthy sandwiches, smoothies, and milkshakes—the best around.

BARHOPPING

Note: Avalon doesn't have listed street addresses, but all these bars are within stumbling distance of each other on the main drag. The **Chi Chi Club** (✆ 310/510-2828), the "noisy bar in Avalon" referred to in Crosby, Stills, and Nash's song "Southern Cross," is the island's only dance club and quite a scene on summer weekend evenings—the DJ spins an eclectic mix of dance tunes. **Luau Larry's** (✆ 310/510-1919) is Avalon's signature bar that everyone must visit; its tacky Tiki theme and signature Wicky Wack drink kicks you into island mode as soon as you step inside—sure to stumble out. Or go where the locals go and swill beers at the **Marlin Club** (✆ 310/510-0044), Avalon's oldest drinking hole; catch the Dodgers game at **J. L.'s Locker Room** (✆ 310/510-0258); and recover from your hangover with a spicy bloody mary at the rustic bar inside the **Busy Bee** (✆ 310/510-1983).

SHOPPING

Don't worry—you won't have any trouble finding that must-have Catalina key chain or refrigerator magnet, as Crescent Avenue is lined with a myriad of schlocky souvenir shops. There are, however, a few stores that do offer unique and tasteful items. **C. C. Gallagher** (✆ 310/510-1278) carries high-end gifts and also is a flower and coffee shop; they're best for finding beautiful art, music, and jewelry created by local artists. For colorful handmade pottery, stop by **Chet's Hardware** (✆ 310/510-0990), in the Arcade—an arched shopping annex that connects Sumner and Metropole avenues. **Latitude 33** (✆ 310/510-0802) is the place to get your vintage aloha shirts, shorts, hats, and sandals. **Buoys and Gulls** (✆ 310/510-0416) offers men's and women's wear such as Reyn Spooner islander shirts, Nautica, Hurley, and Billabong. The **Steamer Trunk** (✆ 310/510-2600) is loaded with unique gifts to take home to the dog sitter or neighbor who collected your mail. **Leo's Drugstore** (© **310/510-0189**) is the obvious spot to pick up the sunscreen that you forgot to pack. **Von's,** located on Metropole Avenue in the center of town, and Von's Express on Catalina Avenue, are Avalon's main grocery stores where you'll find all your food staples.

4 Santa Barbara ★★

92 miles NW of Los Angeles

Situated between palm-lined Pacific beaches and the sloping foothills of the Santa Ynez Mountains, this prosperous resort community presents a mosaic of whitewashed stucco and red-tile roofs and a gracious, relaxed attitude that has earned it the sobriquet American Riviera. It's ideal for kicking back on gold-sand beaches, prowling the shops and galleries that line the village's historic streets, and relaxing over a meal in one of many top-notch cafes and restaurants.

Downtown Santa Barbara is distinctive for its Spanish-Mediterranean architecture. But it wasn't always this way. Santa Barbara had a thriving Native American Chumash population for hundreds, if not thousands, of years. The European era began in the late 18th century around a Spanish *presidio* (fort) that's been reconstructed in its original spot. The earliest architectural hodgepodge was destroyed in 1925 by a powerful earthquake that leveled the business district. Out of the rubble rose the Spanish-Mediterranean town of today, a stylish planned community that continues to enforce strict building codes.

Visit Santa Barbara's waterfront on a Sunday and you're sure to see the weekly **Arts and Crafts Show,** one of the city's best-loved traditions. Since 1965, artists, craftspeople, and street performers have been lining grassy Chase Palm Park, along Cabrillo Boulevard.

ESSENTIALS

GETTING THERE   By car, U.S. 101 runs right through Santa Barbara; it's the fastest and most direct route from north or south (1½ hr. from Los Angeles, 6 hr. from San Francisco).

By train, **Amtrak** (© **800/USA-RAIL** [800/872-7245]; www.amtrak.com) offers daily service to Santa Barbara. Trains arrive and depart from the **Santa Barbara Rail Station,** 209 State St. (© **805/963-1015**). Fares can be as low as $40 (round-trip) from Los Angeles's Union Station.

ORIENTATION   State Street, the city's primary commercial thoroughfare, is the geographic center of town. It ends at Stearns Wharf and Cabrillo Boulevard; the latter runs along the ocean and separates the city's beaches from touristy hotels and restaurants. Electric shuttles provide frequent service along these two routes if you'd rather leave the car behind.

VISITOR INFORMATION   The **Santa Barbara Visitor Information Center,** 1 Garden St. (off Cabrillo Blvd., across from the beach; © **805/966-9222;** www. santabarbaraca.com), distributes maps, brochures, an events calendar, and information. It's open Monday through Friday from 8:30am to 5pm.

Be sure you pick up a copy of the *Santa Barbara Independent,* a free weekly, with articles and events listings; and *Explore Santa Barbara,* a compact visitor's guide published by the local paper, *New-Press.* Both are also available at shops and sidewalk racks throughout town.

SEEING THE SIGHTS
HISTORIC DOWNTOWN

Following a devastating 1925 earthquake, city planners decreed that all new construction would follow codes of Spanish and mission-style architecture. In time, the adobe-textured walls, rounded archways, glazed tile work, and terra-cotta rooftops came to symbolize the Mediterranean ambience that still characterizes Santa Barbara. The architecture also gave a name to the **Red Tile Tour,** a self-guided walking tour of historic downtown. The visitor center (see "Visitor Information," above) has a map/guide of the tour, which can take anywhere from 1 to 3 hours, including time to visit some of the buildings, and covers about 12 blocks in total. Some of the highlights are destinations in their own right.

Santa Barbara County Courthouse ⓖ★   Built in 1929, this grand "palace" is considered the local flagship of Spanish colonial revival architecture. It's certainly the most flamboyant example, with impressive facades, beamed ceilings, striking murals, an 85-foot-high observation clock tower, and formal sunken gardens. Free guided tours are offered on Monday, Tuesday, and Friday at 10:30am, and Monday through Saturday at 2pm.

1100 Anacapa St. ⓒ **805/962-6464.** www.santabarbaracourthouse.org. Free admission. Mon–Fri 8am–5pm; Sat–Sun 10am–4:30pm.

Santa Barbara Museum of Art ⓖ★   This little jewel of a museum feels more like the private gallery of a wealthy collector. Its leaning is toward early-20th-century Western American paintings and 19th- and 20th-century Asian art, but the best displays might be the antiquities and Chinese ceramics. In addition, there are often visiting exhibits featuring small but excellent collections from other establishments.

1130 State St. ⓒ **805/963-4364.** www.sbmuseart.org. Admission $9 adults, $6 seniors 65 and over, $6 students and children ages 6–17, free for children 5 and under; free for everyone every Sun. Tues–Sun 11am–5pm.

ELSEWHERE IN THE CITY

Ganna Walska Lotusland (Finds   This secluded, lavishly landscaped 37-acre estate is renowned for its exotic plants and mysterious garden paths. Named for the estate's vivacious European-born mistress and the romantic, lotus-filled ponds in her gardens, the estate reflects the late Madame Walska's eccentricity and the skill of her prestigious gardeners. She was especially fond of succulents and cacti, interspersing them artistically among native plants and decorative objects. Assembled when money was no object and import regulations were lenient (mostly in the 1940s), the garden contains priceless rare specimens—even prehistoric plants that are extinct in the wild. Montecito is a 5-minute freeway drive south of downtown Santa Barbara. *Note:* Advance reservations are required and are available up to 6 months in advance.

695 Ashley Rd., Montecito. ⓒ **805/969-9990.** www.lotusland.org. Admission $35 adults, $10 children 5–18, free for children 4 and under. 2-hr. guided tours mid-Feb to mid-Nov Wed–Sat 10am and 1:30pm.

Santa Barbara Botanic Garden (Finds   The Botanic Garden is devoted to indigenous California plants. More than 5½ miles of meandering trails on 65 acres offer glimpses of cacti, redwoods, wildflowers, and much more, many arranged in representational habitats or landscapes. The gardens were established in 1926. You'll catch the very best color and aroma just after spring showers.

1212 Mission Canyon Rd. (a short drive uphill from the mission). ⓒ **805/682-4726.** www.sbbg.org. Admission $8 adults, $6 seniors 60 and over and children 13–17, $4 children 2–12, free for children 1 and under. Daily 9am–5pm (until 6pm Mar–Oct).

Santa Barbara

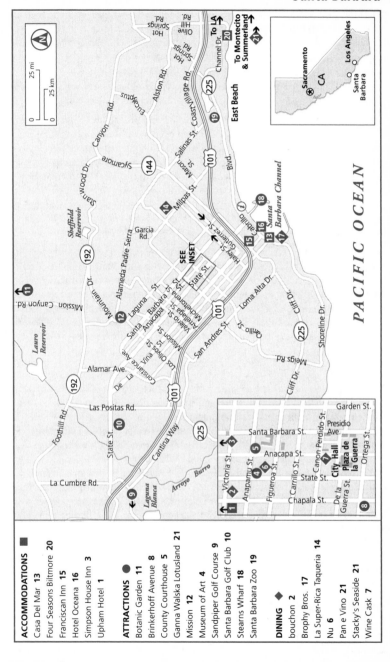

ACCOMMODATIONS ■
Casa Del Mar **13**
Four Seasons Biltmore **20**
Franciscan Inn **15**
Hotel Oceana **16**
Simpson House Inn **3**
Upham Hotel **1**

ATTRACTIONS ●
Botanic Garden **11**
Brinkerhoff Avenue **8**
County Courthouse **5**
Ganna Walska Lotusland **21**
Mission **12**
Museum of Art **4**
Sandpiper Golf Course **9**
Santa Barbara Golf Club **10**
Stearns Wharf **18**
Santa Barbara Zoo **19**

DINING ◆
bouchon **2**
Brophy Bros. **17**
La Super-Rica Taqueria **14**
Nu **6**
Pan e Vino **21**
Stacky's Seaside **21**
Wine Cask **7**

Santa Barbara Mission ⬧ Established in 1786 by Father Junípero Serra and built by the Chumash Indians, this is a rare example in physical form of the blending of Indian and Hispanic spirituality. This hilltop structure is called the Queen of the Missions for its twin bell towers and beauty. It overlooks the town and the Channel Islands beyond. Self-guided tour booklets are available in six languages.

2201 Laguna St. (at Los Olivos St.). ℂ **805/682-4149.** www.sbmission.org. Admission $4 adults, free for children 11 and under. Daily 9am–5pm.

Santa Barbara Zoo ⬧ *(Kids)* When you're driving around the bend on Cabrillo Boulevard, look up—you might spot the head of a giraffe poking through the palms. This zoo is an appealing, pint-size place, where all 700 animals can be seen in about 30 minutes. Most live in natural, open settings. There are also a children's Discovery Area, a miniature train ride, and a small carousel. The picnic areas (with barbecue pits) are underused and are especially recommended.

500 Niños Dr. (off Cabrillo Blvd.). ℂ **805/962-5339** or 805/962-6310 for recorded information. www.santabarbara zoo.org. Admission $11 adults, $8 seniors and children 2–12, free for children 1 and under. Daily 10am–5pm. (Last admission is 1 hr. before closing.) Closed Thanksgiving and Christmas. Parking $4.

Stearns Wharf ⬧ California's oldest working wharf attracts visitors for strolling, shopping, and dining. There's also a Sea Center with aquariums, an outdoor touch-tank, and other exhibits. Although the wharf no longer functions for passenger and freight shipping as it did when built in 1872 by local lumberman John C. Stearns, you might still see local fishing boats unload their daily catch. Consider taking a narrated sunset harbor cruise aboard the *Harbour Queen* at **Captain Don's** (ℂ **805/969-5217**). Public parking is available on the wharf; it's free with merchant validation.

At the end of State St.

BEACHES

East Beach is Santa Barbara's favorite beach, stretching from the Santa Barbara Zoological Gardens to Chase Palm Park and the wharf. Nearer the pier you can enjoy manicured lawns, tall palms, and abundant facilities; to the east are many volleyball courts, plus the Cabrillo Pavilion, a recreational center, bathhouse, and architectural landmark dating from 1925. Picnic areas with barbecue grills, showers, and clean, well-patrolled sands make this beach a good choice for everyone.

On the other side of Santa Barbara Harbor is **Leadbetter Beach,** less sheltered than those to the south and popular with surfers. It's reached by following Cabrillo Boulevard after it turns into Shoreline Drive. This beach is also a great place to watch pleasure boats entering or leaving the harbor. Leadbetter has basic facilities, including restrooms, picnic areas, and a metered parking lot.

Two miles west of Leadbetter is secluded but popular **Arroyo Burro Beach County Park,** also known as Hendry's Beach. This gem has a grassy park beneath the cliffs and a white crescent beach with great waves for surfing and bodysurfing. There are volleyball nets, picnic areas, restrooms, and a free parking lot.

OUTDOOR ACTIVITIES

BIKING & SURREY CYCLING   A relatively flat, palm-lined 2-mile coastal pathway, perfect for biking, runs along the beach. More adventurous riders can pedal through town (where painted bike lanes line many major routes, including one up to the mission). These routes and many more are outlined in the *Santa Barbara County*

Bike Map, a free and comprehensive resource available at the visitor center or by calling **Traffic Solutions** at © 805/963-7283 or logging onto www.trafficsolutions.info.

Wheel Fun Rentals, 101 State St. (just off Cabrillo Blvd.; © **805/966-2282;** www.wheelfunrentals.com), rents well-maintained beach cruisers, mountain bikes, tandem bikes, and an Italian four-wheel surrey that seats three adults; rates vary. It's open daily from 8am to 8pm.

BOATING   The **Santa Barbara Sailing Center,** 133 Harbor Way at the Santa Barbara Harbor (© **800/350-9090** or 805/962-2826; www.sbsail.com), rents sailboats from 21 to 50 feet in length, as well as paddleboats, kayaks, and motorboats. Both skippered and bareboat charters are available by the day or hour. Sailing instruction for all levels of experience is also available. Coastal, island, whale-watching, dinner-cruise, and adventure tours are offered on the 50-foot sailing catamaran *Double Dolphin.* Open daily 9am to 6pm.

GOLF   At the **Santa Barbara Golf Club,** 3500 McCaw Ave., at Las Positas Road (© **805/687-7087**), there's a great 6,009-yard, 18-hole course and a driving range. Unlike many municipal courses, the Santa Barbara Golf Course is well maintained and presents a moderate challenge for the average golfer. Greens fees are $31 Monday through Friday and $41 on weekends. Optional carts rent for $13 for 18 holes, and $10 for 9.

The 18-hole, 7,000-yard **Sandpiper,** at 7925 Hollister Ave. (© **805/968-1541;** www.sandpipergolf.com), is a scenic oceanside course that's rated as one of the top public courses in the U.S. It also has a driving range. Weekday (Mon–Thurs) greens fees are $124, weekends (Fri–Sun) $149, and the cart fee is $16.

HIKING   The foothill trails in the Santa Ynez Mountains above Santa Barbara are perfect for day hikes. In general, they aren't overly strenuous. Trail maps are available at **Pacific Travelers Supply,** 12 W. Anapamu St. (at State St.; © **888/PAC-TRAV** [888/722-8728] or 805/963-4438), at the visitor center (see "Visitor Information," above), and from **Traffic Solutions** (© **805/963-7283**).

One of the most popular hikes is the **Seven Falls/Inspiration Point Trail,** an easy trek that begins on Tunnel Road, past the mission, and skirts the edge of Santa Barbara's Botanic Garden (which contains some pleasant hiking trails itself).

SKATING   The paved beach path that runs along Santa Barbara's waterfront is perfect for rollerblading. **Wheel Fun Rentals,** 101 State St. (just off Cabrillo Blvd.; © **805/966-2282;** www.wheelfunrentals.com), rents skates and all the requisite protective gear. It's open daily from 8am to 8pm.

WHALE-WATCHING   Whale-watching cruises are offered between late December and late March, when Pacific gray whales pass by on migratory journeys from their breeding lagoons in Baja California, Mexico, to their Alaskan feeding grounds. **Shoreline Park,** west of the harbor, has high bluffs ideal for land-based whale-spotting. Sea excursions are offered by both **Captain Don's Harbor Tours** (© **805/969-5217;** www.captdon.com), on Stearns Wharf; and by the **Condor** (© **888/77-WHALE** [888/779-4253] or 805/882-0088; www.condorcruises.com), located at 301 W. Cabrillo Blvd. in the Santa Barbara Harbor.

SHOPPING

State Street from the beach to Victoria Street is the city's main thoroughfare and has the largest concentration of shops. Many specialize in T-shirts and postcards, but there are a number of boutiques as well. If you get tired of strolling, hop on one of the electric shuttle buses (25¢) that run up and down State Street.

Also check out **Brinkerhoff Avenue** (off Cota St., btw. Chapala and De La Vina sts.), Santa Barbara's "antiques alley." Most shops here are open Tuesday through Sunday from 11am to 5pm. **El Paseo** (814 State St.) is a picturesque shopping arcade reminiscent of an old Spanish street. It's built around an 1827 adobe home and is lined with charming shops and art galleries. **Paseo Nuevo,** on the other side of State Street, is a modern outdoor mall, featuring familiar chain stores and cafes, and anchored by a Nordstrom department store.

WHERE TO STAY

Before you even begin calling around for reservations, keep in mind that Santa Barbara's accommodations are expensive—especially in summer. Then decide whether you'd like to stay beachside (even more expensive) or downtown. Santa Barbara is small, but not small enough to happily stroll between the two areas.

The free one-stop reservations service **Hot Spots** (© **800/793-7666** or 805/564-1637; www.hotspotsusa.com) keeps an updated list of availability for about 90% of the area's hotels, motels, inns, and B&Bs. The service will have the latest information on who might be looking to fill last-minute vacancies at reduced rates. Reservationists are available Monday through Saturday from 9am to 9pm, and Sunday from 9am to 4pm. There's no charge for using the service.

VERY EXPENSIVE

Four Seasons Biltmore ✪✪✪   This gem of the American Riviera manages to adhere to the most elegant standards of hospitality without making anyone feel unwelcome. It's easy to sense the ghosts of golden-age Hollywood celebs like Greta Garbo, Errol Flynn, and Bing Crosby, who used to play croquet or practice putting on the hotel's perfectly manicured lawns and then head over to the private Coral Casino Beach & Cabana Club—because that's exactly what today's privileged guests are *still* doing. The Four Seasons company acquired this Spanish-style hacienda (ca. 1927) in 1987 and restored the 20-acre property without spoiling a bit of its historical charm. Rooms have an airy feel, heightened by white plantation shutters, light-wood furnishings, and full marble bathrooms with all the modern amenities. Guests can amuse themselves with a putting green, shuffleboard courts, and croquet lawn. In addition to two acclaimed dining rooms, the Biltmore offers a no-holds-barred Sunday brunch that draws folks from 100 miles away. The hotel's most recent addition is the Spa, a multimillion-dollar, 10,000-square-foot Spanish-style annex that houses numerous treatment rooms, a swimming pool and two huge whirlpool baths, a state-of-the-art fitness center and, for the big spenders, 10 oceanview deluxe suites with fireplaces, in-room bars, changing rooms, and twin massage tables (essentially, your own private treatment room).

1260 Channel Dr. (at the end of Olive Mill Rd.), Santa Barbara, CA 93108. © **800/819-5053** or 805/969-2261. Fax 805/565-8323. www.fourseasons.com/santabarbara. 207 units. $550–$8,000 double; from $1,250 suite. Extra person $55. Children ages 18 and under stay free in parent's room. Special midweek and package rates available. AE, DC, MC, V. Valet parking $29; free self-parking. **Amenities:** Restaurant; 2 lounges; 2 outdoor heated pools; 3 lit tennis courts; health club; salon/spa services; whirlpool; complimentary bikes; 24-hr. room service; laundry service; dry cleaning. *In room:* A/C, TV/DVD w/pay movies, high-speed Internet, minibar, hair dryer, iron, safe, complimentary morning paper, robes.

EXPENSIVE

Simpson House Inn Bed & Breakfast ★★★   The Simpson House is truly something special. Rooms within the 1874 Historic Landmark main house are decorated to Victorian perfection, with extras ranging from a claw-foot tub and antique brass shower to skylight and French doors opening to the manicured gardens. Romantic cottages are also nestled throughout the grounds. The rooms have everything you could possibly need, but most impressive are the extras: the gourmet Mediterranean hors d'oeuvres and Santa Barbara wines served each afternoon, the enormous video library, and the full gourmet breakfast (delivered, for detached cottages, on delicate china). Fact is, the Simpson House goes the distance—and then some—to create the perfect stay. Although this property is packed into a relatively small space, it still manages an ambience of country elegance and exclusivity—especially if you book one of the cottages.

121 E. Arrellaga St. (btw. Santa Barbara and Anacapa sts.), Santa Barbara, CA 93101. ✆ **800/676-1280** or 805/963-7067. Fax 805/564-4811. www.simpsonhouseinn.com. 14 units. $235–$615 double; $595–$605 suite and cottage. 2-night minimum on weekends. Rates include full gourmet breakfast, evening hors d'oeuvres, and wine. AE, DISC, MC, V. **Amenities:** Complimentary bikes; concierge; in-room massage. *In room:* A/C, TV/VCR, minibar, hair dryer, iron, robes.

MODERATE

Casa del Mar Inn at the Beach *Value*   A half-block from the beach (sorry, no views), Casa del Mar is an excellent-value Spanish-architecture motel with one- and two-room suites. The largish rooms have relatively new furnishings, with plenty of pastels. The flower-sprinkled grounds are well maintained, with an attractive sun deck (but no swimming pool), and the staff is eager to please. Many rooms have kitchenettes, and a dozen different room configurations guarantee something to suit your needs (especially families). Guests get discounts at a nearby day spa, and golf packages can be arranged. *Tip:* Despite the hotel's multitude of rates, rooms can often be an unexpected bargain. Also check the website for Internet-only specials.

18 Bath St., Santa Barbara, CA 93101. ✆ **800/433-3097** or 805/963-4418. Fax 805/966-4240. www.casadelmar.com. 21 units. $229–$249 double; from $264 suite. Rates include continental breakfast and wine-and-cheese social. Extra person $10. AE, DC, DISC, MC, V. Free parking. Pets accepted with $10 fee. From northbound U.S. 101, exit at Cabrillo, turn left onto Cabrillo, and head toward the beach; Bath is the 2nd street on the right after the wharf. From southbound U.S. 101, take the Castillo exit and turn right on Castillo, left on Cabrillo, and left on Bath. **Amenities:** Jacuzzi; in-room massage; laundry service; dry cleaning. *In room:* TV, kitchen or kitchenette and fridge in some units, coffeemaker, hair dryer, iron.

Hotel Oceana ★★   If you're going to vacation in Santa Barbara, you might as well stay in style and on the beach—ergo, at the Hotel Oceana, a "beach chic" hotel with an oceanfront setting and an L.A. makeover. The 2.5-acre Spanish mission–style property consists of four adjacent motels built in the 1940s that have been merged and renovated into one sprawling hotel. The result is a wide range of charmingly old-school accommodations—everything from apartments with real daybeds (great for families) to inexpensive courtyard rooms and deluxe oceanview suites with bright modern furnishings. Each guest room, decorated by renowned interior designer Kathryn Ireland, is smartly appointed with soft Frette linens, down comforters (the beds are fantastic), ceiling fans, CD players, cozy duvets, and Aveda bath products. Along with the size and location of your room, you get to choose from four color schemes—soothing blue or green, racy red, and a cheery yellow (my preferred choice). The beach and jogging path are right across the street, and there's a huge lawn area that's perfect for picnic lunches.

202 W. Cabrillo Blvd., Santa Barbara, CA 93101. ✆ **800/965-9776** or 805/965-4577. Fax 805/965-9937. www.hotel oceanasantabarbara.com. 122 units. $185–$360 double. 2-night minimum for weekend reservations. AE, DC, DISC, MC, V. **Amenities:** Denny's restaurant adjacent; 2 swimming pools; fitness room; spa; whirlpool; large lawn area; sun deck. *In room:* A/C, TV, high-speed Internet, Wi-Fi, fridge, hair dryer, iron, CD player.

The Upham Victorian Hotel and Garden Cottages   This conveniently located inn combines the intimacy of a B&B with the service of a small hotel. Built in 1871, the Upham is the oldest continuously operating hostelry in Southern California. Somewhere the management made time for upgrades, though, because guest accommodations are complete with all the modern comforts. The hotel is constructed of redwood, with sweeping verandas and a Victorian cupola on top. It also has a warm lobby and a cozy restaurant.

1404 De La Vina St. (at Sola St.), Santa Barbara, CA 93101. ✆ **800/727-0876** or 805/962-0058. Fax 805/963-2825. www.uphamhotel.com. 50 units. $195–$265 double; from $275 suite and cottage. Rates include continental breakfast and afternoon wine and cheese. AE, DC, MC, V. **Amenities:** Restaurant; laundry service; dry cleaning. *In room:* TV.

INEXPENSIVE

All the best buys fill up fast in the summer months, so be sure to reserve your room—even if you're just planning to stay at the reliable **Motel 6,** 443 Corona del Mar Dr. (✆ **800/466-8356** or 805/564-1392; www.motel6.com), near the beach.

Franciscan Inn   The Franciscan is situated in a quiet neighborhood just a block from the beach, near Stearns Wharf. This privately owned and meticulously maintained hotel is an affordable retreat with enough frills that you'll still feel pampered. The small but comfy rooms feature a country-tinged decor and finely tiled bathrooms. Services include morning newspaper and free local calls. Most second-floor rooms have unobstructed mountain views, and some suites feature fully equipped kitchenettes. The inn stacks up as a great family choice that's classy enough for a romantic weekend, too.

109 Bath St. (at Mason St.), Santa Barbara, CA 93101. ✆ **800/663-5288** or 805/963-8845. Fax 805/564-3295. www. franciscaninn.com. 53 units. Summer (mid-May to mid-Sept) $150–$170 double, $175–$195 suite; winter $120–$150 double, $135–$165 suite. Extra person $10. Rates include continental breakfast and afternoon refreshments. AE, DC, MC, V. Free parking. **Amenities:** Heated outdoor pool; whirlpool; coin-op laundry; laundry service; dry cleaning. *In room:* A/C, TV/VCR, dataport, coffeemaker, hair dryer, iron.

WHERE TO DINE
EXPENSIVE

bouchon ★★ CALIFORNIA   You can tell this warm and inviting restaurant is passionate about wine just from the name—*bouchon* is the French word for "wine cork." And not just any wines, but those of the surrounding Santa Barbara County. There are 50 different Central Coast wines available by the glass; have some fun by enhancing each course with a glass (or half-glass) of wine—knowledgeable servers help make the perfect match. The seasonally composed—and regionally inspired—menu has included dishes such as smoked Santa Barbara albacore "carpaccio," arranged with a tangy vinaigrette and shaved imported Parmesan; luscious sweetbread and chanterelle ragout cradled in a potato-leek basket; local venison sliced and laid atop cumin spaetzle in a shallow pond of green peppercorn–Madeira demiglace; or monkfish saddle fragrant with fresh herbs and accompanied by a creamy fennel-Gruyère gratin. Request a table on the heated front patio, and don't miss the signature chocolate soufflé for dessert.

9 W. Victoria St. (off State St.). ✆ **805/730-1160.** www.bouchonsantabarbara.com. Reservations recommended. Main courses $22–$35. AE, DC, MC, V. Daily 5:30–10pm.

Nu ★★ CALIFORNIA CUISINE   *Nu* is French for naked, which explains why the entire staff here works totally naked. Just kidding. Proprietor and executive chef David Cecchini picked the name to convey that his restaurant "strips away" any preconceived notions you may have about dining in Santa Barbara. Metaphors aside, I love everything about Nu, from its pleasant, woodsy neo-Tuscan decor to the exceptional service, plant-filled courtyard seating, and weekend jazz sessions. But the food is really the thing here. You might want to start with lobster risotto, featuring a carrot-infused crème fraîche and orange demiglace, or the yellowfin tuna tartare, then move on to a citrus-spiced swordfish, served with beet-infused toasted quinoa, cabbage fondue, shiitake mushrooms, and saffron nage. If all this sounds slightly fussy, it is, but it works, and beautifully. *Tip:* If you're not in the mood for a full sit-down dinner, visit the cocktail lounge, with its own menu of appetizers, including great pizzas made in a wood-burning oven.

1129 State St., Santa Barbara. © 805/965-1500. www.restaurantnu.com. Main courses $10–$11 lunch, $22–$28 dinner. AE, DC, DISC, MC, V. Lunch Mon–Fri 11:30am–2:30pm; dinner Mon–Thurs and Sun 5:30–10pm, Fri–Sat 5:30–11pm.

Wine Cask ★★ CALIFORNIA   Take a 20-year-old wine shop, a large 1920s landmark dining room with a big stone fireplace, an outdoor dining patio, and outstanding Italian fare, mix them with an attractive staff and clientele, and you've got the Wine Cask—the most popular upscale dining spot in Santa Barbara. Here you'll be treated to Chef John Pettitt's comforting creations, such as pan-roasted artic char in a Dijon-artichoke emulsion. Other options include Australian lamb chops, or pasta with chanterelle mushrooms, baby artichokes, and gold beets. The wine list reads like a novel, with more than 2,000 wines ($14–$1,400), and has deservedly received the *Wine Spectator* award for excellence. There's also a happy hour at the beautiful maple bar from 4 to 6pm daily.

In El Paseo Center, 813 Anacapa St., Santa Barbara. © 800/436-9463 or 805/966-9463. www.winecask.com. Reservations recommended. Lunch $12–$17; dinner main courses $29–$36. AE, DC, MC, V. Mon–Thurs 11:30am–2pm and 5:30–10pm; Fri 11:30am–2pm and 5:30–11pm; Sat 5:30–11pm; Sun 5:30–10pm.

MODERATE

Brophy Bros. Clam Bar & Restaurant ★★ SEAFOOD   This place is best known for its unbeatable view of the marina, but the dependable fresh seafood keeps tourists and locals coming back. Dress is casual, portions are huge, and favorites include New England clam chowder, cioppino, and any one of an assortment of seafood salads. The scampi and garlic–baked clams are consistently good, as is all the fresh fish, which come with soup or salad, coleslaw, and pilaf or french fries. A great deal is the hot-and-cold shellfish combo platter for $13. Ask for a table on the narrow deck overlooking the harbor. *Be forewarned:* The wait at this small place can be up to 2 hours on a weekend night.

119 Harbor Way (off Cabrillo Blvd. in the Waterfront Center). © 805/966-4418. www.brophybros.com. Reservations not accepted. Main courses $9–$19. AE, MC, V. Sun–Thurs 10am–10pm; Fri–Sat 10am–11pm.

Pane e Vino ★ ITALIAN   This popular Italian trattoria offers food as authentic as you'd find in Rome. The simplest spaghetti topped with basil-tomato sauce is so good it's hard to understand why diners would want to occupy their taste buds with more complicated concoctions. But this kitchen is capable of almost anything. Pasta puttanesca, with tomatoes, anchovies, black olives, and capers, is always tops. Pane e Vino gets high marks for its reasonable prices, service, and casual atmosphere. Although many diners prefer to eat outside on the patio, some of the best tables are in the charming, cluttered dining room.

1482 E. Valley Rd., Montecito (a 5-min. drive south of downtown Santa Barbara). © **805/969-9274.** Reservations required. Main courses $10–$22. AE, MC, V. Mon–Thurs 11:30am–10:30pm; Fri–Sat 11:30am–11:30pm; Sun 5–10:30pm.

INEXPENSIVE

La Super-Rica Taqueria ★★ MEXICAN   Looking at this humble street-corner shack, you'd never guess it was blessed with an endorsement by the late Julia Child. The tacos here are authentic and no-nonsense, with generous portions of filling piled onto fresh, grainy corn tortillas. My favorites are the *adobado* (marinated pork), *gorditas* (thick corn *masa* pockets filled with spicy beans), and flank steak. A dollop of housemade salsa and green or red hot sauce is the only adornment required. Sunday's special is *pozole*, a stew of pork and hominy in red-chile sauce. On Friday and Saturday, the specialty is freshly made tamales. (If the Dover sole tamales are one of the specials, order them—they're incredible.) *Tip:* Always check the daily specials first, and be sure to ask for extra tortillas, no matter what you order.

622 N. Milpas St. (btw. Cota and Ortega sts.), Santa Barbara. © **805/963-4940.** Most menu items $3–$7. No credit cards. 11am–9pm daily.

Stacky's Seaside SANDWICHES   This ivy-covered shack filled with fishnets, surfboards, and local memorabilia has been a local favorite for years. A classic seafood dive, its menu of sandwiches is enormous, as are most of their pita pockets, hoagies, and club sandwiches. A sign proudly proclaims HALF OF ANY SANDWICH, HALF PRICE— NO PROBLEM, and Stacky's has made a lot of friends because of it. Choices include the Santa Barbaran (roasted tri-tip and melted jack cheese on sourdough), the Rincon pita (jack and cheddar cheeses, green Ortega chiles, onions, and ranch dressing), and a hot pastrami hoagie with Swiss cheese, mustard, and onions. Heck, they even serve a PB&J for $3. And if you like fish and chips, they nail it here. Stacky's also serves breakfast, featuring scrambled-egg sandwiches and south-of-the-border egg dishes. An order of crispy fries is enough for two.

2315 Lillie Ave., Summerland (5 min. on the freeway from Santa Barbara—take the Summerland exit, turn left under the freeway, and then take the 1st right). © **805/969-9908.** Most menu items under $8. AE, DISC, MC, V. Mon–Fri 6:30am–7:30pm; Sat–Sun 7am–7:30pm.

Appendix: Fast Facts, Toll-Free Numbers & Websites

1 Fast Facts: Los Angeles

AMERICAN EXPRESS In addition to those at 327 N. Beverly Dr., Beverly Hills (© **310/274-8277**), and at the Beverly Connection, 8493 W. 3rd St., Los Angeles (© **310/659-1682**), offices are located throughout the city. To locate the one nearest you, call © **800/221-7282.**

AREA CODES Within the past 20 years, L.A. has gone from having a single area code (213) to a whopping seven. Even residents can't keep up. As of press time, here's the basic layout: Those areas west of La Cienega Boulevard, including Beverly Hills and the city's beach communities, use the **310** area code. Portions of Los Angeles County east and south of the city, including Long Beach, are in the **562** area. The San Fernando Valley has the **818** area code, while points east—including parts of Burbank, Glendale, and Pasadena—use the newly created **626** code. What happened to 213, you ask? The Downtown business area still uses **213.** All other numbers, including Griffith Park, Hollywood, and parts of West Hollywood (east of La Cienega Blvd.) now use the area code **323.** If it's all too much to remember, just call directory assistance at © **411.**

ATM NETWORKS & CASHPOINTS See "Money & Costs," p. 40.

AUTOMOBILE ORGANIZATIONS Motor clubs will supply maps, suggested routes, guidebooks, accident and bail-bond insurance, and emergency road service. The **American Automobile Association (AAA)** is the major motor club in the United States. If you belong to a motor club in your home country, inquire about AAA reciprocity before you leave. You may be able to join AAA even if you're not a member of a reciprocal club; to inquire, call AAA (© **800/222-4357**). AAA is actually an organization of regional motor clubs; so look under "AAA Automobile Club" in the White Pages of the telephone directory. AAA has a nationwide emergency road service telephone number (© **800/AAA-HELP** [800/222-4357]).

BABYSITTERS If you're staying at one of the larger hotels, the concierge can usually recommend a reliable babysitter. If not, contact the **Baby-Sitters Guild** in Glendale (© **310/837-1800** or 818/552-2229), L.A.'s oldest and largest babysitting service.

BUSINESS HOURS Offices are usually open weekdays from 9am to 5pm. Banks are open weekdays from 9am to 3pm or later and sometimes Saturday mornings. Stores typically open between 9 and 10am and close between 5 and 6pm from Monday through Saturday. Stores in shopping complexes or malls tend to stay open late: until about 9pm on weekdays and weekends, and many malls and larger department stores are open on Sundays.

CAR RENTALS See "Toll-Free Numbers & Websites," p. 328.

DRINKING LAWS The legal age for purchase and consumption of alcoholic beverages is 21; proof of age is required and often requested at bars, nightclubs, and restaurants, so it's always a good idea to bring ID when you go out. Supermarkets and convenience stores in California sell beer, wine, and liquor.

Most restaurants serve alcohol, but some only serve beer and wine—it depends on the type of liquor license they own. By law all bars, clubs, restaurants, and stores cannot sell or serve alcohol after 2am, and "last call" tends to start at 1:30am. There are no county or calendar alcohol restrictions in California.

Do not carry open containers of alcohol in your car or any public area that isn't zoned for alcohol consumption. The police can fine you on the spot. And nothing will ruin your trip faster than getting a citation for DUI ("driving under the influence"), so don't even think about driving while intoxicated.

DRIVING RULES   See "Getting There & Getting Around," p. 31.

ELECTRICITY   Like Canada, the United States uses 110 to 120 volts AC (60 cycles), compared to 220 to 240 volts AC (50 cycles) in most of Europe, Australia, and New Zealand. Downward converters that change 220–240 volts to 110–120 volts are difficult to find in the United States, so bring one with you.

EMBASSIES & CONSULATES   All embassies are located in the nation's capital, Washington, D.C. Some consulates are located in major U.S. cities, and most nations have a mission to the United Nations in New York City. If your country isn't listed below, call for directory information in Washington, D.C. (© **202/ 555-1212**) or check **www.embassy.org/ embassies**.

The embassy of **Australia** is at 1601 Massachusetts Ave. NW, Washington, DC 20036 (© **202/797-3000;** www.aust emb.org). There are consulates in New York, Honolulu, Houston, Los Angeles, and San Francisco.

The embassy of **Canada** is at 501 Pennsylvania Ave. NW, Washington, DC 20001 (© **202/682-1740;** www.canadian embassy.org). Other Canadian consulates are in Buffalo (New York), Detroit, Los Angeles, New York, and Seattle.

The embassy of **Ireland** is at 2234 Massachusetts Ave. NW, Washington, DC 20008 (© **202/462-3939;** www. irelandemb.org). Irish consulates are in Boston, Chicago, New York, San Francisco, and other cities. See website for complete listing.

The embassy of **New Zealand** is at 37 Observatory Circle NW, Washington, DC 20008 (© **202/328-4800;** www.nz emb.org). New Zealand consulates are in Los Angeles, Salt Lake City, San Francisco, and Seattle.

The embassy of the **United Kingdom** is at 3100 Massachusetts Ave. NW, Washington, DC 20008 (© **202/588-7800;** www.britainusa.com). Other British consulates are in Atlanta, Boston, Chicago, Cleveland, Houston, Los Angeles, New York, San Francisco, and Seattle.

EMERGENCIES   Call © **911** to report a fire, call the police, or get an ambulance anywhere in the United States. This is a toll-free call (no coins are required at public telephones).

If you encounter traveler's problems, call the Los Angeles chapter of the **Traveler's Aid Society** (© **310/646-2270;** www.travelersaid.org), a nationwide, nonprofit, social service organization that helps travelers in difficult straits. Its services might include reuniting families separated while traveling, providing food and/or shelter to people stranded without cash, and even emotional counseling.

GASOLINE (PETROL)   At press time, in the U.S., the cost of gasoline (also known as gas, but never petrol), is unusually high (about $4.60 per gallon at press time). Taxes are already included in the printed price. One U.S. gallon equals 3.8 liters or .85 imperial gallons. Fill-up locations are known as gas or service stations.

HOLIDAYS   Banks, government offices, post offices, and many stores, restaurants, and museums are closed on the following legal national holidays: January 1 (New Year's Day), the third Monday in January (Martin Luther King, Jr., Day), the third Monday in February (Presidents' Day), the last Monday in May (Memorial Day), July 4 (Independence Day), the first Monday in September (Labor Day), the second Monday in October (Columbus Day), November 11 (Veterans Day/Armistice Day), the fourth Thursday in November (Thanksgiving Day), and December 25 (Christmas). The Tuesday after the first Monday in November is Election Day, a federal government holiday in presidential-election years (held every 4 years, and next in 2008).

For more information on holidays see "Los Angeles–Area Calendar of Events," in chapter 3.

HOSPITALS   The centrally located (and world-famous) **Cedars-Sinai Medical Center,** 8700 Beverly Blvd., Los Angeles (© **310/423-3277**), has a 24-hour emergency room staffed by some of the country's finest MDs.

INSURANCE   Medical Insurance   Although it's not required of travelers, health insurance is highly recommended. Most health insurance policies cover you if you get sick away from home—but check your coverage before you leave.

International visitors to the U.S. should note that unlike many European countries, the United States does not usually offer free or low-cost medical care to its citizens or visitors. Doctors and hospitals are expensive, and in most cases will require advance payment or proof of coverage before they render their services. Good policies will cover the costs of an accident, repatriation, or death. Packages such as **Europ Assistance's "Worldwide Healthcare Plan"** are sold by European automobile clubs and travel agencies at attractive rates. **Worldwide Assistance**

Services, Inc. (© **800/777-8710;** www.worldwideassistance.com) is the agent for Europ Assistance in the United States. Though lack of health insurance may prevent you from being admitted to a hospital in nonemergencies, don't worry about being left on a street corner to die: The American way is to fix you now and bill the daylights out of you later.

If you're ever hospitalized more than 150 miles from home, **MedjetAssist** (© **800/527-7478;** www.medjetassistance.com) will pick you up and fly you to the hospital of your choice in a medically equipped and staffed aircraft 24 hours day, 7 days a week. Annual memberships are $225 individual, $350 family; you can also purchase short-term memberships.

Canadians should check with their provincial health plan offices or call **Health Canada** (© **866/225-0709;** www.hc-sc.gc.ca) to find out the extent of their coverage and what documentation and receipts they must take home in case they are treated in the United States.

Travelers from the U.K. should carry their European Health Insurance Card (EHIC), which replaced the E111 form as proof of entitlement to free/reduced cost medical treatment abroad (© **0845 606 2030;** www.ehic.org.uk). Note, however, that the EHIC only covers "necessary medical treatment," and for repatriation costs, lost money, baggage, or cancellation, travel insurance from a reputable company should always be sought (www.travelinsuranceweb.com).

Travel Insurance   The cost of travel insurance varies widely, depending on the destination, the cost and length of your trip, your age and health, and the type of trip you're taking, but expect to pay between 5% and 8% of the vacation itself. You can get estimates from various providers through **InsureMyTrip.com**. Enter your trip cost and dates, your age, and other information, for prices from more than a dozen companies.

U.K. citizens and their families who make more than one trip abroad per year may find an annual travel insurance policy works out cheaper. Check **www.money supermarket.com**, which compares prices across a wide range of providers for single- and multitrip policies.

Most big travel agents offer their own insurance and will probably try to sell you their package when you book a holiday. Think before you sign. **Britain's Consumers' Association** recommends that you insist on seeing the policy and reading the fine print before buying travel insurance. The **Association of British Insurers** (☎ **020/7600-3333**; www.abi.org.uk) gives advice by phone and publishes *Holiday Insurance,* a free guide to policy provisions and prices. You might also shop around for better deals: Try **Columbus Direct** (☎ **0870/033-9988;** www.columbusdirect.net).

Trip Cancellation Insurance Trip-cancellation insurance will help retrieve your money if you have to back out of a trip or depart early, or if your travel supplier goes bankrupt. Trip cancellation traditionally covers such events as sickness, natural disasters, and State Department advisories. The latest news in trip-cancellation insurance is the availability of **expanded hurricane coverage** and the **"any-reason"** cancellation coverage—which costs more but covers cancellations made for any reason. You won't get back 100% of your prepaid trip cost, but you'll be refunded a substantial portion. **Travel-Safe** (☎ **888/885-7233;** www.travel safe.com) offers both types of coverage. Expedia also offers any-reason cancellation coverage for its air-hotel packages. For details, contact one of the following recommended insurers: **Access America** (☎ 866/807-3982; www.accessamerica.com); **Travel Guard International** (☎ 800/826-4919; www.travelguard.com); **Travel Insured International** (☎ 800/

243-3174; www.travelinsured.com); and **Travelex Insurance Services** (☎ 888/457-4602; www.travelex-insurance.com).

LEGAL AID If you are "pulled over" for a minor infraction (such as speeding), never attempt to pay the fine directly to a police officer; this could be construed as attempted bribery, a much more serious crime. Pay fines by mail, or directly into the hands of the clerk of the court. If accused of a more serious offense, say and do nothing before consulting a lawyer. Here the burden is on the state to prove a person's guilt beyond a reasonable doubt, and everyone has the right to remain silent, whether he or she is suspected of a crime or actually arrested. Once arrested, a person can make one telephone call to a party of his or her choice. International visitors should call your embassy or consulate.

LOST & FOUND Be sure to tell all of your credit card companies the minute you discover your wallet has been lost or stolen and file a report at the nearest police precinct. Your credit card company or insurer may require a police report number or record of the loss. Most credit card companies have an emergency toll-free number to call if your card is lost or stolen; they may be able to wire you a cash advance immediately or deliver an emergency credit card in a day or two. Visa's U.S. emergency number is ☎ **800/847-2911** or 410/581-9994. American Express cardholders and traveler's check holders should call ☎ **800/221-7282.** MasterCard holders should call ☎ **800/307-7309** or 636/722-7111. For other credit cards, call the toll-free number directory at ☎ **800/555-1212.**

If you need emergency cash over the weekend when all banks and American Express offices are closed, you can have money wired to you via **Western Union** (☎ **800/325-6000;** www.westernunion.com).

MAIL   At press time, domestic postage rates were 27¢ for a postcard and 42¢ for a letter. For international mail, a first-class letter of up to 1 ounce costs 90¢ (69¢ to Canada and Mexico); a first-class postcard costs the same as a letter. For more information go to **www.usps.com** and click on "Calculate Postage."

If you aren't sure what your address will be in the United States, mail can be sent to you, in your name, c/o General Delivery at the main post office of the city or region where you expect to be. (Call © **800/275-8777** for information on the nearest post office.) The addressee must pick up mail in person and must produce proof of identity (driver's license, passport, and so on). Most post offices will hold your mail for up to 1 month, and are open Monday to Friday from 8am to 6pm, and Saturday from 9am to 3pm.

Always include zip codes when mailing items in the U.S. If you don't know your zip code, visit www.usps.com/zip4.

MEASUREMENTS   See the chart on the inside front cover of this book for details on converting metric measurements to nonmetric equivalents.

MEDICAL CONDITIONS   If you have a medical condition that requires **syringe-administered medications,** carry a valid signed prescription from your physician; syringes in carry-on baggage will be inspected. Insulin in any form should have the proper pharmaceutical documentation. If you have a disease that requires treatment with **narcotics,** you should also carry documented proof with you—smuggling narcotics aboard a plane carries severe penalties in the U.S.

For **HIV-positive visitors,** requirements for entering the United States are somewhat vague and change frequently. For up-to-the-minute information, contact **AIDSinfo** (© **800/448-0440** or 301/519-6616 outside the U.S.; www.aidsinfo.nih.gov) or the **Gay Men's Health**

Crisis (© **212/367-1000;** www.gmhc.org).

NEWSPAPERS & MAGAZINES   The *Los Angeles Times* (www.latimes.com) is a high-quality daily with strong local and national coverage. Its Sunday "Calendar" section (www.calendarlive.com) is an excellent guide to entertainment in and around L.A., and includes listings of what's doing and where to do it. The *L.A. Weekly* (www.laweekly.com), a free weekly listings magazine, is packed with information on current events around town. *Los Angeles* magazine (www.lamag.com) is a city-based monthly full of news, information, and previews of L.A.'s art, music, and food scenes. **World Book & News Co.,** at 1652 N. Cahuenga Blvd. (© **323/465-4352**), near Hollywood and Vine and Grauman's Chinese Theatre, stocks lots of out-of-town and foreign papers and magazines. No one minds if you browse through the magazines, but you'll be reprimanded for thumbing through the newspapers. It's open 24 hours.

PASSPORTS   The websites listed provide downloadable passport applications as well as the current fees for processing applications. For an up-to-date, country-by-country listing of passport requirements around the world, go to the "International Travel" tab of the U.S. State Department at **http://travel.state.gov**. International visitors to the U.S. can obtain a visa application at the same website. *Note:* Children are required to present a passport when entering the United States at airports. More information on obtaining a passport for a minor can be found at http://travel.state.gov. Allow plenty of time before your trip to apply for a passport; processing normally takes 4–6 weeks (3 weeks for expedited service) but can take longer during busy periods (especially spring). And keep in mind that if you need a passport in a hurry, you'll pay a higher processing fee.

For Residents of Australia You can pick up an application from your local post office or any branch of Passports Australia, but you must schedule an interview at the passport office to present your application materials. Call the **Australian Passport Information Service** at © **131-232,** or visit the government website at www.passports.gov.au.

For Residents of Canada Passport applications are available at travel agencies throughout Canada or from the central **Passport Office,** Department of Foreign Affairs and International Trade, Ottawa, ON K1A 0G3 (© **800/567-6868;** www.ppt.gc.ca). *Note:* Canadian children who travel must have their own passport. However, if you hold a valid Canadian passport issued before December 11, 2001, that bears the name of your child, the passport remains valid for you and your child until it expires.

For Residents of Ireland You can apply for a 10-year passport at the **Passport Office,** Setanta Centre, Molesworth Street, Dublin 2 (© **01/671-1633;** www.irlgov.ie/iveagh). Those under age 18 and over 65 must apply for a 3-year passport. You can also apply at 1A South Mall, Cork (© **21/494-4700**) or at most main post offices.

For Residents of New Zealand You can pick up a passport application at any New Zealand Passports Office or download it from their website. Contact the **Passports Office** at © **0800/225-050** in New Zealand or 04/474-8100, or log on to www.passports.govt.nz.

For Residents of the United Kingdom To pick up an application for a standard 10-year passport (5-year passport for children 15 and under), visit your nearest passport office, major post office, or travel agency or contact the **United Kingdom Passport Service** at © **0870/521-0410** or search its website at www.ukpa.gov.uk.

POLICE In an emergency, dial © **911.** For nonemergency police matters, call © **213/485-2121;** in Beverly Hills, dial © **310/550-4951.**

SMOKING Heavy smokers are in for a tough time in Los Angeles. There is no smoking in public buildings, sports arenas, elevators, theaters, banks, lobbies, restaurants, offices, stores, bed-and-breakfasts, most small hotels, and bars. That's right—as of January 1, 1998, you can't even smoke in a bar in California. The only exception is a bar where drinks are served solely by the owner. You will find, however, that many neighborhood bars turn the other cheek and pass you an ashtray.

TAXES In the United States, there is no value-added tax (VAT) or other indirect tax at the national level. Every state, county, and city has the right to levy its own local tax on all purchases, including hotel and restaurant checks, airline tickets, and so on, and it is not included in the price tags you'll see on merchandise. This tax is not refundable. Sales tax in Los Angeles is 8%. Hotel tax is charged on the room tariff only (which is not subject to sales tax) and is set by the city, ranging from 12% to 17% around Southern California.

TELEPHONES Generally, hotel surcharges on long-distance and local calls are astronomical, so you're better off using your **cellphone** or a **public pay telephone.** Many convenience groceries and packaging services sell **prepaid calling cards** in denominations up to $50; for international visitors these can be the least expensive way to call home. Many public phones at airports now accept American Express, MasterCard, and Visa credit cards. **Local calls** made from public pay phones in most locales cost either 25¢ or 35¢. Pay phones do not accept pennies, and few will take anything larger than a quarter.

Most long-distance and international calls can be dialed directly from any phone. **For calls within the United States and to Canada,** dial 1 followed by the area code and the seven-digit number. **For other international calls,** dial 011 followed by the country code, city code, and the number you are calling.

Calls to area codes **800, 888, 877,** and **866** are toll-free. However, calls to area codes **700** and **900** (chat lines, bulletin boards, "dating" services, and so on) can be very expensive—usually a charge of 95¢ to $3 or more per minute, and they sometimes have minimum charges that can run as high as $15 or more.

For **reversed-charge or collect calls,** and for person-to-person calls, dial the number 0, then the area code and number; an operator will come on the line, and you should specify whether you are calling collect, person-to-person, or both. If your operator-assisted call is international, ask for the overseas operator.

For **local directory assistance** ("information"), dial 411; for long-distance information, dial 1, then the appropriate area code and 555-1212.

Telegraph and telex services are provided primarily by Western Union. You can telegraph (wire) money, or have it telegraphed to you, very quickly over the Western Union system, but this service can cost as much as 15% to 20% of the amount sent.

Most hotels have **fax machines** available for guest use (be sure to ask about the charge to use it). Many hotel rooms are even wired for guests' fax machines. A less expensive way to send and receive faxes may be at stores such as the **UPS Store** (formerly Mail Boxes Etc.).

TELEGRAPH, TELEX & FAX Telegraph and telex services are provided primarily by **Western Union** (℗ **800/325-6000;** www.westernunion.com). You can telegraph (wire) money, or have it telegraphed to you, very quickly over the Western Union system, but this service can cost as much as 15% to 20% of the amount sent.

Most hotels have **fax machines** available for guest use (be sure to ask about the charge to use it). Many hotel rooms are wired for guests' fax machines. A less expensive way to send and receive faxes may be at stores such as the **UPS Store.**

TIME Los Angeles is in the Pacific Standard Time zone, which is 8 hours behind Greenwich Mean Time and 3 hours behind Eastern Standard Time. The continental United States is divided into **four time zones:** Eastern Standard Time (EST), Central Standard Time (CST), Mountain Standard Time (MST), and Pacific Standard Time (PST). Alaska and Hawaii have their own zones. For example, when it's 9am in Los Angeles (PST), it's 7am in Honolulu (HST),10am in Denver (MST), 11am in Chicago (CST), noon in New York City (EST), 5pm in London (GMT), and 2am the next day in Sydney.

Daylight saving time takes effect at 2am the second Sunday in March until 2am the first Sunday in November, except in Arizona, Hawaii, the U.S. Virgin Islands, and Puerto Rico. Daylight saving moves the clock 1 hour ahead of standard time.

For the correct time, call ℗ **853-1212** (in any L.A. area code).

TIPPING Tips are a very important part of certain workers' income, and gratuities are the standard way of showing appreciation for services provided. (Tipping is certainly not compulsory if the service is poor!) In hotels, tip **bellhops** at least $1 per bag ($2–$3 if you have a lot of luggage) and tip the **chamber staff** $1 to $2 per day (more if you've left a disaster area for him or her to clean up). Tip the **doorman** or **concierge** only if he or she has provided you with some specific service (for example, calling a cab for you or obtaining difficult-to-get theater tickets).

Tip the **valet-parking attendant** $1 every time you get your car.

In restaurants, bars, and nightclubs, tip **service staff** 15% to 20% of the check, tip **bartenders** 10% to 15%, tip **checkroom attendants** $1 per garment, and tip **valet-parking attendants** $1 per vehicle.

As for other service personnel, tip **cabdrivers** 15% of the fare; tip **skycaps** at airports at least $1 per bag ($2–$3 if you have a lot of luggage); and tip **hairdressers** and **barbers** 15% to 20%.

TOILETS   You won't find public toilets or "restrooms" on the streets in most U.S. cities, but they can be found in hotel lobbies, bars, restaurants, museums, department stores, railway and bus stations, and service stations. Large hotels and fast-food restaurants are often the best bet for clean facilities. If possible, avoid the toilets at parks and beaches, which tend to be dirty; some may be unsafe. Restaurants and bars in resorts or heavily visited areas may reserve their restrooms for patrons.

USEFUL PHONE NUMBERS

- Los Angeles weather information
  © 213/554-1212
- Los Angeles beach conditions
  © 310/457-9701
- Los Angeles traffic reports
  © 888/922-5482
- U.S. Dept. of State Travel Advisory
  © 202/647-5225 (staffed 24 hr.)
- U.S. Passport Agency
  © 202/647-0518

- U.S. Centers for Disease Control International Traveler's Hotline
  © 404/332-4559

VISAS   For information about U.S. visas go to **http://travel.state.gov** and click on "Visas." Or go to one of the following websites:

Australian citizens can obtain up-to-date visa information from the **U.S. Embassy Canberra,** Moonah Place, Yarralumla, ACT 2600 (© **02/6214-5600**) or by checking the U.S. Diplomatic Mission's website at **http://usembassy-australia.state.gov/consular.**

British subjects can obtain up-to-date visa information by calling the **U.S. Embassy Visa Information Line** (© **0891/200-290**) or by visiting the "Visas to the U.S." section of the American Embassy London's website at **www.usembassy.org.uk.**

Irish citizens can obtain up-to-date visa information through the **Embassy of the USA Dublin,** 42 Elgin Rd., Dublin 4, Ireland (© **353/1-668-8777;** or by checking the "Consular Services" section of the website at **http://dublin.us embassy.gov.**

Citizens of **New Zealand** can obtain up-to-date visa information by contacting the **U.S. Embassy New Zealand,** 29 Fitzherbert Terrace, Thorndon, Wellington (© **644/472-2068**), or get the information directly from the website at **http://wellington.usembassy.gov.**

2 Toll-Free Numbers & Websites

MAJOR U.S. AIRLINES
(*flies internationally as well)

Alaska Airlines/Horizon Air
© 800/252-7522
www.alaskaair.com

American Airlines*
© 800/433-7300 (in U.S. and Canada)

© 020/7365-0777 (in U.K.)
www.aa.com

Cape Air
© 800/352-0714
www.flycapeair.com

Continental Airlines*
℗ 800/523-3273 (in U.S. and Canada)
℗ 084/5607-6760 (in U.K.)
www.continental.com

Delta Air Lines*
℗ 800/221-1212 (in U.S. and Canada)
℗ 084/5600-0950 (in U.K.)
www.delta.com

Frontier Airlines
℗ 800/432-1359
www.frontierairlines.com

Hawaiian Airlines*
℗ 800/367-5320 (in U.S. and Canada)
www.hawaiianair.com

JetBlue Airways
℗ 800/538-2583 (in U.S.)
℗ 080/1365-2525 (in U.K. or Canada)
www.jetblue.com

Midwest Airlines
℗ 800/452-2022
www.midwestairlines.com

Nantucket Airlines
℗ 800/635-8787
www.nantucketairlines.com

North American Airlines*
℗ 800/371-6297
www.flynaa.com

Northwest Airlines
℗ 800/225-2525 (in U.S.)
℗ 870/0507-4074 (in U.K.)
www.flynaa.com

Pan Am Clipper Connection
℗ 800/359-7262
www.flypanam.com

PenAir (The Spirit of Alaska)
℗ 800/448-4226 (in U.S.)
www.penair.com

United Airlines*
℗ 800/864-8331 (in U.S. and Canada)
℗ 084/5844-4777 (in U.K.)
www.united.com

US Airways*
℗ 800/428-4322 (in U.S. and Canada)
℗ 084/5600-3300 (in U.K.)
www.usairways.com

Virgin America*
℗ 877/359-8474
www.virginamerica.com

CAR RENTAL AGENCIES

Advantage
℗ 800/777-5500 (in U.S.)
℗ 021/0344-4712 (outside of U.S.)
www.advantagerentacar.com

Alamo
℗ 800/GO-ALAMO (800/462-5266)
www.alamo.com

Auto Europe
℗ 888/223-5555 (in U.S. and Canada)
℗ 0800/2235-5555 (in U.K.)
www.autoeurope.com

Avis
℗ 800/331-1212 (in U.S. and Canada)
℗ 084/4581-8181 (in U.K.)
www.avis.com

Budget
℗ 800/527-0700 (in U.S.)
℗ 087/0156-5656 (in U.K.)
℗ 800/268-8900 (in Canada)
www.budget.com

Dollar
℗ 800/800-4000 (in U.S.)
℗ 800/848-8268 (in Canada)
℗ 080/8234-7524 (in U.K.)
www.dollar.com

Enterprise
℗ 800/261-7331 (in U.S.)
℗ 514/355-4028 (in Canada)
℗ 012/9360-9090 (in U.K.)
www.enterprise.com

Hertz
℗ 800/645-3131
℗ 800/654-3001 (for international reservations)
www.hertz.com

Kemwel
℗ 877/820-0668
www.kemwel.com

National
ⓒ 800/CAR-RENT (800/227-7368)
www.nationalcar.com

Payless
ⓒ 800/PAYLESS (800/729-5377)
www.paylesscarrental.com

MAJOR HOTEL & MOTEL CHAINS

Best Western International
ⓒ 800/780-7234 (in U.S. and Canada)
ⓒ 0800/393-130 (in U.K.)
www.bestwestern.com

Clarion Hotels
ⓒ 800/CLARION (800/252-7466) or 877/424-6423 (in U.S. and Canada)
ⓒ 0800/444-444 (in U.K.)
www.choicehotels.com

Comfort Inns
ⓒ 800/228-5150
ⓒ 0800/444-444 (in U.K.)
www.ComfortInnChoiceHotels.com

Courtyard by Marriott
ⓒ 888/236-2427 (in U.S.)
ⓒ 0800/221-222 (in U.K.)
www.marriott.com/courtyard

Crowne Plaza Hotels
ⓒ 888/303-1746
www.ichotelsgroup.com/crowneplaza

Days Inn
ⓒ 800/329-7466 (in U.S.)
ⓒ 0800/280-400 (in U.K.)
www.daysinn.com

Doubletree Hotels
ⓒ 800/222-TREE (800/222-8733) (in U.S. and Canada)
ⓒ 087/0590-9090 (in U.K.)
www.doubletree.com

Econo Lodges
ⓒ 800/55-ECONO (800/552-3666)
www.choicehotels.com

Embassy Suites
ⓒ 800/EMBASSY (800/362-2779)
www.embassysuites.hilton.com

Rent-A-Wreck
ⓒ 800/535-1391
www.rentawreck.com

Thrifty
ⓒ 800/367-2277
ⓒ 918/669-2168 (international)
www.thrifty.com

Fairfield Inn by Marriott
ⓒ 800/228-2800 (in U.S. and Canada)
ⓒ 0800/221-222 (in U.K.)
www.marriott.com/fairfieldinn

Four Seasons
ⓒ 800/819-5053 (in U.S. and Canada)
ⓒ 0800/6488-6488 (in U.K.)
www.fourseasons.com

Hampton Inn
ⓒ 800/HAMPTON (800/426-4766)
www.hamptoninn.hilton.com

Hilton Hotels
ⓒ 800/HILTONS (800/445-8667) (in U.S. and Canada)
ⓒ 087/0590-9090 (in U.K.)
www.hilton.com

Holiday Inn
ⓒ 800/315-2621 (in U.S. and Canada)
ⓒ 0800/405-060 (in U.K.)
www.holidayinn.com

Howard Johnson
ⓒ 800/446-4656 (in U.S. and Canada)
www.hojo.com

Hyatt
ⓒ 888/591-1234 (in U.S. and Canada)
ⓒ 084/5888-1234 (in U.K.)
www.hyatt.com

InterContinental Hotels & Resorts
ⓒ 800/424-6835 (in U.S. and Canada)
ⓒ 0800/1800-1800 (in U.K.)
www.ichotelsgroup.com

La Quinta Inns and Suites
ⓒ 800/642-4271 (in U.S. and Canada)
www.lq.com

Loews Hotels
ⓒ 800/23LOEWS (800/235-6397)
www.loewshotels.com

Marriott
ⓒ 877/236-2427 (in U.S. and Canada)
ⓒ 0800/221-222 (in U.K.)
www.marriott.com

Motel 6
ⓒ 800/4MOTEL6 (800/466-8356)
www.motel6.com

Omni Hotels
ⓒ 888/444-OMNI (888/444-6664)
www.omnihotels.com

Quality
ⓒ 877/424-6423 (in U.S. and Canada)
ⓒ 0800/444-444 (in U.K.)
www.qualityinn.com

Radisson Hotels & Resorts
ⓒ 888/201-1718 (in U.S. and Canada)
ⓒ 0800/374-411 (in U.K.)
www.radisson.com

Ramada Worldwide
ⓒ 888/2-RAMADA (888/272-6232)
(In U.S. and Canada)
ⓒ 080/8100-0783 (in U.K.)
www.ramada.com

Red Carpet Inns
ⓒ 800/251-1962
www.bookroomsnow.com

Red Lion Hotels
ⓒ 800/RED-LION (800/733-5466)
www.redlion.rdln.com

Red Roof Inns
ⓒ 866/686-4335 (in U.S. and Canada)
ⓒ 614/601-4075 (international)
www.redroof.com

Renaissance
ⓒ 888/236-2427
www.renaissancehotel.com

Residence Inn by Marriott
ⓒ 800/331-3131
ⓒ 800/221-222 (in U.K.)
www.marriott.com/residenceinn

Rodeway Inns
ⓒ 877/424-6423
www.rodewayinn.com

Sheraton Hotels & Resorts
ⓒ 800/325-3535 (in U.S.)
ⓒ 800/543-4300 (in Canada)
ⓒ 0800/3253-5353 (in U.K.)
www.starwoodhotels.com/sheraton

Super 8 Motels
ⓒ 800/800-8000
www.super8.com

Travelodge
ⓒ 800/578-7878
www.travelodge.com

Vagabond Inns
ⓒ 800/522-1555
www.vagabondinn.com

Virgin America
ⓒ 877/359-847446
www.virginamerica.com

Westin Hotels & Resorts
ⓒ 800/937-8461 (in U.S. and Canada)
ⓒ 0800/3259-5959 (in U.K.)
www.starwoodhotels.com/westin

Wyndham Hotels & Resorts
ⓒ 877/999-3223 (in U.S. and Canada)
ⓒ 050/6638-4899 (in U.K.)
www.wyndham.com

Index

See also Accommodations and Restaurant indexes, below.

The new way to
get AROUND town.

Make the most of your stay. Go Day by Day!

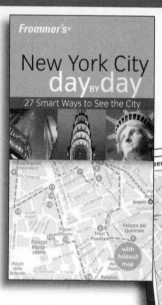

The all-new Day by Day series shows you the best places to visit and the best way to see them.

- Full-color throughout, with hundreds of photos and maps
- Packed with 1–to–3–day itineraries, neighborhood walks, and thematic tours
- Museums, literary haunts, offbeat places, and more
- Star-rated hotel and restaurant listings
- Sturdy foldout map in reclosable plastic wallet
- Foldout front covers with at-a-glance maps and info

The best trips start here.

Frommer's®